# Study Guide
## Melinda Hickman, J.D.
*Fort Hays State University*

# Contemporary Business and Online Commerce Law
*Sixth Edition*

# Henry R. Cheeseman

PEARSON

Prentice Hall

Upper Saddle River, New Jersey 07458

**Editor-in-Chief**: Eric Svendsen
**Project Manager, Editorial**: Kierra Kashickey
**Project Manager, Production:** Kerri Tomasso
**Buyer**: Michelle Klein

**Pearson Prentice Hall**™ **is a trademark of Pearson Education, Inc.**

10  9  8  7  6  5  4  3  2

ISBN-13: 978-0-13-601503-1
ISBN-10:    0-13-601503-4

# Table of Contents

## Chapter 1

# LEGAL HERITAGE
# AND THE INFORMATION AGE

## Chapter Overview

Rules that govern the actions of individuals, businesses, and other organizations are imposed by every society. The law of the United States is essentially derived from English common law, but has been influenced by Spanish and French civil law. The law in the United States has several sources, which include the U.S. and state constitutions, federal and state statutes, ordinances, rules and regulations of administrative agencies, executive orders, and federal and state judicial decisions. Businesses organized in and operating within the United States are subject to its laws, and business people owe a duty to act in a responsible and ethical manner. This chapter introduces the history and sources of U.S. law, the nature and definition of law, and the tenets of critical legal thinking that are applied by courts in deciding cases.

## Objectives

Upon completing the exercises that follow, you should be able to:

1.  Describe law based upon its function.
2.  Recognize and compare the major schools of jurisprudence.
3.  Recognize and compare the Common Law and Civil Law systems of law.
4.  Differentiate between a law court, equity court and merchant court.
5.  Recognize the sources of modern law in the United States.
6.  Understand and recognize key terminology when briefing a case.
7.  Understand how to recognize legal and ethical issues when briefing a case.

## Practical Application

You should be able to recognize the need for law, a flexible interpretation of law, and a framework by which laws are established. You should be able to understand the legal history of the United States and the sources from which it derives its laws. You should be able to distinguish between the common law legal system and the civil law legal system. You should be able to recognize the key terminology used when briefing a court case and see the legal and ethical issues within these cases.

## Helpful Hints

You should read each chapter read the corresponding study tips. A "Refresh Your Memory" exercise will help you to determine the materials on which you need to place more emphasis. The "Critical Thinking" exercise will help to assess your ability to analyze and apply the legal concepts you have learned to the facts presented in the exercise. A "Sample Quiz", consisting of true/false, multiple choice and short answer questions, is provided as a means of assessing your mastery of the chapter.

## Essentials for a Well-Written Critical Thinking Exercise

Critical Thinking Exercises should be approached in a methodical way. Each exercise should be read twice: first to get a feel for the facts and to determine what is being asked of you, and second to spot the issues presented. Once you know what the question is asking you to do, mark up the facts with a pen and place possible applicable legal terms from the chapter you have just studied next to the fact to which they pertain. It is useful to outline the answer to the exercise. State your issues to be discussed and place them in the order in which they will be presented. Demonstrate how the facts in your exercise meet the requirements of the legal principle(s) you are discussing.

Every argument has two sides. When applicable, give reasoning for both sides. When applying case law which you have studied, show how the case(s) apply to the facts you have been given, based upon the similarity of both scenarios. If the case is not supportive of your analysis, indicate this point with a brief explanation and continue with the issues for which you have strong support.

Utilize all of the relevant facts and apply the pertinent law in analyzing these facts. Your reasoning and application chapter materials will help to determine your competency with the information given to you. If you approach these types of exercises as challenging, fun and practical, you can appreciate their usefulness in your everyday life. A sample answer is given at the end of the chapter and is to be used as a guide. Answers will vary based on the law and analysis applied by individual students.

## Study Tips

### What is Law?

The law is a set of rules imposed by society that controls the behavior of individuals, businesses, and other organizations.
- It protects people and property.
- It forbids undesirable activities.

**Definition of Law.** Law is a set of standards and rules by which we justify our conduct and actions, and the violation of which is subject to consequences and sanctions.

**Functions of the Law.** Functions of the law include the following:
- To keep the peace.
- To shape moral standards.
- To promote social justice.
- To maintain the status quo.
- To facilitate orderly change.
- To facilitate planning.
- To provide a basis for compromise.
- To maximize individual freedom.

**Fairness of the Law.** The U.S. legal system, despite some instances of misuse, mistake, and unequal application of the law, is considered to be a comprehensive, fair, and democratic system of law.

**Flexibility of the Law.** The law in the U.S. is designed to evolve and change when society, technology, and commerce change in the U.S. and in the world.

# Schools of Jurisprudential Thought

Various scholars have stated their philosophies on the development of the law. Jurisprudence is the science or philosophy of the law. There are several schools of jurisprudential thought, which may be remembered by using the following mnemonic: **A** **C**ranky **S**quirrel **C**ommands **N**atural **H**istory!

<u>A</u>   The **A**nalytical School asserts that the law is formed by logic.
<u>C</u>   The **C**ritical Legal Studies School does not believe in rules for settling disputes, but advocates applying rules of fairness to each circumstance.
<u>S</u>   The **S**ociological School believes that law is a way to form social behavior and attain sociological goals.
<u>C</u>   The **C**ommand School espouses that the law is handed down from a ruling party and changes when the ruler changes.
<u>N</u>   The **N**atural Law School maintains that the basis of law should be morality and ethics.
<u>H</u>   The **H**istorical School believes that changes in societal norms are eventually demonstrated in the law. These scholars rely on precedent to solve modern problems.

**Natural Law School.** Philosophers of this school emphasize a moral theory of law.
- The law is founded on what is correct.
- Law is "discovered" through reasoning and making choices.

**Historical School.** Philosophers of this school see law an aggregate of social customs and tradition.
- Changes in society will eventually be mirrored in the law.
- Precedent, or past law, is used to solve present problems.

**Analytical School.** Philosophers of this school view law as being shaped by logic.
- The logic of the result is more important than how the result is obtained.

**Sociological School.** Philosophers of this school find law to be a means of achieving and advancing sociological goals.
- These realists aren't likely to look to the precedent of past law to solve problems.

**Command School.** Philosophers of this school see law as being a set of rules that are developed, communicated, and enforced by a ruling party or person.
- Law changes when the ruler changes.
- Law does not reflect society or changes to society.

**Critical Legal Studies School.** Philosophers of this school view legal rules as being unnecessary.
- Rules are used by the powerful to keep the status quo.
- Disputes should be solved with arbitrary rules based on fairness.

**Law and Economics School.** Philosophers of this school, begun at the University of Chicago, believe that the promotion of market efficiency is the central goal of legal decision making.

# History of American Law

The American common law was derived from England and its laws. The English system of law was the foundation that helped to build our common law in America.

**English Common Law.** These laws were developed from judge issued opinions that became precedent upon which other judges would decide similar cases.

*Law Courts.* Courts where judges, appointed by the king or queen, sought to apply the law in a uniform manner.
- Emphasized the form, or legal procedure, over the substance, or merit, of a case.
- The only relief available was monetary damages.

*Chancery (Equity) Courts.* Courts developed under the authority of the Lord Chancellor, whose decisions were based on fairness.
- Inquired into the merits of a case, rather than emphasizing the legal procedure.
- Equitable remedies other than money damages could be awarded.

*Merchant Courts.* Courts which dealt with just the law of merchants. Eventually this court was combined with the regular law court system.
- Dealt with common trade practices and usage.

**Adoption of English Common Law in America.** The law of all states, except for Louisiana, is based on English common law.
- Law, equity, and merchant courts are merged in the U.S.
- Aggrieved parties can generally seek both law and equitable remedies in one court.

**The Civil Law System.** The Romano-Germanic civil law system, dating from 450 B.C, upon which the state law of Louisiana is based.
- Rome first adopted the code of the Twelve Tables, then developed the Corpus Juris Civilis.
- Two national codes are models for countries adopting civil codes:
  - The French Civil Code of 1804 – The Napoleonic Code was developed to be read and used by the people, without needing special training.
  - The German Civil Code of 1896 – Is highly technical and requires special training to read and use it.
- The Civil Code and parliamentary statutes that expand and interpret it are the only sources of law.
  - The adjudication of a case is the application of the statute to the facts.

## Sources of Law in the United States

Over the time since the United States began and the English common law was adopted, lawmakers have shaped a considerable body of law from several sources.

**Constitutions.** The Constitution of the United States is the supreme law of the land, outlining broad and adaptable principles that give this document the description of being a "living document."
- The U.S. Constitution provides for the structure of the federal government
  - The legislative branch, with the power to make laws.
  - The executive branch, with the power to enforce laws.
  - The judicial branch, with the power to interpret laws.
- State constitutions provide the same structure for state governments as the US Constitution does for the federal government.

**Treaties.** These are compacts or agreements between two or more nations.
- Part of the supreme law of the land.
- The president, with the advice and consent of the Senate, may enter into treaties.

**Codified Law.** Statutes are sets of state or federal laws that describe conduct that must be followed by those the statute was designed to protect.

- Federal statutes include anti-trust, securities, bankruptcy, labor, and environmental laws.
- State statutes address corporation, partnership, and Uniform Commercial Code laws.
- Ordinances are laws that are created and enforced by local governments including counties, school districts and municipalities.

**Executive Orders.** These are laws that are made, under express and implied delegation of legislative powers, by the President or state governors.

**Regulations and Order of Administrative Agencies.** Laws promulgated for purposes related to the specific mission of an agency created by Congress or state legislatures.

**Judicial Decisions.** Federal and state issued decisions about individual lawsuits in which the judge explains the legal reasoning used in deciding the case.

*The Doctrine of Stare Decisis.* This doctrine of adhering to precedent encourages uniformity of law and makes it easier for individuals and businesses to determine what the law is.
- Past court decisions become precedent for deciding future cases.
- Lower courts must follow decisions of higher courts.
- The courts of one jurisdiction are not bound by the decisions of another jurisdiction.
    - These decisions can be used as guidance.

**Priority of Law in the United States.**
- The United States Constitution and treaties take precedence over all other laws in the U.S.
    - Federal statutes take precedent over federal regulations.
    - Valid federal law takes precedence over conflicting state or local law.
- State constitutions are the highest state law.
    - State statutes take precedence over state regulations.
    - Valid state law takes precedence over local law.

## Briefing a Case – The IRAC Method

A judge must specify the legal reasoning used in reaching a decision. This critical legal thinking looks at the issue presented, the key facts, the applicable law, and applies the law to the specific case to derive a conclusion that addresses the issue presented.
- Analytical and interpretative skills are essential in deciding legal cases.

**Key Terms.** There are several key terms necessary for reading and analyzing cases.
- Plaintiff – The party who originally brings the lawsuit.
- Defendant – The party who is being sued or against whom the suit is brought.
- Petitioner or Appellant – The party (plaintiff or defendant) who has appealed the decision of the lower court or trial court.
- Respondent or Appellee – The party (or person) who must answer the appeal brought by the petitioner or appellant. The respondent or appellee may be either the plaintiff or defendant, based on which party is the petitioner.

**Briefing a Case Using the IRAC Method.** A case brief can clarify legal issues and foster better understanding of the case. One procedure uses the IRAC method:
- I – What is the legal **I**ssue in the case?
- R – What is the **R**ule (law) of the case?
- A – What is the court's **A**nalysis and rationale?

- C – What was the <u>C</u>onclusion or outcome of the case?
- The procedure for this method includes:
  - o Summarize the court's decision in 600 words or less.
  - o The format is highly structured, with five specific parts.

**Elements of a Case Brief.** A case brief requires a designation of the case and a summary of five parts.
- Case name, citation and the court.
  - o The case name contains the names of the parties to the lawsuit.
  - o The citation includes a designated number and the year in which the case was decided.
  - o The court names the court where the case was decided.
- Important case facts briefly and concisely stated.
- Issues presented to the court.
  - o Once sentence question that can be answered as "yes" or "no".
- Rules of law.
- Analysis of the facts with incorporation of the law.
  - o This rationale states the reasons for the court's decision.
  - o Rephrase pertinent opinions while excluding nonessential points.
- Conclusion or holding of the court hearing the case
  - o This holding should be the "yes" or "no" answer to the stated issue.

# Refresh Your Memory

The following exercises will help to test your memory regarding the principles given in this chapter. Read each question twice, then place your answer in the blank provided for each question. Review the chapter material for any questions you are unable to answer or remember.

1.    Audrey has been given a set of rules and consequences for breaking those rules if she does not follow them. These legally binding guidelines are referred to as the _____.

2.    Realists from the _____ _____ of jurisprudential thought, believe that the purpose of law is to shape social behavior.

3.    The _____ _____ of jurisprudential philosophy would apply if decisions on laws were enforced by a ruling party.

4.    Philosophers of the _____ _____ view law as being shaped by logic.

5.    The English _____ law is the system of law used in most of the states of the U.S.

6.    The _____ _____ dealt primarily with merchants.

7.    The Court of _____ was charged with administering the law in a uniform manner.

8.    The Court of _____ addressed cases where the law remedies were unfair or inappropriate.

9.    The state of _____ bases its law on the _____ law system.

10.    State and federal _____ are written laws enacted by the legislative branch of government.

11. Laws enacted by local government such as traffic laws, building codes and zoning laws are known as _____.

12. A(n) _____ _____ created an Office of Homeland Security in the Executive Office.

13. Past court decisions that are used in deciding future cases become _____.

14. The doctrine that helped establish uniformity of law is known as the Doctrine of _____ _____.

15. Alex has an appellate lawsuit served on Sylvia, which makes Alex's role that of _____.

## Critical Thought Exercise

Following the genocide, torture, rape, and murder of thousands of civilians in Rwanda in 1994, sixty-three individuals were tried for genocide and crimes against humanity. Numerous persons were sentenced to life sentences.

Many of those prosecuted objected to being tried outside Rwanda for acts committed within Rwanda. The accused further objected to being prosecuted for acts that were not deemed criminal by their own leaders or national laws.

You are asked to address a large convention sponsored by a nationalist group that argues against any person ever being subjected to criminal punishment by an international court for acts committed within their home country.

Your argument should address the following issues while trying to explain whether or not you feel prosecutions by an international body are lawful and justified:
1. What law is being violated when someone commits a crime against humanity?
2. Who has the authority to enforce laws against genocide and crimes against humanity?
3. Should a citizen of a sovereign nation be subjected to punishment by an international tribunal for acts committed within their home country?
4. Who is responsible for the prosecution of these crimes?

*Please compose your answer on a separate sheet of paper or on your computer.*

## Practice Quiz

### True/False

1. ___ Laws consist of rules that govern the conduct of individuals, but not businesses and organizations that function with it.

2. ___ Businesses are not like individuals, however they still owe no duty to society.

3. ___ The U.S. Constitution is often called "a living document" as it is so flexible and adaptive.

4. ___ The term *stare decisis* has nothing to do with precedence or predictability of law for businesses or individuals.

5. ___ The Constitution of the United States gave all power to the federal government thereby leaving states with their own constitutions to establish state power.

6. \_\_\_ Legal philosophers who use past legal decisions to solve contemporary problems follow the beliefs of the Law of Economics.

7. \_\_\_ *Brown v. Board of Education* challenged the separate school systems of four states.

8. \_\_\_ An equity court emphasized the procedure of a case versus the merits of a case.

9. \_\_\_ A merchant court emphasized legal procedure in order to grant an appropriate remedy.

10. \_\_\_ Judicial opinions are written opinions that often interpret statutes as well as ordinances.

11. \_\_\_ One function of the law is to maintain the status quo, allowing the freedom to overthrow the government through force.

12. \_\_\_ The law of the U.S. was designed to change as society, technology, and commerce changes.

13. \_\_\_ The U.S. Constitution is an example of a document that reflects the Natural Law theory.

14. \_\_\_ The Romano-Germanic common law system began in 450 B.C. with the adoption of the code of the Twelve Tables by the Romans.

15. \_\_\_ In the common law system, laws are derived from the civil code and parliamentary statutes that expand and interpret this code, whereas in the civil law system, laws are created by the judicial system and through legislation.

## Multiple Choice

16. Some of the primary functions of the law in our country are:
    a. promoting social justice, encouraging legal decisions, and interpreting judicial decisions.
    b. facilitating change, providing a basis for compromise and developing legal reasoning.
    c. keeping the peace, shaping moral standards, maximizing individual freedom.
    d. none of the above.

17. The Sociological School of Jurisprudence maintains that
    a. the law is a set of rules enforced by the ruling party; the law changes when the ruler changes.
    b. the rules of law are unnecessary and subjective decisions made be judges are permissible.
    c. the purpose of law is to achieve, advance and shape social behavior.
    d. the law is an evolutionary process.

18. The term codified law refers to
    a. statutes enacted by the legislative branches of state and federal governments that are arranged by topic in code books.
    b. a written agreement made between the United States and another nation.
    c. administrative rules and regulations.
    d. all of the above.

19. The term stare decisis means:
    a. to interpret statutes and make a decision.
    b. to predict the legal decision in a case.
    c. to stand by the decision.

    d.   to adopt and regulate the conduct of others.

20. Provisions of state established constitutions are valid unless
    a. they are patterned after the U.S. Constitution .
    b. they have an executive branch of their governments.
    c. they apply to evolving social, technological and economic conditions.
    d. they conflict with the U.S. Constitution or any valid federal law.

21. When briefing a court case using the IRAC method, the following components must be present:
    a. 1) the case name, citation, and court; 2) summary of key facts; 3) the amount of the judgment; 4) the rule of law; 5) summary of rationale; and 6) the holding.
    b. 1) the case name and court; 2) summary of key facts; 3) the issue; 4) the rule of law; 5) summary of rationale; and 6) the holding.
    c. 1) the case name, citation, and court; 2) summary of key facts; 3) the issue; 4) the rule of law; 5) summary of rationale; and 6) the holding.
    d. 1) the case name and court; 2) summary of key facts; 3) the amount of the judgment; 4) the rule of law; 5) summary of rationale; and 6) the holding.

22. The petitioner or appellant is the party
    a. who originally brought the lawsuit.
    b. who has appealed the decision of the trial court or lower court.
    c. against whom the lawsuit has been brought.
    d. who must answer the appeal.

23. Administrative agency rules and orders are
    a. created by agencies.
    b. enacted by Congress and state legislatures.
    c. enacted by municipalities and local government entities.
    d. issued by the president and governors of states.

24. The Constitution of the United States provides for three branches of government:
    a. The Chancery, the Legislative, and the Judicial.
    b. The Executive, the Legislative, and the Chancery.
    c. The Chancery, the Executive, and the Judicial.
    d. The Executive, the Legislative, and the Judicial.

25. Two national codes are models for countries adopting civil codes for civil law systems:
    a. The Corpus Juris Civilis and the U.S. Constitution.
    b. The Corpus Juris Civilis and the German Civil Code.
    c. The French Civil Code and the German Civil Code.
    d. The French Civil Code and the U.S. Constitution.

## Short Answer

26. What was the primary example that was set in the case of *Brown v. Board of Education?*
    _____
    _____

27. Distinguish between a law court and a Chancery (equity) court.
    _____
    _____

28. On what were the rules known as the Law of Merchants based?

    _____

29. What is Jurisprudence?

    _____

30. Which school of jurisprudential thought promotes market efficiency as being the central goal of legal decision making?

    _____

31. Why will treaties become increasingly more important to business?

    _____

32. Administrative agencies are created to enforce and interpret statutes. Give two examples of these types of federal agencies.

    _____

33. Which state bases its law on the French Civil Code?

    _____

34. What is a judicial decision?

    _____

35. What purpose do administrative agencies serve?

    _____

36. Which doctrine provides for adherence to precedence?

    _____

37. Which court emphasized legal procedure over the merits of the case?

    _____

38. Distinguish between Common Law and Civil Law.

    _____

    _____

39. What jurisprudential school of thought do realists follow?

    _____

40. Which two national codes became models for countries that adopted civil codes?

    _____

## Answers to Refresh Your Memory

1.  law  [p 3-4]
2.  Sociological School  [p 8]
3.  Command School  [p 8]
4.  analytical  [p 8]
5.  common  [p 10]

# Critical Thought Exercise Model Answer

**The Origins of Law**. Law is comprised of the rules created by the controlling authority of a society, usually its government. These rules are given legal force and effect and control the actions of the individuals within the society. Most law is created by each society within a country and is referred to as national law. Law that is created by way of treaties, customs, and agreements between nations is international law.

For most countries, national law finds its foundation in the philosophies of legal positivism, which assumes that there is no law higher than the laws created by the government, and legal realism, which stresses a realistic approach that takes into account customary practices and present day circumstances.

In the area of international law, the philosophy of natural law plays an important role. Natural law holds that there is a universal law that is applicable to all human beings that is higher than any law created by an individual society or government. Certain conduct, such as genocide and crimes against humanity are deemed to be without any possible moral justification, regardless of the existence or nonexistence of any national law concerning these types of acts.

When a nation or segment of a society within a nation engages in conduct that violates natural law, it is no defense to this conduct that the government or society advocates or condones the conduct.

**Justification for International Criminal Tribunals and an International Criminal Court**. The nations of the world have collectively agreed for over 50 years that international courts capable of resolving disputes and addressing crimes against humanity are needed. This need has been filled by the United Nations.

The members of the United Nations consent to the jurisdiction of the international courts as a way to advance their rights in the international arena. Until 1998, The International Court of Justice (ICJ) was the principal judicial organ of the United Nations. The ICJ, located in The Hague, Netherlands, began operating in 1946. The prior court had been in the same location since 1922. In 1998, The International Criminal Court (ICC) was also created.

The ICJ operates under a Statute that is part of the Charter of the United Nations. The ICJ lacks power to address situations such as the Holocaust and genocide in Cambodia because it can only hear cases between states. It has no jurisdiction over individuals.

Prior to the formation of the ICC, United Nations members formed criminal tribunals to address war crimes and crimes against humanity committed during specific periods of time. These tribunals were given authority to prosecute individuals who were responsible for these severe criminal acts.

The overall purpose of these tribunals was to pursue peace and justice in the affected areas. The International Criminal Tribunal for Rwanda was established for the prosecution of persons responsible for genocide and other serious violations of international humanitarian law committed in the territory of Rwanda between 1 January 1994 and 31 December 1994. The tribunal was also authorized to prosecute Rwandan citizens responsible for genocide and other such violations of international law committed in the territory of neighboring States during the same period.

An international criminal court has been called the missing link in the international legal system. The International Court of Justice handles only cases between States, not individuals. Without an international criminal court for dealing with individual responsibility as an enforcement mechanism, acts of genocide and egregious violations of human rights often go unpunished. No one was held accountable for the over 2 million people killed by the Khmer Rouge in Cambodia in the 1970s. The same was true for murders of men, women and children in Mozambique, Liberia, El Salvador and other countries.

**Defining International Crimes.** When each case of genocide or crimes against humanity has taken place, a specific statute had to be created to set up the tribunal and define the crimes to be prosecuted. The jurisdiction of the tribunal only extends to those crimes and that time period covered in the statute.

In the statute establishing the International Criminal Tribunal for Rwanda, specific definitions for genocide, crimes against humanity, and violations of the Geneva Convention were set forth in detail. To address crimes against humanity, the ICTR statute established "...the power to prosecute persons responsible for the following crimes when committed as part of a widespread or systematic attack against any civilian population on national, political, ethnic, racial or religious grounds: (a) Murder; (b) Extermination; (c) Enslavement; (d) Deportation; (e) Imprisonment; (f) Torture; (g) Rape; (h) Persecutions on political, racial and religious grounds; (i) Other inhumane acts." (ICTR Statute, Article 3)

**Need for International Prosecution.** Without the international tribunals, those responsible could easily flee to other countries and avoid being held accountable for their acts of genocide. This was particularly true in the case of Rwanda, where the perpetrators simply went across the border into neighboring countries to hide when pursued. They would then reenter Rwanda and continue the killing when they were able. Rwanda was unable to handle the apprehension and prosecution of those responsible because the government of Rwanda had broken down and lacked the power to enforce peace. The need for international prosecution arises when the controlling government and its leaders are the perpetrators, such as in Yugoslavia. The government in power may actually mandate that the criminal acts be carried out as part of an "ethnic cleansing." This was true in both Nazi Germany and in Yugoslavia in the 1990s.

**Deterrence and Responsibility for Prosecutions in the Future.** Nations agree that criminals should normally be prosecuted by national courts in the countries where the crimes are committed. When the national governments are either unwilling or unable to act to restore peace and seek justice, there needs to be an institution in place to address the horrors of genocide and crimes against humanity. In the past, perpetrators had little chance of being caught, much less prosecuted. The new ICC seeks to create a deterrent effect. Those responsible for murder, terrorism, genocide, and violations of the Geneva Convention will know that they will be pursued throughout the world. Additionally, the loopholes inherent in the tribunal process will be eliminated. The ineffective nature of the ICTR is shown by the fact that the murder of thousands of people from 1995-1999 will go unpunished because the ICTR was only authorized to prosecute those crimes committed in 1994.

Without an international institution to address crimes such as those committed in Rwanda, the perpetrators of the worst crimes in history would go unpunished. The members of the United Nations have decided that they desire the protection afforded by an international criminal court.

# Answers to Practice Quiz

## True/False

1.  False   Laws consist of rules that govern the conduct of individuals, businesses and organizations that function within it. [p 3]
2.  False   Businesses are not like individuals, but still owe an ethical duty to society. [p 3]
3.  True    Specific laws cannot be written to cover every possible situation. [p 12]

4.    False    The term stare decisis refers to a doctrine that promotes uniformity of law within a jurisdiction, makes the court system more efficient, and makes the law more predictable for individuals and businesses. [p 15]

5.    False    Powers not given to the federal government by the Constitution are reserved for the states. [p 12]

6.    False    Legal philosophers who use past legal decisions to solve contemporary problems follow the beliefs of the Historical School of jurisprudence. [p 8]

7.    True     The 1954 case of *Brown v. Board of Education* challenged the separate school systems of Kansas, South Carolina, Virginia, and Delaware. [p 6]

8.    False    The Chancery (Equity) Courts inquired into the merits of the case as opposed to placing emphasis on legal procedure. The Equity Court was a place where a person could go if a law court could not give an appropriate remedy. [p 10]

9.    False    A Merchant Court is one that was developed to solve the disputes of merchants who traveled through Europe and England. [p 10]

10.   True     Judicial opinions are written opinions where the judge or justice usually explains the legal reasoning used to decide the case. These opinions often include interpretations of statutes, ordinances, and administrative regulations and the announcement of legal principles used to decide the case. [p 14]

11.   False    One function of the law is to maintain the status quo, preventing the overthrow of the government through force. [p 4]

12.   True     U.S. law was designed to change as society, technology, and commerce   change. [p 5]

13.   True     The U.S. Constitution is a document that reflects the Natural Law theory. [p 8]

14.   False    The Romano-Germanic civil law system began in 450 B.C. with the adoption of the code of the Twelve Tables by the Romans. [p 11]

15.   False    In the common law system, laws are created by the judicial system and through legislation, whereas in the civil law system, laws are derived from the civil code and parliamentary statutes that expand and interpret this code. [p 11]

## Multiple Choice

16.   C    Some of the primary functions of the law in our country are keeping the peace, shaping moral standards, and maximizing individual freedom. A is incorrect because even though we would like for legal decisions to be made, it is not a main function of law. B is incorrect as compromise comes as a result of negotiation as opposed to a function of law. Further, legal reasoning is not a function of the law, but is developed by applying the law to facts. Therefore, C is the best answer. [p 4]

17.   C    The Sociological School maintains that the law is an avenue of attaining and advancing certain sociological goals. A is incorrect as this premise asserts the belief of the Command School. B is incorrect as this belief coincides with the Critical Legal Studies School. D is incorrect as this premise is maintained by the Historical School. [p 8]

18.   A    Answer A is correct, as it correctly defines codified law. B is incorrect, as it is a definition of a treaty. C is incorrect, as administrative rules and regulations help interpret the statutes that the administrative agencies enforce. D is incorrect for the reasons stated above. [p 12]

19.   C    C is correct, as this is the true meaning of this Latin phrase. Answers A, B, and D are wrong as the meaning is incorrectly stated. [p 15]

20.   D    Answer D is correct, as the Constitution is the supreme law of the land. The states must follow it as opposed to creating conflicting provisions in their constitutions. Answer A is incorrect, as many state constitutions mirror the United States Constitution. Answer B is incorrect, as state constitutions establish an executive branch of government. Answer C is correct, as it refers to the law and its flexibility toward evolving technological, social, and economic conditions. However, it is incorrect to say that the law is invalid because of these changes. [p 15]

21. C Answer C is correct, as it lists all required components of an IRAC brief. Answer A is incorrect, as the amount of the judgment is not a component and the component of the issue is not present. Answer B is incorrect, as the citation from the first component is missing. Answer D is incorrect, as the citation from the first component is missing and the amount of the judgment is not a component and the component of the issue is not present. [p 19-20]

22. B Answer B is correct, as the petitioner or appellant is the party who has appealed the decision of the trial court or lower court. Answer A is incorrect, as it is the plaintiff who is the party who originally brought the lawsuit. Answer C is incorrect, as it is the defendant who is the party against whom the lawsuit has been brought. Answer D is incorrect, as it is the respondent or appellee who must answer the appeal. [p 19]

23. A Answer A is correct, as administrative agency rules and orders are created by agencies. Answer B is incorrect, as statutes are enacted by Congress and state legislatures. Answer C is incorrect, as ordinances are enacted by municipalities and local government entities. Answer D is incorrect, as executive orders are issued by the president and governors of states. [p 14]

24. D Answer D correctly states the branches of government outlined in the U.S. Constitution. [p 12]

25. C Answer C is correct, as the French (Napoleonic) Code and the German Civil Code are models for countries adopting civil codes. Answer A is incorrect, as the Corpus Juris Civilis is the compilation of Roman law from which civil law is derived and the U.S. Constitution is a source of U.S. law, which is a common law system. Answer B is incorrect, as the Corpus Juris Civilis is the compilation of Roman law from which civil law is derived. Answer D is incorrect, as the U.S. Constitution is a source of U.S. law, which is a common law system. [p 11]

## Short Answer

26. This case demonstrates the law leading the people as well as the law's response to social changes by overturning the "separate but equal doctrine." This doctrine approved of separate schools for black and white children. [p 6]

27. The only relief available from a law court was an award of money for damages. An equity court inquired as to the merits of the case and could award other remedies tailored to the circumstances. Remedies in an equity court were based on fairness and took precedence over law courts. [p 10]

28. The Law of Merchants was based on common trade practices and usage [p 10]

29. the philosophy or science of the law. [p 8]

30. The Law and Economics School. [p 8]

31. As more agreements are reached between nations, economic relations between these nations will also increase, thereby increasing their importance to business. [p 12]

32. The Securities and Exchange Commission (SEC) and the Federal Trade Commission (FTC) [p 13]

33. Louisiana. [p 11]

34. A judicial decision is a court issued statement of the holding of the case and the basis for reaching the decision in the case. [p 14]

35. Their purpose is to enforce and interpret statutes enacted by Congress. [p 13-14]

36. The Doctrine of Stare Decisis. [p 15]

37. Law [p 10]

38. In the Common Law system, laws are created by the judicial system as well as by congressional legislation. In the Civil Law system, the Civil Code and parliamentary statutes that expand and interpret it are the sole sources of the law. [p 10-11]

39. The Sociological School. [p 8]

40. The French Civil Code of 1804 (the Napoleonic Code) and the German Civil Code of 1896. [p 11]

# Chapter 2

# CONSTITUTIONAL LAW
# FOR BUSINESS AND E-COMMERCE

## Chapter Overview

Prior to the thirteen original colonies declaring independence from England, they operated as separate sovereign governments under the rule of England. After the American Revolution, these colonies began the republic of the United States of American. The U.S. Constitution establishes the legal framework under which the federal government works and the powers delegated to that government by the states. It reserves powers to each state and guarantees fundamental rights to the people. This chapter looks at the provisions of and amendments to the U.S. Constitution and how they affect commerce in this country.

## Objectives

Upon completion of this chapter's exercises, you should be able to:

1. Recognize the function of the powers granted to the state and federal governments.
2. Realize the importance and application of the Supremacy Clause of the U.S. Constitution.
3. Understand the authority of the federal government to regulate interstate commerce.
4. Discuss the protection that speech is afforded under the First Amendment.
5. Differentiate between substantive and procedural due process.
6. Identify the constitutional standards applicable in equal protection cases.

## Practical Application

You should be able to recognize the importance of the Supremacy Clause in the federalism of the United States. You should be able to understand the importance of the Commerce Clause in the regulation of commerce. You should be able to appreciate the protections and limitations on speech. You should be able to identify and apply the standards of review in equal protection cases.

## Helpful Hints

As you review the chapter, weigh the governmental interest against the interests of the individual and the rights being protected.

## Study Tips

### Constitution of the United States of America

The federal government of the U.S. was formed with the adoption of the Articles of Confederation by the original thirteen states. The federal government was reinforced with the adoption of the Constitution.

- The U.S. Constitution serves two functions:
    - o It creates the executive, legislative, and judicial branches of the federal government.
    - o It limits the power of the federal government to impinge on individual rights.
- The U.S. Constitution provides that it may be amended.

**Federalism and Delegated Powers.** Federalism refers to our country's form of government, where the states and the federal government share powers.

- The states granted enumerated powers to the federal government, such as authority over national and international affairs.
- All powers not granted to the federal government are reserved for the states.

**Doctrine of Separation of Powers.** The federal government has three branches.

- The legislative branch.
    - o Established by Article I of the U.S. Constitution.
    - o Provides for bicameral Congress, composed of the Senate and the House of Representatives.
- The executive branch.
    - o Established by Article II of the U.S. Constitution.
    - o Provides for the election of the president and vice president.
- The judicial branch.
    - o Established by Article III of the U.S. Constitution.
    - o Provides for the Supreme Court and the creation of other federal courts.

**Checks and Balances.** The U.S. Constitution provides several types of checks and balances so that no one branch of the government becomes too powerful.

- The judicial branch can evaluate the actions of the executive and legislative branches to verify that those actions are constitutional.
- The legislative branch must be consulted and then approve whether the executive branch can enter into treaties.
- The legislative branch can create federal courts and decide on their jurisdiction, and it can enact statutes that change judicially made law.

## Supremacy Clause

This clause of the U.S. Constitution establishes that the supreme law of the land is composed of the U.S. Constitution, treaties, federal laws, and federal regulations.

- The preemption doctrine states that federal law will take precedence over state or local law.
    - o State and local governments usually have concurrent jurisdiction.
    - o Any state or local law that conflicts with the federal law will be preempted.
    - o Congress can direct that a specific federal statute will exclusively regulate a certain area or activity.

## Commerce Clause

This clause of the U.S. Constitution gives Congress the power to regulate commerce.

- It is meant to encourage the development of a national market and free trade among the states.

**Commerce Regulation with Native American Tribes.** Before the United States spread across the breadth of North America, there were many Native American nations within the original states and outside these states, in the territories that would eventually become the United States.

- The original states gave the federal government the power to enter into treaties with these nations.

o   This power endures to the present.

*Native American Law.*  Many larger tribes entered into treaties with the U.S. that allowed them to keep their own government, under the protection of the U.S. Government.
- Native American tribes are treated as domestic dependent nations with limited sovereignty.
- Tribal councils are the governing authority on Indian reservations.
  o   Legal matters that cannot be handled within the tribe are taken to federal courts.
  o   State courts do not have jurisdiction over matters on Indian land.

**Foreign Commerce Clause.**  The federal government is given exclusive power to regulate commerce with foreign nations under the U.S. Constitution.
- A state or local regulation that unduly burdens foreign commerce is unconstitutional.

**Interstate Commerce.**  The federal government is given the power to regulate interstate commerce by the U.S. Constitution.
- The difference between interstate and intrastate commerce is that interstate commerce involves instrumentalities of trade moving across state borders and intrastate commerce is commerce moving within the state.
- Traditionally, courts viewed this to mean that only commerce that moved *in* interstate commerce could be regulated by the federal government.
- The modern rule allows the regulation of activities that *affect* interstate commerce.
  o   The activity does not have to be in interstate commerce.
  o   The activity only has to have an effect on interstate commerce.

*No Undue Burden on Interstate Commerce.*  The states, through their police power, retained the power to regulate intrastate commerce and a significant amount of interstate business activity within their borders.
- States can make laws to protect or promote the public health, safety, morals, and general welfare.
- These laws are unconstitutional if they unduly burden interstate commerce.

## Bill of Rights

The Bill of Rights, the first ten amendments to the United States Constitution, guarantees several fundamental rights and protects them from governmental intrusion.
- Most of these rights have been applied to artificial persons, as well as natural persons.
- The rights were originally only protected from federal government action.
  o   The Due Process Clause of the Fourteenth Amendment limited state and local government actions.
  o   The Incorporation Doctrine applies most of the guarantees to state and local governments.

## Freedom of Speech

This freedom extends only to speech and not conduct.  Speech is divided into three categories:  fully protected, limited protected, and unprotected speech.

**Fully Protected Speech.**  Speech under this category cannot be prohibited or regulated by the government.
- Political speech is fully protected.

**Limited Protected Speech.**  Speech under this category cannot be forbidden by the government, but can be limited in time, place, and manner.

- Offensive speech is that which offends many people, though not obscene, and can be limited by time, place, and manner restrictions.
- Commercial speech, such as advertising, was once unprotected; it is now protected, but can be limited in time, place, and manner.

**Unprotected Speech.** Speech in this category is unprotected and can be banned by the government.
- Dangerous speech
- Fighting words
- Speech that incites to the violent or revolutionary overthrow of the government
- Defamatory language
- Child pornography
- Obscene speech
  - o The Supreme Court has defined obscene speech as
    - Speech which appeals to the average person's prurient interest,
    - Speech where the work is patently offensive in its description or depiction of sexual conduct as defined under state law, and
    - Speech where the work fails to provide serious literary, artistic, political or social value.
  - o The states can define the meaning of obscene speech.

## Freedom of Religion

The Constitution mandates that the local, state and federal governments be neutral regarding religion. The religion clauses in the First Amendment are the Establishment Clause and the Free Exercise Clause.

**The Establishment Clause.** This clause prohibits the government from establishing a state religion or promoting one religion over another.

**The Free Exercise Clause.** This clause prevents the government from making laws that inhibit or prohibit people from participating in or practicing their chosen religion.

## The Equal Protection Clause

This clause of the Fourteenth Amendment prohibits discriminatory and unfair government action.

**Federal, State, and Local Government Action.** The Equal Protection Clause declares that a state cannot, "deny to any person within its jurisdiction the equal protection of the laws."
- This clause primarily applies to state and local governments, but it also applies to federal government action.
- Similarly situated persons cannot be treated differently.
- Artificial persons are also protected.
- The classification of individuals is not unlawful per se.

**Standards of Review.** There are three standards of review in equal protection cases:
- The Strict Scrutiny Test is applied when there is a classification that is a suspect class, like race.
- The Intermediate Scrutiny Test is applied when the classification is based on a protected class that is not race, such as age and sex.
- The Rational Basis Test is applied when neither a suspect nor protected class is involved, where all that is needed is a justifiable reason for the law being reviewed.

## Due Process Clause

Both the Fifth and Fourteenth Amendments to the Constitution include a due process clause. The crux of this clause is that no individual shall be deprived of life, liberty or property without due process of law.

- The Fifth Amendment applies to the federal government.
- The Fourteenth Amendment applies to state and local government.
- The government is not prohibited from taking life, liberty or property, but must follow certain procedures to do so.

**Substantive Due Process.** Substantive due process refers to the content of the law, where the law must be clear and not too broad.

- The law must be worded in such a way that a "reasonable person" could understand the law in order to obey it.

**Procedural Due Process.** Procedural due process requires a person be given notice and an opportunity to be heard before his/her life, liberty or property is taken.

- The Just Compensation Clause states that the government must pay to the owner just compensation for taking an individual's property under eminent domain.

## Privileges and Immunities Clause

This clause prohibits states from enforcing laws that unduly favor their own residents, thereby resulting in discrimination against residents of other states.

- If states were to enact statutes that favor their own residents, nationalism will be crushed.

# Refresh Your Memory

The following exercises will help to test your memory regarding the principles given in this chapter. Read each question twice, then place your answer in the blank provided for each question. Review the chapter material for any questions you are unable to answer or remember.

1. The type of government under which the United States operates is known as _____.

2. The powers delegated to the federal government by the ratification of the Constitution by the states are known as _____ _____.

3. The three branches of government into which the federal government is divided are the _____, the _____, and the _____ branches.

4. The system of _____ and _____ built into the United States Constitution prevents any one of the three branches of the federal government from becoming too powerful.

5. The _____ Clause ensures that the federal Constitution, treaties, federal laws, and federal regulations are the supreme law of the land.

6. The _____ Clause has greater impact on business than any other provision of the Constitution.

7. _____ commerce refers to commerce that moves between states or that affects commerce between the states.

8. _____ commerce refers to local commerce that also does not affect commerce between states.

9. The power retained by the states that allows the states to regulate both private and business activity within their borders is known as _____ _____.

10. Under the _____ Doctrine, many of the fundamental guarantees set forth in the Bill of Rights are also applied to state and local government action.

11. The Freedom of Speech Clause of the First Amendment protects _____ and not _____.

12. The _____ Doctrine refers to federal law taking precedence over state and local law.

13. The _____ Clause of the First Amendment bars the government from establishing a state religion or promoting one religion over another.

14. The _____ _____ Clause of the First Amendment bars the government from enacting laws that either prohibit or inhibit individuals from participation in or practice of chosen religions.

15. The _____ _____ Clause contained in the Fourteenth Amendment bars state, local, and federal governments from passing laws that classify and treat "similarly situated" persons differently.

# Critical Thought Exercise

Larry Brown is a very religious person who is very active in the anti-abortion movement. While Brown travels the streets of his hometown of Westerfield, Illinois, he plays taped sermons and spiritual music that support his religious and political views. The City of Westerfield enacted an ordinance that prohibited the playing of car sound systems at a volume that would be "audible" at a distance greater than fifty feet. Brown was arrested and convicted for violating the ordinance. Brown appealed his conviction on the grounds that the ordinance violated his right to free speech and free exercise of his religious beliefs. The City of Westerfield countered that noise coming from Brown's car could pose a hazard if he and other drivers were unable to hear emergency vehicles as they approached, and as such, the ordinance was a proper exercise of the police power possessed by the State of Illinois.

Was the playing of sermons by Brown protected by the Free Speech and Free Exercise Clauses of the First Amendment to the United States Constitution?

*Please compose your answer on a separate sheet of paper or on your computer.*

# Practice Quiz

## True/False

1. ___ State laws may burden interstate commerce.

2. ___ The part of government that consists of Congress is the legislative branch.

3. ___ The Equal Protection Clause also applies to federal government action.

4. ___ Commercial speech is subject to proper time, place and manner restrictions.

5. ___ Government classifications based on a suspect class are subject to the strict scrutiny test.

6. ___ Substantive due process requires the government to give a person proper notice and a hearing before depriving the person of life, liberty, or property.

7. ___ The Free Exercise Clause prohibits the government from either establishing a state religion or promoting one religion over another.

8. ___ The Bill of Rights, plus 17 other amendments, have been added to the U.S. Constitution.

9. ___ Police power permits states to enact laws that regulate the conduct of business.

10. ___ Speech and conduct are protected by the First Amendment.

11. ___ Enumerated powers are those powers retained by the states to regulate public health, safety, morals, and general welfare.

12. ___ Checks and balances are built into the U.S. Constitution to prevent one branch of the government from becoming too powerful.

13. ___ The state governments retained the right to make treaties with the Indian nations.

14. ___ The federal government can only regulate commerce that actually moves *in* interstate commerce under the Commerce Clause of the U.S. Constitution.

15. ___ The first ten Amendments to the U.S. Constitution are known as the Bill of Rights.

## Multiple Choice

16. Enumerated powers are
    a. the part of the government that consists of the Supreme Court and other federal courts.
    b. sequentially numbered laws.
    c. powers delegated to the federal government by the states.
    d. None of the above.

17. The Commerce Clause is intended to
    a. deregulate commerce with foreign nations.
    b. foster development of a national market and free trade among the states.
    c. authorize state governments to regulate trade with the Indian tribes.
    d. be the supreme law of the land.

18. The concept of federal law taking precedence over state or local law is called
    a. the supremacy clause.
    b. interstate commerce regulation.
    c. the preemption doctrine.
    d. All of the above

19. Intrastate commerce refers to
    a. commerce that crosses state borders.
    b. commerce that occurs within a state.
    c. commerce that occurs across state borders and within a state.

    d.   commerce that occurs only in a limited local area.

20.    Offensive speech is an example of
    a.   speech that is given excessive protection.
    b.   speech that has time, place and manner restrictions.
    c.   speech that will incite the overthrow of the government.
    d.   speech that is fully protected.

21.    The test of whether substantive due process has been met is whether
    a.   proper notice and a hearing have been given.
    b.   Laws are clear and are not overly broad in what they cover.
    c.   a reasonable person could understand the law and comply with it.
    d.   none of the above

22.    The privileges and immunities clause prohibits
    a.   states from giving the same privileges to out-of-state residents.
    b.   prevents out-of-state residents from owning property in other states.
    c.   the government from enacting laws that unduly discriminate in favor of their own residents.
    d.   the federal government from regulating commerce that moves in interstate commerce.

23.    The Commerce Clause of the U.S. Constitution gives the federal government the
    a.   redundant power to regulate commerce with foreign nations.
    b.   reserved power to regulate commerce with foreign nations.
    c.   exclusive power to regulate commerce with foreign nations.
    d.   elusive power to regulate commerce with foreign nations.

24.    The Commerce Clause of the U.S. Constitution gives the federal government the power to regulate interstate commerce.
    a.   The traditional interpretation of this power allowed the federal government to regulate activities that affect interstate commerce, whereas the modern view allows the federal government to only regulate commerce that moved in interstate commerce.
    b.   The traditional interpretation of this power allowed the federal government to only regulate commerce that moved in interstate commerce, whereas the modern view allows the federal government to regulate activities that affect interstate commerce.
    c.   The traditional interpretation of this power allowed the federal government to regulate activities that affect intrastate commerce, whereas the modern view allows the federal government to only regulate commerce that moved in intrastate commerce.
    d.   The traditional interpretation of this power allowed the federal government to only regulate commerce that moved in intrastate commerce, whereas the modern view allows the federal government to regulate activities that affect intrastate commerce.

25.    Speech under the First Amendment to the U.S. Constitution is divided into three categories with three different levels of protection:
    a.   Fully protected speech, which cannot be prohibited or regulated by the government, and includes political speech. Limited protected speech, which can be limited as to time, place, and manner, and includes offensive speech. Unprotected speech, which can be prohibited by the government; it includes obscene speech.
    b.   Fully protected speech, which cannot be prohibited or regulated by the government, and includes political speech. Limited protected speech, which can be limited as to time, place, and manner, and includes obscene speech. Unprotected speech, which can be prohibited by the government; it includes offensive speech.

c. Fully protected speech, which cannot be prohibited or regulated by the government, and includes offensive speech. Limited protected speech, which can be limited as to time, place, and manner, and includes political speech. Unprotected speech, which can be prohibited by the government; it includes obscene speech.

d. Fully protected speech, which cannot be prohibited or regulated by the government, and includes obscene speech. Limited protected speech, which can be limited as to time, place, and manner, and includes political speech. Unprotected speech, which can be prohibited by the government; it includes offensive speech.

## Short Answer

26. What do the Due Process Clauses of the Fifth and Fourteenth Amendments to the Constitution state?

_____

27. To what does the Due Process Clause of the Fifth Amendment to the U.S. Constitution apply?

_____

28. To which classifications is the intermediate scrutiny test applied?

_____

29. What does the substantive due process clause require of government statutes, ordinances, regulations or other laws?

_____

30. When is the Rational Basis test used?

_____

31. To what action is offensive speech subject?

_____

32. What government action does the Free Exercise Clause prevent?

_____

33. What does the Privileges and Immunities Clause prohibit?

_____

34. What is required of the government under the Just Compensation Clause?

_____

35. Give six (6) examples of unprotected speech.

_____

36. Which clause to the U.S. Constitution was intended to encourage the development of a national market and free trade among the states?

_____

37. Which level of government has the authority to regulate commerce with the Indian tribes?

_____

38. What power does the Commerce Clause to the U.S. Constitution give the federal government?

_____

39. Distinguish between interstate and intrastate commerce.

_____

_____

40. What is the meaning of police power?

_____.

## Answers to Refresh Your Memory

1.  federalism  [p 30]
2.  enumerated powers  [p 30]
3.  legislative, executive, judicial  [p 30]
4.  checks, balances  [p 32]
5.  Supremacy  [p 32]
6.  Commerce  [p 33]
7.  interstate  [p 38]
8.  intrastate  [p 38]
9.  police power  [p 41]
10. Incorporation  [p 43]
11. speech, conduct  [p 43]
12. Preemption  [p 32]
13. Establishment  [p 48]
14. Free Exercise  [p 50]
15. Equal Protection  [p 51]

## Critical Thought Exercise Model Answer

States possess police powers as part of their inherent sovereignty. These powers may be exercised to protect or promote the public order, health, safety, morals, and general welfare. Free Speech that has political content, such as the speech being used by Brown, has traditionally been protected to the fullest extent possible by the courts. Free speech includes the right to effective free speech. Amplification systems can be used as long as the speech does not harass or annoy others in the exercise of their privacy rights at an inappropriate time or in an inappropriate location. Thus, Brown would have greater leeway to play his sermons in a commercial district during the day than he could to blast then in a residential neighborhood at midnight. The Free Exercise Clause provision in the First Amendment to the Constitution prohibits Congress from making a law "prohibiting the free exercise" of religion. The free exercise clause guarantees that a person can hold any religious belief that he or she wants. When religious practices are at odds with public policy and the public welfare, the government can act. Brown has the absolute right to listen to his sermons and preach them to others. However, he cannot engage in this activity if it causes a danger to the safety of others. The question that is not answered by the facts is whether the distance of fifty feet is to prevent annoyance or a danger to drivers upon the streets and highways. Without a showing by Westerfield that music and speech that is audible from fifty feet is actually dangerous to drivers, Brown is free to play his sermons and spiritual music in a manner that is annoying to others.

# Answers to Practice Quiz

## True/False

1.  False    State laws may not burden interstate commerce. [p 41]
2.  True     The part of government that is comprised of Congress is the legislative branch. The executive branch is made up of the President and Vice-President. The judicial branch is comprised of the Supreme Court and other federal courts. [p 30]
3.  True     The equal protection clause also applies to federal government action. [p 51]
4.  True     Commercial speech is subject to proper time, place and manner restrictions. [p 44]
5.  True     When a government classification is based on a suspect class, it is subject to the strict scrutiny test. [p 51]
6.  False    Substantive due process requires that the government laws, ordinances and regulations must be clear on their face and not overly broad in scope. It is procedural due process that requires the government give a person proper notice and a hearing before that person is deprived of his or her life, liberty or property. [p 51-52]
7.  False    The Free Exercise Clause prohibits the government from interfering with the free exercise of religion in the United States. This clause prevents the government from enacting laws that either prohibit or inhibit individuals from participating in or practicing their chosen religion. The Establishment Clause of the First Amendment bars the government from establishing a state religion or promoting one religion over another. [p 48, 50]
8.  True     Seventeen other amendments have been added to the U.S. Constitution in addition to the Bill of Rights. [p 42]
9.  True     Businesses may be regulated under a state's police power. [p 41]
10. False    Speech, not conduct, is protected by the First Amendment. [p 43]
11. False    Police powers are those powers retained by the states to regulate public health, safety, morals, and general welfare. Enumerated powers are those powers delegated to the federal government by the states. [p 30, 41]
12. True     Checks and balances are built into the U.S. Constitution to prevent one branch of the government from becoming too powerful. [p 32]
13. False    The state governments gave to the federal government the right to make treaties with the Indian nations. [p 33-34]
14. False    Traditionally, the federal government can only regulate commerce that actually moves in interstate commerce under the Commerce Clause of the U.S. Constitution. However, the modern rule allows the government to regulate commerce that affects interstate commerce. [p 38]
15. True     The first ten Amendments to the U.S. Constitution are known as the Bill of Rights. [p 42]

## Multiple Choice

16. C    Answer C is correct, as the states delegated powers to the federal government when they ratified the Constitution thereby calling them enumerated powers. Answer A is incorrect, as this refers to the legislative branch of the government. Answer B is incorrect, as it does not make any sense. Answer D is incorrect for the reasons given above. [p 30]
17. B    Answer B is correct, as the Commerce Clause has a greater impact on business than any other clause in the Constitution. Answer A is incorrect, as Congress has the authority to regulate commerce with foreign nations under the Commerce Clause. Answer C is incorrect, as Congress regulates commerce with the Indian tribes, not the state. Answer D is incorrect, as the Constitution is the supreme law of the land. [p 33]
18. C    Answer C is correct, as the question provides the definition of the preemption doctrine. Answer A is incorrect, as the Supremacy Clause provides that federal regulations, federal laws, treaties

25

and the federal Constitution are the supreme law of the land. Answer B is incorrect, as the regulation of interstate commerce is only one aspect of permissible regulation under federal law and does not embody an entire concept of priority over various types of state laws. Answer D is incorrect for the reasons given above. [p 32]

19. B  Answer B is correct, as intrastate commerce is commerce that moves within a state. Answer A is incorrect, as this refers to interstate commerce. Answer C is incorrect, as it combines the concepts of interstate and intrastate commerce. Answer D is incorrect, as it is an incorrect statement of law. [p 38]

20. B  Answer B is correct, as offensive speech is subject to time, place and manner restrictions. Answer A is incorrect, as it makes no sense. Answer C is incorrect, as speech inciting overthrow of the government is an example speech that is not protected under the First Amendment. [p 44]

21. A  Answer C is correct, as it correctly states the test on whether due process has been met. For this reason answers A, B and D are all incorrect, as they have nothing to do with whether a reasonable person could understand the law and comply with it. [p 52]

22. C  Answer C is correct, as this is the main premise of the Privileges and Immunities Clause. Answer A is incorrect, as the Privileges and Immunities Clause encourages nationalism and favor states giving other states the same privileges as its own residents enjoy and benefit from. Answer B is incorrect, as it would unduly discriminate in favor of the states own residents owning property, which would defeat the concept of nationalism. Answer D is incorrect, as the Privileges and Immunities Clause is not applicable to regulation of interstate commerce. [p 52]

23. C  Answer C is correct, as this correctly states the federal government's power to regulate foreign commerce. Answers A, B, and D are incorrect statements of the type of power given to the federal government in regulating foreign commerce. [p 36]

24. B  Answer B is correct, as this correctly states the interpretation of the power of the federal government to regulate interstate commerce. Answer A is incorrect, as this statement is exactly opposite as the correct statement. Answer C and D are incorrect, as they are stating incorrect interpretations of intrastate commerce, rather than interstate commerce. [p 38]

25. A  Answer A is correct, as this correctly states the categories of speech and the levels of protection outlined by the U.S. Supreme Court. Answers B, C, and D are incorrect, as they do not correctly state these categories and protections. [p 43-47]

## Short Answers

26. that no person shall be deprived of "life, liberty, or property" without due process of the law. [p 51]
27. federal government action. [p 51]
28. To protected classes other than race. [p 51]
29. That they not be overly broad in scope and that they be clear on their face. [p 51]
30. In reviewing Equal Protection cases that do not involve a suspect or protected class. [p 51]
31. time, place and manner restrictions. [p 44]
32. from enacting laws that prohibit or inhibit individuals from adhering to their chosen religion. [p 50]
33. states from enacting laws that unduly discriminate in favor of their residents. [p 52]
34. must pay the owner for taking his or her property under eminent domain. [p 52]
35. dangerous, defamatory language, fighting words, child pornography, obscene speech, speech inciting the violent overthrow of the government [p 46]
36. The Commerce Clause. [p 33]
37. The federal government. [p 33-34]
38. The exclusive power to regulate commerce with foreign nations. [p 36]
39. Interstate commerce involves instrumentalities of trade moving across state borders and, intrastate commerce is commerce moving within the state [p 39]
40. Police power is the power retained by the states to regulate public health, safety, morals, and general welfare. [p 41]

# *Chapter 3*

# COURT SYSTEMS AND JURISDICTION

## Chapter Overview

The United States has two major court systems, the federal court system and the court systems of the states and the District of Columbia. There are basic requirements, such as standing to sue, that must be met before a plaintiff can file a court case. There are additional requirements, such as jurisdiction and venue, which must be met before a specific court can hear a case. At the Supreme Court level, some decisions must be followed by all lower courts, whereas a few decisions will not have this effect. Certain contract clauses can specify the court in which a case will be heard and the law which will be applied to the case. This chapter outlines the federal and state court systems and addresses the requirements of jurisdiction, venue, and standing to sue. It distinguishes between different types of Supreme Court decisions and shows how parties can specify which court and what law will be used in contract disputes.

## Objectives

After completing the exercises that follow, you should be able to:

1. Compare the state court systems and the federal court system.
2. Recognize jurisdictional issues and their application to state and federal court.
3. Explain the concepts of standing to sue and venue.
4. Define the various types of decisions given by the Supreme Court and explain the future ramifications of each.
5. Distinguish between forum-selection clauses and choice-of-law clauses.

## Practical Application

You should be able to define when a party has standing to sue and where venue should rest. You should be able to recognize which is the proper court and system to hear particular cases using the different types of jurisdiction under which courts are empowered to hear cases. You should be able to understand the various types of decisions given by the Supreme Court and the future effects of each. You should be able to distinguish the difference between a forum-selection clause and a choice-of-law clause and how each is used in contracts.

## Helpful Hints

You should diagram the state and federal court systems, branching each of the various courts off of the applicable state or federal court system. You should place two to four main points next to each type of court. For example, if you are working on the state court systems, in particular the limited-jurisdiction trial court, you may want to note that they are sometimes called inferior trial courts, hear matters that are specialized and list some of the examples of the types of cases that are heard in this type of court. As you proceed in this manner, you will create a flow chart of the courts that will be easy to visualize when determining the answers to text and real life situations. Review this chapter's Study Tips, complete the Refresh Your Memory exercise and the Critical Thought Exercise, and work through the Sample Quiz.

# Study Tips

## State Court Systems

Every state, as well as the District of Columbia, has a state court system. The majority of states have at least four types of courts.

**Limited -Jurisdiction Trial Court.** These trial courts, also called inferior trial courts, in most cases can hear specialized cases such as those involving family law, probate, traffic matters, juvenile issues, misdemeanors, and civil cases that do not exceed a set dollar amount.
- A party may introduce evidence and solicit testimony.
- If the case does not result in a favorable outcome for one of the parties to the lawsuit, that party may appeal his/her case to an appellate court or a general-jurisdiction court.
- Many states also have a small claims court
    - A party, on his/her own behalf, brings a civil case worth a small dollar amount.
    - If a party in a small claims case loses, then that party may also appeal to the general-jurisdiction trial court or an appellate court.

**General-Jurisdiction Trial Court.** A general-jurisdiction trial court can be found in every state. This court hears felonies, cases above a certain dollar amount and cases not heard by the inferior trial courts.
- These courts are called courts of records because the trial testimony and evidence is preserved.
- A party may introduce evidence and solicit testimony.
- If the case does not result in a favorable outcome for one of the parties to the lawsuit, that party may appeal his/her case to an intermediate appellate court or the state supreme court.

**Intermediate Appellate Court.** This court hears appeals from trial courts and decides if the trial court erred thereby justifying a reversal or modification of the decision.
- The entire trial court record or just the important parts of the record may be reviewed.
- A party may not introduce new evidence or testimony.
- The decision of this appellate court may be appealed to the highest state court.

**Highest State Court.** The majority of states have a supreme court, which is the highest court in the state court system. The job of a state supreme court is to hear appeals from the intermediate appellate court.
- No new evidence or testimony is allowed.
- Once this court has made its decision, it becomes final.
    - However, if there is a question of law that is appealable, then the decision of the state supreme court might be granted review by the U.S. Supreme Court.

## Federal Court System

Article III of the U.S. Constitution states the judicial power of the federal government lies with the Supreme Court. In addition to this judicial power, Congress was allowed to establish inferior or special courts that include the U.S. District Court and the U.S. Courts of Appeal.

**Special Federal Courts.** These courts hear limited types of cases such as those involving federal tax laws, law suits against the United States, international commercial disputes, cases involving bankruptcy, and appeals from members of the armed services and decisions by the Department of Veterans Affairs.

**U.S. District Courts.** These courts are the federal system's general jurisdiction courts, empowered to impanel juries, receive evidence, hear testimony, and decide cases.
- There is at least one federal district court in each state and the District of Columbia.
- The geographical area served by each court is called a district.

**U.S. Courts of Appeal.** These courts are the intermediate appellate courts of the federal court system. The U.S. Courts of Appeals hear appeals from the cases already heard by the U.S. District Courts.
- The geographical area served by each court is called a circuit.
- There are thirteen circuits in the federal court system.
- As with the state court systems, no new evidence or testimony may be introduced by a party.

*Court of Appeals for the Federal Circuit.* Even though this is a United States Appellate Court, its jurisdiction is special as it is able to review the decisions made in the Patent and Trademark Office, the Court of International Trade and the Claims Court.

## United States Supreme Court

This highest court of our land is made up of nine nominated justices. It is administered by a chief justice, appointed by the president, and includes eight associate justices.

**Jurisdiction of the U.S. Supreme Court.** This court hears cases from the federal circuit courts of appeals, from some federal district and special federal courts, as well as from the highest state courts.
- No new evidence or testimony may be introduced at this level.
- The Court's decision is final.

**Decisions by the U.S. Supreme Court.** Except in rare cases that require mandatory review, the Supreme Court has discretion to decide which cases it will hear.
- A petition for certiorari must be made to the Supreme Court if a petitioner wants his/her case reviewed.
- If the court decides to review the case, then a writ of certiorari is issued, provided there is a constitutional or other important issue involved in the case.

*Unanimous Opinion.* This type of decision requires that all of the justices hearing the case agree on the outcome and reasoning of the decision.
- Unanimous decisions are precedent for later cases.

*Majority Opinion.* This type of decision requires that the majority of justices hearing the case agree on the outcome and reasoning of the decision.
- A majority decision becomes precedent for later cases and has the same force of law as a unanimous decision.

*Plurality Opinion.* This type of decision requires that a majority of the justices hearing the case agree on the outcome of the case, but not the reasoning for the decision.
- A plurality decision settles the case but is not precedent for later cases.

*Tie Vote.* This type of decision can happen when the Court sits without all nine justices.
- A tie vote affirms the decision of the lower court, but is not precedent for later cases.

*Concurring Opinion.* This type of opinion occurs when a justice chooses to write a separate opinion that agrees with the outcome of the Court decision, but sets out an alternative reasoning for that decision.

*Dissenting Opinion.* This type of opinion occurs when a justice chooses to write a separate opinion that sets out the reasoning for not agreeing with the Court decision.

## Jurisdiction of Federal and State Courts

Article III of the U.S. Constitution specifies the jurisdiction of federal courts, which have limited jurisdiction to hear cases involving a federal question or cases based on diversity of citizenship.

**Federal Question.** A case involving a federal question deals with treaties, federal statutes and the U.S. Constitution.
- There need not be a set dollar amount to bring this type of case.

**Diversity of Citizenships.** Federal diversity of citizenship jurisdiction was intended to prevent state court bias against nonresidents.
- Cases must involve one of three situations:
  o Be between citizens of different states or
  o Be between a citizen of a foreign country and a citizen of a state or
  o Be between a citizen of a state and a foreign country, with the foreign country acting as the plaintiff in a law suit.
- A corporation is a citizen of the state in which it is incorporated and in which it has its principal place of business.
- These types of cases require that the controversy exceed $75,000.00.
  o If the dollar amount isn't met, then the appropriate state court must hear the case.

**Exclusive Jurisdiction.** In cases involving federal crimes, antitrust, bankruptcy, patent and copyright cases, suits against the U.S., and most admiralty cases, the Federal courts have exclusive jurisdiction.

**Jurisdiction of State Courts**. State courts hear cases that federal courts do not have jurisdiction to hear. These cases involve state law, such as real estate law, corporate law, partnership law, limited liability company law, contract law, sales and lease contracts, negotiable instruments, and other non-federal question matters that do not involve diversity of citizenship.

*Concurrent Jurisdiction.* States share jurisdiction with federal courts in cases involving diversity of citizenship and federal questions which are not under exclusive federal jurisdiction.
- Such a case brought by a plaintiff in federal court will remain in federal court.
- Such a case brought in a state court can be moved to the federal court if the defendant chooses.

## Personal Jurisdiction of Courts

In order to bring a lawsuit, a person must have a stake in the outcome of the lawsuit, the court must have personal jurisdiction over the case, and the court must be the proper venue for the case.

**Standing to Sue.** The plaintiff must have some stake in the outcome of the lawsuit.
- Hypothetical questions will not be heard.

*In Personam* **Jurisdiction**. A court must have personal jurisdiction over both the plaintiff and defendant in a lawsuit.
- The plaintiff gives the court jurisdiction when the lawsuit is filed.
- The court acquires jurisdiction over a defendant by serving a summons within state boundaries.

- A court has jurisdiction over a corporation in the state in which it is incorporated, has its principal office, and is doing business.

*In Rem* **Jurisdiction**. A court can have jurisdiction over property that is the subject of the lawsuit because that property is located within the jurisdiction of the court.

**Long-arm Statutes**. These statutes extend jurisdiction to nonresidents who have had some minimum contact with the state.
- The nonresident has committed torts within the state.
- The nonresident has entered into a contract in the state or that affects the state.
- The nonresident has transacted business in the state that caused injury.

**Venue.** Lawsuits must be heard by the court with jurisdiction that is closest to where the incident happened or where the parties live.

**Forum-Selection and Choice-of-Law Clauses.** Parties to a contract can agree as to which courts will hear a lawsuit and what law will be used in the lawsuit.
- In Forum-Selection Clauses, parties to a contract specify the state, federal, or nation's court that will have jurisdiction if there is a dispute related to the contract.
- In Choice-of-Law Clauses, parties to a contract specify which state's or country's law will be applied in resolving any dispute related to the contract.

# Refresh Your Memory

The following exercises will help to test your memory regarding the principles given in this chapter. Read each question twice, then place your answer in the blank provided for each question. Review the chapter material for any questions you are unable to answer or remember.

1. The two major _____ systems in the United States are the federal _____ system and the _____ systems of the 50 states and the District of Columbia.

2. State limited-jurisdiction trial courts are also known as _____ trial courts.

3. Trial courts allow _____ to be introduced and _____ to be given.

4. State general-jurisdiction courts are often referred to as _____ _____ _____.

5. State _____-jurisdiction trial courts hear cases that are not within the jurisdiction of state _____-jurisdiction trial courts, such as felonies and civil cases over a certain dollar amount.

6. _____ _____ courts hear civil cases involving small dollar amounts.

7. _____ courts review the _____ court record to determine any trial errors that would mandate reversal or modification of the trial court decision.

8. The Court of _____ for the Federal _____ has special appellate jurisdiction to review cases involving Claims Court decisions, Patent and Trademark Office decisions, and Court of International Trade decisions.

9.  Name four types of special federal courts that have limited jurisdiction: _____, _____, _____, _____.

10. The geographical area served by a U.S. District Court is called a(n) _____ and the area served by a U.S. Court of Appeals is called a(n) _____.

11. The _____, appointed by the president, is responsible for the administration of the Supreme Court.

12. A(n) _____ decision of the Supreme Court requires that a majority of the justices agree as to the outcome and reasoning used to decide a case.

13. _____ cases are those arising under the U.S. Constitution, treaties, and federal statutes and regulations.

14. When a plaintiff has a stake in the outcome of a lawsuit, he or she has _____ _____.

15. When a plaintiff files a lawsuit with a court, he or she gives the court _____ _____ jurisdiction over him- or herself.

## Critical Thought Exercise

You are a District Manager of marketing for Intestine Smart, Inc., a California corporation, makers of Colon Grenade, a colon-cleansing drug. You have negotiated the sale of over 4 million dollars worth of this product from Prescript Co, another California corporation, which operates pharmacies under the names of Col On, Goodstuff Co. and Drugs 2 Go. These pharmacies are located primarily in California, but Prescript Co has now expanded into 22 states, including Utah.

Enticed by a Goodstuff ad in the Utah Free Press for Colon Grenade, Alice Thinstone bought the drug at Goodstuff Co. Within a week of using it, Thinstone suffered a ruptured colon. Alleging that the injury was caused by Colon Grenade, Thinstone sued Prescript Co and Intestine Smart in a Utah state court.

You have received a letter from the CEO of Intestine Smart, Ms. Sheila Snob, threatening to fire you and demanding to know why Intestine Smart is being subjected to a lawsuit in Utah, since she has never been informed of any sales of the product to companies outside of California.

Your assigned task is to draft a memo to your boss, Ms. Snob, and explain to her whether Intestine Smart must respond to the suit and defend against it in Utah. Explain the legal theory and the reasons for your opinion.

*Please compose your answer on a separate sheet of paper or on your computer.*

## Practice Quiz

### True/False

1. ____ A court of record is only allowed to review the trial court record to determine whether an error has been made at trial that would merit reversal or modification of the trial court's decision.

2. ____ Evidence, but not testimony can be introduced into an appellate court.

3. \_\_\_ The function of a state's highest court is to hear appeals from intermediate state courts and certain trial errors.

4. \_\_\_ Decisions of highest state courts can always be appealed to the US Supreme Court.

5. \_\_\_ The geographical area served by each federal district court is referred to as a circuit.

6. \_\_\_ The U.S. Supreme Court usually hears cases concerning major constitutional questions.

7. \_\_\_ A plurality opinion of the US Supreme Court decides a case, but is not precedent.

8. \_\_\_ There is a set dollar amount on federal question cases that can be brought in Federal Court.

9. \_\_\_ *Writs of certiorari,* issued by the US Supreme Court in deciding to review a case, are granted in all types of cases.

10. \_\_\_ Andy's friend, Wanda, is injured when a wrecking ball, controlled by Bart, is dropped on her. Wanda has standing to sue Bart.

11. \_\_\_ A court may not hear a case unless it has personal jurisdiction.

12. \_\_\_ Long arm statutes limit a state's jurisdiction to residents who have moved out of state.

13. \_\_\_ A forum-selection clause in a contract designates a certain court to hear any dispute concerning a breach of the contract.

14. \_\_\_ A change of jurisdiction will be granted if prejudice would occur because of pretrial publicity.

15. \_\_\_ If a plaintiff brings a case involving concurrent jurisdiction in state court, the defendant cannot have the case removed to federal court.

## Multiple Choice

16. State jurisdiction is limited to
    a. bankruptcy cases.
    b. small claims cases.
    c. matters not subject to federal jurisdiction.
    d. suits against the United States.

17. A party who disputes the jurisdiction of a court cannot
    a. enter a claim in the forum state's small claims court to recover expenses of the dispute.
    b. make a special appearance in that court to argue against the merits.
    c. appeal to the state supreme court and ask that the suit be dismissed.
    d. be served a complaint if he or she makes a special appearance in the court to argue against imposition of jurisdiction.

18. The U.S. District Courts
    a. are the federal court system's trial courts of general jurisdiction.
    b. serve a geographical area known as a district.

c. are empowered to impanel juries, receive evidence, hear testimony, and decide cases.

d. all of the above.

19. The U.S. Courts of Appeals

a. are the federal court system's trial courts of limited jurisdiction.

b. serve a geographical area known as a circuit.

c. are empowered to impanel juries, receive evidence, hear testimony, and decide cases.

d. all of the above.

20. A majority decision of the U.S. Supreme Court

a. becomes precedent for later cases.

b. settles the case, but is not precedent for later cases.

c. causes the lower court decision to be affirmed.

d. causes the lower court decision to be overturned.

21. Congress has given the U.S. Supreme Court discretion to decide the cases it will hear.

a. A petitioner must file a writ of certiorari asking the Court to hear the case. If the Court decides to review the case, it will issue a petition for certiorari.

b. A petitioner must file a petition for pleading asking the Court to hear the case. If the Court decides to review the case, it will issue a writ of pleading.

c. A petitioner must file a petition for certiorari asking the Court to hear the case. If the Court decides to review the case, it will issue a write of certiorari.

d. A petitioner must file a writ of pleading asking the Court to hear the case. If the Court decides to review the case, it will issue a petition for pleading.

22. A plurality decision of the U.S. Supreme Court requires that

a. all of the justices agree as to the outcome and reasoning used to decide a case.

b. a majority of the justices agree as to the outcome of the case but not as to the reasoning for the decision.

c. a majority of the justices agree as to the outcome and reasoning used to decide a case.

d. an equal number of justices agree and disagree as to the outcome of the case.

23. A case may be brought in federal court if there is diversity of citizenship, which occurs if a lawsuit involves

a. citizens of the same state or a citizen of a state and a citizen or subject of a foreign country.

b. citizens of the same state or citizens of different states.

c. citizens of different states or a citizen of a state and a citizen or subject of a foreign country.

d. citizens of different states or a citizens of different foreign countries.

24. A concurring opinion occurs when

a. a justice agrees with the outcome of a case but not the reasoning and issues an opinion setting forth his or her reasoning.

b. a justice does not agree with the outcome of a case and issues an opinion setting forth his or her reasons for disagreement.

c. a majority of the justices agree as to the outcome and reasoning used to decide a case.

d. a majority of the justices agree as to the outcome of the case but not as to the reasoning for the decision.

25. States share jurisdiction with federal courts in cases involving diversity of citizenship and federal questions which are not under exclusive federal jurisdiction.

a. Such a case brought by a plaintiff in federal court will remain in federal court.

b. Such a case brought in a state court can be moved to the federal court if the defendant chooses to do so

c. Both a and b.

d. None of the above.

## Short Answer

26. Kerry is injured when Joe fails to stop at a pedestrian crossing while Kerry is crossing the street in downtown Chicago, Illinois. Joe immediately returns to his home of St. Louis, Missouri. Kerry, having incurred more than $100,000 in damages. Under what theory can Kerry choose to sue Joe in a federal court?

_____

27. To what does *in rem* jurisdiction refer?

_____

28. Kerry is injured when Joe fails to stop at a pedestrian crossing while Kerry is crossing the street. Jane, a good friend of Kerry, is very upset and wants to sue Joe for Kerry's injuries. What will preclude Jane from suing Joe?

_____

29. To what does a concurring opinion refer?

_____

_____

30. Under concurrent jurisdiction, if a case does not qualify to be brought in federal court

_____

31. What does a choice-of-law clause in a contract designate?

_____

32. Kerry is injured when Joe fails to stop at a pedestrian crossing while Kerry is crossing the street in downtown Chicago, Illinois. Joe immediately returns to his home of St. Louis, Missouri. Kerry wishes to sue Joe in Illinois. What tool can the Illinois courts use to extend the state's jurisdiction to Joe?

_____

33. Simone won her case at the federal Court of Appeal, but her opponent has appealed the case to the U.S. Supreme Court, which has granted *certiari*. One of the justices for the U.S. Supreme Court dies suddenly, so only eight justices hear Simone's case. Four justices vote for Simone's cause and four justices vote against Simone. What will be the effect of this tie vote?

_____

34. What does a forum selection clause in a contract designate?

_____

35. Kerry is injured when Joe fails to stop at a pedestrian crossing while Kerry is crossing the street in downtown Chicago, Illinois. Joe immediately returns to his home of St. Louis, Missouri. Kerry,

having incurred more than $100,000 in damages, sues Joe in a state court. Under what theory can Joe choose to have the case removed to a federal court?

_____

36.    Why are general-jurisdiction courts often referred to as courts of record?

_____

37.    What type of court is the U.S. Court of Federal Claims?

_____

38.    Under what circumstances can a party make a special appearance in a court?

_____

39.    Under what circumstances may a change of venue be granted?

_____

_____

40.    What is the name of the recently created 13th Court of Appeals which has jurisdiction to review decisions of the Court of Federal Claims, the Patent and Trademark Office, and the Court of International Trade?

_____

## Answers to Refresh Your Memory

1.    court, court, court  [p 59]
2.    inferior  [p 59]
3.    evidence, testimony  [p 59]
4.    courts of record  [p 59]
5.    general, limited  [p 59]
6.    small claims  [p 59]
7.    Appellate, trial  [p 60]
8.    Appeals, Circuit  [p 64]
9.    Name four of the following: U.S. Tax Court, U.S. Court of Federal Claims, U.S. Court of International Trade, U.S. Bankruptcy Court, U.S. Court of Appeals for the Armed Services, U.S. Court of Appeals for Veterans Claims  [p 63]
10.    district, circuit  [p 64]
11.    chief justice  [p 65]
12.    majority  [p 68]
13.    Federal Question  [p 69]
14.    standing to sue  [p 70]
15.    *in personam* (or personal)  [p 71]

## Model Answer to Critical Thought Exercise

To:       Ms. Snob
From:    Student, District Manager, Intestine Smart Inc.
Re:       Response to Lawsuit in Utah State Court

This is a question involving jurisdiction, which is the authority of a court to hear a case. There are two pertinent types of jurisdiction: 1) *In personam* jurisdiction, whereby the court has jurisdiction over the parties to a lawsuit; and 2) *In rem* jurisdiction, whereby the court has jurisdiction to hear a case because of jurisdiction over the property involved in the lawsuit.

Even though we were never informed of any sales of Colon Grenade outside of the state of California, we may be required to respond to the suit and defend against it in Utah based on the following reasons:

1) Even though our company wasn't physically located in Utah when Alice Thinstone suffered a ruptured colon, she may apply the principles surrounding the theory set forth in *International Shoe Co. v. Washington,* 326 U.S. 310, wherein the court said that "the Due Process Clause permits jurisdiction over a defendant in any state in which the defendant has 'certain minimum contacts' such that the maintenance of the suit does not offend traditional notions of fair play and substantial justice." Arguably, by selling our product to Prescript Co., which operates in 22 states, including Utah, we are receiving the benefit of increased sales, albeit indirectly, from Utah resident Alice Thinstone. Further, as was expressed in the court's ruling in *Calder v. Jones*, 465 U.S. 783, 104 S.Ct. 1482, 79 L.Ed.2d 804 (1984), Intestine Smart should "reasonably anticipate being hauled into court" in Utah as it is reasonably foreseeable that Colon Grenade would be sold in different states given the fact that Prescript Co. operates in 22 states, with Utah being one of them. If it is found that Intestine Smart, Inc. had sufficient minimum contacts with the forum State of Utah and that the sale of its product there afforded Intestine Smart the benefits of the laws of the forum state, then we will be required to defend ourselves in a suit in Utah state court.

2) It may be argued that we assumed the risk that our product would be sold to an out-of-state resident as we knowingly and voluntarily negotiated the sale of the Colon Grenade product with Prescript Co., a business operating in several states. Also, we should not be allowed to reap only the benefits of profit from our sales and shirk our corporate ethical responsibility to not harm those to whom our product is sold.

In conclusion, it would be in our best interest to respond to the lawsuit filed against us. If we are able to show that there was some other intervening act (such as improper use of Colon Grenade by Ms. Thinstone, some other medical condition that could have had the same result, etc.) responsible for Ms. Thinstone's ruptured colon and that Colon Grenade in no way caused her injury, we may be successful in defending against the suit. We could really secure a feather in our cap if we could demonstrate that, despite an alleged forseeability of the injury alleged, the use of Colon Grenade could not have possibly caused the result complained of by Ms. Thinstone. *(Note: A higher degree of understanding is demonstrated by a student who incorporates the reasoning given in this paragraph, as this material is not addressed until later in the text.)*

# Answers to Practice Quiz

## True/False

1. False    An appellate court is only allowed to review the trial court record to determine whether an error has been made at trial that would merit reversal or modification of the trial court's decision. A court of record is a trial court that accepts the evidence and testimony necessary to make the trial court record. [p 59-60]

2.  False    Neither evidence nor testimony can be introduced into an appellate court, which only reviews the record of the trial court to determine whether an error has been made at trial that would merit reversal or modification of the trial court's decision. [p 60]

3.  True     The function of a state's highest court is to hear appeals from intermediate state courts and certain trial errors. [p 60]

4.  False    Decisions of highest state courts are final unless a question of law is involved that is appealable to the US Supreme Court. [p 60]

5.  False    The geographical area served by each federal district court is referred to as a district. [p 64]

6.  True     The U.S. Supreme Court hears appeals from federal circuit courts of appeals and, under certain circumstances, from deferral district courts, special federal courts, and the highest state courts. It is the supreme law of the land, responsible for evaluating the constitutionality of legislation and is the final authority concerning major constitutional questions. [p 67]

7.  True     A plurality opinion of the US Supreme Court decides a case but is not precedent. [p 67]

8.  True     The dollar amount of the controversy must exceed $75,000. [p 69]

9.  False    *Writs* are granted only in cases involving constitutional and other important issues. [p 67]

10. True     Since Wanda has an interest in the result of the case, as she was the injured one, she does have standing to sue. [p 70]

11. True     A court may not hear a case unless it has personal jurisdiction. [p 70-71]

12. False    Long arm statutes extend a state's jurisdiction to nonresidents who were not served a summons within a state. [p 72-73]

13. True     A forum-selection clause in a contract designates a certain court to hear any dispute concerning a breach of the contract. [p 73]

14. False    A change of venue will be granted if pretrial publicity would cause prejudice. [p 73]

15. False    If a plaintiff brings a case involving concurrent jurisdiction in state court, the defendant can let the case be decided by the state court or have the case removed to federal court. [p 70]

## Multiple Choice

16. C    Bankruptcy, antitrust cases and suits against the United States are matters over which the federal courts have exclusive jurisdiction. Answer C is correct because states have exclusive jurisdiction over matters not subject to federal jurisdiction. [p 70]

17. B    A party may make a special appearance to dispute jurisdiction and service of process may not take place during this appearance. Answer A makes no sense, as a party who suffers expenses of a lawsuit would ask for the appropriate remedy in his/her prayer for relief of his/her complaint. Further, expenses to the lawsuit may or may not be allowed depending upon the cause(s) of action being brought. Answer C is incorrect as the function of the state supreme court is to hear appeals from intermediate state courts. The facts do not indicate that the issue of jurisdiction was one that had been tried and that a judgment against the party had been made at an intermediate court level. Answer D is incorrect, as a party may not be served with a complaint in court when the purpose of the party being in court is to dispute jurisdiction. [p 71]

18. D    All of the answers are correct. [p 64]

19. B    The U.S. Courts of Appeals serve a geographical area known as a circuit. A is incorrect because these courts are the federal system's intermediate appellate courts. C is incorrect because, as appeals courts, the courts are only allowed to review the trial court record to determine whether an error has been made at trial that would merit reversal or modification of the trial court's decision. D is incorrect because only B is correct. [p 64]

20. A    A majority decision of the US Supreme Court becomes precedent for later cases. B is incorrect

because a plurality decision settles the case, but is not precedent for later cases. C is incorrect because a tie decision causes the lower court decision to be affirmed. D is incorrect because only unanimous or majority decisions can become precedent for later cases. [p 68]

21.    C    Answer C is correct, as a petitioner must file a petition for certiorari asking the Court to hear the case. If the Court decides to review the case, it will issue a write of certiorari. Answer A is incorrect, as it is opposite of the correct answer. Answers B and D are incorrect, as a petition for and writ of pleading do not exist. [p 67]

22.    B    Answer B is correct, as a plurality decision is where a majority of the justices agree on the outcome, but not on the reasoning for the decision. Answer A is incorrect, as a unanimous decision is where all of the justices agree on the outcome and reasoning used to decide a case. Answer C is incorrect, as a majority decision is where a majority of the justices agree on the outcome and reasoning used to decide a case. Answer D is incorrect, as a tie decision is where an equal number of justices agree and disagree on the outcome of the case. [p 68]

23.    C    Answer C is correct, as diversity of citizenship requires that the parties be citizens of different states or a citizen of a state and a citizen or subject of a foreign country. Answers A, B, and D are incorrect, as they do not correctly define diversity of citizenship. [p 69]

24.    A    Answer A is correct, as a concurring opinion occurs when a justice agrees with the outcome of a case but not the reasoning and issues an opinion setting forth his or her reasoning. Answer B is incorrect, as a dissenting opinion occurs when a justice does not agree with the outcome of a case and issues an opinion setting forth his or her reasons for disagreement. Answer C is incorrect, as a majority decision is where a majority of the justices agree as to the outcome and reasoning used to decide a case. Answer D is incorrect, as a plurality decision is where a majority of the justices agree as to the outcome of the case but not as to the reasoning for the decision. [p 68]

25.    C    Answer C is correct, as both A and B are correct statements of what can happen a case that is subject to concurrent jurisdiction by federal and state courts. Answers A and B are incorrect, as both answers are correct. Answer D is incorrect, as both A and B are correct. [p 70]

## Short Answer

26. Diversity of citizenship [p 69-70]
27. *In rem* jurisdiction refers to a court's jurisdiction over the thing [p 72]
28. Jane lacks standing to sue. [p 70]
29. A concurring opinion refers to a judicial opinion that allows a justice who agrees with the outcome of a case, but not the reason, to set out his/her reasons for deciding the case. [p 68]
30. it must be brought in the appropriate state court. [p 70]
31. What state's law or country's law will apply in resolving a dispute. [p 73]
32. The state's long-arm statute. [p 72-73]
33. that Simone remains the winner because she won at the Court of Appeals, but the decision does not set precedent for later cases. [p 68]
34. Which court will hear any dispute concerning nonperformance of the contract. [p 73]
35. Diversity of citizenship [p 69]
36. These courts record and store testimony and evidence for future reference. [p 59]
37. It is a special federal court. [p 63]
38. A party who disputes the jurisdiction of a court can make a special appearance in that court to argue against imposition of jurisdiction. [p 71]
39. When there has been substantial pretrial publicity that may prejudice jurors located in the proper venue, a change of venue may be requested so that a more impartial jury can be found. [p 73]
40. Court of Appeals for the Federal Circuit [p 64]

# Chapter 4

# JUDICIAL, ADMINISTRATIVE, ALTERNATIVE, AND ONLINE DISPUTE RESOLUTION

## Chapter Overview

Litigation is the bringing, maintaining, and defending of a lawsuit which involves complex rules that make the process difficult, time-consuming, and expensive. In an effort to cut costs, alternative dispute resolution has been developed to resolve commercial disputes. Federal and state legislative and executive branches of government have formed administrative agencies to help with imposing laws that regulate business. Operations of these agencies are governed by administrative law. This chapter examines the judicial litigation process, introduces alternative dispute resolution, and defines administrative law.

## Objectives

After completing the exercises that follow, you should be able to:

1. Consider various factors in conducting a cost-benefit analysis for bringing or defending a lawsuit.
2. Understand the pre-trial litigation process.
3. Comprehend the stages of a trial.
4. Discuss the process for the appeal of a trial court decision.
5. Be aware of nonjudicial alternatives for settling disputes.
6. Explain the functions of administrative agencies and the definition of administrative law.

## Practical Application

You should have a broader understanding of the pre-trial litigation process and its various procedural requirements. You should be able to discuss the sequence of events in a trial and be aware of available nonjudicial alternatives. You should be able to explain the appeals process. You should be able to evaluate the costs and benefits of bringing and defending a lawsuit. You should be able to define the functions of administrative agencies and administrative law.

## Helpful Hints

This chapter is easily organized for review. Diagram the pretrial litigation process, branching the flow chart where there are multiple alternative steps or decisions, and giving a short explanation of each step. For the primary process and the cross-complaint, diagram two separate but related flow charts proceeding simultaneously. Diagram the appeal process in a similar manner. For the different types of alternative dispute resolution, place this information into a table that allows specification of the main features of each type in one column, notation of how each type is distinguished from the other types in a separate column, and commentary on the best use of each type in another column.

# Study Tips

## Pretrial Litigation Process

The litigation process, or litigation, is the bringing, maintaining, and defending of a lawsuit, which has four major phases: pleadings, discovery, dismissals and pretrial judgments, and settlement conference.

**Pleadings.** The documents filed with the court to commence and counter a lawsuit are the complaint, answer, the cross-complaint, and the reply.

*Complaint and Summons.* A plaintiff begins a lawsuit by filing a complaint with the appropriate court which names the parties, alleges the facts and the violation of law, and requests a remedy from the court.
- The court will issue a summons, directing defendant to appear in court and answer the complaint.

*Answer.* A defendant files an answer with the court that admits or denies the allegations in the complaint.
- The case proceeds when the defendant denies any of the allegations.
- If the defendant fails to answer the complaint, a default judgment is entered for any damages proven by the plaintiff.
- The answer can state affirmative defenses to the allegations in the complaint.

*Cross-complaint and Reply.* The defendant can also file a cross-complaint against the plaintiff if there has been alleged injury done by the plaintiff to the defendant.
- The plaintiff must file a reply to the cross-complaint with the court which admits or denies the allegations of the cross-complaint.
- The reply can include affirmative defenses.

*Intervention and Consolidation.* Others with an interest may intervene and become parties to the lawsuit.
- The court can consolidate the cases of several plaintiffs stemming from the same circumstances into one case, if doing so will not cause undue prejudice to the parties.

*E-filings.* Many courts have e-filing of pleadings, briefs, and other documents related to lawsuits.
- This process uses CD-ROMs for briefs, scanning evidence and documents for storage and retrieval, and e-mailing correspondence and documents to the court and opposing counsel.
- Conferences are held via telephone conferences and e-mail.

**Statute of Limitations.** These statutes establish the period during which a plaintiff must bring a lawsuit.
- The plaintiff loses the right to sue if the lawsuit is not filed within this time.

**Discovery.** During discovery, each party works to discover facts of the case from the other party and witnesses before the trial.
- This process prevents surprise at trial and allows thorough preparation for trial by the parties, preserves the evidence, saves court time, and promotes the settlement of cases prior to trial.

*Deposition.* This is the verbal testimony given under oath by a party or witness before the trial.
- This type of discovery is used to preserve evidence and impeach testimony of witnesses at trial.

*Interrogatories.* These are written questions given by one party to another party in a lawsuit.
- These questions must be answer within a specified time and the answers signed under oath.

*Production of Documents.* One party may request that the other party to the lawsuit produce all documents relevant to the case before trial.

- The requesting party may be required to examine the documents at the other party's premises.

*Physical and Mental Examination.* A court can compel a party to submit to physical or mental exams.

**Dismissals and Pretrial Judgments.** Parties to a lawsuit can make several pretrial motions to dispose of all or part of a lawsuit before trial.

*Motion for Judgment on the Pleadings.* This motion is made by either party once pleadings are complete.
- It alleges that if all facts presented are true, the party making the motion would win the lawsuit.
- The judge cannot consider any facts outside the pleadings.

*Motion for Summary Judgment.* This motion states that there are no factual disputes to be decided and that the judge should decide the case.
- It is supported by evidence outside the pleadings.

**Settlement Conference.** Most court rules allow the court to direct that a settlement conference or pretrial conference be conducted.
- If no settlement is reached, the hearing can identify major trial issues and other relevant factors.

*Cost-Benefit Analysis of a Lawsuit.* Decisions of whether or not to bring or defend a lawsuit should be approached like other business decisions, including a cost-benefit analysis.
- In most civil lawsuits, each party must pay its own attorneys' fees.
- In civil or criminal lawsuits, attorneys may represent clients on an hourly or project-fee basis.
- In civil lawsuits, plaintiffs' attorneys often work under a contingency fee arrangement, where the lawyer receives a percentage of the amount received after the case is won or settled.
- Lawyers for defendants are usually paid an hourly fee.
- Some factors that should be evaluated include the following: The probability of winning or losing and the amount to be won or lost, The costs and opportunity costs of litigation, The long-term effects, and The stress of the lawsuit

## Trial

The Seventh Amendment to the U.S. Constitution guarantees a right to a jury trial in a case in federal court. Most states have similar guarantees.
- Both parties can waive their right to a jury, in which case the judge will sit as the trier of fact.
- Each party usually submits a trial brief that states the legal support for its side of the case.

**Phases of a Trial.** A trial can last less than a day or many months. It is usually divided into stages.

*Jury Selection.* Individuals are selected, usually from voter or vehicle registrations, to hear specific cases through a process called *voir dire*.
- Prospective jurors are questioned to verify their open-mindedness; biased jurors can be excluded.
- After selection, jurors are impaneled and sworn in, and can be sequestered if necessary.

*Opening Statements.* Attorneys for each side are allowed to summarize the main issues of the case and the positions of their clients prior to the presentation of evidence and testimony.
- This statement is not considered to be evidence.

*The Plaintiff's Case.* The plaintiff has the burden of proof of the merits of his or her case and must present witnesses and evidence to that end.
- Witnesses are called by the plaintiff's attorney to give testimony.

- Documents can be introduced during this presentation.
- Once the defendant's attorney is allowed to cross-examine each witness, the plaintiff's attorney can ask additional questions under redirect examination.

*The Defendant's Case.* Once the plaintiff's case is done, the defendant presents a similar case:
- It must rebut the evidence given.
- Prove any affirmative defenses.
- Prove any cross-complaints made by the defendant.

*Rebuttal and Rejoinder.* Once the defendant's case is concluded, the plaintiff is allowed to call witnesses and present evidence to rebut the defendant's case.
- After this rebuttal is completed, the defendant is allowed to call witnesses and present evidence in rejoinder to counter the plaintiff's rebuttal.

*Closing Arguments.* Once evidence and testimony are concluded, each party's attorney makes a statement to the jury reiterating the strengths of their own case and the weaknesses of their opponent's case.
- This statement is not considered to be evidence.

*Jury Instructions.* After the completion of closing arguments, the judge reads the instructions to the jury regarding what law to apply when they decide the case.

*Jury Deliberation and Verdict.* After being given their instructions, the jury goes to the jury room to deliberate and, after deliberation of a few minutes to several weeks, reaches a verdict.

*Entry of Judgment.* Once the verdict is returned by the jury, the judge enters the judgment in the record.
- The court may overturn the verdict with a "judgment notwithstanding the verdict" if it finds bias or jury misconduct.
- The judge may reduce the damage award in civil cases under *"remittitur"* if he or she finds the jury to be biased, emotional, or inflamed.
- The trial court usually issues a written memorandum of its reasoning which, with the trial transcript and evidence introduced at trial, makes up the permanent record of the trial.

## Appeal

Either party in a civil case, or the defendant in a criminal case, can appeal the trial court's decision.
- A notice of appeal must be filed within a designated time period.
- Parties:
  - The appealing party is called the appellant or petitioner.
  - The responding party is called the appellee or respondent.
- The parties may decide to submit all or part of the trial record for review.
- An appellate court will reverse a lower court decision if there is an error of law in the record.
  - It will not reverse the lower court decision for a finding of fact unless such finding is unsupported by the evidence or is contradicted by the evidence.

## Alternative Dispute Resolution

Using the court system to resolve disputes is expensive and time-consuming, and causes disruption for businesses. Businesses have turned to methods of alternative dispute resolution (ADR), which include negotiation, arbitration, mediation, conciliation, minitrial, fact-finding, and a judicial referee.

**Negotiation.** The simplest form of ADR involves negotiation between the parties to allow them to come to a voluntary agreement to settle a dispute.

- The parties usually make offers and counteroffers to one another, and may provide information to the other side that would assist the other side in reaching an agreement.
- Negotiation can happen before or after a lawsuit is filed, or before other forms of ADR are tried.
- Many courts require parties to a lawsuit to conduct settlement discussions prior to trial.
- If a settlement agreement is reached, a settlement agreement is drafted, signed, and filed.

**Arbitration.** In arbitration, the parties choose an impartial third party to hear and decide the dispute.

- Many contracts have an arbitration clause that requires parties to decide a dispute via arbitration.
- The parties, if there is no arbitration clause, can choose to enter into a submission agreement where they agree to settle the dispute using arbitration.
- The Federal Arbitration Act promotes arbitration of disputes at the federal level, and about half the states have adopted the Uniform Arbitration Act, which promotes arbitration at state level.
- Many federal and state courts refer disputes to arbitration and other forms of ADR.

*Arbitration Providers.* Private organizations, or individuals who qualify to hear and decide certain disputes, usually provide ADR services.

- The American Arbitration Association is the largest provider of ADR services.

*Arbitration Procedure.* A description of specific procedures that must be followed in the event of a dispute between the parties is usually contained in an arbitration agreement, which may address such things as the notice that must be given and how an arbitrator will be chosen.

- When a dispute occurs, the parties usually agree on the date, time, and place of the arbitration.
- During arbitration, the parties call witnesses and introduce evidence to support their case, and refute the other party's case.
- Generally, rules similar to those used in federal courts will apply.

*Decision and Award.* At the end of the hearing, the arbitrator makes a decision and gives an award.

- If the parties agree to be bound by the arbitrator's decision and remedy, it is a binding arbitration and the decision cannot be appealed to the courts.
  - If a party does not adhere to the arbitrator's decision, the other party may sue in court to have the decision enforced.
- If the arbitration is not binding, the parties can appeal to the courts.
  - Courts give great credence to an arbitrator's decision and award.

**Mediation.** This is a form of negotiation in which a neutral third party, the mediator, aids the disputing parties in reaching a settlement, but does not make a decision or an award.

- The mediator is selected by the parties to act as an intermediary.
- The mediator usually meets with each party to discuss the case, transmit offers between the parties, and encourage settlement by pointing out strengths and weaknesses of each case.
- The mediator can propose a reasonable settlement of the case, but the parties are not required to accept this proposal.
- If a settlement is reached, an agreement is drafted and signed by the parties to end the dispute.

**Conciliation.** Conciliation is very similar to mediation in that the conciliator acts as an intermediary to the parties in dispute.

- The primary difference between a mediator and a conciliator is that a conciliator is often an interested party, rather than a neutral party.

- The conciliator transmits information between the parties and carries offers and counteroffers for settlement between the parties.
- The conciliator cannot make a decision or award.
- If the parties do reach a settlement, the agreement is drafted and executed by the parties.

**Minitrial.** This is a voluntary private proceeding where the lawyers for each side present a truncated case to the representatives of both sides, who have authority to settle the dispute.
- Often, the parties hire a neutral third party to preside over the minitrial and who is called upon to give an opinion as to how a court might decide the case.
- If the parties come to a settlement, an agreement is drafted and executed to end the dispute.
- Minitrials serve to show the strengths and weaknesses of each party as a real trial would, but are much less expensive and time-consuming for the parties.

**Fact-Finding.** Sometimes, the parties will employ a neutral third party to act as a fact-finder to investigate the dispute.
- This person is to investigate, gather and prepare evidence, and prepare reports of findings.
- A fact-finder does not have power to make a decision or award, but may recommend settlement.
- The parties may use the evidence and findings in negotiating a settlement of the dispute.

**Judicial Review.** A court, if the parties agree, may appoint a judicial referee to conduct a private trial and give a judgment.
- Referees have most powers of a trial judge and their decisions become a judgment of the court.
- Parties usually keep their right to appeal the decision.

# Administrative Law

Administrative agencies are created by governments; there are more than one-hundred administrative agencies at the federal level and thousands of other administrative agencies at the state and local levels.
- When Congress enacts a statute, it often creates an administrative agency to administer and enforce the statute, or gives this authority to an existing agency.

**Federal Administrative Agencies.** These agencies are created by the legislative or the executive branch of the federal government.
- Congress has established many federal administrative agencies which have broad regulatory powers, such as the Securities and Exchange Commission (SEC).
- The President also creates administrative agencies, such as the U.S. Department of Justice.

**State Administrative Agencies.** All states have created agencies, such as a corporation department, to enforce and interpret state law.
- Local governments and municipalities create agencies, such as zoning commissions.

**Government Regulation.** Administrative agencies regulate businesses and industries collectively.
- Some agencies regulate specific industries, such as the Federal Aviation Administration (FAA).

**Administrative Law.** Administrative law combines substantive and procedural law.
- An administrative agency enforces the law that has been created, or the substantive law.
- The agency must follow certain procedural laws to enforce these laws.

**Administrative Procedure Act.** This Act establishes administrative procedures that must be followed by federal administrative agencies in conducting their affairs.

- It gives notice and hearing requirements, rules for adjudication, and procedures for rule making.
- Most states have similar acts for state agencies.

**Administrative Law Judge.** Administrative Law Judges (ALJs) are employees of the agency who preside over administrative proceedings and decide questions of law and fact.
- In administrative proceedings, both the agency and the respondent may have attorneys.
- Witnesses may be examined and evidence introduced.
- The ALJs decision is called an order and must state the reasons for the decision.
- The order is final, unless appealed.

**Delegation of Powers.** Administrative agencies are delegated certain legislative, judicial, and executive powers on creation under the delegation doctrine. This combined power has been held as constitutional.
- An agency acting outside its specifically delegated powers has acted unconstitutionally.

*Rule Making.* This legislative power authorizes an administrative agency to make substantive rules, which are much like a statute.
- Violations invoke civil or criminal liability.
- Agencies can issue interpretive rules, and statements of policy.

*Licensing Power.* Those entering certain industries or professions are often required to obtain a license.
- Most administrative agencies have the power to grant or deny licenses.
    o It accepts applications, listens to comments from interested parties, and holds hearings.

*Judicial Power.* Many administrative agencies have the authority to adjudicate cases through administrative proceedings, which begin when the agency serves a complaint on someone believed to have violated a statute or rule.
- The agency must comply with the requirements of the Due Process Clause of the Constitution.
    o The respondent be given proper notice and an opportunity to present evidence.

*Executive Power.* Administrative agencies are often granted powers that allow them to investigate and prosecute violations of statutes and rules.
- Agencies can issue an administrative subpoena to obtain information not supplied voluntarily.
- The agency can seek judicial enforcement if the party does not comply with the subpoena.

**Judicial Review of Administrative Actions.** Administrative agencies are subject to judicial review.
- Where federal statutes do not expressly provide for this review, the Administrative Procedure Act authorizes judicial review of federal administrative agency actions through federal courts.
- Decisions of state administrative agencies can be appealed through the state courts.

# Refresh Your Memory

The following exercises will help to test your memory regarding the principles given in this chapter. Read each question twice, then place your answer in the blank provided for each question. Review the chapter material for any questions you are unable to answer or remember.

1.      The process of bringing, maintaining and defending a lawsuit is known as _____.

2.      To initiate a lawsuit, the plaintiff must file a(n) _____ and the defendant must then file a(n) _____ with the court.

3. A(n) _____ _____ _____ establishes the period during which a plaintiff must file a lawsuit.

4. During _____, the parties to a lawsuit work to uncover facts and witnesses before trial.

5. A(n) _____ is the oral testimony given by a party or witness prior to trial.

6. _____ are written questions submitted by one party to a lawsuit to another party, which must be answered under oath.

7. One party to a lawsuit may file a(n) _____ _____ _____ that requests that the other party produce all documents that are relevant to the case prior to trial.

8. A(n) _____ _____ _____ _____ asserts that there are no factual disputes to be decided by the jury, and that the judge should apply the relevant law to the undisputed facts and decide the case.

9. The primary purpose of a(n) _____ _____ is to facilitate settlement of a court case.

10. _____ is a form of alternative dispute resolution where the parties choose an impartial third party to hear and decide the dispute.

11. _____ is a form of alternative dispute resolution where the parties choose an impartial third party to facilitate the settlement of their dispute.

12. _____ is a form of alternative dispute resolution where the parties choose a third party, who may be an interested party, to facilitate the settlement of their dispute.

13. When Congress enacts a statute, it can choose to create or assign to an existing _____ _____ the task of administering and enforcing the statute.

14. The Securities and Exchange Commission is a(n) _____ _____ agency.

15. When an administrative agency is created, it is delegated certain _____, _____, and _____ powers.

# Critical Thought Exercise

You are the night manager at the Giddy-Up-N-Go, a convenience store in a small town in Oklahoma. Two weeks ago, one of your employees reported that there had been an incident on their shift where a customer had slipped and fallen when a large cup of coffee had been spilled near the cash register. The coffee had been spilled by the customer immediately ahead of the customer who had slipped and fallen. Since your employee was the only employee on duty at the time, she had finished the transaction for the customer, logged off of the cash register, and asked the remaining customer to wait while she went to the back of the store to retrieve a mop to clean up the spill and warned the customer to avoid the spill. When the employee returned, that customer was on the floor after slipping in the spilled coffee. Your employee offered to call an ambulance, but the customer declined and left the store to return to their car and drive away.

You have been called to a meeting with the owner, who has just received a letter from an attorney for Ms. Emma Payne, who is the customer who slipped and fell in your store. Ms. Payne is demanding that your store pay damages for the injuries she sustained when she slipped and fell in your store. She maintains that she has sustained back, neck, hip, knee, and ankle injuries as result of this accident with medical bills in the amount of $2,500. She states that she has missed work, incurring $2,240 in lost income. She asserts that she has been unable to care for her two children on her own and has incurred $1,600 in paying for unanticipated child care. She states that she has been unable to drive and has sustained $480 in hiring taxis to take her to necessary medical appointments. Additionally, she claims that there are other miscellaneous expenses related to her injuries, as well as the pain and suffering and inconvenience that cannot be quantified, that she believes to be compensable at $3,000. The total amount of damages she is demanding is $9,820.

The owner of the Giddy-Up-N-Go has asked that you review Ms. Payne's demands and advise him as to how you think he should proceed, since the incident happened on your watch. He has held a preliminary consultation with his attorney of one hour. His lawyer has estimated that an immediate settlement could be made for the amount requested for no additional fee on his part. A negotiated settlement could require 20 to 30 hours of his time. Taking the case to court could take 100 hours or more of his time in preparation and an additional 10 hours in court. His attorney charges $150 per hour, with a charge of $300 for court time.

Write a memo to the owner outlining how you think the owner should reply to Ms. Payne's demands and explaining your reasons for your advice.

*Please compose your answer on a separate sheet of paper or on your computer.*

# Practice Quiz

## True/False

1. ___ The bringing, maintaining, and defense of a lawsuit are generally referred to as the pleadings.

2. ___ Paperwork filed with the court to begin and respond to a lawsuit is referred to as the pleadings.

3. ___ Once a summons has been filed, the court issues a complaint.

4. ___ The affirmative defense is where the defendant admits or denies the allegations contained in the plaintiff's complaint.

5. ___ A deposition is oral testimony given by a party or witness before trial.

6. ___ Interrogatories are the legal process whereby the parties engage in activities to discover facts and witnesses before the trial.

7. ___ When one party requests that the other party produce all documents that are relevant to the case prior to trial, it is known as a production of documents.

8. ___ A judge who decides a motion for Judgment on the pleadings cannot consider any facts extraneous to the pleadings.

9. ___ One of the purposes of a pretrial hearing is to organize and address the issues of the case so that the trial will be professionally presented.

10. ___ The Fifth Amendment to the U.S. Constitution guarantees that a party to an action at law has the right to a jury trial in a case in federal court.

11. ___ The defendant bears the burden of proof to persuade the trier of fact on the merits of the case.

12. ___ Once the defendant's attorney has finished calling witnesses, the plaintiff's attorney can call witnesses and present evidence in rejoinder.

13. ___ A court may not overturn a verdict if mere bias is shown.

14. ___ In the appeal of the trial court's decision, the appealing party is called the appellee and the responding party is called the appellant.

15. ___ Many contracts, like labor union agreements and franchise agreements, include an arbitration clause that requires all disputes arising out of the contract to be submitted to arbitration.

## Multiple Choice

16. The bringing, maintaining, and defense of a lawsuit is known as
    a. discovery
    b. litigation
    c. a cross-complaint
    d. a summons

17. A law establishing the period within which a plaintiff must bring a lawsuit against the defendant is
    a. a statute of limitations
    b. a complaining period
    c. an e-filing of pleadings
    d. none of the above

18. A deposition is
    a. written testimony given by a party or witness prior to trial
    b. oral testimony given by a party or witness prior to trial
    c. a pleading alleging ultimate allegations of fact
    d. all of the above

19. Which of the following situations refers to the production of documents
    a. Alice's attorney submits written questions to Jeff, the party to whom she is suing.
    b. Ed brings a motion for a mental and physical examination of Bob, a party to the lawsuit.
    c. Jan brings a motion for the assembly of legal documents
    d. Fred, one party to a lawsuit requests that Barney, the other party produce all documents that are relevant to the case prior to trial.

20. The term rejoinder refers to
    a. when the plaintiff's attorney calls witnesses and brings evidence to rebut the defendant's case.
    b. the making of a closing argument by each party's attorney
    c. the reading of jury instructions to the jury
    d. the calling of added witnesses and introduction of other evidence countering plaintiff's rebuttal

21. When a court overturns a verdict based on bias or jury misconduct, this is known as
    a. a judgment on the pleadings
    b. an entry of judgment

    c.  a judgment notwithstanding the verdict
    d.  all of the above.

22.  The responding party in an appeal is known as
    a.  the respondent
    b.  the appellant
    c.  the defendant
    d.  the plaintiff

23.  Mediation is a form of alternative dispute resolution that
    a.  is a procedure where the parties engage in discussions to reach a voluntary settlement of their dispute.
    b.  is a procedure where the parties choose an impartial third party to hear and decide the dispute.
    c.  is a procedure where the parties choose an impartial third party to act as a facilitator in reaching a settlement of their dispute.
    d.  is a procedure where the parties choose an interested or impartial third party to act as a facilitator in reaching a settlement of their dispute.

24.  Administrative Law Judges (ALJs)
    a.  preside over court proceedings.
    b.  decide questions of law and fact concerning a case.
    c.  cannot be an employee of the administrative agency.
    d.  All of the above.

25.  A contingency fee arrangement is where
    a.  in a criminal lawsuit, the plaintiff's attorney receives a percentage of the amount recovered for the plaintiff upon winning or settling the case.
    b.  in a criminal lawsuit, the defendant's attorney receives a percentage of the amount paid to the plaintiff upon winning or settling the case.
    c.  in a civil lawsuit, the plaintiff's attorney receives a percentage of the amount recovered for the plaintiff upon winning or settling the case.
    d.  in a civil lawsuit, the defendant's attorney receives a percentage of the amount paid to the plaintiff upon winning or settling the case

## Short Answer

26.  What does the term "discovery" mean?

27.  What are interrogatories?

28.  What is the term for a request by one party in a lawsuit to another party to produce all documents relevant to the case prior to trial?

29.  What are the motions a party can make to try to dispose of all or part of a lawsuit prior to trial?

30. What term is used for the jury in a jury trial and the judge where there is not a jury trial?

31. What is the person called who chosen as a neutral third party to act as a conveyor of information between the parties and help them to try and reach a settlement of the dispute?

32. What is the person called who the parties hire as a neutral person to investigate the dispute?

33. What is an agreement called where the lawyer receives a percentage of the amount recovered for the plaintiff upon settling or winning the lawsuit?

34. At what time is a summons issued?

35. When must the defendant final an answer?

36. What may the defendant assert when answering the plaintiff's complaint?

37. Give an example of when an appellate court may find an error of law.

38. Which branch(es) of the government can create federal administrative agencies?

39. What is the role of an administrative law judge (ALJ)?

40. What is the delegation doctrine?

# Answers to Refresh Your Memory

1. litigation [p 81]
2. complaint, answer [p 82]
3. statute of limitations [p 83, 86]
4. discovery [p 87]
5. deposition [p 87]
6. Interrogatories [p 87]
7. production of documents [p 88]
8. Motion for Summary Judgment [p 88]
9. settlement conference (or pretrial hearing) [p 90]
10. Arbitration [p 96]
11. Mediation [p 97]
12. Conciliation [p 98]

13.   administrative agency  [p 100]
14.   federal administrative  [p 101]
15.   legislative, judicial, executive  [p 102]

# Model Answer to Critical Thought Exercise

Essentially, this is what is called a "nuisance suit", because a business will often settle, as the costs for defending suits of this kind generally outweigh any "savings" of winning in court.

The report given by our employee shows that Ms. Payne was aware of and warned of the spill. No one saw her fall, as she was on floor when the employee returned with the mop. Ms. Payne declined medical attention at the time, and walked away with no apparent injury.

Documentation of Ms. Payne's purported injuries and related expenses is necessary to ensure that her injuries are legitimate and the result of this accident. This information can be used to quash an unfounded claim, to negotiate a fair settlement based on accurate data, or as discovery for a court case.

If Ms. Payne provides some or all of the requested documentation, we would then need to evaluate whether agreeing to a settlement would be less expensive than defending against her claim in court. Our attorney has estimated that it would cost between $1,500 and $4,500 for his services in the event of a settlement. He estimates that his services would cost at least $10,500 if the case were to go to court. There would also be the costs for additional wages and lost time to be in court for employees acting as witnesses or representing the store, transportation costs, clerical costs, and other miscellaneous expenses.

An initial request for documentation from Ms. Payne could be made by us, rather than the attorney. If her claim is spurious, such a request may be sufficient for her to drop her claim. A letter from our attorney could add weight to our request for documentation and provide additional discouragement for any bogus claims. The time required for such a letter would be minimal.

If Ms. Payne proceeds with her claim and provides the necessary documentation, it would appear that a settlement would be in our best interests, as attorney fees alone would make the defense against this claim in court more expensive than is the proposed amount of the settlement.

It is imperative that Ms. Payne provide documentation of her injuries and related expenses prior to negotiating a settlement. We must not settle a claim unless that claim is legitimate, or we will have many such claims by those looking for an easy windfall.

# Answers to Practice Quiz

## True/False

1.   False   The bringing, maintaining, and defense of a lawsuit are referred to as litigation.  [p 81]
2.   True    Paperwork filed with the court to begin and respond to a lawsuit are the pleadings.  [p 82]
3.   False   Once a complaint has been filed, the court issues a summons.  [p 82]
4.   False   The answer is where the defendant admits or denies the allegations contained in the plaintiff's complaint.  [p 82-83]
5.   True    A deposition is the oral testimony given by a party or witness prior to trial.  [p 87]
6.   False   Discovery is the legal process whereby the parties engage in activities to discover facts and witnesses before the trial. Interrogatories are written questions asked by one party and answered in writing, under oath, by the other party.  [p 87]
7.   True    When one party requests that the other party produce all documents that are relevant to the case prior to trial, it is known as a production of documents.  [p 88]
8.   True    Facts extraneous to the pleadings may not be considered once a judge decides a motion for judgment on the pleadings.  [p 88]
9.   False   One of the major purposes of a pretrial hearing is to facilitate settlement of the case.  [p 90]

10.    False    The Seventh Amendment to the U.S. Constitution guarantees that a party to an action at law has the right to a jury trial in a case in federal court. [p 91]

11.    False    Plaintiff bears the burden of proof to persuade the trier of fact on merits of the case. [p 91]

12.    False    Once the defendant's attorney has finished calling witnesses, the plaintiff's attorney can call witnesses and present evidence in rebuttal. Once the plaintiff's attorney has completed rebuttal, the defendant's attorney can call additional witnesses and present evidence in rejoinder. [p 91-92]

13.    False    A court may overturn a verdict if bias is shown. This is called a judgment notwithstanding the verdict. [p 92]

14.    False    In the appeal of the trial court's decision, the appealing party is called the appellant and the responding party is called the appellee. [p 93]

15.    True    Many contracts, including labor union agreements and franchise agreements, include an arbitration clause that requires all disputes arising out of the contract to be submitted to arbitration. [p 96]

## Multiple Choice

16.    B    Answer B is correct, as litigation is the process of bringing, maintaining, and defending a lawsuit. Answer A is incorrect, as discovery is a detailed pretrial procedure that allows both parties to discover facts of the case from the other party and witnesses before trial. Answer C is incorrect, as a cross-complaint is a pleading usually filed by a defendant who is now suing a plaintiff who filed the original complaint against him/her. The cross-complaint is usually filed at the same time as the defendant's answer to the plaintiff's complaint. Answer D is incorrect, as a summons is a court order indicating that the defendant must appear before the court and answer the complaint against him or her. [p 81]

17.    A    Answer A is correct, as a statute of limitations is a law that establishes the time period which a plaintiff must bring a lawsuit against the defendant. Answer B in incorrect, as there is no such thing as a complaining period. Answer C is incorrect, as an e-filing of pleadings refers to the technology currently available for electronic filing of pleadings and other legal documents as they pertain to a lawsuit. Answer D is incorrect for the reasons given above. [p 86]

18.    B    Answer B gives the correct definition of a deposition. Answer A is incorrect, as it tries to confuse you by incorporating the written aspect of interrogatories with the oral facet of testimony which is associated with depositions. Answer C is incorrect, as it is referring to the pleading known as a complaint. Answer D is incorrect for the reasons given above. [p 87]

19.    D    Answer D states the correct explanation of the discovery form known as production of documents. Answer A is incorrect, as this is the definition for interrogatories. Answer B is incorrect, as this is the explanation for discovery requesting a party to submit to a physical or mental examination. Answer C is incorrect, as it does not make sense as applied to the legal aspect of discovery. [p 88]

20.    D    Answer D gives the correct explanation for the term rejoinder. The important aspect to remember is that rejoinder is a term that is used when the defendant is attempting to counter the plaintiff's rebuttal of the defendant's case. Answer A is incorrect, as this explains the term rebuttal. Answer B is incorrect, as this in an incorrect explanation of the term. Answer C is incorrect, as the reading of jury instructions refers to the aspect of the trial that occurs once the closing arguments by each party are completed. [p 92]

21.    C    Answer C gives the correct terminology for a verdict overturned for bias or jury misconduct. Answer A is incorrect, as a motion for judgment on the pleadings is made once the pleadings are complete. In essence it is asking for the judge to dispose of all or part of the lawsuit before trial, as compared to overturning a verdict after the trial as in a judgment notwithstanding the

verdict. Answer B is incorrect, as the entry of judgment refers to the court's official decision of the successful party based upon the verdict, not on overturning the verdict. [p 92]

22.   A   Answer A is correct, as the responding party in an appeal is known as the respondent and is also referred to as the appellee. Answer B is incorrect, as the appellant is the party who is bringing the appeal. The appellant is also known as the petitioner. Answer C is incorrect, as the term respondent is usually used at the appellate level whereas the term defendant is used at the trial court level. Answer D is incorrect, as the plaintiff is the party to the original lawsuit who has initiated the action against the defendant. [p 93]

23. C   Answer C is correct because mediation is a form of alternative dispute resolution where the parties choose an impartial third party to act as a facilitator in reaching a settlement of their dispute. Answer A is incorrect because negotiation is where the parties engage in discussions to reach a voluntary settlement of their dispute. Answer B is incorrect because arbitration is where the parties choose an impartial third party to hear and decide the dispute. Answer D is incorrect because conciliation is where the parties choose an interested or impartial third party to act as a facilitator in reaching a settlement of their dispute. [p 97]

24.   B   Answer B is correct because Administrative Law Judges (ALJs) decide questions of law and fact concerning a case before the administrative hearing. Answer A is incorrect because the ALJ presides over administrative proceedings, not court proceedings. Answer C is incorrect because the ALJ is an employee of the administrative agency. Answer D is incorrect for the reasons stated above. [p 102]

25.   C   Answer C is correct, as a contingency fee arrangement is where, in a civil lawsuit, the plaintiff's attorney receives a percentage of the amount recovered for the plaintiff upon winning or settling the case. Answers A and B are incorrect, as contingency fee arrangements are not used in criminal proceedings. Answer D is incorrect, as defendant's attorneys in civil suits are usually paid on an hourly basis. [p 90]

## Short Answer

26.   Discovery is the process of engaging in various activities to discover facts of the case from the other party and witnesses prior to trial in order to prevent surprise, prepare for trial, preserve evidence, save court time and encourage the settlement of cases. [p 87]

27.   Interrogatories are written questions given by one party to a lawsuit to another party, which must be answered in writing and under oath. [p 87]

28.   A production of documents. [p 88]

29.   A Motion for Summary Judgment and a Motion for Judgment on the Pleadings. [p 88]

30.   The trier of fact. [p 88]

31.   A mediator. [p 97]

32.   The fact finder. [p 98]

33.   A contingency fee arrangement. [p 90]

34.   A summons is issued once a complaint has been filed with the court. [p 82]

35.   The defendant must file an answer once he/she is served with the complaint.   [p 82]

36.   Affirmative defenses. [p 83]

37.   An error of law can occur if the jury was improperly instructed, if prejudicial evidence was admitted when it should have been excluded, if prejudicial evidence was obtained with an unconstitutional search and seizure. [p 93]

38.   The legislative and the executive branches. [p 100]

39.   An administrative law judge (ALJ) presides over administrative proceedings and decides questions of law and fact. [p 102]

40.   The delegation doctrine states that an administrative agency has only the legislative, judicial, and executive powers delegated to it by the legislative or executive branch of government. [p 102]

# Chapter 5

# TORTS AND STRICT LIABILITY

## Chapter Overview

Tort law, derived from common law and expanded through statutes, provides remedies for various types of injuries. It allows parties to seek compensation through civil lawsuits, requesting monetary damages to compensate for injuries such as medical expenses, loss of wages, pain and suffering, mental distress, and wrongful death. Punitive damages and equitable remedies may also be available. This chapter examines tort laws for intentional and unintentional torts, strict liability, and cyber torts.

## Objectives

Upon completion of this chapter's exercises, you should be able to:

1.  Differentiate between intentional torts against persons and intentional torts against property.
2.  Understand the elements necessary to prove negligence and recognize the associated defenses.
3.  Appreciate the special negligence doctrines and how they differ from one another.
4.  Understand the business torts of disparagement and fraud.
5.  Appreciate the doctrine of strict liability and recognize its application.

## Practical Application

You should be able to identify the different intentional torts and distinguish them from negligence. You should be able to apply the elements of each tort to real and hypothetical situations. You should have a greater understanding of strict liability, and the situations where punitive damages are requested.

## Helpful Hints

The information in this chapter is easily organized for study. You can sort the intentional torts by their application to individuals, property or business. The elements of the tort of negligence can be organized by listing the elements vertically and diagramming causation horizontally.

## Study Tips

### Intentional Torts Against Persons

The law protects people from unauthorized touching, restraint, or contact, and protects the individual's reputation and privacy.

**Assault.** The intentional threat of immediate harm or offensive contact, or any action that arouses reasonable apprehension of imminent harm.
- Future threats are not actionable.

- The victim must be fearful of what appears to be an inevitable contact.
- The victim must be aware of the tortuous act.
- The victim's reaction must be one of fear as opposed to laughter, or there is no apprehension.

**Battery.** The intentional, unauthorized and harmful or offensive touching of another, without consent or legal privilege.
- The touching of an accessory attached to the victim may be enough to satisfy this element.
- Merchant's protection statutes sometimes have a role in the privilege arena of this tort.
- The victim does not have to be aware of the battery in order for the tort to occur.
  o The victim may be sleeping when it happens or have his or her back turned.
- Battery and assault can occur together.

*Transferred Intent Doctrine.* If an individual intends to injure a person but instead injures another individual, the law transfers the perpetrator's intent from the original target to the actual victim.
- The actual victim may bring a lawsuit against the wrongdoer.

**False Imprisonment** – Intended mental or physical detention of another without consent or legal right.
- An assertion of legal authority or intimation by one in a superior position may be sufficient.
- Physical confinement may include barriers or threats of physical harm.
  o Future threats or moral pressure are not sufficient.
- If a merchant is involved, the lack of legal privilege may be difficult to prove.

*Merchant Protection Statutes.* Since many merchants lose thousands of dollars every year from shoplifters, many states have enacted statutes to protect them.
- These statutes are often referred to as shopkeeper's privilege.
- There are three important aspects of this type of statute that will absolve a merchant from liability of false imprisonment allegations:
  o There must be reasonable grounds for detaining and investigating the shoplifter.
  o The suspected shoplifter can be detained for only a reasonable time.
  o The investigations must be conducted in a reasonable manner.

**Misappropriation of the Right to Publicity.** This tort is an attempt by another to appropriate a living person's name or identity for commercial purposes.

**Invasion of the Right to Privacy.** A violation of an individual's right to live his/her life without unwarranted or undesired publicity.
- Truth is not a defense to this tort, as the fact does not have to be untrue.
- If the fact is one of public record, this tort cannot be claimed.
- Placing someone in a "false light" is an invasion of privacy.
  o Falsely assigning beliefs or actions to another can violate this right .

**Defamation of Character.** This tort involves an intentional or accidental untrue statement of fact made about an individual to a third party.
- The truth is always a defense.
- A third party must see or hear the untrue statement, and it may be overheard accidentally.
- Libel is written defamation.
- Slander is oral defamation.
- Opinions are not actionable, as they are not considered to be an untrue statement of fact.

*Public Figures as Plaintiffs.* Public figures such as movie stars, celebrities and other famous people must show that the statement was knowingly made or with reckless disregard of the statement's falsity.
- Malice must be shown.

**Disparagement or Trade Libel.** This tort of product disparagement or trade libel involves an untrue statement made by a person or business about the reputation, services, or products of another business.
- The plaintiff must show that
  - The defendant made an untrue statement about products, services, property, or reputation.
  - The statement was heard or seen by a third party.
  - The defendant knew the statement was untrue.
  - The statement was made maliciously, with intent to injure.

**Intentional Misrepresentation (Fraud).** This tort, also known as deceit, happens when one person deceives another person out of something of value. The following mnemonic will assist you in remembering its elements. The mnemonic is MIS JD.

M   Misrepresentation of material fact that was false in nature
I   Intentionally made to an innocent party
S   Scienter (knowledge) of the statement's falsity by the wrongdoer
J   Justifiable Reliance on the false statement by the innocent party
D   Damages were suffered by the injured party

**Intentional Infliction of Emotional Distress.** This tort is the intentional or reckless conduct by one individual against another that causes severe emotional distress.
- The conduct must be extreme and outrageous and must go beyond the bounds of decency.
- Many states require a physical injury, illness or discomfort.

**Malicious Prosecution.** In this tort, the plaintiff in the original lawsuit becomes the defendant in a civil case which asserts that there was probably no cause for the original lawsuit, that the plaintiff in the original lawsuit instituted the action with malice, and that the defendant in the original lawsuit suffered injury because of the original lawsuit.
- Malice is difficult to prove and courts consider these lawsuits to inhibit legitimate lawsuits.

## Intentional Torts Against Property

The two torts in this area are trespass to land, which is real property, and trespass to personal property, which involves those items that are movable.

**Trespass to Land.** Involves intentional entry onto the land of another without consent or legal privilege.
- It is not intentional if someone else pushes an individual onto someone else's land.
- Rescuing someone from danger is not considered trespass.
- Remaining on someone's land after the invitation has expired is trespass.

**Trespass to and Conversion of Personal Property.**
- Trespass to Personal Property involves the intentional injury or interference with another's enjoyment of his or her personal property.
- Conversion of Personal Property involves intentionally depriving a true owner of the use and enjoyment of his or her personal property.
  - The failure to return borrowed property may be sufficient.
  - The rightful owner can bring a cause of action to get the property back.
    - If the property is destroyed or lost, the true owner can recover the value.

# Unintentional Torts (Negligence)

A person is responsible for the foreseeable consequences of his or her actions. Negligence is taking action that a reasonable person would not or failing to act when a reasonable person would. In order to be successful in a cause of action for negligence, one must show four elements:
- That a duty of care was owed to the plaintiff,
- That the defendant breached this duty,
- That the plaintiff suffered injury (damages), and
- That the defendant was the actual and proximate cause of the plaintiff's injuries.

**Duty of Care.** The general duty of care states that we all owe one another a duty of due care so as to not subject others to an unreasonable risk of harm.
- This general duty of care is based on the reasonable person standard.
    - A person must exercise the same care as a reasonable person in the same circumstances.
    - Children are measured against other children of similar age and experience.
- There are certain situations where a higher standard of care is owed.

**Breach of Duty.** If a duty, either general or special, has been established and it is found that the defendant has not acted as a reasonable person would, the court may find a breach of the duty of care.
- Passersby are not usually expected to rescue others to save them from harm.

**Injury to Plaintiff.** The plaintiff must have actually suffered an injury or damages.
- Recoverable damages depend on how the injury affects the life or profession of the plaintiff.

**Actual Cause.** The plaintiff must show that the defendant was the actual (factual) cause of the injuries.
- If more than one person is liable for negligently causing injuries to the plaintiff, all can be liable.

**Proximate Cause.** The defendant must be the proximate (legal) or direct cause of the plaintiff's injuries.
- If plaintiff cannot show a direct cause, he or she must show that the injuries were foreseeable.
    - The injuries are the type expected from the activity in which the defendant was engaged.

*Causation.* It is best to diagram this element horizontally in order to remember its nuances. Please see below.

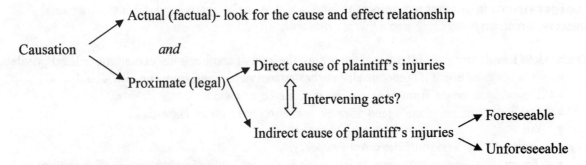

# Special Negligence Doctrines

Many special negligence doctrines have been developed by the courts.

**Professional Malpractice.** Professionals are held to the standard of a reasonable professional.
- Liability for injury in the case of professionals is known as malpractice.

**Negligent Infliction of Emotional Distress.** This is a tort that is not only against individuals, but is one that some courts are recognizing when a defendant's negligent conduct causes the plaintiff to suffer severe emotional distress. This tort requires that
- The plaintiff's relative was injured or killed and
- That the plaintiff suffered severe distress at the same time he or she observed the accident.
  - Some jurisdictions require that the plaintiff suffer some sort of physical injury.

**Negligence per se.** This involves the violation of a statute that proximately causes the plaintiff's injuries.
- There must be a statute that was enacted to prevent the type of injury suffered by the plaintiff and
- The plaintiff must be within the class of persons the statute was designed to protect.

**Res ipsa loquitur.** This doctrine means, "the thing speaks for itself."
- There is a presumption of negligence where
  - The plaintiff proves that the defendant had exclusive control of the instrumentality or circumstances that caused the plaintiff's injuries and
  - The injury that the plaintiff suffered wouldn't have ordinarily occurred, "but for" someone's negligence.

**Good Samaritan Laws.** Because many health-care professionals were reluctant to stop and render aid in emergency situations for fear of incurring liability, almost all states have enacted Good Samaritan laws.
- These statutes relieve medical professionals from liability for injury caused by their ordinary negligence in circumstances where they stop and render aid to victims in emergency situations.
- There is no relief for gross negligence or reckless or intentional conduct.

**Dram Shop Acts.** Taverns and bartenders are liable to third parties who are injured by a patron who was served too much alcohol or who was served alcohol when he/she was already intoxicated.

**Guest Statutes.** When a driver voluntarily, and without compensation, gives a ride to another person, the driver is not liable for injuries caused by the driver's ordinary negligence.

**Fireman's Rule.** A fireman who is injured while putting out a fire may not sue the person who caused the fire because the job implies that injury may occur.
- People would be reluctant to call for help if they thought they might be sued for doing so.

**"Danger Invites Rescue" Doctrine.** This doctrine allows those who are injured while going to someone's rescue to sue the person who caused the dangerous situation.

**Social Host Liability.** Social Hosts are liable for injuries by guests who are served too much alcohol.

**Liability of Landowners.** There is a general duty of care is owed by the owner/tenant of a property to invitees and licensees.
- An invitee is one who is invited onto the land of another for the mutual benefit of both people.
- A licensee is one who, with consent, comes onto the land of another for his or her own benefit.
- An owner/tenant does not owe a general duty of care to a trespasser.
  - An owner of property does owe a duty not to willfully or wantonly injure a trespasser.

**Liability of Common Carriers and Innkeepers.**
- Common carriers owe a duty of utmost care for their guests.
- Innkeepers owe a duty of utmost care and have to provide security for their guests.

## Defenses Against Negligence

There are several defenses that a defendant can raise in a negligence lawsuit.

**Superseding or Intervening Event**. A person is liable only for foreseeable events.
- An event that interferes with the normal course of events and causes an unforeseen result can be raised as a defense to liability.

**Assumption of the Risk**. This is a defense that a defendant may assert indicating that the plaintiff knowingly and voluntarily entered into a risky activity that resulted in injury.

**Contributory Negligence**. This doctrine states that if a plaintiff is partially at fault for causing his or her own injuries, then the plaintiff is barred from recovering damages.
- The "Last Clear Chance Rule" states the defendant has a duty to avoid the accident if possible.

**Comparative Negligence**. This doctrine, known as pure comparative negligence, assesses damages by the plaintiff's percentage of fault.
- If the plaintiff is in a jurisdiction that adopts the partial comparative negligence doctrine, then the plaintiff must be less than fifty percent negligent in causing his or her injuries.
  - o If the plaintiff is over 50 % negligent, then recovery is barred and defendant is not liable.

## Strict Liability

This is a category of tort that involves liability without fault if the activity that the defendant is engaged in places the public at risk of injury, despite reasonable care being taken.
- Examples of activities that qualify for this categorization include fumigation, storage of explosives, keeping wild animals as pets, and blasting.
- Punitive damages are also recoverable in strict liability cases.

# Refresh Your Memory

The following exercises will help to test your memory regarding the principles given in this chapter. Read each question twice, then place your answer in the blank provided for each question. Review the chapter material for any questions you are unable to answer or remember.

1. Tort is a French word that means _____.

2. The main purpose that punitive damages are awarded is to _____ the defendant.

3. The tort of assault requires reasonable apprehension of _____ _____.

4. The Doctrine of _____ _____ applies when an individual acts with the intent to injure one person but actually injures another.

5. Actual malice means that the defendant made the false statement knowingly or with _____ _____ of its falsity.

6. Slander is a(n) _____ defamatory statement.

7. The tort of misappropriation is also known as the tort of _____.

8. _____ is an example of an action constituting the tort of invasion of the right to privacy.

9. Interference with an owner's right to exclusive possession of land constitutes the tort of _____ to _____.

10. _____ of _____ refers to the obligation not to cause any unreasonable harm or risk of harm to others.

11. When proving causation in a negligence action, both causation _____ _____ and _____ cause must be proved before the plaintiff may prevail.

12. A professional who breaches the reasonable professional standard may be found liable based on _____ _____.

13. The doctrine of res ipsa loquitur raises the _____ of negligence.

14. Under _____ _____ Acts a tavern and bartender may be held civilly liable for serving too much alcohol.

15. Keeping a tiger as a pet will subject the owner to _____ liability.

## Critical Thought Exercise

Chip North is a 22-year-old racing enthusiast who went to a car race at Trona International Speedway. North was excited because he had obtained a seat close to the track near the finish line. North's ticket came with five others in a sealed envelope that was imprinted in a large font with the following:

**"WARNING!**
Your seating for this event is in a very
DANGEROUS AREA
Debris and fluids from race cars may be ejected or sprayed from the
race surface into your seating area in the event of a crash or malfunction
of a race vehicle. Please ask to change your seating if you do not desire to
ASSUME THE RISK OF SERIOUS INJURY."

The envelope is opened by North's younger brother, who does not pay any attention to the envelope and discards it after removing the tickets. During the race, a car crashes into the wall in front of North's seat and sprays him with burning gasoline, causing severe injuries. North sues Trona Speedway for negligence for subjecting him to a known danger by seating him and others so close to the racetrack. Trona Speedway denies any liability based upon the warning on the envelope and the known risk that spectators take when attending a race.

At trial, which side should prevail?

*Please compose your answer on a separate sheet of paper or on your computer.*

## Practice Quiz

### True/False

1. ___ Fred can sue Sam for assault if Sam threatens to beat Fred to a pulp right now.

2. ___ Direct physical harm between the perpetrator and the victim is needed when proving the tort of battery.

3. ___ Truth is not an absolute defense to a charge of defamation.

4. ___ Angie attempts to use Jennifer Aniston's picture to advertise her new real estate agency without Jennifer's permission. Jennifer does not have any cause of action to sue Angie, as she should assume her popularity will be used in such things as advertising.

5. ___ Threats of future harm as well as moral pressure are both considered to be forms of false imprisonment.

6. ___ The tort of conversion can not happen when someone who initially was given possession of personal property fails to return it.

7. ___ A person who is the cause of a car accident because he or she fell asleep while driving is not liable for any resulting injuries caused by his or her carelessness as his or her actions were not intentional.

8. ___ Under the reasonable person standard, the courts try to determine how a subjective, careful, and unconscious person would have acted in the same circumstances, and then measure the defendant's conduct against this standard.

9. ___ Actual cause is the same principle as proximate cause.

10. ___ Since there have been an increase in malpractice law suits, almost all states have enacted the Good Samaritan laws that relieve medical professionals from liability for injury caused by their ordinary negligence in circumstances where they stop and render aid to victims in emergency situations.

11. ___ Dram Shop Acts do not hold tavern and bartenders civilly liable for injuries caused to or by patrons who are served too much alcohol.

12. ___ The fireman's rule provides that a fireman may not sue the party whose negligence caused the fire for any resulting injuries from putting out the fire.

13. ___ Under the social host liability rule, a social host is liable for injuries caused by guests who are served alcohol at a social function.

14. ___ Common carriers and innkeepers owe a duty of utmost care to their passengers and guests.

15. ___ If a plaintiff knows of and voluntarily enters into or participates in a risky activity that results in injury, the law acknowledges that the plaintiff assumed the risk involved.

## Multiple Choice

16. A tort that states that a person whose extreme and outrageous conduct intentionally or recklessly causes severe emotional distress is known as
    a. intentional infliction of emotional distress.
    b. res ipsa loquitur.

   c.  extreme negligence.
   d.  invasion of right to privacy.

17.  Jane spray painted George's red corvette purple and dented the passenger door. Which tort has Jane committed?
   a.  false imprisonment.
   b.  trespass to personal property.
   c.  stinginess.
   d.  negligence.

18.  If Jane borrowed George's red Corvette and sold it, this would be considered the tort of
   a.  trespass to personal property.
   b.  conversion of personal property.
   c.  trespass to land.
   d.  strict liability.

19.  In determining the standard of care owed by an attorney, the court will measure the defendant's conduct against
   a.  a reasonable person.
   b.  a reasonable brain surgeon.
   c.  a reasonable attorney.
   d.  a reasonable child.

20.  A breach of duty of care is
   a.  a fulfillment to act as a reasonable person under the same or similar circumstances.
   b.  an expectation in certain circumstances.
   c.  the failure to act as a reasonable person would.
   d.  immaterial in assessing liability.

21.  If two or more individuals are liable for negligently causing the plaintiff's injuries, both or all can be held liable to the plaintiff if each of their acts is a
   a.  proximate cause of plaintiff's injuries.
   b.  substantial factor in causing the plaintiff's injuries.
   c.  inconsequential cause of plaintiff's injuries.
   d.  None of the above.

22.  Sally, a bystander who witnessed the injury of Charlie, her brother, that was caused by Kaitlin's negligent conduct may bring a cause of action against Kaitlin for
   a.  negligent death.
   b.  intentional infliction of emotional distress.
   c.  battery.
   d.  negligent infliction of emotional distress.

23.  Liability for a surgeon who braches the reasonable professional standard of care is known as
   a.  negligence per se.
   b.  res ipsa loquitur.
   c.  professional malpractice.
   d.  social host liability.

24.  Violation of a statute that proximately causes an injury is referred to as
   a.  negligence per se.

    b.  negligent infliction of emotional distress.

    c.  the "Danger Invites Rescue" doctrine.

    d.  unfair competition.

25.  If Andrea Smith, a registered nurse, sees Ida Victim laying helplessly in the line of traffic and decides to render aid, but, in doing so causes her ankle to be bruised, which statute will relieve Andrea of liability for Ida's injuries?

    a.  Assumption of the risk

    b.  Dram shop acts

    c.  Good Samaritan law

    d.  Strict liability

## Short Answer

26.  If Terry wants to sue Cyrina for defamation of character, what must Terry prove?

27.  Briefly describe the difference between real property and personal property.

28.  What are the necessary elements that Shelly must prove in order to establish a cause of action for negligence against Andrew?

29.  What is the difference between actual cause and proximate cause?

30.  Why isn't opinion actionable in terms of defamation of character?

31.  If Harold wants to sue Archie for Intentional Misrepresentation, what elements must Harold prove?

32.  What must a plaintiff show in order to succeed in a cause of action for disparagement?

33.  If Wendy intended to hit Marie, but hit Jeff instead, what must Jeff show under the Doctrine of Transferred Intent?

34.  Explain the liability concept under a cause of action for strict liability.

35. Define negligence per se.

_____

36. The Doctrine of Res Ipsa Loquitur raises what presumption?

_____

37. What is the difference between an invitee and a licensee?

_____

_____

38. What duty of care does a landowner owe to a trespasser?

_____

39. What is the difference between contributory negligence and comparative negligence?

_____

_____

40. What is the Last Clear Chance Rule?

_____

## Answers to Refresh Your Memory

1. wrong  [p 113]
2. punish  [p 113]
3. imminent harm  [p 113]
4. Transferred Intent  [p 114]
5. reckless disregard [p 116]
6. oral  [p 116]
7. appropriation  [p 115]
8. Wiretapping, reading another's e-mail, secretly taking photos  [p 115]
9. trespass, land  [p 120]
10. duty, care  [p 121]
11. in fact, proximate  [p 126-127]
12. professional malpractice  [p 128]
13. presumption  [p 130]
14. Dram Shop[p 131]
15. strict  [p 138]

## Critical Thought Exercise Model Answer

The tort of negligence occurs when someone suffers injury because of the failure of another to exercise the standard of care that a reasonable person would exercise in similar circumstances. The operator of a facility where a sporting event takes place has a duty to provide safe seating for the spectators, unless the risk of injury is assumed and accepted by the spectators. Spectators at a baseball game assume the risk that a ball may be hit into the stands and strike them. A plaintiff who voluntarily enters into a risky situation, knowing the risk involved, will not be allowed to recover. This is the defense of assumption of risk. The requirements of this defense are (1) knowledge of the risk and (2) voluntary assumption of the risk. If North had actually been given knowledge of the risk, he may have voluntarily assumed that risk by sitting close to the racetrack. However, six tickets were placed in one envelope that was opened by someone other than North. Trona speedway cannot argue that North voluntarily assumed a risk for which he was not given notification. The knowledge of risk may be implied from the general knowledge of spectators at a particular type of event, such as baseball. There is no indication that North or any other spectator would know of the danger associated with sitting in a seat for which a ticket was sold. Because North did not assume the risk of being injured by burning gasoline while a spectator at the race, Trona is still liable for negligence.

# Answers to Practice Quiz

## True/False

1. True    Threatening to punch someone right now creates immediate apprehension, thereby creating a cause of action for assault. [p 113]
2. False    Direct physical contact between the victim and the perpetrator is not needed. [p 114]
3. False    Since defamation, by its very definition, involves an untrue statement, truth is an absolute defense to a defamation allegation. [p 116]
4. False    Misappropriating a living person's name or identity for commercial gain is actionable under the tort of misappropriation of the right to publicity. [p 115]
5. False    A threat of future harm or moral pressure is not considered false imprisonment. [p 114]
6. False    When the true owner of property is deprived of the use and enjoyment of his or her personal property by another taking over such property and exercising ownership rights over it, this is known as conversion of personal property. The failure to return borrowed property is also considered conversion. [p 120]
7. False    The unintentional tort of negligence bases liability for harm on that which is a foreseeable consequence of his or her actions. Therefore, it is foreseeable that injuries may result from a driver who is asleep at the wheel. Under the doctrine of negligence, intent has no applicability. [p 121]
8. False    The courts use an objective standard against which to measure the defendant's actions. The defendant's subjective intent has no bearing in determining liability. [p 121]
9. False    Proximate cause is determined by forseeability, which places a limitation on liability. Actual cause pertains to the factual circumstances of the case. [p 126-127]
10. True    Nearly all states have passed Good Samaritan laws that relieve medical professionals from liability for injury caused by their ordinary negligence in such circumstances. [p 130]
11. False    The bartender and tavern are liable to third parties injured by the patron and for the injuries suffered by the patron. [p 131]
12. True    A fireman may not sue a party whose negligence caused the fire he or she was injured in while putting out the fire. [p 131]
13. True    A social host is liable for injuries caused by guests who are served alcohol at a social function. [p 131]
14. True    Common carriers and innkeepers owe a duty of utmost care to passengers and guests. [p 132]
15. True    The plaintiff must know and voluntarily enter into or participate in a risky activity that causes injury before the court will find that the plaintiff assumed the risk involved. [p 135]

## Multiple Choice

16. A    A is the correct answer, as the statement given is the definition of intentional infliction of emotional distress. Answer B is incorrect, as res ipsa loquitur involves an instrumentality that is in the exclusive control of the defendant and would not have occurred but for someone's

negligence. Answer C is incorrect, as there is no such thing as extreme negligence. Answer D is incorrect, as the question gives an incorrect definition of invasion of the right to privacy. [p 118]

17. B  Answer B is the correct answer, as trespass to personal property involves one person's interference with another person's personal property. Answer A is incorrect, as false imprisonment is the intentional mental or physical confinement of another without consent or legal privilege. Answer C is incorrect, as stinginess is not a tort. Answer D is incorrect, as trespass to property is an intentional tort, not a tort involving negligence. [p 120]

18. B  Answer B is the correct answer, as the question concerns conversion of personal property. Answer A is incorrect, as the tort of trespass to personal property involves only the interference of a person's use and enjoyment of his or her property. Answer C is incorrect, as trespass to land involves real property. Answer D is incorrect, as strict liability is liability without fault that is often utilized in cases involving abnormally dangerous activities. [p 120]

19. C  Answer C is correct, as defendants who have a particular expertise or competence are measured against a reasonable professional standard which, in this case, would be that of a reasonable attorney. Answer A is not the best answer, as the reasonable person standard is usually used in circumstances where a general duty of care is owed and professionals or those having a special duty are not involved. Answer B is incorrect, as measuring an attorney's duty against that of a brain surgeon would not accurately indicate the conduct of a reasonable attorney in the field. Answer D is incorrect, as comparing an attorney to a child would not be an indicator of the conduct of another attorney of similar expertise or competence. [p 122]

20. C  Answer C is correct, as the duty of care is measure against how an objective, careful and conscientious person would act in similar circumstances. As such, the breach of the duty of care is the failure to act as a reasonable person would. Answer A is incorrect, as the concepts of breach and fulfillment are not synonymous with one another, as breach connotes failure. Answer B is incorrect, as breach does not imply expectation, regardless of the circumstances. Answer D is incorrect, as it is an untrue statement because the breach of duty is what helps to begin the process of proof in a negligence cause of action. [p 122]

21. B  Answer B is the correct answer, as two or more individuals can be held liable to the plaintiff if each of their negligent acts is a substantial factor in causing the plaintiff's injuries. Answer A is incorrect, as proximate cause is only one of the two types of causation that must be shown before liability can be established. Answer C is incorrect, as it is an untrue statement. Answer D is incorrect for the reasons given above. [p 126]

22. D  Answer D is correct, as some jurisdictions have allowed the tort of emotional distress to include the negligent infliction of emotional distress of which the question addresses emotional distress as a result of a negligent act. Answer A is incorrect, as death may result from a negligent act, however, there is no such thing as negligent death. Answer B is incorrect, as negligent conduct is involved and not intentional. Answer C is incorrect, as battery is an intentional tort and the facts indicate that negligent conduct is involved. [p 128]

23. C  Answer C is correct, as the breach of the reasonable professional standard of care is known as professional malpractice. Answer A is incorrect, as negligence per se involves the violation of a statute that was designed to prevent the type of injury suffered. Answer B is incorrect, as res ipsa loquitor refers to an instrumentality that was in the control of the defendant that negligently caused another's injuries. Answer D is incorrect, as this rule allows for social host liability for injuries caused by guests who are served too much alcohol at a social function. [p 128]

24. A  Answer A is correct, as negligence per se is a special negligence doctrine that establishes the duties owed by one person to another by use of a statute that is to prevent the type of injury suffered. The injured individual must have been within the class of individuals the statute was designed to protect. Answer B is incorrect, as negligent infliction of emotional distress is not what constitutes a violation of statute that proximately causes injuries of an individual. Answer C is incorrect, as the Danger Invites Rescue Doctrine speaks to liability in terms of the person who caused the dangerous situation. Note that the individual injured in a dangerous situation may not

be afforded protection of a statute. Answer D is incorrect, as state unfair competition laws protect businesses from disparaging statements made by competitors or others. [p 130]

25. C    Answer C is correct, as most states have passed Good Samaritan laws that relieve professionals of liability for injuries caused by their ordinary negligence. If the court finds that Ida's bruised ankle was a result of Andrea's ordinary negligence, then she will be relieved of liability. Answer A is incorrect, as the defense of assumption of the risk has no applicability as Ida did not knowingly and voluntarily assume the risk that her ankle would be bruised by Andrea. Answer B is incorrect, as dram shop acts refer to the civil liability that can be assessed to tavern and bartenders for injuries caused to or by patrons who are served too much alcohol. Answer D is incorrect, as strict liability refers to liability without fault. Andrea's actions would not be considered a hazardous activity to be able to qualify under a strict liability theory. [p 130]

## Short Answer

26. Terry needs to show that the Cyrina made an untrue statement of fact about Terry and the statement was accidentally or intentionally published to a third party. [p 116]
27. Real property involves land and personal property concerns tangible, moveable items such as a car or personal belongings. [p 120]
28. Shelly must establish the following elements in a cause of action for negligence against George: a) The defendant must owe the plaintiff a duty of care. b) The defendant must have breached that duty to the plaintiff. c) The defendant was the actual (factual) as well as proximate (legal) cause of plaintiff's injuries. d) Damages. [p 121]
29. Actual cause is the factual cause of plaintiff's injuries whereas proximate cause is the legal cause of the plaintiff's injuries. Proximate cause is based on forseeablity of the injury based upon the defendant's actions. [p 126-127]
30. The publication of an untrue statement of fact is not the same as the publication of an opinion. The publication of opinions is usually not actionable as they are not necessarily facts. [p 116]
31. The elements for the tort of intentional misrepresentation are: a) A misrepresentation of a material fact is made to the plaintiff. b) This misrepresentation was intentionally made. c) The defendant had knowledge of the statement's falsity when he or she made it. d) The plaintiff justifiably relied upon the misrepresentation. e) The plaintiff suffered damages as a result of the misrepresentation. [p 118]
32. In a cause of action for disparagement, the plaintiff must show: a) The defendant made an untrue statement about the plaintiff's products or services, etc.; b) The defendant published this untrue statement to another individual; and c) The defendant knew the statement that was made was false; and d) The defendant made the statement maliciously intending to hurt the plaintiff. [p 117]
33. The doctrine of transferred intent transfers the wrongdoer's intent from the original target to the actual victim of the act. Jeff must show that Wendy intended to do the act, regardless of the fact that he wasn't her original target. [p 114]
34. Strict liability is liability without fault. A participant in a covered activity will be held liable for any injuries caused by that activity, even if he or she was not negligent. [p 138]
35. Negligence per se is the violation of a statute that proximately causes an injury. [p 130]
36. The Doctrine of Res Ipsa Loquitur raises the presumption of negligence, requiring the defendant to prove that he or she was not negligent. [p 130]
37. An invitee is someone who has been expressly or impliedly invited onto the owner's premises for their mutual benefit. A licensee is someone who enters onto the premises, with the express or implied consent of the owner, for his or her own benefit. [p 132]
38. A landowner generally does not owe a duty of ordinary care to a trespasser, but owes a duty to not willfully or wantonly injure a trespasser. [p 132]
39. Under the Doctrine of Contributory Negligence, a plaintiff who is partially at fault for his or her own injury cannot recover damages from the negligent defendant. Under the Doctrine of Comparative Negligence, damages are apportioned according to fault. [p 137]
40. The "Last Clear Chance Rule" states a defendant has a duty to avoid the accident if possible. [p 137]

# Chapter 6

# Criminal Law and White-Collar Crime

## Chapter Overview

Criminal laws promote peaceful coexistence and thriving commerce by encouraging people to act reasonably and by imposing penalties for violation of these laws. The U.S. criminal justice system is unique in that the accused is presumed innocent until proven guilty, the government must prove the guilt of the accused and a jury must agree with that guilt, and the Constitution provides many safeguards for those accused of crimes. White-collar crimes are those crimes, like fraud and bribery, which are more often committed by businesses. The internet and computer technology has opened the way for new crimes and for new ways of committing old crimes. This chapter introduces crimes and crimes affecting business, white-collar crimes, criminal procedure and penalties, and Constitutional safeguards.

## Objectives

Upon completion of this chapter's exercises, you should be able to:

1. Explain the difference between a felony and a misdemeanor.
2. Describe the elements of various crimes and identify white-collar crimes.
3. Discuss criminal procedure, beginning with the arrest and ending with the trial.
4. Explain corporate criminal liability.
5. Appreciate the Constitutional safeguards inherent in the Fourth, Fifth, Sixth and Eighth Amendments.

## Practical Application

You should be able to identify the different types of crimes, and white-collar crimes, and the elements necessary to establish liability for these crimes. You should be able to discuss the criminal process, from the arrest through to trial. You should be able to discuss the application of Constitutional safeguards.

## Helpful Hints

Distinguish between the elements necessary to establish a felony and those necessary to establish a misdemeanor. It may be helpful to draw a horizontal time line listing the various stages of the criminal process. You should be aware of statutes like the Racketeer Influenced and Corrupt Organization Act.

## Study Tips

### Definition of a Crime

A crime is a violation of a duty owed to society that has legal consequences and which requires the individual to make amends to the public.

**Penal Codes and Regulatory Statutes.**  Statutes are the main source of criminal law.
- Penal codes are detailed definitions of criminal activities, specifying punishment for violations.
  o Federal crimes are defined in a federal criminal code.
  o State and federal regulatory statutes define violations and penalties.
- Penalties include fines, imprisonment, or both.
  o Imprisonment incapacitates the criminal, provides means for rehabilitation, deters others, and inhibits personal retribution by victim.

**Parties to a Criminal Action.**  The government is the plaintiff in a criminal action, represented by an attorney called a prosecutor.
- The accused is the defendant in a criminal action, represented by a defense attorney.

**Classification of Crimes.**  There are three classifications of crime:  felony, misdemeanor, and violation.

*Felony.*  They are the most serious types of crimes and are inherently evil (mala in se).
- They are usually punished with imprisonment for more than one year.
  o The death penalty is imposed in some jurisdictions for the crime of first-degree murder.
  o A number of statutes provide for the degrees of crime and the penalties for each degree.
- Violation of regulatory statutes can be a felony if the violation is serious.

*Misdemeanor.*  They are less serious than felonies and are prohibited by society (mala prohibita).
- They are punished with imprisonment for less than a year and/or a fine.

*Violations.*  They are neither a felony nor a misdemeanor.
- They are punished with a fine, unless a jury trial is granted.

**Elements of a Crime.**  Two elements must be shown for a person to be guilty of a crime: act and intent.

*Criminal Act (Actus Reus).*  The defendant must have performed the wrongful act.
- The performance of or failure to perform a certain act can satisfy this element.
  o A thought of doing the crime will not satisfy the criminal act element.
- The wrongful act must have been carried out.

*Criminal Intent (Mens Rea).*  The defendant must have the necessary state of mind when he or she performed the act.
- The jury may deduce the type of intent based upon the defendant's actions.
  o Specific intent is demonstrated when the accused intentionally or with knowledge or purposefully performs the prohibited act.
  o General intent is proven where there is a lesser amount of culpability.
- There is no crime where there is no mens rea.

**Non-Intent Crimes.**  Most states have made provision for certain types of crimes which do not require proof of intent for punishment to be imposed.
- Reckless conduct that violates a statute may be sufficient to find a defendant guilty of a crime.

**Criminal Acts as the Basis for Tort Actions.**  Criminal acts that cause injury to another party can bring about separate civil law actions that have their basis in tort.

## Criminal Procedure

Pretrial procedures, involving the arrest, indictment, arraignment and plea-bargaining, lead to the trial.

**Arrest.** The police must have a warrant based upon probable cause before a person can be arrested.
- Probable cause requires that there be considerable likelihood that the person either committed or is about to commit a crime.
- A search without a warrant is allowed
  - When the crime is in progress.
  - Those involved in the crime are fleeing from the scene.
  - There is a great chance that the evidence will be destroyed.
  - Probable cause is still required even in the absence of a warrant.
- After the accused is arrested they are booked.
  - Recording of the arrest, the standard fingerprinting, and other administrative procedures.

**Indictment or Information.** The indictment or information involves the formal charges that must be brought against the accused before being brought to trial.
- For those charged with serious crimes, a grand jury considers the evidence in most cases.
  - If there is enough evidence, an indictment is then issued and the accused is held for trial.
- For crimes with a lesser magnitude, a judge will determine if there is sufficient evidence to hold the accused for trial.
  - An information is issued with sufficient evidence and the accused is held over for trial.

**Arraignment.** Once an information or indictment is issued, the accused is brought before a court, informed of the charges against her or him, and is requested to enter a plea.
- The accused may enter a guilty, not guilty or *nolo contendere* plea.
  - If the latter is chosen, the accused does not admit guilt, but agrees to a penalty.

**Plea Bargaining.** This involves an agreement between the government and the accused whereby the accused admits to a lesser offense in exchange for the government's imposition of a lesser penalty.
- The rationale behind plea bargaining is to minimize overcrowding of prisons, to avoid trial risks, and to save costs associated with trial.

**The Criminal Trial.** All jurors must agree unanimously before the accused is found guilty.
- If one juror disagrees the jury is "hung" and the accused will not be found guilty.
  - The government then has the option to retry the case before a new jury or judge.
- The defendant may appeal if he or she is found to be guilty.
- If the defendant is found not guilty, the government can not appeal.

## Common Crimes

There are many crimes committed against business property, each of which has necessary elements that must be proved.

**Murder.** At common law, the unlawful killing of a human being by another with malice aforethought.

*Felony Murder Rule.* Covers a murder committed during the commission of another crime, even when there is no intent to kill during the original crime.
- Most state hold the accused liable for the crime of murder, as well as the original crime.
- The intent to commit the murder is inferred from the intent to commit the other crime.
- Many states hold accomplices liable under this rule

**Robbery.** At common law, the taking of personal property of another using fear or force.
- A pickpocket does not qualify as a robbery as there is no fear or force.

**Burglary.** At common law, the "breaking and entering a dwelling at night" with the intent to commit a felony therein.
- The modern expansion includes daytime thefts of offices and commercial buildings.
- The "breaking in" element is no longer a requirement in many jurisdictions.
  - An unauthorized entry through an unlocked door or window will be sufficient.

**Larceny.** At common law, the "wrongful and fraudulent taking of another person's personal property."
- Personal property includes trade secrets, computer programs, tangible property and other types of business property.
- The perpetrator need not use force or go into a building in order to commit this crime.

**Theft.** In those jurisdictions that do not categorize their crimes in terms of robbery, larceny and burglary, the crimes of this nature are under the heading of theft.

**Receiving Stolen Property.** If a person knowingly receives stolen property with the intent to deprive its rightful owner of that property, they may have committed the crime of receiving stolen property.
- The stolen property may be personal property, money, stock certificates or anything tangible.
- The element of knowledge may be inferred from the circumstances.

**Arson**. At common law "the malicious or willful burning of the dwelling house of another person."
- Modernly, the term "dwelling" includes all buildings including public, commercial and private.

# White-Collar Crime

Some crimes are commonly committed by businesspersons and are known as white-collar crimes. Generally, these crimes are those of cunning and deceit, rather than force.

**Forgery.** This crime involves the fraudulent making or alteration of a written document, which affects the legal liability of another person.
- Examples include falsifying public records and counterfeiting as well as imitating another person's signature on a check or altering the amount of the check.

**Embezzlement.** A statutory crime involving the fraudulent conversion of property by a person to whom another individual's property was entrusted.
- Employer's representatives, agents or employees usually commit this crime.
- The property was entrusted to the individual whom ultimately absconded with it.

**Bribery.** Exists when one individual gives money, property, favors or anything of value to another in exchange for a favor, often referred to as a kickback or a payoff.
- Intent is an essential element of this crime.
- Exists when the offeror tenders the bribe.
- Exists when the offeree accepts the bribe.
- The offeror can be guilty of the crime without the offeree accepting the bribe.

*The Foreign Corrupt Practices Act of 1977.* American companies may not bribe a foreign official, political party or candidate to influence new business or in the retention of a continuing business.
- Requires firms to keep accurate records as they pertain to foreign transactions.
- Knowledge is a key element in making this type of conduct a crime.
- Defenses:

o The accused can show the payment was lawful under the written laws of that country.
o The accused can show the payment was a reasonable and bonafide expenditure.

**Extortion.** Extortion involves the obtaining of property of another, with his or her consent, by use of actual or threatened force, violence, or fear.
- Extortion occurs when one person threatens another that a piece of information will be exposed unless money or property is given to the extortionist.
- Extortion of a private person is known as blackmail.
- Extortion of public officials is referred to as extortion "under color of official right."

**Criminal Fraud.** This crime of false pretenses or criminal fraud or deceit occurs where the accused obtains title to property through trickery.

*Mail Fraud and Wire Fraud.* Where the mail or wires are used to defraud another individual.
- These statutes are often used where there is insufficient evidence to prove the primary crime.
- The maximum penalty for violations of these statutes is 20 years in prison.

**The Racketeer Influenced and Corrupt Organizations Act (RICO).** This Act was originally intended to fight organized crime. Its broad language allows use against non-organized crime defendants.

*Criminal RICO.* It is a federal crime to acquire or maintain an interest in or conduct or participate in an "enterprise" through a "pattern" of "racketeering activity."
- An "enterprise" can be a corporation, partnership, sole proprietorship, business or organization, or the government.
- Criminal penalties include fines, imprisonment, and forfeiture of any property or business interests that were obtained as a result of the RICO violations.
- Civil penalties include business reorganization, dissolution, and the dissolution of the defendant's interest in an enterprise as part of civil penalties for RICO violations.

*Civil RICO.* Injuries to third parties can be addressed through a private civil action against the violator.
- Plaintiffs can recover treble damages, or three times the actual loss, plus attorney's fees.

**Criminal Conspiracy.** Occurs when two or more individuals enter into an agreement to commit a crime.
- An overt act in furtherance of the crime is needed, but the actual crime need not be committed.

**Money Laundering.** Criminals use legitimate businesses as a means of "washing" money gained from illegal activities so as not to alert the government to their illegal activities.
- The legitimate business will make false entries into its financial records showing faked expenditures and receipts that bury the origins of the illegal monies.
- Legitimate businesses often used for these laundering activities include restaurants, motels, and other cash businesses.

*Money Laundering Control Act.* Makes it a criminal action to knowingly make a monetary transaction through a financial institution which involves illegal property valued at more than $10,000. Such activities would include deposits and withdrawals from a bank account.
- Makes it a criminal action to knowingly make a financial transaction that involves the proceeds of an illegal transaction.
- Punishment can include a fine of up to $500,000 or double the value of the property involved, and can include up to 20 years in prison.
- Any property involved in or linked to the offense is subject to forfeiture to the government.

**Corporate Criminal Liability.** A corporation is a fictitious legal person that cannot act on its own behalf and must act through its managers, representatives, and employees.
- At common law, the courts held that corporations lacked the *mens rea* needed to commit a crime.
- Modernly, corporations are held criminally liable for acts of managers, employees, and agents.
  - Since imprisonment is not feasible, they are fined or have their franchise or license taken.
  - The corporate officers, employees or directors are held personally liable for crimes that they personally commit regardless if it was done for personal gain or for the corporation.
  - If a corporate manager fails to appropriately supervise his or her subordinate, the manager may be held criminally liable for the subordinate's criminal activities.

## Protection Against Unreasonable Search and Seizure

The **Fourth Amendment** protects corporations and persons from *unreasonable searches and seizures* by the government. "It permits people to be secure in their person, houses, papers and effects."
- Search warrants are necessary and must be based on "probable cause".
- Searches may not go beyond the area specified in the warrant.
- Warrantless searches are allowed in limited situations and must meet "probable cause" standard.

**Exclusionary Rule.** Evidence obtained by an unreasonable search or seizure, will be considered tainted.
- This evidence may not be used against the accused, but can be used against other individuals.
- The "good faith" exception to the exclusionary rule states that illegally obtained evidence may be used against the accused if the police officers that obtained the evidence believed in good faith that they were acting in accordance with a lawful search warrant.

**Searches of Business Premises.** Search warrants are necessary and must be based on "probable cause".
- Regulated businesses, as well as those that are involved in hazardous industries, are subject to warrantless searches.

**Federal Antiterrorism Act.** Congress enacted this legislation in response to the terrorist attacks against the World Trade Center in New York and the Pentagon in Washington, DC on September 11, 2001.
- The Act authorizes the issuance of expanded wiretap orders and subpoenas to obtain evidence of suspected terrorism through the Special Intelligence Court.
- The Act provides for a nationwide search warrant to acquire evidence of terrorist activities.
- The Act allows "roving wiretaps" on those suspected of terrorist involvement.
- The Act provides governmental authority for detention of nonresidents in the United States for a limited period without filing charges against that person.

## Fifth Amendment Privilege Against Self-Incrimination

The Fifth Amendment states "no person shall be compelled in any criminal case to be a witness against himself."
- The *privilege against self-incrimination* applies to individuals, not corporations and partnerships.
- Business records are not protected from disclosure under this privilege.
- Private papers, such as personal diaries of businesspersons, are protected from disclosure.

***Miranda* Rights.** The Supreme Court in this case stated that the privilege against self-incrimination was not useful unless a criminal suspect has knowledge of this right.
- The Supreme Court required that all criminal suspects be given a specific warning prior to being interrogated by the police or other government officials.

- Any statements or confessions obtained prior to a suspect being given this warning can be excluded from evidence at trial.

**Attorney-Client Privilege and Other Privileges.** These privileges are provided in the Fifth Amendment
- The accused in a criminal case must feel safe to discuss his or her case with their attorney without fear that the attorney will be called as a witness against them.
- The Fifth Amendment also recognizes the psychiatrist/psychologist-patient privilege, priest/minister/rabi-penitent privilege, spouse-spouse privilege and parent-child privilege.
- The Supreme Court does not recognize an accountant-client privilege under federal law.
  o Some states do recognize this privilege.

**Immunity from Prosecution.** The government agrees not to use evidence given by the individual against that person.
- Immunity is granted when the government wants information to prosecute more important criminal suspects.
  o If immunity is granted, the individual loses his or her Fifth Amendment protection.

## Other Constitutional Protections

The U.S. Constitution provides many other protections for the criminal process.

**Fifth Amendment Protection Against Double Jeopardy.** The Fifth Amendment states that a person may not be tried twice for the same crime.
- If the accused has committed several crimes with the same act, they may be tried for each of the crimes without being in violation of the double jeopardy rule.
- If the acts are violations in different jurisdictions, each jurisdiction may try the accused.

**Sixth Amendment Right to a Public Jury Trial.** The Sixth Amendment gives the accused the right to be tried by an impartial jury, to cross-examine witnesses against the accused, to have a lawyer's assistance and to have a speedy trial.

**Eighth Amendment Protection Against Cruel and Unusual Punishment.** This Amendment protects the accused from abusive or torturous punishments, but does not prohibit capital punishment.

# Refresh Your Memory

The following exercises will help to test your memory regarding the principles given in this chapter. Read each question twice, then place your answer in the blank provided for each question. Review the chapter material for any questions you are unable to answer or remember.

1.    A(n) _____ is defined as any act done by an individual in violation of those duties that he or she owes to society and for the breach of which the law provides that the wrongdoer shall make amends to the public.

2.    The _____ is represented by an attorney called the prosecutor in a criminal lawsuit.

3.    Felonies are the _____ _____ kinds of crimes.

4.    _____, _____, and _____ are three examples of felonies that are usually punishable by imprisonment.

5. _____ are crimes that are less serious than felonies.

6. The two elements that must be shown for a person to be found guilty of most crimes are criminal _____ and criminal _____.

7. When the police obtain an arrest warrant, it usually must be based upon _____ _____.

8. _____ persons must be formally charged with a crime before they can be brought to trial.

9. If a grand jury determines that there is enough evidence to hold the accused for trial, it will issue a(n) _____.

10. _____ is the taking of personal property from another person by the use of fear or force.

11. The wrongful and _____ taking of another person's personal property is the definition for the crime of larceny.

12. The _____ Amendment protects the rights of the people from unreasonable search and seizure by the government.

13. The _____ Rule prohibits evidence from an unreasonable search and seizure from being introduced at trial or an administrative proceeding against the person searched.

14. The _____ Amendment guarantees criminal defendants the right to trial by impartial jury.

15. The _____ _____ _____ of 2001 assists the government in detecting and preventing terrorist activities and prosecuting businesses.

# Critical Thought Exercise

Build-Rite Construction Company of Santa Maria, Jamaica receives a copy of an invoice for $160,000 of supplies from Hayward Lumber. Tom Cheat, owner of Build-Rite, notices that the invoice states that the company name is Build-Right Contractors and gives the company office address as Santa Maria, California. The invoice contains three different account numbers that Cheat discovers are all assigned to Build-Right. Cheat pays the invoice but does nothing to correct the account numbers.

During the next 14 months, Cheat has his employees order over $800,000 worth of materials from Hayward Lumber via the Internet, using the account numbers assigned to the California company. When the bills come due each month, Build-Right pays for the materials sent to Build-Rite, thinking that they have been shipped to one of their own construction sites. Cheat builds over 200 luxury vacation homes in Jamaica and has the funds from the sale of the homes send to his accounts in the Bahamas, where his brother runs a one-person bank. The credit of Build-Right is ruined when they discover the misuse of their account numbers and refuse to pay the balance of over $300,000 charged to their accounts. Several banks pull their funding of Build-Right projects and equipment is seized. Build-Right has to temporarily lay off 180 employees.

What crime, if any, has been committed by Tom Cheat or his company? Who may be prosecuted? What law will apply? What steps should Build-Right take to help it recover financially and prevent this from happening again in the future?

*Please compose your answer on a separate sheet of paper or on your computer.*

# Practice Quiz

## True/False

1. ___ In a criminal lawsuit, the government is the defendant.

2. ___ The actual performance of the criminal act is called the mens reus.

3. ___ General intent is where there is a showing of a higher degree of mental culpability or recklessness.

4. ___ To be found guilty of a crime, the state of mind of the accused when the act was committed is relevant.

5. ___ Cody Cop, a policeman arrived at an apartment building where Sam Speed was burglarizing Doris' apartment. Cody may arrest Sam Speed even if he does not have a warrant to do so.

6. ___ If the defendant is not found guilty, he or she may not appeal.

7. ___ Robbery is defined as the forceful and fraudulent taking of another person's personal property.

8. ___ If Randy lies to Wanda in order to get her new Microsoft computer program, Wanda may be able to have Randy charged with larceny.

9. ___ Anne signed her soon-to-be ex-husband George's paycheck one Friday evening, knowing she wanted to take him for as much as she could. Anne has not committed any crime, as she and George are not divorced yet.

10. ___ The fraudulent conversion of property by a person to whom the property was entrusted is known as embezzlement.

11. ___ Under the exclusionary rule, evidence that is tainted cannot be prohibited from introduction at a trial or administrative proceeding against the person searched.

12. ___ Any confessions or statements obtained from a suspect before he or she is read his or her Miranda rights may be included as evidence at trial.

13. ___ When a suspect is offered immunity from prosecution, the government agrees to use the evidence given by a person granted immunity against that person.

14. ___ The Eighth Amendment prohibits capital punishment.

15. ___ The government may deny immunity from prosecution if a suspect asserts his or her Fifth Amendment privilege against self-incrimination.

## Multiple Choice

16. What type of crimes has Edna committed if she has traffic violations and has jaywalked?

    a.  Violations

    b.  Felonies

    c.  Misdemeanors

    d.  Trespass

17.  A magistrate who finds there is enough evidence to hold the accused for trial of a lesser crime will issue an

    a.  information.

    b.  indictment.

    c.  injunction.

    d.  intentional tort.

18.  Carol has purchased real estate with money she obtained from robbing a local bank.  Which act has Carol violated?

    a.  Identity Theft and Assumption Deterrence Act of 1998

    b.  The Racketeer Influenced and Corrupt Organization Act

    c.  Money Laundering Control Act

    d.  Civil False Claims Act

19.  Warrantless searches are allowed only when

    a.  they are incident to an arrest.

    b.  where evidence is in "plain view."

    c.  where it is likely that evidence will be destroyed.

    d.  all of the above.

20.  If Trenton threatens to tell Kyle's wife about Kyle's affair unless Kyle gives him money, this is an example of

    a.  Forgery

    b.  Extortion

    c.  Receiving stolen property

    d.  Larceny

21.  Jones walks into a convenience store with a gun. He points the gun at the clerk and instructs her to empty the cash register into a bag and hand the bag to him.  As the clerk hands the bag of money to Jones, a customer enters the store and accidentally knocks against Jones, causing Jones to fire the gun and instantly kill the clerk.  When Jones is apprehended, he is charged with what crime(s)?

    a.  Robbery.

    b.  Murder.

    c.  Both a and b.

    d.  None of the above.

22.  Lisa works for her father's company, The L'il Keg, a microbrewery.  One day, Lisa decides to visit the offices of their main competitor, Hop'n Pilsner, to have a look around.  She dresses in jeans and a t-shirt and walks around to the delivery entrance, where she slips into the building unnoticed.  As she wanders around, she comes across a recipe for a new specialty beer that Hop'n Pilsner is developing for release.  Lisa makes a copy of the recipe and quietly exits the building.  What crime(s) has Lisa committed?

    a.  Burglary.

    b.  Larceny.

    c.  Robbery.

    d.  Forgery.

23. Karl is in charge of the office petty cash fund. He finds himself short of cash one week and borrows $20 from the fund, planning to pay it back the next week. What crime(s) has Karl committed?
    a. Bribery.
    b. Larceny.
    c. Robbery.
    d. Embezzlement.

24. Evidence obtained from an unreasonable search and seizure
    a. is considered to be tainted evidence.
    b. can generally be prohibited from introduction at trial against the person searched.
    c. Both a and b.
    d. None of the above.

25. In regards to searches of business premises,
    a. the government, generally, has the right to search business premises without a search warrant.
    b. certain hazardous and regulated industries are given extra protection from government searches.
    c. Both a and b.
    d. None of the above.

## Short Answer

26. What is the usual punishment for felonies?

27. What are the two elements that must be proven for a person to be found guilty of most crimes?

28. Why would a person injured by a criminal act not sue the criminal to recover civil damages?

29. Who usually evaluates the evidence of serious crimes?

30. Please tell what it means when the government grants a suspect immunity from prosecution.

31. What is the definition for the crime of robbery?

32. What is required for the crime of receiving stolen property?

33. Mr. Sly convinces Suzy Sweet to withdraw all of her money and invest in his water well that he claims to bottle as the water of youth. He has Suzy believe that her investment will triple in a month. Mr. Sly takes her money and flees the country to live in Barbados. What crime has Mr. Sly committed?

34. From what does the Fourth Amendment protect persons and corporations?

35. How may an accused be prosecuted twice or more without violating the double jeopardy clause of the Fifth Amendment?

36. What does the Sixth Amendment guarantee to criminal defendants?

37. Against what does the Eighth Amendment protect criminal defendants?

38. Define probable cause.

39. How does the modern definition of arson differ from the common law definition?

40. What types of crimes are referred to as white-collar crimes?

## Answers to Refresh Your Memory

1. crime  [p 148]
2. government  [p 149]
3. most serious  [p 149]
4. Choose three:  murder, rape, embezzlement, and bribery  [p 149]
5. Misdemeanors  [p 149]
6. act, intent  [p 150]
7. probable cause  [p 152]
8. Accused  [p 153]
9. indictment  [p 153]
10. robbery  [p 159]
11. fraudulent  [p 159]
12. Fourth  [p 164-165]
13. Exclusionary  [p 165]
14. Sixth  [p 172]
15. Federal Antiterrorism Act  [p 169]

## Critical Thought Model Answer

Obtaining title to property through deception or trickery constitutes the crime of theft by false pretenses, commonly referred to as fraud. When the fraud is accomplished by the use of mails or wires, a federal offense has taken place. Because Cheat assumed the identity of Build-Right, the offense of identity theft may have been committed. The use of new technology, especially computers and the Internet make this offense hard to prevent and extremely damaging to the victim. To combat such fraud, Congress passed the Identity Theft and Assumption Deterrence Act of 1998. Identity theft is a federal felony punishable by a sentence of up to 25 years. The act also appoints the Federal Trade Commission to help victims restore their credit and erase the impact of the imposter.

Cheat may be both criminally and civilly liable under the Racketeer Influenced and Corrupt Organization Act (RICO). RICO makes it a federal crime to acquire or maintain an interest in, use income from, or conduct or participate in the affairs of a criminal enterprise through a pattern of racketeering activity. The commission of two or more enumerated crimes within a ten-year period establishes the pattern of activity. The enterprise can be a corporation, partnership, sole proprietorship, business, or organization. The Build-Rite construction company suffices as a criminal enterprise. The use of the Internet previously created a problem if wires were not used for transmission of the fraudulent communication. The statutes concerning wire fraud have been amended to include Internet activity within the definition of wire fraud. If the profits from the building of the condominiums had been invested in or maintained by Build-Rite, the assets would have been subject to forfeiture.

Unfortunately, the funds have been transferred to a bank in the Bahamas. The Bahamas have joined the Cayman Islands as a location where the bank secrecy laws protect the identity and amount of account deposits. The assets of Build-Rite are subject to forfeiture as are the proceeds sent to the Bahamas. Cheat is liable for multiple criminal offenses, if he can be apprehended. The employees of Build-Rite will incur criminal liability only if they knew that the account numbers were being misused. To remedy the situation, Build-Right should create a secure electronic signature for all account transactions. They can insist that all orders over a certain amount be confirmed by a separate e-mail with a password. The FTC should be consulted for advice and help in getting equipment released and credit with the banks restored.

# Answers to Practice Quiz

## True/False

1. False   In a criminal lawsuit, there is not a private party; the government is the plaintiff. [p 149]
2. False   Actus reus means guilty act, which references the criminal nature of the act. [p 150]
3. False   General intent is less than that of specific intent where an accused purposefully and intentionally or with knowledge commits a prohibited act. General intent indicates a degree of recklessness. [p 150]
4. True    There is no crime if the requisite state of mind cannot be proven. [p 150]
5. True    Warrantless arrests are judged by the probable cause standard. Cody Cop may arrest Sam Speed as Cody has arrived during the commission of a crime and there would be no time for him to obtain an arrest warrant. [p 152]
6. True    If the defendant is found not guilty, he or she would be innocent and have no need for an appeal. [p 154]
7. False   Robbery is the taking of personal property from another by the use of fear or force. Fraud is not an element. [p 159]
8. True    Most personal property, including tangible property, trade secrets, computer programs, and other business property is subject to larceny. [p 159]
9. False   Regardless of the fact that Anne and George are not divorced yet, Anne has committed the crime of forgery as she had the intent to defraud him, since she wanted to "take him for as much money as she could." If Anne and George were happily married, forgery would not be committed provided that Anne deposited the check into a joint checking or savings account at a bank. [p 160]
10. True   Embezzlement is most commonly committed by an employer's employees, agents or representatives, thus to people whom property is entrusted. The embezzlement occurs when the entrusted individual(s) convert the property for their own use. [p 160]
11. False  Tainted evidence can be prohibited at a trial or administrative hearing if it is against the accused, however, this tainted evidence may be used against other individuals. [p 165]

12. False   The Supreme Court requires that the Miranda rights be read to a criminal suspect before he or she is interrogated. The Fifth Amendment privilege against self-incrimination cannot be utilized unless a suspect is aware of this right. [p 170]

13. False   When the government grants an individual immunity from prosecution, this means that the government agrees not to use any evidence given by a person granted immunity against that person. [p 171]

14. False   The Eighth Amendment protects against cruel and unusual punishment but does not prohibit capital punishment. [p 172]

15. False   The government may offer immunity from prosecution in cases where the suspect has asserted his or her Fifth Amendment privilege against self-incrimination. The policy behind this offer is for the government to obtain information that will lead to the prosecution of other more important criminal suspects. [p 171]

## Multiple Choice

16.   A.   Answer A is correct, as jaywalking and traffic violations are neither misdemeanors nor felonies. Answer B is incorrect, as felonies are the most serious crimes in which jaywalking and traffic violations are not included. Answer C is incorrect, as misdemeanors are less serious than felonies, but more serious than jaywalking or traffic violations. Answer D is incorrect, as trespass is an intentional tort with nothing to do with jaywalking or traffic violations. [p 149]

17.   A.   Answer A is correct as a magistrate (judge) decides whether there is sufficient evidence to hold the accused for trial of a lesser crime and will then issue an information. Answer B is incorrect as the grand jury issues an indictment if they decide there is sufficient evidence to hold the accused for trial of a serious crime. Answer C is incorrect as an injunction is an equitable remedy that has nothing to do with the finding of evidence to hold an accused for trial. Answer D is incorrect, as a magistrate cannot issue an intentional tort or wrong; torts are civil in nature and the issuance of an indictment or an information are both criminal in nature. [p 153]

18.   C.   Answer C is correct as per the federal Money Laundering Control Act wherein narcotics activities and almost every white-collar crime are considered unlawful under this act. Answer A is incorrect as this act criminalizes identity fraud. Answer B is incorrect as this Act provides for making the participation in or maintenance of an interest, use of income or conducting affairs in a "pattern" of racketeering activity a federal crime. Answer D is incorrect as it protects against corrupt government contractors and their employees who defraud the government. [p 164]

19.   D.   Answer D is correct, as answers A, B, and C all state when warrantless searches are allowed. [p 152]

20.   B.   Answer B is correct as extortion involves the procurement of another's property with or without their consent, induced by an improper use of actual or threatened force, fear or violence. Answer A is incorrect as forgery involves the fraudulent making or altering of a written document that alters the legal liability of another person. Answer C is incorrect as receiving stolen property is where an individual knowingly receives stolen property and intends to deprive the rightful owner of that property. Answer D is incorrect as larceny is the intentional taking and carrying away of the personal property of another without consent or legal privilege. With the crime of larceny, there is no force as there can be with the crime of extortion. [p 162]

21.   C   Answer C is correct, as Jones has committed robbery by taking personal property by force and murder under the felony murder rule because he does not need to intend to kill while committing another crime, the intent to commit the original crime is sufficient. Answer A is incorrect, as Robbery is only one of the crimes Jones committed. Answer B is incorrect, as Murder is only one of the crimes Jones committed. Answer D is incorrect, for the reasons stated above. [p 157, 159]

22.  B  Answer B is correct, as larceny is the wrongful and fraudulent taking of another's person's personal property.  Answer A is incorrect, as burglary is the breaking and entering with the intent to commit a felony.  Answer C is incorrect, as robbery is the taking of personal property from another by use of force or fear.  Answer D is incorrect, as Forgery is fraudulently making or altering of a document that affects the legal liability of another.  [p 159]

23.  D  Answer D is correct, as embezzlement is the fraudulent conversion of property to whom that property was entrusted.  Answer A is incorrect, as bribery is the giving or receiving of anything of value in corrupt payment for an official act.  Answer B is incorrect, as larceny is the wrongful and fraudulent taking of another's person's personal property.  Answer C is incorrect, as robbery is the taking of personal property from another by use of force or fear.  [p 160-161]

24.  C  Answer C is correct, as both of these statements regarding the exclusionary rule are correct.  Answer A and B are incorrect, as they are each only one of two correct statements.  Answer D is incorrect for the above reasons.  [p 165]

25.  D  Answer D is correct, as neither A or B are correct.  Answer A is incorrect, as the government, generally, does not have the right to search business premises without a search warrant.  Answer B is incorrect, as certain hazardous and regulated industries are subject to warrantless searches if proper statutory procedures are met.  Answer C is incorrect for the above reasons.  [p 168]

## Short Answer

26.  Imprisonment. [p 149]

27.  A criminal act and criminal intent are the two elements that must be proven for a person to be found guilty of most crimes. [p 150]

28.  Because the criminal is often judgment proof and does not have the money to pay the civil judgment. [p 150]

29.  The grand jury usually evaluates the evidence of serious crimes. [p 153]

30.  Immunity from prosecution means that the government agrees not to use any evidence given by a person granted immunity against that person. [p 171]

31.  Robbery is the taking of personal property from another by the use of fear or force. [p 159]

32.  A person must knowingly receive stolen property and intend to deprive the rightful owner of that property. [p 159]

33.  Mr. Sly has committed criminal fraud as he obtained Suzy Sweets's money through deception by convincing her to withdraw and invest all of her money in non-existant water. [p 162]

34.  The Fourth Amendment protects persons and corporations from unreasonable searches and seizures by the government. [p 164-165]

35.  If the accused has committed several crimes with the same act or if the acts are violations in different jurisdictions, they may be tried for each of the crimes without being in violation of the double jeopardy rule. [p 171]

36.  The Sixth Amendment guarantees that an accused will be tried by an impartial jury be allowed to confront witnesses, have the assistance of counsel, and have a speedy trial. [p 172]

37.  The Eighth Amendment protects criminal defendants from cruel and unusual punishment, but does not prohibit capital punishment. [p 172]

38.  Probable cause is the substantial likelihood that the person either committed or is about to commit a crime. [p 152]

39.  At common law, arson was defined as the malicious or willful burning of the dwelling of another person.  The modern definition expands this to include the burning of all types of private, commercial, and public buildings. [p 159]

40.  These are crimes typically committed by businesspersons which involve cunning and deceit, rather than physical force. [p 160]

# Chapter 7

# Intellectual Property and Piracy

## Chapter Overview

Rights in intellectual property are valuable, especially with the pervasiveness of computers and the Internet. Trade secrets are integral to many businesses and must be protected from misappropriation. Patents, copyrights, and trademarks are protected by federal and international laws. This chapter explores how rights in intellectual property, like trade secrets, patents, copyrights, and trademarks, are protected.

## Objectives

Upon completion of this chapter's exercises, you should be able to:

1. Explain the business tort of misappropriating a trade secret.
2. Describe patent infringement under federal patent laws.
3. Explain copyright protection and the penalties for copyright infringement.
4. Describe trademarks and service marks and the penalties for trademark infringement.
5. Discuss the protection of patents, copyrights, and trademarks internationally.

## Practical Application

You should be able to identify the different categories of intellectual property, and the statutes that impose penalties for their infringement. You should be able to discuss the steps a business or individual can take to protect rights in intellectual property. You should be able to discuss the protection this type of property has internationally.

## Helpful Hints

Distinguish between the different categories of intellectual property. It may be helpful to construct a table with the categories of intellectual property in one column, the specific types of property that fit into each of these categories in a second column, and the U.S. laws and international laws that apply to each category of intellectual property in a third column.

## Study Tips

### Trade Secrets

Trade secrets, such as product formulas, can be instrumental in making a business successful.
- These secrets may not qualify for patent, copyright, or trademark.
- State unfair competition laws allow the owner to bring a suit for misappropriation against anyone who steals a trade secret.
    - The defendant must have obtained the trade secret through unlawful means.

- o The owner of a trade secret is required to take all reasonable actions to prevent the discovery of the secret by others.
- o A successful plaintiff
    - ▪ Can recover profits.
    - ▪ Can recover for damages.
    - ▪ Can obtain an injunction barring the offender from disclosing or using the secret.

**The Economic Espionage Act.** This Act makes the theft of another's trade secret a federal crime.
- It is criminal to convert a trade secret to offender's benefit or the benefit of others
    - o Knowing or intending to injure the owner.
- Intended to address the ease of stealing trade secrets through computer espionage and Internet.
- Penalties
    - o Fines of $5 to $10 million dollars.
    - o Prison terms of 15 to 25 years.

# Patents

The U.S. Constitution provides for the protection of the work of inventors and writers.

**Federal Patent Statute.** This law encourages inventors to invent and make their inventions public and protects patented inventions from infringement.
- Federal patent law is exclusive.
- Applications for patents must be filed with the U.S. Patent and Trademark Office (PTO).

**U.S. Court of Appeals for the Federal Circuit in Washington, D.C.** This court was established to hear patent appeals.
- It was created to promote uniformity in patent law.

**Patent Period.** Congress changed U.S. patent law in 1995 to agree with laws of other developed nations.
- Patents are valid for 20 years.
    - o Design patents are valid for 14 years.
    - o The patent term begins to run from the date the application is filed.
- When the term runs out, the invention or design becomes public domain.
- The U.S. follows the first-to-invent rule.
    - o The first person to invent is awarded the patent.
    - o Some other countries follow the first-to-file rule

**Patenting an Invention.** An invention must be novel, useful, and nonobvious.
- Subject matters that can be patented include:
    - o Machines.
    - o Processes.
    - o Compositions of matter.
    - o Improvements to existing machines, processes, or compositions of matter.
    - o Designs for an article of manufacture.
    - o Asexually reproduced plants.
    - o Living material invented by a person.
- Abstractions and scientific principles generally are not patentable.
- A patent application must contain a written description and be filed with the PTO
    - o If a patent is granted, the invention receives a patent number.
        - ▪ A patent holder places "patent" or "pat." and the patent number on the article.
    - o If a patent is pending, the applicant places "patent pending" on the article.

- The issuance of a patent or the validity of an existing patent can be challenged.

**One Year "On Sale" Doctrine.** This public use doctrine states that a patent may not be granted if the public had use of the invention for more than one year prior to filing the patent application.

**The American Inventors Protection Act.** This Act permits inventors to file a provisional application with the PTO and grants provisional rights for three months.
- The PTO is required to issue a patent within three years.
- Non-patent holders may challenge a patent for being overly broad.
  - o Reexamination of the patent application will be by the PTO.
  - o The decision of the PTO can be appealed to the US Court of Appeals.

**Patent Infringement.** This occurs when someone makes unauthorized use of another's patent.
- A patent holder successful in a suit for infringement can recover
  - o Money damages equal to a reasonable royalty,
  - o Other damages, like loss of customers,
  - o An order to destroy the infringing article,
  - o An injunction preventing future infringement.
- The court can award treble damages if the infringement was intentional.

# Copyrights

The U.S. Constitution gives Congress the power to protect the works of writers for limited times.
- The Copyright Revision Act institutes the requirements for obtaining a copyright and protects copyrighted works from infringement.
  - o Federal copyright law is exclusive.
  - o This Act increases the number of creative works available.
    - Protects works from unauthorized use.
    - Provides a financial incentive for authors to create.
- Only tangible writings, those that can be physically seen, can be copyrighted.

**Registration of Copyrights.** A work must be original to be protected under federal copyright law.
- A copyright is created at the time a work is produced.
  - o Works may be registered with the U.S. Copyright Office.
    - Registration is permissive and voluntary.
- The U.S. signed the Berne Convention, an international copyright treaty, in 1989.
  - o The need to place the symbol © or the word "copyright" or 'copr." on copyrighted works was eliminated.
- Sonny Bono Copyright Term Extension Act extends individual protection to life plus 70 years.
  - o Businesses are protected for 95 years from first publication or 120 from creation, whichever is shorter.
- Once the copyright period closes, the work becomes public domain.

**Computer Software Copyright Act.** This Act amends the Copyright Act of 1976 and includes computer programs in the list of items protected by copyright law.
- The creator of a software program obtains automatic copyright protection.

*Semiconductor Chip Protection Act.* This Mask Work Act provides more protection for hardware components of a computer by protecting masks that are used to create computer chips.
- Notice is optional.
  - o When used, notice must use "mask work" or "*M*" or "(M)" and the owner's name.

**Copyright Infringement.** This happens when a significant or material part of a copyrighted work is copied without permission.
- Copying need not be verbatim or the entire work.
- A copyright holder successful in an infringement suit can recover:
    o Profit made by the infringer,
    o Damages,
    o An order to impound and destroy the infringing works,
    o An injunction preventing future infringement.
- A court can award statutory damages for willful infringement in lieu of actual damages.

**The Fair Use Doctrine.** This doctrine allows some unauthorized use of copyrighted materials.
- Several uses are allowed under this doctrine:
    o A quotation for review or criticism or in a scholarly or technical work,
    o Use in a parody or satire,
    o A brief quotation in a news report,
    o Reproduction of a small part to illustrate a lesson for a teacher or student,
    o Incidental reproduction in a newsreel or broadcast of an event being reported,
    o Reproduction in legislative or judicial proceedings.
- The copyright holder cannot recover for infringement if fair use is found.

**The NET Act: Criminal Copyright Infringement.** The No Electronic Theft Act (NET Act) criminalizes willful infringement of a copyright.
- The Act prohibits infringement
    o For commercial or financial gain, or
    o Without commercial or financial gain if the retail value exceeds $1,000.
- Criminal penalties include imprisonment and fines up to $100,000.

**Digital Millennium Copyright Act.** This Act criminalizes the cracking of wrappers and selling of technology of copyrighted digital works.
- This Act prohibits circumvention of wrapper or encryption on copyrighted digital works.
    o The information need not be misused.
- This Act prohibits the manufacture and distribution of means designed to circumvent wrappers and encryption on copyrighted digital works.
    o Multipurpose devices that can be used in other ways do not violate the Act.
- There are exceptions to this Act:
    o Software developers seeking compatibility with the protected work.
    o Law enforcement conducting criminal investigations.
    o Parents protecting their children from harmful materials on the internet.
    o Internet users disabling cookies and other identification devices.
    o Nonprofit libraries, educational institutions, archives reviewing the work for acquisition.
- This Act provides both civil and criminal penalties:
    o Civil penalties include actual and treble damages, costs and attorney fees, destruction of illegal items, and injunction against future violations OR statutory damages of $2,500 to $25,000 per act.
    o Criminal penalties include fines of $500,000 to $1 million, imprisonment of 5-10 years.

## Trademarks

Companies spend millions to gain market recognition through company names, slogans, and logos.

**Federal Lanham Trademark Act.** This Act protects the owner's investment and goodwill embodied in a mark and prevents confusion of consumers as to the origin of goods and services.

- The PTO is the place where trademarks are registered.
  - The original registration is good for 10 years.
  - Renewal registration is good for an unlimited number of 10 year periods.
  - Registration is national.
  - Registration gives notice that the mark is personal property.
  - Trademark holder may use the ®, but it is not required.
- The mark can be registered if it has been used in the sale of goods or services.
  - The mark can be registered six months before its proposed use.
  - It will be cancelled if not used during this time.
- A third party can oppose a proposed registration or the cancellation of a registered mark.

**Marks That Can Be Trademarked.** The term "mark" refers to several separate types of marks.

- Trademarks are distinctive marks, symbols, names, words, mottos, or devices that identify the goods of a specific business.
- Service marks are used to distinguish the services of a specific business.
- Certification marks are used to verify that goods and services are of a specified quality or originate from a specific geographical area.
- Collective marks are sued by cooperatives, associations, and fraternal organizations.
- Some marks cannot be trademarked:
  - Flags or coats of arms of any state, municipality, or foreign nation.
  - Marks which are immoral or scandalous.
  - Geographical names alone.
  - Surnames alone.
  - Marks resembling any already registered.

**Distinctiveness of a Mark.** A mark must be distinctive or it must have obtained a "secondary meaning."

- Descriptions without a secondary meaning cannot be trademarked.

**Trademark Infringement.** Unauthorized use of a mark can subject the offender to a suit by the owner.

- Trademark infringement requires that
  - The mark was used in an unauthorized manner by the defendant.
  - There would be public confusion, mistake, or deception from this use.
- The successful owner can recover damages from the defendant.
  - Profits made by the defendant.
  - Damages to plaintiff's business and reputation.
  - Destruction of all goods with unauthorized mark.
  - Injunction against future infringement.
  - The Court can award treble damages if the infringement is intentional.

**Trade Dress.** The Lanham Act protects some forms of how the product looks and feels, the packaging, or a service establishment.

**Generic Names.** A generic word, name, or slogan cannot be registered as a trademark.

- A trademark or trade name that becomes a common term for a particular product or service, rather than for the individual seller, loses its trademark protection.

**Federal Dilution Act.** This Act protects famous marks from dilution.

- The mark must be famous.
- The use by the other party must be commercial.

- The use must cause dilution.
  - o Dilution is the lessening of the ability of the mark to identify and distinguish the goods and services of the mark holder.

*Trademark Dilution Revision Act.* This Act states that a dilution plaintiff need not show actual harm.
- The Act helps define dilution, blurring, and tarnishment.
- The Act allows comparative advertising and fair use.

**International Protection of Intellectual Property Rights.** Countries began signing treaties and conventions to protect intellectual property rights in the late 1800s.
- The Paris Convention protects patents and trademarks.
- The Berne Convention protects copyrights.

*The World Intellectual Property Organization (WIPO).* This is a specialized agency of the United Nations founded to promote and protect intellectual property rights worldwide.
- The WIPO Copyright Treaty protects copyrights to computer programs and data compilations.
- The WIPO Phonogram Treaty gives performers and producers the exclusive right to broadcast, reproduce, and distribute copies of their performances.

# Refresh Your Memory

The following exercises will help to test your memory regarding the principles given in this chapter. Read each question twice, then place your answer in the blank provided for each question. Review the chapter material for any questions you are unable to answer or remember.

1. A(n) _____ _____ can be a product formula, pattern, design, compilation of data, or customer list.

2. State unfair competition laws give the owner of a trade secret the ability to sue someone who steals a trade secret for _____.

3. The owner of a trade secret must take all _____ _____ to prevent discovery of the trade secret by others.

4. The _____ _____ _____ criminalizes the theft of another's trade secrets and was intended to address such thefts through computer espionage and the Internet.

5. Applications for patents must be filed with the United States _____ _____ _____ _____ in Washington, D.C.

6. An invention or design enters the _____ _____ once the patent period runs out.

7. The U.S. uses the _____ _____ _____ Rule, which states that the first person to invent is given the patent protection over a party who is first to file an application.

8. An invention must be _____, _____, and _____ to be patented.

9. Under the _____ _____ _____ _____ Doctrine a patent may not be granted if the public has had use of the invention for more than one year before filing of the application.

10. Patent _____ happens with the unauthorized use of another's patent.

11. Only _____ _____ are subject to copyright registration and protection.

12. A(n) _____ is created when a work is produced by an author.

13. A(n) _____ is a distinctive mark, symbol, name, word, motto, or device that identifies the goods of a specific business.

14. A mark must be _____ or must have acquired a "secondary meaning" to qualify for trademark protection.

15. A trademark that becomes a common term for a product or service is a(n) _____ _____ and loses its protection under federal trademark law.

## Critical Thought Exercise

Mary's Marketing has been a one-woman business from its beginnings in June of 1985 when Mary graduated from business school with an MBA in Marketing. This small business has developed a reputation for designing innovative and cost-effective marketing strategies for small- and medium-sized businesses. Mary has spent years developing and maintaining good working relationships with her clients. An outgrowth of her having maintained many long-term business relationships is a very detailed client list and potential client list. This list contains the usual information of owner names, company names, addresses, business product and/or service lines, primary employees, and target markets. The list also contains outline strategies that Mary develops as she learns of new or changing circumstances for the individuals, companies, and markets. She uses this type of information to approach established clients and prospective clients about possible marketing campaigns. Because of how she develops information within this list, Mary knows her list is very unique and highly important to the success of her business.

On July 21 of 2006, Mary hired an administrative assistant to organize the increasing amount of paperwork coming into her office, to answer and ever-increasing number of telephone calls while she was in meetings, and to run business errands when necessary. Mary has not told this assistant of the existence of her client list. The business is still run from a dedicated office in Mary's home. Mary keeps a working copy of her client list on her computer, which is password protected, and keeps a back-up copy in a locked safe in her office.

In a few weeks, Mary plans to move her office to a professional office complex at the edge of the swiftly growing industrial and professional park in town. She will be sharing a suite of offices with two other small professional businesses. All three businesses will share a common reception area and receptionist. A separate room to the rear of the reception area will house a common copy room and break room. There will be one large office and one small office for each business, but all clients would have to walk through the reception area to reach any of the offices. Mary expects that the larger office will be hers, as she will be meeting with clients. The smaller office will be for her administrative assistant.

Mary has often helped the local university with student projects and has volunteered time to help develop marketing strategies for the business department and the university as a whole. She has asked the business department to look at her situation and comment on how she can ensure the safety of her valuable client list and minimize any losses from the theft of that list. The head of the business department has asked you to draft comments and suggestions to Mary.

*Please compose your answer on a separate sheet of paper or on your computer.*

# Practice Quiz

## True/False

1. ___ Trademarks include product formulas, patterns, designs, and compilations of data.

2. ___ Misappropriation is the theory under which the owner can bring a lawsuit against someone who stole a trade secret.

3. ___ The Federal Patent Statute of 1952 encourages writers to create and make their creations public and to protect these creations from infringement.

4. ___ Once a patent period has run out, the invention or design enters the public domain.

5. ___ The U.S. follows the first-to-file rule in that the first person to file an application for patent will be given the patent.

6. ___ Abstractions and scientific principles are easily patented as part of the tangible environment.

7. ___ An invention that is used by the public for more than one year prior to the filing of the patent application may not be granted patent protection.

8. ___ The Copyright Revision Act of 1976 establishes what is needed to obtain a copyright and protects copyrighted works from infringement.

9. ___ Only intangible writings are subject to copyright registration and protection.

10. ___ An author must register a work with the U.S. Copyright Office before a copyright is issued.

11. ___ The Trademark and Patent Act protects the owner's investment in a mark and prevents consumers from being confused as to the origin of goods and services.

12. ___ The original trademark registration is valid for 70 years, with one renewal allowed for 10 years.

13. ___ The flag of the United States cannot be trademarked.

14. ___ A mark, to qualify for federal protection, must be distinctive or have acquired a "primary meaning."

15. ___ The Berne Convention protects patents and trademarks internationally.

## Multiple Choice

16. The owner of a trade secret is required to take all reasonable precautions to prevent the discovery of the secret by others.
    a. Fencing in buildings, placing locks on doors, and hiring security guards are methods to protect a trade secret.
    b. Failure to take appropriate actions in protecting a trade secret will remove that secret from the protection of state unfair competition statutes.
    c. Both a and b.
    d. None of the above.

17. Federal patent law is
    a. exclusive.
    b. inclusive.
    c. concurrent.
    d. subjective.

18. Jane files a patent application for Herrowine, an asexually reproducing plant, on May 21, 2007. Jane invented this plant on April 30, 2007. George files a patent application for Halovine, an asexually reproducing plant identical to Herrowine, on June 8, 2007. He invented this plant on March 15, 2007. Who will receive the U.S. patent for their plant?
    a. Jane will receive the patent for Herrowine under the first-to-file rule, because she filed her application for a patent on May 21 and George filed his application on June 8.
    b. George will receive the patent for Halovine under the last-to-file rule, because he filed his application for a patent on June 8 and Jane filed her application on May 21.
    c. George will receive the patent for Halovine under the first-to-invent rule, because he invented his plant on March 15 and Jane invented her plant on April 30.
    d. Jane will receive the patent for Herrowine under the last-to-invent rule, because she invented her plant on April 30 and George invented his plant on March 15.

19. Simone invents a device on July 7, 2005 and sells that device to the public. On August 8, 2006, she files an application for patent for the device with the Patent and Trademark Office. Will her patent be granted?
    a. Yes, so long as her device is novel, useful, and nonobvious.
    b. No, as the one-year "on sale" rule applies and she did not file her application for patent until more than one year after she invented her device.
    c. Yes, as the one-year "on sale" rule applies and she met the requirement of having the device on the market at least one year before applying for a patent.
    d. No, as her device is not novel nor useful nor nonobvious.

20. Phillip is a talented storyteller who tells stories to schoolchildren and community organizations. The stories he tells are those of his own imagination. He has never written down his stories, as his memory is phenomenal, nor does he allow his storytelling sessions to be videotaped or recorded. Herbert, who has heard Phillip tell his stories several times, writes down one of the stories and has it published under his own name. Phillip sees this story selling in a local bookstore and is very upset. If Phillip sues Herbert for copyright infringement, will he be successful?
    a. Yes. The story was created by Phillip and heard by Herbert, who published it knowing it was not his own work.
    b. Yes. The story was published by Phillip when he told it to groups of schoolchildren and community organizations, so he can prove that Herbert stole his work.
    c. No. Under the first-to-publish rule, Herbert will be given the copyright to the story.
    d. No. Phillip created the story, but he never wrote down the story and did not allow his storytelling sessions to be recorded or videotaped. He had no tangible record of his work, thus cannot have a copyright for that work.

21. Carmine publishes a novel that sells well and earns him a good living for the 60 years after he publishes the novel to the time that he dies. At his death, Carmine's novel is still selling well and the publisher expects that it will continue to sell for many years. Stella is Carmine's niece and only heir. What benefit, if any, will Stella receive from Carmine's novel?
    a. Stella, as the only heir, will receive the royalty from the novel for 70 years after Carmine's death, as Carmine's copyright was for his life plus 70 years. If she dies before then, her heirs will receive the royalty for the remainder of the 70 years.

b. Stella, as the only heir, will receive the royalty from the novel for 10 years after Carmine's death, as Carmine's copyright is for 70 years from date of publication. If she dies before then, her heirs will receive the royalty for the remainder of the 10 years.

c. Stella will receive nothing, as Carmine's copyright dies with him and his novel will become public domain.

d. Stella will receive nothing, as Carmine's copyright does not pass to his estate and heirs, but goes to the publisher.

22. Lyle successfully sues Fred for copyright infringement. Which of the following can Lyle recover?
   a. The profit made by Fred from the infringement, and damages suffered by Lyle.
   b. An order directing the impoundment and destruction of the infringing materials.
   c. An Injunction preventing future infringement by Fred.
   d. All of the above.

23. Which of the following uses is permitted under the Fair Use Doctrine of copyright?
   a. Reproduction of a work by a teacher to write a teaching manual.
   b. Documentation of the work on a public television program.
   c. Use of the work in a parody or satire.
   d. All of the above.

24. Steve's Save-a-Lot registers a trademark with the Patent and Trademark Office on February 2, 2004, though the business does not plan to conduct business until April. Due to various unforeseen problems, Steve's Save-a-Lot does not begin business until November 1, 2004. What is the status of the trademark registered by Steve's Save-a-Lot?
   a. The trademark is registered for 10 years, Steve's Save-a-Lot is not required to use it during that 10 years.
   b. The trademark was registered prior to its proposed use, thus Steve's Save-a-Lot had six months to use the mark before that mark was lost. The mark is no longer protected by that registration.
   c. The trademark was registered prior to its proposed use, therefore the 10 year registration period does not begin until Steve's Save-a-Lot actually uses the mark.
   d. None of the above.

25. Which of the following lists the types of marks protected as trademarks:
   a. Trademarks, service marks, certification marks, and cooperative marks.
   b. Trademarks, service marks, criminal marks, and collective marks
   c. Trademarks, social marks, certification marks, and collective marks.
   d. Trademarks, service marks, certification marks, and collective marks.

## Short Answer

26. What types of items may be considered to be trade secrets?

_____

27. For a lawsuit for misappropriation to be actionable, what must the plaintiff prove?

_____

28. What types of precautions must an owner of a trade secret take to protect the secret from discovery?

_____

29. What can a successful plaintiff in a trade secret action recover?

_____

30. What is the meaning of public domain?

31. What is the first-to-invent rule?

32. What types of subject matter are patentable?

33. What is the Public Use Doctrine?

34. What can a successful plaintiff in a patent infringement suit recover?

35. What does federal copyright law protect?

36. When is a copyright effective?

37. What is the Berne Convention?

38. What did the Sonny Bono Copyright Term Extension Act grant individuals?

39. What can a successful plaintiff in a copyright infringement suit recover?

40. What uses of copyrighted material are protected under the Fair Use Doctrine?

## Answers to Refresh Your Memory

1. trade secret  [p 182]
2. misappropriation  [p 182]
3. reasonable precautions  [p 182]
4. Economic Espionage Act  [p 183]
5. Patent and Trademark Office  [p 184]
6. public domain  [p 184]
7. First-to-Invent  [p 185]

8.   novel, useful, nonobvious  [p 186]
9.   one-year "on sale" [p 188]
10.   infringement  [p 190]
11.   tangible writings  [p 192]
12.   copyright  [p 192]
13.   trademark  [p 200]
14.   distinctive  [p 201]
15.   generic name  [p 206]

# Critical Thought Model Answer

The client list for Mary's Marketing is a very valuable trade secret. As such, it is important that all reasonable precautions be taken to ensure that this trade secret is not discovered by her competitors. If reasonable precautions to keep this secret safe are not taken, then this client list will not be protected as a trade secret and Mary's Marketing will be unable to sue for damages in the event that the list is taken.

Mary has made a good start in keeping her client list secret. She keeps her working copy on her password protected computer, and she keeps a back-up copy in her office safe. These actions show that she does consider the client list to be valuable and secret and has taken measures to keep it safe.

However, she can improve these basic precautions. She can improve the protection of the computer file by encrypting the information. She can program the computer to automatically shut down after a very short time to minimize the ability of others to accidentally see this information. She may wish to keep her working copy on a removable device so that the entire device can be locked in her office safe. She should consider measures that require her, or anyone she allows to work with this list, to shut down the computer when stepping away from the computer or to remove the storage device and lock it in the safe when stepping out of the office for any reason. Additionally, Mary should have two back-up copies of her current list in secure places away from her office. Now that she is moving to an office outside of her home, she can store one back-up copy in her home safe and a second back-up copy in a bank safety deposit box. If her working copy is damaged or stolen, or if the office is destroyed, she can retrieve a copy of her list from a separate location.

Moving to an office outside of her house poses some security issues for her client list, as she will not be on the premises outside of working hours. She should consider installing a security system for her office area. She should also consider a security system in her home to protect her back-up copy. The fact that all visitors must walk through the reception area to access the offices is good for Mary, so long as there is a receptionist on duty to keep track of visitors. It may be a good idea to install a security alarm that will notify people in the offices when a visitor enters the reception area.

Mary should tell her administrative that she has a confidential client list and specify the security measures that the assistant will have to follow in regards to the list. Failure to do so could make it appear that she did not really consider the list to be valuable, therefore it would not be protected as a trade secret.

Overall, Mary needs to keep in mind that her client list is a valuable trade secret and that she must take precautions to keep her client list a secret.

# Answers to Practice Quiz

## True/False

1.   False   Trade secrets include product formulas, patterns, designs, and compilations of data. [p 182]
2.   True   Misappropriation is the theory under which the owner can bring a lawsuit against someone who stole a trade secret. [p 182]

3.   False   The Federal Patent Statute of 1952 encourages inventors to invent and make their inventions public and to protect these patented inventions from infringement. [p 184]
4.   True    Once a patent period has run out, the invention or design enters the public domain. [p 184]
5.   False   The U.S. follows the first-to-invent rule in that the first person to invent is given patent protection, rather than the party that was first to file an application for patent. [p 185]
6.   False   Abstractions and scientific principles cannot be patented unless they are part of the tangible environment. [p 186]
7.   True    An invention that is used by the public for more than one year prior to the filing of the patent application may not be granted patent protection. [p 188]
8.   True    The Copyright Revision Act of 1976 establishes what is needed to obtain a copyright and protects copyrighted works from infringement. [p 191]
9.   False   Only tangible writings are subject to copyright registration and protection. [p 192]
10.  False   A copyright is created when an author produces his or her work; registration is voluntary. [p 192]
11.  False   The Lanham Act protects the owner's investment in a mark and prevents consumers from being confused as to the origin of goods and services. [p 200]
12.  False   The original registration of a trademark is valid for 10 years, with unlimited renewals allowed of 10 years each.[p 200]
13.  True    The flag of the United States cannot be trademarked. [p 201]
14.  False   A mark, to qualify for federal protection, must be distinctive or have acquired a "secondary meaning." [p 201]
15.  False   The Berne Convention protects copyrights internationally. [p 209]

## Multiple Choice

16.  C.   Answer C is correct, as both A and B are correct statements regarding the protection of trade secrets. Answers A and B are incorrect, as each of these statements are correct. Answer D is incorrect, for the reasons stated above. [p 182]
17.  A.   Answer A is correct, as only the federal government has authority to legislate patent law. Answer B is incorrect, as the term has no pertinence to legislation of patent law. Answer C is incorrect, as concurrent authority would mean that the federal and state governments shared authority to legislate patent law, which is untrue. Answer D is incorrect, as the term has no pertinence to legislation of patent law. [p 184]
18.  C.   Answer C is correct, as the U.S. follows the first-to-invent rule and George invented his plant on March 15 and Jane invented her plant on April 30. Answer A in incorrect, as the U.S. does not follow the first-to-file rule, as do many other countries. Answer B is incorrect, as there is no last-to-file rule for filing patents. Answer D is incorrect, as there is no last-to-invent rule for filing patents. [p 185]
19.  B    Answer B is correct, as the one-year "on sale" rule applies since she did not file her application for patent until more than one year after she invented her device. Answers A and D are incorrect, as there are insufficient facts to show whether or not her device is novel, useful, and nonobvious. Answer C is incorrect, as the one-year "on sale" rule requires the application for patent be filed no later than one year after the device is made available for public use, not that the device must be in public use at least a year before filing an application for patent. [p 188]
20.  D    Answer D is correct, as copyright protection is only give to tangible writings, writings that can be physically seen. Phillip never made a tangible copy of his work. Answer A is incorrect, as Phillip never made a copyrightable version of his work, thus Herbert did not use the story in an illegal manner. Answer C is incorrect, as there is no first-to-publish rule for copyright. [p 192]
21.  A    Answer A is correct, as this is a correct statement of the copyright protection given a work of the author's life plus 70 years. Answers B, C, and D are incorrect, as all of these answers are not accurate statements. [p 192]

22. D   Answer D is correct, as answers A, B, and C are all correct statements of the recovery Lyle can make. [p 193]

23. C   Answer C is correct, as the Fair Use Doctrine allows the use of a work in a parody or satire. Answer A is incorrect, as this is an incorrect statement of the allowed use by a teacher or a student of a small part of the work to illustrate a lesson. Answer B is incorrect, as this is an incorrect statement of the allowed use of an incidental reproduction of a work in a newsreel or broadcast of an event being reported. Answer D is incorrect for the above reasons. [p 196]

24. B   Answer B is correct, as trademark was registered prior to its proposed use, thus Steve's Save-a-Lot had six months to use the mark before that mark was lost. The mark is no longer protected by that registration. Answer A and B are incorrect, as they are each incorrect statements. Answer D is incorrect for the above reasons. [p 200]

25. D   Answer D is correct, as it correctly lists the types of marks that are protected under trademark laws. Answer A, B, and C are incorrect, as they are each incorrect listings. [p 200-201]

## Short Answer

26. Product formulas, patterns, designs, compilations of data, customer lists may be trade secrets. [p 182]

27. That the defendant obtained the trade secret through unlawful means, such as theft, bribery, or industrial espionage. [p 182]

28. All reasonable precautions, which can include fencing of buildings, placing locks on doors, hiring security guards. [p 182]

29. The profits made by the offender in using the trade secret, damages, an injunction prohibiting the offender from divulging or using the trade secret. [p 182]

30. Public domain means that anyone can produce and sell the invention without paying the prior patent holder, or publish a work without paying the prior copyright holder. [p 184, 193]

31. The first-to-invent rule states that the first person to invent an item or a process is given patent protection over another party who was first to file a patent application. [p 185]

32. Machines, processes, compositions of matter, improvements to existing machines processes, or compositions of matter, designs for an article of manufacture, asexually reproduced plants, and living material invented by a person. [p 186]

33. The Public Use Doctrine, or the One-year "On Sale" Doctrine, states that a patent may not be granted if the invention was used by the public for more than one year prior to the filing of the patent application. [p 188]

34. Money damages equal to a reasonable royalty rate on the sale of the infringed items, other damages, an order requiring destruction of the infringing article, and an injunction preventing future infringement by the offender. [p 190]

35. Federal copyright laws protect the work of authors and other creative persons from unauthorized use of their copyrighted materials and provide a financial incentive to write. [p 191]

36. A copyright is created at the time an author produces his or her work.[p 192]

37. The Berne Convention is an international copyright treaty which eliminated the need to place a symbol or words designating a copyright on copyrighted works. [p 192]

38. This act granted individuals copyright protection for their life plus 70 years. [p 192-193]

39. Profit made from the copyright infringement; damages; an order for impoundment and destruction of the infringing works; an injunction against future infringement by the offender. [p 193]

40. Quotation of the copyrighted work for review or criticism or in a scholarly or technical work; use in a parody or satire; brief quotation in a news report; reproduction by a student or teacher of a small part of the work to illustrate a lesson; incidental reproduction of a work in a newsreel or broadcast of an even being reported; reproduction of a work in a legislative or judicial proceeding. [p 196]

# *Chapter 8*

# ETHICS OF MANAGERS AND SOCIAL RESPONSIBILITY OF BUSINESS

## Chapter Overview

Businesses that are organized in the U.S. must follow its laws are required to follow the laws of other countries in which they operate. Businesspersons have a duty to act in an ethical manner and businesses have a social responsibility to not harm society. Though law is often based on standards of ethical behavior, not all of these standards have become law. The basic premise of law is that is defines a minimum degree of conduct for persons and businesses in society. Ethics is more stringent. Ethics and social responsibility of business are presented in this chapter.

## Objectives

Upon completion of the exercises that accompany this chapter, you should be able to:

1. Describe how law and ethics interweave.
2. Define and compare the five main moral theories of business ethics.
3. Compare the traditional role of social responsibility of business to the modern trend.
4. Describe corporate citizenship.
5. Describe the corporate social audit and discuss its importance in business today.

## Practical Application

You should be able to recognize the types of ethical behavior being utilized in business based upon your knowledge of the various ethical theories. You should develop a greater appreciation for the history of this area of the law.

## Helpful Hints

You should become familiar with the key terms and phrases associated with ethics and be familiar with a case example for the theory you are trying to remember. The study tips given below have been organized by theory and come with a case or an example to enforce the principles to which it applies.

## Study Tips

### Ethics and the Law

There are three basic relationships of the law to ethics:
- When the law and ethics demand the same response.

- o Taking someone's property through fraud would be wrong under the law and ethics.
- When the law would permit conduct that ethics would forbid.
  - o Failing to provide promised retirement benefits to employees may be legal, but is not ethical.
- When the law demands certain conduct and ethics demands the opposite.
  - o An employer is ordered to garnish the wages of an employee when the employer knows that the employee's child has been undergoing expensive treatment for cancer which is only partially covered by health insurance. The garnishment is legal, but garnishing wages from this employee would not seem ethical.

## Business Ethics

Though ethics are hard to measure and very personal to an individual, there are some rules regarding ethical conduct that appear to be universal.

**Ethical Fundamentalism.** Under this theory, an individual looks to an outside source, such as the Bible and Koran or Karl Marx, for guidance and rules for ethical conduct.
- Criticism: This theory does not allow individuals to decide right and wrong for themselves.
- Taken to an extreme, ethical conduct under this theory could be considered unethical under most other ethical theories.
- Example: As noted in the text, the Bible specifies the maxim "an eye for an eye."
  - o Following this maxim would allow retaliation.
  - o If Joe runs over Mary's cat with his car, then Mary should be allowed to run over Joe's cat with her car.

**Utilitarianism.** The actions or rule that provides the greatest good to society should be chosen.
- This does not mean the most good to the most people.
- Criticism: This theory treats morality as an impersonal mathematical calculation, a "cost-benefit" analysis.
- Example: The case of Charter *Township of Ypsilanti Michigan v. General Motors Corporation,* No. 161245 (Mich. App. 1993) involved a General Motors Chevrolet production plant that decided to move from Ypsilanti, Michigan to Arlington, Texas.
  - o The Charter Township of Ypsilanti brought a suit against General Motors alleging that it had given the automaker $13 million dollars in tax abatements, and that without the plant 4,500 people would be out of work.
  - o The trial judge appeared to apply the concept of utilitarianism in this case by ruling that just because General Motors thinks it can make the cars cheaper elsewhere does not make it right to desert the workers and their families.
  - o The tax abatements given to the automaker could have been given toward education.
  - o Unfortunately, the appellate court reversed, holding that there was no quid pro quo (this for that) agreement between the parties.

**Kantian Ethics.** This is a duty ethics theory where moral duties, grounded on universal rules, are owed.
- Ethical decisions are reached through reasoning.
- Behavior is based on the categorical imperative: "Do unto others as you would have them do unto you."
- The universal rules are based on two principles:
  - o Consistency, with all cases being treated alike.
  - o Reversibility, where one is judged by the rules one used to judge others.
    - ▪ If you make an exception, that exception becomes the new rule.
- Criticism: Consensus on what universal rules should be is difficult to reach.

- Example: A teacher has a rule that allows students one hour to complete an examination. If the teacher allows one student to have an extra five minutes to complete the examination, all other students must be given an extra five minutes to complete the examination.

**Rawls's Social Justice Theory.** There is a presumption that each person has entered into a social contract with all others in society to obey necessary moral rules to keep the peace.
- Involves an implied contract, "I will keep the rules if everyone else does."
- These moral rules are used to resolve conflict between interests in society.
- Fairness is the essence of justice.
    - Principles would be chosen by those unaware of their place in society.
        - Those with a "veil of ignorance."
    - Rules chosen under this veil would be the fairest possible.
- Least advantaged in society must receive special assistance to realize their potential.
- Criticism:
    - The real world does not allow the original position screened from prejudice.
    - Many would not choose to maximize the benefit to the least advantaged.
- Example: The Sears and Robuck Co. "bait and rip off" scheme wherein Sears distributed discount brake job coupons to consumers and upon redemption of the same would convince the consumer that he or she needed additional repairs.
    - The customers presumed that Sears would act ethically until many became upset with being overcharged.
    - Thereafter California officials became aware of the situation and threatened to revoke Sears auto repair license.
    - Sears settled all lawsuits against it.
    - In this case forty-one states voiced complaints thereby evoking anger and conflict versus peace and harmony as per this ethical theory.

**Ethical Relativism.** Ethical behavior is based on the feelings of right or wrong of an individual.
- There are no universal rules to guide conduct.
    - There can be no criticism if a person meets his or her own moral standard in a decision.
- Criticism: If an individual does not consider particular behavior to be unethical, then taking that action would not be unethical.
- Few philosophers consider this theory as an acceptable method for determining ethical behavior.
- Example: The case of *McNeil-P.C.C. inc. v. Bristol-Meyers Squibb Co. 938F.2d 1544 (1991)* illustrates this theory as McNeil sued Bristol –Meyers based upon the theory of false advertising.
    - Bristol Meyers had advertised that Excederin worked better than Tylenol.
    - After testing both products, it was found that they were basically the same and that Bristol-Meyers violated the Lanham Act, which prohibits false advertising.
    - If Bristol-Meyers were applying ethical relativism to their claims regarding their product, they may claim that in their opinion, its products is better than that of McNeil-P.C.C. and that there should be no conflict on this point based upon how they feel.
    - Therefore, even though the court found that fraud was committed, under this theory, Bristol-Meyer's actions would in fact be ethical.

## Social Responsibility of Business

Many business decisions in the past were founded on cost-benefit analysis and how they affected profits. Decisions with this basis often caused harm to others. Today, businesses are expected to behave with a degree of social responsibility in their actions.

**Maximizing Profits.** This is the traditional view of social responsibility for business, that of a duty to gain the most profit for shareholders.

- The interests of others are unimportant.
- Milton Friedman advocated this theory.
  - o A business should use its resources to increase profits.
  - o So long as it stays within the rules of the game.
    - ▪ Open and free competition.
    - ▪ Without deception or fraud.
- Example: The case of *Mangini v. R.J. Reynolds Tobacco Company* involved R.J. Reynolds Tobacco Company's use of Joe Camel, a cartoon character that attorney and plaintiff Janet Mangini claimed was using unfair business practices.
  - o The defendant utilized the defense of freedom of speech under the First Amendment.
  - o However, the plaintiff showed that R.J. Reynold's advertising was targeted at youth who were unable to make an informed choice knowing what the health risks are.
  - o R.J. Reynold's marketing ploy was designed to make money regardless of the existing and potential harm it was causing to those it wanted to sell to.
  - o It appears that this case is a classic example of the theory of maximizing profits.

**Moral Minimum.** This theory states that the social responsibility of business is met as long as it either avoids or corrects any social injury it causes.

- A corporation may make a profit
  - o If it does not cause harm to others while doing so.
- Example: The case of In re Union Carbide Corporation Gas Plant Disaster at Bhopal, India, in December 1984, 634 F.Supp. 842 (S.D.N.Y. 1986); 804 F.2 195 *(2d Cir. 1987); cert. Denied, 484 U.S. 871 (1987)* involved a leakage of Methyl isocyanate, a toxic gas used to produce pesticides.
  - o The winds blew the gas into a heavily populated residential area causing many deaths and over 200,000 people to be injured.
  - o After determining that the Indian legal system would decide the cause of the event, Union Carbide was ordered to set up a fund of $470 million dollars for the claimants.
  - o Many issues were raised in this case, however, the main ethical one appears to be, did this fund correct the injuries it caused?
  - o Opponents argue that it did not, as the settlement amounted to less than a thousand dollars per claimant.

**Stakeholder Interest.** In this theory, businesses have to consider the impact its actions will have on its stakeholders, which include stockholders, employees, suppliers, customers, creditors and the community.

- All of these individuals have a stake in the business.
- Criticism: It is difficult to synchronize the conflicting stakeholder interests.
- Example: As per the text, if employees of a business were seen only as a means to acquire wealth for the stockholders, this would not take into consideration the impact it would have on those employees.

**Corporate Citizenship.** Under this theory, a business has a responsibility to do well.

- Businesses are under a duty to help solve social problems with which it had minimum or no association.
  - o The rationale is that a duty is owed because of the social power society has given to businesses.
- Criticism: Society will always have some sort of social problem that needs to be solved, and businesses have limits to their funds.
- Taken to an extreme, potential investors may be reluctant to invest.

- Example: Corporations owe a duty to fund a cure for a local child suffering from a rare disease.

**Sorbanes-Oxley Act.** This Act has prompted public companies to adopt code of ethics.
- Enacted in the wake of massive financial frauds perpetrated by senior officers of companies.
- Encourages senior officers of companies to act ethically.
- Requires disclosure of whether or not a company has adopted a code of ethics.

**The Corporate Social Audit.** Audits are usually conducted to examine the financial health of a business, but a moral check up may be conducted as well.
- Corporations subject to such an audit would be more likely to prevent unethical and illegal conduct by managers, employees, and agents.
- An ethical check up would include
  - An examination of employee adherence to the company's code of ethics.
  - Whether the corporation has fulfilled its duty of social responsibility.
    - Promotion of worker safety.
    - Employment opportunities for protected classes.
    - Environmental protection.
- It may be difficult to conceptualize what is being audited and the results are difficult to measure.
- An independent firm should conduct the audit for autonomy and objectivity.
- Corporate personnel should cooperate fully.
- Findings should be reported directly to the Board and the Board should review these results.

**United Nations Code of Conduct for Transnational Corporations: Respect for National Sovereignty.** Transnational corporations will respect the sovereignty of countries in which they operate.
- These corporations should act in conformity with the development policies, objectives, and priorities of these governments.
- These corporations should cooperate with these governments to contribute to the development process
- These corporations should work toward establishing mutually beneficial relations.

*Adherence to Sociocultural Objectives and Values.* Transnational corporations should respect the social and cultural objectives, values, and traditions of the countries in which they operate.
- These corporations should be positive to requests for consultations from these governments.

*Respect for Human Rights and Fundamental Freedoms.* Transnational corporations shall respect human rights and fundamental freedoms in the countries in which they operate.
- These corporations shall conform to policies extending quality of opportunity and treatment.

*Abstention from Corrupt Practices.* Transnational corporations shall refrain from actions of bribery.

# Refresh Your Memory

The following exercises will help to test your memory regarding the principles given in this chapter. Read each question twice, then place your answer in the blank provided for each question. Review the chapter material for any questions you are unable to answer or remember.

1. The _____ establishes a minimum degree of conduct; _____ demands more.

2. With the theory of _____ _____, a person looks to outside sources for ethical rules.

3. The moral theory of _____ states that people must choose the actions or follow the rule that provides the greatest good to society.

4. _____ _____ is being implemented if Cathy believes that by treating others with respect, they should treat her in the same manner.

5. A theory that promulgates that each person is presumed to have entered into a social contract with all others in society to obey moral rules that are necessary for people to live in peace and harmony is known as _____ _____ _____ Theory.

6. If Willy, a customer of Food Inc., sees Fred drop a $20.00 bill while checking out of the store and Willy's first instinct is to inform Fred, Willy would be applying the ethical theory of _____ _____.

7. If a sewage treatment plant that causes damage to a local lake and camp site offers to clean the lake and camp site, the plant would be applying the theory of _____ _____.

8. The social responsibility owed by businesses that states that business should maximize profits is known as the _____ view.

9. The stakeholder theory states that a corporation should consider the effects that its _____ have on other _____.

10. A business' responsibility to help solve social problems that it may not have caused would have its foundation in the theory known as _____ _____.

11. The corporate social audit refers to an audit of the corporation's _____ health.

12. If Mary looks to the Bible for ethical rules or commands to guide her, she would be supporting the theory of _____ _____.

13. Corporations have some degree of _____ _____ for their actions.

14. The theory that a corporation's duty is to make a profit while avoiding causing harm to others is known as the _____ _____ theory.

15. The corporate citizenship theory of social responsibility states that businesses have a(n) _____ to do _____.

# Critical Thought Exercise

You are an employee in the public relations department of Preciso, the luxury European automobile manufacturer. Preciso's sales have skyrocketed since the handcrafted vehicles were introduced to the United States ten years ago. Preciso's president has announced that Preciso will stop buying wood products from endangered forests following the example last year of Challenger Motor Company. Preciso will immediately stop buying wood from Canada's Great Bear Forest in British Columbia and phase out purchases of other wood from endangered forests. Instead, Preciso would like to use a "manmade wood-like product" for the interior parts (steering wheels, door panels, shifter knobs, etc.) of the autos it designs and builds.

There is no law against using wood from endangered forests and it is highly profitable to include these rare woods as part of the interiors of Preciso's cars. Shareholders are furious with the decision and are considering suing the Board of Directors and the officers of Preciso for wasting profits.

You are asked by the President of Preciso to draft a speech that she will deliver at the annual shareholders meeting which will explain the ethical business decision that was made and persuade the shareholders to not pursue a suit against the company.

*Please compose your answer on a separate sheet of paper or on your computer.*

# Practice Quiz

## True/False

1. ____ The corporate social audit should be designed to inspect the corporation's moral health.

2. ____ The moral minimum theory states that a corporation's social responsibility is to rectify the social injury that it causes.

3. ____ When a person looks to an outside source such as the Koran or the Bible for ethical rules, he or she is utilizing ethical fundamentalism.

4. ____ Under Rawl's Social Justice Theory, one must enter into a formal written contract in order to enforce rules that are necessary for people to live in peace and harmony.

5. ____ Kantian ethics refers to an individual's own feelings as to what is right or wrong.

6. ____ The United Nations has drafted a Code of Conduct for Transnational Corporations.

7. ____ Under the maximizing profits theory, the interest of others such as employees, suppliers, and local residents are not important in and of themselves.

8. ____ A stakeholder audit examines how well a corporation has met its duty of social responsibility.

9. ____ If a corporation pollutes the waters and then refuses compensation to those whom it injures, it has met its moral minimum duty of social responsibility.

10. ____ The stakeholder interest theory is criticized as it is challenging to harmonize the conflicting interests of the stakeholders.

11. ____ In the past, many businesses have made business decisions utilizing a small factor analysis.

12. ____ Ethical relativism would apply in the situation of one company making what it feels is an honest comparison to a competitor's product even though the comparison is actually invalid.

13. ____ It is unethical for a company to purposefully create partnerships to appear profitable and use these partnerships in an effort to borrow money to engage in speculative business dealings.

14. ____ Proponents of the corporate citizenship theory contend that the duty of a corporation to do good is limited and cannot be expanded beyond certain limits.

15. ___ Consistency and reversibility are two main principles espoused in Kantian universal rules.

## Multiple Choice

16. A moral theory that states that people must choose the actions that will provide the greatest good to society is
    a. Kantian ethics.
    b. maximizing profits.
    c. Utilitariansim.
    d. corporate social audit.

17. Which theory proposes a social contract theory of morality?
    a. Stakeholder interest
    b. Rawl's Social Justice Theory
    c. Ethical relativism
    d. Ethical fundamentalism

18. Which theory indicates that the use of fraud is all right if the perpetrator honestly thought it was in fact ethical?
    a. Rawl's social justice theory
    b. Maximizing profits
    c. Moral minimum
    d. Ethical relativism

19. Edward brought a $15.00 discount coupon off of his next oil change to Sam Slick's garage. Fred, an employee of Sam Slick's garage convinces Edward to have a variety of other services performed, which in turn causes Edward's final bill to be over $500.00. What ethical theory would Sam Slick allege if his "bait and switch" scheme is questioned?
    a. Utilitarianism
    b. Ethical fundamentalism
    c. Ethical relativism
    d. Stakeholder interest

20. If a computer manufacturer decided to close one of its manufacturing plants in Burlington, Vermont because the employees were not assembling the computers fast enough which was causing sales to drop, which ethical theory would this manufacturer be violating?
    a. Stakeholder interest
    b. Utilitarianism
    c. Kantian ethics
    d. All of the above

21. Under which ethical theory could an individual be considered to act unethically if he or she went to extremes in following the code of conduct promulgated by this theory?
    a. Ethical fundamentalism
    b. Maximizing profits
    c. Corporate citizenship
    d. Corporate audit

22. Which ethical theory is based on universal rules and a categorical imperative of "Do unto others as you would have them do unto you"?
    a. Ethical fundamentalism
    b. Utilitarianism

    c. Kantian Ethics

    d. Rawl's Theory of Social Justice

23. What is the traditional view of social responsibility?
    a. Ethical fundamentalism
    b. Maximizing profits
    c. Corporate citizenship
    d. Corporate audit

24. The text refers to *Dodge v. Ford Motor Company* where Henry Ford stated that his ambition in reducing the price of his cars was to employ more men, to spread the benefits of industry to the greatest number, and to help people build their lives and homes. Into which theory of ethics does his argument fit?
    a. Ethical fundamentalism
    b. Utilitarianism
    c. Kantian Ethics
    d. Rawl's Theory of Social Justice

25. The text refers to *Dodge v. Ford Motor Company* where Henry Ford stated that his ambition in reducing the price of his cars was to spread the benefits of industry to the greatest number. The court ruled that the duty of Mr. Ford to the shareholders was to carry on the business for profit. Into which theory of social responsibility does this ruling fit?
    a. Ethical fundamentalism
    b. Maximizing profits
    c. Corporate citizenship
    d. Corporate audit

## Short Answer

26. Define Kantian Ethics.

_____

27. What will corporations that conduct social audits likely prevent?

_____

28. Define Utilitarianism.

_____

29. On what two basic principles are the universal rules of Kantian ethics founded?

_____

30. If Cigarette Co. uses a thirteen year old smoking a cigarette at a party in one of its ads, what ethical theory might it be utilizing?

_____

31. The Environmental Safe Company promotes the safe dumping of toxic materials into our nation's waters. On one particular instance, Environmental caused the deaths of hundreds of sea lions. Its only response to the tragedy was that there are plenty of sea lions to mate with one another, so the population will be back in no time. If Environmental had met its duty of social responsibility by cleaning up the waters where the toxic materials were dumped and provide for safe dumping in the future so that other marine life are saved, it would have subscribed to what ethical theory?

_____

32. Which theory says that a corporation must consider the effects its actions have on individuals other than its stockholders?

    _____

33. What is the code of conduct that includes the respect for national sovereignty as well as adherence to socio-cultural objectives and values called?

    _____

34. Define the corporate citizenship theory of social responsibility.

    _____

35. What did the Sarbanes-Oxley Act prompt public companies to do?

    _____

36. Why is it important to have an independent firm conduct the social audit of a corporation?

    _____

37. What are the three relationships between law and ethics mentioned in the text?

    _____

    _____

38. What type of ethical theory is based on seeking sources such as the Bible and Koran or Karl Marx for ethical rules?

    _____

39. Action 1 will return 34 units of benefit to society. Action 2 will return 33 units of benefit to society. Action 3 will return 37 units of benefit to society. Using the utilitarian theory, which action should be taken?

    _____

40. The text refers to the case of *Dodge v. Ford Motor Company.* Briefly state Henry Ford's position and the court's ruling in that case.

    _____

    _____

# Answers to Refresh Your Memory

1. law, ethics  [p 217]
2. ethical fundamentalism  [p 218]
3. utilitarianism  [p 219]
4. Kantian ethics  [p 221]
5. Rawl's Social Justice  [p 223]
6. ethical relativism  [p 225]
7. moral minimum  [p 229]
8. traditional  [p 226]
9. actions, stakeholders  [p 229-230]
10. corporate citizenship  [p 231]
11. moral  [p 233]
12. ethical fundamentalism  [p 218]
13. social responsibility  [p 226]

14.  moral minimum  [p 229]
15.  responsibility, well  [p 231]

# Critical Thought Exercise Model Answer

Traditionally, it was perceived that the duty to shareholders took precedence over all other duties owed by the corporation and that the primary duty and goal of a company was to maximize profits. However, as corporations have developed global markets and society has changed, corporations have come to realize that they have several other duties that must be fulfilled. Employers have an ethical duty to employees to provide a safe workplace, to pay a decent wage, and to provide employment opportunities to present and future employees. As society has changed, the corporation has had to take into account ethical concerns such as equal pay for equal work and the prevention of sexual harassment. The company has had to change its policies to comply with laws such as the Family Medical Leave Act and the Americans With Disabilities Act. A corporation also has a duty to the persons who use its products. We must make a safe product that is economical and gives good value to the consumer for their investment and faith in us. We have a duty to our suppliers to maintain good business relations and use good faith and fair dealing in our contracts with them. We have a duty to the community where our facilities and offices are located. What we do as a corporation affects the tax base of the community and the quality of the schools, services, and collateral businesses in the area. Lastly, we have a duty to society at large to be the most ethical citizen possible. This means complying with environmental protection laws, preservation of scarce natural resources, and being part of the solution to very big problems instead of a cause. This corporation is in a unique position because of our wealth and power. We have a responsibility to society to use that wealth and power in socially beneficial ways. We should promote human rights, strive for equal treatment of minorities and women in the workplace, preserve and protect the environment, and not seek profits at the expense of ethics. If a corporation fails to conduct its operation ethically or respond quickly to an ethical crisis, its goodwill and reputation, along with profits, will suffer. Instead of aiming for maximum profits, we should aim for optimum profits—profits that can be realized while staying within legal and ethical limits set by government and society. For all these reasons, we have a duty to refrain from using wood from endangered forests to decorate our product. The manmade products we will substitute are more economical and will not detract from the overall look. Conversely, if we are known as the company that abuses scarce resources, consumers will support our competitors who are concerned about their corporate ethics.

# Answers to Practice Quiz

## True/False

1.  True    The corporate social audit should be designed to prevent unethical and illegal conduct by mangers, employees and agents. The purpose of the social audit is to examine a company's moral health. [p 233]
2.  True    The moral minimum theory contends that it is a corporation's duty to make a profit while avoiding causing harm to others. [p 229]
3.  True    When an individual looks to an outside source for ethical rules or commands, the individual is said to be adhering to the theory of ethical fundamentalism. [p 218]
4.  False   Under Rawl's Social Justice Theory, a person is presumed to have entered into an implied social contract with all others in society to obey the moral rules that are needed for people to live in peace and harmony. [p 223]
5.  False   The question states the principle behind ethical relativism. Kantian ethics basic premise is that people owe more duties that are based on universal rules. [p 221]

6. True   The UN Code of Conduct for Transnational Corporations addresses the issue of Respect for National Sovereignty. [p 233]

7. True   The traditional view of business and the social responsibility owed is that a business should maximize its profits for its shareholders regardless of the interests others may hold.[p 226-227]

8. False  A corporate social audit examines how well a corporation has met its duty of social responsibility. [p 233]

9. False  The moral minimum theory of corporate social responsibility asserts that a corporation's duty is to make a profit while avoiding harm to others. Compensation for the harm caused by the pollution meets the moral minimum as it acts as a corrective measure. [p 229]

10 True   The stakeholder interest theory is criticized due to the difficulty in harmonizing the stakeholders' conflicting interests. [p 230]

11. False Traditionally the "bottom line" is all that mattered and as such the cost-benefit analysis was utilized to determine the profit that was to be made. [p 226]

12. False Ethical relativism is based on an individual's own feelings of what is right or wrong. So, even though one company is making an invalid product comparison to that of its competitor, under this theory, it would not be unethical if the company making the comparison thought it was ethical to do so despite the lack of validity. [p 225]

13. True  This is a classic example of what has happened to the Enron Corporation. It would be far reaching to even apply ethical relativism to this situation in light of the fact that speculative business dealings were involved, which most business people should know are not the sort of ventures in which a secure company would engage itself. [p 231-232]

14. False Those who promote the corporate citizenship theory contend that corporations owe a duty to promote the same social goals as individual members of society and that they should make the world a better place because of the social power placed upon them. Critics contend that there is a limit to corporate duty and funds. [p 231]

15. True  An actor must live by the rule he or she uses to judge someone else's morality based on that person's conduct and an actor must be consistent in his or her treatment of others. [p 221]

## Multiple Choice

16. C   Answer C is correct, as utilitarianism dictates that individuals must select the actions or abide by the rule that provides the greatest good to society. Answer A is incorrect, as Kantian ethics dictate that people owe moral duties based upon universal rules. Answer B is incorrect, as the maximizing profit theory bases its theory upon the maximum amount of profits that business can make for its shareholders regardless if it is good or bad for others with an interest. Answer D is incorrect, as the corporate social audit involves checking on a corporation's moral health. [p 219]

17. B   Answer B is correct, as Rawl's Social Justice Theory believes that each person is presumed to have entered into an implied social contract with others to obey rules that are necessary for people to live in peace and harmony. Answer A is incorrect, as the stakeholder interest theory contends that a corporation must consider the effects its actions have on other stakeholders. Answer C is incorrect, as ethical relativism bases its theory upon an individual's feelings on whether the action he or she is taking is right or wrong. Answer D is incorrect, as those following the theory of ethical fundamentalism look to an outside source for ethical guidelines. [p 223]

18. D   Answer D is correct, as actions that are usually viewed as unethical, such as fraud, would not be considered unethical if the perpetrator thought the action taken was ethical. Under ethical relativism, individuals must decide what is ethical based on their own feelings of what is right or wrong. Answer A is incorrect, as in Rawl's social justice theory, fairness is the crux or justice. Answer B is incorrect, as this theory is mainly concerned with the maximum amount of profits that can be made for the shareholders regardless of the effect it has on other interested parties. Answer C is incorrect, as the moral minimum requires that businesses make a profit while not doing harm to others. [p 225]

19. C    Answer C is correct, as this moral theory leaves little room for criticism if that it is subjective in nature. If Sam truly believes that Edward should have the additional auto services even though Edward came in for a discounted oil change, then Sam has met his own moral standards based on what he feels are right or wrong. Therefore, ethical relativism would be Sam's best theory to allege. Answer A is incorrect, as utilitarianism involves choosing the best alternative that would provide the greatest good to society. The greatest good would be the subject of debate depending on whom you were trying to do the greatest good for, Sam or Edward. Therefore this would not be the best answer. Answer B is incorrect, as ethical fundamentalism involves looking to an outside source for what is right or wrong. By finding other automotive services to convince Edward of, some might contend that Sam was stealing or "ripping off" Edward in contradiction to an outside source's commandment for example of "Thou shall not steal." Answer D is incorrect, as the stakeholder interest theory would favor Edward more as the social responsibility includes considering the interests of customers. Arguably, Edward's interests as a customer trying to save a little bit of money by using a coupon are not being considered. [p 225]

20. A    Answer A is correct, as the stakeholder interest theory would require that the computer manufacturer considers the effects of its actions on the other stakeholders. Since the amount of sales seems to be its main concern, it appears that the only value it sees in its employees is their ability to make money. The closing of the plant and its effects on unemployment do not appear to be a factor. Answer B is incorrect, as closing the plant would not provide the greatest good to society, which is the premise underlying utilitarianism. Instead, closing the plant appears to be detrimental in nature. Answer C is incorrect, as followers of Kantian ethics believe that people owe moral duties based upon universal rules. As such, even though the employees are not producing fast enough to create larger profits, the parties have a contract. Under Kantian ethics, this contract needs to be honored regardless of the drop in profits and the detriment suffered by the company's owners. Answer D is incorrect, for the reasons stated above. [p 229-230]

21. A    Answer A is correct, as critics do not favor ethical fundamentalism since people take the outside source's meaning and guidelines literally, which can make people go to extremes and act unethically, despite the belief in an ethical principal. Answer B is incorrect, as the theory of maximizing profits was the traditional view of social responsibility whereby business should maximize its profits for the shareholders, and any other interests associated with the business are not important in and of themselves. Ignoring the other interests by itself does not necessarily constitute going to extremes that would qualify as being unethical. Answer C is incorrect, as corporate citizenship involves a business' responsibility to do good and solve social problems regardless if the business caused the problems or not. The solving of social problems hardly constitutes unethical behavior. Answer D is incorrect, as the corporate audit involves a moral or values check up of a business that would not be unethical in and of itself. [p 218]

22. C    Answer C is correct, as Kantian Ethics is based on universal rules and a categorical imperative of "Do unto others as you would have them do unto you." Answer A is incorrect, as ethical fundamentalism involves looking to an outside source for what is right or wrong. Answer B is incorrect, as utilitarianism dictates that individuals must select the actions or abide by the rule that provides the greatest good to society. Answer D is incorrect, as Rawl's social justice theory believes that each person is presumed to have entered into an implied social contract with others to obey rules that are necessary for people to live in peace and harmony. [p 221]

23. B    Answer B is correct, as the theory of maximizing profits was the traditional view of social responsibility whereby business should maximize its profits for the shareholders, and any other interests associated with the business are not important in and of themselves. Answer A is incorrect, as ethical fundamentalism involves looking to an outside source for what is right or wrong. Answer C is incorrect, as corporate citizenship involves a business' responsibility to do good and solve social problems regardless if the business caused the problems or not. Answer D is incorrect, as the corporate audit involves a moral or values check up of a business that would not be unethical in and of itself. [p 226]

24. B    Answer B is correct, as utilitarianism dictates that individuals must select the actions or abide by the rule that provides the greatest good to society. Answer A is incorrect, as ethical fundamentalism involves looking to an outside source for what is right or wrong. Answer C is incorrect, as Kantian Ethics is based on universal rules and a categorical imperative of "Do unto others as you would have them do unto you." Answer D is incorrect, as Rawl's social justice theory believes that each person is presumed to have entered into an implied social contract with others to obey rules that are necessary for people to live in peace and harmony. [p 219, 227]

25. B    Answer B is correct, as the theory of maximizing profits is that a business should maximize its profits for the shareholders, and any other interests associated with the business are not important in and of themselves. Answer A is incorrect, as ethical fundamentalism involves looking to an outside source for what is right or wrong. Answer C is incorrect, as corporate citizenship involves a business' responsibility to do good and solve social problems regardless if the business caused the problems or not. Answer D is incorrect, as the corporate audit involves a moral or values check up of a business that would not be unethical in and of itself. [p 226-227]

## Short Answer

26.    Kantian Ethics is a set of universal rules that establishes ethical duties. [p 221]
27.    They will be more likely to prevent illegal and unethical conduct by employees, managers, and agents. [p 233]
28.    Utilitarianism dictates that individuals must select the actions or abide by the rule that provides the greatest good to society. [p 219]
29.    Consistency and reversibility. [p 221]
30.    Maximizing profits. [p 226-227]
31.    Moral minimum. [p 229]
32.    Stakeholder interest. [p 229-230]
33.    The United Nations Code of Conduct for Transnational Corporations. [p 233]
34.    This theory states that business has a responsibility to do well; it should help solve social problems, even when it did nothing to cause these problems. [p 231]
35.    This Act prompted public companies to adopt code of ethics. [p 231-232]
36.    An independent auditor helps to ensure autonomy and objectivity in the audit. [p 233]
37.    Where law and ethics demand the same response. When law permits something that ethics would not permit. Where law demands certain conduct and ethics demands the opposite. [p 217]
38.    Ethical fundamentalism. [p 218]
39.    Action 3, as it yields the greatest benefit to society. [p 219]
40.    Henry Ford contended that reducing the price of his cars would do the most good to society, as it would allow the benefits of industrialization to be spread out. The court ruled that Ford's duty was to maximize profit for the shareholders. [p 227]

# Chapter 9

# NATURE OF TRADITIONAL
# AND ONLINE CONTRACTS

## Chapter Overview

Contracts provide the method by which people and businesses sell and transfer property, services, and other rights. Commerce would crumple without contracts. Parties enter into contracts voluntarily and the terms of the contract become private law between the parties. Some contracts are unenforceable, though most contracts are legally enforceable. Most of these contracts are performed without the parties resorting to the court system for enforcement. The definition of a contract, the requirements for forming a contract, sources of contract law, and the classifications of contracts are examined in this chapter.

## Objectives

Upon completion of the exercises in this chapter, you should be able to:

1.    Define a contract.
2.    Describe the necessary elements that form a valid contract.
3.    Differentiate between a bilateral and unilateral contract.
4.    Differentiate between an implied-in-fact contract and an express contract.
5.    Distinguish between a valid, void, voidable and an unenforceable contract.

## Practical Application

You should be able to recognize whether or not a contract has been formed. When a contract has been formed, you should be able to ascertain the type of contract that is involved and whether that contract can be enforced. You should be able to identify whether or not equity will play a role in the contract.

## Helpful Hints

It is helpful to know what constitutes a contract and the necessary requirements for its formation. It is useful to list the various types of contracts, with an example of each, to help you remember and differentiate between them. It is important that you read the hypotheticals and/or cases line by line, being careful to examine the facts, as they may or may not be controlled by the contract principles that you have learned. Slight variations in wording or in a sequence of events can change the outcome of a case.

## Study Tips

### Definition of Contract

A contract is an agreement between two or more parties that is enforceable in equity or a court of law.

**Parties to a contract**. At least two parties are involved in every contract.
- The person making an offer to enter into a contract is known as the offeror.
  o The offeror promises to do, or not do, something.
- The individual to whom the offer to enter into a contract is made is known as the offeree.
  o The offeree has the power to create the contract by accepting the offer.

**Elements of a Contract.** An enforceable contract has four requirements:

*Agreement.* An offer and acceptance, with mutual assent, comprise an agreement.

*Consideration.* Consideration is a legally sufficient bargained-for-exchange.
- Gift promises, moral obligations, past consideration and illusory promises are considered insufficient consideration.

*Contractual Capacity.* The parties must have contractual capacity to enter into the contract.
- Minors, intoxicated individuals and those who have been adjudged insane may not have the requisite capacity to understand the nature of the transaction into which they are entering.

*Lawful Object.* Contracts to accomplish illegal goals are contrary to public policy and are void.
- A contract entered into to kill another individual in order to receive the proceeds from an insurance policy would be an illegal contract because the object of the contract is illegal.

**Defenses to the Enforcement of a Contract.** There are two defenses that can be used against the enforcement of a contract:

*Genuineness of Assent.* The parties to a contract must genuinely assent to entering into the contract.
- Consent made under duress, undue influence, or fraud is not genuine assent.

*Writing and Form.* Certain contracts must be in writing or must conform to a specific form.
- A contract for the sale or lease of real property must be in writing.

## Sources of Contract Law

Contract law in the United States comes from several sources:

**Common Law of Contracts**. This law was developed from early court decisions that eventually became precedent for subsequent decisions.
- It is primarily made from state court decisions, thus there is some variation between the states.

**Uniform Commercial Code (U.C.C.).** The purpose of this law is to establish a uniform system of commercial law in the United States.
- The U.C.C. takes precedence over common law.
- There are nine main articles in the U.C.C., two of which are important to contract law:
  o Article 2 (Sales) gives uniform rules for the creation and enforcement of sales contracts.
  o Article 2A (Leases) gives uniform rules for the creation and enforcement of lease contracts.

**Restatement (Second) of Contracts.** This compilation of contract law principles is not law, but is often used as a guide, due to its stature.

**Objective Theory of Contracts**. This theory states that the intent of the parties to enter into an express or an implied-in-fact contract is judged by the reasonable person standard, taking into consideration the words and conduct of the parties and the circumstances of the incident.
- Offers made in jest, anger, or undue excitement will not produce valid contracts.
- Subjective intent is irrelevant as it is the objective intent based on the reasonable person standard that will be examined.

**Uniform Computer Information Transactions Act (UCITA)**. This act targets a majority of the legal issues that are faced when conducting e-commerce over the Internet.
- Though this Act has not been adopted by most states, it has served as a model Act for states enacting their own statutes for governing e-commerce.

## Classifications of Contracts

There are a variety of contracts, each of which has differences in formation, enforcement, performance, and discharge.

**Bilateral and Unilateral Contracts.** These contracts are differentiated by how the offeree must accept the offer of the offeror.

*Bilateral Contract*. This type of contract involves a promise for a promise.
- For example, "I promise to wash your car if you promise to take me to the movies."
  - o Acceptance is in the form of a promise.

*Unilateral Contract*. This type of contract involves a promise for performance.
- For example, "If you mow the lawn, I will pay you $10.00."
  - o There is no contract until the offeree performs the requested act of mowing the lawn.
  - o Acceptance is in the form of performance.

*Incomplete or Partial Performance*. An offer to create a unilateral contract cannot be revoked if the offeree has begun or has substantially completed performance.

**Express and Implied-in-Fact Contracts.** Either an express or an implied-in-fact contract constitutes an actual contract.

*Express contract*. These are either oral or written agreements between two parties.
- An example would be an oral agreement to buy someone's radio and a written agreement to buy someone's home.

*Implied-in-fact contracts*. The conduct of the parties implies this type of contract.
- Certain requirements must be met before a court will find that this type of contract exists:
  - o The plaintiff gave services or property to the defendant.
  - o The plaintiff expected compensation for the property or services.
    - ▪ In other words the property or services were not gifts.
  - o Even though the defendant could have refused to accept the property or services given by the plaintiff, he or she did not.

**Quasi-contracts (Implied-in-Law Contracts).** The term quasi-contract is an equitable one where the Court will create a contract, even though there is not an actual contract between the parties, if the plaintiff provided goods or services to the defendant without compensation.

- Further reinforcement for the creation of a quasi-contract exists when it is shown that it would be unjust not to require the defendant to pay for the benefit received.

**Formal and Informal Contracts**. These contracts are differentiated by whether or not they require a special form or method to create them.

*Formal Contracts*. A formal contract is one requiring a special method or form to create it. The *Restatement (Second) of Contracts* identifies several of these types of contracts:
- Negotiable Instruments.
  - o Include checks and notes.
  - o Require a special form and language to be created.
  - o Must meet specific U.C.C. requirements to be transferred.
- Letters of Credit.
  - o Are agreements by an issuer of the letter to pay a sum of money when an invoice and other documents are received.
  - o Are governed by the U.C.C.
- Contracts Under Seal.
  - o A contract where a seal is attached.

*Informal Contracts*. All contracts that do not require a special form or method to create are considered informal contracts.

**Valid, Void, Voidable, and Unenforceable Contracts.** Contracts can be placed in several categories.

*Valid Contract*. A valid contract is one that meets all of the required elements to establish a contract.
- It is enforceable by at least one of the parties.

*Void Contract*. A void contract is one that does not have any legal affect.

*Voidable Contract*. A voidable contract is one that enables one party to avoid his or her contractual duties.
- Examples of where this situation may exist, absent certain exceptions, are
  - o Contracts entered into by minors.
  - o Insane individuals.
  - o Intoxicated persons
  - o Those acting under undue influence.
  - o Duress.
  - o Fraud.
  - o Where there is a mutual mistake.

*Unenforceable Contract.* If there is a legal defense to the enforcement of the contract, the contract is unenforceable.
- An example of this would be where the purchase of real estate is required to be in writing as per the Statute of Frauds.
  - o Failure to have a written contract would make the contract unenforceable.

**Executed and Executory Contracts.**

*Executed Contract*. If both parties have performed their required obligations under the contract, the contract is said to be executed.

*Executory Contract.* If only one side has fully performed his or her obligations of the contract, the contract is said to be executory.

- If both sides of the contract are not fully performed, the contract is said to be executory.

## Equity

The equity courts of England developed a set of rules whose foundation was premised on fairness, moral rights, and equality.

- Equity principles were applied when the remedy at law was not adequate or in the interest of fairness, and equitable principles had to be applied.
- The doctrine of equity is sometimes applied in contract cases.

## The United Nations Convention on Contracts for the International Sale of Goods (CISG)

The CISG gives rules for the formation, performance, and enforcement of international contracts.

- It incorporates rules from all of the prominent legal systems.
   - It is substantially similar to the Uniform Commercial Code of the United States.
   - Developed, developing, and Communist countries have given this Convention widespread support.
- It applies to contracts for the sale of goods between a buyer and seller with places of business in different countries.
   - Both of the nations must be parties to the CISG or
   - The contract must specify that the CISG controls.
   - The parties can agree to exclude or modify application of the CISG.

## Refresh Your Memory

The following exercises will help to test your memory regarding the principles given in this chapter. Read each question twice, then place your answer in the blank provided for each question. Review the chapter material for any questions you are unable to answer or remember.

1.  A(n) _____ is an agreement between two parties that is enforceable in equity or law.

2.  The two parties to a contract are the _____ and the _____.

3.  The four basic elements of a contract are: _____, _____, _____ _____, and a(n) _____ _____.

4.  Two defenses to the enforcement of a contract are _____ _____ _____ and _____ _____ _____.

5.  List three sources of contract law: _____ _____, _____ _____ _____, and the _____ _____ _____ _____.

6.  A(n) _____ contract consists of an offeror's promise answered with the offeree's promise of acceptance.

7.  A(n) _____ contract is where the offeror's offer can be accepted only by the performance of an act.

8. An actual contract may be either _____ or _____ _____ _____ .

9. Contracts that are stated in oral or written words are known as _____ contracts.

10. A(n) _____ _____ _____ contract is implied by the actions of the parties.

11. A(n) _____ contract requires a special form or method of creation.

12. A(n) _____ contract does not require any special form or method of creation.

13. The equity courts developed a set of rules based on _____ , equality, moral rights, and natural law that were applied in settling disputes.

14. The goal of the _____ _____ _____ is to create a uniform system of law among the 50 states.

15. A(n) _____ contract is meant to prevent unjust enrichment and unjust detriment.

# Critical Thought Exercise

Ricky Boggs, a 27-year-old country singer was severely injured in an automobile accident. Boggs was airlifted by Bishop County Air Ambulance to Bishop Trauma Center for surgery and treatment. Boggs slipped into a coma and after seven weeks was transported to Bishop County Extended Care Hospital. Boggs remained in the hospital for fourteen months before he died without ever having regained consciousness. The total charges assessed by Bishop County for the care of Boggs exceeded $370,000.00. After he died, Bishop County sued the Boggs estate to recover the expenses of the air ambulance, trauma treatment, surgery, hospital stay, and extended care.

Was there a contract between Bishop County and Boggs? If so, how much can Bishop County recover from the estate?

*Please compose your answer on a separate sheet of paper or on your computer.*

# Practice Quiz

## True/False

1. ___ The Restatement (Second) of Contract is law that does not take precedence over the common law of contracts.

2. ___ Under the objective theory of contracts, the subjective intent of either party who enters into a contract does not play an important role in determining the true intentions of the parties.

3. ___ Every contract involves at least two parties.

4. ___ Consideration is defined as bargained-for exchange that is legally sufficient.

5. ___ The contract is bilateral if the offeror's offer can be accepted only by the offeree's promise of acceptance.

6. \_\_\_ If there is an ambiguity as to whether a contract is bilateral or unilateral, it will be presumed to be a unilateral contract.

7. \_\_\_ The theory of quasi-contract applies to actual contracts between two parties.

8. \_\_\_ The Uniform Commercial Code usually does not take precedence over the common law of contracts.

9. \_\_\_ If a contract is required to be in writing but it is not, the contract is unenforceable because of the legal defense to enforcement of the contract.

10. \_\_\_ A contract is voidable where at least one party has the option to avoid his or her contractual obligations.

11. \_\_\_ A void contract is one that meets all of the essential elements to establish a contract.

12. \_\_\_ An executed contract is one that has not been fully performed on both sides.

13. \_\_\_ The CISG applies to contracts for the international sale of services.

14. \_\_\_ The doctrine of equity can sometimes be applied to contract cases.

15. \_\_\_ A contract to kill someone would be an example of a contract with an illegal object.

## Multiple Choice

16. The four basic requirements to have an enforceable contract are
    a. duty, breach, causation, and damages.
    b. bilateral, unilateral, executed and executory.
    c. agreement, consideration, capacity, and lawful object.
    d. offeror, offeree, offer and acceptance.

17. A bilateral contract is
    a. a promise for performance.
    b. a promise for money.
    c. a promise for a promise.
    d. a promise for an offer.

18. Two types of defenses that may be raised to the enforcement of a contract are
    a. writing and form and genuineness of assent.
    b. uniform commercial code and common law of contracts.
    c. contributory negligence and assumption of the risk.
    d. unilateral and bilateral promise.

19. A contract to commit a crime is
    a. valid.
    b. void.
    c. voidable.
    d. informal.

20. The Uniform Computer Information Transaction Act will be useful in acting as
    a. a quasi-contract.
    b. the reasonable person standard.
    c. the basis for establishing legally sufficient consideration.
    d. the basis for the creation and enforcement of cyberspace contracts and licenses.

21. An oral agreement to purchase a neighbor's gardening tools is an example of
    a. an implied-in-fact contract.
    b. an express contract.
    c. an executory contract.
    d. a void contract.

22. James and Rory enter into an oral contract for James to purchase Rory's double-wide mobile home and one-half acre of land. Before James has paid any money, he decides he doesn't want to purchase Rory's property. Can Rory enforce the contract against James?
    a. Yes. They have a bilateral contract where James promised to pay Rory for his property and Rory promised to sell his property to James.
    b. Yes. They have a valid contract with all four required elements: agreement, consideration, capacity, and legality.
    c. No. They have a unilateral contract that has not been accepted by James.
    d. No. They have a valid, bilateral contract, but James can raise the defense that the contract for land must be in writing to be enforceable. The contract was for the sale of land and it was not in writing.

23. A voidable contract is
    a. a contract inferred from the conduct of the parties.
    b. a contract for which a party has the option of voiding or enforcing the contract.
    c. a contract that is not fully performed by one or both parties.
    d. a contract that cannot be enforced because of a legal defense.

24. An informal contract is
    a. a contract implied by law to prevent unjust enrichment.
    b. a contract that requires a special form or method of creation.
    c. a contract that requires no special form or method of creation.
    d. a contract that cannot be enforced because of a legal defense.

25. A valid contract is
    a. a contract that meets all of the essential elements for establishing a contract.
    b. a contract expressed in oral or written words.
    c. a contract that exchanges a promise for a promise.
    d. a contract that requires a special form or method of creation.

## Short Answer

26. What does the equitable doctrine of quasi-contract allow a court to do?

   _____

   _____

27. What do formal contracts require?

   _____

28. Differentiate between a void and a voidable contract?

_____

29. What is a contract implied by law to prevent unjust enrichment?

_____

30. To what does the United Nations Convention on Contracts for the International Sales of Goods (CISG) apply?

_____

31. If Kate tells her son Tony that she will give him everything she owns if he loves her for the rest of her life, would a valid contract exist between the two?

_____

32. Jan Ruiz, a business owner says to Mary Munoz, a decorator, "If you promise to wallpaper my waiting room by December 1, I will pay you $600.00." Mary promises to do so. What type of contract has been created?

_____

33. Which act is expected to become the basis for the creation and enforcement of cyberspace contracts and licenses?

_____

34. What type of contract is formed where Gio says to Paul, "I will give you $10,000 if you help my friend Clyde murder his wife Bonnie?

_____

35. Why is the Uniform Commercial Code important to the law of contracts?

_____

36. Why was the Uniform Computer Information Transactions Act developed?

_____

37. If Ellen has painted Max's entire house except for the front door, may Max revoke his offer to pay Ellen for painting his house?

_____

38. Mary purchased a car from Ajax Autos. Mary has paid for the car, but Ajax has not yet delivered the car. What type of contract do they have?

_____

39. Mary purchased a car from Ajax Autos. Mary has paid for the car, and Ajax has delivered the car. What type of contract do they have?

_____

40. Mary purchased a car from Ajax Autos. Mary has not yet paid for the car, and Ajax has not yet delivered the car. What type of contract do they have?

_____

## Answers to Refresh Your Memory

1.  contract  [p 241]
2.  offeror, offeree  [p 241]
3.  agreement, consideration, contractual capacity, lawful object  [p 242]
4.  genuineness of assent, writing and form  [p 242]
5.  Common Law, Uniform Commercial Code, Restatement (Second) of Contracts [p 243]
6.  bilateral  [p 247]
7.  unilateral  [p 247]
8.  express, implied-in-fact  [p 248]
9.  express  [p 248]
10. implied-in-fact  [p 248]
11. formal  [p 251]
12. informal  [p 251]
13. fairness  [p 253]
14. Uniform Commercial Code  [p 243]
15. quasi-  [p 250]

## Critical Thought Exercise Model Answer

For parties to have an express contract, the terms of the agreement must be fully and explicitly stated in words, either oral or written.  If there is no express agreement, an implied-in-fact contract may be created in whole or in part from the conduct of the parties, rather than their words.  In this case, Boggs was unconscious, so he never manifested an assent to any agreement to pay for services, either by his words or conduct.  In this type of situation, a plaintiff may have to rely upon a theory of quasi contract.  A Quasi contract is a fictional contract imposed on parties by a court in the interests of fairness and justice.  Quasi contracts are usually imposed to avoid unjust enrichment of one party at the expense of another.  Society wants medical personnel to come to the aid of injured persons without regard to the existence of a contract before services are rendered.  This is especially true in an emergency situation where life may be in jeopardy.  Though Boggs never consented to an agreement, it would be unfair for Bishop County to render medical treatment to Boggs to save his life and then receive no compensation.  Boggs would then be unjustly enriched at the expense of Bishop County.  The amount of recovery, however, is not dependent upon the charges assessed by the county.  Because Boggs was never able to bargain for the amount or extent of services, the court will only allow Bishop County to recover the reasonable value of the medical services rendered.  The $370,000.00 in bills will be scrutinized by the court and reduced if they exceed a reasonable cost for Boggs' treatment.

## Answers to Practice Quiz

### True/False

1.  False    The Restatement of the Law of Contracts is not law, but instead acts as a guide.  The Uniform Commercial Code takes precedence over the common law of contracts.  [p 244]
2.  True     The subjective intent of a party to enter into a contract is immaterial. Under the objective theory of contracts, intent is judged by whether a reasonable person would conclude that the parties intended to make a contract.  [p 244]
3.  True     There are at least two parties, the offeror and the offeree, to every contract.  [p 241]
4.  True     Consideration is bargained-for exchange that is legally sufficient.  [p 242]

5.    True    A bilateral contract involves a promise for a promise. [p 247]

6.    False    Though the offeror's promise must be carefully examined, the courts usually hold that ambiguities as to whether a contract is bilateral or unilateral will usually result in a finding of the contract to be bilateral. [p 247]

7.    False    Quasi-contracts are also called implied-in-law contracts and are created in the interest of fairness because there is no actual contract. [p 250]

8.    False    The Uniform Commercial Code usually does take precedence over the common law of contracts. [p 243]

9.    True    An unenforceable contract is one where some legal defense to the enforcement of the contract exists, such as a contract that is required to be in writing not being in writing. [p 242]

10.    True    Where at least one party has the option to avoid his or her contract obligations, the court will find that the contract is voidable. [p 252]

11    False    A void contract is one that has no legal effect. A valid contract on the other hand is one that meets the essential elements to establish a contract. [p 252]

12.    False    If both parties have performed each of their obligations to the contract, the contract is said to be executed. [p 252]

13.    False    The CISG applies to contracts for the international sale of goods. [p 254]

14.    True    The doctrine of equity can sometimes be applied to contract cases. [p 253]

15.    True    A contract to kill someone would be an example of a contract with an illegal object. [p 242]

## Multiple Choice

16.    C    Answer C correctly states the requirements to have an enforceable contract. Answer A is incorrect, as these are the necessary requirements for a negligence cause of action. Answer B is incorrect, as these are four types of contracts as opposed to requirements. Answer D is incorrect, as it states the two parties to a contract and only part of what is required to form a contract. [p 242]

17.    C    Answer C correctly defines a bilateral contract as it is a promise for a promise. Answer A is incorrect, as this is the definition of a unilateral contract. Answer B is incorrect, as the way it is phrased could imply either a bilateral or a unilateral contract. Answer D is incorrect, as a promise for an offer could imply a unilateral contract. [p 247]

18.    A    Answer A correctly states the two types of defenses that may be raised to the enforcement of a contract. Answer B is incorrect, as the Uniform Commercial Code and the common law of contracts are both sources of contract law not defenses. Answer C is incorrect, as these are defenses to a negligence cause of action. Answer D is incorrect, as unilateral and bilateral refer to the types of contracts verses defenses to the enforcement of a contract. [p 242]

19.    B    Answer B is correct, as a contract to commit a crime has no legal effect and is therefore void, as though no contract had ever been created. Answer A is incorrect, as contracting to commit a crime is not a lawful object, which would make the contract void. Answer C is incorrect, as a contract is only voidable when one party has the option of performing or not performing. In the situation where the main object of the contract is to commit a crime, this option is not available. Answer D is incorrect, as an informal contract is one that does not qualify as a formal contract. A contract to commit a crime is not a contract at all and as such would not fall under either the formal or informal categorization of contracts. [p 242]

20.    D    Answer D is correct, as it succinctly states the purpose of the Uniform Computer Information Transaction Act. Answer A is incorrect, as a quasi-contract is an equitable remedy that is enforced to prevent unjust enrichment. Further, the UCITA does not need to be present in order to enforce a quasi-contract. Answer B is incorrect, as the UCITA was not designed to define the reasonable person standard. Answer C is incorrect, as even though the act will help address issues such as consideration in the formation of cyberspace contracts, that is not the sole purpose or issue to be addressed by the act. [p 244]

21. B    Answer B is correct, as this is a primary example of an oral, express contract. Answer A is incorrect, as implied-in-fact contracts are implied from the conduct of the parties. The facts are silent as to any conduct, but instead state that there was an oral agreement. Answer C is incorrect, as an executory contract is one that is not fully performed by one or both of the parties. There is nothing in the facts that would indicate nonperformance by either or both parties. Answer D is incorrect, as a void contract is one that has no legal effect and is against public policy. In the example given, purchasing a neighbor's gardening tools is not a crime nor is it against public policy. [p 248]

22. D    Answer D is correct, as they have a valid, bilateral contract, but James can raise the defense that the contract for land must be in writing to be enforceable. The contract was for the sale of land and it was not in writing. Answers A and B are incorrect, as the do not consider the defense available to James. Answer C is incorrect, as a unilateral contract is a promise for an act and their verbal contract was a promise for a promise. [p 242]

23. B    Answer B is correct, as a voidable contract is a contract for which a party has the option of voiding or enforcing the contract. Answer A is incorrect, as an implied-in-fact contract is a contract inferred from the conduct of the parties. Answer C is incorrect, as an executory contract is a contract that is not fully performed by one or both parties. Answer D is incorrect, as an unenforceable contract is a contract that cannot be enforced because of a legal defense. [p 252]

24. C    Answer C is correct, as an informal contract is a contract that requires no special form or method of creation. Answer A is incorrect, as a quasi-contract is a contract implied by law to prevent unjust enrichment. Answer B is incorrect, as a formal contract is a contract that requires a special form or method of creation. Answer D is incorrect, as an unenforceable contract is a contract that cannot be enforced because of a legal defense. [p 251]

25. A    Answer A is correct, as a valid contract is a contract that meets all of the essential elements for establishing a contract. Answer B is incorrect, as an express contract is a contract expressed in oral or written words. Answer C is incorrect, as a bilateral contract is a contract that exchanges a promise for a promise. Answer D is incorrect, as a formal contract is a contract that requires a special form or method of creation. [p 251]

## Short Answer

26.    It allows a court to award monetary damages to a plaintiff for providing work or services to a defendant even though no actual contract existed between the parties. [p 250]
27.    Formal contracts require a special form or method of creation. [p 251]
28.    No contract exists if the contract is void. A voidable contract is where a party has the option of voiding or enforcing the contract. [p 252]
29.    Quasi-contract or an implied-in-law contract. [p 250]
30.    Contracts for the international sale of goods. [p 254]
31.    Probably not as moral obligations, such as loving one's mother, would not be construed as bargained-for consideration that is legally sufficient. [p 242]
32.    A bilateral contract was created the moment Mary promised to wallpaper the waiting room. [p 247]
33.    The Uniform Computer Information Transactions Act (UTICA) [p 244]
34.    A void contract, as entering into a contract to commit a crime has no legal effect. [p 242]
35.    It helps to establish a uniform system of commercial law among the 50 states. [p 243]
36.    It was developed to establish uniform legal rules for the formation and enforcement of electronic contracts and licenses. [p 244]
37.    No, Max may not revoke his offer, as Ellen has substantially completed the entire house with the exception of the front door. [p 247]
38.    An executory contract. [p 252]
39.    An executed contract. [p 252]
40.    An executory contract. [p 252]

# Chapter 10

# AGREEMENT AND CONSIDERATION

## Chapter Overview

Contracts are voluntary agreements, where one party makes an offer to another party, who then accepts the offer. Contracts require mutual assent, which can be express or implied. Enforceable contracts must be supported by consideration. This chapter explores the agreement and mutual assent, consideration, promises that lack consideration, and promises without consideration that may be enforced.

## Objectives

Upon completion of the exercises in this chapter, you should be able to:

1. Define an offer and acceptance.
2. Discuss what a counteroffer is and its impact.
3. Discuss the various ways an offer may be terminated.
4. Describe what the mailbox rule is and how it is applied.
5. Define consideration, the meaning of legal value, and the definition of bargained-for-exchange
6. Describe when promises lacking consideration are enforceable
7. Define an accord and satisfaction and the effect it has on the original contract.
8. Discuss the doctrine of promissory estoppel.

## Practical Application

You should be able to recognize whether or not a valid offer has been made, whether or not the essential terms are included within it, and whether or not an offer has been properly terminated. You should be able to determine whether there has been an acceptance of an offer and whether the mailbox rule affects the outcome. You should be able to identify whether there is sufficient consideration in a contractual situation and what type of consideration is being given. If consideration is lacking, you should be able to determine whether a contract will or will not be enforceable.

## Helpful Hints

Each chapter, especially in the area of contracts, builds one on top of another. It is vital that you understand the information given in each chapter and know how to apply it to given fact situations. There are several questions you can ask yourself while analyzing a potential contract situation:

- Has there been an offer? What is required to establish a valid offer? If one of the elements is missing, is there a rule of law that may apply to satisfy that missing element.
- Is this a special offer such as a reward, an advertisement, auction or counteroffer. Do any special rules apply to these types of offers?
- Has the offer has been terminated.

- Has there been an acceptance to the offer? Was the acceptance proper? Did the offer specify the means of and time for acceptance, and method of communication? Does the mailbox rule apply?
- Has there been consideration given? Was the consideration legally sufficient? Was the consideration bargained-for?

# Study Tips

## Agreement

An agreement is the expression by the parties of the substance of a contract.
- There must be an offer, made by the offeror.
- There must be an acceptance, made by the offeree.

## Offer

The definition of an offer, as stated in Section 24 of Restatement (Second) of Contracts, is "The manifestation of willingness to enter into a bargain, so made as to justify another person in understanding that his assent to that bargain is invited and will conclude it."
- Three elements are required to make an offer effective:
    - The offeror must objectively intend to be held to the offer.
    - The offer's terms must be definite or reasonably certain.
    - The offer has to be communicated to the offeree.
        - Without communication, there can be no acceptance.

**Objective Intent.** Objective intent is gauged against a reasonable person in the same or similar circumstances.
- A question asked by the offeror, as opposed to making a statement of intent to bargain, is likely an invitation to make an offer and not indicative of the offeror's present intent to contract.
- An offer made in anger, jest or undue excitement, is missing the objective intent and the offer cannot result in a valid contract.
- Offers made as an expression of opinion are not enforceable promises.

**Definiteness of Terms.** The terms of the offer must be clear so that the offeree was able to accept or reject the terms of the offer.
- The offer must contain an
    - Identification of the parties.
    - Identification of the subject matter.
    - The consideration to be paid.
    - The time for performance.

**Implied Terms.** Under Common Law, if any of the terms were missing, the offer would fail. The Modern Law has more leniency:
- The court will supply a missing term if a reasonable term can be implied, such as for price and time of performance.

**Communication.** If an offer is not communicated to the offeree, there can be no acceptance.

**Advertisements.** These are treated as invitations to make an offer.

- Exception: if the offer is so definite or specific that it is obvious that the advertiser had the present intent to be bound by the advertisement, then it will be considered to be an offer.

**Rewards.** An offer to pay a reward is an offer to form a unilateral contract. The two requirements to accept a reward are that:
- The offeree had knowledge of the reward before completing the requested act and
- He or she performed the requested act.

**Auctions.** Usually a seller uses an auctioneer to offer to sell his or her goods.
- Auctions are generally with reserve, as they are considered an invitation to make an offer. The seller can withdraw his or her goods from the sale and refuse the highest bid.
- If the auction is without reserve, the seller must accept the highest bid and cannot take his or her goods back.

## Termination of Offers

Offers may be terminated either by the actions of the parties or by operation of law.

**Revocation of an Offer by the Offeror.** At common law, the offeror could revoke his or her offer any time before the offeree accepted.
- The revocation may be express or implied by the offeror or a third party.
- The majority of states rule that the revocation is not effective until it is received.
- Revocation of an offer made to the public may be revoked by communicating in the same way that the offer was made for the same length of time.

**Rejection of an Offer by the Offeree.** The rejection may be express or implied by the offeree's conduct.
- The rejection is not effective until it is received.
- An acceptance by the offeree after the offeree has rejected the offer is taken as a counteroffer.

**Counteroffer by the offeree.** It terminates the original offer.
- It creates a new offer that the original offeror is now free to accept or reject.

**Destruction of the Subject Matter.** The offer is terminated if the subject matter of the offer is destroyed through no fault of either party before the offer is accepted.

**Death or Incompetency of the Offeror or Offeree.** Death of either the offeror or offeree terminates the offer. Incompetency of the offeror or offeree terminates the offer.
- Notice of the death or incompetency is not a requirement.
- Death or incompetency will not terminate an option contract, unless it was for personal services.

**Supervening Illegality.** If the object of the offer is made illegal before the offer is accepted, the offer terminates. Many times statutes are enacted that make the object of the offer illegal.

**Lapse of Time.** The offer sometimes limits the time in which it can be accepted.
- The time begins to run from the time it is actually received by the offeree and extends until the stated time period ends.
- If no time is stated in the offer, then the offer terminates within a "reasonable time" and on a case-by-case basis.
- An offer made over the telephone or face to face usually terminates after the conversation.

**Option Contracts.** Prevention of revocation by the offeror is accomplished through an option contract.
- The offeree usually pays the offeror money to keep the offer open for an agreed-upon time.
- During this time the offeror agrees not to sell the subject matter of the offer to anyone else.
- Death or incompetency does not terminate the option contract, unless it was for personal services

## Acceptance

An acceptance is an outward manifestation of assent to be bound by the terms of the offer as assessed by the reasonable person standard.
- Unilateral contracts can be accepted only by performance.
- Bilateral contracts can be accepted by a promise to perform.

**Who Can Accept an Offer?** Only the offeree can accept the offer to create a contract.
- If an offer is made to more than one person, each person has the power to accept the offer.
- If an acceptance is made by one party, it terminates the offer as to the other individuals to whom the offer was made.
- If a joint offer has been made, the offer must be accepted jointly.

**Unequivocal Acceptance.** The Mirror Image Rule states that the offeree must accept the offeror's terms as stated in the offer.
- Grumbling acceptances do form contracts.
- Acceptances that add conditions to them are not unequivocal and thus fail.

**Silence as Acceptance.** The general rule is that silence is not held to be an acceptance despite the offeror stating it is. There are several exceptions to the general rule:
- Where the offeree by his words intended his silence to mean acceptance
- A signed agreement by the offeree allowing continued delivery until notice was given.
- Prior course of dealings by the parties where silence is construed as an acceptance.
- The offeree accepts the benefit of goods or services given by the offeror even though the offeree had the opportunity to reject the services or goods.

**Time of Acceptance.** The Mailbox Rule states that acceptance of a bilateral contract happens when the offeree dispatches the acceptance by an authorized means of communication. This rule is also known as the acceptance-upon-dispatch rule.
- Acceptance is effective when it is placed in the mailbox, or dispatched, even if it gets lost.
- The rule does not apply if a rejection is sent first and then an acceptance is mailed.

**Mode of Acceptance.** The acceptance has to be properly dispatched. In other words, it has to be properly addressed, packaged and have proper postage applied. Under common law, if the acceptance wasn't properly dispatched, it wasn't effective unless received by the offeror.
- The usual rule is that the offeree must accept by an authorized mode of communication.
- The offer can state how it is to be accepted. This is called express authorization. If the offeree uses a different means to communicate his or her acceptance instead of the means stipulated to be the parties, then the acceptance is ineffective.
- Implied authorization may apply where it is customary in similar transactions between the parties, or prior dealings or usage of trade. Implied authorization will be allowed "by any medium reasonable in the circumstances." Section 30 of the Restatement Second.

# Consideration

Consideration is defined as "Something of legal value," which can include money, property, forbearance of a right, the provision of services or anything else of legal value.
- A written contract is presumed to be supported by consideration.

**Requirements of Consideration.** There are two requirements for consideration:

*Legal Value.* Something of legal value must be given.
- This is found if the promisee suffers a legal detriment or the promisor receives a legal benefit.

*Bargained-for Exchange.* There must be a bargained-for exchange.
- This refers to the exchange that parties engage in that leads to an enforceable contract.

**Gift Promises.** Gift promises and gratuitous promises by themselves are not enforceable.
- If the promissee offers to do something in exchange for either of these two types of promises, then consideration is established.

**When Is Consideration Inadequate?** Generally, parties are free to agree on the consideration for the contract, and courts do not look into the adequacy of that consideration. Some states make an exception on a case-by-case basis:
- Courts look to whether the inadequacy of the consideration "shocks the conscience of the court."
- The court will look to the value of the item or service, the amount of consideration, the relationship of the parties, and other facts and circumstances.

# Contracts Lacking Consideration

Some contracts appear to be supported by consideration, but are not.

**Illegal Consideration.** A contract based on illegal consideration is void.
- A promise to refrain from doing an illegal act will not be enforceable as illegal consideration is part of the bargained-for exchange.
- Example: "If you pay me $5,000, I will not damage your brand new car!"

**Illusory Promises.** If the parties enter into a contract, but one or both of them can choose not to perform, then consideration will be lacking.
- Example: Fred says to Jim, "I will paint your garage if I feel like it."

**Moral Obligations.** The general rule regarding moral obligations is that they lack consideration.
- The minority rule however allows for the enforcement of moral obligations.
- Deathbed promises or contracts based on affection and love are promises of moral obligation.

**Preexisting Duty.** If a person promises to perform an act or do something he or she is already under an obligation to do, then the promise is unenforceable because no new consideration has been given.
- The individual had a preexisting duty.
- Exception: If a party encounters substantial unforeseen difficulties while performing his or her contractual duties and the parties modify their contract to accommodate these difficulties, no new consideration is necessary.

**Past Consideration.** When a party to a contract promises to compensate another for work that has been performed in the past, then the situation involving past consideration exists.

- A contract must be supported by new consideration in order to be binding.

**Special Business Contracts.** Court tolerate more uncertainty in business contracts that they will in personal contracts, because business contracts are seen as being between sophisticated parties who know how to protect themselves when negotiating contracts.
- Contracts, such as output, requirements, and best-efforts contracts, are allowed a higher degree of uncertainty.
- The law imposes an obligation of good faith in the performance of these contracts.

*Output Contracts.* The seller agrees to sell all of its production to one buyer.

*Requirements Contract.* The buyer agrees to buy all of the requirements for an item from a single seller.

*Best Efforts Contract.* The contract contains a clause that usually states that one or both of the parties will use their best efforts to achieve the objective of the contract.

**Settlement of Claims.** Voluntary settlement of disputes is encouraged, as this saves judicial resources and benefits the parties of the dispute.
- Sometimes, one party to a contract believes that he or she did not receive what he or she was due and the parties agree to compromise, called an accord and satisfaction.
  - An accord is an agreement where both parties agree to accept something different in satisfaction of the original contract.
  - A satisfaction is the performance of the accord.

## Promissory Estoppel

The purpose of promissory estoppel is to give a remedy to a person who has justifiably relied upon another's promise, but that person takes back his or her promise.
- Because there is no agreement or consideration, the recipient of the promise cannot sue based on breach of contract.
- This doctrine estops the promisor from revoking his or her promise, thereby preventing unjust enrichment by the promisor.
- To use the Doctrine of Promisory Estoppel, four elements must be shown:
  - There was a promise made by the promisor.
  - There was a reasonable expectation by the promisor that the promisee would rely on that promise.
  - The promise actually relied on the promise and was harmed because of that reliance.
  - An injustice would occur if the promise were not enforced.

# Refresh Your Memory

The following exercises will help to test your memory regarding the principles given in this chapter. Read each question twice, then place your answer in the blank provided for each question. Review the chapter material for any questions that you are unable to answer or remember.

1.   A(n) _____ is the manifestation by two or more individuals of the substance of a contract.

2.   If June says to Monica, "I will give you ten dollars to wash my car." _____ is the offeree.

3.   The offeror must _____ intend to be bound by the terms of the offer.

4. The terms of the offer must be definite or _____ _____.

5. The _____ _____ _____ _____ is used in determining whether the parties intended to enter into a contract.

6. Under the modern law of contracts, two terms of an offer – _____ and _____ _____ _____ – may be implied.

7. _____ are usually viewed as invitations to make an offer.

8. A(n) _____ _____ _____ provides that the seller must accept the highest bid and cannot withdraw the goods from sale

9. An offer is terminated if the offeree _____ it.

10. A(n) _____ by the offeree both terminates the offeror's offer and creates a new offer.

11. The offer terminates by operation of law if the _____ _____ of the offer is destroyed through no fault of either party before its acceptance.

12. The offeree's acceptance must be _____.

13. Under the mailbox rule, acceptance is effective upon _____.

14. Usually an offeree must accept an offer by a(n) _____ means of communication.

15. Only the _____ has the power to accept an offer and create a contract.

## Critical Thought Exercise

Gus Vincent sent invitations to a number of potential buyers to submit bids for the mineral rights to his 2,000-acre parcel of land in upstate New York on the outskirts of the City of Hudson. Seven bids were received, including the highest bid from International Mining and Cement Company, LTD. (IMC). Vincent then decided to hold onto the land for a few more years and never responded to any of the bidders. IMC claimed that a contract had been formed by submission of its winning bid and sued Vincent for breach of contract.

Did a contract exist?

*Please compose your answer on a separate sheet of paper or on your computer.*

## Practice Quiz

### True/False

1. ___ The objective theory of contracts will determine whether there was an intent to enter a contract.

2. ___ The owner of the Z store shouts in frustration, "For even $50,000, I'd sell the whole business along with its company cars!" This statement will not be considered a valid offer.

3. \_\_\_ An offer may be accepted even though it has not been communicated.

4. \_\_\_ Generally speaking, price and time of performance can be implied even if these terms are not present.

5. \_\_\_ An advertisement is considered an offer if it is so definite or specific that it is obvious that the advertiser has the present intent to be bound by the terms of the ad.

6. \_\_\_ An auction with reserve is not considered an invitation to make an offer.

7. \_\_\_ A majority of states do not require receipt of an offeror's revocation in order to be effective.

8. \_\_\_ Rejection of an offer is effective upon receipt.

9. \_\_\_ A counteroffer by the offeree doesn't terminate the original offer, as it is considered to be a mere inquiry.

10. \_\_\_ If a snowmobile being purchased by Sam is destroyed after Jan makes the offer, but before Sid accepts, the offer is terminated.

11. \_\_\_ Generally speaking, a grumbling acceptance is a valid, legal acceptance.

12. \_\_\_ Silence may also be considered an acceptance if the offeree has demonstrated that silence means assent.

13. \_\_\_ Under the mailbox rule, acceptance is effective upon receipt.

14. \_\_\_ An offeree must accept an offer by an authorized means of communication.

15. \_\_\_ Unilateral contracts may only be accepted by the offeree's performance.

## Multiple Choice

16. Sam Brown stated to Mary Powers, "I will buy your house for $350,000." His statement was
    a. valid offer.
    b. a preliminary question.
    c. an opinion.
    d. a bilateral contract.

17. A car dealer tells his customer that he feels the car she is interested in buying is the best car on his lot and will probably give her a lifetime of happiness. If the customer buys the car and immediately has problems, the customer may
    a. enforce the car dealer's promise.
    b. return the car for her money back.
    c. not enforce the promise.
    d. none of the above

18. To be considered a valid offer, the communication must contain
    a. an offer, acceptance and consideration.
    b. protection against potential breach.
    c. the parties, consideration, time for performance and identification of the subject matter.

d.  a provision against communications made in jest or anger.

19.  In order to be entitled to collect on an offer to pay a reward, the offeree must
    a.  return the lost property or capture the criminal.
    b.  offer the goods for sale through an auctioneer.
    c.  let the offeror know that he or she is there to collect the reward.
    d.  have knowledge of the reward before completing the requested act and perform the requested act.

20.  Under common law, an offeror could revoke his or her offer
    a.  any time prior to its acceptance by the offeree.
    b.  once a counteroffer has been made by the offeree.
    c.  upon dispatch into a U.S. mailbox.
    d.  by an authorized means of communication.

21.  Two ways to terminate an offer by operation of law are
    a.  by rejection and revocation.
    b.  death or incompetency of the offeror or offeree.
    c.  rewards and auctions.
    d.  intoxication and incapacity.

22.  The ABC Corporation mailed an offer of employment to Ernest.  The offer stated that acceptance of the job was to be by certified mail.  Ernest was so elated about the idea of working for the ABC Corporation, that he flew to the city ABC was located in and hand delivered his acceptance within the time stated in the offer.  Has a contract been formed between ABC and Ernest?
    a.  No, because Ernest used an unauthorized means of communication to give his acceptance.
    b.  Yes, as an offeree may accept an offer by an unauthorized means of communication.
    c.  No, because the Restatement (Second) of Contracts permits implied authorization by "any medium reasonable in the circumstances."
    d.  Yes, because adherence to the comity principle requires that ABC respect the law that Ernest is applying

23.  In order for an offer to be effective, which elements must be established?
    a.  The offeror must objectively intend to be bound by the offer.
    b.  The terms of the offer must be definite and reasonably certain.
    c.  The offer must be communicated to the offeree.
    d.  All of the above.

24.  Implied authorization for acceptance of an offer may be
    a.  inferred by properly addressing and packaging and dispatching the acceptance.
    b.  expressly stating that acceptance is not effective until received.
    c.  inferred from prior dealings, trade usage, or what is customary from similar transactions.
    d.  by stipulation that acceptance must be by specified means.

25.  Mrs. Sweet, the President of Sweetest Things Corporation, puts an offer to sell the packaging division in writing to Mr. Baker but does not send it.  Thereafter, Mrs. Baker stops in to visit Mrs. Sweet and notices the written offer on Mrs. Sweet's desk.  She then goes home and tells Mr. Baker about the offer.  Can Mr. Baker accept the offer to buy the packaging division of the Sweetest Things Corporation?
    a.  Yes, as Mrs. Baker was acting as a proxy for Mr. Baker.
    b.  No, as Mrs. Baker did not tell Mr. Baker all of the particulars of the offer.

c. Yes, as a wife, Mrs. Baker steps into the shoes of her husband and may convey the message to Mr. Baker.

d. No, because Mrs. Sweet never communicated the offer to Mr. Baker and therefore there is no offer to be accepted.

## Short Answer

26. Why is the statement, "I will purchase your mountain bike for $350.00" a valid offer?

27. Hilda and Mildred are having a fun dinner together complete with wine and laughter. Hilda, in a hysterical fit of laughter, tells Mildred, "Since you are my funniest friend, I'll sell you my California farm for $30,000." Has Hilda made a valid offer to Mildred?

28. If Tom, a tractor salesperson places an advertisement in a local circular that reads, "like new, 2002, Edwards Co. tractor, serial no. 3478942, $6,200." Is this an offer?

29. Sean accidentally leaves his grandfather's top hat in a fancy restaurant he was dining at. He places an ad in the Bradley News Gazette stating, "$500.00 reward for the return of an old, black top hat left in Patrano's Italian Restaurant on March 15, 2003, at approximately 8 p.m. Call 911-555-1212. Dawn, who has not seen the offer, finds Sean's top hat and also notes that there is a phone number on a tag inside of it. She telephone's Sean and determines that she has found his top hat. Dawn's friend Sally thereafter tells Dawn that there is a reward for finding the hat as she had seen the ad in the paper and recognized that the number in the newspaper is the same as the number inside of the hat. Is Dawn entitled to the reward money?

30. What type of auction is considered to be an invitation to make an offer?

31. If Marcia places an ad in the Sunset News Press offering a reward for her lost cat Barney and she lets the ad run for five weeks, what must she do to revoke the ad?

32. If Sue says to Julius, "I think $3,500 is too high for your old truck. I will pay you $2,500 instead." What is the effect of Sue's statement?

33. What is the result if a flood from a broken pipe destroys the bolts of silk fabric Martha was intending to buy?

34. If Omar decides to sell Jane his motor home for $60,000, provided she decides by May 1, and Omar is adjudged insane before Jane makes her decision, what is the effect of Omar's insanity?

35. What does the mirror image rule require?
   _____

36. What is an option contract?
   _____
   _____

37. What happens if a person waits too long to accept an offer?
   _____

38. Why is silence usually not considered an acceptance even if the offeror states that it is?
   _____

39. What is another name for an offer that stipulates that acceptance must be by a specified means of communication?
   _____
   _____

40. What is the effect of a supervening illegality on an offer?
   _____

## Answers to Refresh Your Memory

1. agreement [p 259]
2. Monica [p 259]
3. objectively [p 259]
4. reasonably certain [p 259]
5. Objective Theory of Contracts [p 260]
6. price, time for performance [p 260]
7. Advertisements [p 262]
8. auction without reserve [p 264]
9. rejects [p 266]
10. counteroffer [p 266]
11. subject matter [p 267]
12. unequivocal [p 267]
13. dispatch [p 271]
14. authorized [p 272]
15. offeree [p 269]

## Critical Thought Exercise Model Answer

To have an offer that is capable of acceptance, three elements must be present: (1) There must be a serious, objective intention by the offeror; (2) The terms of the offer must be reasonably certain, or definite, so that the parties and the court can ascertain the terms of the contract; and, (3) The offer must be communicated to the offeree. There appears to be sufficient information in the bid to find definite terms. Sending the request for a bid to IMC fulfilled the communication requirement. The issue centers on whether the request for a bid was accompanied by a serious intent to be bound by the offeror. Intent is not determined by the subjective intentions, beliefs, or assumptions of the offeror. What meaning Vincent attached to his invitation to bid is not relevant. Intent is determined by what a reasonable person in the offeree's position would conclude the offeror's words and actions meant. A request or invitation to negotiate is not an offer. It only expresses a willingness to discuss the matter and possibly enter into a contract after further negotiations. A reasonable person in the position of IMC would not conclude that the invitation evidenced an intention to enter into a binding agreement. As in construction contracts, an invitation to submit a bid is not an offer, and the bidding party does not bind the party who requests bids merely by submitting a bid. The party requesting the bids is free to reject all the bids or not act at all. Vincent was not bound by the bid of IMC merely because it was the highest bid submitted. Vincent never manifested an intent to be bound by the invitation to bid and he remained free to reject the bid of IMC or simply change his mind and take no action at all.

# Answers to Practice Quiz

## True/False

1. True    The basis of the objective theory of contracts is whether a reasonable person viewing the situation would conclude that the parties intended to be legally bound. [p 260]

2. True    Offers made in jest, anger, or undue excitement cannot result in a valid contract as a reasonable person would conclude that in light of the circumstances, the parties did not intend to be bound. [p 260]

3. False    An offer cannot be accepted if it is not communicated to the offeree by the offeror or an agent or representative of the offeror. [p 262]

4. True    Price will be implied if there is a market or source to determine the price of the item or service. The time for performance will be implied based on what is reasonable under the circumstances. [p 260]

5. True    Generally advertisements are treated as invitations to make an offer. However, if the offer is so definite and specific that it is obvious that the advertiser has the present intent to bind himself or herself to the terms of the advertisement, it will be considered an offer. [p 262]

6. False    An auction with reserve is an invitation to make an offer. In this situation, the seller keeps the right to refuse the highest bid and may withdraw the goods from sale. [p 264]

7. False    Most states provide that in order for the revocation to be effective, it must be received by the offeree or the offeree's agent. [p 266]

8. True    A rejection is not effective until it is actually received by the offeror. [p 266]

9. False    The effect of a counteroffer is that it terminates the offeror's offer and creates a new offer. [p 266]

10. True    The offer terminates if the subject matter, in this case the snowmobile, of the offer is destroyed through no fault of either party prior to its acceptance. [p 267]

11. True    The offeree may feel discontented; a grumbling acceptance is a legal acceptance, as he or she is not adding any conditions to the offer before accepting. [p 269]

12. True    This is an exception to the general rule that silence usually is not considered acceptance even if the offeror states that it is. If the offeree has indicated that silence means assent, then it will be construed as an acceptance. A classic example is when someone indicates that if you haven't heard from them by a date certain, then go ahead and send the order. [p 270]

13. False    Under the mailbox rule, acceptance is effective upon dispatch, not receipt. [p 271]

14. True    This is the general rule that an offeree must accept an offer by an authorized means of communication. [p 272]

15. True    Unilateral contracts may only be accepted by the offeree's performance of the required act. Compare this to a bilateral contract where it can only be accepted by an offeree who promises to perform the requested act. [p 269]

# Multiple Choice

16. A   Answer A is correct as Sam's statement indicates his present intent to enter into a binding contract with Mary.  Answer B is incorrect as there is not any question involved, but rather a statement.  Answer C is incorrect as there is nothing in the statement that states what Sam believes in order to classify it as an opinion.  Answer D is incorrect as this is a one-sided statement that is impossible to determine if a return promise is forthcoming to create a bilateral contract.  [p 260]

17. C   Answer C is correct as the car dealer expressed his opinion that he felt the car was the best car on his lot and would probably give her a lifetime of happiness.  Traditionally expressions of opinions are not actionable as promises as they do not satisfy the intent requirement of the formation of a contract.  Answer A is incorrect for the reason stated above.  Answer B is incorrect as her grounds for rescission only appear to be based on the car dealer's opinion, which would not substantiate granting her money back.  Answer D is incorrect for the reasons stated above.  [p 260]

18. C   Answer C is correct as it states what is needed in order to establish a valid offer.  Answer A is incorrect as these elements are part of what composes a valid contract.  Answer B is incorrect as it makes no sense and it is not an element to establish a valid offer.  Answer D is incorrect for the same reasons that answer B is incorrect.  [p 260]

19. D   Answer D correctly states what is required of an offeree in order to collect a reward that is being offered.  Answer A is incorrect, because even though the return of lost property or the capturing of a criminal may be the requested act to be performed, these do not address the two basic elements of knowledge of the reward and performance of the act that is required.  Answer B is comical at best as it also does not address the requirements of an offeree in order to collect a reward.  Answer C is incorrect as there is nothing to indicate that the individual had knowledge of the reward or performed a requested act before notifying the offeror that he or she is there to collect the reward.  [p 264]

20. A   Answer A is correct as revocation at common law could be accomplished any time prior to the offeree's acceptance.  Answer B is incorrect as a counteroffer terminates a prior offer and creates a new offer, therefore disposing of the need for revocation of the original offer.  Answer C is incorrect as this states the mailbox rule, which applies to acceptance.  Hence acceptance is effective upon dispatch.  Answer D is incorrect as not all offers may be revoked by any authorized means of communication.  For example, an offer to the public must be revoked by the same means and for the same length of time as the offer itself.  [p 266]

21. B   Answer B is correct as death or incompetency of the offeree or offeror are two ways by operation of law that an offer may be terminated.  Answer A is incorrect as rejection and revocation are ways that the parties may terminate an offer.  Answer C is incorrect, as it does not make any sense.  Answer D is incorrect as intoxication and incapacity are defenses to the enforcement of a contract not ways to terminate an offer.  [p 267]

22. A   Answer A is correct as an offer may stipulate that acceptance must be by a specified means of communication, such as registered mail.  Further, since Ernest used an unauthorized means of communication by hand delivering his acceptance, the acceptance of employment is not effective even if it is received by the ABC Corporation in a timely manner because the means of communication was a condition of acceptance.  Ernest should have accepted by certified mail as stated in the offer from the ABC Corporation.  Answer B is incorrect as the general rule states that an offeree must accept an offer by an authorized means of communication, not an unauthorized means of communication.  Answer C is incorrect as implied authorization usually applies in circumstances of prior dealings between the parties, or it is implied from what is customary in similar transactions or usage of trade.  Accepting employment does not appear to fit within any of the categories given for an implied authorization situation.  Answer D is incorrect as the comity principle is an ethical rule that states that nations will respect other nation's laws.  This principle does not apply in this particular case.  [p 272]

23. D  Answer D is correct as answers A, B, and C all correctly state the necessary elements to establish a valid offer. [p 259]

24. C  Answer C is correct, as implied authorization may be inferred from prior dealings between the parties, usage of trade and from what is customary in similar transactions. Answer A is incorrect, as this states the proper dispatch rule. Answer B is incorrect, as it not only is contradictory in that authorization cannot be implied and expressed at the same time. Further, the general rule regarding acceptance is that it is effective upon dispatch, unless there was a stipulation by the parties that acceptance was effective upon receipt. Answer D is incorrect as, once again, the answer is phrased in contradictory terms to the question. Authorization may not be implied and stipulated to at the same time. [p 272]

25. D  Answer D is correct, as an offer may not be accepted if it is not communicated to the offeree by the offeror or a representative or agent of the offeror. Since Mrs. Sweet did not communicate the offer to Mr. Baker, he cannot accept the offer to buy the packaging division of the Sweetest Things Corporation. Answer A is incorrect, as the rule does not apply to representatives or agents of the offeree, but rather representatives or agents of the offeror. Answer B is incorrect as the fact that Mrs. Baker did not tell Mr. Baker all of the offer's particulars is irrelevant, as she cannot communicate the offer to her husband. Answer C is incorrect, as even though she, as a manner of speaking, may wear the shoes in their family, she may not make the offer to her husband. Mrs. Sweet as the offeror must make the offer to Mr. Baker, the offeree. [p 262]

## Short Answer

26. It indicates the offeror's present intent to enter into a contract. [p 260]

27. No, as offers made in jest do not satisfy the element of intent to be bound by the terms of the offer as judged by a reasonable person under the same circumstances. [p 260]

28. Yes, as the advertisement was definite and specific enough to demonstrate that Tom intended to bind himself to the terms of the advertisement. [p 263]

29. No, because Dawn did not have prior knowledge of the reward before she found Sean's missing top hat. [p 264]

30. An auction with reserve. [p 264]

31. Marcia must communicate the revocation in the Sunset News Press for five weeks as the general rule is that revocation of offers made to the public must be by the same means and for the same length of time as the original offer. [p 266]

32. Sue has made a counteroffer that in effect terminated the original offer from Julius and created a new offer. [p 266]

33. The offer is automatically terminated by operation of law as the subject matter, here the bolts of silk fabric was destroyed through no fault of either party (flooding from a broken pipe) prior to the offer being accepted. [p 267]

34. The offer automatically terminates since there is no contract prior to Omar being adjudged insane. [p 267]

35. The mirror image rule requires the offeree to accept the offeror's terms. Acceptance must be unequivocal. [p 269]

36. An option contract is one in which an offeror is prevented from revoking his or her offer by receiving compensation from the offeree to keep the offer open for an agreed-upon period of time. [p 268]

37. An offer terminates when a stated time period ends. If no time is stated, an offer terminates after a reasonable time. [p 268]

38. Because this rule is intended to protect offerees from being legally held to offers because they did not respond. [p 270]

39. Express authorization. [p 272]

40. It terminates the offer. [p 268]

# Chapter 11

# CAPACITY AND LEGALITY

## Chapter Overview

Parties to a contract are generally presumed to have the necessary contractual capacity. Minors, insane persons, and intoxicated persons do not have this capacity and are protected by law from having contracts enforced against them. Contracts must have a lawful object or they are void. Contracts that are unconscionable, or so oppressive and manifestly unfair as to make them unjust, are not enforceable. This chapter explores capacity to contract and the lawfulness of contracts.

## Objectives

Upon completion of the exercises contained in this chapter, you should be able to:

1. Describe and recognize situations where the infancy doctrine applies.
2. Describe legal insanity and explain its impact on contractual capacity.
3. Recognize and explain illegal contracts that are contrary to statutes.
4. Explain what a covenant not to compete is and recognize when they are lawful.
5. Explain the reasons for exculpatory clauses and explain when they are lawful.
6. Describe what an unconscionable contract is and when it is unlawful.

## Practical Application

You should be able to determine whether or not the rules of law regarding the infancy doctrine, legal insanity, and intoxication will have an impact on particular contractual situations. You should be able to determine whether or not an incapacitated individual will be responsible for the execution of a contract. You should be able to determine whether or not covenants not to compete and exculpatory clauses are lawful, and whether or not a contract may be unconscionable, void or voidable.

## Helpful Hints

This chapter lends itself to organization, based on who is involved in a contractual situation and the type of clause with which the parties are concerned. Explore the critical legal thinking cases at the end of the chapter in the text and answer the critical thought exercise contained herein. The more exposure you have to situations involving capacity and legality, the easier it will be for you to recognize these issues.

## Study Tips

### Minors

The law seeks to protect those too young to have the maturity, experience, or sophistication to enter into contracts with adults.

- Under common law, females under 18 years of age and males under 21 years of age are minors.
- Most states have statutes specifying the age of majority.
- Most prevalent age of majority is 18 years old for males and females.
- Any age below the statutory age of majority is called the period of minority.

**Infancy Doctrine.** This gives minors the right to disaffirm most contracts entered into with adults.
- It serves as a minor's protection against unscrupulous adults who may want to take advantage of a minor.
  - It is an objective standard.
- A minor may choose whether or not to enforce the contract.
  - If both parties are minors, both parties have the right to cancel the contract.
- A minor cannot disaffirm as to part of the contract and affirm as to another part of the contract.

**Disaffirmance.** A minor in may disaffirm a contract in writing, orally or by conduct.
- No formalities are needed.
- It must be done prior to reaching the age of majority or a reasonable time thereafter. Reasonable is assessed on a case-by-case basis.

**Minor's Duty of Restoration.** If either party has not performed the contract, the minor only needs to disaffirm the contract.

*Competent Party's Duty of Restitution.* If the minor has given consideration to the competent party before disaffirming, the competent party must place the minor in the status quo.
- He or she must give the minor back his or her money to make him or her whole again.

*Minor's Duty of Restoration.* Upon disaffirmance of the contract, the minor must return the goods to the adult, even if the goods are lost, destroyed, consumed or have depreciated in value.

**Minor's Duty of Restitution.** In a majority of states, the minor will be required to put the adult in status quo upon disaffirming the contract if the minor was intentionally or grossly negligent in his or her conduct thereby causing the adult's property to lose value.
- Most states require that minors who misrepresent their age must put the adult in status quo upon disaffirming the contract.
- Some states require the minor to make restitution of the reasonable value of the item when disaffirming any contract.

**Ratification.** Ratification means "to accept" and may be express or implied by conduct.
- A minor may ratify a contract before reaching the age of majority or a reasonable time thereafter.
- If disaffirmance does not occur in this time frame, it is considered accepted.

**Parents' Liability for Their Children's Contracts.** If the parents have not sufficiently provided for their children's necessaries of life, then they are liable for their children's contracts.
- Exception: If a minor becomes emancipated by voluntarily leaving home and living apart from his or her parents and can support him or herself, then the parents have no duty to support their child. This is looked at on a case-by-case basis.

**Necessaries of Life.** Minors are required to pay for the necessaries of life for which they contract.
- There is no standard definition for "necessaries", but food, clothing, tools of the trade, medical services, and education are typical examples.

- The minor is required to pay the reasonable value of the services or goods under the Doctrine of Quasi-contract, rather than on the contract itself.
- Statutes exist that make minors liable for certain contracts, which include child support, education, medical, surgical and pregnancy care.

## Mentally Incompetent Persons

The law seeks to protect those suffering from substantial mental incapacity from having contracts enforced against them because they may not understand the consequences of their actions in entering into a contract.

- The person must have been legally insane at the time he or she entered into the contract.
- Legal insanity is determined by using the *objective cognitive understanding test* which involves determining whether the person was incapable of understanding or comprehending the nature of the transaction.
- Delusions, light psychological or emotional problems, or weakness of intellect do not qualify.

**Adjudged Insane.** The court, on the request of an interested party, will determine that a person is legally insane and will appoint a guardian to act on behalf of the insane person.

- Only the court-appointed guardian has legal authority to enter into contracts on behalf of the adjudged insane person.
- Any contract entered into by the adjudged insane person will be void.

**Insane, But Not Adjudged Insane.** Any contracts made by a person who suffers from a mental impairment that makes him or her legally insane are voidable by the insane person.

- For those mentally impaired persons who suffer alternating periods of sanity and insanity:
  - Contracts made during a lucid period are enforceable.
  - Contracts made during an insane period are voidable.
- The other party does not have the option to avoid the contract, unless that party doesn't have the contractual capacity either.
- The other party must put the insane party back to the status quo.
  - The sane party must also be placed back to the status quo if he or she was unaware of the other party's insane condition.
- Under a quasi-contract, insane individuals are liable for the reasonable value for the necessaries of life that they receive.

## Intoxicated Persons

Contracts entered into by individuals intoxicated by alcohol or drugs are voidable by that person.

- The contract is voidable only if the person was so intoxicated that he or she was incapable of understanding or comprehending the nature of the transaction.
  - Some states will only allow the person to disaffirm the contract if he or she was forced to become intoxicated.
- The other party does not have the option to avoid the contract, unless that party doesn't have the contractual capacity either.
- The intoxicated one must be returned to the status quo.
  - The intoxicated person must return the consideration under the contract thereby making restitution to the other party and returning him or her to the staus quo.
- These individuals are liable in quasi-contract to pay the reasonable value for the necessaries that they receive.

# Legality

The object of a contract must be lawful. If the object is illegal, then the contract is void and unenforceable.

**Contracts Contrary to Statutes.** Statutes at both federal and state levels prohibit certain activities.
- Contracts to perform activities that are contrary to statute are illegal.
- Such contracts are void and unenforceable.

**Usury Laws.** These laws set an upper limit on the annual rate that can be charged on certain loans.
- They are enacted to protect borrowers from loan sharks.
- Consequences for violating these laws include criminal and civil penalties.
- Most states exempt certain types of lenders and loan transactions.

**Sabbath Laws.** These blue laws or Sunday laws prohibit or limit certain secular activities on Sundays.
- Only certain states enact these laws.
- Contracts for "necessaries" are exempt.
- Many states do not enforce these laws.
    o These laws have been found unconstitutional in some states.

**Contracts to Commit Crimes.** These contracts are void.
- If the object of the contract became illegal after the contract was entered into because of a governmental statute, both parties no longer have to perform under the contract.
- The contract is only illegal if the parties agree to go forward and complete it.

**Contracts Contrary to Public Policy.** If the contract has a negative impact on society or impacts public safety or welfare, it is void.
- Immoral contracts may be against public policy, such as a contract that requests sexual favors.
    o Societal beliefs and practices are used as a guide in determining what constitutes immoral conduct.

**Gambling Statutes.** All states have some sort of regulation or prohibition concerning gambling, Lotteries, wagering and games of chance.
- Consequences for violating these laws also include criminal and civil penalties.
- Risk-shifting contracts, such as property insurance, are distinguished from gambling contracts.
- Statutory exceptions include games of chance under a certain dollar amount, bingo games, dog and horse racing, and lotteries conducted for charity.

**Effect of Illegality.** Generally speaking one cannot enforce an illegal contract. However, there are circumstances that are exempt from this general rule:
- Innocent persons who justifiably relied on the law or fact making the contract illegal.
- Persons who were induced to enter into a contract.
- Persons who withdrew from the illegal act prior to its being performed.
- Persons who were less at fault that the other party.

# Special Business Contracts

The issue of whether a contract is lawful applies to several special business contracts.

**Contracts in Restraint of Trade.** Capitalism favors competition.

- Contracts that unreasonably restrain trade are unlawful.

**Licensing Statutes.** All states require that certain occupations and professions, such as lawyers, doctors, and hairdressers, be licensed in order to practice.
- A license signifies that the person has the proper schooling, experience and moral character.

*Regulatory Statutes.* These statutes concern those that protect the public.
- Unlicensed persons may not collect payment for services that a regulatory statute requires a licensed person to provide.

*Revenue-raising Statutes.* These statutes are made to raise money for the government.
- Protecting the public is not a consideration with this type of statute.
- Unlicensed persons can collect payment for services that a revenue-raising statute requires a licensed person to provide.

**Exculpatory Clauses.** An exculpatory clause relieves one or both parties from tort liability under a contract.
- This type of clause can relieve a party from ordinary negligence but not be used in cases of gross negligence, intentional torts, fraud, or willful conduct.
- Courts do not condone exculpatory clauses unless the parties have equal bargaining power.

**Covenant Not to Compete.** To protect goodwill after the sale of a business, the seller often agrees not to engage in a similar business or occupation within a specified area for a specified time.
- These contracts are ancillary to the legitimate sale of a business or employment contract.
- These contracts are lawful if reasonableness can be demonstrated based on
  o the line of business protected
  o the duration of the restriction
  o the geographical area that is being protected
- The court can refuse to enforce it or alter it to make it reasonable.

## Unconscionable Contracts

Some otherwise lawful contracts are unconscionable, or so unfair that they are unjust.
- The public-policy-based doctrine of unconscionablility allows the courts to
  o Refuse to enforce the contract
  o Refuse to enforce the unconscionable clause but enforce the rest of the contract or
  o Limit the application of any unconscionable clause to avoid an unconscionable result.

**Elements of Unconscionability.** Three elements must be shown to prove that a contract, or clause, is unconscionable.
- The parties possessed severely unequal bargaining power.
- The dominant party unduly used its unequal bargaining power to obtain unfair contract terms.
- The subservient party had no reasonable alternative

## Refresh Your Memory

The following exercises will help to test your memory regarding the principles given in this chapter. Read each question twice, then place your answer in the blank provided for each question. Review the chapter material for any questions that you are unable to answer or remember.

1.  The law presumes the parties to a contract have the requisite contractual _____ to enter into the contract.

2.  Any age below the statutory age is called the _____ _____ _____.

3.  The infancy doctrine is a(n) _____ standard whereby the court will not inquire into an individual's knowledge, sophistication or experience.

4.  Under the infancy doctrine, the contract is _____ by the minor.

5.  If both parties to the contract are minors, both parties have the right to _____ the contract.

6.  A minor can expressly disaffirm a contract _____, in _____, or by the minor's _____.

7.  Minors who misrepresent their age must place the adult in _____ _____ if they disaffirm the contract.

8.  To ratify means to _____.

9.  Parents owe a duty to provide _____ _____ _____ for their minor children.

10. _____ occurs when a minor leaves home voluntarily and lives apart from his or her parents.

11. A person is _____ _____ if a court, after hearing evidence at a formal hearing, makes that person a ward of the court and appoints a guardian to act on their behalf.

12. Some states allow an intoxicated person to _____ a contract only if they were forced to become intoxicated or did so unknowingly.

13. _____ _____ are enacted to protect the public from those who may not have met the state standard for a particular profession and to raise revenue for the state.

14. Contracts that have a negative impact on society or interfere with public safety and welfare are _____ _____ _____ _____ _____.

15. The Doctrine of _____ is based on public policy and allows the courts to declare some oppressive and manifestly unjust contracts to be unenforceable.

# Critical Thought Exercise

You manage a small bicycle shop and sell a very good product, with some bikes costing $2,000. A young man comes into your store and wants to buy a mountain bike for $1,200. He has the cash. You are very happy to sell it to him. He tells you that he is an ambitious high school student who is taking classes at the local university and needs a bicycle that is capable of handling the large hills between the high school and college so that he can make it to class.

Two years later, the young man comes into the shop and tells you that yesterday was his 18th birthday and after drinking a great deal of alcohol, he rode his bike down the Cuesta Grade and crashed into a Ford Expedition. He hands you a piece of bent frame and states that this is all that was left of the bicycle when he went back to the accident scene this morning. He asks for his $1,200 back as he now "desires to undue the contract."

Will you agree to the full refund? Why or why not?

*Please compose your answer on a separate sheet of paper or on your computer.*

# Practice Quiz

## True/False

1. ___ Unconscionable contracts are enforceable.

2. ___ Minors do not always have the maturity and experience they need to enter into contracts with adults.

3. ___ The law does recognize the infancy doctrine.

4. ___ Contracts for the necessities of life are exempt from the infancy doctrine.

5. ___ If both parties are minors when entering into a contract, only one party may disaffirm the contract.

6. ___ The infancy doctrine is an objective standard in most states.

7. ___ A minor may not affirm one part of the contract and disaffirm another part.

8. ___ A minor may disaffirm a contract if neither party has performed and the minor's contract is executory.

9. ___ The competent party to a contract must return the minor to status quo if the minor transferred consideration, money, property or other valuables to the competent party before disaffirming the contract.

10. ___ A minor is not required to put the adult in status quo upon disaffirmance of the contract if the minor's intentional or grossly negligent conduct caused the loss of value to the adult's property.

11. ___ To ratify is another term for affirm.

12. ___ A minor's ratification may be accomplished by express, oral or written words or implied from the minor's conduct.

13. ___ Minors are obligated to pay for the necessaries of life for which they contract.

14. ___ Minors are not responsible for such things as shelter, clothing, food, or medical services.

15. ___ Parents do not owe a legal duty to provide food, clothing, shelter and other necessaries of life for their minor children.

## Multiple Choice

16.   Parents owe a legal duty to their children to provide
      a.   a good post secondary education so that they can get a good job.
      b.   a place to live until they get married.
      c.   food, clothing, shelter and other necessaries of life.
      d.   tools of the trade for the occupation in which they are interested.

17.   People who are suffering from substantial mental incapacity will be protected from having contracts enforced against them because
      a.   they may have emotional problems rendering them legally insane.
      b.   they may have been intoxicated.
      c.   they may be delusional when entering into the contracts.
      d.   they may not understand the consequences of their actions in entering into a contract.

18.   Any contract entered into by a person who has been adjudged insane is
      a.   valid.
      b.   void.
      c.   voidable.
      d.   enforceable.

19.   A person who has contracted with an insane person must place that insane person
      a.   in status quo if the contract is void or voided by the insane person.
      b.   in pari delicto with the competent party to the contract.
      c.   in counseling to help him or her out.
      d.   in status quo if the contract is void or voided by the sane person.

20.   Most states hold with regard to intoxication that a contract is voidable only if the person
      a.   was so intoxicated when he or she entered into the contract that he or she was aware of how many drinks he or she had consumed.
      b.   was so intoxicated that a subjective individual would be able to validate the nature of his or her transaction.
      c.   was so intoxicated that he or she could not remember where he or she was.
      d.   was so intoxicated that he or she was incapable of understanding or comprehending the nature of the transaction.

21.   The amount of drugs or alcohol that is necessary to be consumed for an individual to be considered legally intoxicated to disaffirm contracts
      a.   is usually two or more alcoholic beverages.
      b.   is a reasonable amount.
      c.   varies from case to case.
      d.   none of the above.

22.   An individual who disaffirms a contract using intoxication as his or her basis must
      a.   be awarded punitive damages against the server of alcohol or drugs.
      b.   be returned to status quo.
      c.   understand or comprehend the nature of the transaction.
      d.   pass a breathalyzer test.

23.   Ratification
      a.   relates back to the inception of the contract.
      b.   can be by express oral or written words.

   c.  can be implied from the minor's conduct.
   d.  All of the above.

24.  State usury laws
   a.  set a lower limit on the annual interest rate that can be charged on certain types of loans.
   b.  are intended to protect unsophisticated lenders from loan sharks and others who charge exorbitant rates of interest.
   c.  exempt certain types of lenders and loan transactions involving legitimate business transactions.
   d.  All of the above.

25.  An exculpatory clause
   a.  is a contractual provision that relieves one or both parties to a contract from tort liability.
   b.  can relieve a party of liability for ordinary negligence.
   c.  cannot be used in a situation involving willful conduct, intentional torts, fraud, recklessness, or gross negligence.
   d.  All of the above.

## Short Answer

26.  What is a covenant not to compete?

_____

_____

_____

27.  Define an unconscionable contract.

_____

28.  What is the Infancy Doctrine?

_____

29.  Define disaffirmance.

_____

30.  How are the items that comprise "necessaries" determined?

_____

31.  What is emancipation?

_____

_____

32.  What is an immoral contract?

_____

33.  Define the period of minority.

_____

34.  What does the minor's duty of restitution require?

_____

_____

35. What does the minor's duty of restoration require?

_____

_____

36. What is the objective cognitive "understanding" test?

_____

_____

37. What is the contractual effect of a person being adjudged insane?

_____

38. What is the contractual effect of a person with alternating periods of sanity and insanity?

_____

39. Joe's Loans made a loan to Silly Sally with the following stipulation: "the interest on this loan is 360 percent per annum, payable monthly". Joe doesn't want his loans declared unenforceable if the limits on interest are lowered. How can he rephrase this to keep the contract valid?

_____

40. How are judges to define morality when faced with a purportedly immoral contract?

_____

# Answers to Refresh Your Memory

1. capacity  [p 292]
2. period of minority  [p 292]
3. objective  [p 292]
4. voidable  [p 293]
5. disaffirm  [p 293]
6. orally, writing, conduct  [p 293]
7. status quo  [p 294]
8. accept  [p 294]
9. necessaries of life  [p 295]
10. Emancipation  [p 295]
11. adjudged insane  [p 297-298]
12. disaffirm  [p 300]
13. licensing statutes  [p 305]
14. contracts contrary to public policy  [p 302]
15. Unconscionability  [p 308]

# Critical Thought Exercise Model Answer

In almost all states, the age of majority for contractual purposes is eighteen years old. With some exceptions, the contracts entered into by a minor are voidable at the option of the minor. For a minor to exercise their option to disaffirm a contract, he or she only needs to manifest an intent not to be bound by the contract. The contract can normally be disaffirmed at any time during minority, or for a reasonable time after attaining the age of majority. When a minor disaffirms a contract, all property that has been given to the adult as consideration must be returned to the minor. Upon disaffirmance, most states require that the minor need only return the goods or money that were the subject of the contract, provided that the minor still has the goods or money. The minor may disaffirm the contract even if the goods are lost, stolen, damaged, or destroyed. A minor may disaffirm a contract for necessaries, such as food, clothing, shelter, and medical services. However, the minor remains liable for the reasonable value of the goods used when the goods are deemed a necessary. Transportation is normally not considered a necessary. The young man who purchased the bike told me that he was only in high school. This should have put me, as the agent for the store, on notice that I was dealing with a minor. It is irrelevant that the minor drank alcohol before he crashed the bicycle. I will be obligated to return the total purchase price unless my store is in one of the few states that require the minor to put me in the same position as before the contract. In that state, the minor would only be entitled to a refund of the purchase price minus the cost of the damage to the bicycle. Since the bicycle was destroyed, no refund would be warranted.

# Answers to Practice Quiz

## True/False

1. False    A contract that is so oppressive or manifestly unfair that it would be unjust to enforce it is unconscionable and hence unenforceable. [p 292]
2. True    Minors do not always have the maturity, experience or sophistication they need to enter into contracts. [p 292]
3. True    The law does recognize the infancy doctrine so that minors are protected and allowed to disaffirm most contracts that they have entered into. [p 292]
4. True    Minors are obligated to pay for the necessaries of life that they contract for. [p 293]
5. False    Both parties have the right to disaffirm the contract. [p 293]
6. True    The infancy doctrine is an objective standard. [p 292]
7. True    A minor may not affirm one part of the contract and disaffirm another part. [p 293]
8. True    If the minor has not yet performed and neither party has performed, the minor may disaffirm the contract. [p 293]
9. True    If the minor has transferred consideration to the competent party before disaffirming the contract, that party must place the minor in status quo. [p 293]
10. False    A majority of jurisdictions hold that the minor must put the adult in status quo upon disaffirmance of the contract, even if the minor's intentional or grossly negligent conduct cause the loss of value to the adult's property. [p 294]
11. True    Ratify means to accept not disaffirm. [p 294]
12. True    Ratification may be accomplished by express, oral or written words or implied by the minor's conduct. [p 294]
13. True    Minors are obligated for contracts they enter into involving the necessaries of life. [p 296]
14. False    Though necessary of life has not been defined by the court, items such as shelter, clothing, food or medical services are found to be necessaries of life. [p 296]
15. False    Parents do owe a legal duty to provide for the necessaries of life (such as food, shelter and clothing) for their minor children. [p 295]

## Multiple Choice

16. C    Answer C is correct as parents do owe a legal duty to provide clothing, food, shelter and other necessaries of life for their minor children. Answer A is incorrect as parents are not responsible for their children's post-secondary education. Answer B is incorrect as parents are not obligated to their children for a place to live once they marry. Answer D is incorrect as parents are not responsible for tools of the trade in which their children are interested. [p 295]
17. D    Answer D is correct as those suffering from substantial mental incapacity may be legally insane and may be incapable of understanding or comprehending the nature of the contracts they

are a part of. Answer A is incorrect as emotional problems do not constitute legal insanity under the law. Answer B is incorrect as the question is directed toward insanity and not intoxication. Answer C is incorrect, as delusions do not constitute insanity under the law. [p 297]

18. B    Answer B is correct as a person who is adjudged insane becomes a ward of the court and any contract entered into by the insane individual is void. Answer A is incorrect because a contract entered into by an individual who has been adjudicated as insane cannot be valid. Answer C is incorrect as a contract is voidable if the individual is insane but not adjudged Insane. Answer D is incorrect for the reason that answer A is incorrect. [p 297-298]

19. A    Answer A is correct as a majority of states hold that a party who was unaware that he or she was dealing with an insane individual must return the insane individual to status quo if the contract is either void or voided by the insane person. Answer B is incorrect, as it makes no sense since in pari delicto means that both parties are equally at fault in an illegal contract. There is no such situation in the present fact situation concerning contracting with insane individuals. Answer C is incorrect as, though this is an admirable thing to do, under contract law an individual is not responsible for placing the insane person in counseling to help him or her out. Answer D is incorrect as the contract must be void or voided by the insane individual not the sane person. [p 298]

20. D    Answer D is the correct answer as this states the majority rule of law with regard to whether a contract will be enforceable or not in situations involving intoxication. Answer A is incorrect because, if the person was so intoxicated, how could he or she be aware of how man drinks that he or she consumed? Therefore, this answer does not make sense. Answer B is incorrect, as the factors that are considered in determining whether a person is legally intoxicated include the user's physical characteristics and his or her ability to tolerate or hold intoxicants, not someone else's validation of the nature of the transaction that had been entered into. Answer C is incorrect, as it is not whether the intoxicated individual could remember where he or she was at, but rather was he or she so intoxicated that he or she was incapable of understanding or comprehending the nature of the transaction? [p 299]

21. C    Answer C is correct as the amount of alcohol or drugs to be considered legally intoxicated varies from case to case, taking the user's physical characteristics and ability to hold intoxicants into consideration. Answer A is incorrect, as not every individual becomes intoxicated on two or more alcoholic beverages, as it is determined on a case-by-case basis. Answers B and D are incorrect, based on the reasoning given in Answer C. [p 300]

22. B    Answer B is correct, as the disaffirming party claiming intoxication as a reason for not accepting the terms of the contract must be returned to the status quo. Answer A is incorrect, as generally an individual may not receive punitive damages in a cause of action based on contract law. Answer C is incorrect because, if the individual understood or comprehended the nature of the transaction, he or she would not be able to disaffirm the contract based on intoxication. Answer D is incorrect, as there is nothing in contract law that would require an individual utilizing intoxication as a reason for disaffirming a contract to pass a breathalyzer test. [p 300]

23. D    Answer D is correct, as all three answers are correct statements regarding ratification. Answers A, B, and C are incorrect, as each of them is a correct statement. [p 294]

24. C    Answer C is correct, as usury laws exempt certain types of lenders and loan transactions involving legitimate business transactions. Answer A is incorrect, as usury laws set an upper limit on the annual interest rate that can be charged on certain types of loans. Answer B is incorrect, as usury laws are intended to protect unsophisticated borrowers from loan sharks and others who charge exorbitant rates of interest. Answer D is incorrect for the above reasons. [p 301]

25. D    Answer D is correct, as all three answers are correct statements regarding exculpatory clauses. Answers A, B, and C are incorrect, as each of them is a correct statement. [p 306]

## Short Answer

26. A covenant not to compete is an ancillary agreement between parties to the sale of a business or employment contract whereby the seller agrees with the buyer not to engage in a similar business or occupation within a specified geographical area for a specified period of time upon sale of the business or departing the employment situation. All aspects must be reasonable to be enforceable. [p 307]

27. A contract that is so oppressive or manifestly unfair that it would be unjust to enforce it. [p 308]

28. A doctrine that gives minors the right to affirm or disaffirm a contract entered into with an adult. [p 292]

29. Disaffirmance is the act of a minor to rescind a contract under the infancy doctrine. [p 293]

30. The minor's age, lifestyle and status in life are what are looked at in determining what are necessaries as they pertain to contracts the minor has entered into. [p 296]

31. Emancipation is when a minor voluntarily leaves home and lives apart from his or her parents. The courts will view a minor's ability to be self-supportive in determining emancipation. [p 295]

32. One whose objective is the commission of an act that is considered immoral by society. [p 302]

33. Any age below the statutory age of majority. [p 292]

34. That the minor must put the adult in status quo upon disaffirmance of the contract if the minor's intentional or grossly negligent conduct caused the loss of value to the adult's property. [p 294]

35. A minor is obligated only to return the goods or property he or she has received from the adult in the condition it is in at the time of disaffirmance, even if it has been consumed, lost, or destroyed or has depreciated in value. [p 293]

36. This test is used to determine legal insanity. It requires that the person's mental incapacity renders that person incapable of understanding or comprehending the nature of the transaction. Mere weakness of intellect, slight psychological or emotional problems, or delusions do not constitute legal insanity. [p 297]

37. Any contract such a person enters into will be void. Only the court-appointed guardian can enter into contracts on this person's behalf. [p 298]

38. Any contracts made by such a person during a lucid period are enforceable. Contracts made while the person is insane can be disaffirmed. [p 298]

39. Joe can rephrase this stipulation to read "the interest on this loan is 360 percent per year, or the highest rate allowable by law, payable monthly." [p 301]

40. Judges are not free to define morality based on their own views. They must look to the practices and beliefs of society when defining immoral conduct. [p 302]

## Chapter 12

# GENUINENESS OF ASSENT
# AND STATUTE OF FRAUDS

## Chapter Overview

An enforceable contract requires that the parties give voluntary assent. Genuine assent may be lost when a party enters a contract due to mistake, fraud, duress, or undue influence. Some contracts must be in writing to be enforceable. This chapter discusses genuineness of assent, the writing requirement of the Statute of Frauds for some contracts, integration of other documents into a contract, when parol evidence can be considered, and interpretation of contract language.

## Objectives

Upon completion of the exercises in this chapter, you should be able to:

1. Discuss genuineness of assent.
2. Explain how a mutual mistake of fact excuses performance.
3. Explain undue influence and its applicability to contracts
4. Describe the contracts that must satisfy the Statute of Frauds.
5. Discuss the impact of the failure to adhere to the Statute of Frauds.
6. Explain the Parol Evidence Rule and its exceptions.

## Practical Application

You should be able to discuss the requirements of genuine assent, and whether a mistake is a unilateral or a mutual, by analyzing given facts. You should be able to decide whether or not a fraudulent misrepresentation or other fraud exists and the remedies that are available for fraud. You should be able to understand the impact of both physical and economic duress, and undue influence upon a contractual situation. You should be able to recognize when the Statute of Frauds applies to certain situations, and whether or not the writing requirement can be satisfied in the absence of a writing. You should be able to determine which documents comprise a contract, and whether there are any issues regarding parol evidence and if any exceptions exist.

## Helpful Hints

The five main areas with which you should be familiar are categorized in the Study Tips section. Since differentiating between the different types of fraud can be confusing, it is important to gain exposure to as many cases and examples as possible. The exercises provided for this chapter will help to enhance the exercises given at the end of the chapter in your text.

# Study Tips

## Mistake

Mistakes occur when one or both of the parties have an incorrect belief about the subject matter, value or some other area of the contract.
- Mistakes can be either unilateral or mutual.
- Some contracts made in mistake can be rescinded.

**Unilateral Mistakes.** This occurs where one party is mistaken about a material fact concerning the subject matter of the contract.
- The general rule is the mistaken party usually will not be allowed to rescind the contract.
- There are three exceptions to this rule:
  o If one party is mistaken and the other party knew or should have known of the mistake, then the mistake is treated as a mutual mistake and rescission is allowed.
  o If a unilateral mistake is made because of a clerical or mathematical error and is not because of gross negligence.
  o The gravity of the mistake makes enforcing the contract unconscionable.

**Mutual Mistakes.** A mistake made by both parties concerning a material fact that is important to the subject matter of the contract.
- The general rule is that either party may rescind the contract if there has been a mutual mistake of a past or existing material fact.
- There are two types of mutual mistake:
  o Mutual mistake of fact, where the contract may be rescinded because there has been no meeting of the minds between parties as the subject matter is in dispute.
  o Mutual mistake of value, where the contract remains enforceable because the subject matter is not in dispute and the parties are only mistaken as to the value.

## Fraud

When fraudulent misrepresentation is used as an inducement to enter into a contract, the innocent party's assent is not genuine and the contract is voidable.

**Proving Fraud.** There are four elements necessary to show fraud:
- A false representation of material fact was made.
- There was intent to deceive the innocent party.
- There was justifiable reliance on the misrepresentation by the innocent party.
- There was injury to the innocent party.

The mnemonic you utilized in chapter 4 is also applicable here. The mnemonic is MISJD

**M** - **M**isrepresentation of a material fact that was false in nature
**I** - **I**ntentionally made to the innocent party
**S** - **S**cienter (knowledge) of the statement's falsity by the wrongdoer
**J** - **J**ustifiable reliance on the false statement by the innocent party
**D** - **D**amages were suffered by the injured party

*Material Misrepresentation of Fact.* Misrepresentation can happen through words or by conduct.

- It must be of a material fact.
- It must have played a major role in inducing the innocent party to enter into a contract.
- Opinion or predictions are not sufficient to show fraud.

*Intent to Deceive.* The persons creating the misrepresentation must have knowledge of the falsity or insufficient knowledge of the truth; this is called *scienter*.
- The misrepresentation must be made with the intent to deceive; intent can be inferred.

*Reliance on the Misrepresentation.* The innocent party must have justifiably relied on the misrepresentation. This reliance is usually found unless
- The innocent party knew the falsity of the misrepresentation, or
- The misrepresentation was so extravagant as to be obviously false.

*Injury to the Innocent Party.* The innocent party must prove economic injury.
- Damages are the difference between the value of property as represented and actual value
- Alternatively, the buyer can rescind the contract and recover the purchase price.

**Fraud in the Inception.** Fraud in the factum, is when a person is deceived on what is signed.
- The contract is void.

**Fraud in the Inducement.** Happens when the person knows what he or she is signing, but has been fraudulently induced to enter into the contract.
- The contract is voidable by the innocent party.

**Fraud by Concealment.** One party specifically conceals a material fact from the other party.

**Silence as Misrepresentation.** If nondisclosure would cause death or bodily injury or there is a fiduciary relationship or statutes require that a fact be disclosed, then fraud may be implied.
- The *Restatement (Second) of Contracts* states that nondisclosure is misrepresentation if it would show a failure to act in "good faith."

**Misrepresentation of Law.** The general rule is that this is not actionable as fraud.
- If one party is a professional who should know the law and intentionally misrepresents the law to a less knowledgeable party, this will allow rescission of the contract.

**Innocent Misrepresentation.** This occurs when a party makes a statement of fact that he or she honestly believes is true even though it is not.
- The injured party may rescind the contract but may not seek damages.

## Undue Influence

Rescission for undue influence is allowed if shown that one person took advantage of another person's mental, emotional, or physical weakness to influence that person to enter into a contract.
- Two elements must be shown:
  - There was a fiduciary or confidential relationship between the parties.
  - The dominant party unduly used his or her influence to induce the servient party to enter into the contract.
- This contract is voidable by the innocent party.

## Duress

Duress happens when one person threatens to do some wrongful act unless another person enters into a contract.

- Threats to cause physical harm or extortion are duress.
- Threats to bring, or not drop, a criminal lawsuit can be duress.
- Threats to bring, or not drop, civil lawsuits do not constitute duress, unless the suit is frivolous or brought in bad faith.
- Duress makes the contract unenforceable due to lack of genuine assent.

**Economic Duress.** Business compulsion or economic coercion occurs if one party refuses to perform duties unless the other party pays more money and enters into a second contract.

- Innocent party must show no choice but to pay the extra money and yield to the threat.

## Statute of Frauds

Certain kinds of contracts must be in writing in order to memorialize the significant terms and prevent misunderstanding or fabrications, otherwise known as fraud.

**Writing Requirement.** The Statute of Frauds requires certain contracts to be in writing.

- Those involving land
- Those that cannot possibly be performed within one year
- Collateral contracts
- Those made in consideration of marriage
- Those for the sale of goods over $500
- Those for the services of a real estate agent
- Those for the services of an agent where the underlying contract must be in writing
- Those promising to write a will
- Those to pay debts barred by bankruptcy or a statute of limitations
- Those to pay for services provided in negotiation the purchase of a business
- Those involving finders fees

The mnemonic below is an easy way to remember which contracts are required to be in writing.

<u>M</u>r. <u>D</u>ibbles <u>P</u>laces <u>M</u>any <u>F</u>ancy <u>R</u>eal <u>E</u>state <u>A</u>ds.

| | | |
|---|---|---|
| **M**r. | – | Contracts in consideration of **M**arriage |
| **D**ibbles | – | **D**ebt of another |
| **P**laces | – | **P**art Performance |
| **M**any | – | **M**ust be performed within one year |
| **F**ancy | – | **F**or goods $500 or more |
| **R**eal **E**state | – | Transfers of ownership interests in **R**eal **E**state such as mortgages, leases |
| **A**ds | – | **A**gency contracts |

*Enforcement of Writing Requirement.* The general rule is that contracts required to be in writing under the Statute of Frauds must be in writing to be enforced.

- If an executory contract is not in writing, even if required to be, it is unenforceable.

- If an oral contract should have been in writing under the Statute of Frauds but has already been executed, neither party can have the contract rescinded.

**Contracts Involving Interests in Land.** Contracts that transfer an ownership interest in land must be in writing. Real property includes the land, its buildings, trees, soil, minerals, timber, plants, crops, and permanently affixed things to the buildings (fixtures).
- Mortgages are an interest in real property given as security for repayment of a loan.
- Leases transfer the right to use real property for a specified period of time.
- Life Estates give a person an interest in real property for their lifetime, whereupon that interest will transfer to another party on that person's death.
- Easements give the right to use another person's land without owning or leasing it.

*Part Performance Exception.* This involves the situation where there is an oral contract for the sale of land or other transfer of interest in real property and there is partial performance.
- In order to use the equitable doctrine of part performance as an exception, many courts require that the purchaser either take possession of the property and pay part of the purchase price or make valuable improvements on the land.
- If part performance can be shown, the oral contract will be ordered to be specifically performed in order to prevent an injustice

**One-Year Rule.** Intended to prevent disputes over terms near the end of a long-term contract.
- If a contract cannot be performed by its own terms within one year, it must be in writing.
- If it can be performed within one year, the contract can be oral.

**Guaranty Contracts.** This type of contract allows one person to answer for the debts or duties of another. There are at least three parties and two contracts in any guaranty contract:
- First Contract, also known as the original or primary contract is between the debtor and the creditor and does not have to be in writing
- Second Contract, also called the guaranty contract is between the guarantor, the person who agrees to pay the debt if the primary debtor does not, and the original creditor and does have to be in writing

*The "Main Purpose" Exception.* A leading object exception to the Statute of Frauds occurs when the primary reason of the transaction and an oral contract is to provide financial benefit to the guarantor and treats the collateral contract as an original contract, which need not be in writing.

**Contracts for the Sale of Goods.** The Uniform Commercial Code requires contracts for the sale of goods that cost $500 or more to be in writing in order to be enforceable.
- Modifications that cause goods to escalate in price to $500 or more must be in writing.

**Agents' Contracts.** The *equal dignity rule* requires agent's contracts must be in writing.

**Promises Made in Consideration of Marriage.** A unilateral promise to pay money or give property in consideration of marriage must be in writing.

**Promissory Estoppel.** This is an equitable doctrine which is also known as equitable estoppel.
- It involves an oral promise that is enforceable if three conditions are met:
  - The promise induces action or forbearance of action by another.
  - The reliance on the oral promise was foreseeable, and
  - Injustice can be avoided only by enforcing the oral promise.

## Formality of the Writing

A written contract needs to be a writing containing essential terms of the parties' agreement.
- A contract does not have to be drafted by a lawyer or formally typed to be binding.
- A contract can be a letter, telegram, invoice, sales receipts, checks and even handwritings on scraps of paper.

**Required Signature.** The contract must be signed by the party to be charged.
- The signature of the person enforcing the contract is not necessary.
- A written contract can be enforced against one party, but not the other.

*Signatures.* A signature may appear anywhere on the writing.
- It need not be a full name and can be a nickname, initial, a symbol, and even an 'X'.

*Signatures in Foreign Countries.* In Japan, China, and other countries of Asia, individuals may follow the tradition of using a stamp as their signature.
- A stamp with a set of characters on the end of it, called hanko in Japan, chop in China.
- Hankos and chops are registered with the government.

**Integration of Several Writings.** A writing need not be a single document to be enforceable.
- Incorporation by reference may be by an express reference in one document that refers to and incorporates another document.
- Several writings can be combined to form a single written contract.

**Interpreting Contract Words and Terms.** Courts often interpret the meaning of contract terms.
- The parties may explain the words and terms used in the contract.
- Some contracts contain a glossary that defines the terms and used in a contract.
- If words and terms are not defined, the courts will interpret using the following standard:
  - Ordinary words- given the meaning as stated in the dictionary.
  - Technical words – given their technical meaning.
  - Specific terms qualify general terms.
  - Typed words prevail over preprinted words.
  - Handwritten words prevail over preprinted and typed.
  - An ambiguity will be resolved against the party who drafted the contract.
  - If both parties are in the same sort of trade, then the words used in the trade will be given their meaning as per trade usage.
  - Interpretation will be to advance the object of the contract.

**Merger, or Integration, Clause.** Contracts may include a clause that stipulates that the contract is a complete integration and exclusive expression of agreement and bars use of parol evidence.

## Parol Evidence Rule

Any words outside of the four corners of the contract are called parol evidence. The parol evidence rule states that if a written contract is a complete and final expression of the parties' agreement, any prior oral or written statements that alter, contradict, or are in addition to the terms of the written contract are inadmissible in any court proceeding concerning the contract.
- A completely integrated contract is the best evidence of the terms of the agreement.

**Exceptions to the Parol Evidence Rule.** Parol evidence may be admitted to court if:
- It shows that a contract is void or voidable.
- It explains ambiguous language.
- It concerns a prior course of dealing or course of performance, or a usage of trade.
- If fills the gaps in a contract.
- If it corrects an obvious clerical or typographical error.
  - The court can reform the contract to reflect the correction.

# Refresh Your Memory

The following exercises will help to test your memory regarding the principles given in this chapter. Read each question twice, then place your answer in the blank provided for each question. Review the chapter material for any questions that you are unable to answer or remember.

1. The two types of mistake are _____ and _____.

2. When only one party is mistaken about a material fact regarding the subject matter of the contract, this is known as a(n) _____ mistake.

3. If Bart, a contractor, tells Mary, a homeowner, that he will not finish her room addition on her home unless she agrees to pay him an additional $10,000 and Mary feels pressured to give him the additional compensation, this may be seen as _____ _____.

4. Undue influence occurs when one person takes advantage of another person's _____, _____, or _____ weakness and unduly persuades that person to enter a contract

5. All states have enacted a(n) _____ _____ _____ that requires that certain types of contracts be in writing.

6. A(n) _____ contract that is not in writing, but is required to be under the Statute of Frauds, is not enforceable by either party.

7. Any contract that transfers an ownership interest _____ _____ must be in writing under the Statute of Frauds.

8. Give three examples of real property as it pertains to the Statute of Frauds: _____, _____, and _____.

9. The _____ _____ _____ helps to prevent disputes about contract terms that might occur toward the end of a long-term contract.

10. The _____ must distinguish between a mutual mistake of value and a mutual mistake of fact.

11. Fraud in the _____ is not the same as fraud in the _____.

12. _____ _____ will be found in a cause of action for fraud even if the innocent party did not know that the misrepresentation was false.

13. A(n) _____ _____ occurs when someone consciously induces another to rely and act on a misrepresentation.

14. Attaching several documents together by a staple is an example of _____.

15. _____ words prevail over _____ and _____ words in a contract

## Critical Thought Exercise

At Rip-Off Motors, an exotic used car dealership, you are the general manager and Slick is your dishonest salesman. Slick told a potential customer, Dupe, that the Porsche he was interested in purchasing had been driven only 25,000 miles in four years and had never been in an accident. Dupe hired Grease, a mechanic, to appraise the condition of the car. Grease said that the car probably had at least 75,000 miles on it and probably had been in an accident. In spite of this information, Dupe still thought the car would be a good buy for the price, which was still lower than a Porsche with 75,000 miles. Dupe bought the car and it immediately developed numerous mechanical problems which would cost over $10,000 to repair. Dupe has now come back to Rip-Off Motors and is seeking to have you rescind the contract on the basis of Slick's fraudulent misrepresentations of the car's condition. If you rescind the contract, it will cause the dealership to lose over $13,000.

Write a letter to either:

A) Dupe, if you are refusing to rescind the contract, or

B) Mr. Big, the owner of Rip-Off Motors, if you intend to rescind the contract and suffer the loss.

Explain the reasons for your decision, citing authority for your action.

*Please compose your answer on a separate sheet of paper or on your computer.*

## Practice Quiz

### True/False

1. ____ Either party may rescind a contract if there has been a mutual mistake of past or existing material fact.

2. ____ If Brandon asks his mother to take him to the store to buy a new mouse and she takes him to the pet store when he wanted to go to the electronics store for a computer mouse, any contract between the two of them may not be rescinded as there has not been a mutual mistake of fact.

3. ____ If Chad fails to tell Cory about the wobbly frame on a bike he just bought from him and William loses control of the steering on his first ride resulting in a broken leg and collar bone, William may bring suit under the theory of silence as misrepresentation.

4. ____ John calls Funco Inc. to inquire about one of their arcade games and is told that it costs thirty-two fifty. Thereafter John tells the representative of Funco, "That's a great price.

Put my name on it and I'll be right there to pick it up. Upon arrival he is told that the game costs three thousand two hundred and fifty dollars. Despite this fact, John will be able to purchase the arcade game for thirty-two dollars and fifty cents.

5. ___ A misrepresentation of law will be allowed as a ground for rescission of a contract even if one of the parties to a contract is a professional who should know what the law is and intentionally misrepresents the law to a less knowledgeable contracting party.

6. ___ The innocent party to a contract may not rescind the contract based on fraud and obtain restitution or enforce the contract and sue for damages.

7. ___ Fraudulent misrepresentation is not the same as fraud.

8. ___ A party's assent to a contract needs to be genuine.

9. ___ Intent in a cause of action based on fraud may be inferred from the circumstances.

10. ___ The signature of the person enforcing a contract is not necessary to enforce a contract.

11. ___ The placing of several documents in a tube may indicate integration.

12. ___ The U.C.C. does allow several writings to be integrated to form a single document.

13. ___ A written contract must be in writing, contain the essential terms and need not be drafted by a lawyer in order to be binding.

14. ___ In Japan, individuals use their hand written signatures to sign legal documents.

15. ___ Handwritten words prevail over preprinted and typed words in a contract.

## Multiple Choice

16. If an innocent misrepresentation has been made, what action may the innocent party bring?
   a. An action for fraudulent misrepresentation.
   b. An action for specific performance.
   c. An action based on undue influence.
   d. An action for rescission of the contract without damages.

17. If Walter threatens to bring a criminal lawsuit against Joshua if Joshua doesn't sign a fencing contract giving Walter the job, this would constitute
   a. a misunderstanding between the parties.
   b. duress.
   c. undue influence over Joshua.
   d. mutual mistake of fact.

18. If a unilateral mistake happens because of a mathematical or clerical error that is not the result of gross negligence, a contract between the parties will
   a. be enforced.
   b. be deemed unconscionable.
   c. not be enforced.
   d. rewritten to reflect the correction.

19. An innocent party's assent to a contract is not genuine when
    a. the innocent party has made a unilateral mistake.
    b. a fraudulent misrepresentation is used to induce the innocent party to enter into the contract.
    c. the innocent party knew that the misrepresentation was false or so extravagant to be obviously false.
    d. the innocent party has participated in the fraudulent misrepresentation.

20. A clause in a contract that stipulates that it is the complete integration and the exclusive expression of the parties agreement is known as a(n)
    a. promissory estoppel clause.
    b. marital clause.
    c. incorporation by reference clause.
    d. merger clause.

21. Real property as it pertains to the Statute of Frauds includes
    a. timber, crops., fixtures, soil and buildings.
    b. stocks, bonds, money and certificates.
    c. timber, inoperable automobiles, plants and minerals.
    d. fixtures, crops, and farm equipment.

22. Which aspect of the Statute of Frauds is intended to prevent disputes about contract terms that may otherwise occur toward the end of a long-term contract?
    a. the part performance exception
    b. the guaranty contract rule
    c. the one year rule
    d. goods for $500 or more

23. A collateral guaranty contract happens where
    a. contracts for the sale of goods $500 or more are present.
    b. one person agrees to answer for the debts or duties of another person.
    c. electronic commerce agreements are a second means of enforcement to contracts.
    d. the most recent agreement of the parties is integrated with the former contract thereby guaranteeing its enforcement.

24. Jane and John enter into a contract for the purchase of Jane's computer, with delivery set for December 15. Upon signing the contract, John discovers that a price has not been set. Which rule would best assist the parties in enforcing the contract?
    a. the Kelly Blue Book rule
    b. the promissory estoppel rule
    c. the parol evidence rule
    d. the equal dignity rule

25. Cameron expressly grants Jennifer the right to use his land from her land to the boat dock adjacent to the end of his property. If Cameron decides that Jennifer cannot use his land, what must Jennifer show in order to enforce the right to use Cameron's land?
    a. that an easement was created
    b. that she was given a right to use Cameron's land
    c. that the right to use Cameron's land was in writing
    d. all of the above

## Short Answer

26. What are the three situations when a contract made with a unilateral mistake will not be enforced?

_____

_____

_____

27. What are the elements necessary for proving fraudulent misrepresentation?

_____

_____

28. What is the measure of damages in a cause of action for fraud?

_____

29. What is meant by the term undue influence?

_____

_____

30. When a party takes specific action to hide a material fact from another, what is this called?

_____

31. Briefly define the meaning of fixtures as they pertain to real estate.

_____

32. What type of contract has been formed if Stephanie agrees to pay Sally's debt to Visa?

_____

33. If Bert decides to sell his golf cart to Maria for $900.00, what will be required?

_____

34. What is the rule that says that agent's contracts to sell property covered by the Statute of Frauds must be in writing to be enforceable?

_____

35. Explain why telegrams that are not signed may still be enforceable contracts.

_____

36. What is meant by the term rescission?

_____

37. What is a mutual mistake of fact?

_____

38. When will a threat to bring or drop a civil lawsuit not be considered duress?

_____

39. At what price do contracts for the sale of goods have to be in writing?

_____

40.    How does the doctrine of promissory estoppel apply to oral contracts for the sale of land?

_____

_____

## Answers to Refresh Your Memory

1.    unilateral, mutual  [p 316]
2.    unilateral  [p 316]
3.    economic duress  [p 324]
4.    mental, physical, emotional  [p 323]
5.    Statute of Frauds  [p 326]
6.    executory  [p 326]
7.     in land  [p 326]
8.    Any three of the following:  trees, timber, minerals, plants, crops, and fixtures [p 326]
9.    One-year Rule [p 328]
10.    Courts  [p 318]
11.    inception, inducement  [p 319]
12.    Justifiable reliance  [p 319]
13.    intentional misrepresentation  [p 318]
14.    integration  [p 332]
15.    Handwritten, preprinted, typed  [p 333]

## Critical thought Exercise Model Answer

Because of the circumstances of this case, it would be more appropriate to write a letter to Mr. Dupe refusing to rescind the contract. The following letter outlines the reasons for this decision and why it would be inappropriate for Rip-Off Motors to rescind the contract.

Dear Mr. Dupe:

My salesman, Slick, did make representations to you concerning the mileage and condition of the Porsche you purchased. However, you took the car to an independent mechanic, Grease, who informed you that the car had greater mileage than represented by Slick and had probably been in an accident. You decided that the car was still a good value despite this additional information.

In order for you to rescind the contract as a result of the tort of fraud, you must show: (1) a misrepresentation of a material fact; (2) an intent on the part of Slick to deceive you; and, (3) you, the innocent party, must have justifiably relied on the misrepresentation.

You did not rely upon the representations of my salesman when you purchased the car. You relied on the independent assessment of a mechanic as to the condition of the car to evaluate whether you should make the purchase before making the decision to purchase the car. As a result, you are not entitled to rescind the agreement nor are you entitled to any other damages.

Yours truly,
General Manager

# Answers to Practice Quiz

## True/False

1. True   Both parties may rescind the contract on the ground that no contract has been formed because there is no meeting of the minds between the parties. [p 318]

2. False   Because Brandon and his mother were each referring to a different type of mouse, there can be no binding contract and rescission would be an option since there was no meeting of the minds between the parties. [p 318]

3. True   William may bring a cause of action under the theory of silence as misrepresentation since Chris's failure to tell William of the wobbly frame resulted in bodily injury, here a broken leg and collarbone. [p 319]

4. True   Two meanings were obviously applied to the term thirty-two fifty whereby the difference between what each party meant was significant. To quote the language utilized in *Konic International Corp v. Spokane Computer Services, Inc. 708P.2d932 (1985),* "The mutual understanding of the parties was so basic and so material that any agreement the parties thought they had reached was merely an illusion." John will not be able to enforce the agreement. [p 316-317]

5. True   The basic rule regarding misrepresentation of law is that it is not actionable as fraud. However, the exception to the rule is that if one of the parties to the contract is a professional who should know what the law is and intentionally misrepresents the law to a less knowledgeable individual, then the misrepresentation will be grounds for rescission. [p 321]

6. False   The remedy when a fraudulent misrepresentation is used to induce another to enter into a contract is to either rescind the contract and obtain restitution or enforce the contract and sue for damages. [p 318]

7. False   Fraudulent misrepresentation is also known as fraud. [p 318]

8. True   There can be no contract if the assent is not genuine. [p 316]

9. True   If a party's assent to a contract is not genuine, the courts will permit the innocent party to avoid the contract. If a party's assent is not genuine, other individuals make get away with claiming mistake, committing fraud, utilizing duress and undue influence to get what they want. [p 319]

10. True   The U.C.C. requires the written contract to be signed by the party against whom enforcement is sought; it does not require that the party seeking enforcement have signed the contract. [p 332]

11. True   The placing of several documents together in a container may be implied integration thereby forming a single written contract. [p 332]

12. True   The Uniform Commercial Code does allow several writings to be integrated to form a single written contract. [p 332]

13. True   As long as all of the essential terms are contained in a contract, it need not be drafted by a lawyer to be binding. [p 332]

14. False   The Japanese often use a stamp called a *hanko*. [p 333]

15. True   Handwritten words do prevail over preprinted and typed words. [p 333]

## Multiple Choice

16. D   Answer D is correct, as an action based on innocent misrepresentation warrants rescission without relief for damages. Answer A is incorrect, as an innocent misrepresentation does not warrant a cause of action for fraudulent misrepresentation since the person making a statement of fact in the former situation honestly and reasonably believes the statement

he or she has made is true. Compare this to a fraudulent misrepresentation whereby the person making the statement intends to deceive the innocent party. Therefore, one type of statement does not warrant a cause of action based on a theory that is opposite. Answer B is incorrect, as the equitable remedy of specific performance is utilized when the remedy at law is not adequate which, in the case of an innocent misrepresentation, rescission would be sufficient. Answer C is incorrect, as an action based on undue influence has no relation to an action based on innocent misrepresentation. [p 321]

17. B   Answer B is correct, as Walter is threatening to do the wrongful act of bringing a criminal lawsuit against Joshua unless Joshua gives him the fencing contract. This constitutes duress. Answer A is incorrect, as there is nothing in the facts that indicates there is a misunderstanding between the parties. Answer C is incorrect, as even though the facts indicate that Walter was threatening Joshua, there is nothing to indicate that Walter took advantage of Joshua's mental, emotional or physical weakness or that the parties had a fiduciary or confidential relationship. Answer D is incorrect, as a mutual mistake of fact exists where both parties are mistaken as to the subject matter of the contract, which is not supported by the facts given. [p 324]

18. C   Answer C is correct, as it is one of the exceptions to the general rule that a contract based on a unilateral mistake will not be enforced. Answer A is incorrect, as this is one of the exceptions where a contract based on a unilateral mistake will not be enforced. Answer B is incorrect, as there is nothing in the facts that would "shock the conscience" of the courts to deem it unconscionable. Answer D is incorrect because, as an exception to the general rule of enforcing contracts based on unilateral mistakes, rewriting the contract would be antagonistic to not enforcing the contract based upon the exception. [p 316]

19. B   Answer B is correct, as the use of a fraudulent misrepresentation to induce another to enter into a contract is unenforceable. Answer A is incorrect, as the making of a unilateral mistake does not have a bearing on assent unless of course the mistake was based on one of the exceptions to the general rule regarding the enforcement of contracts based on unilateral mistakes. The facts are silent on this point. Answer C is incorrect, as acquiescence to false representation is an acceptance that qualifies as an assent, since the innocent party knew of the misrepresentation thereby giving the innocent party a chance to make an informed decision. Answer D is incorrect, as once again participating in the fraudulent misrepresentation would probably constitute acceptance of the terms being represented and hence genuine assent. [p 318]

20. D   Answer D is correct, as the question explains what a merger clause is, which expressly restates the parol evidence rule. Answers A and B are incorrect, as there is no such thing as a promissory estoppel clause or a marital clause. Answer C is incorrect, as an incorporation by reference clause refers in one document to another document and incorporates the outside document into the original one. [p 333]

21. A   Answer A is correct, as timber, crops, fixtures, soil and buildings are considered real property for the Statute of Frauds. Answer B is incorrect, as these are not real property and are considered intangible property under some legal circumstances. Answer C is incorrect, as inoperable automobiles are not considered real property. Answer D is incorrect, as farm equipment is personal property and not real property. [p 326]

22. C   Answer C is correct, as an executory contract that cannot be performed by its own terms within one year of formation must be in writing so as to avoid disputes that may occur toward the end of a long-term contract. Answer A is incorrect, as the part performance exception is primarily used in situations involving oral contracts and land. Answer B is incorrect, as this refers to answering the debt of another. Answer D is incorrect, as the statement does not reflect a measure to prevent disputes, but rather states part of a type of contract that needs to be in writing according to the Statute of Frauds. [p 328]

23. B   Answer B is correct, as it correctly states what a collateral or guaranty contract is. Answer A is incorrect, since the goods may in fact cost over $500, there is no dollar amount requirement when it comes to answering for another's debts. Answer C is incorrect, as it does not make any sense. Answer D is incorrect, as integrating one agreement with another agreement does not necessarily guarantee its enforcement nor does it correctly explain what a collateral or guarantee agreement is. [p 328-329]

24. C   Answer C expresses the rule that would help the parties the most, as an exception to the parol evidence rule is that if there is a gap such as price in the contract, the court may fill in that price. Answer A is incorrect, as there is no such thing as the Kelly Blue Book Rule. Answer B is incorrect, as the doctrine of promissory estoppel is utilized in oral contract situations where enforcement is necessary to prevent an injustice. The facts indicate that there is a written contract that was signed. Answer D is incorrect, as the equal dignity rule concerns the requirement that an agents' contract to sell property must be in writing in order to be enforceable. [p 333]

25. D   Answer D is correct as answers A, B, and C all state what Jennifer must show in order to enforce the right to use Cameron's land. [p 327]

## Short Answer

26.   1) Where one party makes a unilateral mistake of fact and the other party knew (or should have known that a mistake was made. 2) Where a unilateral mistake occurs because of a clerical or mathematical error, which is not the result of gross negligence. 3) Where the mistake is so serious that enforcing the contract would be unconscionable. [p 316]

27.   The elements for proving fraudulent misrepresentation are: 1) The wrongdoer made a false misrepresentation of material fact. 2) The wrongdoer intended to deceive the innocent party 3) The innocent party justifiably relied on the misrepresentation. 4) The innocent party was injured. [p 318]

28.   The measure of damages is the difference between the value of the property as represented and the actual value of the property. [p 319]

29.   Undue influence is when one individual takes advantage of another's mental, emotional or physical weakness and unduly persuades that person to enter into a contract. [p 323]

30.   fraud by concealment. [p 319]

31.   Fixtures are personal property that is permanently adhered to the real property such as the lights on the ceiling in a house. [p 326]

32.   A guaranty contract [p 328]

33.   It will be required to be in writing under the Statute of Frauds, as the golf cart costs more than $500. [p 329]

34.   The Equal Dignity Rule [p 329]

35.   Because the name of the parties printed on the telegram itself may be sufficient to constitute a signature. [p 332]

36.   Rescission is an action to undo an act. [p 318]

37.   A mutual mistake of fact is one both parties are mistaken about which pertains to the subject matter of the contract. [p 318]

38.   When such a suit is frivolous or brought in bad faith. [p 324]

39.   The Uniform Commercial Code requires that contracts for the sale of goods costing $500 or more must be in writing in order to be enforceable. [p 329]

40.   The purchaser must either pay part of the purchase price as well as take possession of the property or make valuable improvements on the land. [p 330]

# Chapter 13

# THIRD-PARTY RIGHTS
# AND DISCHARGE

## Chapter Overview

The parties to a contract share privity of contract and are obligated to perform the duties specified in the contract. This duty can be discharged by agreement, excuse, or operation of law. If one party fails to perform their obligations, the other party can enforce the contract and sue for breach. Third parties do not have rights under other people's contracts, except in two instances: assignees, to which rights are transferred, and intended beneficiaries. The rights of third parties, conditions to performance, and discharge of contracts are discussed in this chapter.

## Objectives

Upon completion of the exercises contained in this chapter, you should be able to:

1.  Define the meaning of assignment of contracts and what contract rights are assignable.
2.  Define delegation of duties and discuss the liability of the parties in a delegation.
3.  Define an intended beneficiary and discuss his or her rights under a contract.
4.  Differentiate between conditions precedent, conditions subsequent, concurrent conditions.
5.  Distinguish between objective impossibility and commercial impracticability of a contract.
6.  Discuss the various ways that contracts are discharged by operation of law.

## Practical Application

Upon mastering the concepts in this chapter, you should be able to recognize whether or not a contract may be assigned or delegated, and discuss any liabilities that may have been incurred as a result of the delegation or assignment. You should be able to identify whether or not a third party to a contract has any rights as a beneficiary to the contract. You should be able to analyze questions and real life situations about the various ways a contract may be discharged by law.

## Helpful Hints

Since it can be difficult to keep the parties straight in contracts involving more than two parties, it is helpful to diagram the transaction either in box form, as is displayed in your text, or by use of a triangle, or by any other means that may be useful to you. It is helpful to imagine yourself as the person being given an assignment, or right, and a delegation, or duty. If you substitute yourself into the question or hypothetical situations, the concepts become clear.
Do not get burdened by the titles assignee and assignor, delagatee and delegator, or obligor and obligee. It is much easier to learn the concept behind the titles first, then the titles, and who is doing what, then its impact will become second nature to you.

# Study Tips

## Assignment of Rights

The transfer of contractual rights by the obligee to another party is called an assignment of rights or an assignment.

**Form of Assignment.** No formalities are necessary to assign rights under a contract, but words such as transfer, give and convey have been used to express intent in an assignment. Public policy favors free commerce, thus most contract rights are assignable.
- The party who owes a duty of performance is the obligor.
- The party who is owed a right is the obligee.
- The obligee who transfers the right to performance is the assignor.
- The party to whom the right is transferred is the assignee.
- The assignee can assign the right to a subsequent assignee or subassignee.

**Special Problems for Assignment.** Some types of contracts have unique issues for assignment:

*Personal Service Contracts.* These contracts generally cannot be assigned.
- The parties can agree to allow the contract to be assigned.
- Contracts of professional athletes may contain a clause permitting assignment.

*Assignment of Future Rights.* The general rule is that a person may not assign a currently non-existing right that he or she is expecting in the future.

*Contracts Where Assignment Would Materially Alter the Risk.* The contracts cannot be assigned.
- Example: Assigning your homeowner's insurance to a friend who cannot afford it.

*Assignment of Legal Actions.* An individual may not assign the right to sue in legal actions involving personal rights.
- One can assign a legal right that arises out of a breach of contract.

**Effect of an Assignment of Rights.** The assignee stands in the shoes of the assignor.
- The assignor is entitled to performance by the obligor.
- The assignment extinguishes all rights of the assignor against the obligor.
- The assignee has no more rights under the contract that the assignor had.
- The obligor can assert any defenses he or she had against the assignor or assignee.
- The obligor can raise any personal defenses against the assignee.

**Notice of Assignment.** The assignee has a duty to notify the obligor that the assignment has happened and the performance by the obligor must be given to the assignee.
- Without notice the obligor can continue performing under the contract to the assignor.
  - The assignee's only recourse is to sue the assignor for damages.
- If obligor is notified of assignment but continues performing under contract to assignor
  - The assignee can sue and recover payment from the obligor.
  - This makes the obligor pay twice.
  - The obligor's only recourse is to sue the assignor for damages.

**Anti-Assignment and Approval Clauses.**  The anti-assignment clause prohibits the assignment of rights under the contract.
- An approval clause is one in which the obligor must approve any assignment.
  - o  Many states prohibit unreasonable withholding of approval.

**Successive Assignment of the Same Right.**  When an obligee fraudulently or mistakenly assigns the same right to a number of assignees, there are several rules that may be applied to decide which assignee has the legal right to the assigned right.

*The American Rule (New York Rule).*  This rule states that the first assignment in time prevails.
- The majority of states use this rule.

*The English Rule.*  This rule states that the first to give notice prevails.

*The Possession of Tangible Token Rule.*  Under either the American or English rule, if the assignor makes a successive assignment of a contract right that is represented by a tangible token, the first assignee who receives delivery of the tangible token prevails over subsequent assignees.

## Delegation of Duties

The transfer of contractual duties by the obligor to another party for performance is called delegation of duties or delegation.  Generally, parties can delegate duties to other parties, unless otherwise agreed.  No special words or formalities are necessary to delegate duties.
- The obligor who transferred his or her duty is the delegator.
- The party to whom the duty has been transferred is the delegatee.
- The party to whom the duty is owed is the obligee.

**Duties That Can and Cannot be Delegated.**  When contracts are entered into with companies or firm, rather than individuals, any qualified employee can perform the contract.
- If the obligee has an important interest in the obligor performing the duties of the contract, the duties cannot be transferred.

*Personal Service Contracts.*  Contracts that require the discretion, expertise and the exercise of personal skills cannot be delegated.

*Material Variance of Performance.*  Contracts whose performance would materially vary if the obligor's duties were delegated cannot be delegated.

**Effect of Delegation of Duties.**  The delegator remains legally liable for the performance of the contract, thereby being subjected to a lawsuit if the delegatee does not perform properly.

*Assumption of Duties.*  If the word assumption or a similar term is contained in the delegation, then there has been an assumption of duties.
- The delegate is responsible to the obligee for nonperformance.
- The obligee can sue the delegator or the delegate.

*Declaration of Duties.*  If a delegatee has not assumed the duties under the contract, then this is called a declaration of duties.
- The delegatee is not obligated to the obligee for nonperformance.
- The obligee can only sue the delegator.

**Anti-Delegation Clause.** This clause indicates that duties for a contract cannot be delegated.
- These clauses are usually enforced.
- Some courts hold that duties that are totally impersonal in nature can still be delegated.

**Assignment and Delegation.** This occurs when there is a transfer of both rights and duties.
- Modern View: When a transfer contains only language of an assignment, there is a corresponding delegation of duties.

## Third-Party Beneficiaries

Third parties who claim rights under contracts are either intended or incidental.

**Intended Beneficiaries.** Parties to a contract can agree that the performance of one of the parties will be made to or directly benefit a third party.
- This beneficiary can be expressly named or can be identified by other means.
- This beneficiary can enforce the contract against the party obligated to perform.
- Intended beneficiaries are either donee or creditor beneficiaries.
    - o The *Restatement (Second) of Contracts* no longer makes this distinction.

*Donee Beneficiaries.* A contract that confers a benefit or gift on an intended third party is called a donee beneficiary contract.
- Parties:
    - o The party who directs that the benefit be conferred is the promisee.
    - o The party who agrees to confer performance for the benefit of the third person is the promisor.
    - o The third party on whom the benefit is conferred is the donee beneficiary.
- If the promisor does not perform the contract, the donee beneficiary can sue the promisor.

*Creditor Beneficiaries.* This type of contract usually arises when
- A debtor borrows money to purchase some item.
- The debtor signs an agreement to pay the amount of the loan, plus interest.
- The debtor sells the item to another person before the loan is paid in full.
- The new buyer promises to the debtor to pay the remainder of the loan.
- Parties:
    - o The original debtor is the promisee.
    - o The new party is the promisor.
    - o The original creditor is the creditor beneficiary.
- If the promisor fails to perform, the creditor beneficiary can
    - o Enforce the original contract against the debtor-promisee.
    - o Enforce the new contract against the promisor.
    - o The creditor can collect only once.

**Incidental beneficiary.** This beneficiary is one who is unintentionally benefited by other people's contracts and cannot enforce or sue under the contract.

## Covenants and Conditions

Parties to contracts make definite promises to each other, which may be classified as covenants and conditions.

**Covenant.** An unconditional promise to perform is known as a covenant.
- Nonperformance of a covenant equals a breach of contract, giving the other party the right to sue.

**Conditions of Performance.** A conditional promise, which is not as definite as a covenant, is known as a condition.
- The promisor's duty only arises if the condition does, or does not, occur.
- The condition becomes a covenant if the condition is met.
- *If, on condition that, provided that, when, after*, and *as soon as* indicate a condition.
- There are three conditions of performance: Condition precedent, Condition subsequent, and Concurrent conditions.

*Condition Precedent.* The occurrence or nonoccurrence of an event before a party is obligated to perform under the contract.
- The happening, or not, of the event triggers the contract or duty of performance.
- If the event does not happen, no duty arises.

Condition precedent based on satisfaction. Contracts can specify that a party pays for services only if they meet that party's "satisfaction." There are two tests to determine satisfaction:
- The personal satisfaction test is a subjective test whereby the person is to act in good faith in matters involving personal taste and comfort.
- The reasonable person test is an objective test that is used to judge contracts involving mechanical fitness and most commercial transactions. This is used when a third person is involved who is used to judge another's work.

Time of performance as a condition precedent. If a contract is not performed when due, there is a breach of contract.
- If a party is not jeopardized by a delay, this will be considered a minor breach.
- If *"time is of the essence,"*performance by the stated time is an express condition. This will be considered a breach of contract if performance is not rendered by the stated date.

*Condition Subsequent.* This exists when a contract provides that the occurrence or nonoccurrence of a certain event automatically excuses the performance of an existing duty to perform.
- In the Restatement (Second) of Contracts, there is no distinction between a condition precedent and a condition subsequent.

*Concurrent Conditions.* This occurs when both parties render performance at the same time.

*Implied Conditions.* Any of the above conditions may be considered to be express or implied.
- It is implied from the situation surrounding the contract and the parties' conduct.

## Discharge of Performance

There are three ways to discharge a party's duty under a contract: by mutual agreement of the parties, by impossibility of performance, or by operation of law.

**Discharge by agreement.** The parties to a contract can mutually decide to discharge their duties.

*Mutual Rescission.* The parties can mutually agree to discharge or end their contractual duties.

- The parties enter into a second contract that specifically terminates the first one.
- Unilateral rescission of a contract is a breach.

*Substituted contract.* The parties can enter into a new contract, called a substituted contract, that revokes and discharges a prior contract.
- Failure to perform under the substituted contract allows the nonbreaching party to sue to enforce its terms.
- The prior contract cannot be enforced, as it has been discharged.

*Novation.* This agreement substitutes a new party for one of the original contracting parties. All three must be in unison regarding the substitution.
- The existing party is relieved of liability, while the newly substituted party has an obligation to perform the contract.

*Accord and Satisfaction.* The settlement of a contract dispute where the parties accept something different than originally agreed upon and performance of the same.
- The new agreement is called an accord.
- The performance of the accord is called a satisfaction.
- If an accord is not satisfied when it is due, the injured party may enforce either the accord or the original agreement.

**Discharge by Impossibility.** Nonperformance of contractual duties can be excused because of impossibility of performance.

*Impossibility of Performance.* This excuse for nonperformance becomes valid if the contract becomes objectively impossible to perform, rather than subjectively impossible to perform.
- Death or incapacity of a promissory in a personal service contract excuses performance.
- Destruction of the subject matter prior to performance excuses performance.
- A supervening illegality that makes performance illegal excuses performance.

*Force Majeure Clauses.* These type of clauses are where the parties agree in their contract as to the events that will excuse nonperformance of the contract.
- The typical force majeure clause excuses nonperformance caused by natural disasters.
- Modernly, labor strikes, and shortages of materials excuse performance.

*Commercial Impracticability.* This excuse for nonperformance indicates that if an extreme or unexpected development or expense makes it impractical for the promissory to perform, then this excuse may be recognized.

**Discharge by Operation of Law.** The legal rules that discharge parties from performing their duties under their contracts are as follows:

*Statute of Limitations.* A time frame set by statute, within which a plaintiff must bring a lawsuit.
- Many states set a time of one to five years to bring an action for breach of contract.
- The U.C.C. indicates that four years is the time frame to bring a cause of action based on breach of contract.

*Bankruptcy.* If the debtor's assets are inadequate to pay all creditors' claims, then the debtor receives a discharge of the unpaid debts and is relieved of liability to pay the discharged debts.

*Alteration of the Contract.* This occurs when a party to the contract intentionally alters the contract 's material terms, such as price or quantity.

- Innocent party may discharge the contract or enforce it on its original or modified terms.

# Refresh Your Memory

The following exercises will help to test your memory regarding the principles given in this chapter. Read each question twice, then place your answer in the blank provided for each question. Review the chapter material for any questions that you are unable to answer or remember.

1.   The state of two specified parties being in contract is known as _____ _____ _____.

2.   A transfer of contractual rights by an obligee to another for receipt of performance is a(n) _____ _____ _____.

3.   A(n) _____ owes a duty of performance.

4.   A(n) _____ is owed a right under a contract.

5.   A(n) _____ who transfers the right to receive performance is called a(n) _____.

6.   A(n) _____ has had a contractual right transferred to them.

7.   A transfer of contractual duties by the obligor to another party for performance is a(n) _____ _____ _____.

8.   A(n) _____ who transfers his or her duty is called a(n) _____.

9.   A(n) _____ is the person to whom a duty has been transferred.

10.  A(n) _____ is the person to whom the duty is owed.

11.  There are two types of intended beneficiaries to a contract: a(n) _____ beneficiary, and a(n) _____ creditor beneficiary.

12.  A(n) _____ beneficiary is someone who is unintentionally benefited under a contract.

13.  A(n) _____ is an unconditional promise to perform.

14.  There are three types of conditional promises to perform a contract: _____ _____, _____ _____, and _____ _____.

15.  There are three ways that that performance under a contract can be discharged: _____ _____, _____ _____ _____, or _____ _____ _____.

# Critical Thought Exercise

The Rocky Mountain Plumbing Company (RMP), which you manage, is very successful and has an excellent reputation. It is known for its fairness, prompt performance and superior work. After a severe earthquake that measured 7.4 on the Richter scale, billions of dollars worth of pipe damage occurred to hundreds of structures within the area serviced by your company. RMP has signed several huge contracts to repair or replace plumbing for government buildings, hospitals, and three hotels owned by Alexis. Each of these contracts will be for $800,000 or more.

You are uncertain if RMP will be able to meet the deadlines set in the contracts, as the urgency of the work needing to be done to so many buildings might call for more time.

You have the option of assigning some of the work to Bob's Plumbing, a far less reputable company, or making other arrangements with the county, the hospital district, and Alexis. You are afraid that if you inform people that RMP is unable to perform the contracts on time, it may lose the contracts along with the huge profits they will bring.

Your partners share your skepticism about meeting the deadlines and want to hire Bob's Plumbing immediately without mentioning it to any of the parties involved.

RMP's partners request that you draft a memorandum advising them of the options and risks involved with each option.

*Please compose your answer on a separate sheet of paper or on your computer.*

# Practice Quiz

## True/False

1. ___ The unconditional assignment of a contract right extinguishes all the assignor's rights, including right to sue the obligor directly for nonperformance.

2. ___ The assignee has a duty to notify the obligor of the assignment and about to whom performance must be rendered.

3. ___ Mandy hires Dr. Saran, a plastic surgeon to give her a new nose. Thereafter Dr. Saran delegates his contract with Mandy to Dr. Foiler, another plastic surgeon. This is not acceptable delegation of duties.

4. ___ If a delegatee does not perform his or her duties under a delegation, then the obligee can sue the obligor-delegator.

5. ___ A declaration of duties is present when the delegatee has not yet performed the duties under a contract.

6. ___ When there has been a transfer of both rights and duties under a contract, an assignment as well as delegation has occurred under the contract.

7. ___ When a person enters into a contract with the intent to confer a benefit or a gift on an third party, the contract is called a donee beneficiary contract.

8. ___ In a creditor beneficiary situation, the creditor is the new intended creditor beneficiary to a second contract.

9. ___ When the parties to a contract unintentionally benefit a third party, this third party is referred to as a donee beneficiary.

10. ___ A covenant is an unconditional promise to perform.

11. ___ Commercial impracticability does not excuse performance under a contract if an unforeseeable event makes it impractical for the promisor to perform.

12. ___ The Uniform Commercial Code provides that the statute of limitations for a breach of a sales or lease contract is one year after the cause of action accrues.

13. ___ A condition precedent is present when the occurrence or nonoccurrence of a specific event automatically excuses the performance of an existing duty to perform.

14. ___ A condition subsequent is present when the occurrence or nonoccurrence of a specific event must occur before a party is obligated to perform a contractual duty.

15. ___ A concurrent condition is present when the parties to a contract must render performance simultaneously.

## Multiple Choice

16. Which two exceptions allow third parties to acquire rights under other parties' contracts?
    a. A force majeure clause and an approval clause
    b. An assignment and a discharge of duties
    c. An assignment and a third-party beneficiary contract
    d. An assignment and a conveyance of personal or real property

17. An obligee who transfers the right to receive performance is called
    a. a delegator.
    b. an assignor.
    c. a delegatee.
    d. a lessor.

18. An assignee is
    a. the party who transfers the right to receive performance.
    b. the party who transfers the right to suspend performance.
    c. the party to whom the right has been transferred.
    d. the party to whom the right has been delegated.

19. Tom's Tourist Shop is located on the beach next to where a new high-rise hotel is going in. There are supposed to be sixteen floors to the hotel, however, Charter Construction Company decides to stop building at the thirteenth floor. Since the beginning of the project, the owner of Tom's has noticed a definite increase in business. He knows that once the hotel is complete, his profits will escalate due to the patrons staying at the hotel. Tom decides to bring a cause of action against the Charter Construction Company for breach of contract, as he is claiming that his tourist shop was a beneficiary of the hotel and Charter Construction Company contract. What will be the probable result?
    a. Tom will win because his shop is a donee beneficiary under the hotel and Charter Construction Company.

b. Tom will lose, as his shop is merely an incidental beneficiary as his business unintentionally benefited from the contract just by being located next to the new hotel.

c. Tom will win because if it were not for Tom, the area surrounding the hotel would be unappealing to tourists.

d. Tom will lose because he did not give notice of the benefit to Charter Construction.

20. There are three methods for discharging a contract by operation of law:
a. Condition precedent, condition subsequent, and concurrent conditions.
b. Commercial impracticability, force majeure, and impossibility.
c. Mutual rescission, novation, accord and satisfaction.
d. Statute of limitations, bankruptcy, and alteration of the contract.

21. A substituted contract is
a. Where the parties to a contract have entered into a new contract that revokes and discharges a prior contract.
b. Where the parties to a wholly or partially executory contract have agreed to cancel the contract.
c. Where all parties have agreed to substitute a third party for one of the original contracting parties, relieving the departing original party of liability.
d. Where the parties agree to accept something different in satisfaction of the original contract.

22. Which of the following are examples of objective impossibility that will excuse nonperformance of a contract:
a. The death or incapacity of the promisor prior to the performance of a personal service contract.
b. The destruction of the subject matter of a contract prior to performance.
c. A supervening illegality, which makes performance of the contract illegal.
d. All of the above.

23. A concurrent condition exists
a. when the occurrence or nonoccurrence of a specific event automatically excuses the performance of an existing duty to perform.
b. when the occurrence or nonoccurrence of a specific event must occur before a party is obligated to perform a contractual duty.
c. when the parties to a contract must render performance simultaneously.
d. when an unexpected or extreme circumstances or expense makes it impractical for the promisor to perform.

24. A contract clause in a contract that indicates that the duties of the contract cannot be delegated is called a(n)
a. anti-assignment clause.
b. anti-delegation clause.
c. accord and satisfaction.
d. declaration of duties.

25. A covenant is
a. when the occurrence or nonoccurrence of a specific event automatically excuses the performance of an existing duty to perform.
b. when the occurrence or nonoccurrence of a specific event must occur before a party is obligated to perform a contractual duty.

c. when the parties to a contract must render performance simultaneously.

d. none of the above.

## Short Answer

26. What is a transfer of contractual rights called?

_____

27. Can Julie transfer her sailboat insurance to her roommate Liz? Why or why not?

_____

28. From whom is an assignee entitled to receive performance?

_____

29. Which rule states that the first assignment in time prevails?

_____

30. What are the three ways that a party's duty of performance may be discharged?

_____

31. Alice is suing Roger for injuries she sustained when his tractor plowed into the back of her small sports car she was driving. She is tired of the delays in getting the case to trial and assigns her legal action to her best friend Stephanie. What is the effect of the assignment?

_____

32. What is the effect of an unconditional assignment of a contract right?

_____

33. Which rule regarding assignments provides that the first assignee to give notice to the obligor prevails?

_____

34. If Sid assigns his savings passbook to Marla and then assigns the same savings passbook to Claude but delivers the actual passbook to Claude, who is entitled to the savings account and why?

_____

35. What is the obligee's role under the contract?

_____

36. What is the obligor's role under the contract?

_____

37. Why can Joseph not assign his expected right to receive inheritance from his living grandmother?

_____

38. When an assignor makes an assignment of a right under a contract, the assignee is under a duty to do what?

_____

39. If an obligor does not want to deal with or render performance to an unknown third party, what type of clause may he or she use?

_____

40. What is an approval clause?

_____

## Answers to Refresh Your Memory

1. privity of contract  [p 344]
2. assignment of rights  [p 344]
3. obligor  [p 344]
4. obligee  [p 344]
5. obligee, assignor  [p 344]
6. assignee  [p 344]
7. delegation of duties  [p 348]
8. obligor, delegator  [p 348]
9. delegatee  [p 348]
10. obligee  [p 348]
11. donee, creditor  [p 349]
12. incidental  [p 351]
13. covenant  [p 352]
14. condition precedent, condition subsequent, concurrent conditions  [p 352]
15. mutual agreement, impossibility of performance, operation of law  [p 354]

## Critical Thought Exercise Model Answer

To:    RMP Partners
From: Your Partner
RE:    Options for performing the contracts

The obligor in a contract must be careful to refrain from informing the obligee that he or she is unable to perform. This may cause the obligee to treat the statement as an anticipatory repudiation and a breach. Therefore, RMP should pursue an option that does not create a breach. It is lawful to transfer the duties under a contract to another party. This delegation of duties does not relieve the party making the delegation of the obligation to perform in the event that the party to whom the duty has been delegated does not perform the duties of the contract.

No special form is required to create a valid delegation of duties. Some duties cannot be delegated, such as when performance depends upon the special skills of the obligor, when the contract expressly prohibits delegation, when special trust has been placed in the obligor, or when performance by a third party will vary materially from that expected by the obligee.

These contracts were awarded to us because we are capable of handling the work. This does not mean that Bob's Plumbing is incapable of performing the same duties. RMP would be within its rights to delegate the duties under one or more of the contracts to Bob's Plumbing. RMP would remain liable for any breach of the contract by Bob's Plumbing. Because Bob's Plumbing is a far less reputable company than RMP, we may expose ourselves to greater liability.

Alternatively, we could maintain some oversight of the work done by Bob's Plumbing in this situation and, thus, retain some control over the quality of work performed.

Another option is to enter into a novation with one or more of the obligees and Bob's Plumbing, which will allow a new contract to be formed between Bob's Plumbing and an obligee and then extinguish our contract. This will relieve us of any liability under that particular contract, but it will also cause us to lose the profit from the contract and hurt our reputation. Additionally, because Bob's Plumbing is less reputable than RMP, our reputation may become tarnished by convincing our clients to use Bob's Plumbing if the work is substandard. It is also likely that our clients will refuse to form a new contract with the less-reputable company.

Our reputation will be hurt more if we become embroiled in a contract dispute with the schools and hospital, not to mention a very influential businessperson, Alexis. We should calculate how much of the business we can handle and then approach the parties involved in the smaller contracts and suggest a novation. If the novation is refused, we will then have no choice but to delegate some of the work to Bob's Plumbing.

# Answers to Practice Quiz

## True/False

1. True     Where there has been a valid assignment of rights, the assignee "stands in the shoes of the assignor." Thus the unconditional assignment of a contract right extinguishes all the assignor's rights, including the right to sue the obligor directly for nonperformance. [p 345-346]

2. True     The assignee is under a duty to notify the obligor of the assignment and that performance is to be rendered to the assignee. [p 347]

3. True     Obligations under personal service contracts calling for the exercise of personal skills, discretion, or expertise such as in this case with a plastic surgeon are not delegable. [p 348]

4. True     The obligee can sue the obligor-delegator for damages. [p 348]

5. False    If the delegatee has not assumed the duties under a contract, this delegation of duties is a mere declaration of duties wherein the delegatee is not legally liable to the obligee for nonperformance. [p 348-349]

6. True     An assignment and a delegation occurs where there is a transfer of duties and rights under a contract. [p 349]

7. True     A contract with the intent to confer a benefit or gift on a third party is called a donee beneficiary contract, not a creditor beneficiary contract. [p 349]

8. True     In a creditor beneficiary contract, the orginal creditor becomes a beneficiary under the debtor's new contract with another party. [p 350]

9. False    A party who is unintentionally benefited by other individual's contracts is an incidental beneficiary. [p 351]

10 True     A covenant is an unconditional promise to perform. [p 352]

11. False   Nonperformance that is excused if an unexpected or extreme circumstances or expense makes it impractical for the promisor to perform is known as commercial impracticability. [p 356]

12. False   The Uniform Commercial Code provides that a breach of sales or lease contract must be brought within four years after the cause of action accrues. [p 357]

13. False   A condition subsequent is present when the occurrence or nonoccurrence of a certain event automatically excuses performance of an existing duty to perform. [p 352]

14. False   A condition precedent is present when the occurrence or nonoccurrence of a specific event must occur before a party is obligated to perform a contractual duty. [p 353]

15. True   A concurrent condition is present when the parties to a contract must render performance simultaneously. [p 352]

## Multiple Choice

16. C   Answer C is correct, as assignments and third-party beneficiary contracts allow third parties to acquire rights under other parties' contracts. Answer A is incorrect, as a force majeure clause involves an agreement between the parties regarding events that will excuse non-performance under a contract. Further, an approval clause permits the assignment of a contract only upon the receipt of the obligor's approval. Answer B is incorrect, as it is only partially correct in stating an assignment. The discharge of duties, however, is incorrect as this would discharge performance, as opposed to acquire a right under another's contract. Answer D is incorrect, as it is only partially correct with respect to the assignment. However, the conveyance of personal or real property is incorrect in terms of acquiring rights under other parties' contracts. [p 344]

17. B   Answer B is correct, as an assignor is also an obligee that transfers the right to performance. Answer A is incorrect, as a delegator is one who transfers duties under a contract. Answer C is incorrect, as a delegatee is one who receives duties under a contract. Answer D is incorrect, as a lessor is inapplicable in terms of transferring the right to receive performance. [p 344]

18. C   Answer C is correct, as the party to whom a right has been transferred is referred to as the assignee. Answer A is incorrect, as the party who transfers the right to receive performance is the assignor. Answer B is incorrect, as there is not a name for a party who attempts to suspend performance nor is this a legally recognized right. Answer D is incorrect, as the party to whom the right has been delegated is confusing terminology as it mixes terms associated with assignments and delegations. [p 344]

19. B   Answer B is correct, as Tom's Tourist Shop was unintentionally benefited by the hotel and Charter Construction Company Contract since there is nothing to indicate at the inception of their contract or thereafter that the parties intended to benefit the shop. Answer A is incorrect, as the hotel and the Charter Construction Company did not intend to confer a benefit or gift on Tom's Tourist Shop. Therefore, the shop is not a donee beneficiary. Answer C is incorrect, as the appeal of the surrounding area has no bearing on whether Tom should win. Answer D is incorrect, as giving notice is not a requirement to receiving benefits especially in a situation involving an incidental beneficiary. [p 351]

20. D   Answer D is correct, as statute of limitations, bankruptcy, and alteration of the contract are the ways that performance is discharged through operation of the law. Answer A is incorrect, as condition precedent, condition subsequent, and concurrent conditions are the types of conditions for performance. Answer B is incorrect, as commercial impracticability, force majeure, and impossibility ways that a contract may be discharged through impossibility of performance. Answer C is incorrect, as mutual rescission, novation, accord and satisfaction are ways that a contract may be discharged through mutual agreement of the parties. [p 357]

21. A   Answer A is correct, as a substituted contract is where the parties to a contract have entered into a new contract that revokes and discharges a prior contract. Answer B is incorrect, as mutual rescission is where the parties to a wholly or partially executory contract have agreed to cancel the contract. Answer C is incorrect, as a novation is where all parties have agreed to substitute a third party for one of the original contracting parties, relieving the departing original party of liability. Answer D is incorrect, as an

accord and satisfaction is where the parties agree to accept something different in satisfaction of the original contract. [p 354]

22. D  Answer D is correct, as each of answers A, B, and C are correct examples of objective impossibility that will excuse nonperformance of a contract. [p 355]

23. C  Answer C is correct, as a concurrent condition exists when the parties to a contract must render performance simultaneously. Answer A is incorrect, as a condition subsequent exists when the occurrence or nonoccurrence of a specific event automatically excuses the performance of an existing duty to perform. Answer B is incorrect, as a condition precedent exists when the occurrence or nonoccurrence of a specific event must occur before a party is obligated to perform a contractual duty. Answer D is incorrect, as commercial impracticability occurs when an unexpected or extreme circumstances or expense makes it impractical for the promisor to perform. [p 353]

24. B  Answer B is correct, as an anti-delegation clause indicates that the duties of the contract cannot be delegated. Answer A is incorrect, as an anti-assignment clause prohibits the assignment of rights under contracts. Answer C is incorrect, as an accord and satisfaction is where the parties agree to accept something different in satisfaction of the original contract. Answer D is incorrect, as a declaration of duties is where the delegatee has not yet assumed the contract duties and cannot be held liable for performance. [p 349]

25. D  Answer D is correct, as none of the other answers are correct. Answer A is incorrect, as a condition subsequent exists when the occurrence or nonoccurrence of a specific event automatically excuses the performance of an existing duty to perform. Answer B is incorrect, as a condition precedent exists when the occurrence or nonoccurrence of a specific event must occur before a party is obligated to perform a contractual duty. Answer C is incorrect, as a concurrent condition exists when the parties to a contract must render performance simultaneously. [p 352]

## Short Answer

26. An assignment of rights. [p 344]
27. No, because an assignment of the right to sailboat insurance would materially alter the risk and duties of the insurance company. [p 345]
28. The obligor. [p 344-346]
29. The American Rule. [p 347]
30. A party's duty of performance may be discharged by agreement of the parties, impossibility of performance, or by operation of law. [p 354]
31. The assignment is ineffective; legal actions involving personal rights cannot be assigned. [p 345]
32. It extinguishes all of the assignor's rights, including the right to sue the obligor directly for nonperformance. [p 345-346]
33. The English Rule. [p 347]
34. Claude is entitled to the savings account under possession of tangible token rule. [p 347]
35. The obligee is the party owed a right under a contract. [p 344]
36. The obligor is the party who owes the duty of performance. [p 344]
37. This would be an assignment of a future right, not yet in existence. [p 345]
38. Notify the obligor that the assignment ahs been made and performance must be rendered to the assignee. [p 347]
39. An anti-assignment clause. [p 347]
40. An approval clause is one that permits the assignment of the contract only upon receipt of an obligor's approval. [p 347]

# Chapter 14

# REMEDIES FOR BREACH OF TRADITIONAL AND ONLINE CONTRACTS

## Chapter Overview

Contracts can be performed at three levels. Complete performance discharges all duties under the contract. Substantial performance provides a minor breach of the contract. Inferior performance provides a material breach of the contract. Breach of a contract allows the nonbreaching party to receive monetary damages and equitable remedies. The concepts of breach of contract and the remedies available for that breach are discussed in this chapter.

## Objectives

Upon completion of the exercises in this chapter, you should be able to:

1. Discuss complete performance in relation to discharging contractual duties.
2. Explain inferior performance, as well as material breach of contract.
3. Explain and differentiate between compensatory, consequential and nominal damages.
4. Discuss the equitable remedies of injunction and specific performance.
5. Explain the torts that are associated with contracts.

## Practical Application

You should be able to determine whether a minor or material breach has occurred in a contract and what legal or equitable remedies may be available for the breach. You should be able to identify what is necessary to seek the equitable remedies of specific performance and injunction. You should be able to recognize the torts that sometimes accompany contracts.

## Helpful Hints

You should list and learn the legal remedies for breach of contract separately from the equitable remedies. Mnemonics for the equitable remedies of injunction and specific performance should help you to remember the requirements of these remedies.

## Study Tips

### Performance and Breach

A contracting party owes an absolute duty to perform if the duty has not be discharged or excused. There are three types of performance in a contract: complete, substantial, and inferior.

**Complete Performance.** Complete performance, or strict performance, happens when a party to a contract gives performance exactly as outlined in the parties' contract.
- If the contract is fully formed, it is said to be executed.
- A contracting party's unconditional and absolute offer, or tender, to perform will discharge a party's obligations under the contract.

**Substantial Performance: Minor Breach.** Substantial performance happens when a party to a contract gives performance that only has a little bit left to do before it will be considered completely performed. The non-breaching party has several options available to him or her.
- To convince the breaching party to lift performance to completion of the contract.
- To deduct costs of repair from the contract price.
- If the breaching party has been paid, to sue to recover the cost of repair.

**Inferior Performance: Material Breach.** A material breach occurs when a party gives such inferior performance of contractual obligations, that the contract purpose is destroyed or impaired
- Courts will examine each case to determine whether the breach is minor or material.
- The non-breaching party may rescind the contract and seek restitution of monies paid.
  o The non-breaching party is excused from further performance.
- Alternatively, the non-breaching party can sue for contract breach and ask for damages.

**Anticipatory Breach.** Anticipatory repudiation happens when one party lets the other know in advance that either he or she will not or may not perform the contractual duties when due.
- The repudiator may expressly state this or his or her conduct may show it.
- The non-breaching party's obligations are discharged immediately and he or she may sue for breach of contract immediately without waiting for performance to become due.

## Monetary Damages

Monetary damages can be recovered by the nonbreaching party. Several types of damages are available: compensatory, consequential, liquidated, and nominal.

**Compensatory Damages.** These damages pay a non-breaching party for the loss of the bargain.
- These were designed to "make the person whole again."
- The court determines how much will be awarded by the type of contract involved.

*Sale of Goods.* The measure of compensatory damages for a breach of sales contract is the difference between the contract price and market price at the time and place of delivery of goods.
- These damages are governed by the Uniform Commercial Code (U.C.C.)

*Construction Contracts.* The amount of compensatory damages available for breach depends upon the status of the construction project itself.
- The contractor may recover the profits that he or she might have made on the contract if the owner breaches before the construction begins.
- The owner can recover the increased cost to have the contract completed if the builder breaches before or during construction.

*Employment Contracts.* Recovery based on an employer breaching equals lost wages or salary as compensatory damages.

- If the employee breaches, the employer can recover the costs of hiring a new employee plus any salary increase to pay the replacement.

*Mitigation of Damages.* The law places a duty on the non-breaching party to avoid and reduce, or mitigate, the resulting damages.
- A party's duty of mitigation will be based on the type of contract involved.

**Consequential Damages.** These special damages are foreseeable damages that happen because of circumstances not related to the contract itself.
- The breaching party must be aware or have reason to know that the breach will cause special damages to the other party.

**Liquidated Damages.** Sometimes the parties to a contract agree in advance as to the amount of damages that will be payable in the event of a breach, which are known as liquidated damages.
- It must be shown that
  - o the actual damages are difficult or impracticable to determine
  - o the liquidated amount must be reasonable in the circumstances.
- This is an exclusive remedy regardless of how much the actual damages are later assessed
- A liquidated damages clause is seen as a penalty if the actual damages are clearly able to be determined in advance and if the liquidated damages are unconscionable or excessive.
  - o When a liquidated damages clause is viewed as a penalty, it is unenforceable.
  - o Actual damages may be recovered by the nonbreaching party.

**Nominal Damages.** These damages are awarded based on principle and are usually a very small amount. No real financial loss is suffered when a party brings a suit based upon principle.

**Enforcement of Remedies.** Once a judgment has been rendered, an attempt to collect it is made. If the breaching party fails to satisfy the judgment, then the court may issue a Writ of Attachment or Issue a Writ of Garnishment.

*Writ of Attachment.* The writ orders the sheriff to seize the breaching party's property that he or she has in his or her possession and to sell the property to satisfy the judgment.

*Writ of Garnishment.* Wages, bank account and other property owned by the breaching party that is being handled by a third party, such as a bank, must be paid to the non-breaching party.
- Federal and state laws limit the amount of wages or salary that can be garnished.

## Rescission and Restitution

Rescission is an action to undo a contract where there has been a material breach of contract due to fraud, duress, undue influence or mistake. The parties must make restitution of the consideration they received under the contract if they are going to rescind it.
- Parties must return goods, property, money or other consideration received from the other
- Notice of the rescission is a requirement.
- Together, rescission and restitution restore the parties their status prior to the contract.

## Equitable Remedies

If the remedy at law is not adequate, then the equitable remedies of specific performance, quasi-contract, injunction and reformation may be available so that an injustice may be prevented.

**Specific Performance**. This is a discretionary remedy where the courts may order the breaching party to perform the contract.

- The subject matter must be unique.
- A personal service contract cannot be involved.
- The following mnemonic is a practical application memory device for analyzing whether specific performance applies:  **C**athy **A**lways **E**ats **M**uch **C**andy **D**uring **E**aster

  **C** - Was there a **contract** for unique goods or land between the parties?
  **A** - The remedy at law was not **adequate.**
  **E** - The contract may only be **enforced** by this remedy.
  **M** - The remedy is **mutual**; both the buyer and seller may ask for it.
  **C** - All **conditions** have been satisfied by the party asking for the remedy.
  **D** - A discussion of any **defenses** is also brought to light.
  **E** - A reminder that this is an **equitable** remedy.

**Reformation**. This equitable remedy allows a court to rewrite the contract to reflect true intent.

**Injunction**. This equitable remedy is where the court prohibits a person from doing a certain act.

- The requesting party must show irreparable harm if the injunction is not granted.
- The following mnemonic is a practical application memory device for determining whether an injunction may be sought:  **T**ed **A**lways **E**njoys **P**otatoes and **H**am at **D**inner

  **T** - Usually a **tort** is involved which must first be proven.
  **A** - The remedy at law was not **adequate**.
  **E** - The tortuous conduct may only be **enforced** by this remedy.
  **P** - There is a **property** right involved.
  **H** - A **hardship** will be suffered if this remedy is not enforced.
  **D** - A discussion of **defenses** is shown if they apply.

## Torts Associated With Contracts

If a party shows a contract-related tort has occurred, tort damages will be available, including compensation for pain and suffering, emotional damages, punitive damages, and personal injury.

- Punitive damages are usually not available for breach of contract.
  - They are available for tortuous conduct such as fraud and intentional conduct.
  - They are awarded in addition to actual damages.
  - They are awarded to punish the defendant, deter the defendant from future similar conduct, and set an example for others.

**Intentional Interference with Contractual Relations**. This occurs when a third party induces one contracting party to breach the contract with another party.

- The nonbreaching party must show the following elements:
  - The contracting parties had a valid, enforceable contract.
  - The third-party knew of this contract.
  - The third-party induced the other party to breach the contract.
- The third-party does not need to act in bad faith or with malice.
- The third party will not be held to have induced a breach if the breach already existed.

**Breach of Implied Covenant of Good Faith and Fair Dealing**. This tort of bad faith is implied in some contracts where the parties are held to act in "good faith" and deal fairly in all aspects in obtaining the contract's objective.

- A breach of this covenant of good faith allows the recovery of tort damages.

# Refresh Your Memory

The following exercises will help to test your memory regarding the principles given in this chapter. Read each question twice, then place your answer in the blank provided for each question. Review the chapter material for any questions you are unable to answer or remember.

1. _____ performance, or _____ performance of a contract occurs when a party renders performance exactly as required.

2. A fully performed contract is a(n) _____ contract.

3. When there has been substantial performance of a contract, one of the parties has committed a(n) _____ breach.

4. When there is a material breach of contract, _____ performance has been rendered.

5. When there is a material breach, the non-breaching party may _____ the contract.

6. _____ breach of contract occurs when one contracting party informs the other party in advance the he or she will not perform the contract when due.

7. _____ damages help to compensate a non-breaching party for the loss of the bargain.

8. The usual measure of damages for a(n) _____ _____ _____ _____ contract is the difference between the contract price and the market price of the goods.

9. _____ _____ _____ places a duty on the nonbreaching party to make reasonable efforts to avoid and reduce the resulting damages from a breach of contract.

10. _____ damages are foreseeable damages arising from conditions outside a contract.

11. _____ damages are damages the parties to a contract agree to in advance, payable upon a breach of the contract.

12. _____ damages are usually awarded in a small amount, such as a $1 in cases which are brought on principle, rather than for financial loss resulting from a breach.

13. An award of _____ _____ orders the breaching party to perform the acts promised in a contract.

14. _____ is an equitable doctrine that allows the court to rewrite a contract to express the true intentions of the parties.

15. A(n) _____ is a court order that prohibits a person from doing a certain act.

## Critical Thought Exercise

The Cheersville Fire Department (CFD) entered into a written contract on 2-17-02 with American Emergency Truck Co. (AET) for the purchase of a $290,000.00 ladder/pump truck. The contract set forth a delivery date of September 1, 2002, as insisted upon by CFD. According to CFD Chief Sam Miller, their 1932 pumper truck was not going to last beyond that date and time was of the essence. On August 1, 2002, the CFD truck died and could not be repaired. The Cheersville Town Council voted to wait until the new truck arrived on September 1, 2002 instead or renting another old truck from Friendsville Fire District. On August 15, 2002, AET notified CFD that the truck would not be ready for delivery until October 1, 2002. The Town Council again decided to wait without renting another truck. Cheersville notified AET that its truck was out of service and the new truck was desperately needed by September 1, 2002. On September 15, 2002, a major fire damaged the Cheersville School. The fire started in the kitchen and could have easily been controlled with normal fire fighting equipment. The damage to the school was estimated to be approximately $2,800,000. The truck was delivered by AET on October 5, 2002.

AET denies any liability. You are on the Cheersville Town Council and have been assigned the task of drafting a memorandum for the council detailing the following:
1. Whether Cheersville has grounds to sue American Emergency Truck.
2. What damages would be recoverable from AET.
3. What defenses AET may assert.

*Please compose your answer on a separate sheet of paper or on your computer.*

## Practice Quiz

### True/False

1. \_\_\_\_ Monetary damages are not available for breach of contract.

2. \_\_\_\_ Equitable remedies are premised on the idea of monetary compensation.

3. \_\_\_\_ A material breach of contract does not occur when performance deviates only slightly from complete performance.

4. \_\_\_\_ Compensatory damages help defer costs associated with a breach of contract, as they compensate a non-breaching party for the loss of the bargain.

5. \_\_\_\_ The standard measure of damages for a breach of sales contract involving goods is the difference between the contract price and the market price.

6. \_\_\_\_ If an employee breaches an employment contract, the employer can recover the costs to hire a new employee, but must absorb any increase in salary paid to the replacement.

7. \_\_\_\_ A liquidated damages clause may act as a penalty if there were actual damages that could have been assessed in advance.

8. \_\_\_\_ Nominal damages may be awarded in amounts up to but not exceeding $125,000.

9. ___ To mitigate means to avoid or reduce.

10. ___ The court may not issue a Writ of Attachment in order to assist in the collection of a judgment.

11. ___ The remedy of rescission is unavailable if there has been fraud, undue influence or mistake involved with regard to the parties' contract.

12. ___ A party may not seek the remedy of specific performance for all contracts he or she is having difficulty enforcing.

13. ___ Specific performance of personal service contracts is usually granted.

14. ___ An equitable doctrine that allows the court to rewrite the parties contract to reflect their true intentions is known as reformation.

15. ___ A party may seek damages for a breach of the tort of bad faith.

## Multiple Choice

16. Suppose Manny Musolf contracts with The Snowy Construction Company to have Snowy build a recreation building for $20 million. The architectural plans indicate that installation of special insulation that is four times that of normal is required for this building, as it will be located in northern Rhode Island. Snowy constructs the building according to specification except that Snowy forgets to put in the insulation. It will cost five million dollars to blow in proper insulation, and will lose them time that they have already promised to give to other jobs. What may Manny sue Snowy for if Snowy does not elevate its level of performance under the contract?
    a. Manny may deduct the cost to have the building repaired (insulated) from the contract price and remit the difference to Snowy.
    b. Nothing, as Snowy did the best they could under the winter conditions.
    c. Manny may sue for the cost of standard insulation if Snowy has substantially performed.
    d. None of the above.

17. Where there is anticipatory repudiation in a contract, the non-breaching party's obligation under the contract
    a. is partially fulfilled
    b. remains in tact
    c. is discharged immediately
    d. is rescinded

18. Suppose Mogul Bear's Fun Land enters into a written contract to employ a manager for five years at a salary of $4,000 per month. However, before work is to begin, the manager is informed that he or she will not be needed after all. Thereafter, the manager finds another job, but it pays only $2,000 per month. How much will the manager be able to recover from Mogul Bear's Fun Land if a law suit is brought?
    a. Nothing, as the manager "assumed the risk" of job loss when he or she agreed to work for Mogul Bear's Fun Land.
    b. liquidated damages

    c.   Nominal damages, as it was an at will contract

    d.   $120,000.

19.   Hillside Resort contracted to buy a piece of ice resurfacing equipment from The Zamboni Company for $80,000, however the equipment never gets delivered. Hillside decides to purchase the equipment from another seller, but must do so at $100,000 due to an increase in the market price. What may Hillside recover?

    a.   $20,000.

    b.   $180,000.

    c.   Nothing, as inflation is implied in contracts involving goods.

    d.   $65,000.

20.   The Random Engineering Corporation has hired Lisa Sharpe as a robotics engineer to design housekeeper robots. Lisa contracted with Random to give her an initial annual income of $132,000 plus benefits. Additionally, if she can design a microchip to place in the robot which will enable it to garden as well, Random will give Lisa a percentage of the profits and a twelve percent salary increase. Lisa works for Random for two months and Random decides to downsize and use engineers who have been employed with them for twenty or more years to design the housekeeper/gardener robots. Lisa is told she will need to find another place to work. If Lisa brings a lawsuit against Random based on breach of her employment contract, what does she need to do in order to mitigate her damages?

    a.   She will need to gather as much information about Random as possible.

    b.   She will need to try to find comparable, substitute employment.

    c.   She will need to beg to be given a second chance, as she is the best person for the job.

    d.   She will need to ask for specific performance based upon her skills and experience.

21.   If the liquidated damages are excessive or unconscionable and the actual damages are clearly able to be determined in advance, the liquidated damages clause will be considered to be

    a.   an adhesion clause.

    b.   enforceable.

    c.   a penalty.

    d.   compensation for a breach of contract.

22.   In order to obtain an injunction, the requesting party must show that he or she

    a.   will suffer irreparable harm unless the injunction is issued.

    b.   deserves the injunction more than the other party.

    c.   requires recovery of compensation even though no enforceable contract exists.

    d.   needs the contract to be rewritten to reflect the true intentions of the parties.

23.   In order to recover for the tort of intentional interference with contract relations, what must be shown?

    a.   The third party had knowledge of a valid enforceable contract between contracting parties.

    b.   A valid, enforceable contract between the contracting parties existed.

    c.   The third party induced one of the parties to breach the contract.

    d.   All of the above.

24.   Specific performance can be used in which of the following situations?

    a.   In the performance of a personal service contract.

    b.   In the sale of a piece of land.

c. In the sale of a mass-produced poster.

d. All of the above.

25. Under the covenant of good faith and fair dealing, the parties to a contract

a. the parties are held to the express terms of the contract.

b. the parties are required to act in good faith and deal fairly in all respects of the contract.

c. the parties can recover damages for the tort of bad faith for breaching this covenant.

d. All of the above.

## Short Answer

26. What does a Writ of Attachment order?

27. When will punitive damages be awarded in a contract situation?

28. What must the parties do in order to rescind a contract?

29. When are equitable remedies available?

30. Give examples of restitution.

31. What may the court do if a judgment is entered against a breaching party and the breaching party refuses to pay it?

32. What is a Writ of Garnishment?

33. What is one purpose that an equitable remedy might have?

34. What is an injunction?

35. What is the function of the equitable remedy called specific performance?

36. What are the three levels of performance of a contract?

37. What are the equitable remedies available for breach of contract?

38.  What duty does a contracting party owe if a contractual duty has not been discharged or excused?

_____

39.  What are the compensatory damages for a breach of contract involving the sale of goods?

_____

40.  What damages are available to an employee when an employer has breached his or her employment contract?

_____

## Answers to Refresh Your Memory

1.  Complete, strict  [p 365]
2.  executed  [p 365]
3.  minor  [p 366]
4.  inferior  [p 366]
5.  rescind  [p 366]
6.  Anticipatory  [p 367]
7.  Compensatory  [p 368]
8.  breach of a sales  [p 369]
9.  Mitigation of damages  [p 369]
10. Consequential  [p 371]
11. Liquidated  [p 371]
12. Nominal  [p 374]
13. specific performance  [p 377]
14. Reformation  [p 379]
15. injunction  [p 379]

## Critical Thought Exercise Model Answer

Before either party to a contract has a duty to perform, one of the parties may make an assertion or do an act that indicates they will not perform their obligations under the contract at a future time. This called an anticipatory repudiation of the contract and is treated as a material breach. The non-breaching party may immediately bring an action for damages, wait to see if the breaching party changes their name, or may seek specific performance by the breaching party. When AET notifies CFD that it will not be able to deliver the truck as promised, CFD must decide what course of action it will take. The damages that may be sought would be any increase in cost that CFD as to pay to obtain the truck from another seller plus any consequential or incidental damages. In this situation, CFD needs the truck more than it needs money damages. The CFD had a duty to protect the citizens of Cheersville and another truck is not readily obtainable. The truck that was being built for CFD by AET was somewhat unique and failure to perform the contract would create great hardship for CFD. However, CFD had to make an election at the time of the breach, which took place on August 15, 2002. Because CFD failed to elect to pursue specific performance, they will be left with an action for damages. Specific performance is not available at this late point in time because the truck was actually delivered on October 5, 2002. CFD will seek consequential damages for the damage caused to the Cheersville School. AET will be liable for those damages if they were reasonably foreseeable at the time of the breach or fire occurred. CFD had previously notified AET that their truck was old and would not last in service beyond September 1, 2002. CFD again told AET of the urgency when the truck was taken out of service on August 1, 2002. Knowing the need for the truck and the fact that CFD was without a truck after August 1, 2002, AET continued to promise to perform the contract. The damages to the school were probably foreseeable because they are the exact type of damages that would occur if the CFD was without a truck.

AET will have two possible defenses to the contract. The most obvious is that Cheersville failed to fulfill its duty of mitigation of damages. This rule requires the plaintiff to have done whatever was reasonable to minimize the damages caused by the defendant. CFD failed to take any action to mitigate their damages. The city council decided to not rent a replacement truck, even after their only truck was taken out of service. Because they failed to mitigate their damages, Cheersville will have their damages reduced by those amounts they could have prevented. In this case, the facts state that the damages to the school could have been minimized if a temporary replacement truck had been obtained. A rental was available from Friendsville and Cheersville failed to mitigate their damages by renting the truck.

The second defense that AET may assert is that Cheersville agree to a modification of the contract when they did not pursue any action when notified of the delay in the delivery date. This defense is weak because Cheersville notified AET that it desperately needed the truck by the original contract date of September 1, 2002. Cheersville did nothing that could be deemed as acquiescence in the request by AET to extend the delivery date. Therefore, no modification of the original agreement was ever accomplished.

Cheersville will prevail in their breach of contract suit, but the amount of damages will be relatively small due to Cheersville's failure to mitigate damages.

# Answers to Practice Quiz

## True/False

1.  False   Monetary damages, which are often termed the "law remedy", are the most common remedy for a breach of contract cause of action. [p 365]
2.  False   Legal remedies are based on monetary awards and equitable remedies are based on fairness. [p 365]
3.  True   A material breach occurs when there has been inferior performance under the contract. [p 366]
4.  True   Compensatory damages do compensate a non-breaching party for the loss of the bargain. [p 368]
5.  True   In contracts involving the sales of goods, the difference between the contract price and the market price is the standard measure of damages in a breach of contract cause of action. [p 369]
6.  False   The costs to hire a new employee as well as an increase in salary paid to that new employee are recoverable by an employer if an employee has breached an employment contract. [p 369]
7.  True   A liquidated damages clause may act as a penalty if there were actual damages that could have been assessed in advance. [p 371]
8.  False   Nominal damages are based on principle and therefore awarded in small amounts. [p 374]
9.  True   To mitigate means to avoid or reduce. [p 369]

10. False   The Writ of Attachment is a court order directing the sheriff to seize property in the possession of the breaching party that he or she owns. Then the sheriff is to sell the property at the auction in order to satisfy the judgment. [p 375]

11. False   Rescission is an available remedy for a material breach of contract where fraud, undue influence, duress or mistake is involved. [p 375]

12. True   Courts have been prone to enforcing the remedy of specific performance in situations involving unique goods or land. Thus, it is not an available remedy for any contract that the parties are having difficulty in enforcing. [p 377-378]

13. False   The courts would find it very difficult or impracticable to supervise or monitor the performance of a personal service contract. [p 378]

14. True   Reformation permits the court to rewrite a contract to express the parties' true intentions. [p 379]

15. True   The tort of the implied covenant of good faith and fair dealing allows for the recovery of damages. [p 381]

## Multiple Choice

16. A   Answer A is the correct answer as it properly states the damages that Manny may recover from Snowy if Manny has to hire someone else to put in proper insulation. Answer B is incorrect, as doing its best would be expected regardless of the winter conditions. Answer C is incorrect, as the cost of standard insulation is not a correct statement of damages that Manny could receive. Answer D is incorrect for the reasons given above. [p 369]

17. C   Answer C is the correct answer as, the nonbreaching party's obligations under a contract are discharged immediately where there is anticipatory repudiation. Answer A is incorrect, as it makes no sense. Answer B is incorrect, as it misstates the law. Answer D is also an incorrect statement of law, as the nonbreaching party's obligations do not have to fully mature. [p 367]

18. D   Answer D is correct as the $2,000 monthly difference multiplied by the duration of the contract, sixty months equals $120,000. This will place the manager in the same situation as if the contract with Mogul Bear's Fun Land had been performed. Answer A is incorrect, as there is no risk to assume with the job. Answer B is incorrect, as nothing in the facts indicated that the parties had agreed to a liquidated damages clause. Answer C is incorrect, as nominal damages are awarded as a matter of principle and where there are no actual damages. Clearly, based on the facts, damages do exist. [p 369]

19. A   Answer A is correct, as Hillside may recover $20,000, which represents the difference between the market price paid ($100,000) and the contract price ($80,000) in compensatory damages. Answers B and D are incorrect, as they do not represent what the law would allow under the circumstances and facts given. Answer C is incorrect, as inflation is not an implied term which would negate damages as a result of a breach of contract. [p 369]

20. B   Answer B is correct, as an employee owes a duty to mitigate damages by trying to find substitute employment that is comparable to that which they had. Answer A is incorrect, as gathering information about Random will not assist her in mitigating her damages though it may assist her in the discovery process should she decide to sue. Answer C is incorrect, as begging for a second chance will not be a factor that the court will consider in determining whether Lisa has mitigated her damages. Answer D is incorrect, as the courts usually do not grant specific performance where contracts of personal service are involved. Arguably, this would be a personal service contract that would be nearly impossible for the court to monitor. [p 370]

21. C  Answer C is correct, as the liquidated damages clause will be considered to be a penalty if actual damages are clearly able to be determined in advance or if they are excessive or unconscionable. Answer A is incorrect, as an adhesion clause speaks to only the aspect of unconscionablility and not to the ability to assess actual damages. Answer B is incorrect, as the clause will not be enforceable if the damages are excessive or unconscionable or able to be determined in advance. Answer D is incorrect, as under the facts as presented the clause would not be considered compensation for breach of contract since it would be a penalty. [p 371]

22. A  Answer A is correct, as the court will grant the equitable remedy of injunction if the party can show that irreparable harm will come if it is not granted. Answer B is incorrect, as demonstration of need over another is not a requisite in obtaining the enforcement of an injunction. Answer C is incorrect, as this answer is mixing a legal remedy involving compensation with the equitable remedy of injunction as stated in the facts. Answer D is incorrect, as it speaks to the equitable remedy of reformation and not injunction. [p 379]

23. D  Answer D is correct, as answers A, B, and C are all things that must be shown in order to recover for the tort of intentional interference with contract relations. [p 380]

24. B  Answer B is correct, as specific performance is available to enforce land contracts because every piece of real property is considered to be unique. Answer A is incorrect, as the courts will not grant specific performance of a personal services contract, as supervision would be difficult. Answer C is incorrect, as specific performance is reserved for items that are unique, and a mass-produced poster would generally be unique. Answer D is incorrect, for the reasons stated above. [p 378]

25. D  Answer D is correct, as answers A, B, and C are all correct statements with regard to the covenant of good faith and fair dealing. [p 381]

## Short Answer

26.  It orders the sheriff to seize property in the possession of the breaching party that he or she owns, and to sell the property at auction to satisfy the judgment. [p 375]

27.  They will be awarded when certain tortuous conduct is associated with the nonperformance of a contract. [p 380]

28.  Make restitution of the consideration received under the contract. [p 375]

29.  If there has been a breach that cannot be adequately compensated through a legal remedy. [p 377]

30.  Returning goods, property, money or other consideration received from the other party. [p 375]

31.  The court may issue a Write of Attachment or a Writ of Garnishment. [p 375]

32.  An order that garnishes wages, bank accounts or other property of the breaching party that is in a third parties hands to be paid over to the non-breaching party. [p 375]

33.  To prevent unjust enrichment. [p 377]

34.  A court order that prohibits a person from doing a certain act. [p 379]

35.  A court order that orders the breaching party to perform the acts promised in a contract. [p 377-378]

36.  Complete, substantial and inferior. [p 365]

37.  Specific performance, reformation, and injunction. [p 377] Quasi contract is an equitable remedy discussed in Chapter 9.

38.  An absolute duty to perform. [p 365]

39.  The difference between the contract price and the market price. [p 369]

40.  Lost wages or salary as compensatory damages. [p 369]

## Chapter 15

# E-CONTRACTS, INTERNET LAW, AND CYBER CRIMES

## Chapter Overview

Both large and small businesses use e-commerce to sell goods and services over the internet using websites and domain names. Businesses and individuals can register domain names, which can be protected from infringement by others. Software licenses can be obtained through purchase, installation, or downloading of the software. Concerns regarding the applicability of traditional contract law to internet transactions and the licensing of software and information led to the creation of the Uniform Computer Information Transactions Act (UCITA), as well as federal statutes that regulate this new area of law. The topics of Internet law, domain names, e-contracts, licenses of software, privacy laws, and criminal laws for the internet and online commerce are introduced in this chapter.

## Objectives

Upon completion of the exercises in this chapter, you should be able to:

1. Explain how freedom of speech applies to the Internet using the rationale expressed in the case of *Reno v. American Civil Liberties Union.*
2. Explain the procedure for procuring Internet domain names.
3. Discuss what a license is and the parties to a licensing agreement.
4. Explain the provisions of the Federal Electronics Signature Act and the Electronic Signature in Global and National Commerce Act for e-commerce.
5. Discuss the importance of the Uniform Computer Information Transactions Act (UCITA)

## Practical Application

You should have a clearer understanding of the various electronic and computer information acts that apply to the Internet and web businesses. You should have a better understanding of e-commerce created licensing contracts and what necessary steps you may need to take if confronted with an Internet domain name dispute.

## Helpful Hints

Since this chapter involves technology and the Internet, it would be helpful to become familiar with the technical terminology associated with the Information Age. It is imperative to learn the acts that protect and guide your conduct on the Internet in order to responsibly do business with the world. Learning the various acts will give a better understanding of what is expected in transactions on the Web.

# Study Tips

## Vocabulary

- **Authenticate** – This means executing an electronic symbol, sound or message linked to a record or signing the contract.
- **Computer formatting** – This refers to the use of common code languages such as Java and Hypertext Markup Language (HTML).
- **Domain name** – This identifies and differentiates one web site from another. Suffixes, or endings that are often used are *com* for commercial use, *org* for organizations, *edu* for educational institutions and *net* for networks.
- **Electronic communication** – This involves any writing, images, sound, data, transfer of signals or any intelligence that is communicated electronically.
- **E-mail** – Electronic mail; written communication between individuals whose computers are connected to the Internet.
- **Exclusive License**- This license gives the licensee exclusive rights in the information as described in the license for a specified period of time.
- **Internet** – a collection of millions of computers that enable a network of electronic connections to exist between computers.
- **Internet Corporation for Assigned Names and Numbers (ICANN)** – This is an organization whose job is to regulate the issuance of domain names on the Internet.
- **License**- This grants the contractual rights that are expressly stated in the license and the right to use any informational rights within the licensor's control that are necessary to exercise the expressly described rights. [UCITA Sec.307]
- **Licensee**- The party who is given limited rights in or access to the informational rights or intellectual property.
- **Licensing Agreement** – A very detailed agreement between licensor and licensee that sets forth the terms of their agreement concerning the uses granted with respect to the intellectual property and informational rights.
- **Licensor**- The party who owns the informational rights or the intellectual property and obligates him or herself to transfer rights in the property or information to the licensee.
- **Title to Copy** – This is established by the license as the licensor may reserve title to the copy or the copy can transfer to the licensee.
- **Uniform Dispute Resolution Policy** – Mandates that all ICANN registered domain name users agree to utilize this dispute resolution policy as part of their accreditation.
- **Web site**- A combination of Web pages stored on various servers throughout the world.
- **World Wide Web**- The connection between millions of computers that enforces a standard set of rules for exchanging information referred to as Hypertext Transfer Protocol (HTTP).

## The Internet

Millions of computers worldwide collectively form the network called the Internet, or Net. Hundreds of millions computer users use the Internet for communication of information and data.

**The World Wide Web.** Standardized rules and coding enable businesses and individuals to connect to the Web through service providers.
- These users can have their own websites, with their own unique online address.

- The Web facilitates online commercial activities and has allowed both traditional and e-commerce-based businesses access to this e-environment.

**Free Speech and the Internet.** In *Reno v. American Civil Liberties Union* [521 U.S. 844, 117 S.Ct. 2329, 138 L.Ed.2d 874, Web 1997 U.S. Lexis 4037 (Supreme Court of the United States)] parts of the Communications Decency Act, meant to keep minors from "indecent transmissions", were found to be unconstitutional, violating the Free Speech Clause of the First Amendment.
  - Internet users should have the highest level of Constitutional protection for free speech.
  - Past justifications for the regulation of broadcast media of radio and television do not apply to the Internet.
  - Parents can control Internet access and the material available to their children.
  - The evidence shows that systems to block sexually explicit images will soon be available.
  - It is not the place of the government to reduce the information available to the adult population only to material that is fit for children.

**E-Mail.** E-mail allows individuals around the world to instantly communicate with each other.
  - Individuals can have unique e-mail addresses.
  - The use of e-mail continues to replace the use of telephone and paper correspondence.

## Domain Names

E-commerce is conducted by using Web sites identified by a unique Internet domain name.
  - Databases of domain names are maintained by InterNIC or Network Solutions.

**Domain Name Anticybersquatting Act.** This Act was aimed at those who register domain names of the famous and demand high payments from the famous to obtain the domain name.
  - It requires that the name be famous and the domain name be registered in bad faith.

## E-Contracts

An online contract is much like that of a written one in that the same elements of offer, acceptance and consideration must be satisfied.
  - Evidence is made by printing out an e-mail, Web contract, prior e-mails or negotiations.

**E-Contracts Writing Requirement.** Electronic Signature in Global and National Commerce Act provides electronic commerce with the same credence as written contracts in the U.S.
  - It provides that electronic contracts satisfy writing requirements of the Statute of Frauds.
  - It provides that e-contracts with electronic signatures cannot be denied effect.
  - Record retention requirements are fulfilled by electronically stored records.
  - It makes provisions for consumer protection:
    - o The Consumer must consent to the receipt of electronic records and contracts.
    - o Demonstrable access to electronic records must be provided by the Consumer.
    - o Consumer must be informed that they have a right to hard-copy documents.

**E-Signatures.** The Electronic Signature in Global and National Commerce Act recognizes an e-signatures, or electronic signatures, with the same significance as pen-inscribed signatures.
  - A digital signature is an electronic technique that identifies a person.
  - The act provides three ways to verify a digital signature:
    - o By something the signatory knows, such as the answer to a personal question.

o By something the person has that stores personal information.
o By the use of biometrics.

## Software and E-Licensing

E-commerce provides a challenge in the formation of contracts, enforcement of contracts, and the provision of consumer protection.

- The Uniform Computer Information Transaction Act (UCITA) provides an exhaustive set of uniform rules that sets the standard for performance and enforcement of computer information transactions.
  o A computer information transaction is an agreement to create, transfer, or license computer information or informational rights. [UCITA Sec.102 (a)(11)].
  o Most states have statutes like the UCITA for computer transactions and licensing.

**Licensing.** A license allows the owner of an intellectual property right to transfer limited rights to other parties for specified purposes and duration.

- Parties:
  o The owner of the intellectual property right who transfers limited rights in this property is the licensor.
  o The licensee is granted limited rights in or access to the intellectual property.
- A license gives express contractual rights and the right to use information rights within the licensor's power that may be necessary to implement the expressly given rights.
- An exclusive license grants the licensee sole rights to use the information
  o The licensor cannot grant any other person rights in the same information.

**Click-Wrap Licenses.** These are contracts used by many software companies to sell their products, either over the Internet or in packages to be downloaded later.

- Dialogue boxes are displayed prior to installation that state the terms of the agreement.
  o These terms are nonnegotiable.
  o The licensee accepts the license by clicking the appropriate button on the screen.
- Courts consider agreements to be enforceable when the user clicks the "I Agree" button.
- The Uniform Computer Information Transaction Act (UCITA) provides that a licensee is bound by agreement if they give assent before or during initial use or access to software.

**Licensing Agreement.** A licensing agreement expressly states the terms of the agreement between the licensor and licensee.

- These agreements, usually written, are detailed and comprehensive.
- These agreements are specific about the limited uses granted.

**Counteroffers Ineffectual Against Electronic Agents.** The Uniform Computer Information Transaction Act (UCITA) provides that a contract is formed when a person causes an electronic agent, which is a telephone or computer system set up by a seller to take orders, to institute performance or a promise of benefits.

- Electronic agents cannot accept or make counteroffers.
- Counteroffers are not effective against electronic agents. [UCITA Sec. 206(a)]

**Breach of License Agreements.** The nonbreaching party in a licensing agreement has the right to recover damages, or other remedies.

- Adequate assurance is akin to anticipatory repudiation whereby an aggrieved party may suspend performance if he or she has reasonable grounds to believe that the performance from the other party is not going to be forthcoming.
  o The aggrieved party may demand adequate assurance of performance.
- If a licensor tenders a defective copy, the licensee may refuse the defective tender, accept the tender or accept any commercially reasonable units and refuse the rest.
- If a licensee has accepted a defective tender, the licensee may revoke acceptance if
  o He or she could not have reasonably discovered the nonconformity at the time of acceptance or
  o The nonconformity was discovered upon acceptance and the licensor agreed to cure the defect but it was not reasonably cured.

**Consumers Saved from Electronic Errors.** The Uniform Computer Information Transaction Act (UCITA) protects consumers if they make an electronic error in contracting.

- This Act provides that consumers are not bound if they learn of the error and tell the other party.
  o The consumer must not derive any benefit from the information.
  o The consumer must deliver all copies of the information to the third party or destroy the information as per the third party's instruction.
  o The consumer must pay all shipping and processing costs. [UCITA Sec. 217]
- The consumer is not relieved of the consequences of their error if the other party gives a reasonable way of detecting and correcting, or avoiding, the error.
  o Having the buyer verify the information, usually by clicking the order button a second time before the order is processed, strips the consumer of this defense.
- The common law of contracts or the Uniform Commercial Code (U.C.C.) applies to electronic errors of non-consumers.

**Remedies.** The Uniform Computer Information Transaction Act (UCITA) provides to nonbreaching party certain remedies when a licensing agreement is breached.

- A party cannot recover more than once for the same loss, nor for more than the loss.
- Suit must begin within one year of when the breach was or should have been discovered.
- The suit cannot commence more than five years after the breach actually happened.

*Cancellation.* This is the ending of a contract by a contracting party upon the material breach of contract by the other party.

- It is effective upon notification.
- Breaching party must return materials or hold for disposal as instructed by other party.
- All executory obligations are discharged.
- The licensor has the right to return of all materials to prevent continued use of materials.

*Licensor's Damages.* The licensor may sue a licensee who is in breach and seek monetary damages caused by the breach, as well as any consequential and incidental damages.

*Licensor's Right to Cure.* Under UCITA, a licensor may, if notice is given, cure a breach

- If the time for performance under the contract has not expired, or
- If it has expired, the licensor had reasonable grounds to feel that the performance would be acceptable and would cure within a reasonable time, or
- If the licensor makes a conforming performance before cancellation by the licensee.

*Electronic Self-Help.* If the licensee does not pay the license fee, the licensor can give at least a 15 day notice and activate a disabling bug that is embedded in the software or information that will prevent further access to the same.

- Proper notice to enable the licensee to make lawful adjustment must be made.
- Self-help is not available if it causes public health or safety issues or personal injury.

*Licensee's Damages.* A licensee can sue and recover money damages from a breaching licensor.

- Damages depend on the facts of the situation.
- Licensee may cover by engaging in a commercially reasonable substitute transaction, or
- The licensee may recover the value of the performance.
- The licensee can also receive consequential and incidental damages.

*Limitations of Remedies.* Parties may limit which remedies are available in the event of a breach.

- Remedies can be restricted to the return of copies, the repayment of the licensing fee, the repair or replacement of the copy.
- Limitation of remedies is enforceable unless they are unconscionable.

## Online Privacy

Because electronic communications provide unique issues in privacy, the Electronic Communications Privacy Act (ECPA) was enacted by the federal government.

- It is a crime to intercept "electronic communication" at any stage of its delivery.
- There are exceptions to the ECPA that allow access to stored electronic communications without being in violation of the act. They are:
  - The individual providing the service.
  - Government and law enforcement agencies that are investigating suspicious illegal activity are allowed if a valid search warrant is in place.

## Cyber Crimes

The use of the computer and the Internet have led to a new type of crime known as "cyber crimes," which allow criminals to commit traditional crimes through a new medium.

- Fraud is committed over the Internet.
- New crimes have been created by criminals.
- Congress has enacted statutes to address these crimes.
- Courts have interpreted new statutes and applied old statutes to these crimes.

**Counterfeit Access Device and Computer Fraud and Abuse Act.** This Act makes it a federal crime to use phony or unauthorized devices to obtain items of value or funds or to deal in such.

- It is a crime to knowingly access a computer to obtain the following:
  - Restricted government information.
  - Records of financial institutions.
  - Reports from consumer reporting agencies.

**Electronic Funds Transfer Act.** This Act regulates electronic funds transfers for the payment and deposit of funds.

- It is criminal to wrongly use ATM cards, codes, or other related devices.
- The Act provides for criminal penalties of imprisonment and fines.

**Cyber Identity Fraud.** Identity theft can be very lucrative to the criminal, but leaves the victim with stolen funds, damaged credit, and significant credit repair costs.

- The Identity Theft and Assumption Deterrence Act makes it a federal crime to commit identity theft.

**Information Infrastructure Protection Act (IIP Act).** This Act criminalizes the intentional and unauthorized access and acquisition of information from a protected computer.

**State Criminal Laws.** Many states have updated or amended laws to criminalize certain computer-based activities.

- Larceny statutes have often covered only tangible property, where computer software, programs, and data are intangible and their theft has not been covered.
- Modern statutes cover computer trespass, unauthorized use, tampering, and unauthorized duplication of materials.

# Refresh Your Memory

The following exercises will help to test your memory regarding the principles given in this chapter. Read each question twice, then place your answer in the blank provided for each question. Review the chapter material for any questions you are unable to answer or remember.

1. The _____, or _____, is a collection of millions of computers providing a network of electronic connections between computers.

2. The _____ _____ _____ consists of millions of computers supporting standardized rules for the exchange of information.

3. _____ _____, or _____, is a widely used application for communication over the Internet.

4. A(n) _____ _____ is a unique name that signifies an individual's or a company's Web site.

5. The _____ _____ _____ Act was specifically aimed at those who register domain names of the famous and hold them hostage for exorbitant ransom.

6. If all of the elements necessary to establish a contract are present, a(n) _____ or _____ contract is valid and enforceable.

7. One of the main features of the _____ _____ _____ _____ _____ _____ _____ Act is the recognition of electronic contracts as meeting the writing requirements of the Statute of Frauds for most contracts.

8. The _____ _____ _____ _____ Act establishes uniform and comprehensive rules to govern the creation, performance, and enforcement of computer information transactions.

9. An agreement that is used to transfer limited rights in property or information to parties for specified purposes and limited duration is called a(n) _____.

10. The _____ is the party who owns the intellectual property or information rights and agrees to transfer rights to the _____.

11. The _____ is the party who is granted limited rights in or access to the intellectual property or information rights.

12. If there has been a material breach of a licensing contract that has not been cured or waived, the aggrieved party may _____ the contract.

13. A licensor can recover _____ _____ caused by the licensee's failure to accept or complete performance of the contract.

14. _____ _____ _____ can consist of activating disabling bugs and time bombs embedded in software to prevent the licensee from further using the software or information.

15. _____ is the act of engaging in a commercially reasonable substitute transaction in the even of a breach of contract by the other party.

## Critical Thought Exercise

The James Co. of New York has been in the business of retail chocolate and confection sales since 1923. As the Internet has developed, James has commenced doing business by e-mail. Mrs. Dubyah communicates with James by numerous e-mails, negotiating the sale of 300 one-pound chocolate Easter eggs. They agree that the price will be $18 per egg and they will be shipped for arrival in Maryland 10 days before Easter. James produces the eggs and ships them in a timely manner. At the last minute, Mrs. Dubyah decides to order her Easter gifts from another company. When the shipment arrives in Maryland, Mrs. Dubyah wants to reject the shipment and order her eggs from her friend in Oklahoma. As the business secretary for Mrs. Dubyah, you are responsible for advising her on business matters and executing her contracts as instructed.

Write a brief memorandum to Mrs. Dubyah, explaining whether she can rely on the Statute of Frauds as a defense to a claim by James Co. and whether the shipment should be accepted.

*Please compose your answer on a separate sheet of paper or on your computer*

## Practice Quiz

### True/False

1. ___ Domain names cannot be registered.

2. ___ Electronic contracts do meet the Statute of Frauds requirements.

3. ___ The license does not govern a licensee's right to possess, control and use a copy of the licensed software.

4. ___ The Internet Corporation for Assigned names is responsible for regulating the issuance of domain names on the Internet.

5. ___ Mary has entered into an electronic contract with Watson for the purchase of Watson's motorcycle. Mary authenticates the contract by using an electronic symbol. Mary's means of authentication will be sufficient to constitute a signing.

6. ___ Electronic agents usually do not have the ability to evaluate and accept counteroffers or to make counteroffers.

7. ___ One of the benefits of the Electronic Signature in Global and National Commerce Act is that the act does not provide for verification of digital signatures.

8. ___ Under UCITA, if a licensing agreement is breached, the statute of limitations is open ended due to the electronic nature of the transaction.

9. ___ The licensee may not sue and recover monetary damages from the licensor when the licensor breaches a contract.

10. ___ The parties to an agreement may limit the remedies available for breach of the contract under the Electronic Communications Privacy Act (ECPA).

11. ___ A licensor cannot use electronic self-help if the license agreement is breached.

12. ___ The UCITA gives a licensor the right to cure a breach of a license in some situations.

13. ___ If there has been a minor breach of a contract that has not been cured or waived, the aggrieved party may cancel the contract.

14. ___ A party may recover more than once for the same loss caused by a breach of a license.

15. ___ An electronic agent is any telephonic or computer system that has been established by a seller to accept orders.

## Multiple Choice

16. Which of the following is one of the most widely used means of Internet communication?
    a. Licensing agreements
    b. Electronic mail
    c. Chat rooms
    d. None of the above

17. What was the court's opinion regarding the Communications Decency Act and the freedom of speech in the case of *Reno v. American Civil Liberties Union?*
    a. The act is effective in allowing freedom of speech.
    b. The act is vague and has a chilling effect on free speech.
    c. The act is specific and protects our children from sexually oriented speech.
    d. The act appropriately protects all that are concerned.

18. Who is the owner of intellectual property or informational rights who transfers rights in the property or information to the license?

a. The licensee
b. The licensor
c. The obligor
d. The obligee

19. Which of the following established a uniform comprehensive set of rules to govern the creation, performance, and enforcement of computer information transactions?
a. the Uniform Computer Information Transactions Act
b. the express warranty
c. the Federal Electronics Signatures Act
d. all of the above

20. Which of the following is a function of InterNIC?
a. to establish an extension for U.S. Web sites
b. to establish a uniform international code among nations using the Internet
c. to maintain a "Whois" database that contains the domain names that have been registered.
d. to enable organizations unrestricted global name recognition

21. When is cancellation of a contract effective?
a. when the breaching party notifies the canceling party of the cancellation
b. when the canceling party notifies the breaching party of the cancellation
c. when it is obvious that the contract must be canceled due to a material breach
d. none of the above

22. What may a licensor recover for a licensee's failure to accept or complete performance of a contract?
a. lost wages
b. unemployment insurance
c. discretionary damages
d. lost profits

23. Which legislative Act provides that a licensor can use electronic self-help if a breach of the license agreement occurs?
a. The Anticybersquatting Consumer Protection Act.
b. The Electronic Signature in Global and National Commerce Act.
c. The Uniform Computer Information Transactions Act.
d. The Electronic Communications Privacy Act.

24. Under the Electronic Signature in Global and National Commerce Act, how can an electronic signature be verified?
a. By something the signatory knows, like a password.
b. By something a person has, like a smart card.
c. By biometrics, through devices recognizing information like fingerprints.
d. All of the above.

25. Which of the following statements about click-wrap licenses is true?
a. The terms of this license are generally negotiable.
b. This license is typically provided through a mail-in form.
c. These licenses are enforceable.
d. None of the above.

## Short Answer

26. What type of penalties are provided for by the Electronic Communications Privacy Act?

_____

27. What role does the licensee have in the license agreement?

_____

28. Which act lets a court issue cease-and-desist orders and injunctions and to award monetary damages against those who register a domain name of a famous name in bad faith?

_____

29. What is a licensor liable for if he or she uses electronic self-help improperly?

_____

30. When may remedies be restricted under UTICA?

_____

31. What does the term cover mean?

_____

32. What may an aggrieved party do if he or she thinks that prior to the performance date the other party might not deliver performance?

_____

33. What may a licensee do when a defective tender of a copy has been made to them?

_____

34. What is the Internet?

_____

35. Define e-mail.

_____

_____

36. Which act makes it a crime to intercept an "electronic communication"?

_____

37. What is the purpose of the Anticybersquatting Consumer Protection Act?

_____

38. Who is responsible for regulating the issuance of domain names on the Internet?

_____

39. What is a license?

_____

40. Which act establishes a uniform and exhaustive set of rules that rule the creation, performance and enforcement of computer information transactions?

_____

# Answers to Refresh Your Memory

1. Internet, Net  [p 389]
2. World Wide Web  [p 389]
3. Electronic mail, e-mail  [p 391]
4. domain name  [p 392]
5. Anticybersquatting Consumer Protection  [p 393]
6. e-mail, Web  [p 396]
7. Electronic Signature in Global and National Commerce  [p 396]
8. Uniform Computer Information Transactions  [p 397]
9. license  [p 397]
10. licensor, licensee  [p 397]
11. licensee  [p 397]
12. cancel  [p 400]
13. lost profits  [p 400]
14. Electronic self-help  [p 400]
15. Cover  [p 401]

# Critical Thought Exercise Model Answer

E-mail is a convenient way to negotiate and agree on contract terms and to ultimately agree on a final contract. Assuming that all the elements to establish a valid contact are present, the fact that the contract is communicated by e-mail does not prevent the agreement from being valid and enforceable. In this instance, the subject matter, parties, price, and delivery terms have all been negotiated and agreed upon. While this is a contract for goods exceeding $500 that requires a written contract, there is no reason why the e-mails cannot be printed and used as the required writing. The e-mails will amply demonstrate the parties' intent and desire to enter into the agreement. The ordering of the eggs by Mrs. Dubyah by e-mail will have no less effect than a written letter. Thus, e-mail contracts meet the writing requirements for enforceable contracts.

Mrs. Dubyah is therefore advised to accept the shipment and pay for it as agreed. The Statute of Frauds will not give a viable defense and it would be unethical to cancel the order on a whim.

# Answers to Practice Quiz

## True/False

1. False   Domain names can be registered with a domain name registration service by paying the applicable fee. [p 392]
2. True    Since parties to an e-mail contract can print a paper copy of the electronic contract, the writing requirement of the Statute of Frauds is met. [p 396]
3. False   The license states the terms of the party's agreement, which includes the licensee's right to possess, control and use a copy of the licensed software. [p 397]
4. True    It is responsible for regulating the issuance of domain names on the Internet. [p 392]

5. True    Mary may authenticate her contract with Watson by using the electronic symbol that is attached to, included in, or linked with the record as provided for under the Uniform Computer Information Transactions Act. [p 396-397]

6. True    Under the Uniform Computer Information Transactions Act, limits of e-commerce are acknowledged thereby providing that a contract is formed if a person takes action resulting in the electronic agent causing performance or a promise of benefits to the individual, making counteroffers ineffectual against electronic agents. [p 398]

7. False   The act does in fact provide three ways to verify a digital signature. [p 396-397]

8. False   A cause of action must be brought within one year after the breach was or should have been discovered, but no more than five years after the breach occurred. [UTICA Sec.805] [p 399-400]

9. False   The licensee may sue and recover monetary damages from the licensor when the licensor breaches a contract. [p 401]

10. False  The parties to an agreement may limit the remedies available for breach of contract under the Uniform Computer Information Transactions Act (UCITA). [p 401]

11. False  A licensor is allowed to use electronic self-help if a breach of the license agreement happens. [p 400]

12. True   The UCITA provides that a licensor has the right to cure a breach of a license in some circumstances. [p 400]

13. False  If there has been a material breach of a contract that has not been cured or waived, the aggrieved party may cancel the contract. [p 400]

14. False  A party may not recover more than once for a loss from a breach of license. [p 399]

15. True   An electronic agent is any telephonic or computer system that has been established by a seller to accept orders. [p 398]

## Multiple Choice

16. B    Answer B is the correct answer, as electronic mail is the most widely used means of communication over the Internet. Answer A is incorrect, as licensing agreements are not a typical means of communication that are widely used. Answer C is incorrect, as even though chat rooms are popular, electronic mail is more widely used. Answer D is incorrect for the reasons given above. [p 391]

17. B    Answer B is the correct answer, as the court's opinion stated that the Computer Decency Act is a content-based regulation of speech which raised special First Amendment concerns due to its chilling effect on free speech. Also, the criminal nature of the act will stifle communication that might be entitled to protection. Answer A is an incorrect statement in light of the court's analysis in the case. Answer C is incorrect, as the act is not specific nor does it appear to protect our children from sexually oriented speech. Answer D is blatantly incorrect in light of the rationale for the answers given above as well as the court's lengthy reasoning given in the case. [p 390-391]

18. B    Answer B is correct, as the owner of informational rights who transfers rights is the licensor. Answer A is incorrect, as the licensee receives the rights. Answers C and D do not make sense in this question, as even though duties and possible rights might be inferred from the terms obligor and obligee, there is nothing to indicate a license is involved with respect to an oligor and obligee. [p 397]

19. A    Answer A is correct, as the Uniform Computer Information Transaction Act established a uniform, comprehensive set of rules to govern the creation, performance, and enforcement of computer information transactions. Answer B is incorrect, as it does not make any sense. Answers C and D are incorrect for the reasons given above. [p 397]

20. C    Answer C is correct, as one of the functions of the InterNIC is to maintain a "Whois" database of domain names that have been registered. Answer A is incorrect, as this

answer is indicative of an explanation of a business domain name. Answers B and D are incorrect, as they do not make any sense. [p 392]

21. B  Answer B is correct, as cancellation is effective when the canceling party notifies the breaching party of the cancellation. Answer A is incorrect, as it is not the breaching party who notifies of a cancellation when there has been a material breach of a contract. Answer C is incorrect, as it may not be obvious to one or both parties that the contract must be canceled. Answer D is incorrect based on the reasons given above. [p 400]

22. D  Answer D is correct, as a licensor may recover lost profits for a licensee's failure to accept or complete performance of a contract. Answer A is incorrect, as lost wages does not have anything to do with a license agreement. Answer B is incorrect, as unemployment insurance also has nothing to do with a license agreement. Answer D is incorrect, as it does not state the proper type of damages allowed under the law. [p 400]

23. C  Answer C is correct, as the Uniform Computer Information Transactions Act provides that a licensor can use electronic self-help if a breach of the license agreement occurs. Answer A is incorrect, as the Anticybersquatting Consumer Protection Act is aimed at those who register domain names of the famous and hold those names hostage for ransom. Answer B is incorrect, as the Electronic Signature in Global and National Commerce Act recognizes electronic contracts as meeting the writing requirement of the Statute of Frauds. Answer D is incorrect, as the Electronic Communications Privacy Act makes it criminal to intercept electronic communications. [p 400]

24. D  Answer D is correct, as all three answers A, B, and C are correct methods for verifying an electronic signature under this Act. [p 397]

25. C  Answer C is correct, as click-wrap license have been held by courts to be enforceable, and the UCITA provides for their enforceability. Answer A is incorrect, as the terms of this license are generally not negotiable. Answer B is incorrect, as this license is usually provided via a series of dialogue boxes prior to installation of the software. Answer D is incorrect, for the reasons stated above. [p 398]

## Short Answer

26.  Both civil and criminal penalties. [p 403]
27.  The licensee is the party who is granted limited rights or access to intellectual property or informational rights. [p 397]
28.  The Anticybersquatting Consumer Protection Act. [p 393]
29.  A licensor is liable for damages. [p 400]
30.  When the parties agree to it and the limitations are not unconscionable. [p 401]
31.  Cover means "engaging in a commercially reasonable substitute transaction." [p 401]
32.  The aggrieved party may make a demand for adequate assurance of due performance from the other party. [p 399]
33.  The licensee may refuse the tender, accept the tender, or accept any commercially reasonable units and refuse the rest. [UCITA Sec. 704] [p 399]
34.  The Internet is "a collection of millions of computers that provide a network of electronic connections between the computers." [p 389]
35.  Electronic mail, or e-mail is a form of communication via electronic writing between individuals whose computers are connected to the Internet. [p 391]
36.  The Electronic Communications Privacy Act. [p 402]
37.  To oust cybersquatters who register Internet domain names of famous people and companies, holding them hostage for ransom money. [p 393]
38.  The Internet Corporation for Assigned Names and Numbers. [p 392]
39.  A contract that transfers limited rights in informational and intellectual property. [p 397]
40.  Uniform Computer Information Transaction Act (UCITA) [p 397]

# Chapter 16
# FORMATION OF SALES, LEASES, AND E-CONTRACTS

## Chapter Overview

Rules for enforcing agreements and resolving disputes in the exchange of goods developed in the medieval fairs of Europe as the "Law Merchant." These rules were eventually brought into the common law. England codified these rules in 1880, and the U.S. created the Uniform Sales Act in 1906. The Uniform Commercial Code (U.C.C.) was enacted in 1949 as a broad statutory scheme covering commercial transactions. Article 2 and Article 2A of this Act govern Sales and Leases, while the common law continues to cover transactions not addressed in the U.C.C. Sales and Lease contracts, as well as other articles of the U.C.C. are discussed in this chapter.

## Objectives

Upon completion of the exercises in this chapter, you should be able to:

1.   Explain what sales contracts are governed by Article 2 of the UCC.
2.   Explain lease contracts as governed by Article 2A of the UCC.
3.   Apply the principles of good faith and reasonableness as per the UCC
4.   Discuss how sales and lease contracts are formed.
5.   Explain the UCC's additional terms rule and how to apply it to the "battle of the forms"

## Practical Application

You should be able to determine what is necessary and acceptable to form valid sales or lease contracts. Your studies should provide you with the knowledge you need to modify, explain or validate either of these types of contracts should the need arise.

## Helpful Hints

The basic contract principles apply to sales and lease contracts. You should review the basic elements contract formation and add in the principles of sales and lease contracts. The U.C.C. is lenient in forming sales and lease contracts. When you analyze a fact situation, or a contract, it is advisable to read and analyze each line separately so that you do not miss any potential issues.

## Study Tips

### Uniform Commercial Code (UCC)

The UCC is a model act drafted to provide uniform rules for commercial transactions.

- The UCC is organized into articles which each addresses a specific part of commerce.
- The UCC is often revised for changes in modern commercial practice and technology.
- States must adopt the UCC as their commercial law statute before it becomes law
  - Nearly every state has adopted all or most of the UCC.

## Article 2 (Sales)

Louisiana is the only state which has not adopted some version of this Article. It is also applied to sales contracts governed by federal law.

**What Is a Sale?** A sale is the passing of title from a seller to a buyer for a price.

**What Are Goods?** Goods are tangible things that are movable when they are identified.
- Some things that are not considered to be goods are money, bonds, patents, and stocks.
- Land is not a tangible good, as it is not movable.
- Things severable from the land can be goods, such as minerals, structures, and crops.

**Goods versus Services.** Services are not covered under Article 2
- A mixed sale of both goods and services, if the goods dominate the transaction, is covered by Article 2.

**Who Is a Merchant?** Article 2 applies to all sales, regardless of a person's status of being or not being a merchant. Some provisions apply only to merchants, or require greater duty of merchants
- A merchant is defined as
  - Someone who deals in the kind of goods involved in the transaction, or
  - Someone who, by his or her occupation, represents themselves as having knowledge or skill specific to the goods involved in the transaction.

## Article 2A (Leases)

This article applies to personal property leases, which include consumer leases of vehicles or equipment and commercial leases of aircraft and industrial machinery.
- This Article addresses the formation, performance and default of leases.

**Definition of Lease.** A lease is the conveyance of the right to the possession and use of the named goods for a set time period in return for certain consideration.
- The lessor is the person who transfers right of possession and use of goods under a lease.
- The lessee obtains the right to possession and use of goods under a lease.

**Finance Lease.** This lease involves three parties, the lessor, the lessee, and the vendor (supplier).
- The lessor is not a manufacturer or supplier of goods, but still acquires title to the goods or the right to use and possess in connection with the lease terms.

## Formation of Sales, Leases, and E-Contracts:  Offer

An offer and an acceptance are required to form sales and lease contracts. The UCC rules for these elements can be significantly different that those in common law.
- These contracts can be made in any manner that shows agreement, including the conduct.
- An agreement can be found even when the moment of its making cannot be determined.

**Open Terms.** At common law, all necessary terms needed to be in place. The UCC allows gap-filling, where if a term is left open, the courts will look at the parties' intent and determine if there is a reasonably certain basis for giving an appropriate remedy.

- Open Price term – The court will imply a "reasonable price" at the time of delivery.
  - Price can be fixed by a market rate, set by a third party, or by another standard.
    - The price can be fixed either upon delivery or on specified date.
    - If the standard is unavailable, a reasonable price is implied at delivery.
  - The party reserving the right to fix the price must act in good faith.
  - When one of the parties fails to fix the price, the other party may opt to
    - Treat the contract as being cancelled, or
    - Fix a reasonable price.
- Open Payment Term – Payment is due when and where the buyer is to receive the goods.
  - Delivery by title document, payment is due when and where buyer receives title.
- Open Delivery Term – Delivery is to take place at the seller's place of business.
  - Delivery is to be made at the seller's residence if there is no place of business.
  - Delivery is to be made where the goods are located if located elsewhere.
  - The seller must make reasonable shipping arrangements in good faith when the goods are to be shipped by an unnamed shipper,
- Open Time Term – The contract must be performed within a reasonable time.
- Open Assortment Term –Buyer is given option of choosing goods from an assortment.

**UCC "Firm Offer" Rule.** The common law allows offeror to revoke an offer at any time before acceptance, with the exception being an option contract. The UCC also allows the firm offer rule.

- A merchant cannot revoke an offer for the stated time, or a reasonable time, when
  - The merchant offers to buy, sell, or lease goods and
  - Gives a written and signed assurance on a separate form.

**Consideration.** Consideration is required in formation of sales and lease contracts like common law, but the UCC indicates modification of sales and lease contracts needs no consideration.

- Modifications do require the element of good faith.
- Modifications cannot bind the parties when made through fraud, duress, or extortion.

## Formation of Sales and Lease Contracts: Acceptance

At common law and under the UCC, a contract is created when the buyer or lessee sends his or her acceptance to the offeror, not upon receipt.

**Methods of Acceptance.** Acceptance may be accomplished in any manner and by any reasonable medium of acceptance.

- If a buyer makes an offer, then the seller's acceptance is signified by either
  - the seller's prompt promise to ship or
  - his or her prompt shipment of conforming or nonconforming goods.
- Acceptance of the goods by the buyer occurs if after the buyer has a reasonable opportunity to inspect the goods, and either
  - indicates that the goods are conforming, or
  - signifies that he or she will keep the goods regardless of their nonconformity or
  - if he or she fails to reject goods within a reasonable period of time after delivery.

**UCC Permits Additional Terms.** With the common law mirror image rule, acceptance must be on the same terms as the offer, or the acceptance is a counteroffer. The UCC is more liberal, allowing definite and timely expression of acceptance or confirmation to act as an acceptance.
- When both parties are merchants, the additional terms become part of the contract unless
    - the acceptance is expressly conditional on assent to the terms of the offer or
    - the additional terms materially alter the terms of the original contract or
    - the offeror notifies the offeree that he or she is rejecting the additional terms
- When one or both parties are nonmerchants, additional terms are proposed terms.
    - If the terms are accepted, they become part of the contract.
    - If the terms are not accepted, the contract forms from the original offer.

**Accommodation Shipment.** A shipment of nonconforming goods is not considered acceptance if seller reasonably notifies buyer that shipment is being offered as an accommodation to buyer.
- An accommodation shipment is considered a counter offer from the seller to the buyer.
- The buyer can accept or reject the counteroffer.

**"Battle of the Forms."** When negotiating sales contracts, merchants exchange preprinted forms which contain "boilerplate" language that favors the drafter. The offer will contain one set of "boilerplate", the acceptance another set. The UCC provides guidance on which terms will apply.
- Both parties are merchants, additional terms in acceptance become part of contract unless
    - The offer limits acceptance to the terms of the offer, or
    - The terms materially alter the terms of the offer, or
    - The offeror notifies the offeree of his or her objections within a reasonable time.
- There is no contract if additional terms alter terms so much that parties cannot agree.

## UCC Statute of Frauds

Statute of Frauds provisions in the UCC apply to all sales and lease contracts.
- Goods costing $500 or more and lease payments of $1,000 or more must be in writing.
    - The writing must be sufficient to show a contract has been made.
    - The agreement must be signed by the party to be charged.

**Exceptions to the Statute of Frauds.** These sale and lease situations do not have to meet the writing requirement of the Statute of Frauds:
- Specially Manufactured Goods
    - If the good are unsuitable for others in the ordinary course of business.
    - If substantial beginning to manufacture or procurement of goods has been made.
- Admissions in Pleadings or Court
    - If the party to be charged with an oral contract admits in court that a contract was made, the contract is enforceable.
    - The contract can be enforced only for the quantity admitted.
- Part Acceptance
    - If goods have been received and accepted, the contract is enforceable to the extent of those goods.

**UCC Written Confirmation Rule.** If both parties are merchants and one of the parties to the oral contract sends written confirmation within a reasonable time and the other merchant does not object within ten days of his or her receipt of the confirmation, the Statute of Frauds is satisfied.
- The confirmation must be sufficient.
- The party in receipt must have reason to know its contents.

**When Written Modification is Required.** If the parties state that the modification must be in writing, then it has to be.

- In general, an oral modification is sufficient, if it does not violate the Statute of Frauds.

**Parol Evidence.** A rule that states that a written contract is the complete and final expression of the parties' agreement.

- Any prior or contemporaneous oral or written statements to the contract may not be introduced to alter or contradict or add to the written contract.
- Exceptions to the parol evidence rule: When the contract's express terms are unclear, the court may consider as outside sources to clarify the terms of the parties' agreement
  - the course of performance,
  - the course of dealing, and
  - usage of trade.

# Refresh Your Memory

The following exercises will help to test your memory regarding the principles given in this chapter. Read each question twice, then place your answer in the blank provided for each question. Review the chapter material for any questions that you are unable to answer or remember

1.  The _____ _____ _____ is a comprehensive statutory scheme that includes laws that cover most aspects of contract transactions.

2.  Article 2 of the Uniform Commercial Code provides rules to govern the _____ _____ _____.

3.  Article 2A of the Uniform Commercial Code is mainly concerned with _____ _____ _____.

4.  A(n) _____ is the passing of title from a seller to a buyer for a price.

5.  _____ are tangible, movable things at the time of their identification to a contract.

6.  A sale that involves both the provision of a good and a service is called a(n) _____ _____.

7.  A(n) _____ is a person who deals in the goods of the kind involved in the transaction or who holds him- or herself out as having knowledge or skill peculiar to those goods.

8.  A(n) _____ is a transfer of the right to the possession and use of named goods for a set term in return for certain consideration.

9.  The U.C.C. will affix a(n) _____ price to a good if none is stated.

10. If one or both parties to a sales contract are both nonmerchants, any additional terms would be considered _____ _____ to the contract.

11. Oral modifications to sales and lease contracts are binding if they do not violate the

    _____ _____ _____.

12. Part of the _____ _____ rule states that "when a sales or lease contract is evidenced by a writing that is intended to be a final expression of the parties' agreement … the terms of the writing may not be contradicted by evidence…"

13. _____ _____ _____ is the previous conduct of the parties regarding the contract in question.

14. A practice or method of dealing that is generally used in a place, vocation, trade, or industry is known as _____ _____ _____.

15. The maximum time permitted under the firm offer rule is _____ _____.

## Critical Thought Exercise

Apex Mattress Company, for whom you are the vice-president of material acquisition, entered into an oral agreement with Davis Wool Ranch (DWR), a wool supplier, in which DWR agreed to sell Apex 800 bundles of wool, each weighing 350 pounds. Shortly after your conversation with Dan Davis of DWR, you sent Davis an e-mail confirming the terms of the oral contract. Davis did not respond to the e-mail or offer any objection to the terms stated in the e-mail. When the delivery date arrived four months later, you contacted DWR to finalize the delivery terms. DWR stated that there was no agreement and DWR had sold the 800 bundles to Fluffy-Air Mattress because the price of wool had doubled on the open market since the date of the oral agreement. The board of directors of Apex requests that you inform them of your position in regards to bringing suit against DWR and the likelihood that Apex will prevail.

Write a memo to the board setting forth your position and authority for your conclusion.

*Please compose your answer on a separate sheet of paper or on your computer.*

## Practice Quiz

### True/False

1. ____ A lessee is a person who transfers a right of use and possession of goods under a lease.

2. ____ Goods are tangible things, mobile at the time of their identification to the contract.

3. ____ Stocks, bonds, patents and money are intangible goods.

4. ____ Article 2 of the U.C.C. governs equipment, computers and other transactions in goods.

5. ____ Under the UCC, an agreement sufficient to constitute a contract for the sale or lease of goods may be found even if the moment of its making is undetermined.

6. ____ Under a finance lease, the lessor selects, manufactures or supplies the goods.

7. ___ Sale and lease contracts require only an offer and acceptance to be binding.

8. ___ The UCC is very strict with open contract terms.

9. ___ Under the UCC rules, a court will fill in gaps if terms are missing.

10. ___ A seller or buyer who reserves the right to fix a price must do so in bad faith.

11. ___ If Jon, a seller and Nathan, a buyer do not agree on payment terms, payment is due at the time and place Nathan receives the goods.

12. ___ When goods are to be shipped but the shipper is not named, the buyer is obligated to make the shipping arrangements.

13. ___ The firm offer rule states that a merchant who offers to buy, sell, or lease goods and gives a separate signed, written assurance that the offer will be held open cannot revoke the offer for the time stated, or if no time is stated, for a reasonable time, not to exceed three months.

14. ___ Generally, contracts for specially manufactured goods need to be in writing.

15. ___ If an oral modification brings a contract within the Statute of Frauds, then the contract must be in writing in order to be enforceable.

## Multiple Choice

16. Goods for $500 or more and lease payments of $1,000 or more must
    a. be insured.
    b. be in writing.
    c. be inspected.
    d. all of the above.

17. Goods that are severable from real estate include
    a. stocks, patents, bonds.
    b. money, coins.
    c. dental services and legal services.
    d. minerals, structures, and growing crops.

18. Which of the following properly defines what a merchant is?
    a. A person who deals in the good of the kind involved in the transaction.
    b. A person by his or her occupation holds him or herself out as having knowledge or skill peculiar to the good involved in the transaction.
    c. Neither a or b.
    d. answers a and b.

19. Article 2 applies to
    a. merchants.
    b. nonmerchants.
    c. sales contracts.
    d. all of the above.

20. How may the Statute of Frauds requirement be met if both parties to an oral lease or sales contract are merchants?
    a. One of the parties to the oral agreement sends a written confirmation within a reasonable time after contracting and the other party does not give written notice of an objection within 10 days of receiving the confirmation.
    b. One of the parties may send an oral confirmation.
    c. One of the parties to the oral agreement may send a written confirmation.
    d. One of the parties may have his or her agent or broker send an oral confirmation.

21. Suppose Joey's Hardware store contracts to purchase 1,000 wrenches from Ed's Wholesale Hardware Supply Co. The contract is silent as to the assortment of sizes of wrenches. What must Joey's Hardware do when choosing the sizes of wrenches from Ed's stock?
    a. make the selection in good faith and within limits set by commercial reasonableness
    b. ask that the contract guarantee more choices for future transactions
    c. request document of title regardless of whether the goods chosen are actually received
    d. pay for what is chosen and ask that the contract thereafter be cancelled

22. Which of the following does not apply to the firm offer rule?
    a. The rule applies to merchants.
    b. A merchant must give a written and signed assurance on a separate form that the offer will be held open.
    c. A merchant cannot revoke the offer for the time stated.
    d. The maximum amount of time permitted under this rule is six months.

23. Both the common law and the UCC state that a contract is created when
    a. the lessor sends an acceptance to the lessee.
    b. the lessee receives the acceptance from the lessor.
    c. the offeree sends an acceptance to the offeror.
    d. the offeror sends an acceptance to the lessee or buyer.

24. Julie, a buyer offers to purchase 400 pairs of purple gloves from Debbie, a seller. The seller's purple gloves are temporarily out of stock. Debbie sends Julie 400 pairs of red gloves and notifies her that the gloves are being sent as an accommodation. What may Julie do under the circumstances?
    a. not respond to Debbie's substitution of goods.
    b. accept or reject Debbie's counteroffer
    c. She has no choice but to accept the different colored gloves, as the product type remained the same.
    d. none of the above

25. Norman, a veterinarian contracts to purchase dog treats for his patients' owners to purchase from the Eat Right Dog Food Company. Eat Right delivers byproduct dog treats to Norman's office. Norman rejects the dog treats and demands delivery of all natural treats that are specifically formulated for natural digestion. If Norman and Eat Right had prior dealings, what would be the parties' primary source of interpretation of the agreement?
    a. usage of trade
    b. course of performance
    c. the express terms of the parties contract
    d. the usage of the term dog treats in their prior dealings

## Short Answer

26.  What does the lessee acquire under a lease?

_____

27.  What is a finance lease?

_____

28.  What is meant by gap filling rules?

_____

29.  Define the term "goods" as it applies to contracts.

_____

30.  State the mirror image rule.

_____

31.  What is a lease?

_____

32.  How may an offer for a contract for the sale or lease of goods be formed?

_____

33.  Explain the type of acceptance permissible under the Uniform Commercial Code.

_____

34.  The Statute of Frauds requires what types of sales and lease contracts be in writing?

_____

35.  What three situations involving a sales or lease contract will still warrant their enforcement, despite the fact that they are not in writing as per the Statute of Frauds?

_____

36.  What guidance does the U.C.C. provide for deciding cases based on mixed sales?

_____

37.  What are five examples of terms that are commonly left open in sales and lease contracts?

_____

38.  What is the effect of proposed additions to a sales contract between nonmerchants?

_____
_____

39.  When the express terms of written contracts are not clear, reference may be made to which three sources outside the contract?

_____

40.  When is a shipment of nonconforming goods not an acceptance?

_____

# Answers to Refresh Your Memory

1. Uniform Commercial Code  [p 413]
2. sale of goods  [p 414]
3. personal property leases  [p 416]
4. sale  [p 414]
5. Goods  [p 415]
6. mixed sale  [p 415]
7. merchant  [p 416]
8. lease  [p 417]
9. reasonable  [p 419]
10. proposed additions  [p 420]
11. Statute of Frauds  [p 422]
12. parol evidence  [p 423]
13. Course of performance  [p 423]
10. usage of trade  [p 423]
15. three months  [p 419]

# Critical Thought Exercise Model Answer

If both parties to an oral sales contract are merchants, the Statute of Frauds requirement can be satisfied if one of the parties to the oral agreement sends a written confirmation of the sale within a reasonable time after making the agreement and the other merchant does not give written notice of an objection to the contract within 10 days after receiving the confirmation. If both merchants are within the United States, UCC section 2-201(2) will control. If one of the merchants is a foreign entity, then the 1980 United Nations Convention on Contracts for the International Sale of Goods (CISG) will apply. Under the CISG, Article 11, an international sales contract "need not be concluded in or even evidenced by writing and is not subject to any other requirements as to form."

When the confirming e-mail was sent to DWR, they did not respond within a ten-day period or voice any objections to the contents of our e-mail. Modernly, an e-mail can serve as a writing. Thus, Apex had a legally binding contract with DWR. The failure of DWR to tender delivery of the 800 bundles of wool on the delivery date put them in breach. The fact that DWR desired to sell the wool for a larger profit hurts their position and helps us because of the requirement that they deal with us in good faith.

Lastly, we will have to obtain the wool from another source and may be required to pay a premium for the wool because of the urgency that we face due to the actions of DWR. We should be able to recover damages in an amount equal to the difference between the contract price and market price at the time we enter into a new contract with a different wool supplier.

# Answers to Practice Quiz

## True/False

1. False   An individual who transfers the right of possession and use of goods under a lease is called the lessor, not the lessee.  [p 417]
2. True   Goods are tangible things that are mobile (not immobile) at the time of their identification to the contract.  [p 415]

3. True   These are all examples of intangible things. [p 415]
4. True   Article 2 of the UCC governs sales of goods not leases. [p 414-415]
5. True   The UCC provides that an agreement that is adequate to constitute a sale or lease of goods may still be found despite not knowing when it was made. [p 418]
6. False   The lessor acquires title to the good or the right to their possession and use in connection with the terms of the lease. [p 417]
7. False   Under the UCC, sales and lease contracts require an offer, acceptance and consideration to be binding. [p 419]
8. False   The UCC will utilize gap-filling rules when there are missing terms and is very lenient in this area. [p 418]
9. True   As was stated in the previous answer, if there is a missing term, the court will read certain terms into a sales or lease contract if the parties intended to make a contract and there is a reasonably certain basis for giving an appropriate remedy. [p 418]
10. False   UCC 2-305 (2) states that when a seller or buyer reserves the right to set a price, he or she must do so in good faith. [p 419]
11. True   Payment is due at the time and place that Nathan is to receive the goods. [p 419]
12. False   The seller is obligated to make the shipping arrangements where the goods are to be shipped, but the shipper is not named. [p 419]
13. True   UCC 2-205, 2A-205 states requirements and time limits of firm offer rule. [p 419]
14. False   The case of specially manufacture goods is a situation in which a contract will be enforceable despite not being in writing, if the goods are not suitable for sale or lease to others in the ordinary course of the lessor's or seller's business and the seller or lessor has made commitments for their procurement or a substantial beginning of their manufacture. [p 421]
15. False   Modification must be written if contract is brought within Statute of Frauds. [p 422]

## Multiple Choice

16. B   Answer B is correct, as the Statute of Frauds requires goods for $500 or more to be in writing. Answer A is incorrect, it might be a good idea to insure the goods, but it is not a requirement. Answer C is incorrect, as there is no rule that correlates a dollar amount and an inspection. Answer D is incorrect for the reasons given above. [p 421]
17. D   Answer D is correct, as mineral, structures and growing crops are severable as per Article 2 of the UCC. Answer A is incorrect, as stocks, patents and bonds are intangible items that do not fall within the UCC's definition of goods. Answer B is incorrect, as money and coins also do not fall within the UCC's definition of goods. Answer C is incorrect, as contracts for provision of services are not covered by Article 2 of the UCC. [p 415]
18. D   Answer D is correct, as both answer A and answer B correctly define a merchant. Answer C is incorrect, as answers A and B correctly define a merchant. [p 416]
19. D   Answer D is correct as Article 2 applies to merchants and nonmerchants and is primarily concerned with sales contracts, making Answers A, B, and C all correct choices. [p 416]
20. A   Answer A is correct as it properly states the law with regard to merchants and the Statute of Frauds. Answer B is incorrect as sending an oral confirmation will not satisfy the Statute of Frauds. Answer C is incorrect as sending a written confirmation is not enough to satisfy the Statute of Frauds. Answer D is incorrect as sending a party's agent or broker with an oral confirmation is insufficient under the Statute of Frauds. [p 422]
21. A   Answer A is correct based on the UCC's rule concerning open assortment terms. If the assortment of goods to a sales contract is left open, the buyer is given the option of choosing those goods provided that his or her selection is made in good faith and within limits set by commercial reasonableness [ UCCC 2-311 (2) ]. Answers B,C, and D are

incorrect as none of them have any basis in law under the open assortment term of the UCC. [p 419]

22. D   Answer D is correct as the maximum amount of time an offer may remain open under the firm offer rule is three, not six months. Answers A, B, and C all correctly state provisions associated with the firm offer rule. [p 419]

23. C   Answer C is correct as it properly states when a contract is created. Answer A is incorrect, as a lessor cannot send an acceptance to the lessee to create a contract as the lessor is the offeror. Further, the facts are silent whether this is a counteroffer, in which case, the fact would have told you that the lessor was also the lessee. Answer B is incorrect, as it misstates the law that acceptance is effective upon dispatch, not upon receipt under both common law as well as the UCC. Answer D is incorrect for the reasons that Answer A is incorrect. [p 420]

24. B   Answer B is correct since the accommodation offered by Debbie is a counteroffer, Julie as buyer is free to accept or reject Debbie's offer for the different colored gloves. Answer A is incorrect, as silence may be a means of acceptance. However, this answer does not fully state what Julie may do, hence accept or reject under the circumstances. Answer C is an incorrect statement of law. Answer D is incorrect for the reasons given above. [p 420-421]

25. D   Answer D is correct, as the parties had prior dealings with the usage of the terms. Answer A is incorrect, as the question does not concern the parties practice or method of dealing. Answer B is not correct, as the previous conduct of the parties is not in issue. Answer C is incorrect, as the express term of the party's contract do not appear to be clear. As such, these terms must be interpreted. [p 423]

## Short Answer

26. The right to possession and use of goods. [p 417]
27. A three-party transaction with the lessor, the lessee and the vendor (supplier). [p 417]
28. When open terms are read into a sales or lease contract. [p 418]
29. Tangible things that are made moveable at the time of identification to the contract. [p 415]
30. The offeree's acceptance must be the same as the offer. [p 420]
31. A transfer of the right to possession and use of the named goods for a set term in return for a specified consideration. [p 417]
32. A contract for the lease or sale of goods may be made in any manner adequate to show agreement. [p 418]
33. Any reasonable manner or method of communication. [p 420]
34. Contracts for the sale of goods $500 or more and lease contracts involving payments of $1,000 or more must be in writing. [p 421]
35. Specially manufactured goods, admissions in pleadings or court, part acceptance. [p 421]
36. The UCC provides no guidance for mixed sales cases; the courts decide on a case-by-case basis. [p 415]
37. Price, payment, delivery, time, assortment. [p 419]
38. The proposed additions do not constitute a counter-offer or extinguish the original offer. If the additions are accepted by the original offeror, they become part of the contract. If they are not accepted, the contract will be formed with the terms of the original offer. [p 420]
39. Course of performance, course of dealing, and usage of trade. [p 423]
40. When the seller reasonably notifies the buyer that the shipment is offered only as an accommodation to the buyer. [p 420]

# Chapter 17

# PERFORMANCE OF SALES, LEASES, AND E-CONTRACTS

## Chapter Overview

The rights and duties of buyers, sellers, and third parties were defined in common law by who had technical title to goods. Specific rules for the passage of title are given in Article 2 of the Uniform Commercial Code (UCC). The risk of loss at common law was on the party holding title to goods, while Article 2 of the UCC stipulates rules that are not coupled with title. Parties with insurable interests are allowed to insure goods against loss. This chapter looks at title, risk of loss, and insurable interest.

## Objectives

Upon completion of the exercises in this chapter, you should be able to:

1.  Distinguish between shipment and destination contracts and discuss when title passes in each.
2.  Discuss the different shipment and delivery terms.
3.  Identify who bears the risk of loss when goods are damaged or lost in shipment.
4.  Determine who bears the risk of loss when goods are stolen and resold.
5.  Explain the meaning of a good faith purchaser for value.

## Practical Application

You should be able to determine what type of contract has been formed as you analyze shipping terms. You should be able to determine who bears the risk of loss in situations involving damaged, lost or stolen and resold goods. You should gain some familiarity with the laws involving consignments.

## Helpful Hints

You should keep in mind who is receiving the most benefit from type of contract into which the parties are entering. The seller begins with the letter "s" and usually will want a shipment (also begins with the letter "s") contract as the carrier that the goods are placed on will then bear the risk of loss. A buyer will want the contract to be a destination contract as the seller will bear the risk of loss up until the time that the buyer receives the goods. One of the easiest ways to analyze facts in this area is to ask the following questions in the following order:
- Who are the parties?
- Have the goods been identified to the contract?
- Do the parties have a shipment or a destination contract?
- Who bears the risk of loss in light of the type of contract that exists?
- What if anything has happened to the goods?
- Are there any third parties involved? If so, what is their capacity or role in the facts?
- Are there any special rules of law that apply?

# Study Tips

## Identification and Passage of Title

Identification of goods in a contract sets apart those goods from other goods held by seller or lessor.
- The risk of loss remains with the sellor or lessor until they are identified to a contract.
- Title to goods cannot pass to the buyer unless they are identified to a contract.
- The lessor, or a third party, retains title to leased goods.

**Identification of Goods.** This can occur at any time and in any manner. If no time is specified, then the UCC will state when it occurs.
- Already existing goods are identified at the contract's inception.
- Goods that are part of a bulk shipment are identified when specific merchandise is designated.
- Future goods, which do not yet exist and other than corps or livestock, are identified when the goods are shipped, marked, or otherwise designated.

**Passage of Title.** After identification, goods can be transferred to the buyer from the seller.
- Parties can agree on the manner and conditions under which title will pass.
- If the parties do not agree on a specific time, title passes when and where delivery is completed.

**Shipment and Destination Contracts**.
- The seller is obliged to ship the goods to the buyer through a common carrier in a shipment contract.
  - The seller must make suitable shipping provisions.
  - The seller must deliver the goods to the carrier.
  - Title passes to the buyer when and where shipped.
- The seller is obliged to deliver the goods to the buyer's place of business or another specified destination in a destination contract.
  - Title passes to the buyer when and where seller tenders delivery at the proper destination.

**Delivery of Goods Without Moving Them.** Sales contracts can consent to the delivery of goods without the seller having to move them, requiring the buyer to pick up the goods from the seller.
- If a document of title is required, title passes when and where the document is delivered to buyer.
- If no document of title is required and the goods are identified, title passes when and where the contract is made.

## Risk of Loss:  No Breach of Sales Contract

The UCC changes the common law rule that put the risk of loss on the party who held title to goods.
- Parties can agree as to who will bear the risk of loss.
- If the parties fail to agree, the UCC mandates who will bear the risk of loss.

**Carrier Cases: Movement of Goods.** Goods shipped through a carrier are understood to be sent by a shipment contract or a destination contract.
- Sales contracts are presumed to be shipment contracts rather than destination contracts.

*Shipment Contracts.* This requires the seller to ship and deliver goods to the buyer via a common carrier.
- Risk of loss passes to the buyer when conforming goods are delivered to the carrier.

- Creation is accomplished in one of two ways:
  - by using the term shipment contract or
  - using delivery terms such as F.O.B., F.A.S., C.I.F. or C.& F

*Destination Contracts.* This requires the seller to deliver the goods to buyer's place of business or another specified destination.
- Risk of loss does not pass until the goods are tendered at the specified destination.
- The seller is required to replace any goods lost in transit.
- Creation is accomplished in one of two ways:
  - by using the term destination contract or
  - using delivery like F.O.B. place of destination, ex-ship, or no-arrival, no-sale contract.

*Shipping Terms.* Some shipping terms are commonly used.
- F.O.B. (free on board) point of shipment – The seller arranges shipment and delivers goods to carrier. Risk is seller's until the goods are delivered to the carrier.
- F.A.S. (free alongside) or F.A.S. (vessel) port of shipment – The seller delivers and tenders goods alongside the vessel or on the dock. Risk is seller's until this is done.
- C.I.F. (cost, insurance, and freight) and C. & F. (cost and freight) – The seller is responsible for the specified costs. Risk is seller's until goods are loaded.
- F.O.B. place of destination – The seller must tender delivery at the specified destination. Risk is seller's until goods are tendered.
- Ex-ship (from carrying vessel) – The seller must unload the goods at the port of destination. Risk is seller's until this is done.
- No-arrival, no-sale contract – The seller is responsible for transportation. The seller is not required to replace goods that do not arrive.

**Noncarrier Cases: No Movement of Goods.** Sales contracts can stipulate that the buyer is to pick up the goods. The UCC gives two rules for whom bears the risk of loss in this type of arrangement.
- Merchant-Seller – Risk of loss does not pass until the goods are received.
- Nonmerchant-Seller – Risk of loss occurs when there is a tender of delivery of the goods.
  - Seller makes the goods available to the buyer, and
  - Seller notifies the buyer.

*Goods in the Possession of a Bailee.* Goods are sometimes held by a bailee, such as a warehouse, and will be delivered without actually moving them
- The buyer assumes the risk of loss when
  - He or she receives the negotiable document of title, or
  - The bailee recognizes the buyer's right of possession, or
  - He or she receives a nonnegotiable document of title and has a reasonable time to present the document to the bailee to demand the goods.
- The seller retains the risk of loss if the bailee refuses to honor the document of title.

## Risk of Loss: Conditional Sales

Buyers often take possession of goods on a trial basis. These types of transactions are categorized as sales on approval, sales or returns, and consignments.

**Sale on Approval.** A sale does not occur unless the buyer accepts the goods.
- The situation presents itself when a merchant allows a buyer to take the goods home for a specified period of time to determine if it meets the customer's needs.
- Acceptance is shown by:

     o   expressly accepting the goods.

     o   failing to notify the seller of buyer's rejection.

     o   use of the goods inconsistently with the purpose of the trial.

- Risk of loss and title stay with the seller and do not pass until the buyer accepts the goods.
- Goods are not subject to buyer's creditor's claims until buyer accepts them.

**Sale or Return.** The seller delivers the goods to the buyer letting the buyer know that he or she may return them if they are not used or resold within a stated period of time.

- If the buyer doesn't return them within a reasonable time, the goods are considered sold.
- *Risk of loss* and title pass when the buyer takes possession of the goods.
- Buyer's creditors may make claims against the buyer while the goods are in buyer's possession.

**Consignment.** A buyer-consignee sells goods on behalf of the seller-consignor for a fee paid by the seller-consignor if and when the goods sell.

- It is treated as a sale or return.
- If the seller-consignee files a financing statement per Article 9 of the UCC, the goods are subject to claims of the seller-consignor's creditors.
- If the seller-consignee fails to file a financing statement, the goods are subject to the buyer-consigee's creditors.

## Risk of Loss: Breach of Sales Contract

Separate rules for risk of loss apply when there is a breach of a sales contract.

**Seller in Breach.** Breach occurs when the seller tenders nonconforming goods to the buyer.

- If the buyer has the right to reject the goods, the *risk of loss* stays with the seller until the nonconformity or defect is cured or the buyer accepts the non-conforming goods.

**Buyer in Breach.** Breach occurs where the buyer refuses to take delivery of conforming goods, if the buyer repudiates the contract, or otherwise breaches the contract.

- The *risk of loss* rests on the buyer for a commercially reasonable time.
- Buyer is liable for any loss in excess of insurance covered by the seller.

## Risk of Loss: Lease Contracts

The parties may agree who will bear the risk of loss if the goods are lost or destroyed.

- If there is no provision, the UCC states that in an ordinary lease, the *risk of loss* stays with the lessor. If it is a finance lease, then the *risk of loss* passes to the lessee. [UCC 2A-219]
- If tender of delivery of goods fails to conform to the lease contract, the *risk of loss* stays with the lessor or supplier until acceptance or cure. [UCC 2A-220(1)(a)].

**Insuring Against Loss of Goods.** The parties to sales and lease contracts should purchase insurance against loss of goods through damage, destruction, loss or theft.

- A party must have an insurable interest to purchase insurance.
  - o  A seller has this interest while title or security interest in goods is retained.
  - o  A lessor has this interest during the lease term.
  - o  A buyer or lessee has this interest when goods are identified.

## Sales by Nonowners

This category involves individuals who sell goods that they do not have good title to.

**Void Title and Lease: Stolen Goods.** Where the buyer purchases goods from a thief, title to the goods does not pass and the lessee does not require any leasehold interest in the goods.
- The real owner of the goods may reclaim the goods from the buyer or lessee. Title is void.

**Voidable Title: Sales or Lease of Goods to Good Faith Purchasers for Value.** A seller has voidable title to goods if the goods were obtained by fraud, dishonored check, or impersonation of another person.
- An individual with voidable title may transfer good title to goods to a good faith purchaser for value or a good faith subsequent lessee.
- A good faith purchaser for value is one who pays consideration or rent for the goods to one he or she honestly believes has good title to those goods.
- The real owner cannot reclaim the goods from this type of purchaser.

**Entrustment Rule.** If an owner entrusts the possession of his or her goods to a merchant who deals in the particular type of goods, the merchant may transfer all rights to a buyer in the ordinary course of business.
- The real owner cannot reclaim the goods from this type of buyer.

## Refresh Your Memory

The following exercises will help to test your memory regarding the principles given in this chapter. Read each question twice, then place your answer in the blank provided for each question. Review the chapter material for any questions that you are unable to answer or remember.

1. Excluding crops and unborn children, future goods are identified when the goods are _____, _____, or otherwise designated by seller or lessor as goods referred to in the parties' contract.

2. A(n) _____ contract requires the seller to ship goods to the buyer via common carrier.

3. A(n) _____ contract requires the seller to deliver the goods either to the buyer's place of business or to another destination set forth in the sales contract.

4. Sales contracts are presumed to be _____ contracts rather than _____ contracts, unless otherwise indicated.

5. In a shipment contract, the _____ bears the risk of loss during transportation.

6. In a destination contract, the risk of loss does not pass until the goods are tendered to the buyer at a(n) _____ _____.

7. The shipping term C.I.F. stands for _____, _____, and _____, which are costs that the seller is responsible for.

8. A(n) _____ _____ _____ _____ contract requires the seller to bear the expense and risk of loss of goods during transportation, but not to deliver replacement goods.

9. A holder of goods who is not a seller or a buyer is a(n) _____.

10. In a sale on approval, the risk of loss remains with the _____.

11.  A seller breaches a sales contract if he or she tenders _____ goods.

12.  A buyer breaches a sales contract if he or she refuses to _____ _____ of conforming goods.

13.  If the goods are so nonconforming that the _____ has the right to reject them, the risk of loss remains on the _____ until the defect or nonconformity is cured, or the _____ accepts the nonconforming goods.

14.  In the case of an ordinary lease, the risk of loss is kept by the _____.

15.  A seller or lessor has _____ _____ to goods if the goods were obtained by fraud, if a check is later dishonored, or if he or she impersonates another person.

# Critical Thought Exercise

Bristol Physical Therapy (BPT) contracted with Summit Pools, Inc. for the purchase of a "fully installed portable therapy whirlpool" for the sum of $14,000. The price included all labor and parts, but the order form was not itemized. The freight carrier hired by the manufacturer delivered the pool to the parking lot just outside the building occupied by BPT. A receptionist for BPT signed the delivery invoice and immediately called Summit Pools. When the installation crew for Summit Pools arrived five days later to install the whirlpool, it was gone.

In this situation, had the risk of loss of the whirlpool passed from Summit Pools to BPT?

*Please compose your answer on a separate sheet of paper or on your computer.*

# Practice Quiz

## True/False

1.  ___ The Uniform Commercial Code does not have any impact on the time of when the identification of goods occurs.

2.  ___ The buyer or lessee retains the risk of loss of the goods until the goods are identified to the contract.

3.  ___ Goods such as unborn young animals and crops to be harvested can be identified to a contract.

4.  ___ Once the goods exist and are identified, the seller may not pass title to the buyer.

5.  ___ The time and place of passage of title will be different if a document of title is required.

6.  ___ The UCC places the risk of loss of goods on the party who has title to the goods.

7.  ___ The UCC is reluctant to allow the parties to a sales contract too much leniency in determining who will bear the risk of loss if the goods subject to the contract are lost or destroyed.

8.  ___ Sales contracts are recognized as being destination contracts rather than shipment contracts.

9. ___ The delivery terms to a contract do not dictate the risk of loss of goods while they are being transported.

10. ___ Marla's Magnificent Creations, a large Oklahoma clothing manufacturer, places the term, F.O.B. Atlanta when shipping an order of clothes to Tamara's Boutique in Atlanta, Georgia. Marla's will not bear the expense and risk of loss until Tamara's Boutique has the goods tendered upon it.

11. ___ In a consignment situation, the consignee delivers goods to a consignor to sell.

12. ___ A buyer does not breach a sales contract if he or she refuses to take delivery of conforming goods.

13. ___ Betty purchases goods from Slick, a thief who has stolen them. Betty does not acquire title to these goods. However, Slick has a leasehold interest in the goods.

14. ___ A good faith purchaser or lessee for value is someone who pays sufficient consideration or rent for goods to the person he or she honestly believes has good title to those goods.

15. ___ A sale on approval happens when a merchant lets a customer take goods for a specified time to try them out.

## Multiple Choice

16. Future goods that are not yet in existence are identified when
    a. they are conceived or have yet to be harvested.
    b. they are shipped, marked or otherwise designated by the seller or lessor.
    c. they are part of a larger mass of goods.
    d. it is mandated that they be identified.

17. A buyer orders 5,000 toy racecars that light up when pushed along a flat surface. The contract between the parties was a shipment contract. The cars that were shipped were plain racecars that did not have the light up feature. The toy cars are smashed flat while in transit. Who will bear the risk of loss in this situation?
    a. The buyer will as it is a shipment contract passing the risk of loss to the buyer.
    b. The buyer will as he or she did not purchase insurance to cover potential loss.
    c. The seller will as he or she did not ship conforming goods.
    d. Both the buyer and seller are responsible due to the nature of their transaction.

18. Jacob wants to purchase insurance to protect against financial loss in case the goods that he sells are damaged, destroyed, lost or stolen. He is told that he must have an insurable interest in the goods. What does this mean?
    a. He must have a valid driver's license with no convictions against him.
    b. He must retain title or have a security interest in the goods.
    c. He must sell the goods to a good faith purchaser for value.
    d. He must not have an insurable interest at the same time as the buyer.

19. If Joe steals an entire shipment of computers that are owned by Computer City and resells them to Computer Land, who does not know that they are stolen, Computer City may reclaim the goods from Computer Land because
    a. it found out where the goods were located.
    b. Computer Land was a good faith purchaser for value.

    c.   as a seller with an insurable interest in the computers, Computer City is protected.

    d.   Joe had no title in the goods and title was not transferred to Computer Land.

20.   A person to whom a lease interest can be transferred from a person with voidable title is

    a.   a good faith purchaser for value.

    b.   a lessee.

    c.   an insured interested party.

    d.   a good faith subsequent lessee.

21.   A buyer orders 500 musical teapots from a seller. The contract is a shipment contract. The seller ships nonconforming teapots that will not play music when the water becomes heated. The goods are destroyed in transit. Who bears the risk of loss?

    a.   the seller

    b.   the buyer

    c.   both share the risk of loss equally

    d.   the teapot maker

22.   In a sale or return contract, when does the risk of loss and title to the goods pass to the buyer?

    a.   The risk of loss never passes

    b.   The risk of loss passes when the seller takes possession.

    c.   The risk of loss passes when the buyer takes possession of the goods.

    d.   None of the above

23.   When do non-merchant sellers pass the risk of loss to buyers?

    a.   upon acceptance by the buyer.

    b.   upon tender of delivery of goods

    c.   upon presentation of the document of title

    d.   all of the above

24.   Which of the following does not indicate the acceptance of goods?

    a.   A buyer expressly states acceptance of goods.

    b.   A buyer fails to notify the seller of rejection of the goods within the agreed-upon trial period.

    c.   A buyer inconsistently uses the goods with the purpose of the trial.

    d.   A buyer rejects the goods.

25.   When does title pass if the goods named in the sales contract are located at a warehouse?

    a.   Title passes at the inception of the sales contract.

    b.   Title passes after the buyer's check has cleared the seller's account.

    c.   Title may not pass until the goods are removed from the warehouse.

    d.   Title passes when the seller delivers a warehouse receipt representing the goods to the buyer.

## Short Answer

26.   Where does the shipping term F.A.S. require the seller to deliver and tender goods?

_____

27.   When does a sale on approval occur?

_____

28.   When are goods that are part of a larger mass of goods identified?

_____

29. What are future goods?

_____

30. What types of terms signify a destination contract?

_____

31. Who bears the risk of loss if the goods are stolen or destroyed after the contract date and before the buyer picks up the goods from the seller who is a merchant?

_____

32. When do nonmerchant sellers pass the risk of loss to the buyer?

_____

33. What does the Entrustment Rule state?

_____

_____

34. What are the most widely used trade terms in international contracts?

_____

35. What is a good faith purchaser or lessee?

_____

36. What kind of title can a person with voidable title pass to a good faith purchaser?

_____

37. What kind of title can a person with a void title pass to a good faith purchaser?

_____

38. What is a consignment?

_____

_____

39. What does an ex-ship contract require of the seller?

_____

40. When can already existing goods be identified?

_____

# Answers to Refresh Your Memory

1. shipped, marked  [p 432]
2. shipment  [p 432]
3. destination  [p 432]
4. shipment, destination  [p 433]
5. buyer  [p 433]
6. specified destination  [p 433]
7. cost, insurance, freight  [p 434]
8. No-arrival, no-sale  [p 434]

9.  bailee [p 434]
10. seller [p 435]
11. nonconforming [p 436]
12. take delivery [p 436]
13. buyer, seller, buyer [p 436]
14. lessor [p 437]
15. voidable title [p 437]

## Critical Thought Exercise Model Answer

The goods in this case, a whirlpool, had been delivered to the customer and a representative of BPT had signed for the shipment. The whirlpool had been placed on BPT's property by the common carrier. Normally, the risk of loss passes in a shipment contract when the goods are placed with the common carrier. In this case, however, the goods are being resold by Summit Pools to BPT. Thus, the risk of loss will not pass to BPT until they have been delivered to BPT as dictated by the agreement. In this agreement, the goods were to be fully installed as part of the contract and there was no separation of the goods from the installation services in the agreement.

In a mixed goods and services contract, a court will look to see whether the goods or services are the predominant item to be provided. The whirlpool being sold to BPT is considered a portable unit, so the installation services appear to be a secondary purpose in the sales contract. Risk of loss will therefore not pass to BPT until the whirlpool is fully installed as required by the agreement. The theft or loss of the whirlpool unit will fall upon Summit Pools.

## Answers to Practice Quiz

### True/False

1.  False   In the absence of an agreement indicating the time and manner of the identification of goods, the UCC may mandate when identification occurs. [p 432]
2.  False   The goods must be identified before risk of loss and title will pass from the seller to the buyer. [p 432]
3.  True    Unborn young animals are identified at conception and crops to be harvested are identified when the crops are planted or otherwise become growing crops. [p 432]
4.  False   Title to the goods may be transferred from the seller to the buyer once the goods have been identified. [p 432]
5.  True    The time and passage of title does depend on whether the seller is to deliver a document of title. [p 432-433]
6.  False   This was the law under common law not the UCC. The UCC mandates who will bear the risk of loss. [p 433]
7.  False   Article 2 does allow the parties to a sales contract to agree among themselves who will bear the risk of loss if the goods subject to the contract are lost or destroyed. [p 433]
8.  False   Sales contracts are presumed shipment contracts rather than destination contracts. [p 433]
9.  False   The risk of loss of goods while they are being transported depends on the contract and the delivery terms contained therein. [p 432]
10. False   The shipping term F.O.B. Atlanta indicates that the Oklahoma seller intended to create a destination contract whereby Marla's will have to bear the expense and risk of loss until the goods are tendered at Tamara's Boutique in Atlanta, Georgia. [p 434]
11. False   The consignor delivers goods to the consignee to sell. [p 435]
12. False   A buyer's refusal to take delivery of conforming goods is a breach of contract. [p 436]

13. False    Where a buyer buys goods or a lessee leases goods from a thief who has stolen them, the purchaser, in this case Betty, does not acquire title to the goods and the lessee, here Slick, does not acquire a leasehold interest in the goods. [p 437]

14. True    A good faith purchaser for value is someone who pays sufficient (not insufficient) consideration or rent for the goods to the person he or she honestly believes has good title to those goods. [p 438]

15. True    A sale on approval happens when a merchant lets a customer take goods for a specified time to try them out. [p 434-435]

## Multiple Choice

16. B    Answer B is correct, as future goods other than unborn young and harvested crops are identified when the goods are shipped, marked or otherwise designated by the seller or lessor. Answer A is incorrect based on the reasoning given for answer B. Answer C is incorrect, as it is irrelevant whether the future existing goods are part of a larger mass of goods or not. Answer D is incorrect, as it makes it appear that the only time they have to be identified is if it is mandated in an agreement. [p 432]

17. C    Answer C is correct, as the seller bears the risk of loss since he or she shipped nonconforming goods. Answer A is incorrect, as despite the fact that a shipment contract would ordinarily shift the risk of loss once the seller placed the goods with a carrier, the fact that the seller shipped nonconforming goods is enough to have the risk of loss remain with the seller. Answer B is incorrect, as the fact that the buyer did not purchase insurance to cover the potential loss does not exonerate the seller from the fact that he or she shipped nonconforming goods. Answer D is incorrect, as it is an untrue statement since the buyer does not share in the risk of loss when a seller ships nonconforming goods. [p 433]

18. B    Answer B is correct, as it correctly explains what an insurable interest means. Answer A is incorrect, as this answer is referring to insurance one might get for an automobile not with respect to goods being lost, destroyed or damaged. Answer C is incorrect, as selling the goods to a good faith purchaser for value has no bearing on a seller's retention of title and security interest in goods. Answer D is incorrect, as both the buyer, and seller or lessee and lessor can have an insurable interest in the goods at the same time. [p 437]

19. D    Answer D is correct, as the purchaser, Computer Land, does not acquire title to goods thereby making the title void and the goods subject to reclamation by the real owner, Computer City. Answer A is incorrect, as this does not supply the proper reasoning as to why Computer City may reclaim the goods. Answer B is not correct, as the rules applicable to stolen goods as is the case with this fact situation are different than that of a seller having voidable title whereby a good faith purchaser for value is involved which in turn precludes the original owner from reclaiming the goods. Answer C is incorrect, as the insurable interest would provide reimbursement from the insurance company for the loss of the goods verses the right to reclaim the goods. [p 437]

20. D    Answer D is correct, as a good faith subsequent lessee can acquire a lease interest from a person with voidable title. Answer A is incorrect, as the term good faith purchaser for value refers to one paying for goods versus the transferring of a lease interest from a person with voidable title. Answer B is incorrect, as it is only partially correct by the terminology lessee. Answer C is incorrect, as it makes no sense that a lease interest could be transferred from an insured interested party with voidable title. [p 437-438]

21. A    Answer A is correct, as the seller bears the risk of loss because he breached the contract by shipping non-conforming goods. Answer B is an incorrect statement, as the buyer did not ship non-conforming goods. Answer C is an incorrect statement of law. Answer D makes no sense except from a products liability standpoint, which is not the issue for this question. [p 436]

22. C    Answer C is correct, as the risk of loss and title to the goods pass to the buyer when the buyer takes possession of the goods in a sale or return contract. Answer A is an absurd statement, as

risk of loss always passes. Answer B is incorrect, as it is the buyer who would take possession, not the seller. Answer D is incorrect based on the reasons given above. [p 435]

23. B    Answer B is correct, as non-merchant sellers pass the risk of loss to the buyer upon tender of delivery of the goods. Answer A is an incorrect statement of law. Answer C is incorrect, as the presentation of the document of title has nothing to do with non-merchant sellers and the risk of loss. Answer D is incorrect based on the reasons given above. [p 434]

24. D    Answer D is correct, as the buyer's rejection of goods obviously does not signify an acceptance of those goods. Answers A, B, and C are all incorrect, as all indicate acceptance of goods. [p 435]

25. D    Answer D is correct, as UCC 2-401(3)(a) provides that if a document of title is required, title passes when and where the seller delivers the document to the buyer. Answers A, B, and C are all incorrect as they have no basis in law. [p 434]

## Short Answer

26.    Alongside the named vessel or on the dock designated and provided by the buyer. [p 433]
27.    When a merchant allows a customer to take the goods home for a specified time. [p 434-435]
28.    When the specific merchandise is designated. [p 432]
29.    Goods not yet in existence. [p 432]
30.    F.O.B. place of destination, ex-ship, or no-arrival, no-sale contract. [p 433]
31.    A merchant-seller bears the risk of loss between the time of contracting and the time that the buyer picks up the goods. [p 434]
32.    Non-merchant sellers pass the risk of loss to the buyer on tender of delivery of the goods. [p 434]
33.    That if an owner entrusts the possession of his or her goods to a merchant who deals in goods of that kind, the merchant has the power to transfer all rights in the goods to a buyer in the ordinary course of business and the real owner cannot reclaim the goods. [p 438]
34.    The trade terms published by the International Chamber of Commerce called *Incoterms*. [p 440]
35.    Someone who pays sufficient consideration or rent for the goods to the person he or she honestly believes has good title to those goods. [p 438]
36.    A person with voidable title to goods can transfer good title to a good faith purchaser for value. [p 437-438]
37.    A buyer who purchases goods from a thief who has stolen them acquires no title to the goods, as the thief had no title to them. [p 437]
38.    A consignment is where a seller (consignor) delivers goods to a buyer (consignee) to sell. The consignee is paid a fee if the goods are sold on behalf of the consignor. [p 435]
39.    It requires the seller to bear the expense and risk of loss until the goods are unloaded from the ship at its port of destination. [p 434]
40.    These goods are identified when the contract is made and names the specific goods sold or leased. [p 432]

# Chapter 18

# REMEDIES FOR BREACH OF
# SALES, LEASE, AND E-CONTRACTS

## Chapter Overview

The parties to a sales or lease contract are obligated to perform according to their agreement. A general duty to transfer and deliver goods belongs to the seller or lessor. A general duty to accept and pay for the goods belongs to the buyer or lessee. The Uniform Commercial Code provides several remedies to an injured party based on a breach of a sales or lease contract. The performance of obligations and remedies available for a breach are explored in this chapter.

## Objectives

Upon completion of the exercises in this chapter, you should be able to:

1. Describe the seller's and lessor's obligations under a contract.
2. Describe the buyer's and lessee's obligations under a contract.
3. Discuss remedies available to a seller or lessor if a buyer or lessee breaches a contract.
4. Discuss remedies available to a buyer or lessee if a seller or lessor breaches a contract.
5. Discuss agreements and additional terms that could affect remedies of a buyer or seller.

## Practical Application

You should be able to understand what types of obligations are expected of you as a buyer or a seller. You should be able to recognize the remedies that are available to you in the event of a breach of a sales or lease contract if you are a buyer and lessee or a seller and lessor.

## Helpful Hints

You should become familiar with the parties, as well as the concepts that pertain to those parties. You should study the buyer and seller's obligations and the remedies available in the event of a breach by the buyer or seller. The study tips section allows you to learn what each party's obligations are and what remedies are available to each of them in the event of a breach.

## Study Tips

### Seller's and Lessor's Performance

The basic obligation of the seller is to tender delivery in accordance with his or her contract terms with the buyer.

- Tender of delivery requires that the seller or lessor
  - Keep conforming goods at the buyer or lessee's direction and
  - Give buyer or lessee reasonable notice of delivery.
- The parties may agree to the when, where, and how of the delivery.
  - If there is no agreement, delivery must be at a reasonable hour and goods must be kept for a reasonable time.
- Goods must be delivered in one single delivery, unless the parties agree otherwise.
- Payment is due upon tender of delivery.

**Place of Delivery.** The contract may state where delivery is to take place.
- The contract may state that the buyer will pick up the goods.
- If nothing is stated in the contract, the UCC will dictate this term.

*Noncarrier Cases.* If no carrier is involved, then delivery is at the seller's or lessor's business.
- If the parties know the goods are located elsewhere, then that is the place of delivery.
- If the goods are in the possession of a bailee, tender of delivery occurs when the seller:
  - Tenders to the buyer a negotiable document of title, or
  - Produces verification from the bailee of the buyer's right to possession, or
  - Tenders to the buyer a nonnegotiable document of title.
  - All documents must be delivered in correct form.

*Carrier Cases.* If a carrier is involved, it will depend on if the contract is a shipment or a destination contract.
- If it is a *shipment* contract, the seller must deliver the goods to the carrier, obtain proper contract documentation and give the buyer notice.
- If it is a *destination* contract, the seller is required to deliver the goods to the buyer's place of business or wherever is designated in the parties' contract.
  - Delivery must be at a reasonable time and in a reasonable manner accompanied with proper notice and documents of title.

**Perfect Tender Rule.** The seller is under a duty to deliver conforming goods to the buyer.
- If tender is not perfect, the buyer may opt to
  - reject the whole shipment, or
  - accept the whole shipment, or
  - reject part and accept part of the shipment.

*Exceptions to the Perfect Tender Rule.* The UCC changes the perfect tender rule sometimes.
- Agreement of the parties – The parties may agree to limit the application of the perfect tender rule by doing so in their written contract.
- Substitution of carriers – The UCC mandates a commercially reasonable substitute be used if the agreed upon manner of delivery fails or becomes unavailable.
- Cure – If nonconforming goods are delivered, the UCC gives the seller the chance to cure the defective delivery
  - If the time for performance has not expired or the lessor gives the buyer notice that he or she will make a conforming delivery within the time frame stated in the parties' contract.
  - If the seller reasonably believed the delivery would be accepted, the seller or lessor may have additional time to substitute a conforming tender.

**Installment Contracts.** One that requires or authorizes the goods to be accepted or delivered in separate lots.
- The UCC alters the perfect tender rule by letting the buyer reject the entire contract if the noncomformity with respect to any installment(s) basically impairs the entire contract.
- The buyer or lessee may reject any nonconforming installment that cannot be cured.
- The court will view installment contracts on a case-by-case basis.

**Destruction of Goods.** If the destruction of goods is not the fault of either party and the goods have been identified to the contract, the contract will be void.
- If the goods are partially destroyed, the buyer may then inspect and accept the goods or treat the contract as void.
  - If the buyer opts to accept, compensation will be adjusted accordingly.

**Good Faith and Reasonableness.** These two principles rule the performance of lease and sales contracts and apply to both the buyer and the seller.
- There is a higher standard of good faith for merchants than for nonmerchants.
  - Nonmerchants must meet a subjective standard of honesty.
  - Merchants must meet an objective standard of fair dealing in the trade.
- Reasonableness is not specifically defined, but is defined by reference to the course of dealing, the course of performance, or usage of trade.

## Buyer's and Lessee's Performance

The basic obligation of the buyer, if proper tender of delivery is made to the buyer or lessee, is to accept and pay for the goods as per the parties' contract or as mandated by the UCC in the event that there is no contract.

**Right of Inspection.** The buyer has the right to inspect goods that are tendered, delivered or identified to the contract.
- If the goods are shipped, inspection will be at the time the goods arrive.
- If the goods are nonconforming, the buyer may reject the goods and not pay for them.
- Parties may agree as to time, place and manner of inspection.
  - If there is no agreement, then it must be at a reasonable time, place and manner.
    - Reasonable by common usage of trade, prior course of dealings, etc.
  - If the goods conform to the contract, buyer pays for the inspection.
  - If the goods are nonconforming, the seller pays for the inspection.
- C.O.D. deliveries are not subject to buyer inspection until the buyer pays for the goods.

**Payment.** Goods that are accepted must be paid for when the goods are delivered, even if the delivery place is the same as the place where the goods are shipped.
- Goods paid for on credit have a credit period that begins to run from the time that the goods are shipped.
- Goods may be paid for using any acceptable method of payment unless the agreed upon terms involve cash only.
  - If cash is all that a seller will accept from the buyer, then the buyer must be given extra time to procure the cash.
  - Payment by check is conditioned on the check being honored

**Acceptance.** This occurs after the buyer has had a reasonable chance to inspect the goods and takes actions to accept the goods or acts inconsistently with the ownership rights of the seller.

- The buyer must indicate acceptance:
  - o The buyer must communicate to the seller that the goods are conforming or will be accepted despite nonconformity.
  - o The buyer does not reject the goods within a reasonable time.
- Acceptance is for commercial units only.
  - o Commercial usage defines what is embodied in a commercial unit.
  - o Acceptance of any part of a commercial unit is acceptance of the whole.

**Revocation of Acceptance.** Once goods have been accepted, the buyer or lessee can revoke it.
- If the goods are nonconforming,
- The nonconformity is substantial enough to impair the value of the goods, and
- One of the following is present:
  - o The seller or lessor's promise to cure is not met,
  - o The acceptance was made prior to the discovery of the nonconformity, which was difficult to discover, or
  - o The acceptance was made prior to the discovery of the nonconformity and the seller or lessor made assurances that the goods were conforming.
- The seller or lessor must be notified before revocation is effective.
  - o It must occur within a reasonable time.
  - o It must occur before there is substantial damage to the goods.

## Seller's and Lessor's Remedies

The seller and lessor have several remedies if the buyer or lessee breaches the contract.

**Right to Withhold Delivery.** Delivery of the goods may be withheld if the seller is in possession of the goods when the buyer or lessee is in breach.
- If there has been a partial delivery of the goods when the breach occurs, then the seller or lessor may withhold delivery of the remaining part of the goods.
- A buyer or lessee's insolvency will also justify a seller or lessor's withholding of delivery of the goods under the contract.

**Right To Stop Delivery of Goods in Transit.** Goods are in transit when they are in the carrier-bailee's possession.
- If a buyer is discovered to be insolvent while the goods are in transit, the seller may stop the goods while in transit.
- If the buyer or lessee repudiates the contract, delivery can be withheld only if it is a carload, a planeload or a truckload.
- Notice to the carrier or bailee is required.
- The seller must hold the goods for the buyer after the delivery has been stopped.

**Right to Reclaim Goods.** Reclamation refers to a seller or lessor's right to demand the return of goods from the buyer or lessee under certain situations.
- Where the buyer is insolvent, seller has 10 days to demand the return of the goods.
- Where the buyer has misrepresented his or her solvency in writing three months before delivery or presents a check that is later dishonored, reclamation may occur at any time.
- Requirements of reclamation include:
  - o Written notice to the buyer or lessee
  - o Refraining from self-help if the buyer refuses.
  - o Use of legal proceedings must be instituted.

**Right to Dispose of Goods**. If the buyer or lessee breaches or repudiates before the seller or lessor disposes of the goods, then the seller may release or resell goods and recover damages from the buyer or lessee.

- Disposition of the goods must be in good faith and in a commercially reasonable manner.
    o Disposition may be as a unit or in parcels and publicly or privately.
    o Notice must be given.
- Damages incurred as a result of disposition are measured by the disposition price and the contract price.
    o Incidental damages may also be recovered.

*Unfinished Goods.* If a sales or lease contract is breached or repudiated before the goods are finished the seller can:

- Stop manufacturing of the goods and resell them for scrap or salvage value or
- Complete the goods and resell, release or otherwise dispose of them, or
- Recover damages from the buyer or lessee.

**Right to Recover the Purchase Price or Rent**. The UCC allows a seller to sue the buyer for the purchase price or rent as provided in the parties sale or lease contract.

- This remedy is available when:
    o Buyer or lessee accepts the goods but does not pay for them when the rent is due.
    o The buyer or lessee breaches the contract after the goods have been identified to the contract and the seller or lessor cannot dispose of or sell the goods.
    o The goods are damaged or lost after the risk of loss passes to the buyer or lessee.
- The seller must hold the goods for the buyer after the delivery has been stopped.
    o If the seller resells the goods, the amount received must be credited against the judgment procured against the buyer.
    o The seller or lessor may recover incidental damages.

**Right to Recover Damages for Breach of Contract**. A cause of action to recover damages caused by the breach of contract may be brought where the buyer or lessee repudiates a sales or lease contract or wrongfully rejects tendered goods.

- The measure of damages is the difference between the contract price and the market price at the time and place where the goods were delivered plus incidental damages.
    o If this does not place the seller in a position as though the contract was performed, the seller may recover lost profits that would have resulted from full performance plus an allowance for reasonable overhead and incidental damages.

**Right to Cancel a Contract**. The seller or lessor may cancel the contract if the buyer or lessee breaches the contract by revoking acceptance of the goods, rejects the contract or fails to pay for the goods or repudiates all or any part of the contract.

- The cancellation may apply to the entire contract or to only the affected goods.
- The seller or lesser who notifies the buyer or lessee of the cancellation is discharged from any further obligations under the contract.
    o He or she may seek damages against the buyer or lessee for the breach.

## Buyer's and Lessee's Remedies

The buyer or lessee also has many remedies available to him or her upon the breach of a sales or lease contract by the seller or lessor.

**Right to Reject Nonconforming Goods or Improperly Tendered Goods**. If tender of delivery fails, buyer may reject or accept the whole, or accept any commercial unit and reject the rest.
- A buyer who rejects nonconforming goods must identify the defects that are able to be determined by a reasonable inspection.
- Rejection must be within a reasonable time after delivery and in a reasonable manner.
- The seller must be notified.
- The buyer must hold the goods for a reasonable period of time.

**Right to Recover Goods from an Insolvent Seller or Lessor**. If the buyer makes a partial payment to the seller and the seller or lessor becomes insolvent within ten days of the first payment, the buyer or lessee may recover the goods from the seller or lessor.
- This is called capture.

**Right to Obtain Specific Performance**. When the remedy at law is inadequate and the goods are unique, the buyer or lessee may ask for specific performance of the sales or lease contract.

**Right to Cover**. The buyer or lessee may cover if the seller or lessor fails to make delivery of goods or repudiates the contract or the buyer or lessee rightfully rejects the goods or justifiably revokes their acceptance.
- Renting or purchasing substitute goods accomplishes covering.
- A buyer or lessee may sue the seller or lessor to recover damages, which is the difference of the cost of cover and the contract price or rent.
    - A buyer or lessee may also recover incidental and consequential damages.

**Right to Replevy Goods**. A buyer or lessee may recover scarce goods wrongfully withheld by a Seller or lessor by demonstrating that he or she was unable to cover or the attempts to cover will not come to fruition.
- This remedy is only available as to goods identified to the lease or sales contract.

**Right to Cancel a Contract**. Failure to deliver conforming goods, repudiation of the contract by the seller, rightful rejection of the goods, or justifiable revocation of goods that were accepted, all may enable the buyer to cancel with respect to the affected goods or the whole contract if the breach is material in nature.

**Right to Recover Damages for Nondelivery or Repudiation**. The buyer or lessee may recover damages that equate to the difference between the contract price and the market price, along with incidental and consequential damages, less expenses saved if a seller or lessor fails to deliver the goods or repudiates the sales or lease contract.

**Right to Recover Damages for Accepted Nonconforming Goods**. A buyer may seek to recover damages from any loss as a result of the nonconforming goods accepted from the seller.
- Incidental damages as well as consequential damages may be recovered.
- The buyer must give notice of the nonconformity to the seller within a reasonable time of when the breach should have been discovered.

## Additional Performance Issues

Articles 2 and 2A of the Uniform Commercial Code (U.C.C.) have several provisions performance of sales and lease contracts.

**Assurance of Performance**. If one party has reasonable grounds to believe that the other party either will not or cannot perform his or her contractual obligations, the other party may demand assurance for performance in writing.

- The aggrieved party may suspend his or her own performance if it is commercially practicable to do so until the assurance is forthcoming from the potential wrongdoer.

**Anticipatory Repudiation**. The repudiation of a lease or sales contract by one of the parties before the date set for performance.

- Simple wavering of performance does not equate to anticipatory repudiation.
- The aggrieved party may:
    o Await performance for a commercially reasonable time or
    o Treat the contract as breached at the time of the anticipatory repudiation.
    o Both remedies allow the aggrieved party to suspend performance.
- An anticipatory repudiation may be retracted before the aggrieved parties performance is due if the aggrieved party has not:
    o Cancelled the contract or
    o Materially changed his or her position or
    o Otherwise stated that the repudiation is viewed as final.
    o Retraction may be made by any method as long as the intent to perform the contract is clearly expressed.

**Statute of Limitations**. Under the UCC, an action for breach of any written or oral sales or lease contract must be within four years.

- The parties can agree to a one-year statute of limitations.
- It cannot be extended beyond four years.

**Agreements Affecting Remedies.** The parties can agree to additional or substituted remedies to those contained in the UCC.

- Preestablished damages - These are called liquidated damages, which act as a substitute for actual damages.

# Refresh Your Memory

The following exercises will help to test your memory regarding the principles given in this chapter. Read each question twice, then place your answer in the blank provided for each question. Review the chapter material for any questions you are unable to answer or remember.

1.   If the parties have no agreement respecting the time, place and manner of delivery, tender must be made at a(n) _____ hour and the goods must be kept _____ for a reasonable period of time.

2.   In noncarrier cases, the place of delivery is the _____ _____ _____ place of business.

3.   _____ contracts require delivery to be tendered at the buyer's place of business or other specified location.

4.   A seller or lessor is obligated to deliver _____ goods.

5.  The UCC gives a seller or lessor who delivers nonconforming goods a chance to _____ the nonconformity.

6.  A(n) _____ contract requires or authorizes goods to be delivered and accepted in separate lots.

7.  The buyer or lessee has the right to _____ goods that are tendered, delivered, or identified prior to accepting or paying for them.

8.  _____ is due from a buyer when and where the goods are delivered, even if that is the same as the place of shipment.

9.  Buyers and lessees may only accept delivery of a(n) _____ _____.

10. The buyer may reject the goods if a(n) _____ delay or loss is caused by seller's failure to make a proper contract for the shipment of goods or properly _____ the buyer of the shipment.

11. If a buyer pays for goods by check, payment is _____ upon the check being honored when it is presented to the bank for payment.

12. A buyer or lessee may _____ goods from a seller or lessor who is wrongfully withholding them.

13. The buyer or lessee may _____ the sales or lease contract if the seller or lessor fails to deliver conforming goods or repudiates the contract.

14. If John, a party to a contract, has reasonable grounds to believe that Sophie, the other party, will not perform her contractual obligations, a(n) _____ _____ of due performance may be demanded in writing.

15. A pre-established substitute for actual damages is _____ damages.

## Critical Thought Exercise

Sanco Corporation agreed to sell two seven-ton diesel forklifts to Agro-Star, Inc., for $250,000, with an option to purchase four more at $500,000. The forklifts were to be installed in a produce cooling warehouse according to specific design and performance standards. Sanco did not deliver and Agro-Star covered by purchasing different forklifts from Power Arm Lifts for $200,000, plus an additional $300,000 for testing and development by Power Arm Lifts. Agro-Star also bought the four additional lifts that they needed from Power Arm Lifts for $350,000. At trial, Agro-Star is awarded $250,000, the difference between Sanco's price for the first two forklifts and the cost of the first two Power Arm forklifts.

As an officer in Sanco Corporation, you must decide whether to pay the judgment or pay an additional $20,000 in attorney's fees and appeal the judgment. Will you authorize the appeal? Why? Is it fair for Sanco to benefit from a bargain struck by Agro-Star when they covered?

*Please compose your answer on a separate sheet of paper or on your computer.*

# Practice Quiz

## True/False

1. ____ If Eb's Furniture Store calls Charlene Jones at 2:00 a.m. to let her know the delivery truck will be at her home in 30 minutes, Charlene does not have to allow Eb to tender delivery of the goods.

2. ____ If goods are delivered in lots, payment is calculated by the entire delivery.

3. ____ If a seller or lessor does not have a place of business, then the place of delivery is the warehouse where the goods are kept.

4. ____ Under a shipment contract, one thing that the seller must do is put the goods in the buyer's possession and contract for the safe and proper transportation of the goods.

5. ____ In a destination contract, delivery of the goods is to be tendered at the seller's place of business or other location designated in the sales contract.

6. ____ A contract is void if identified goods to a lease or sales contract are totally destroyed through no fault of either party before the risk of loss passes to the buyer or lessee.

7. ____ The parties' prior course of dealing, common usage of trade and the overall circumstances are not considered by the court in determining reasonableness with respect to the buyer's right to inspection.

8. ____ Buyers who agree to C.O.D. deliveries are not entitled to inspect the goods before paying for them.

9. ____ Payment is usually due from a buyer where and when the goods are delivered even if the place of delivery is the same place of shipment.

10. ____ The repudiation of a sales or lease contract by one of the parties after the date set for performance is known as anticipatory repudiation.

11. ____ A buyer contracts to purchase 2,500 tires from a tire manufacturer with delivery set for May 1 and partial payment due March 1. In February the buyer learns that automobile sales have decreased by 38% and assembly line workers have been laid off in the small plant in which he would need the tires. The tire manufacturer contacts the buyer and wants a written demand for adequate assurance on February 18. The buyer fails to give adequate assurance of performance. The tire manufacturer has no recourse and must wait until March 1 when partial payment is due before it can do anything.

12. ____ Delivery of goods may be withheld if the seller or lesser is in possession of them when the buyer or lessee breaches the contract.

13. ___ Liquidated damages are invalid if they are reasonable for the anticipated or actual harm caused by the breach, the difficulties of proving loss, and nonfeasibility of obtaining an adequate remedy.

14. ___ The U.C.C. statute of limitations states that an action for breach of any written or oral sales or lease contract must begin within one year after the cause of the action accrues.

15. ___ Replevin actions are only available as to goods identified in a sales or lease contract.

## Multiple Choice

16. The perfect tender rule is altered when
    a. the parties to the sales or lease contract agree to limit the effect of the rule.
    b. the buyer or lessee rejects the whole shipment of goods.
    c. the buyer or lessee rejects part of the shipment of goods.
    d. the buyer or lessee accepts the entire shipment of goods.

17. Rachel contracted for a crystal chandelier from Phoebe, a crystal dealer. Phoebe agrees to deliver the chandelier to Rachel's home. The truck delivering the chandelier breaks down and the chandelier is stolen while the delivery driver has walked away trying to find help. What effect does the theft of the chandelier have on the parties' agreement?
    a. The risk of loss had already passed to Rachel and she is responsible for payment.
    b. The risk of loss stays with Rachel, but she can get her insurance to cover the damage.
    c. The risk of loss is shared between both parties as the situation involved a thief which requires both parties to share the cost of the damages.
    d. The risk of loss had not yet passed to Rachel and as such, the contract is voided and she does not have to pay for the chandelier.

18. If Jaclyn's Fine Vases begins manufacture of 50 vases all of which have a sculpted form of sea life on them and the buyer, a tourist shop on the ocean, goes out of business before the goods are finished, Jaclyn, the seller, may choose to
    a. open up the buyer's business and try to sell the vases herself.
    b. stop manufacturing the goods and resell them for scrap or salvage value.
    c. use self-help in reclaiming what is due her under the parties' agreement.
    d. obtain an injunction against the buyer to prevent him or her from contracting with her again.

19. A buyer enters into a sales contract to purchase a rare pink diamond ring with a platinum band for $1.3 million. When the buyer tenders payment, the seller refuses to sell the rare ring to the buyer. What type of action may the buyer bring in order to get the ring?
    a. The buyer may bring an action for damages.
    b. The buyer is out of luck and will have to find another jeweler.
    c. The buyer may bring an equity action to obtain a decree of specific performance from the court ordering the seller to sell the ring to the buyer.
    d. The buyer may bring an action in tort for embezzlement.

20. A buyer or lessor who rightfully covers may sue the seller or lessor to recover
    a. the difference between the cost of cover and the contract price or rent.
    b. incidental damages.
    c. consequential damages less expenses saved.
    d. all of the above.

21. The measure of damages a buyer or lessor may recover for a seller or lessor's failure to deliver the goods is
    a. an equitable decree of specific performance.
    b. the difference between the contract price and the market price at the time the buyer or lessee learned of the breach.
    c. the difference between the market price and the contract price at the time the buyer or lessee learned of the breach.
    d. a set amount that is preestablished by using a liquidated damages clause.

22. The UCC provides if goods identified in a sales or lease contract are totally destroyed without fault of either party before risk of loss passes to buyer or lessee, the contract is
    a. void.
    b. voidable.
    c. valid.
    d. all of the above

23. A buyer contracts to buy a red and purple striped, fully loaded corvette for $33,000. When the seller tenders delivery, the buyer refuses to accept the corvette or pay for it. The seller, in good faith and in a commercially reasonable manner, resells the corvette to a third party for $29,000. Incidental expenses of $400 are incurred on the resale. What can the seller recover from the original buyer?
    a. Nothing, as the seller ultimately sold the corvette.
    b. $33,400.
    c. $4,400.
    d. $29,400.

24. What recourse does a buyer or lessee have against a seller or lessor who is wrongfully withholding goods that were identified in the parties sale or lease contract?
    a. The buyer may ask for an injunction.
    b. The buyer may ask for cancellation of the contract
    c. The buyer may bring an action for replevin to recover the goods from the seller.
    d. none of the above.

25. If a seller or lessor fails to deliver goods or repudiates the sales or lease contract, what is the measure of damages that the buyer or lessee may recover?
    a. The buyer may recover the contract price.
    b. The buyer may recover the difference between the contract price and the market price at the time the buyer or lessee learned of the breach.
    c. The buyer may recover incidental and consequential damages, less expenses saved.
    d. Both b and c.

## Short Answer

26. What is an installment contract?

_____

27. What do the initials C.O.D. stand for when used as part of a shipment form?

_____

28. What is a commercial unit?

_____

29. List at least two things must occur in order for a revocation by the buyer to be effective.

_____
_____

30. When may adequate assurance of due performance be demanded of one party by the other?

_____
_____

31. A seller or lessor who discovers that the buyer or lessee is insolvent before the goods are delivered may refuse to deliver as promised unless what?

_____

32. What is the measure of damages a seller or lessor may recover when disposing of goods?

_____

33. What is reclamation?

_____

34. What are the remedies designed to do for the aggrieved party?

_____
_____

35. What is the seller's or lessor's basic obligation under a sales or lease contract?

_____

36. What are liquidated damages?

_____

37. When may a buyer or lessee cancel a sales or lease contract?

_____
_____

38. What must the buyer or lessee show in a replevin action?

_____

39. When may a buyer or lessee obtain specific performance of a sales or lease contract?

_____

40. When may a seller or lessor cancel a sales or lease contract?

_____
_____

# Answers to Refresh Your Memory

1. reasonable, available  [p 447]
2. seller's or lessor's  [p 448]

3.  Destination  [p 448]
4.  conforming  [p 449]
5.  cure  [p 449]
6.  installment  [p 450]
7.  inspect  [p 452]
8.  Payment  [p 452]
9.  commercial unit  [p 452]
10. material, notify  [p 448]
11. conditional  [p 452]
12. recover (replevy)  [p 457]
13. cancel  [p 457]
14. adequate assurance  [p 459]
15. liquidated  [p 460]

# Critical Thought Exercise Model Answer

Yes, I will authorize the appeal.  Under UCC 2-715, the remedy of cover allows the buyer, on the seller's breach, to purchase the goods, in good faith and within a reasonable time, from another seller and substitute them for the goods due under the contract.  If the cost of cover exceeds the cost of the contract goods, the breaching seller will be liable to the buyer for the difference, plus incidental and consequential damages.

In our case, the cost of the contracted forklifts was to be $750,000.  Agro-Star had to pay only $550,000 for the forklifts, plus the incidental damages of $300,000 for further testing and development.  By exercising their right of cover, Agro-Star only suffered damages of $100,000.  The cost of the appeal is only $20,000 and we will likely have the award reduced by $150,000.

It is both fair and ethical for us to take advantage of the cover rule.  The purpose of contract damages is to put the non-breaching party in the same position they would have been if the breach had not occurred.  Damages awarded after the non-breaching party has covered make the buyer whole while avoiding a punitive result to the seller.

# Answers to Practice Quiz

## True/False

1.  True    Charlene does not have to allow Ed the opportunity to fulfill his obligation in that tender must be at a reasonable hour, of which 2:00 a.m. would not be considered reasonable for a furniture delivery.  [p 447]
2.  False   Goods correctly delivered in lots may have payment apportioned for each lot.  [p 450]
3.  False   If a seller or lessor does not have a place of business, then the place of delivery is the seller or lessor's residence.  [p 448]
4.  False   The safe and proper transportation of goods as well as putting the goods in the carrier's transportation is one of the obligations of a seller.  [p 448]
5.  False   Tender of delivery in destination contracts is either the buyer's place of business or other place specified in the parties' contract.  [p 448]
6.  True    If goods that are identified to a lease or sales contract are totally destroyed without either party being at fault before the risk of loss passes to the buyer or lessee, the contract is void.  [p 451]

7. False   The court will consider common usage of trade, prior course of dealings between the parties, and other types of similar factors in determining reasonableness as it pertains to a buyer's right to inspection. [p 452]

8. True   Buyers are not entitled to inspection of goods before paying for them when he or she has agreed to cash on delivery (C.O.D.) deliveries. [p 452]

9. True   The place in which goods are delivered, even if it is the same as the place of shipment, is the place where payment is due from the buyer. [p 452]

10. False   Repudiation of a lease or sales contract by one of the parties prior to the date set for performance is known as anticipatory repudiation. [p 460]

11. True   The tire manufacturer does have recourse as he or she may suspend performance and treat the sales contract as repudiated. [p 459]

12. True   Delivery of the goods may be withheld if the lessor or seller is in possession of them when the lessee or buyer is in breach of the contract. [p 453]

13. False   Liquidated damages are valid if they are reasonable for the anticipated or actual harm caused by the breach, the difficulties of proving loss, and nonfeasibility of obtaining an adequate remedy. [p 460]

14. False   The U.C.C. statute of limitations states an action for breach of written or oral sales or lease contract must begin within four years after cause of action accrues. [p 460]

15. True   Replevy is only available for goods identified in a sales or lease contract. [p 457]

## Multiple Choice

16. A   Answer A is the correct answer, as the UCC alters the perfect tender rule when parties agree to limit the effect of it or in cases of a substitution of carriers. Answers B, C, and D are all incorrect answers, as they pertain to buyer's remedies in certain situations. [p 449]

17. D   Answer D is the correct answer, as the risk of loss had not passed to Rachael. The contract is voided and she does not have to pay for the chandelier. Answer A is incorrect, as the facts are indicative of a destination contract wherein a buyer does not assume the risk of loss until the goods are delivered. Here the goods were not delivered as the chandelier was stolen. Answer B is incorrect, as once again, the risk of loss had not passed. Further, the fact that she has insurance, though a nice benefit, does not assist in the allegation of the risk of loss passing to her, as it did not. Answer C is incorrect, as it is a misstatement of law. [p 451]

18. B   Answer B is the correct answer, as the UCC provides for cessation of the manufacturing of goods where the buyer or lessee has breached or repudiated the contract before the goods are finished. Answer A is incorrect, as this is not an option under the UCC where unfinished goods are involved. Answer C is incorrect, as self-help is also not an option that the seller or lessor has under the UCC. Answer D is incorrect, as an injunction would not be a proper remedy for a sales contract situation. [p 454]

19. C   Answer C is the correct answer, as the good, a rare pink diamond with a platinum band, is unique and the remedy at law would be inadequate. Therefore, the buyer or lessee may obtain specific performance of the sales or lease contract. Answer A is incorrect, as damages would not be an adequate remedy in light of the unique nature of the good. Answer B is incorrect, as it is an untrue statement. Answer D is incorrect, as embezzlement is not a proper cause of action to bring in light of the facts, as the parties involved do not have an employer/employee relationship and the facts state that the parties have a contract to purchase a good (the ring), the fact of which would not establish any element necessary for the tort of embezzlement. [p 457]

20. D   Answer D is the correct answer, as answers A, B, and C all state the remedies available to a buyer or seller who rightfully covers. [p 457]

21. B  Answer B is the correct answer, as a buyer may recover the difference between the contract price and the market price at the time the buyer learns of the breach when a seller or lessor fails to deliver the goods. Answer A is incorrect, as the remedy of specific performance does not involve damages. Answer C is incorrect, as it is worded backwards of the true remedy as stated in answer B. Answer D is incorrect, as liquidated damages would need to be in the parties agreement and liquidated damages are not a standard measure of damages that is available to buyers and lessors who want to bring a cause of action against sellers and lessees for a failure to deliver goods. [p 458]

22. A  Answer A is the correct answer, as the UCC states that if goods identified in a sales or lease contract are totally destroyed without the fault of either party before the risk of loss passes to the buyer or the lessee, the contract is void. Answers B,C, and D are all incorrect based on the reason given above. [p 451]

23. C  Answer C is the correct answer, as the seller can recover $4,400 from the original buyer: the $4,000 difference between the resale price and the contract price and $400 for incidental expenses. [p 454]

24. C  Answer C is the correct answer, as a buyer or lessee may replevy goods from a seller or lessor who is wrongfully withholding them. Answers A, B and D are incorrect, as the inappropriate remedies are given. [p 457]

25. B  Answer B is the correct answer, as the measure of damages is the difference between the contract price and the market price at the time the buyer or lessee learned of the breach. Answers A and C do not state the correct measure of damages and are therefore incorrect. Answer D is incorrect based on the reasoning given above. [p 458]

## Short Answer

26. An installment contract requires or authorizes goods to be delivered and accepted in separate lots. [p 450]

27. A C.O.D. shipment is where the buyer agrees to pay cash on delivery of the goods. [p 452]

28. A commercial unit is a unit of goods that commercial usage deems is a single whole for purposes of sale. [p 452]

29. It must be shown that the goods are nonconforming and the nonconformity substantially impairs the value of the goods to the buyer or lessee. [p 453]

30. An adequate assurance of performance may be demanded of a party if one party to the contract has reasonable grounds to believe that the other party either will or cannot perform his or her contractual obligations. [p 459]

31. The buyer or lessee pays cash for the goods. [p 453-454]

32. A seller may recover the difference between the disposition and contract price. [p 454]

33. Reclamation is the right of a seller or lessor to demand the return of goods from the buyer or lessee under certain situations. [p 453-454]

34. The remedies are designed to place the injured party in as good of a position as if the breaching party's contractual obligations were fully performed. [p 447]

35. To transfer and deliver goods to the buyer or lessee. [p 447]

36. Liquidated damages are established in advance as a substitute for actual damages. [p 460]

37. When a seller or lessor fails to deliver conforming goods, repudiates the contract, or if the buyer or lessee rightfully rejects the goods or justifiably revokes acceptance. [p 457]

38. That he or she was unable to cover or that attempts at cover will be unavailing. [p 457]

39. When the goods are unique or the remedy at law is inadequate.[p 457]

40. If the buyer or lessee breaches the contract by rejecting or revoking acceptance, failing to pay, or repudiates all or part of the contract. [p 455]

# Chapter 19

# WARRANTIES AND PRODUCT LIABILITY

## Chapter Overview

After centuries ruled by *caveat emptor,* or let the buyer beware, the law acknowledged that those who purchased and leased goods should have better protection. Warranties give assurance that the goods meet specific standards, and the Uniform Commercial Code (U.C.C.) and other laws allow the buyer or lessee to sue for their breach. If a product is defective, causing injury, the injured party can recover damages through various tort theories referred to as products liability. This chapter discusses sales and lease warranties and tort principles that permit recovery for injuries caused by defective products.

## Objectives

When you have completed the exercises in this chapter, you should be able to:

1. Identify and describe express and implied warranties.
2. Discuss the concept of strict liability.
3. Determine which parties may be held liable for injuries that are a result of a defective product.
4. Compare and contrast the difference between a manufacture, design and packaging defect.
5. Compare defects associated with a failure to warn and a failure to provide sufficient instructions.
6. Recognize and be able to state applicable defenses in product liability lawsuits.

## Practical Application

You should be able to recognize the different types of legal theories and their elements when confirming a basis for a product liability lawsuit. You should be able to identify the party against whom liability should be assessed, apply potential defenses, and be familiar with the types of damages available.

## Helpful Hints

You should review the concepts of negligence and misrepresentation learned in previous chapters. You should learn the duties that are owed by those who manufacture and sell or lease products that are defective. You should review the necessary elements for the causes of action in a product liability lawsuit and the proper parties against whom suit should be brought.

## Study Tips

### Express Warranty

These warranties are the oldest type, created by the affirmation of a seller or lessor that the goods he or she is selling provide certain levels of quality, performance, condition, or meet a specific description.

- These warranties can be verbal, written, or by inference.
- These warranties can be made by mistake, as they do not require intent.
- These warranties are often made to entice purchase of a product.
- Creation requires an indication that the goods will conform to one of the following:
  o All promises or facts made in regards to the goods.
  o Any description of the goods.
  o Any model or sample of the goods.

**Basis of the Bargain.** If an express warrant was a contributing factor which induced a buyer to purchase or lessee to lease the product, the buyer or lessee can recover for breach.
- The UCC does not define this term so courts apply the concept broadly.
- All statements by the seller or lessor made prior to or contemporaneously with the making of the contract are presumed part of the basis of the bargain, unless shown to the contrary.
- Statements that modify the contract, but made post sale, are part of the basis of the bargain.
- A retailer is liable for any express warranties made by manufacturers of the goods it sells.
  o A manufacturer must authorize or ratify express warranties made by retailers or wholesalers to be held liable.

**Statements of Opinion.** Express warranties can arise from the negotiations between the buyer and seller or lessor and lessee.
- Praise of the goods, or puffing, made by the seller or lessor do not create an express warranty.
  o It is not always easy to distinguish between statements of opinion, which are puffing, and statements of fact, which are warranties.
  o Affirming the value of goods does not create an express warranty.

**Damages Recoverable for Breach of Warranty.** The buyer or lessee can sue the seller or lessor to recover compensatory damages for a breach of warranty.
- The measure of damages is usually the difference between the value of the goods as warranted and the actual value of the goods.
- Recovery can be made for any personal injuries resulting from the breach of warranty.

## Implied Warranties

The law can imply warranties in the sale or lease of goods. Common forms of these warranties include those for merchantability, fitness for human consumption, and fitness for a particular purpose.

**Implied Warranty of Merchantability.** In the case of merchants, the sales contract will contain an implied warranty of merchantability, unless it is expressly disclaimed. This implied warranty does not apply to nonmerchants or casual sales.
- The goods must be fit for the ordinary purposes for which they are used.
- The goods must be adequately contained, packaged, and labeled.
- The goods must be of an even kind, quality, and quantity within each unit.
- The good must conform to any promise or affirmation of fact made on the container or label.
- The quality of the goods must pass without objection in the trade.
- Fungible goods, like grain or ore, must meet a fair average or middle range of quality.

**Implied Warranty of Fitness for Human Consumption.** This warranty was implied at common law to food products and is incorporated within the Uniform Commercial Code (UCC) under the implied warranty of merchantability, with application to food and drink consumed on or off premises.

- Foreign substance test – A food product is unmerchantable when a foreign object in that product causes injury.
- Consumer expectation test – This test is based in what expectations a consumer would have as to the specific product and any dangers it might contain.

**Implied Warranty of Fitness for a Particular Purpose.** Goods must meet the buyer's or lessee's expressed needs.
- The seller or lessor must have reason to know the specific purpose for which the goods are being purchased or leased.
- The seller or lessor must make assurance that the goods will serve this purpose.
- The buyer or lessee must rely on the seller or lessor's skill and judgment.

# Warranty Disclaimer

Disclaimers and limitations of warranties can be made.
- An express warranty can be limited only if the disclaimer and the warranty can reasonably be construed together.
- Disclaimers of implied warranties must include language that clarifies that there are no implied warranties and may be verbal or written.
    - Sales of used products often use terms such as "as is", "with all faults", etc.
    - Without this language, the term "merchantability" must be specified to disclaim the implied warranty of merchantability.
    - General language, rather than the specific term "fitness", can disclaim the implied warranty of fitness for a specific purpose.

**Conspicuous Display of Disclaimer**. Valid written disclaimers must be obvious to a reasonable person.

# Product Liability

Tort actions to recover damages can be brought by those who are injured by products or by the heirs of those killed by products.
- Traditional tort theories, such as negligence and misrepresentation, can be used, as well as the theory of strict liability.
- Plaintiffs can recover compensatory damages and, sometimes, punitive damages.

**Negligence.** An action for negligence can be brought by a person injured by a defective product.
- The plaintiff must first establish that a duty was owed and thereafter breached by the defendant.
- The plaintiff must show the defendant was the actual and proximate cause of his or her injuries.
- Only the party who was actually negligent is liable.
- The plaintiff and defendant do not need to have privity of contract.
- The plaintiff generally must prove that the defendant was negligent.

**Misrepresentation.** A plaintiff bringing a lawsuit based on misrepresentation will do so because of the fraud associated with the quality of the product.
- Only those who relied on the misrepresentation and thereafter suffered injury may bring a cause of action under this tort.
- The plaintiff must show that the seller or lessor made a misrepresentation concerning the product's quality or did not reveal a defect in the product.
- Manufacturers, sellers and lessors are potential defendants for this type of cause of action.

# Strict Liability

The Doctrine of Strict Liability removes many difficulties for the plaintiff caused by other theories.

**Liability Without Fault.**  The basis behind strict liability is to impose liability regardless of fault.
- Strict liability is imposed on lessors and sellers in the business of leasing and selling products.
  - A seller can be found strictly liable even after exercising all possible care in the preparation and sale of a product.
- Casual sellers are exempt from the facet of being in the business of leasing and selling products.
- Strict liability involves products and not services.
  - The court will look at the prevalent element in order to determine whether or not strict liability applies.

**Liability of All in the Chain of Distribution.**  All manufacturers, distributors, wholesalers, retailers, lessors, manufacturers of sub-components may be held strictly liable for injuries caused by the product.
- It is presumed sellers and lessors will spread the cost to consumers by increasing product prices.
- If one or more of the parties in the chain of distribution are held liable in a strict liability lawsuit, the parties may seek indemnification by bringing a separate cause of action against the negligent party.

**Parties Who Can Recover for Strict Liability.**  Strict liability is a tort doctrine that applies whether or not the injured party had a contractual relationship with the defendant.
- Sellers and lessors are liable to the ultimate user or consumer, which include the purchaser or lessee, family members, guests, employees, customers, and passive beneficiaries.
- Bystanders have had this protection statutorily extended to them.

**Damages Recoverable for Strict Liability.**  Various types of damages are available under strict liability.
- Damages for personal injury, with some jurisdictions limiting the dollar amount of the award.
- Damages for property damage, which is recoverable in most jurisdictions.
- Damages for lost income, which is recoverable in some jurisdictions.
- Punitive damages, if the plaintiff can show that the defendant intentionally injured him or her or acted with reckless disregard for his or her safety.

# Defective Product

To recover in strict liability, the injured party must show injury was caused by a defective product.
- They do not have to prove who caused the defect.
- They can name multiple product defects.
- The most common defects are those in manufacture, design, and failure to warn.

**Defect in Manufacture.**  A failure on the manufacturer' part to properly assemble, test or check the product's quality.

**Defect in Design.**  This defect involves the application of a risk-utility analysis.
- The court will weigh several factors:
  - The gravity of the danger from the design
  - The likelihood that injury will result from the design
  - The availability and expense of producing a safer design
  - The utility of the design

*Crashworthiness Doctrine.* The courts have held that automobile manufacturers have a duty when designing automobiles to consider the possibility of a second collision from within the automobile.
- A failure to protect occupants from foreseeable dangers may result in a strict liability lawsuit.

**Failure to Warn.** Manufacturers and sellers have a duty to warn users about the dangerous aspects.
- The warning must be clear and conspicuous on the product.
- A failure to warn may subject those in the chain of distribution to a strict liability lawsuit.

**Defect in Packaging.** A manufacturer has a duty to design and provide safe packages for their products so that they are either tamperproof or indicate if they have been tampered with.
- This type of defect has particular application in the pharmaceutical industry.

**Failure to Provide Adequate Instructions.** The seller is charged with providing adequate instructions so that assembly and use of the product can be done safely.

*Other Defects.* There are other defects that can give rise to a strict liability cause of action, such as the failure to safely assemble a product, failure to adequately test a product or select proper component parts or materials, and failure to properly certify the product.

**Punitive Damages.** A court can award these damages when a defendant's conduct was made with intent or was in reckless disregard of human life.
- These damages are meant to punish and send a message that such behavior will not be tolerated.

## Defenses to Product Liability

There are several defenses that may have applicability in a product liability lawsuit.

**Generally Known Dangers.** Some products are inherently dangerous and are known to be so by the general public.
- Sellers are not strictly liable for failing to warn of these dangers.

**Government Contractor Defense.** A Government contractor must show that the government provided precise specifications for the product, that the contract did in fact conform to those specifications, and that the government was warned by the contractor of any known product defects or dangers.

**Assumption of the Risk.** A defendant may utilize this defense by showing that the plaintiff knew and appreciated the risk involved and voluntarily assumed the risk; this defense is narrowly applied by courts.

**Misuse of the Product.** The main aspect the defendant must prove is that the plaintiff has abnormally misused the product and that such misuse was unforeseeable.
- If the misuse was foreseeable, the seller of the product will remain liable.

**Correction of a Product Defect.** A manufacturer who discovers that a product is defective is required to notify purchases and users of the defect and correct the defect, frequently by recalling the product and repairing or replacing the product. If a user ignores the warning and fails to have the defect corrected, this can be raised as a defense by the seller.
- The seller must make reasonable efforts to notify purchasers and users of the defect and how to have the defect corrected.
- Courts have held that notice is effective even against users who did not see the notice.

**Supervening Event.** No liability exists if the product is materially altered or modified after it leaves the sellers possession and the modification or alteration causes the injury.

- A supervening event removes liability from all prior sellers in the chain of distribution for strict liability.

**Statute of Limitations and Statute of Repose.** A failure to bring a cause of action within the allowed time frame will relieve the defendant of liability.

- Many jurisdictions hold the statute of limitations begins to run when the plaintiff suffers injury.
- Other states have created statutes of repose that limit the liability a seller has by setting a time frame in terms of years from when the product was initially sold.

**Contributory Negligence and Comparative Fault.** If a person is found to have been negligent in contributing to his or her own injuries, this will not prevent him or her from recovering in a strict liability cause of action, as it would under an ordinary negligence cause of action.

- Courts have applied the defense of comparative negligence to strict liability cases, as well as to negligence actions, thereby apportioning the damages on the negligence of each of the parties.

# Refresh Your Memory

The following exercises will help to test your memory regarding the principles given in this chapter. Read each question twice, then place your answer in the blank provided for each question. Review the chapter material for any questions that you are unable to answer or remember.

1. A(n) _____ _____ is created when a seller or lessor represents that the goods he or she is selling or leasing meet certain standards of quality, description, performance, or condition.

2. Under the _____ _____ _____ _____ goods must be fit for the ordinary purposes for which they are used.

3. Using the _____ _____ _____, a food product is unmerchantable if a foreign object in that product causes injury to a person.

4. Warranties can be _____ or limited.

5. Persons injured by products can rely on several traditional tort theories, such as _____ and _____ _____ of the defendant.

6. All parties in the _____ _____ _____ of a defective product are strictly liable for injuries caused by the product.

7. When examining a design defect, the court will apply the _____ _____ analysis.

8. The defense of _____ _____ bars an injured plaintiff from recovering from the defendant in a negligence action.

9. The doctrine of comparative negligence says that a plaintiff who is contributorily negligent for his or her injuries is responsible for a(n) _____ _____ of the damages.

10. When a manufacturer fails to adequately check the quality of the product, this is considered to be a defect in _____.

11. A(n) _____ _____ analysis involves weighing the gravity of the danger posed by a product's design against the utility of the product.

12. If an automobile manufacturer fails to design an automobile to protect the passengers from foreseeable dangers caused by a second collision, the _____ and the _____ are subjected to a lawsuit based on strict liability.

13. If a manufacturer of Get Well Quick drugs places its tablets into bottles that a child could easily twist the cap off of, it may have breached the duty to provide _____ _____ for its products.

14. If Peter leases a boat and the front end is too weighted from the materials used to construct it thereby causing it to sink its first time in the water, Peter may utilize _____ _____ laws in order to recover for the design defect.

15. A(n) _____ and _____ warning placed on the product protects those in the chain of distribution from strict liability.

## Critical Thought Exercise

Bruce Owens bought a Chevrolet Suburban from General Motors Corp. (GMC). Four years later, Owens crashed into the rear of another car while commuting to work. The speed of Owens' vehicle at the time of the crash was estimated to be less than 35 miles per hour. A properly functioning seatbelt will restrain the driver from impacting the steering wheel and the windshield during a crash at 40 miles per hour. During the crash, the seatbelt that Owens was properly wearing broke away from its anchor, causing Owens to be thrust against the steering wheel and into the windshield. Owens received a fractured skull, broken ribs, and a fractured left ankle. Owens sued GMC, Chevrolet, and the dealership that sold the vehicle to him. Owens claimed in his suit that because the seat belt broke, the defendants were strictly liable for his injuries. Investigation determined that the seatbelt anchor was both inadequate to sustain the forces involved in restraining a person during a crash and had been installed in a manner that increased the likelihood of failure during a crash.

Are the defendants strictly liable to Owens?

*Please compose your answer on a separate sheet of paper or on your computer.*

## Practice Quiz

### True/False

1. ___ If a person is injured by a defective product, he or she may not bring a cause of action for negligence against the negligent party.

2. ___ Since most respectable manufacturers, sellers and lessors purposefully misrepresent the quality of their products, misrepresentation is used very often as a basis for a product liability lawsuit.

3. ___ Most states have not adopted the doctrine of strict liability in tort as a foundation for product liability actions.

4. \_\_\_ Strict liability, like negligence, does require the injured person to prove that the defendant breached his or her duty of care.

5. \_\_\_ If Ronnie's Rafts fails to provide a booklet regarding the safe use or assembly of its products, Rhonda Rapids may bring a strict liability cause of action against Ronnie's Rafts for failure to provide adequate instructions, if she is injured.

6. \_\_\_ Everyone in the chain of distribution of a defective product may be held strictly liable for the injuries caused by the product.

7. \_\_\_ There does not have to be privity of contract between the plaintiff and the defendant in a strict liability cause of action.

8. \_\_\_ Bystanders are not afforded the protection of strict liability.

9. \_\_\_ A plaintiff may recover property damage in a strict liability action.

10. \_\_\_ A defendant who is not negligent but who has to pay a strict liability judgment can bring a separate action against the negligent party in the chain of distribution.

11. \_\_\_ Economic loss, such as lost income, is never recoverable in strict liability actions.

12. \_\_\_ A defect in manufacturer occurs when the manufacturer properly tests a product.

13. \_\_\_ Express warranty represents that goods are fit for the ordinary purposes for which they are used

14. \_\_\_ With the consumer expectation test, a food product is unmerchantable if a foreign object in that product causes injury to a person.

15. \_\_\_ Written disclaimers of warranty must be conspicuously displayed to be valid.

## Multiple Choice

16. Under the doctrine of comparative negligence, a plaintiff who is contributorily negligent for his or her injuries is responsible for
    a. a small share of the damages.
    b. a proportional share of the damages.
    c. only the property damage that may have resulted.
    d. replacement of part of the product.

17. Punitive damages are usually allowed in a strict liability action if the plaintiff can prove that
    a. jurisdictions have judicially or statutorily extended protection of strict liability to bystanders.
    b. property damage is recoverable in most jurisdictions.
    c. the defendant either intentionally injured him or her or acted with reckless disregard of his or her safety.
    d. sellers and lessors are liable to the ultimate user or consumer.

18. Which of the following would not be considered a defect in manufacture?
    a. A failure to properly assemble a product.
    b. A failure to place a product in tamperproof packaging.
    c. A failure to properly test a product.
    d. A failure to adequately check the quality of the product.

19. A manufacturer that makes a defective product and thereafter discovers the defect must
    a. notify users and purchasers of the defect and correct the defect.
    b. know and appreciate the risk and voluntarily assume the risk.
    c. file a complaint in accordance with its state's statute of limitations.
    d. prove that the plaintiff has abnormally misused the product.

20. Which doctrine establishes a duty of an automobile manufacturer to design an automobile to account for the possibility of harm from a person's body striking something inside the automobile in case of a car accident?
    a. The collision doctrine
    b. The doctrine of res ipsa loquitur
    c. The negligence per se doctrine
    d. The crashworthiness doctrine

21. Who may be able to recover for his or her injuries as a result of a product's defect?
    a. Sellers, lessors and manufacturers
    b. Purchasers, lessees, users or bystanders
    c. Anyone who witnesses the defect causing the injuries
    d. All of the above

22. Drug manufacturers owe a duty to
    a. place their products on shelves out of a child's reach.
    b. provide nicely packaged containers for their drugs.
    c. properly design easy to swallow pills.
    d. place their products in containers that cannot be opened by children.

23. Which of the following statements are true of the implied warranty of merchantability?
    a. The goods must be fit for the unforeseen purposes for which they are used.
    b. The goods must be inadequately contained, packaged, and labeled.
    c. The quality of the goods must pass with objection in the trade.
    d. None of the above.

24. The implied warranty of fitness for a particular purpose requires that
    a. The seller or lessor has reason to know the particular purpose for which the goods will be used.
    b. The seller or lessor makes a statement that the goods will serve that purpose.
    c. The buyer or lessee relies on the statement and buys or leases the goods.
    d. All of the above.

25. Which of the following tort theories can be relied on by persons injured by products?
    a. Anticipatory repudiation.
    b. Punitive liability.
    c. Negligence.
    d. None of the above.

## Short Answer

26. If a computer manufacturer fails to place instructions on how to put together its brand of computer, and a buyer gets injured from overloading the system due to an improperly installed plug, the consumer may claim that the product defect was the manufacturer's

27. The defense that acknowledges that certain products are inherently dangerous and are known to the general population to be so is known as

_____

28. Who may be sued under the doctrine of strict liability in tort?

_____

29. What doctrine says that automobile manufacturers are under a duty to design automobiles to take into account the possibility of a second collision?

_____

30. When won't sellers of inherently dangerous products be held liable for failure to warn?

_____

31. What is used to determine whether or not the defense of product misuse is effective?

_____

32. What effect does a supervening event have with regard to a product liability action?

_____

33. What type of defect exists if a drug manufacturer fails to place its product in a childproof container?

_____

34. What type of defect exists if a manufacturer constructs a toy with removable parts that are eventually swallowed by five-year old Tommy Toodles?

_____

35. In a strict liability cause of action, what must an injured party show with regard to the product that caused his or her injury?

_____

36. What is contributory negligence?

_____

37. What is comparative fault?

_____

38. What is a statute of repose?

_____

39. What is the Doctrine of Supervening Event?

_____

40. What is the government contractor defense?

_____
_____

# Answers to Refresh Your Memory

1. express warranty  [p 469]

2.  implied warranty of merchantability  [p 472]
3.  foreign substance test  [p 473]
4.  disclaimed  [p 476]
5.  negligence, material misrepresentation  [p 478]
6.  chain of distribution  [p 480]
7.  risk-utility  [p 484]
8.  contributory negligence  [p 496]
9.  proportionate share  [p 496]
10. manufacture  [p 482]
11. risk-utility  [p 484]
12. manufacturer, dealer  [p 486]
13. safe packaging  [p 490]
14. strict liability  [p 483]
15. proper, conspicuous  [p 487]

# Critical Thought Exercise Model Answer

In order to establish strict liability, Owens must establish the following requirements:
(1) *The defendant must sell the product in a defective condition.* The anchor was unable to perform as intended because it was poorly designed and was also installed incorrectly. Either reason makes the product defective. (2) *The defendant was in the business of selling this product.* GMC, Chevrolet, and the dealership are all in the business of selling Suburbans. (3) *The product must be unreasonably dangerous to the user because of its defect.* A vehicle without a safely functioning seatbelt that can properly restrain a passenger during a crash is very dangerous. There is no valid reason for a manufacturer not to install a working seatbelt. (4) *The plaintiff must incur physical injury.* Owens was severely injured. (5) *The defective condition must be the proximate cause of the injury.* We know that Owens was propelled into the steering wheel and windshield because the seatbelt did not restrain him. The speed of the crash was within limits where the seatbelt should have worked properly. (6) *The goods must not have substantially changed from the time of sale to the time of injury.* There are no facts showing any modification to the seatbelt while owned by Owens.

All of the elements needed to establish strict liability for the defective product are present. When a product is defective, all defendants in the chain of distribution, from the manufacturer to the distributor to the dealer, have joint and several liability for the injury to plaintiff. Owens may recover against all the defendants in this case.

# Answers to Practice Quiz

## True/False

1.  False   A successful plaintiff will have proved that the defendant breached a duty of due care to the plaintiff that caused the plaintiff's injuries. Examples of a failure to exercise due care include negligent inspection or testing of the product, negligent packaging, failure to warn of the product's dangerous propensities, negligent product design, and a failure to assemble the product carefully. [p 479]
2.  False   Most manufacturers, lessors or sellers have integrity when they sell their products and do not misrepresent the quality of their products, thereby minimizing the use of fraud as a means of recovery for a product liability action. [p 480]
3.  False   Use of strict liability as a basis for product liability actions has eliminated many of the difficulties associated with the other causes of action of products liability. [p 480]

4. False   Strict liability is imposed regardless of fault.  [p 480]
5. True    Failure to provide adequate instructions for the safe assembly and use of a product subjects those in the chain of distribution to strict liability.  [p 491]
6. True    All who are in the chain of distribution are strictly liable.  [p 480]
7. True    Privity of contract is not required between the plaintiff and defendant because strict liability is a tort defense.  [p 482]
8. False   Bystanders are afforded protection in strict liability cases in most state statutes.  [p 482]
9. True    Property damage may be recovered in a majority of jurisdictions.  [p 482]
10. True   A defendant who is made to pay a strict liability judgment, but who is not negligent, can bring a separate action against the negligent party in the chain of distribution in order to recover its losses.  [p 480]
11. False  A few jurisdictions do allow recovery for economic loss, such as lost income.  [p 482]
12. False  A defect in manufacturer occurs when the manufacturer fails to properly test a product not when the manufacturer properly tests a product.  [p 482]
13. False  An express warranty represents that goods meet certain standards of quality, description, performance, or condition.  [p 469]
14. False  With the foreign substance test, a food product is unmerchantable if a foreign object in that product causes injury to a person.  [p 474]
15. True   Written disclaimers of warranty must be conspicuously displayed to be valid.  [p 476]

## Multiple Choice

16. B   Answer B is correct, as the principle behind comparative negligence is to apportion damages between the plaintiff and the defendant.  Answer A is incorrect, as this is presuming that the plaintiff's negligence was proportionately less than that of the defendant and that the damages would be reduced only slightly.  Answer C is incorrect, as the plaintiff's liability under a comparative negligence statute would include other damages besides property damage as a result of the plaintiff's negligence.  Answer D is incorrect, as it is under the assumption that the plaintiff's negligence was as a result of failing to replace a part of the product.  [p 496]
17. C   Answer C is correct, as punitive damages are designed to punish those who acted maliciously or with a wanton or reckless disregard for the plaintiff.  Answer A is incorrect, as judicial and statutory extensions of protection have no correlation to when punitive damages are allowed.  Answer B is incorrect, as property damage is not the basis of punitive damages.  Answer D is incorrect because punitive damages may be assessed if malice is shown.  However, proving a seller or lessor's liability to an ultimate user or consumer is not equivalent to a wanton or reckless disregard for a plaintiff.  [p 482]
18. B   Answer B is correct, as it describes a defect in packaging as opposed to a defect in manufacture.  Answers A, C, and D are incorrect as all state defects in manufacture.  [p 482]
19. A   Answer A is correct, as it reiterates what the law requires with regard to notifying consumers and users of defects discovered by the manufacturer.  Answer B is incorrect, as the explanation for the defense of assumption of the risk does not apply to the duties placed on a manufacturer upon discovery of a defective product it has produced.  Answer C is incorrect, as the filing of a complaint by a manufacturer who discovered a defect in one of its products is not required to file a complaint as a result of its discovery.  Answer D is incorrect, as abnormal misuse is a potential defense in a products liability lawsuit, not a requirement of proof upon discovery of a manufacturing defect by the manufacturer.  [p 494]
20. D   Answer D is correct, as the crashworthiness doctrine, which is also referred to as the second collision, requires manufacturers to design automobiles with the possibility of a second collision.  Answer A is incorrect, as being crashworthy and the concept of collision by itself are not synonymous.  Answer B is incorrect, as res ipsa loquitur means 'the thing speaks for itself" and is helpful in establishing negligence in a variety of cases, of which the duty to design an automobile taking into account the possibility of harm are contradictory to one another.  Answer C is

incorrect, as negligence per se is also a special negligence doctrine that has its basis in statutory law that is designed to protect a described class of people against a specific type of act. [p 486]

21. B   Answer B is correct, as purchasers, lessees, users and bystanders are those who are protected under product liability law. Answer A is incorrect, as sellers, lessors and manufacturers are in the chain of distribution of a product that makes them prone to liability for injuries resulting from a defective product. Answer C is incorrect, as witnessing is not the same concept as being injured as a bystander and would therefore not be able to recover based on mere observation of the defect causing injuries. Answer D is incorrect for the reasons given above. [p 469]

22. D   Answer D is correct, as the drug manufacturer has a duty to package their products in tamperproof packaging. Answer A is incorrect, as even though this may be a cautionary measure on the manufacturer's part, it is not a duty that if breached would give rise to a cause of action based on product liability. Answer B is incorrect, as the marketing of a manufacturer's drug by use of nicely packaged containers is also not a duty that if reached would give rise to a cause of action based on product liability. Answer C is incorrect, as the manufacturer has no duty to properly design easy to swallow pills. [p 490]

23. D   Answer D is correct, as none of the statements A, B, or C are correct. Correct statements for the implied warranty of merchantability are: the goods must be fit for the ordinary purposes for which they are used; the goods must be adequately contained, packaged, and labeled; and the quality of the goods must pass without objection in the trade. [p 472]

24. D   Answer D is correct, as all three statements A, B, and C are correct. [p 474]

25. C   Answer C is correct, as negligence theory can be used to bring an action for product liability. Answer A is incorrect, as anticipatory repudiation is a contract term. Answer B is incorrect, as punitive liability is a nonsense term. Answer D is incorrect for the above reasons. [p 478]

## Short Answer

26. failure to provide adequate instructions. [p 491]
27. generally known dangers. [p 493]
28. Manufacturers, distributors, wholesalers, retailers, lessors and subcomponent manufacturers. [p 480]
29. The crashworthiness doctrine. [p 486]
30. With generally known dangers. [p 487]
31. whether the misuse was foreseeable. [p 494]
32. It absolves all prior sellers in the chain of distribution from strict liability. [p 494]
33. A defect in packaging. [p 490]
34. A design defect. [p 483]
35. The product was defective. [p 482]
36. Contributory negligence bars a plaintiff who is injured by a defective product if that person contributed to his or her own injuries. [p 496]
37. Comparative fault apportions damages between plaintiff and defendant according to fault. [p 496]
38. A statute of repose limits the seller's liability to a certain number of years from the date when the produce was first sold. [p 495]
39. The original seller is not liable if the product is materially altered or modified after it leaves seller's possession and the alteration or modification causes an injury. [p 494]
40. A government contractor must prove that the precise specifications for the product were provided by the government, that the product conformed to these specifications, and that the contractor warned the government of any known defects or dangers of the product. [p 493-494]

# Chapter 20
# NEGOTIABILILTY
# AND TRANSFERABILITY

## Chapter Overview

Modern commerce could not function without negotiable instruments such as checks and promissory notes. These instruments can be transferred to other parties by negotiation. This chapter looks at the types and creation of negotiable instruments, the negotiation of these instruments, and the types of indorsements used in their creation.

## Objectives

Upon completion of the exercises in this chapter, you should be able to:

1. Differentiate between a negotiable and a nonnegotiable instrument.
2. Discuss drafts and checks and name the parties to these instruments.
3. Explain promissory notes and certificates of deposit and name the parties to these.
4. Explain the difference between instruments payable to order and payable to bearer.
5. Discuss the process for indorsing and transferring negotiable instruments.
6. Differentiate between blank and special indorsements.

## Practical Application

This chapter will help you to better understand negotiable instruments and their importance in conducting personal and business affairs. You will be introduced to the tools that you need to create a negotiable instrument. You should be able to recognize the different indorsements, as well as the requirements and restrictions for each.

## Helpful Hints

This chapter involves negotiable instruments, at least one of which you will likely have used. Keep in mind those which you have used and are familiar with in terms of commercial paper. List the parties and their roles on a separate sheet of paper so as to view how they differ. Try to imagine yourself in one or more of the parties' positions as you work with hypothetical situations.

## Study Tips

### Negotiable Instruments

Article 3 of the Uniform Commercial Code sets out the requirements that must be met for a document to be a negotiable instrument.
- The primary benefit is that these instruments can be used as a substitute for money.

- Negotiation describes the transfer of these instruments to subsequent transferees.
- These are still considered to be ordinary contracts subject to contract law.

**Functions of Negotiable Instruments.** These instruments serve several functions:
- Negotiable instruments act as a substitute for money.
- Negotiable instruments may act as a credit device.
- Negotiable instruments may serve as a record-keeping device.

## Types of Negotiable Instruments

There are four kinds of instruments recognized under Revised Article 3 of the Uniform Commercial Code: drafts, checks, promissory notes, and certificates of deposit.

**Drafts.** A three-party instrument that is an unconditional written order by one party that orders a second party to pay money to the third party.
- The Drawer orders a second party (drawee) to pay money to a third party (payee).
- A time draft is payable at a specified future date.
- A sight draft, or demand draft, is payable on sight.
- A trade acceptance is a sight draft that arises when credit is given with a sale of goods.

**Checks.** A three-party instrument that is a distinct form of draft, unique in that it is drawn on a financial institution and payable on demand.
- The parties:
  - The Drawer is the customer who writes (draws) the check.
  - The Drawee is the financial institution upon which the check is written.
    - Also known as the acceptor because of the obligation to pay the payee instead of the drawer
  - The Payee is the party to whom the check is written.
- There are several types of special checks: certified, cashier's, and traveler's checks.

**Promissory Notes.** An unconditional written promise by one party to pay money to another.
- A note is proof of the extension of credit and the borrower's promise to repay the debt.
- The parties:
  - The Maker is the borrower who makes the promise to pay.
  - The Payee is the lender to whom the promise is made.
- Collateral, which provides security for the lender, is sometimes needed.
- Types of notes:
  - A time note is payable at a specific time.
  - A demand note is payable on demand.
  - An installment note can be paid in a single payment or in installments.
  - Mortgage notes are secured by real estate.
  - Collateral notes are secured by personal property.

**Certificates of Deposit.** A specially created note that is created upon a depositor depositing monies at a financial institution in exchange for the institution's promise to pay the deposited amount back with an agreed upon amount of interest after a set period of time.
- The parties:
  - The maker (borrower) is the financial institution.
  - The payee (lender) is the depositor.

# Creating a Negotiable Instrument

In order to create a negotiable instrument in compliance with UCC 3-104(a), several things must be present and must appear on the face of the instrument:

**Writing.** The instrument must be in writing, must have permanency, and must be portable.
- Oral promises are not clearly transferable in a way that will prevent fraud.
- Most writings on paper, though not tissue paper, are considered permanent.
- Portability ensures free transfer of the instrument.

**Signed by the Maker or the Drawer.** The UCC requires the signature of the maker if it is a not or CD and by the drawer if it is a check or a draft.
- The maker or drawer is not liable without his or her signature on the instrument.
- A signature can be put on the instrument by the maker or drawer or by a valid agent.
  - A signature can be the formal name, informal name, initials, nickname, symbols, typed, printed, lithographed, rubber-stamped or other mechanical signatures.
- The maker or drawer can appoint an agent to sign on his or her behalf.
  - The maker or drawer is liable on the instrument.
  - The properly disclosed agent is not personally liable on the instrument.

**Unconditional Promise or Order to Pay.** It must be an unconditional promise or order to pay.
- Mere debt acknowledgement is not sufficient for this requirement.

*Order to Pay.* A draft or check must contain the drawer's unconditional order for the drawee to pay a payee.
- An order is a direction to pay.
  - Must be more than an authorization or a request to pay.
- The language of the order must be precise and contain the word pay.

*Promise to Pay.* A promissory note must contain the maker's unconditional and affirmative promise to pay.
- An expressly stated promise to pay is negotiable.

*Unconditional Promise or Order.* The promise or order must be unconditional.
- A conditional promise or order is not negotiable because the risk of the condition not occurring would fall on the person holding the instrument.
- A conditional promise or order is not negotiable if it states:
  - An express condition to payment.
  - That it is subject to another writing.
  - The rights or obligations are stated in another writing.
- A conditional promise is subject to normal contract law.
- A promise or order is unconditional even if it refers to another writing for description of rights to collateral, prepayment, or acceleration.

**Payable to Order or to Bearer.** Negotiable instruments are intended to act as a substitute for money, so must be freely transferable to others.
- They must be payable to order or payable to bearer.
  - Those not meeting this requirement are nonnegotiable.
    - They may be assignable.

*Order Instruments.* These are instruments payable to the order of an identified person or to an identified person or orders.

*Bearer Instruments.* These are instruments payable to anyone in physical possession of the instrument who presents it for payment when it is due.

**Fixed Amount of Money.** It must contain a promise or an order to pay a fixed amount of money.
- The fixed amount ensures that the value can be determined with certainty.
- The principal amount of the instrument has to be on the face of the instrument.

*Payable in Money.* Money is a "medium of exchange authorized or adopted by a foreign or domestic government as part of its currency." [UCC 1-201(24)]
- Instruments payable in a medium of exchange other than money are non negotiable.

*Variable Interest Rate Loan.* Variable interest rate notes are negotiable instruments.
- The amount or rate of interest can be found by reference to data outside the instrument.

**Not Require Any Undertaking in Addition to the Payment of Money**. It cannot state any other undertaking by the person promising or ordering payment to do any act in addition to the payment of money.

**Payable on Demand or at a Definite Time.** It must be payable on demand or at a definite time.
- It is necessary to know when the maker, drawee, or acceptor is required to pay.

*Payable on Demand.* Instruments that are payable on demand are demand instruments.
- They are created by language such as "payable on sight," or "payable on demand."
- They can be created with silence as to when payment is due.

*Payable at a Definite Time.* Instruments payable at a definite time are called time instruments.
- These are created if the instrument is payable
  - At a fixed date.
  - On or before a stated date.
  - At a fixed period after sight.
  - At a time readily ascertainable when the promise or order is issued.

*Prepayment, Acceleration, and Extension Clauses.* The inclusion of these clauses in an instrument does not affect its negotiability.
- A prepayment clause allows the maker to pay the amount due before the due date.
- An acceleration clause lets the payee or holder accelerate payment of the principal.
- An extension clause allows the date of maturity to be extended.

## Nonnegotiable Contracts and Assignment

If a promise or order to pay does not meet the requirements discussed under negotiable instruments, then it is a nonnegotiable contract.
- A nonnegotiable contract is neither nontransferable nor nonenforceable.
- A nonnegotiable contract is enforceable under contract law.

**Assignment.** It transfers contract rights of the assignor (transferor) to the assignee (transferee).
- An assignment results when

o   There has been a transfer of a nonnegotiable instrument.
o   There has been a transfer of a negotiable instrument that fails as a negotiation.

## Transfer by Negotiation

Negotiation is the transfer of a negotiable instrument by a person other than the issuer.
- The holder is the person to whom the instrument is transferred.
- A holder in due course has better rights than a holder.
  o   He or she is not subject to defenses that could be raised against the transferor.

**Negotiating Order Paper.** Order paper is an instrument payable to a specific payee or indorsed to a specific indorsee.
- Negotiated by delivery with the necessary indorsement.

**Negotiating Bearer Paper.** Bearer paper is an instrument that is not payable to a specific payee or indorsee.
- Negotiated by delivery.
- There is substantial risk from loss or theft of bearer paper.

## Indorsements

An indorsement is the signature of a signer (not the maker, drawer or acceptor) that is put on an instrument to negotiate it to another person.
- The signature may be
  o   by itself,
  o   state an individual to whom the instrument is to be paid or
  o   be with other words.
- The indorser is the one who indorses the instrument.
- The Indorsee is the payee named in the instrument.
- An indorsement is usually placed on the reverse of the instrument.
  o   An allonge is a separate piece of paper affixed to the instrument that contains indorsements which will not fit on the instrument itself.
- Order paper requires an indorsement.
  o   Bearer paper does not.

**Types of Indorsements.** There are four categories of indorsement: Blank, special, qualified, and restrictive.

*Blank Indorsement.* It does not specify an indorsee and may be just a signature.
- Order paper indorsed in blank becomes bearer paper.

*Special Indorsement.* It contains the signature of the indorser and specifies the indorsee.
- A special indorsement creates order paper, with less risk of loss than bearer paper.
- Words of negotiation are not required.

*Unqualified Indorsement.* It is a promise by the indorser to pay the holder and subsequent indorsers the amount of the instrument if the maker, drawer, or acceptor defaults.
- The order and liability of indorsers is the order in which they indorse the instrument.

*Qualified Indorsement.* It is an indorsements disclaiming or limiting liability on the instrument.

- There is no guaranteed payment of the instrument by the qualified indorser if the maker, drawer, or acceptor defaults on the instrument.
- These are often used by individuals signing instruments as a representative.
- This indorsement protects only the indorser who wrote it on the instrument.
- A special qualified indorsement creates order paper.
- A blank qualified indorsement creates bearer paper.

*Nonrestrictive indorsement.* This is an indorsement without conditions or instructions attached to the payment of the funds.

*Restrictive indorsement.* An indorsement with an instruction from the indorser.
- There are two restrictive indorsements you should be familiar with as provided for under UCC 3-206.
    - o Indorsement for Deposit or Collection is an indorsement that establishes the indorsee as the indorser's collecting agent. For example: "for deposit only."
    - o Indorsement in Trust is an indorsement for the benefit or use of the indorser or another individual.
- An indorsee who does not honor the instructions of the restrictive indorsement is liable to the indorser for all losses this noncompliance causes.

**Misspelled or Wrong Name.** If the payee or indorsee name is misspelled, the payee or indorsee in the negotiable instrument may indorse the instrument in the misspelled name, the correct name or both.

**Multiple Payees or Indorsees.** There are three instances addressed in cases:
- If more than one person are listed as indorsees or payees on a negotiable instrument and are listed jointly, both indorsements are needed to negotiate the instrument.
    - o Pay to Joe Jones and Sam Smith
- If the instrument indicates that one or the other may negotiate the instrument, then each person's signature is sufficient to negotiate the instrument.
    - o Pay to Joe Jones or Sam Smith
- If a *Virgule* (which is a slash mark) is used, then the negotiable instrument may be paid in the alternative.
    - o Pay to Joe Jones/Sam Smith

# Refresh Your Memory

The following exercises will help to test your memory regarding the principles given in this chapter. Read each question twice, then place your answer in the blank provided for each question. Review the chapter material for any questions you are unable to answer or remember.

1. The _____ is the person who issues a draft.

2. The _____ is a person to whom the check is made payable.

3. The financial institution where the drawer's checking account is located is the _____.

4. To be negotiable, an instrument must have a promise or order to pay a fixed _____ _____ _____.

5.  Instruments that are payable on demand are called _____ _____.

6.  A(n) _____ clause allows the date of maturity of an instrument to be extended.

7.  If a promise or order to pay does not meet the UCC requirements of negotiability, it is a(n) _____ _____.

8.  A(n) _____ is the signature of a signer that is placed on an instrument to negotiate it to another person.

9.  Merchants and consumers often use negotiable instruments as a substitute for _____.

10. Ellen owes Grace $100. Grace writes out a draft ordering Ellen to pay the $100 to Bart. Ellen agrees to this change of obligation and accepts the draft. Grace is the drawer and Bart is the _____.

11. A(n) _____ _____ is an unconditional written promise by one party to pay money to another party.

12. A(n) _____ note is one that is payable at a specific time.

13. The party who makes the promise to pay is the maker of the note or the _____.

14. The party to whom the promise to pay is made is the payee of a note or the _____.

15. That it be _____ and _____ _____ _____ are two elements that must be present in order to establish the writing requirement of a negotiable instrument.

## Critical Thought Exercise

The Gold Coast Investment Group (IG) is building a large office building that it is financing itself through its banking arm, Gold Coast Bank (GCB). When payments for the final phase of the building come due, GC issues checks to the contractors with a condition on the front of the check that states:

> *"This instrument valid only after a permit to occupy the building is granted by all governmental agencies from which a permit is mandatory."*

Ace Construction deposits the check with its bank, First City Bank. The occupancy permits are not issued by the city or county entities where the building is located. When presented with the checks by First City Bank, GCB refuses to honor them.

Ace Construction then brings suit against First City Bank, GCB, and IG.

Should GCB be compelled to pay the checks presented to it by First City Bank on behalf of Ace Construction? Was it ethical for IG to put a condition on the negotiation of the instrument?

*Please compose your answer on a separate sheet of paper or on your computer.*

## Practice Quiz

## True/False

1. ___ A check is not a substitute for money.

2. ___ The drawee need not be obligated to pay the drawer money before the drawer can order the drawee to pay this money to the payee.

3. ___ The drawee of a check is not the financial institution where the drawer has his or her account.

4. ___ The party who makes the promise to pay is not the payee.

5. ___ Examples of collateral that may be used as security against repayment of a note to a lender include cars, homes or other property.

6. ___ A maker is not the party to whom the promissory note is made payable which is usually the lender.

7. ___ A maker is the financial institution that issues the certificate of deposit.

8. ___ A writing on Kleenex meets the permanence aspect of the writing requirement of negotiable instruments.

9. ___ A promise to pay that is indented in a steel girder would not qualify as a negotiable instrument because the girder is not freely transferable in commerce.

10. ___ The drawer or maker is liable on the instrument regardless of whether his or her signature appears on it.

11. ___ A negotiable instrument has to contain a promise or order to pay a fixed amount of money.

12. ___ The value of an instrument cannot be determined with certainty by having a fixed amount.

13. ___ After issuance of a negotiable instrument, it may not be transferred to a subsequent party.

14. ___ An assignment cannot take place when a nonnegotiable contract has been transferred.

15. ___ The transfer of a negotiable instrument by an issuer is known as negotiation.

## Multiple Choice

16. Negotiable instruments serve which function
    a. as a substitute for money.
    b. as a credit device.
    c. as a record keeping device.
    d. all of the above.

17. A drawer of a draft is the
    a. person to whom the check is made payable.
    b. person who issues the draft.
    c. person to whom the draft is made payable.
    d. person who owes money to the drawer.

18. To qualify as a negotiable instrument under the UCC, the writing must
    a. contain an unconditional promise to pay.
    b. contain an unconditional order to pay.
    c. contain an unconditional promise or order to pay.
    d. none of the above.

19. A promise or order to pay may include
    a. authorization or power to protect collateral.
    b. a vague amount.
    c. a conditional promise to perform.
    d. an immobile writing.

20. Stewart draws a check payable to the order of Kurt. Kurt indorses the check and negotiates it to Martha. When Martha presents the check for payment, there are insufficient funds in Stewart's account to pay the check. If Kurt is an unqualified indorser and is liable on the check, who may Kurt recover against?
    a. Martha
    b. Henry
    c. Martha's daughter
    d. Stewart

21. An instrument that is not payable to a specific payee or indorsee is
    a. order paper
    b. bearer paper
    c. stationary paper
    d. electronic paper

22. The purpose of a prepayment clause is
    a. to permit the maker to pay the amount due before the due date of the instrument.
    b. to permit the maker to pay the amount due after the due date of the instrument.
    c. to permit the maker to waive one of his or her payments.
    d. all of the above

23. Which of the following is not true with regard to variable interest rate loans?
    a. These loans tie the interest rate to some set measure.
    b. The interest changes during the life of the loan.
    c. Interest may not be stated in an instrument as a fixed or variable amount of money.
    d. Many lending institutions offer variable interest rate loans.

24. An extension clause is
    a. one that permits maker to pay the amount due prior to the due date of the instrument.
    b. a clause that allows the payee or holder to accelerate payment of the principal amount of the instrument, plus accrued interest, upon the happening of an event.
    c. a clause that allows the borrower extra time to secure financing.

d. a clause that allows the date of maturity of an instrument to be extended to some time in the future.

25. Nonrestrictive indorsements do not have
    a. signatures placed on them.
    b. any instructions or conditions attached to the payment of funds.
    c. subsequent indorsers in place of qualified indorsers.
    d. any negotiability attached to them.

## Short Answer

26. What are examples of negotiable instruments?

27. What are three requirements that must be on the face of an instrument in order to be considered a negotiable instrument?

29. What is the definition of money under the UCC?

30. What is the transfer of a negotiable instrument by an individual other than the issuer called?

31. What are the three functions served by negotiable instruments?

32. What is the difference between a time draft and a sight draft?

33. What is an installment note?

34. What makes a certificate of deposit a special kind of note?

35. What are acceptable forms of writing for a negotiable instrument under the UCC?

36. What qualifies as a signature for negotiable instruments under the UCC?

37. If an agent properly signs a negotiable instrument on behalf of the maker, what is the liability of the agent and the maker?

38. Why is a conditional promise not acceptable for a negotiable instrument?

39.  What is the difference in negotiating order paper and bearer paper?

_____

40.  What, if anything, happens to order paper indorsed in blank?

_____

## Answers to Refresh Your Memory

1.   drawer  [p 508]
2.   payee  [p 509]
3.   drawee  [p 509]
4.   amount of money  [p 517]
5.   demand instruments  [p 518]
6.   extension  [p 519]
7.   nonnegotiable contract  [p 520]
8.   indorsement  [p 522]
9.   money  [p 507
10.  payee  [p 508]
11.  promissory note  [p 510]
12.  time  [p 510]
13.  borrower  [p 510]
14.  lender  [p 510]
15.  written, permanent and portable  [p 512]

## Critical Thought Exercise Model Answer

The general rule is that the terms of the promise or order must be included in the writing on the face of a negotiable instrument.  UCC 3-104(a) requires that the terms must also be unconditional.  The terms cannot be conditioned on the occurrence or nonoccurrence of some other event or agreement.

By placing the condition on the face of the instrument, IG prevented the checks from being valid negotiable instruments.  Both First City Bank and GCB would be within their rights to refuse to honor the checks.  A promise to pay that is conditional on another event, such as the issuing of the occupancy permits, is not negotiable because the risk of the other event not occurring would fall on the person who held the instrument.  A conditional promise like the one place on the check by IG is subject to normal contract law.

IG will not have made payment on the required contractual installments and may now be in breach of contract.  Ace Construction will be able to recover against IG for failure to meet its contractual obligations, unless the occupancy permits were a condition of payment contained in the parties' original contract.

The placing of the condition upon the face of the check by GC appears to be unethical.  If the condition were not part of its contract with Ace, it would be unethical to attempt to unilaterally modify the terms of their agreement.  If the purpose of placing the condition on the check were to cause the checks to be dishonored and thus delay payment, this would also be unethical.  IG would be employing a trick to avoid lawful payment, which may damage Ace Construction when it is unable to meet its financial obligations.

# Answers to Practice Quiz

## True/False

1.  False   A check is an example of a substitute for money. [p 507]
2.  False   Before the drawer can order the drawee to pay money to a third party, the drawee must be obligated to pay the drawer money. [p 508]
3.  False   The financial institution where the drawer has his or her account is the drawee of the check. [p 509]
4.  True    The maker of the note is the party who makes the promise to pay. [p 510]
5.  True    Security against repayment of the note that lenders often require may include cars, homes or other security. [p 510-511]
6.  True    A maker is the party who issues the promissory note, which is usually the borrower. [p 510]
7.  True    The maker is the financial institution that issues the certificate of deposit. [p 511]
8.  False   Kleenex does not meet the permanence requirement. [p 512]
9.  True    A steel girder is not freely transferable in commerce. [p 513]
10. False   Unless a drawer or maker's signature appears on an instrument, he or she is not liable. [p 513]
11. True    A negotiable instrument must contain a promise or order to pay a fixed amount of money. [p 517]
12. False   The fixed amount requisite helps to guarantee that the value of the instrument may be assessed with certainty. [p 517]
13. False   Negotiable instruments can be transferred to subsequent parties after they have been issued. [p 507]
14. False   When a nonnegotiable contract is transferred, an assignment results. [p 520]
15. True    Negotiation happens when a transfer of a negotiable instrument by a person other than the issuer takes place. [p 507]

## Multiple Choice

16. D   Answer D is the correct answer, as answers A, B, and C all state the functions that negotiable instruments serve. [p 507-508]
17. B   Answer B is the correct answer, as a person who issues the draft is the drawer of the draft. Answer A is incorrect, as this states the definition of a payee. Answer C is incorrect, as this is also the definition of a payee. Answer D is incorrect, as this states the definition of the drawee. [p 508]
18. C   Answer C is the correct answer, as the writing must contain either an unconditional order or promise to pay. Answer A is incorrect, as this is not the only requirement that the UCC allows in determining whether an instrument is negotiable. Answer B is incorrect, for the same reasoning given with regard to answer A. Answer D is incorrect, based on the reasoning given above. [p 513]
19. A   Answer A is the correct answer, as it correctly states what is allowed under the UCC 3-104. Answer B is incorrect, as vague amounts are not allowed; fixed amounts of money are. Answer C is incorrect, as the instrument must contain an unconditional promise. Answer D is incorrect, as it makes no sense. [p 515]

20. D Answer D is the correct answer, as Kurt may recover against Stewart as the order and liability of the indorsers is presumed to be the order in which they indorse the instrument. Answer A is incorrect, as Martha is not the one who defaulted on the instrument. Answer B is incorrect, as Henry is not involved in the hypothetical. Answer C is incorrect, as Martha's daughter isn't in the hypothetical either. [p 524]

21. B Answer B is the correct answer, as bearer paper is an instrument that is not payable to a specific payee or indorsee. Answer A is incorrect, as order paper is an instrument that is payable to a specific payee or indorsed to a specific indorsee. Answer C is incorrect, as is Answer D, as neither make any sense in terms of negotiable instruments. [p 516]

22. A Answer A is the correct answer, as it correctly states the purpose of a prepayment clause which is to permit the maker to pay the amount due before the due date of the instrument. Answer B is incorrect, as this answer seems to indicate payment of the amount after the due date in which case it should have been called a postpayment clause. Answer C is an incorrect definition and for this reason, answer D is also incorrect. [p 519]

23. C Answer C is the correct answer, as it is the only answer that states what is not true with respect to variable interest loans. Answers A, B and D all are true answers with regard to variable interest loans. [p 517]

24. D Answer D is the correct answer, as it correctly states what an extension clause is. Answers A, B, and C all incorrectly define an extension clause. [p 519]

25. B Answer B is the correct answer, as it properly states what nonrestrictive indorsements do not have. Answers A, C and D are incorrect as these answers pertain to the things that nonrestrictive indorsements do have. [p 525]

## Short Answer

26. Checks and promissory notes. [p 507]
27. Be in writing, be an unconditional promise or order to pay and be signed by the maker or drawer. [p 513]
28. A "medium of exchange authorized or adopted by a domestic or foreign government as part of its currency." [p 517]
30. Negotiation. [p 521]
31. Substitute for money, act as credit devices, and act as record-keeping devices. [p 507-508]
32. A time draft is payable at a designated future date, whereas a sight draft is payable on sight or demand. [p 508]
33. It is a note that can be payable in a single payment or in installments. [p 510]
34. The financial institution is the borrower (maker) and the depositor is the lender (payee), rather than the financial institution being the lender (payee) and the customer being the borrower (maker). [p 511]
35. Preprinted forms; typewritten, handwritten, or other tangible agreements; or a combination of types of writing. [p 512]
36. The use of any name, including a trade or assumed name, or by any work or mark used in the place of a written signature. [p 513]
37. The maker is liable. The agent is not personally liable. [p 513]
38. A promise or an order that is conditional on another promise or event makes the risk of the other promise or event not occurring fall on the person who holds the instrument. [p 514]
39. Negotiating order paper requires delivery with the necessary indorsement, where as bearer paper only requires delivery. [p 521]
40. The order paper becomes bearer paper. [p 523]

# Chapter 21
# HOLDER IN DUE COURSE
# AND LIABILITY OF PARTIES

## Chapter Overview

Commercial paper held by a holder in due course is nearly as good as money. A holder in due course takes the negotiable instrument free of all claims and most defenses, though there are some universal defenses that can be raised. The holder in due course can use the court system to enforce payment. Some parties, both signors and nonsignors, have primary liability on the instrument, while others are secondarily liable. This chapter looks at the rule of a holder in due course, the liability for payment and the discharge of liability on a negotiable instrument.

## Objectives

Upon completion of the exercises in this chapter, you should be able to:

1.    Explain the meaning of a holder and a holder in due course.
2.    Discuss signature liability of makers, drawers, drawees, acceptors, accommodation parties.
3.    Discuss transfer and presentment warranties.
4.    Recognize real defenses that can be asserted against a holder in due course.
5.    Explain the FTC rule that prohibits the holder in due course rule in consumer transactions.

## Practical Application

You should be able to recognize the benefits of holder in due course status for a negotiable instrument. You should be able to understand signature liability and the warranties represented when negotiating instruments. You should be aware of what is involved in discharging liability.

## Helpful Hints

It is helpful to list the requirements of what is necessary to be a holder in due course, as well as the requirements for each of the elements contained within the basic definition. To facilitate your studies in this area, the study tips section has been organized so that you will be able to easily refer to the lists when analyzing the case studies or hypotheticals presented to you.

## Study Tips

### Holder in Due Course (HDC)

Two of the most important concepts of the law regarding negotiable instruments are those of holder and holder in due course.

- A holder is a person in possession of a bearer instrument or an order instrument payable to that person.
  - He or she has same rights as an assignee of an ordinary nonnegotiable contract.
  - Subject to all claims and defenses that can be asserted against the transferor.
- A holder in due course takes an instrument for value, in good faith, and without notice that it is defective or is overdue.
  - He or she takes the instrument free of all claims and most defenses that can be asserted against the transferor.
  - Only real defenses, not personal defenses, may be asserted against him or her.

## Requirements for HDC Status

The UCC sets out the requirements for a transferee to qualify as an HDC. The individual must be a holder of a negotiable instrument that was taken for value, in good faith, without notice of defect, and bearing no apparent evidence of forgery, alterations or irregularity.

**Taking for Value.** The holder must have given value for the instrument. [UCC 3-302(a)(2)(i)]
- If the holder performs the agreed-upon promise.
- Acquires a security interest or lien on the instrument.
- Takes the instrument in payment of or as security for an antecedent claim.
- Gives a negotiable instrument as payment.
- Gives an irrevocable obligation as payment.

**Taking in Good Faith.** A holder must have taken an instrument in good faith.
- Good faith means honesty in fact and applies only to the holder.
  - Honesty is a subjective test as judged by the circumstances.

**Taking Without Notice of Defect.** A holder cannot take instrument with any notice of defect.
- It is overdue.
- It has been dishonored.
- It contains an unauthorized signature or has been altered (the red light doctrine).
- There is a defense against it.

*Overdue Instruments.* An instrument not paid when due implies there is some defect to payment.
- There is notice that the instrument is overdue
  - If one payment of an installment note is not paid.
  - If a demand instrument is acquired after demand.
  - If a demand instrument is acquired an unreasonable length after its issuance.

*Dishonored Instruments.* When an instrument is presented for payment and payment is refused.

*Red Light Doctrine.* If an instrument has an unauthorized signature or has been altered or that there is any adverse claim against or defense to its payment.
- Notice is given when the holder has
  - Actual knowledge of defect
  - Received notice of defect
  - Reason to know from facts and circumstances of the defect
- The filing of a public notice is not notice unless the person actually reads it.

**No Evidence of Forgery, Alteration, or Irregularity.** If the instrument bore apparent evidence of forgery or alteration or was so irregular or incomplete as to call into question its validity.

**Payee as an HDC.** Generally a payee cannot be an HDC because they know of any claim or defenses against the instrument.

**Shelter Principle.** Sometimes a holder does not qualify as an HDC on their own, but can be an HDC because they acquired the instrument through an HDC.
- Holder does not qualify as an HDC on his or her own.
- Holder must acquire instrument from an HDC, or trace title back to an HDC.
- Holder must not have been party to fraud or illegality affecting instrument.
- Holder cannot have notice of defense or claim against payment of instrument.

## Signature Liability

A person can only be held liable on a negotiable instrument if his or her signature is on it.
- A signature identifies who is obligated to pay.
- The location of the signature generally determines the capacity of the signor.
    - Lower-right corner of a check indicates the drawer.
    - Lower-right corner of a note indicates the maker.
    - Indorsements appear on the reverse of an instrument.
- Every signor has either primary or secondary liability on the instrument.

**Signature Defined.** A signature is a name, word, or mark used instead of a written signature.
- A signature is any word, symbol, mark in lieu of written signature that is handwritten, typed, stamped, etc. and adopted or executed by a party to authenticate the writing.
- An unauthorized signature is ineffective as that person's signature, but is effective in favor of an HDC.

**Primary Liability.** Makers of certificates of deposits, promissory notes have primary liability.
- The maker unconditionally promises to render the amount set in the note when due.
- No party is primarily liable when a draft or check is issued since these instruments are merely an order to pay.
- Acceptance of a draft happens when drawee writes "accepted" on the face of the draft.
    - The acceptor (drawee) is primarily liable on the instrument.
    - A certified check is accepted when certified by the bank.

**Secondary Liability.** Secondary liability attaches to the drawers of checks and drafts and unqualified indorsers of negotiable instruments.
- The drawer is obligated to pay an unaccepted draft or check that is dishonored.

*Unqualified Indorsers.* These indorsers have secondary liability on negotiable instruments.
- They must pay a dishonored instrument to the holder or any subsequent indorser.
- Indorsers are liable to each other in the order in which they indorsed the instrument.

*Qualified Indorsers.* These indorsers are not secondarily liable on the instrument.

*Requirements for Imposing Secondary Liability.* A party is secondarily liable on an instrument only if certain requirements are met:
- The instrument must be properly presented for payment.

- The instrument is dishonored.
- Notice of the dishonor is given in a timely manner to person who is secondarily liable.
  - Notice must reasonably identify the instrument.
  - Notice can be given by any commercially reasonable means.

**Accommodation Party.**  A party who signs an instrument and lends his or her credit (and name) to another party to the instrument.
- They are obligated to pay the instrument in the capacity in which they sign.
- They can recover reimbursement from the accommodated party and enforce the instrument against him or her.

*Guarantee of Payment.*  The accommodation party signs an instrument guaranteeing payment.
- He or she is primarily liable on the instrument.

*Guarantee of Collection.*  The accommodation party guarantees collection rather than payment.
- He or she is secondarily liable on the instrument.
- Requirement of payment arises only if:
  - execution of judgment against the other party has been returned unsatisfied,
  - the other party is in an insolvency proceeding or is insolvent,
  - the other party is unable to be served with process, or
  - it is otherwise obvious that payment cannot be received from the other party. [UCC3-419(d)]

*Agent's Signature.*  An individual may sign a negotiable instrument or authorize agent to do so.
- The representative is the agent.
- The represented person is the principal.

*Authorized Signature.*  If an authorized agent properly signs an instrument, the principal is bound as if the signature were made on a simple contract.
- The principal does not need to be identified in the instrument.
- If the signature of the agent unambiguously shows that he or she is acting as an agent for a principal identified in the instrument, he or she is not liable on the instrument.
- If the signature of the agent is not unambiguous in representing him or her as an agent and if the agent cannot prove that the original parties did not intend him or her to be liable, the agent is liable.

**Unauthorized Signature.**  This is a signature made by a purported agent without authority from the alleged principal.
- The purported agent is liable to any individual who in good faith pays the instrument or takes it for value.
- The alleged principal is liable if he or she ratifies the unauthorized signature.

# Forged Indorsement

The general rule is that unauthorized indorsements are inoperative as the indorsement of the person who signed it.
- The loss is born by the party accepting the forged instrument.
- There are two exceptions, the imposter rule and the fictitious payee rule:
  - Imposter rule

- An imposter is one who impersonates a payee and induces the issue of an instrument to the imposter.
- The drawer or maker is liable on the instrument to any person who in good faith pays the instrument or takes it for value or for collection.
- This rule does not apply if wrongdoer poses as agent of drawer or maker.
  o The fictitious payee rule
    - An imposter is one signing as or on behalf of a drawer or maker and intends payee to have no interest in instrument or when payee is fictitious
    - A drawer or maker is liable on an unauthorized or forged indorsement of a fictitious payee.
    - This rule applies if an agent or employee of the drawer or maker supplies the drawer or maker with the name of a fictitious payee.

## Warranty Liability

Transferors can be held liable for breaching certain implied warranties when negotiating instruments
- Warranty liability is placed upon a transferor irrespective of whether or not the transferor signed the instrument.
- These implied warranties shift the risk of loss to the party best positioned to prevent it.

**Transfer Warranties.** Except for its issuance and presentment for payment, any transmission of an instrument is considered a transfer.
- Five warranties are made when one transfers a negotiable instrument for consideration.
  o The transfer of good title to the instrument or authorization to obtain acceptance or payment on behalf of one who does have good title.
  o All signatures are authentic or authorized.
  o The instrument has not been altered materially.
  o No defenses of any party are applicable against the transferor.
  o The transferor is unaware of any insolvency proceeding against the maker, the acceptor, or the drawer of an unaccepted instrument.
- Instruments other than checks may disclaim transfer warranties with the use of an indorsement such as "without recourse" [UCC3-416 (c)]

**Presentment Warranties.** Any person who presents a draft or check for payment or acceptance makes the following warranties to a drawee or acceptor who pays or accepts the instrument in good faith [UCC 3-417(a)]:
- The presenter has good title to the instrument or is authorized to obtain payment or acceptance of the person who has good title.
- The material has not been materially altered.
- Presenter has no knowledge that the signature of the maker or drawer is unauthorized.

## Defenses

There are real and personal defenses that arise from the underlying transaction concerning the creation of negotiable instruments.

**Universal Defenses.** These real defenses can be raised against both holders and HDC.
- If proven, the holder or HDC cannot recover on the instrument.

*Minority.* Infancy is a defense in that it is a defense to a simple contract.
- A minor can disaffirm contracts, including negotiable instruments.

*Extreme Duress.* This requires some form of force or violence.

*Mental Incapacity.* An instrument is void if issued by one adjudicated mentally incompetent.

*Illegality.* This occurs if the instrument arose from an illegal transaction.

*Discharge in Bankruptcy.* Relieve debtors of burdensome debts, including negotiable instruments

*Fraud in the Inception.* This type of fraud happens when someone is deceived into signing a negotiable instrument while believing it is something else.
- There is a duty to use reasonable efforts to ascertain what is being signed.

*Forgery.* An unauthorized signature of a maker, drawer, or indorser is ineffective unless the person whose name is signed ratifies the signature or is precluded from denying it.
- A person can be prevented form raising this defense if his or her own negligence substantially contributed to the forgery.
- The forger is liable on the instrument.

*Material Alteration.* Occurs when any part of a signed instrument is added or deleted or changed.
- Materially altered instruments cannot be enforced by a normal holder.
- If the alteration is not apparent, and HDC can enforce the instrument.

**Personal Defenses.** These defenses can be raised against an ordinary holder, but cannot be raised against an HDC.

*Breach of Contract.* A very common defense against enforcement of a negotiable instrument.

*Fraud in the Inducement.* This occurs when the wrongdoer makes a false statement to head another person to enter into a contract.

*Other Personal Defenses.*
- Mental Illness, usually nonadjudicated, makes a contract voidable.
- Illegality of contract that makes the contract voidable.
- Ordinary duress or undue influence.
- Discharge by payment or cancellation.

## FTC Rule Limits HDC Status

The FTC rule puts the holder of due course of a consumer credit contract on the same level as an assignee of a simple contract.
- The result is the holder of due course of a consumer credit instrument is subject to all of the defenses and claims of the consumer.
- This rule applies to consumer credit transactions that
  o include a promissory note,
  o the buyer signs an installment sales contract that contains a waiver of defenses clause, and
  o the seller arranges consumer financing with a third-party lender.

## Discharge

There are several rules that are specified by the UCC on when and how certain parties are discharged from liability on negotiable instruments. Three ways to relieve parties from liability:
- Payment of the instrument.
- Cancellation
  o by any manner or
  o by destroying or mutilating a negotiable instrument with the intent of getting rid of the obligation.
- Impairment of the right of recourse which is accomplished by
  o Releasing an obligor from liability or
  o Surrendering collateral without consent of the parties who would benefit by it.

# Refresh Your Memory

The following exercises will help to test your memory regarding the principles given in this chapter. Read each question twice, then place your answer in the blank provided for each question. Review the chapter material for any questions you are unable to answer or remember.

1.  A person in possession of an instrument that is payable to an identified person or a bearer in possession of an instrument payable to that person is a(n) _____.

2.  A holder who takes an instrument for value, in good faith, and without notice that is defective or is overdue is a(n) _____ _____ _____ _____.

3.  Steve, a thief steals a negotiable instrument and transfers it to Cindy. Cindy is unaware that the instrument is stolen. Since Cindy meets the good faith test, she will qualify as a(n) _____ _____ _____ _____.

4.  A person cannot qualify as a holder in due course if he or she has _____ that the instrument is defective in certain ways.

5.  An instrument that is payable on a certain date is known as a(n) _____ _____.

6.  _____ is when an instrument is presented for payment and payment is refused.

7.  A person who has been authorized to sign a negotiable instrument on behalf of another person is a(n) _____.

8.  A(n) _____ is a person who authorizes an agent to sign a negotiable instrument on his or her behalf.

9.  A(n) _____ signature is one that is made by a purported agent without authority from the purported principal.

10.  _____ defenses may be asserted against a holder in due course.

11.  A demand instrument is one that is _____ _____ _____.

12. Indorsers who indorse instruments "without recourse" or similar language that disclaims liability are referred to as _____ indorsers.

13. Any passage of an instrument other than its issuance and presentment for payment is known as a(n) _____.

14. Mental incompetency, a(n) _____ defense, can be raised against holders in due course.

15. Breach of contract is a(n) _____ defense that can be raised against enforcement of a negotiable instrument by an ordinary holder.

# Critical Thought Exercise

Betty Smith made out a check to George Bell of Bell Plumbing for $1,500 as a partial payment for plumbing renovation of her kitchen. When it was time for Bell to begin his work, he did not appear, nor could Ms. Smith locate him. Smith immediately ordered her bank to stop payment on the check. Bell had already cashed the check at Redi-Cash. When the check was returned to Redi-Cash marked "payment stopped by account holder," Redi-Cash was contacted by an attorney for Smith who informed Redi-Cash that the plumber did not have a license and that engaging in a contracting trade without a license was a crime. Therefore the contract was void and his client would not honor the check.

As manager of Redi-Cash, will you sue Smith to collect the amount of the check?

*Please compose your answer on a separate sheet of paper or on your computer.*

# Practice Quiz

## True/False

1. ___ If Samantha is in possession of a negotiable instrument that is drawn, issued or indorsed to her, or to bearer, or in blank, she may not be a holder.

2. ___ Under the UCC, value has been given if the holder gives a revocable obligation as payment.

3. ___ Good faith applies to only the holder.

4. ___ A holder cannot qualify as a holder in due course if he or she has notice that the instrument contains an unauthorized signature.

5. ___ Signature liability refers to an individual's contractual liability on a negotiable instrument and whether or not his or her signature appears on it.

6. ___ The signature on a negotiable instrument can be by word, mark, symbol or name.

7. ___ When a person authorizes a representative to sign an instrument on his or her behalf, the authorizing party is the agent.

8. \_\_\_ A signature made by a purported agent without authority from a purported principal is an unauthorized signature.

9. \_\_\_ The makers of promissory notes and certificates of deposit have secondary liability for the instrument.

10. \_\_\_ It is not a requirement that the negotiable instrument be dishonored before imposing secondary liability on it.

11. \_\_\_ The two types of implied warranties are transfer warranties and presentment warranties.

12. \_\_\_ The accommodation party who signs an instrument guaranteeing payment is secondarily liable on the instrument.

13. \_\_\_ Sue Smith is Joe Jones' agent. If Sue signs a check on behalf of Joe as "Joe Jones, by Sue Smith, agent", she will have no personal liability on the check.,

14. \_\_\_ Where an indorsement on an instrument has been forged, the loss falls on the party who first takes the instrument after the forgery.

15. \_\_\_ A fictitious payee is a person who impersonates a payee and induces the maker or drawer to issue an instrument in the payee's name and give it to the fictitious payee.

## Multiple Choice

16. A holder is
    a. a person who takes an instrument for value and in good faith.
    b. a person who takes without notice that it is defective or overdue.
    c. a person in possession of an instrument that is payable to bearer or an identified person who is in possession of an instrument payable to that person.
    d. a person who takes a negotiable instrument free of all claims and most defenses.

17. If Megan promises to perform but has not done so yet and there has been no value given, Megan is not a
    a. holder in due course.
    b. third-party beneficiary.
    c. holder without value.
    d. None of the above.

18. If a time instrument is not paid on its expressed date, then it
    a. becomes effective.
    b. becomes overdue and is defective as to its payment.
    c. is payable on demand.
    d. can be made payable according to business practices.

19. Hugo draws a check on Coast Bank "payable to the order of Lamar Huff." When Lamar presents the check for payment, payment is refused. Lamar can collect from Hugo as
    a. the maker.
    b. the drawee.
    c. the person who ratified the check.
    d. the drawer.

20. A demand for acceptance or payment of an instrument made upon the maker, acceptor, drawee, or other payor by or on behalf of the holder is referred to as
    a. a notice of dishonor.
    b. an unqualified indorser.
    c. the red light doctrine.
    d. presentment.

21. An authorized agent's personal liability on an instrument he or she signs on behalf of a principal depends on
    a. the agent's signature.
    b. information disclosed in the signature.
    c. the unauthorized signature of an unauthorized signer.
    d. none of the above

22. An indorsement that states "without recourse" disclaims
    a. the transfer warranties.
    b. negotiable instrument originally issued.
    c. secondary liability
    d. primary liability

23. Which of the following may give rise to a defense to payment of a negotiable instrument?
    a. extreme duress
    b. discharge in bankruptcy
    c. forgery
    d. all of the above

24. Which of the following is true with regard to a holder in due course?
    a. He or she takes a negotiable instrument free of all claims.
    b. Most defenses can be asserted against the transferor.
    c. A holder in due course can acquire greater rights than a transferor.
    d. all of the above

25. The party who signs an instrument for the purpose of lending his or her name to another party to the instrument is the
    a. guarantor of collection.
    b. ethical party
    c. accommodation party
    d. none of the above

## Short Answer

26. When is an instrument dishonored?

   _____

27. What is an accommodation party?

   _____

28. Suppose Monica draws a check "payable to the order of Greg Wallace" and delivers the check to Greg. Greg indorses the check and gives it as a gift to his son. Can Greg's son

qualify as a holder in due course?

_____

29. Why is it better to be a holder in due course rather than an ordinary holder?

_____

_____

30. From what can a holder's subjective belief be inferred?

_____

31. What is a time instrument?

_____

32. What are the four requirements for a holder to qualify as a holder in due course?

_____

_____

33. What is the Red Light Doctrine?

_____

_____

34. What is a signature?

_____

35. What is a demand instrument?

_____

36. What is the signatory liability of a qualified indorser?

_____

37. Where does the loss fall when an indorsement on a negotiable instrument has been forged?

_____

38. What is the Shelter Principle?

_____

_____

39. What are the three requirements for imposing secondary liability?

_____

_____

40. What are the three implied presentment warranties?

_____

_____

## Answers to Refresh Your Memory

1. holder [p538]
2. holder in due course [p538]

3.    holder in due course  [p 538]
4.    notice  [p 540]
5.    time instrument  [p 540]
6.    dishonored  [p 540]
7.    agent  [p 545]
8.    principal  [p 545]
9.    unauthorized  [p 547]
10.   real  [p 550]
11.   payable on demand  [p 540]
12.   qualified  [p 544]
13.   transfer.  [p 549]
14.   real  [p 550]
15.   personal  [p 552]

## Critical Thought Exercise Model Answer

A holder of a negotiable instrument is a holder in due course (HDC) pursuant to UCC 3-302 if he or she takes the instrument (1) for value; (2) in good faith; and (3) without notice that it is overdue, that it has been dishonored, that any person has a defense against it or claim to it, or that the instrument contains unauthorized signatures, alterations, or is so irregular or incomplete as to call into question its authenticity. Redi-Cash gave value for the instrument when they cashed it for Bell. The UCC defines good faith as "honesty in fact and the observance of reasonable commercial standards of fair dealing." UCC 3-103(4). It is immaterial whether the transferor acted in good faith. There is nothing in the facts to show that Redi-Cash did anything but act in good faith. There appears to have been nothing that would have put Redi-Cash on notice that Smith had a defense against the instrument. The fraud, deceit, or illegality of Bell's actions do not keep Redi-Cash from being a HDC.

Unless the instrument arising from a contract or transaction is, itself, made void by statute, the illegality defense under UCC 3-305 is not available to bar the claim of a holder in due course.

Therefore, Redi-Cash should be viewed as a HDC and actually has rights greater than Bell in regards to this negotiable instrument. Smith should be ordered to pay Redi-Cash the $2,500 that Redi-Cash paid for the instrument. Smith will have to seek recourse against Bell.

## Answers to Practice Quiz

### True/False

1.  False    A holder is an individual in possession of a negotiable instrument that is drawn, issued, or indorsed to him or his order, or to bearer, or in blank. [p 538]
2.  False    A holder giving an irrevocable obligation as payment is one of the things that qualify as value being given under UCC 3-303. [p 539]
3.  True     Good faith only applies to the holder. [p 540]
4.  True     The red light doctrine provides that if a holder has notice that the instrument contains an unauthorized signature or has been altered or has an adverse claim against or defense to its payment, a holder cannot qualify as a holder in due course. [p 540]
5.  True     Signature liability is known as contract liability. [p 542]
6.  True     A signature on a negotiable instrument may be by word, name, mark or any symbol that is handwritten, stamped, typed or otherwise affixed. [p 542]

7. False   One who authorizes another to do an act on his or her behalf is the principal. [p 545]
8. True    One whose signature is made by one without authority from a purported principal is an unauthorized signature. [p 547]
9. False   Makers of certificates of deposit and promissory notes have absolute liability to pay the negotiable instrument, subject to liability known as primary liability. [p 542]
10. False  A party is secondarily liable on negotiable instrument if it is dishonored. [p 543-544]
11. True   Transfer and presentment warranties are the two implied warranties when negotiating instruments. [p 549]
12. False  The accommodation party who signs an instrument guaranteeing payment is primarily liable on the instrument. [p 545]
13. True   The agent has no personal liability if the signature shows unambiguously that it is made on behalf of a principal who is identified in the instrument. [p 545-546]
14. True   Where an indorsement on an instrument has been forged, the loss falls on the party who first takes the instrument after the forgery. [p 547]
15. False  An imposter is a person who impersonates a payee and induces the maker or drawer to issue an instrument in the payee's name and give it to the imposter. [p 548]

## Multiple Choice

16. C   Answer C is correct, as a holder is an identified person who is in possession of an instrument payable to that person or a person in possession of an instrument that is payable to bearer. Answers A and B are incorrect, as they each partially state the definition for a holder in due course. Answer D is incorrect, as it states a fact with regard to an individual who is a holder in due course. [p 538]
17. A   Answer A is the correct answer, as Megan does not meet the requirements of taking for value and performing the agree-upon promise as is required in order to be a holder in due course. Answer B is incorrect, as it makes no sense since third-party beneficiaries need not perform nor give value per se. Answer C is incorrect, as it makes no sense. Answer D is incorrect based on the reasoning given above. [p 539]
18. B   Answer B is the correct answer, as time instruments that are not paid on their due dates become overdue the next day and are indicative of some type of defect in payment. Answer A is incorrect because this is not a true statement. Answer C is incorrect, as an instrument that is payable on demand is somewhat opposite of one where a due date is expressed as in the time instrument. Answer D is incorrect, as making an instrument payable according to business practices refers to what may be used to determine a reasonable time for payment of other demand instruments as per UU 3-304. [p 540]
19. D   Answer D is the correct answer, as Hugo as the drawer is secondarily liable on the dishonored check. Answer A is incorrect, as makers are usually the borrowers who make the promise to pay, which is not the case in this hypothetical. Answer B is incorrect, as Coast Bank would be considered the drawee, as they are the financial institution upon which the check is written. Answer C makes no sense, as Hugo cannot accept his own check if he has given it to Lamar Huff. [p 544]
20. D   Answer D is correct, as a presentment is a demand for acceptance or payment of an instrument made upon the maker, acceptor, drawee, or other behalf of holder. Answer A is incorrect, as notice of dishonor refers to the formal act of letting party with secondary liability to pay a negotiable instrument know that the instrument has been dishonored. Answer B is incorrect, as an unqualified indorser is someone who is secondarily liable on negotiable instruments that they indorse. Answer C is incorrect, as the red light doctrine refers to a holder having notice of an unauthorized signature or an alteration of an instrument or any adverse claim against or defense to its payment. [p 544]

21.  B   Answer B is correct, as an agent's personal liability on an instrument depends on the information disclosed in the signature. Note that the agent does not have any liability if the signature shows unambiguously that it is made on the principal's behalf who is identified in the instrument. Answers A and C are incorrect, as they do not make sense. Answer D is incorrect based on the reasoning given above. [p 545-546]

22.  A   Answer A is the correct choice, as UCC 3-419 states that transfer warranties cannot be disclaimed with respect to checks, but they can be disclaimed with respect to other warranties. As such, "an indorsement that states "without recourse" disclaims the transfer warranties." Answer B is incorrect based on the principles set forth in UCC 3-419. Answers C and D are incorrect, as they refer to whom liability will fall upon as opposed to the applicability of disclaiming transfer warranties. [p 544]

23.  D   Answer D is the correct answer, as answers A, B, and C are all situations that may give rise to a defense against the payment of a negotiable instrument. [p 550-551]

24.  D   Answer D is correct, as answers A, B, and C are true with regard to a holder in due course who "takes a negotiable instrument free of all claims and most defenses that can be asserted against the transferor, and can acquire greater rights than a transferor." [p 538]

25.  C   Answer C is the correct answer, as an accommodation party is "the party who signs an instrument for the purpose of lending his or her name (and credit) to another party to the instrument. Answer A is incorrect, as a guarantor of collection is a type of liability associated with being an accommodation party. Answer B is incorrect, because even though ethics should play some party in lending transactions, it has nothing to do with the signing of an instrument for the lending an individual's name and credit. Answer D is correct based on the reasoning given above. [p 545]

## Short Answer

26.   An instrument is dishonored when it is presented for payment and is refused. [p 544]

27.   They sign instrument and lend name and credit to another party on the instrument. [p 545]

28.   Greg's son may not qualify as holder in due course because he has not given value. [p 539]

29.   A holder is subject to all the claims and defenses that can be asserted against the transferor, whereas the holder in due course takes the instrument free of all claims and most defenses. Only real defenses can be used against the HDC, not personal defenses. [p 538]

30.   From the circumstances. [p 540]

31.   A negotiable instrument payable on a specific due date. [p 540]

32.   The holder must take that instrument for value, in good faith, without notice of defect, and with no apparent evidence of forgery, alterations, or irregularity. [p 539]

33.   A holder cannot qualify as an HDC if there is notice that an instrument has an unauthorized signature, has been altered, or has any adverse claim or defense against payment. [p 541]

34.   A signature can be any name, word, or mark used instead of a written signature. [p 542]

35.   A negotiable instrument which is payable on demand. [p 540]

36.   A qualified indorser is not primarily liable, nor is he or she secondarily liable on the instrument, as they have expressly disclaimed liability. [p 544]

37.   The loss will fall on party who first takes the forged instrument after the forgery. [p 547]

38.   The Shelter Principal states that a holder who does not qualify as an HDC in his or her own right becomes an HDC if he or she acquires the instrument through an HDC. [p 541]

39.   The three requirements for imposing secondary liability are met when the instrument is properly presented for payment, when the instrument is dishonored, and when notice of the dishonor is timely given to person to be held secondarily liable on the instrument. [p 544]

40.   The presenter has good title, the instrument has not been materially altered, and presenter has no knowledge that the signature of the maker or drawer is unauthorized. [p 549]

## Chapter 22

# CHECKS, BANKING SYSTEM, AND E-MONEY

## Chapter Overview

Checks, the most common negotiable instrument in the U.S., are substitutes for money and record keeping devices, but are not used as credit devices. Wire transfers constitute billions of dollars in transactions per day. The different types of checks, the process for paying and collecting checks, the duties and liabilities of banks in the collections process, and the electronic fund transfer function are introduced in this chapter.

## Objectives

Upon completion of the exercises in this chapter, you should be able to:

1. Differentiate between cashier's, certified and traveler's checks.
2. Explain the system of processing and collecting checks through the banking system.
3. Recognize when a bank participates in a wrongful dishonor of a check.
4. Explain the liability of parties when a check has been altered.
5. Explain the term wire transfer and discuss the main provisions of Article4A of the U.C.C.

## Practical Application

Almost everyone will have the opportunity to either have a checking account or purchase one of the various types of checks discussed in this chapter. You should recognize the banking procedures involved in payment and collection of checks, identify the duties and liabilities of banks and other parties in the collection process, and understand electronic fund transfers.

## Helpful Hints

Much of what is presented in this chapter has already been experienced in most individuals' everyday personal and business affairs. You may recognize some terms by definition, but not the specific term, so you should review these carefully.

## Study Tips

### The Bank-Customer Relationship

A creditor-debtor relationship is formed when a customer deposits money into a bank.
- The customer is essentially loaning money to the bank.
  - The customer is the creditor.

- o The bank is the debtor.
- o A principal-agent relationship may also be formed whereby the customer is the principal ordering the bank to collect or pay on the check.
  - ▪ The bank turn is the agent obligated to follow the principal's order.
- The rights and duties of the bank and the customer are contractual.

**The Uniform Commercial Code Banking Provisions.**  The U.C.C. gives rules for creating, collecting, and enforcing checks and wire transfers.
- Article 3 (Negotiable Instruments) gives the requirements for a negotiable instrument
- Article 4 (Bank Deposits and Collections) gives the rules to regulate deposit and collection procedures for checking accounts and check-like accounts.
  - o Article 4 controls when Articles 3 and 4 conflict.
- Article 4A (Funds Transfer) regulates creation, collection, liability for wire transfers.

## Ordinary Checks

When a customer goes to a bank, fills out the proper forms, and makes a deposit, the bank issues checks to him or her.
- The customer uses the checks for his or her purchases.
- The checks are presented to the bank and paid.

**Parties to a Check.**  The U.C.C. defines a check as an order by a drawer to a drawer bank to pay a specific sum of money from the drawer's account to the named payee or holder.
- The drawer is the customer with a checking account.
- The drawee is the bank (or payor) at which the check is drawn.
- The payee is the one to whom the check is written.
  - o Payee can demand payment or
  - o Payee can indorse check to another party.

**Indorsement of a Check.**  This refers to the holder or payee signing the back of the check.
- The payee is the indorser.
- The person to whom the check is indorsed is the indorsee.
  - o Becomes holder who can demand payment or
  - o Indorse to another party.

## Electronic Fund Transfer Systems

The electronic fund transfer systems (EFTS) are electronic payment and collection systems supported by contracts with customers, banks, private clearinghouses, and other third parties.

**Automated Teller Machines.**  Electronic machines located in convenient locations, connected to bank's computers, that allow customers to conduct banking activities away from physical bank.

**Point-of-Sale Terminals.**  Many banks issue debit cards to customers, which allows the customer to make purchases from their checking account without a paper check.
- The customer's account is immediately debited for the amount of the purchase.

**Direct Deposits and Withdrawals.**  The customer's bank and the payee's bank must belong to the same clearinghouse in order to provide the service of paying recurring payments and deposits.

**Pay-by-Internet.** Customers may pay bills from their account using their PIN number and account number, the amount of the bill to be paid, and the account number of the payee.

## Special Types of Checks

Bank checks are special checks considered to be "as good as cash" as the bank is solely or primarily responsible for payment. There are certified checks, cashier's checks, traveler's checks.

**Certified Checks.** With this type of check, the bank agrees in advance to accept the check when it is presented for payment and pay the check out of funds set aside from the customer's account.
- These types of checks are payable at any time from when they are issued.
- The bank writes or stamps the word *certified* across the face of an ordinary check thereby certifying it.
- The date, amount being certified, and individual certifying the check are placed on it.

*Liability on a Certified Check.* Either the drawer or the payee can present a check to the drawee bank for certification.
- If the check is certified, the drawer is discharged from liability on the check.
  - The holder must recover from the certifying bank.
- If the check was altered upward:
  - Before certification, the certifying bank is liable for the certified amount.
  - After certification, the bank is liable for only the certified amount.
- The drawer cannot stop payment on a certified check.

**Cashier's Check** – This is a bank-issued check where the customer has paid the bank the amount of the check and a fee.
- The bank guarantees the payment of the check.
- The bank acts as the drawer and the drawee with the holder as payee.
- The bank debits its own account when the check is presented.

**Traveler's Checks.** This type of check is a two-party instrument where the bank who issues it is both the drawer and the drawee.
- It has two signature lines, one for the purchaser to sign when the checks are purchased and the other for the purchaser to sign when he or she uses the check for purchases.
- It is a safe substitute for cash, as it is not negotiable until it is signed a second time.

## Bank Debit Cards

The Electronic Fund Transfer Act regulates consumer electronic fund transfers. Regulation E to this Act provides some consumer rights.

**Unsolicited Cards.** Bank can only send unsolicited debit cards to a consumer if not valid for use.
- The consumer can specifically validate the cards for use.

**Lost or Stolen Debit Cards.** If a customer notifies the issuing bank of the loss or theft of a debit care within 2 days, they are only liable for $50 for unauthorized use.
- If the customer does not notify within 2 days, the liability increases to $500.
- If the customer does not notify within 60 days, liability increases to more than $500.

**Evidence of Transaction.** The bank must give the customer a written receipt of transactions made through a computer terminal.

**Bank Statements.** The bank must provide the customer with a monthly statement where a transaction occurred during that month, or a quarterly statement.

## Honoring Checks

The customer of a bank agrees to keep enough funds in the account to cover checks written.
- If the customer keeps his or her end of this implied agreement, the bank is under a duty to honor the check and charge the customer (or drawer's ) account for whatever amount(s) the check(s) were written for.

**Stale Checks.** A stale check is one that has been outstanding for more than six months.
- Under UCC 4-404, the bank is not obligated to pay on a stale check.
- If the bank does pay it, it may also in good faith charge the drawer's account.

**Incomplete Checks.** If a drawer fails to provide information on a check, holder may complete the information and bank may charge the customer's account the amount of completed amount.
- The exception to this is if the bank receives notice that the completion was improper.

**Death or Incompetence of a Drawer.** With regard to incompetent customers, the checks may be paid against their accounts until the bank has actual knowledge of the condition and has had a reasonable chance to act on the information given.
- Checks may be paid against the accounts of deceased customers on or prior to the date of death for 10 days after the date of death.
  - Unless a person claiming an interest orders the bank to stop payment.

**Postdated Checks.** This type of check is dated for a future payment date and requires specific steps to require a bank to honor the date on the postdated check.
- The drawer must postdate the check to sometime in the future.
- The drawer must give separate written notice to the bank
  - Describing the check with reasonable certainty and
  - Notifying the bank no to the pay the check until the date on the check.

**Stop-Payment Orders.** Order by drawer of a check to payor bank not to pay or certify a check.
- If it is oral, the order is good for only fourteen days.
- If it is in writing, the order is good for six months, and may be renewed in writing for additional six months periods.

**Overdrafts.** If customer does not have sufficient funds in account to cover amount, payor bank may either dishonor the check or honor the check and create an overdraft in the drawer's account.
- In the event of a dishonor, the payor bank notifies the drawer of the dishonor and returns the check to the holder marked insufficient funds.
  - If the holder resubmits the check and there still are insufficient funds in the customer's account, then the holder may seek recourse against the drawer.

**Wrongful Dishonor.** When the bank fails to honor a check where there are sufficient funds in the drawer's account to pay a properly payable check, it is liable for wrongful dishonor.
- The bank is liable to drawer for damages that were proximately caused by the dishonor

## Forged Signatures and Altered Checks

The U.C.C. rules dealing with checks that are forged or altered apply to all types of negotiable instruments, but are particularly important with checks.

**Forged Signature of the Drawer.** The bank is under a duty to verify the drawer's signature by matching the signature on the check with that of the signature card on file at the bank.
- A forged signature makes the instrument inoperative.
- Bank cannot charge the customer's account if it pays a check over a forged signature.
- The bank's recourse is against the party who presented the check, provided he or she was not aware of the unauthorized signature.
- The forger is liable on the check if he or she can be found.

**Altered Checks.** An unauthorized change in the check that modifies a legal obligation of a party is an altered check.
- The check may be dishonored by the bank if it discovers the alteration.
- If an altered check is paid by the bank, the bank may charge the drawer's account for the original tenor (amount) of the check, but not the altered amount.
- The warranty of presentment applies here, especially if there has been an alteration in a chain of collection.
  - Each party in the chain may collect from the preceding transferor based on a breach of this warranty.

**Receipt of Bank Statement.** If a customer fails to report a series of forgeries or alterations on the same account within 30 days from the date the bank statement was made available to the customer, the bank is not liable on similar transactions after this date and prior to notification.
- If a drawer fails to report a forged or altered check within one year of receiving the bank statement, it relieves the bank of any liability.

## The Collection Process

Banks have a duty to accept deposits into a customer's account. The collection process is ruled by Article 4 of the UCC.
- When an individual receives a check, he or she may go to the drawer's bank or to his or her own bank (known as the depository bank).
  - The depository bank must present the check to the payor bank for collection.
  - Banks not classified as a payor or depository bank are intermediary banks.
- A bank can fill more than one role in the collection process.
- The Federal Reserve System helps banks to collect on checks.
  - Member banks may submit paid checks to Federal Reserve Bank for payment.
  - Member banks pay the Federal Reserve to debit and credit their accounts and to show collection and payment of checks.

**Deferred Posting.** This refers to a daily cutoff for posting checks or deposits.
- Weekends and holidays do not count as business days unless all of the functions of the bank are carried on as usual on those days.
- Deferred posting applies to all banks.

**Provisional Credits.** When a collecting bank gives credit to a check prior to its final settlement.

- Provisional credits may be reversed if the check does not "clear."

**Final Settlement.** A check is deemed finally settled if the payor bank pays the check in cash, settles for the check without having the right to revoke the settlement or fails to dishonor the check within certain time periods. UCC 4-215(a)

*"On Us" Checks.* If drawer and holder have accounts at the same bank, check is an "on us" item.
- The check is considered paid if the bank fails to dishonor the check by business on the second banking day following the receipt of the check.

*"On Them" Checks.* Drawer and holder have accounts at different banks, check is "on them" item
- Each bank must take action prior to its midnight deadline following the banking day it received an "on them" check for collection. UCC 4-104(a)(10)

*Deposit of Cash.* A deposit of money becomes available for withdrawal at the opening of the next banking day following the deposit. UCC 4-215 (a)

**The "Four Legals" that Prevent Payment of a Check.** There are four types of notices or actions that effectively prevent payment of a check by the payer bank.
- Receipt of notice of customer's death, bankruptcy or adjudication of incompentcy.
- Receipt of court order freezing the customer's account.
- Receipt of a stop payment order from the drawer.
- The payor bank's exercise of its right of setoff against the customer's account.

**Failure to Examine Bank Statements in a Timely Manner.** Generally banks send monthly statements to their customers.
- If this does not occur, banks must provide adequate information to allow the customer to be aware of which checks were paid and when and for what amount.
- If checks are not given back to customer, bank must keep checks or copies for 7 years.
- The customer has a duty to examine the statements promptly and with reasonable care.

**Liability of Collecting Banks for Their Own Negligence.** The collecting bank owes a duty to use ordinary care in presenting and sending a check for collection.
- A bank is liable only for losses caused by its own negligence. UCC 4-202

## Commercial Wire Transfers

A commercial wire transfer involves the transferring of money over one or both of the two main wire systems, the Federal Reserve wire transfer network and the New York Clearing House Interbank Payments System.
- Article 4A of the UCC governs wholesale wire transfers.
  o It only applies to commercial electronic fund transfers.
  o If subject to the Electronic Fund Transfer Act, not covered under Article 4A.

**Fund Transfer Procedures.** Commercially reasonable security procedures should be set up.
- If the bank verifies the authenticity of a payment, the customer is bound to pay the order, even if it was not authorized.
  o The customer is not liable if he or she can prove that the unauthorized order was not initiated by an employee or agent or someone who obtained the information from a source controlled by the customer.

## Refresh Your Memory

The following exercises will help to test your memory regarding the principles given in this chapter. Read each question twice, then place your answer in the blank provided for each question. Review the chapter material for any questions you are unable to answer or remember.

1. A(n) _____ _____ relationship is formed upon making a deposit into a bank.

2. Article _____ _____ (_____ _____) of the UCC establishes rules that regulate the creation and collection of and liability for wire transfers.

3. Payee is the _____ and the person to whom the check is indorsed is the _____ .

4. The bank on which the check is drawn is the _____ .

5. Individuals usually purchase _____ _____ to use as a safe substitute for cash while on vacation or other trips.

6. The _____ _____ _____ Act regulates consumer electronic fund transfers.

7. If a check is dishonored because of insufficient funds, it is said to have _____ .

8. A check with a forged drawer's signature is called a(n) _____ _____ .

9. The amount of money a drawer owes a bank after it has paid a check despite insufficient funds in the drawer's account is known as a(n) _____ .

10. An order by a drawer of a check to the payor bank to not pay or certify a check is a(n) _____ _____ _____ .

11. When the drawer and the payee or holder have accounts at the same bank, the check is called a(n) _____ _____ item when it is presented for payment.

12. The _____ _____ _____ assists banks in the collection of checks.

13. A(n) _____ _____ is where an unauthorized change has been made that modifies the legal obligation of a party.

14. A(n) _____ _____ is where a bank does not honor a check when there are sufficient funds in a drawer's account to pay a properly payable check.

15. A check that has been outstanding for more than six months is considered _____ .

## Critical Thought Exercise

Dave Austin of Austin Imports is an antique dealer who often makes purchases without sufficient funds in his account because he must often act quickly to purchase a one-of-a-kind item before another dealer can take advantage of a very profitable sale price. Austin often postdates checks for the purchases of furniture, art, rugs and other items that he resells. Austin has a very good relationship with Everglades Bank in Miami, where his main studio is located. The operations officer of Everglades Bank knows that Austin uses postdated checks for purchases approximately 50-75 times per year out of a total of 1,200 checks written on his account.

When the operations officer at Everglades Bank took a position with another bank, four postdated checks totaling $58,000 were negotiated before the written date, causing 47 other checks to be dishonored.

If Austin sues Everglades Bank to recover incidental and consequential damages for wrongful dishonor, will he prevail?

*Please compose your answer on a separate sheet of paper or on your computer.*

# Practice Quiz

## True/False

1. \_\_\_\_ Checks can act as a substitute for money but cannot serve as a credit function.

2. \_\_\_\_ It is necessary that a traveler's check be signed a second time.

3. \_\_\_\_ The bank need not pay a stale check if it has been outstanding for more than six months

4. \_\_\_\_ Checks may be paid against the accounts of deceased customers.

5. \_\_\_\_ If there are insufficient funds in Joanne's account when a check is properly presented for payment, the bank may honor the check and create an overdraft in her account.

6. \_\_\_\_ Under the Forged Signature Act, a bank is required to verify signatures involving customers who have banked with them for more than ten years.

7. \_\_\_\_ If a payor bank pays on an altered check, it can charge the drawer's account of the original tenor but not the altered amount.

8. \_\_\_\_ A depository bank is the bank where the payee or holder has an account.

9. \_\_\_\_ An intermediary bank is neither the depository bank nor the payor bank in the collection process.

10. \_\_\_\_ Under the deferred posting rule, banks are allowed to fix an afternoon hour as a cutoff for the purpose of processing items.

11. \_\_\_\_ An "on us" item refers to the fact that both the drawer and the payee or holder have accounts at different banks.

12. \_\_\_\_ Article 4A applies only to commercial electronic fund transfers.

13. \_\_\_\_ Depository banks often let their customers withdraw their funds before the final settlement of account.

14. ___ Purchasers of traveler's checks do not need an account at the issuing bank.

15. ___ If a bank fails to pay electronic fund transfer when there are sufficient funds in the customer's account to do so, the bank will not be liable for wrongful dishonor.

## Multiple Choice

16. In order for a bank to provide the service of paying recurring payments and crediting recurring deposits, which of the following is necessary?
    a. The customer's bank and the payee's bank must belong to the same clearinghouse.
    b. The customer must have a computer to pay his or her bills on the Internet.
    c. The customer must qualify for a debit card at the bank that holds his or her money.
    d. None of the above.

17. Which of the following is a type of check where a bank agrees in advance to accept the check when it is presented for payment?
    a. A point-of-sale terminal check
    b. A traveler's check
    c. An automatic withdrawal check
    d. A certified check

18. A stale check is one that
    a. has been left on the counter for a week.
    b. has been presented for payment of a drawer's properly drawn check by drawee bank.
    c. has the risk of loss of an incomplete item on the drawer.
    d. has been outstanding for more than six months.

19. What type of duty does a customer owe when determining if any payment was unauthorized due to alteration of a check or forged signature?
    a. The customer does not owe any duty whatsoever.
    b. The customer owes a duty to change banks.
    c. The customer owes a duty to promptly examine the statements and determine if payment was unauthorized.
    d. The customer owes a duty to apprise the bank of its duty.

20. A check is finally paid when the payor bank
    a. pays the check in cash.
    b. settles for the check without having a right to revoke the settlement.
    c. fails to dishonor the check within certain statutory time periods.
    d. all of the above.

21. What is the banking term that refers to a depositor physically presenting a check for payment at the payor bank?
    a. the four legals
    b. presentment across the counter
    c. on them item
    d. the midnight deadline

22. What type of duty does the collecting bank owe when presenting and sending a check for collection?
    a. duty to use ordinary care
    b. duty to use minimal care
    c. duty to use intermediate care
    d. duty to use strict care

23. In the creditor-debtor relationship involving the customer and the financial institution, who is the creditor?
    a. the financial institution
    b. the Visa organization
    c. the customer
    d. the debtor

24. In the principal-agent relationship involving the customer and the financial institution, who is the agent?
    a. the customer
    b. the principal
    c. the debtor
    d. the financial institution

25. Bank checks include which of the following:
    a. certified checks
    b. traveller's checks
    c. cashier's checks
    d. all of the above

## Short Answer

26. Describe the bank process of certification.
    _____
    _____

27. For what will the bank who is obligated on a cashier's check be held liable?
    _____

28. What is meant by presentment across the counter?
    _____

29. When is the process of posting considered to be complete?
    _____
    _____

30. If Kurt wants to write a post-dated check to Mona, what must he do to accomplish this under the rules of UCC 4-401(c)?
    _____
    _____

31. Wanda, a customer of Mississippi Bank and Trust passes away on January 1. What is the rule regarding the length of time that her bank may pay or certify checks drawn on her account?

_____

_____

32. What types of rules and principles does Article 4 of the UCC regulate?

_____

33. Explain the meaning of a check.

_____

_____

34. Give three examples of bank checks.

_____

35. When is a check considered to be certified?

_____

36. For how long is a written stop-payment order binding?

_____

37. List and define the parties to a check.

_____

_____

38. What are the two actions from which the holder of a check has to choose?

_____

39. What is the drawer's liability on a certified check?

_____

40. What role does the issuing bank serve with a cashier's check?

_____

# Answers to Refresh Your Memory

1. creditor-debtor [p 566]
2. Article 4A (Funds Transfer) [p 567]
3. indorser, indorsee [p 567-568]
4. drawee [p 567]
5. traveler's checks [p 570]
6. Electronic Fund Transfer [p 570]
7. bounced [p 588]
8. forged instrument [p 573]
9. overdraft [p 572]
10. stop-payment order [p 572]
11. On Us [p 579]
12. Federal Reserve System [p 577]

13. altered check  [p 574]
14. wrongful dishonor  [p 572]
15. stale  [p 571]

# Critical Thought Exercise Model Answer

A bank may charge a postdated check against a customer's account as a demand instrument, unless the customer notifies the bank of the postdating in time to allow the bank to act on the notice before the bank commits itself to pay on the check.  If the bank receives timely notice from the customer and nonetheless charges the customer's account before the date on the postdated check, the bank may be liable for any damages incurred by the customer as a result.

The bank had discussed the use of postdated checks with Austin and permitted his practice of postdating a significant number of checks each year.  Everglades Bank will have a difficult time convincing a court that it was not on notice that postdated checks were being written by Austin.  However, the UCC makes it clear that the customer must not only give notice that a postdated check has been issued, but must also describe the postdated check with reasonable certainty.  Austin never contacted the bank to describe the checks with any certainty.  He just relied upon the practice of a prior employee of the bank who examined his checks carefully before charging them to his account.  Under the UCC, Everglades Bank has not received notice concerning the specific checks.  Therefore, Austin should not prevail in a suit to recover damages caused by having the other 47 checks dishonored.

# Answers to Practice Quiz

## True/False

1. True  Even though checks are a substitute for money, they do not serve a credit function. [p 566]
2. True  The purchaser initially signs the traveler's check upon purchase of the same and then must sign the second blank when he or she uses the checks to purchase goods or services. [p 570]
3. True  The bank is under no obligation to pay on a check that has been outstanding for more than six months. [p 571]
4. True  Payment against the accounts of deceased customers is very limited.  The bank may pay or certify checks drawn on the deceased customer's account on or prior to the date of death for 10 days after the date of the death. [p 571]
5. True  UCC 4-401(a) allows for the payor bank to honor a check and create an overdraft in the drawer's account if the drawer does not have enough money in his or her account when a properly payable check is presented for payment. [p 572]
6. False  A bank is under a duty to verify the drawer's signature when the drawer presents a check to the drawer bank for payment.  This duty is not limited to customers of 10 years or more. [p 573]
7. True  The payor bank may charge the drawer's account for the original tenor of the check, but not the altered amount. [p 574]
8. True  The bank where the payee or holder has an account is the depository bank. [p 577]
9. True  An intermediary bank is a bank in the collection process that is not the depository or payor bank. [p 577]

10. True The deferred posting rule allows banks to fix an afternoon hour of 2:00P.M. or later as a cutoff hour for the purpose of processing items. [p 578]

11. False A check that is presented for payment where the depository bank is also the payor bank is an "on us" item. [p 579]

12. True Article 4A governs wholesale wire transfers and applies only to commercial electronic fund transfers. [p 582]

13. True Depository banks often let their customers withdraw their funds before the final settlement of account. [p 578]

14. True Purchasers of traveler's checks do not necessarily have to have an account at the issuing bank. [p 570]

15. False If a customer has sufficient funds in his or her account and the bank fails to pay an electronic fund transfer, it will be liable for wrongful dishonor. [p 571]

## Multiple Choice

16. A Answer A is the correct answer, as it is necessary that the customer's bank and the payee's bank must belong to the same clearinghouse in order to provide the service of paying recurring payments and crediting recurring deposits. Answer B is incorrect, as having a computer to pay bills by the Internet may be convenient, however, it would not accomplish or assist the bank in its role of paying recurring payments and crediting recurring deposits. Answer C is incorrect, as qualifying for a debt card would has no impact on the banks service of paying recurring payments and crediting recurring deposits. Answer D is incorrect based on the reasoning given above. [p 568]

17. D Answer D is the correct answer, as a certified check is one in which the bank agrees in advance to accept the check when it is presented for payment and pay the check out of funds set aside from the customer's account and either placed in a special certified check account or held in the customer's account. Answer A is incorrect, as there is no such thing as a point-of-sale terminal check. Point-of-sale terminal refers to terminals used in conjunction with bank issued debit cards for use in making purchases that are directly debited from the customer's account. Answer B is incorrect, as traveler's checks are used instead of cash when people are on vacation or on other trips. Answer C is incorrect, as once again, there is no such thing as an automatic withdrawal check. [p 569]

18. D Answer D is the correct answer, as a stale check is one that has been outstanding for six months or more. Answer A is incorrect, as this definition is not the correct definition used in the banking industry. Answer B is incorrect, as it indicates that the check has been presented whereas a stale check has not been presented. Answer C is incorrect, as it makes no sense whatsoever. [p 571]

19. C Answer C is the correct answer, as bank customers are under a duty to promptly examine their bank statements to determine if any payment was unauthorized due to alteration of a check or forged signature. Answer A is incorrect, as this is an untrue statement. Answer B is incorrect, as the duty to change banks is not a legally recognized duty. Answer D is incorrect, as not only is it untrue, but customers normally do not let the bank know of its duty as the bank already knows that it has a duty of ordinary care. [p 575]

20. D Answer D is the correct answer, as answers A, B, and C all explain when a check is paid based upon what the payor bank does. [p 579]

21. B Answer B is the correct answer, as presentment across the counter refers to a depositor physically presenting a check for payment at the payor bank. Answer A is incorrect, as the four legals refers to types of notices or actions that effectively prevent payment of a check. Answer C is incorrect, as an "on them item" refers to the drawer and payee or holder having accounts at different banks, hence the payor and depository bank are not

the same bank. Answer D is incorrect, as the midnight deadline refers to the proper action a bank must take on a check as per its collection process. [p 579]

22. A  Answer A is the correct answer, as the collecting bank owes a duty to use ordinary care in presenting and sending a check for collection, as well as sending notices of dishonor, and taking other actions in the collection process. Answers B, C, and D are all incorrect, as they do not state the correct duty of care owed by the collecting bank. [p 580]

23. C  Answer C is correct, as the customer is the creditor since he or she is loaning money to the financial institution when he or she deposits money into his or her account. Answer A is incorrect, as the financial institution is the debtor. Answer B is incorrect, as it does not make sense. Answer D is incorrect, as the debtor cannot be the creditor. [p 566]

24. D  Answer D is correct, as the financial institution is the agent. Answer A is incorrect, as the customer is the principal. Answer B is incorrect, as the principal cannot be the agent in the same relationship. Answer C is incorrect, as it makes no sense. [p 566]

25. D  Answer D is correct, as answers A,B, and C all state what is included when referring to bank checks. [p 568]

## Short Answer

26. The bank process of certification involves the accepting bank writing or stamping the word certified on the ordinary check of an account holder and sets aside funds from the account to pay the check. [p 569]

27. The bank can be held liable for the amount of the check, expenses, and loss of interest resulting from nonpayment. [p 570]

28. Presentment across the counter refers to a depositor physically presenting the check for payment at the payor bank instead of depositing an "on them" check for collection. [p 579]

29. It is considered to be complete when the responsible bank officer has made a decision to pay the check and the proper book entry has been made to charge the drawer's account the amount of the check. [p 580]

30. Kurt must postdate the check to Mona to some date in the future. Also, Kurt must give separate written notice to the bank describing the check with reasonable certainty and notifying the bank not to pay the check until the date on the check. [p 571]

31. Mississippi Bank and Trust may pay or certify checks drawn on Wanda's account on or prior to the date of death for 10 days after the date of Wanda's death. [p 571]

32. It regulates bank deposits and collection procedures for checking accounts offered by commercial banks. [p 567]

33. The UCC 3-104(f) defines a check as "an order by the drawer bank to pay a specified sum of money from the drawer's checking account to the named payee (or holder)." [p 567]

34. Certified, cashier's, and traveler's. [p 568]

35. When the bank stamps or writes the word certified across an ordinary check's face. [p 569]

36. For six months and may be renewed for additional six-month periods. [p 572]

37. The drawer is the customer who has the checking account and writes checks against the account. The drawee is the bank on which the check is drawn. The payee is theparty to whom the check is written. [p 567]

38. The holder can chose to demand payment or to indorse the check to another party. [p 577]

39. Once the drawee bank has certified the check, drawer is discharged from liability. [p 569]

40. The issuing bank is both the drawer and the drawee. [p 569]

## Chapter 23
# CREDIT AND SECURED TRANSACTIONS

## Chapter Overview

The U.S. economy is based on credit. Consumers and businesses use credit to purchase goods and services. Some of these loans require that the debtor give a security interest in some of the debtor's property to secure the loan. Other loans require the debtor to have a third party guarantee the loan before the creditor will make the loan. This chapter looks at the different types of credit, security interests in real and personal property, suretyship, and debtor protection laws.

## Objectives

Upon completion of the exercises in this chapter, you should be able to:

1. Explain unsecured credit verses secured credit.
2. Discuss mortgages and deeds of trust.
3. Explain what a deficiency judgment is.
4. Discuss a secured transaction in personal property and the scope of Article 9 of the UCC.
5. Discuss the difference between a surety and guaranty arrangement.

## Practical Application

You should be able to recognize the various types of credit and security interests in real and personal property. You should be able to understand the available remedies associated with personal property transactions. You should be able to discuss surety and guaranty arrangements and remedies associated with the collection of debts.

## Helpful Hints

It can be helpful to differentiate between the terms associated with secured and unsecured credit, real and personal property, and surety and guaranty arrangements. Once you have a grasp of these main terms, the remedies that are available become easier to understand and learn.

## Study Tips

### Unsecured and Secured Credit

There are two basic types of credit that may be extended to a debtor, unsecured or secured.

**Debtor and Creditor.** There are two necessary parties in a credit transaction.
- The creditor, or lender, is the person extending credit to the debtor.
- The debtor, or borrower, is the person borrowing the money.

**Unsecured Credit.** This type of credit does not need any collateral to protect the debt.

- The creditor relies on the debtor's promise to repay the debt, and interest, when due.

**Secured Credit.** This type of credit does need collateral to secure the payment of the loan.

## Security Interest in Real Property

A security interest in real property happens when the owner borrows money from a lender and pledges the real property as security for the loan.

**Mortgage.** A property owner borrows money from a creditor who thereafter uses a deed as a means of security (collateral) to secure the repayment of the loan.

- The mortgagor is the owner-debtor in a mortgage transaction.
- The mortgagee is the creditor in a transaction involving a mortgage.

**Note and Deed of Trust.** Some states use these instruments in the place of a mortgage.

- The note is a legal instrument that is proof of the borrower's debt to the lender.
- The Deed of Trust is a legal instrument that evinces the creditor's security interest in the debtor's property that is pledged as collateral.

**Recording Statute.** These are state laws that require the mortgage or deed of trust to be recorded in the county recorder's office of the county where the real property is located.

- Failure to record does not affect the rights and obligations of parties to the mortgage.
- Improper recording is not notice to subsequent purchasers or other lienholders.

**Foreclosure.** The mortgagee can assert the entire debt due and payable if the mortgagor defaults.

*Foreclosure Sale.* The debtor's default may trigger a foreclosure action which, if successful, produces a court order that the real property be sold at judicial sale.

*Power of Sale.* Foreclosure by power of sale is allowed in most states.

- Power and procedure must be expressly stated in the mortgage or deed of trust.

*Deficiency Judgment.* A separate legal action to recover a deficiency from the mortgagor brings a deficiency judgment giving the mortgagee the right to recover from the mortgagor's property.

- Prohibited by antideficiency statutes against original purchase of residential property.

*Right of Redemption.* The common law and many states allow the mortgagor to redeem real property after default and before foreclosure.

- Mortgagor must pay the full amount of the debt: principal, interest, and other costs caused by the default.

**Land Sales Contract.** The transfer and sale of real property in accordance with a land sales contract whereby the owner of the real property agrees to sell the property to a buyer, who assents to pay the asking price to the owner-seller over a stated, agreed period of time.

- If purchaser defaults, seller may claim forfeiture and retake possession of the property.
- The right of redemption is allowed in many states.

**Mechanic's Lien.** When an individual provides contracting or a service toward improvement of real property, their investments are protected by statutory law that allow them to file a material person's lien (mechanic's lien) against the improved real property.

*Procedure for Obtaining a Material Person's Lien.* State laws vary, but general requirements for obtaining these liens are similar.
- Lienholder must properly, timely file notice of lien, which states particulars of claim.
- Notice must be given to the owner of the real property.

*Lien Release.* The owner of real property can have material persons who have provided services sign a written release of lien contract attesting to payment and releasing any lien.

## Securied Transactions – Revised Article 9 of the UCC

Tangible and intangible personal property are purchased or leased by both individuals and businesses. This property is often sold on credit.
- Types of personal property:
  - Tangible property is items such as furniture, automobiles, and jewelry.
  - Intangible property is items such as intellectual property, and securities.
- Types of credit:
  - Unsecured credit, the creditor does not take an interest in collateral to secure loan
  - Secured credit is where a creditor agrees to extend credit only if the purchaser pledges personal property as collateral for the loan.

**Revised Article 9.** This article of the UCC governs secured transactions in personal property, and recognizes many aspects of e-commerce.

**Secured Transaction.** The security interest in personal property of the debtor that is taken by the creditor when credit is given to the debtor is the basis for a secured transaction.
- If the debtor defaults, the secured party can foreclose and recover the collateral.

**Definitions Important to Secured Transactions.** Revised UCC 9-102(a) defines some terms.
- A debtor is a person with ownership or other interest in collateral and owes payment of a secured obligation.
- A secured party is a person in whose favor a security interest is created or provided under a security agreement.
- A security interest is an interest in the collateral which secures payment or performance of an obligation.
- A security agreement is an agreement that creates or provides for a security interest.
- Collateral is the property subject to a security agreement.
- A financing statement is the record of an initial financing statement or filed record relating to the initial financing statement.

**A Two-Party Secured Transaction.** This secured transaction occurs when a seller sells goods to a buyer on credit and retains a security interest in the goods.

**A Three-Party Secured Transaction.** This secured transaction occurs when a seller sells goods to a buyer who gets financing from a third-party lender that takes a security interest in the goods.

**Personal Property Subject to a Security Agreement.** Personal property can be collateral.

- Goods include consumer goods, equipment, farm products, inventory, and fixtures.
- Instruments include checks, notes, stocks, bonds and other securities.
- Chattel paper such as a conditional sales contract.
- Documents of Title such as a bill of lading, and warehouse receipt.
- Accounts like accounts receivable.
- General intangibles like patents, copyrights, money franchises and royalties.

## Creating and Perfecting a Security Interest

Requirements to create a security interest in personal property are given in Revised Article 9.

**Security Agreement.** There must be a written security agreement, unless the collateral is in the possession of the creditor.
- It must clearly describe the collateral.
- It must contain the debtor's promise to repay the creditor, including terms.
- It must set forth the creditor's rights upon debtor's default.
- It must be signed by the debtor. [UCC 9-203(1)]

*Attachment.* The creditor has an enforceable security interest against the debtor and can satisfy the debt out of the collateral.
- The debtor must have a present or future legal right in or to possession of the collateral.

*The Floating-Lien Concept.* A security agreement that provides that security interest attaches to property not originally in possession of debtor when agreement was executed is a floating lien.
- After-Acquired Property is acquired by debtor after the security agreement is executed.
- Sale Proceeds occur if a debtor sells, exchanges, or disposes of collateral, and the secured party automatically has the right to receive the proceeds.
- Future Advances occur when a debtor establishes a revolving line of credit, certain personal property is designated as collateral for future loans from the line of credit.

**Perfecting a Security Interest.** This is a legal process that establishes the right of a secured creditor against other creditors who claim an interest in the collateral.

*Perfection by Filing a Financing Statement.* Physical possession of collateral by the creditor is often impractical, so filing a financing statement in the proper government office is the most common method for perfecting a security interest.
- These statements are public and serve as notice of the creditor's claim to the collateral.
- These statements are good for five years and can be continued in five year terms.
- A financing statement must contain the debtor's name and mailing address, the secured party name and address, and a statement identifying the collateral.
- State law specifies the place of filing.

*Perfection by Possession of Collateral.* If the creditor has physical possession of the collateral, no financing statement is required.

*Perfection by a Purchase Money Security Interest in Consumer Goods.* When a creditor gives credit to a consumer to purchase a consumer good under a written security agreement, the creditor has a purchase money security interest in the consumer good, or perfection by attachment.
- The agreement automatically perfects the creditor's security interest at the time of sale.
- No financing statement need be filed.

**Termination Statement.** The secured party must file a termination statement with each filing officer with whom the financing statement was filed once the debt is paid.
- Must be filed within 1 month of debt being paid or within 10 days of written demand.
- Failure to file or send this statement subjects the creditor to liability to debtor.

## Priority of Claims

When two or more creditors claim an interest in the same collateral or property, the priority of these claims is determined by secured status and the time of attachment or perfection.

**UCC Rules for Determining Priority.** UCC gives rules for determining the priority of claims.
- Secured Versus Unsecured Claims. A creditor with the only secured interest has priority over unsecured interests.
- Competing Unperfected Secured Claims. If two or more secured parties claim an interest, but neither has perfected, the first to attach has priority.
- Perfected Versus Unperfected Claims. If two or more secured parties claim an interest, but only one has perfected, the perfected security interest has priority.
- Competing Perfected Secured Claims. If two or more secured parties claim a perfected interest, the first to perfect has priority.
- Perfected Secured Claims in Fungible, Commingled Goods. If a security interest is perfected, but the good are later commingled with other goods with perfected security interests, the security interests rank equally according to the ratio that the cost of goods to which each interest originally attached bears to the cost of the total product or mass.

**Exceptions to the Perfection-Priority Rule.** Perfection does not always protect a secured party from third-party claims, as the UCC recognizes several exceptions to the perfection priority rule.

*Purchase Money Security Interest: Inventory as Collateral.* A perfected purchase money security interest can prevail over perfected nonpurchase money security interest in after-acquired property.
- If collateral is inventory, perfected purchase money security interest wins if purchase money secured party gives written notice of perfection to perfected non-purchase money secured party before debtor receives possession of inventory. [UCC 9-312(3)]

*Purchase Money Security Interest: Noninventory as Collateral.* If collateral is not inventory
- A perfected purchase money security interest would prevail over a perfected non-purchase money security interest in after-acquired property if it was perfected before or within 10 days after the debtor receives possession of the collateral. [UCC 9-312(4)]

*Buyers in the Ordinary Course of Business.* This buyer purchases goods from a merchant and takes the goods free of any perfected or unperfected security interest in the merchant's inventory.

*Secondhand Consumer Goods.* Buyers of these goods take the goods free of security interest if they do not have actual or constructive knowledge of the security interest, give value, and buy the goods for personal, family, or household purposes.
- Filing of a financing statement by the creditor is constructive notice.

## Default and Remedies

Article 9 defines rights, duties and remedies of secured party and debtor in event of default.

- Default is not defined, so parties are free to define it in the agreement.
- The secured party may reduce claim to judgment, foreclose, or other enforcement.

**Taking Possession of the Collateral.** Most secured parties seek to cure a default by repossessing the collateral.
- The secured party can retain the property.
- They can sell or dispose of the property and satisfy the debt from the proceeds.
- They must act in good faith.

*Retention of Collateral.* Notice of proposal to retain the collateral must be sent to debtor.
- For consumer goods, no other notice is needed.
- For other goods, notice must be sent to any other secured party who has given written notice of a claim.
- Retention is not allowed when
  - The secured party receives a written objection from a person entitled to notice.
  - Debt involves consumer goods and debtor has paid 60 % of case price or loan

*Disposition of Collateral.* This may be public or private through commercially reasonable means.
- Creditor must give debtor notice of time and place of disposition.
  - For consumer goods, no other notice is needed.
  - For other goods, notice must be sent to any other secured party who has given written notice of a claim.
  - Perishable or goods of volatile value may not require notice.
- Discharges the security interest and any subordinate security interests or liens.

*Proceeds from Disposition.* Proceeds must be applied in a specific order:
- Reasonable expenses for retaking, holding, and preparing collateral for disposition.
- Satisfaction of the balance of the indebtedness to the secured party.
- Satisfaction of subordinate security interests whose written claims have been received prior to distribution.
- The debtor is entitled to any surplus.

*Deficiency Judgment.* The debtor is personally liable for the deficiency if the proceeds from disposition of the collateral are insufficient.
- The secured party may bring a legal action to recover the deficiency.
- If the transaction was chattel paper or a sale of accounts, the debtor is only liable for a deficiency if the agreement so states.

*Redemption Rights.* The debtor or another secured party may redeem the collateral before the priority lienholder has disposed of it.
- Requires payment of all obligations secured by the collateral.

**Relinquishing the Security Interest and Proceeding to Judgment on the Underlying Debt.** A secured creditor may relinquish his or her security interest and go on to judgment against debtor.
- Rarely chosen, unless the value of collateral has been reduced below amount of secured interest and/or debtor has other assets.

**Cumulative Remedies.** The rights and remedies of Revised Article 9 are cumulative and can be exercised simultaneously.

**Artisan's Liens.** A worker who furnishes services or materials in the ordinary course of business with respect to goods can receive a lien on the goods by statue.

- Super-priority liens, as they prevail over all other security interests.

## Surety and Guaranty Arrangements

When a creditor refuses to extend credit unless a third person agrees to become liable on the debt, the third person's credit becomes the security for the debt.

**Surety Arrangement.** A situation where a third party promises to be primarily liable with the borrower for the payment of the borrower's debt.

- The surety is the third person who agrees to be liable in a surety arrangement.
  - o He or she is often called an accommodation party or a co-signer.
  - o He or she is primarily liable on the debt.

**Guaranty Arrangement.** A situation where a third party promises to be secondarily liable for the payment of another's debt.

- The guarantor is the third person who agrees to be liable in a guaranty arrangement.
- He or she is secondarily liable on the debt.

**Defenses of a Surety or Guarantor.** A surety or guarantor may utilize the same defenses as the principal debtor against the creditor.

## Debtor Protection Law

The federal government has enacted a comprehensive scheme of laws to protect consumer-debtors from abusive, deceptive, and unfair practices by creditors.

**Truth-in-Lending Act (TILA).** This Act requires creditors to make certain disclosures to debtors in consumer transactions and real estate loans on the debtor's principal dwelling.

*Regulation Z.* This regulation sets forth detailed rules for compliance with the TILA.

- TILA and Regulation require detailed financial information about credit being offered.

**Consumer Leasing Act (CLA).** This Act extends TILA coverage to consumer lease terms.

**Fair Credit and Charge Card Disclosure Act.** This Act amended TILA to require disclosure of credit terms on credit and charge card solicitations and applications.

**Equal Credit Opportunity Act (ECOA).** This Act prohibits discrimination in extending credit.

**Fair Credit Reporting Act (FCRA).** As part of TILA, this Act protects consumers by setting out guidelines for consumer reporting agencies.

**Fair Debt Collection Practices Act (FDCPA).** This Act protects consumer-debtors from abusive, deceptive, and unfair practices used by debt collectors.

## Collection Remedies

The creditor may bring a legal action against the debtor when a debt is past due. If successful, the court will award a judgment against the debtor.

**Attachment.** This remedy involves a prejudgment order allowing the seizure of the debtor's property while the lawsuit is pending.

**Execution.** This remedy concerns a postjudgment court order allowing seizure of the debtor's property that is in possession of the debtor.

**Garnishment**. This is also a postjudgment court order. However it allows the seizure of the debtor's property that is in the possession of third parties.

**Title III of the Consumer Credit Protection Act.** This law protects debtors who are subject to a writ of garnishment to keep the greater of 75 percent of their weekly disposable earnings (after taxes) or an amount equivalent to thirty hours of work paid at federal minimum wage.

# Refresh Your Memory

The following exercises will help to test your memory regarding the principles given in this chapter. Read each question twice, then place your answer in the blank provided for each question. Review the chapter material for any questions you are unable to answer or remember.

1. _____ and _____ are the two basis from which credit may be extended.

2. If Bob is not required to have any security to protect the payment of a debt to Fine Lamps, Inc., then it may be said that Bob has _____ credit.

3. When a creditor brings a lawsuit against a debtor to recover on a loan for what the collateral cannot satisfy, the lawsuit is for recovery of a(n) _____ _____.

4. A(n) _____ _____ _____ a legal instrument that gives a creditor a security interest in the debtor's property that is pledged as collateral.

5. A surety is called an accommodation party or a(n) _____.

6. A(n) _____ occurs when a property owner borrows money from a creditor and uses his or her real estate as collateral for the loan.

7. A(n) _____ _____ requires that a mortgage or deed of trust be recorded in the county recorder's office in the county in which the real property is located.

8. If a mortgagor defaults on a mortgage, the mortgagee can enforce his or her right to declare the debt due and payable immediately through _____.

9. Most states allow a mortgagor the right to _____ real property after default and before foreclosure.

10. In a(n) _____ _____ _____, the owner of real property agrees to sell the property to a purchaser, who agrees to pay the purchase price over an agreed period of time.

11. A security interest may be given in personal property that becomes _____ for a loan.

12. _____ means the creditor has an enforceable security interest against the debtor and can assure the debt out of the specified collateral.

13. _____ _____ _____ _____ _____ confirms the right of a secured creditor against other creditors claiming an interest in the collateral.

14. _____ _____ serve as constructive notice to the world that a creditor claims an interest in a property.

15. Most secured parties seek to cure a default by _____ the collateral from the debtor.

## Critical Thought Exercise

Steve and Bonnie West purchased an old Victorian home outside St. Louis and planned to renovate it and sell it for a profit before moving onto another renovation project. Bonnie's brother, Doug Nixon, did most of the major work on the house and hired trades people to assist in areas that are beyond his expertise. Nixon hired Summit Roofing to replace the old shake roof with a fire resistant composite product that matched the house in color and style. The cost of the new roof is $17,400, including all labor and materials. Steve and Bonnie pay Doug $86,500 for the entire project. Doug failed to pay Summit Roofing and absconded with all the funds.

Steve and Bonnie West entered into a real estate purchase agreement with Lucy Rogers to purchase the home for $515,000. The contract between West and Rogers states that the property is free of all encumbrances and escrow will close in 30 days.

Summit Roofing filed a mechanics lean against the property. The West's demanded that Summit Roofing seek payment from Doug Nixon. Summit Roofing gave notice that it was going to foreclose against the property to recover the $17,400 owed to it.

What action should the Wests take to ensure that the sale to Rogers will not be thwarted?

*Please compose your answer on a separate sheet of paper or on your computer.*

## Practice Quiz

### True/False

1. \_\_\_\_ A mechanic's lien becomes the security for payment of improvements.

2. \_\_\_\_ The right of redemption prohibits the mortgagor from paying the full amount of the debt which includes principle, interest and other costs.

3. \_\_\_\_ A deed of trust gives the creditor a security interest in the owner-debtor's real property.

4. \_\_\_\_ A surety arrangement involves a third person who is liable in a guaranty arrangement.

5. \_\_\_\_ A surety is a third person who does not agree to be liable in a surety arrangement.

6. \_\_\_\_ In a guaranty arrangement, the debtor is secondarily liable for the debt of the debtor.

7. ___ Samson purchases a riding lawnmower on credit and Gloria acts as the surety for the debt. Thereafter, both Samson and Gloria discover that the gearshift is defective. Both Samson and Gloria may assert the defect as a defense to liability.

8. ___ An attachment is a prejudgment order permitting seizure of the debtor's property while litigation is still pending.

9. ___ Automobiles, furniture and jewelry are examples of real property.

10. ___ Real estate owners can create security interests in their property.

11. ___ In some states a deed of trust may be used in place of a mortgage.

12. ___ Under a power of sale, the procedure need not be in the mortgage or deed of trust.

13. ___ Several states provide a statutory procedure that must be adhered to foreclose on a land sales contract.

14. ___ Felix, a contractor, files a mechanics' lien against Virginia for laying brick around Virginia's home. Felix may use the improvements as security for payment on the services and materials.

15. ___ The general time frame to foreclose on a lien is anywhere from six months to two years from the date that the lien is filed.

## Multiple Choice

16. A person's ownership interest in real property is usually detailed in writing in
    a. a foreclosure.
    b. a deed.
    c. a lien.
    d. a letter.

17. An improperly recorded mortgage or deed of trust is not effective against
    a. debtors.
    b. subsequent purchasers of real property.
    c. mortgagor.
    d. the original mortgagee.

18. The benefits of a statutory procedure of foreclosing on a land sale contract include
    a. the fact that it is a simpler way to foreclose.
    b. the fact that it is less time consuming.
    c. the fact that it is less expensive than foreclosure on a mortgage or deed of trust.
    d. all of the above.

19. A writ of attachment is a
    a. court order that states that the debtor must pay the creditor an amount equal to 30 hours of work paid at federal minimum wage.
    b. court order that directs the sheriff to seize the debtor's property and authorizes a judicial sale of the property.
    c. prejudgment order allowing seizure of the debtor's property while litigation is pending.

    d.  court order stating that property such as tools of the trade, homestead exemption and clothing are exempt from being levied upon.

20.  The Consumer Credit Protection Act provides that debtors may
    a.  have their wages garnished up to 75 percent of weekly disposable earnings after taxes.
    b.  have their wages garnished up to 30 hours of work paid at federal minimum wage.
    c.  retain up to 75 percent of their weekly disposable earnings or an amount equal to 30 hours of work paid at federal minimum wage, which ever is greater of the two.
    d.  protect debtors from the garnishment of any wages whatsoever.

21.  What type of procedure allows a mortgagee to declare an entire property based debt to be due and payable immediately?
    a.  deficiency judgment procedure
    b.  foreclosure
    c.  right of redemption
    d.  all of the above

22.  In a secured transaction, who is the secured party?
    a.  the debtor
    b.  the redeemer
    c.  the mortgagor
    d.  none of the above

23.  Article 9 of the UCC does not apply to which of the following transactions?
    a.  real estate mortgages
    b.  artisan's liens
    c.  judicial liens
    d.  all of the above

24.  What is meant by after-acquired property?
    a.  property that the debtor acquires after the security agreement is executed
    b.  property that the debtor acquires before the security agreement is executed
    c.  property that the debtor acquires during the security agreement
    d.  none of the above

25.  What is the most common method of perfecting a creditor's security interest in collateral?
    a.  by filing a writ of attachment
    b.  by filing a lawsuit
    c.  by filing a perfection of attachment
    d.  by filing a financing statement

## Short Answer

26.  What purpose does collateral have?

_____

27.  What legal option is available to a mortgagor who has defaulted on a loan but has not yet been foreclosed upon?

_____

28. What types of real property interests are sold using a land sale contract?

_____

29. What must a creditor do in order to obtain a writ of attachment?

_____

30. In a writ of execution, for who are the proceeds from the debtor's property used?

_____

_____

31. What is involved with a foreclosure by power of sale?

_____

32. Explain what role a guarantor plays with regard to a debtor's debt.

_____

33. Explain a deficiency judgment.

_____

_____

34. Which party may also assert the defenses that the principal debtor has against the creditor?

_____

35. Give two examples of personal property that are tangible and two that are intangible.

_____

36. What is an artisan's or mechanic's lien?

_____

_____

37. What is a mortgage?

_____

38. What requires the mortgage or deed of trust to be documented in a county office where real property is located?

_____

39. Edna fails to pay her monthly mortgage payment on the ranch she is purchasing from California Savings and Loan. What legal procedure may California Savings and Loan bring against Edna?

_____

40. What does the Truth-In-Lending Act require?

_____

## Answers to Refresh Your Memory

1. unsecured, secured  [p 593]
2. unsecured  [p 594]

3. deficiency judgment [p 594]
4. deed of trust [p 595]
5. co-signer [p 615]
6. mortgage [p 595]
7. recording statute [p 596]
8. foreclosure [p 598]
9. redeem [p 598]
10. land sales contract [p 599]
11. collateral [p 602]
12. Attachment [p 604]
13. Perfection of a security interest [p 605]
14. Financing statements [p 605]
15. repossessing [p 612]

# Critical Thought Exercise Model Answer

Contractors and laborers who expend time and money for materials that are used for improvements upon real property may protect themselves by filing a mechanic's lien against the real property upon which the improvement was made by the contractor or laborer. In order to obtain a mechanic's lien, the contractor will usually have to meet the following requirements to perfect their lien: (1) File a notice of lien with the county recorder's office in the county where the real property is located; (2) The notice must state the amount of the claim, a description of the real property, the name of the property owner, and the name of the claimant; (3) The notice must be filed within the statutory time as set forth in the statute (usually 30-120 days), and; (4) Notice of the lien must be transmitted to the owner of the real property.

Summit Roofing performed actual work upon the West's house and is entitled to file a mechanic's lien if they are not paid. When Nixon absconded with the funds, the West's may have been defrauded by Nixon, but this does nothing to prevent a proper filing of the lien. The lien will prevent the West's from conveying clear title and is an encumbrance upon the property. The West's will be in breach when the date for closing arrives and they are unable to convey clear title to Rogers. The only recourse that the Wests have in this case is to pay Summit Roofing and obtain a release of lien before the escrow closing date. The West's should be careful to have all the contractors, laborers, and material persons who have worked on their home or supplied materials sign the lien release. The West's can proceed against Nixon to recover their $17,400.

# Answers to Practice Quiz

## True/False

1. True   Mechanics liens are security for the payment of services and materials used in making improvements to real property. [p 599]
2. False   A mortgagor is given right to redeem his or her property but cannot do so in part. He or she must pay the full amount owing on the debt, plus interest and costs. [p 598]
3. True   A deed of trust is the instrument that gives the creditor a security interest in the debtor's property that is pledged as collateral. [p 595]
4. False   A surety arrangement involves a third party who promises to be primarily liable with borrower for payment of the borrower's debt whereas a guaranty arrangement occurs

when a third party promises to be secondarily liable for the payment of another's debt. The third party may be one or the other, but not both at the same time. [p 615]

5. False   A surety arrangement involves a surety who is a third person agreeing to be liable for the borrower's debt. [p 615]
6. False   Debtor may not be secondarily liable for his or her own debt. A third party usually acts as a guarantor who agrees to be secondarily liable for payment of debt. [p 615]
7. True   The defenses that Samson the debtor has against whom he purchased the lawnmower from may also be asserted by Gloria, the surety. [p 616]
8. True   An attachment is a prejudgment order that permits seizure of the property while litigation is pending. [p 620]
9. False   Since automobiles, furniture and jewelry are tangible property, they are considered to be personal property. [p 595, 600]
10. True   Security interests in real estate can be created by the owners of real property. [p 595]
11. True   The deed of trust is the legal instrument that gives the creditor a security interest in the property of the debtor that is pledged as collateral. The deed of trust acts in place of a mortgage in some states. [p 595]
12. False   The power of sale must be expressly conferred in mortgage or deed of trust. [p 598]
13. True   Several states set forth a statutory procedure that must be adhered to when foreclosing on a land sale contract. [p 598]
14. True   The brick around Virginia's home would be considered an improvement that Felix may use as security for the payment of his services and materials. [p 599]
15. True   The statutory period to foreclose on a lien is from six month to two years depending on the jurisdiction the parties are in. [p 599]

## Multiple Choice

16. B   Answer B is correct, as a deed is a written instrument that describes a person's ownership interest in real property. Answer A is incorrect, as a foreclosure involves the sale of a debtor's property in order to satisfy the debt. Answer C is incorrect, as a lien is usually present when there has been some sort of service or goods rendered that improve the property. The lien is security in receiving payment for those goods and services without describing an ownership interest in the real property itself. Answer D is incorrect, as letters do not usually detail a person's ownership interest in real property. [p 595]
17. B   Answer B is correct, as an improperly recorded document is ineffective against later purchasers of real property or other lienholders or mortgages who do not have notice of the prior mortgages. Answer A is incorrect, as a debtor who is the mortgagor is still obligated to pay the amount of the mortgage according to its terms even if mortgage is improperly or not recorded. Answer C is incorrect, as this is a false statement. Answer D is incorrect, as there are too few facts to decide who was/is original mortgagee. [p 596]
18. D   Answer D is correct, as all of the statements given in answers A-C state a benefit of utilizing a statutory procedure for foreclosing on a land sale contract. [p 599]
19. C   Answer C is correct, as a writ of attachment is a prejudgment order allowing seizure of debtor's property while litigation is pending. Answer A is incorrect, as it is an untrue statement. Answer B is incorrect, as it is the explanation for a writ of execution. Answer D is incorrect, as these exemptions are usually for a writ of execution. [p 620]
20. C   Answer C is correct, as it states what the debtors may keep without having their wages abusively garnished. Answer A is incorrect, as the Consumer Credit Protection Act does not allow for debtor's wages to be garnished up to 75 percent of their weekly disposable earnings after taxes. Answer B is incorrect, as this is also an untrue statement under the act since the act allows a debtor to keep up to 30 hours of work paid at federal minimum wage if it is greater than 75 percent of his or her weekly disposable earnings after taxes.

Answer D is incorrect, as the act does protect the debtor from abusive garnishment actions by creditors but does not shield the debtor completely from garnishment. [p 620]

21. B    Answer B is correct, as it correctly defines a foreclosure. Answer A is incorrect, as a deficiency judgment procedure refers to an action to recover a deficiency from the mortgagor after foreclosure. Answer C is incorrect, as this refers to the mortgagor's right to redeem the property after default and before foreclosure. [p 598]

22. D    Answer D is correct. Answers A, B, and C are incorrect terms for secured party. [p 601]

23. D    Answer D is correct, as it is a correct statement of which transactions are not covered under Article 9 of the UCC. Answers A, B, and C are incorrect for this reason. [p 603]

24. A    Answer A is correct, as the point of reference for this type of property is the execution of the security agreement. Only property acquired after this agreement is executed can be after-acquired property. Answer B is incorrect, as it refers to property acquired before the execution of the security agreement. Answer C is incorrect, as it generally refers to property acquired during the security agreement, which does not provide a specific frame of reference. The security agreement is executed or not, there is no during time. Answer D is incorrect for the reasons stated above. [p 604]

25. D    Answer D is correct, as filing a financing statement is the most common method of perfecting the creditor's security interest. Answer A is incorrect, as a writ of attachment is a prejudgment court order permitting seizure of property and is not part of the process of perfecting a claim. Answer B is incorrect, as filing a lawsuit is not part of the process of perfecting a claim. Answer c is incorrect, as the term is nonsense. [p 605]

## Short Answer

26.    Collateral secures payment of the loan. [p 594]

27.    A mortgagor has the option of exercising his or her right to redemption of the property by paying the full amount of the purchase price, plus interest and other costs. [p 598]

28.    Undeveloped property, farms and similar types of property are sold using land sale contracts. [p 599]

29.    A creditor must follow the procedures set forth by state law, give the appropriate notice to the debtor and post a bond with the court. [p 620]

30.    The proceeds are utilized to pay the creditor the amount of the final judgment with any surplus being paid to the debtor. [p 620]

31.    The procedure for the sale must be contained in the mortgage or deed of trust itself. [p 598]

32.    A guarantor agrees to pay the debt of the main debtor should he or she default and not pay on the debt when it is due. [p 615]

33.    A court judgment allowing a secured lender to recover other income or property from a defaulting debtor if the collateral is insufficient to repay the unpaid loan. [p 598]

34.    A surety or guarantor. [p 616]

35.    Tangible property would include furniture and jewelry; intangible property would include copyrights and royalties. [p 600]

36.    An artisan or mechanic's lien is one in which a worker in the ordinary course of business works on or provides materials to another person and by statute are allowed to place on lien on the goods until the work or materials are paid for. [p 599, 614]

37.    A mortgage is a collateral situation where a property owner borrows money from a creditor who uses a deed as collateral for repayment of the loan. [p 595]

38.    A recording statute requires that the mortgage or deed of trust be recorded in the county recorder's office of the county in which the real property is located. [p 596]

39.    California Savings and Loan may bring a foreclosure procedure against Edna. [p 598]

40.    It requires lenders to make certain disclosures to debtors in consumer transactions and real estate loans on the debtor's principal dwelling. [p 617]

## Chapter 24

# BANKRUPTCY AND REORGANIZATION

## Chapter Overview

The U.S. Constitution, gives Congress the authority to create uniform bankruptcy laws. Bankruptcy laws work to balance the rights of debtors and creditors and seek to give ways for debtors to make a "fresh start" through debt relief. The bankruptcy law enacted in 1978 was considered to be "debtor friendly", but the recently enacted law of 2005 is considered to be very "creditor friendly". This chapter looks at federal bankruptcy law and the recent changes to it.

## Objectives

Upon completion of the exercises contained in this chapter, you should be able to:

1. Discuss the procedure for filing for bankruptcy.
2. Explain what is involved in a Chapter 7 liquidation bankruptcy.
3. Discuss a Chapter 12 adjustment of debts of a family farmer or fisherman.
4. Explain business reorganization as it pertains to a Chapter 11 bankruptcy.
5. Discuss a Chapter 13 consumer debt adjustment bankruptcy.

## Practical Application

You should be able to recognize the main purpose of bankruptcy law and be familiar with the different types of bankruptcies. You should have a clearer understanding of the impact of bankruptcy and which creditors take priority with regard to payment of the same.

## Helpful Hints

The concepts in this chapter are easier to learn if you learn each of the types of bankruptcy separately. It may be useful to list each type of bankruptcy, the main attributes of each, and the distinctive differences between them.

## Study Tips

### Bankruptcy Law

Article I, section 8, clause 4 of the U.S. Constitution gives Congress the power to establish uniform bankruptcy laws, which are exclusively federal.

**Bankruptcy Abuse Prevention and Consumer Protection Act of 2005.** This Act amended federal bankruptcy law to make it more difficult for debtors to escape unwanted debt.

- The Bankruptcy Code is federal bankruptcy law and gives bankruptcy procedures.

**Types of Bankruptcy.** The Code is divided into chapters.
- Chapters 1, 3, 5 set forth definitions and provisions that govern case administration.
- Chapter 7 covers liquidation.
- Chapter 11 covers reorganization.
- Chapter 12 covers adjustment of debts of a family farmer or fisherman.
- Chapter 13 covers adjustment of debts of an individual with regular income.

**"Fresh Start".** Granting a bankruptcy allows debtors a fresh start by freeing them from some legal responsibility for past debts. Bankruptcy law is designed to accomplish several things:
- Protect debtors from abusive collection activities.
- Prevent certain creditors from gaining an unfair advantage over others.
- Protect creditors from debtor actions that might diminish value of estate.
- Provide for speedy, efficient, and equitable distribution to creditors.
- Require debtors to repay debts if they have the means.
- Preserve existing business relationships.

**Bankruptcy Courts.** Congress created a system of bankruptcy courts, each attached to a U.S. District Court.
- Bankruptcy judges decide core proceedings regarding bankruptcy issues.
- Noncore proceedings involving the debtor go to the relevant state or federal court.

**U.S. Trustee.** This is a U.S. federal government official with the responsibility of supervising administrative tasks associated with bankruptcy cases.

## Bankruptcy Procedure

The Bankruptcy Code sets out procedures and requirements for filing petitions, defines the estate, provides protections to debtors, and establishes the rights of creditors.

**Pre-Petition and Post-Petition Counseling.** Individuals filing for bankruptcy are required to receive pre-petition and post-petition credit and financial counseling.

**Filing a Bankruptcy Petition.** A case is begun by filing a petition with the bankruptcy court.

*Voluntary Petition.* This petition is filed by the debtor and must state that the debtor has debts.

*Involuntary Petition.* This petition is filed by a creditor or creditors and places the debtor in bankruptcy. It must allege that the debtor is not paying debts as they become due.

**Schedules.** The debtor must submit several schedules detailing financial information upon filing a voluntary petition, all of which must be sworn to under oath and signed by the debtor.

**Attorney Certification.** The debtors' attorney must certify the accuracy of the information in the petition and schedules, under penalty of perjury.

**Order of Relief.** This occurs with the filing of a voluntary or unchallenged involuntary petition.

**Meeting of the Creditors.** After the order for relief, the court must call a meeting of the creditors where the debtor is questioned by his or her creditors without a judge being present.

**Proof of Claim and Proof of Interest.** A creditor must submit a proof of claim stating amounts of his or her claim against the debtor. An equity security holder must file a proof of interest.

**Bankruptcy Trustee.** The trustee is appointed as the legal representative of the debtor's estate.
- Duties include but are not limited to setting aside exempt property, looking into the debtor's finances, investigating the proof of claims and making reports to the debtor, his or her creditor's and the court about the estate's administration.

**Automatic Stay.** This goes into effect upon the filing of an involuntary or voluntary petition.
- It suspends creditors' actions against the debtor or the debtor's property.
- A debtor may have an injunction issued for activity not covered in the automatic stay.
- Actions for domestic support, dissolution of marriage, and child custody are not stayed.
- Criminal actions against the debtor are not stayed.

*Relief from Stay.* A secured creditor may seek relief from stay where the property is depreciating.

**Discharge.** When discharge is granted, the debtor is relieved of duty to pay the discharged debts.

*Exceptions to Discharge.* Nondischargeable debts are not dischargeable in bankruptcy, and include alimony, child support and certain fines payable to federal, local and state authorities.

**Reaffirmation Agreement.** This is an agreement where the debtor agrees to pay a creditor for a debt that is dischargeable in bankruptcy.

## Bankruptcy Estate

The bankruptcy estate involves all of the debtor's legal and equitable interests in all types of property, including community property from the onset of a bankruptcy proceeding.
- If the debtor obtains property after he or she files his or her petition, this property usually is not considered to be part of the estate.

**Exempt Property.** This property may be kept by debtor and is not part of the bankruptcy estate.

*State Exemptions.* The Bankruptcy Code allows states to enact exemptions.

**Homestead Exemption.** Homeowners can claim this exemption for their principal residence.
- If the debtor's equity exceeds the exemption limits, the trustee may sell the property to realize the excess value for the bankruptcy estate.

**Voidable Transfers.** Debtors are prevented from making fraudulent and preferential transfers of property during certain periods of time prior to bankruptcy that would unfairly benefit the debtor or some creditors at the expense of other creditors.

*Preferential Transfers.* The Bankruptcy Court can void certain preferential transfers to insiders that occur during certain time periods.
- The court will look for whether the transfer was for the benefit of a creditor, for an antecedent debt, value received, and solvency of the debtor.

- Exceptions include payments for current consideration, made in the ordinary course of business, for less than specified amounts, and for domestic support obligations.
- If the preferential transfer was part of an alternative repayment schedule created and approved by a nonprofit budgeting and credit counseling agency, it cannot be voided.

*Fraudulent Transfers Before Bankruptcy.* The bankruptcy court can void fraudulent transfers of debtor's property and obligations incurred by debtor within two years of the filing of the petition.
- The court will look for intent to hinder, delay or defraud a creditor, the value received, and the solvency of the debtor at the time of transfer.

*Other Fraudulent Transfers.* The bankruptcy court can void transfers to or for the benefit of an insider under an employment contract and not in the ordinary course of business made within two years of the filing of a petition.
- The court will look to intent to hinder, delay or defraud a creditor, and time of transfer.

## Chapter 7 Liquidation

This is the most common type of bankruptcy and is also referred to as a straight bankruptcy.
- The debtor's nonexempt property is sold to obtain cash and then the money is distributed to the debtor's creditors. Debts that are not paid are then discharged.

**Chapter 7 Procedure.** The procedure to file and maintain a Chapter 7 bankruptcy includes the filing of a petition by either the debtor (voluntary) or by one or more creditors (involuntary).
- A meeting of creditors is held where a permanent trustee is elected.

**The 2005 Act's Changes to Chapter 7.** The 2005 revisions add median income and dollar-based means tests that must be met before a debtor is permitted to obtain a discharge of debts.
- Those that don't qualify can be forced into Chapter 13 debt adjustment which requires debtors to pay some of their debts over a five-year period.

*Abusive Chapter 7 Filing.* The bankruptcy court may dismiss a Chapter 7 liquidation case filed by an individual if it finds granting relief would be an abuse of Chapter 7.

*Median-Income Test.* If the debtor's family income is at or below the state's median income, there is no presumption of abuse, and the means test does not apply.

*Means Test.* The means test is complex calculation that creates a bright-line test to resolve whether the debtor has the means to pay pre-petition debts with post-petition income.

*Calculating the Means Test.* The average current monthly income minus allowed expenses and deductions is multiplied by 60, to represent 5 years, and subtracted from the state's median income for five years. Debtors are then categorized by the result:
- Net amount less than $6,000, abuse is not presumed and debtor is eligible.
- Net amount between $6,000 and $9,999
  - If this is sufficient to pay at least 25 percent of unsecured debt, relief is denied.
  - If this is insufficient to pay 25 percent of unsecured debt, relief is granted.
- Net amount $10,000 or more, abuse is presumed and debtor is ineligible.

*Other Reasons for Denial.* Even if the debtor passes these tests, the court can deny relief if it decides the debtor filed the petition in bad faith or because of the "totality of the circumstances".

**Statutory Distribution of Property.** Nonexempt property has to be distributed to the debtor's unsecured and secured creditors.

*Secured Creditor Claims.* The secured creditors take priority over the unsecured creditors.
- An oversecured secured creditor has collateral worth more than the secured interest.
  - He or she will be paid the amount of the secured interest and the surplus will be put toward satisfying unsecured debt.
- An undersecured secured creditor has collateral worth less than the secured interest.
  - Awarded property and becomes unsecured creditor for the remainder of the debt.

*Secured Personal Property.* If personal property of an individual debtor secures a claim or is subject to an unexpired lease and is not exempt property, the debtor must surrender the property or redeem the property or assume the unexpired lease.

*Priority Unsecured Creditor Claims.* Unsecured claims are satisfied in order of statutory priority.
- Each class must be paid in full before any lower class is paid anything.
- If a class cannot be paid in full it is paid proportionately.

*Nonpriority Unsecured Creditor Claims.* Nonpriority unsecured creditors are paid once priority claims have been paid.

**Chapter 7 Discharge.** After the property has been distributed to satisfy the claims that are allowed, then the debtor is no longer responsible for the remaining unpaid claims.

**Acts That Bar Discharge.** If a discharge is obtained through fraud of the debtor, any party of interest can file a motion to have the bankruptcy revoked.

## Chapter 13 Adjustment of Debts of an Individual with Regular Income

The court may oversee the debtor's plan for installment payments of his or her unpaid debts.
- Chapter 13 is beneficial to both the debtor and creditor.
  - The debtor's costs are less more property can be kept than under Chapter 7.
  - The creditors are able to elicit a greater amount of debts that are owing to them.

**Filing the Petition.** The debtor must file a petition claiming that he or she is insolvent or not able to pay his or her debts when they are due.
- A debtor may ask for more time (an extension) to pay his or her debts or
- A debtor may ask for a composition which reduces his or her debts.

**Limitations on Who Can File for Chapter 13 Bankruptcy.** Only an individual with regular income and primarily consumer debt may file for this type of bankruptcy.

**Chapter 13 Procedures.** Subsequent to the filing of the petition, the debtor has to give the court a list of his or her creditors, liabilities and assets.
- Then there is a meeting of creditors where the debtor must be present.
- A trustee is then appointed to confirm the plan.
- Once a debtor files a petition, an automatic stay is in place regarding liquidation bankruptcy proceedings, creditors' judicial and nonjudicial actions and creditors' collection activities for consumer debt.

**Property of the Estate.** This estate includes all nonexempt property of the debtor at the start of the case and acquired after commencement but before the case is closed.

- It includes earnings and future income after the start of the case but before it closes.

**Chapter 13 Plan of Payment.** The debtor must file a plan of payment, which may go either three or five years, within 90 days after the order of relief.

**Modification of the Rights of Creditors.** The plan of payment may modify the rights of unsecured creditors and some secured creditors.

*Secured Creditors.* The plan must be submitted to secured creditors for acceptance.

- The plan will be confirmed if the secured creditor accepts it.
- The court can confirm the plan if the secured creditor does not accept it
  - o If the plan allows the creditor to retain his or her lien,
  - o If the debtor surrenders the property to the creditor.

*Unsecured Creditors.* The plan will be confirmed if the unsecured creditor accepts it.

- The court can confirm the plan if the unsecured creditor does not accept it
  - o If the plan proposes to pay the amount of the claim,
  - o If debtor agrees to commit all disposable income to pay unsecured creditors.

**Confirmation of a Chapter 13 Plan of Payment.** The court can confirm a plan if the prior requirements are met and if the plan is made in good faith, is feasible, is in the best interests of the creditors, all domestic support obligations are met, and the debtor has filed all tax returns.

**Chapter 13 Discharge.** When the debtor has made all payments under the plan, the court will discharge the debtor from all unsecured unpaid debts.

## Chapter 11 Reorganization

In this type of bankruptcy, the court assists the debtor reorganize his or her financial affairs.

**Chapter 11 Reorganization Proceeding.** Individuals, corporations, nonincorporated associations, railroads and partnerships are able to utilize this type of bankruptcy. Corporations use Chapter 11 bankruptcies the most.

**Debtor in Possession.** A unique feature about this type of bankruptcy is that the debtor is left to run his or her business while the reorganization proceeding is taking place.

- The debtor-in-possession has authority to enter into contracts and operate the business.

**Creditors' Committees.** The court will appoint a creditors' committee of representatives of the class of unsecured creditors, and may appoint additional committees of secured creditors and equity holders. They appear at court, participate in plan negotiations, and assert objections.

**Automatic Stay in Chapter 11.** This stay suspends actions by creditors to recover the debtor's property, which allows the business to reorganize and stay in business.

**Executory Contracts and Unexpired Leases.** The debtor is given the opportunity to accept or reject certain executory contracts and unexpired leases without liability.

**Labor Union and Retiree Benefits Contracts.** The court may order the rejection of a collective bargaining agreement or modification of retiree benefits if it finds that the "balance of equities" favors rejection or modification.

**Chapter 11 Plan of Reorganization.** The debtor has a right to file a plan of reorganization within 120 days of the order for relief.
- The reorganization plan describes the debtor's proposed new capital structure that indicates the different classes of claims and interests.
- The creditors and equity holders must be given a court approved disclosure statement.

**Confirmation of a Chapter 11 Plan of Reorganization.** The court must confirm the debtor's plan for reorganization in order for it to become effective.
- Confirmation may be accomplished by giving the different classes of creditors the chance to accept or reject the plan.
  - o The court looks at whether the plan is in the best interests of each class of claims, if the plan is feasible, if at least one class has accepted the plan and whether or not each class of claims and interests is nonimpaired.
- Confirmation may also be achieved using the cram down method.
  - o The plan has to be fair and equitable to the impaired class.
  - o The impaired class can be forced to take part in the plan of reorganization.

**Individuals Filing for Chapter 11 Reorganization.** Individuals may file for reorganization.

**Chapter 11 Discharge.** The debtor is given a discharge of all claims not a part of the plan.

## Chapter 12 Family Farmer and Family Fisherman Bankruptcy

The 2005 Act made Chapter 12 a permanent part of the Bankruptcy Code and created special definitions and rules to allow family farmers and fisherman to file for bankruptcy reorganization.

**Family Farmer.** Chapter 12 defines a family farmer.
- An individual, and spouse, with a debt of no more than $3,273,000, which is at least 50 percent farming, and whose gross income was at least 50 percent earned from farming.
- A corporation that is at least 50 percent owned by one family who conduct the farming, more than 80 percent of the assets are related to farming, and the business's total debt is no more than $3,273,000 which is at least 50 percent related to farming.

**Family Fisherman.** Chapter 12 defines a family fisherman.
- An individual, and spouse, with a debt of no more than $1,500,000, which is at least 80 percent related to commercial fishing, and whose gross income was at least 50 percent earned from commercial fishing.
- A corporation that is at least 50 percent owned by one family who conduct the commercial fishing, more than 80 percent of the assets are related to commercial fishing and the business's total debt is no more than $1,500,000 which is at least 50 percent related to commercial fishing.

**Procedure and Estate.** Debtor may file voluntary petition; involuntary petitions are not allowed.
- A trustee is appointed and the farmer or fisherman is a debtor-in-possession.
- An automatic stay goes into effect when the action is filed.

- In addition to the usual property included in the bankruptcy, the estate includes
  - o Property acquired after start of the case and before reorganization is complete.
  - o Earnings from services performed after start of case and before plan is complete.

**Chapter 12 Plan of Reorganization.** Family farmer or fisherman must file plan within 90 days.
- The plan generally provides for payments to creditors for three years.
  - o The plan must be confirmed by the court.

*Secured Claims.* A debtor's plan can be confirmed for a secured creditor if the plan has been accepted, or the debtor surrenders the property to the creditor, or the plan provides that the creditor retains the mortgage or lien and the distribution is at least the allowed amount.

*Priority Secured Claims.* The debtor and an unsecured creditor can agree to the settlement of an unsecured creditor's priority claim.
- With no agreement, the plan must provide for full payment of the claim or provide for less where all the debtor's disposable income will be applied to payments.

*Nonpriority Unsecured Claims.* The debtor and an unsecured creditor can agree to the settlement of an unsecured creditor's nonpriority claim.
- With no agreement, the plan can modify claims as necessary to attain reorganization.

*Executory Contracts.* The plan can provide for the assumption or rejection of executory contracts and unexpired leases.

**Confirmation of a Chapter 12 Plan.** The bankruptcy court will confirm a plan that was proposed in good faith, is in the best interests of unsecured creditors, is feasible, and the debtor must submit all or part of future income to the trustee for the plan.

*Cram-Down Provision.* The plan can be confirmed over objections if it provides any of these:
- The unsecured creditor is paid the discounted present value of his or her claim.
- The debtor's projected disposable income is applied to make payments under the plan.
- The value of property distributed is not less than the disposable income of the debtor.

**Chapter 12 Discharge.** When the debtor has made all payments under the plan, the court will discharge the debtor from all debts provided for by the plan.

## Special Forms of Bankruptcy

The Bankruptcy Code and other federal laws allow special forms of bankruptcy.
- Railroad reorganization.
- Municipality adjustment of debts.
- Stockbroker and commodities broker liquidation.
- Commercial banks, savings banks, and credit unions are overseen by federal agencies.

# Refresh Your Memory

The following exercises will help to test your memory regarding the principles given in this chapter. Read each question twice, then place your answer in the blank provided for each question. Review the chapter material for any questions you are unable to answer or remember.

1.  Federal bankruptcy law discharges the debtor from cumbersome debts and gives the debtor a(n) _____ _____ by relieving them from legal responsibility for past debts.

2.  A Chapter 7 liquidation bankruptcy is also referred to as a(n) _____ _____.

3.  Once a debtor's nonexempt property is sold for cash, the money is given to the creditors, and any unpaid debts are _____.

4.  The debtor begins a Chapter 7 bankruptcy by filing a(n) _____.

5.  A(n) _____ _____ is filed by the debtor's creditors that states that the debtor is not paying his or her debts as they become due.

6.  Allowing creditor claims and confirming plans of reorganization are examples of _____ _____ that bankruptcy judges decide.

7.  Personal injury, divorce and other civil proceedings that are resolved in federal or state court are considered to be _____ _____ _____.

8.  The debtor must appear at the _____ _____ _____ _____ to answer questions by the creditors.

9.  Creditors must file _____ _____ _____ stating the amount of their claim against the debtor.

10. A(n) _____ _____ suspends certain legal actions against the debtor or the debtor's property.

11. A(n) _____ is an order of the court that relieves a debtor of his or her legal liability to pay his or her debts that were not paid in the bankruptcy proceeding.

12. _____ _____ is the equity in debtor's home that the debtor is allowed to retain.

13. _____ _____ determines the order in which nonexempt property of the bankruptcy estate is distributed to creditors.

14. A plan of payment may be _____ if the debtor's circumstances materially change.

15. The _____ _____ _____ is left in place to operate the business during the reorganization proceeding.

## Critical Thought Exercise

Nancy Mills attended two different institutions of higher learning. She received educational loans totaling $22, 480. After graduation, Mills was employed, but her monthly take-home pay was less than $1200. The monthly expenses for herself and her four children were approximately $1650. Mill's husband had abandoned the family and provided no financial support. Mills received no public assistance and had no possibility to increase her income. A neighbor paid her telephone, water, and gas bills for the two months prior to filing a petition in bankruptcy. Mills also had substantial medical bills and had not been well for months. In her bankruptcy petition, Mills sought to discharge her educational loans.

Are the educational loans owed by Mills dischargeable in bankruptcy? Why was the Bankruptcy Code amended to generally prohibit the discharge of student loans?

*Please compose your answer on a separate sheet of paper or on your computer.*

# Practice Quiz

## True/False

1. ___ Federal bankruptcy law serves the main purpose of obligating the debtor to make good on his or her debts.

2. ___ There is a set time frame for filing a proof of claim in a Chapter 7 bankruptcy.

3. ___ There is a bankruptcy estate upon the commencement of a Chapter 7 proceeding.

4. ___ Property obtained after filing a Chapter 7 petition does not become part of the bankruptcy estate.

5. ___ Dividends, rents and interest payments are not deemed part of the bankruptcy estate.

6. ___ States that have Homestead Declarations as an exemption require that the debtor file this document after the bankruptcy.

7. ___ A debtor's use of a preferential lien is a way of demonstrating a debtor's favoritism toward certain unsecured creditors.

8. ___ The court may not void preferential liens made to relatives, partners, partnerships, officers and directors of corporations or anyone else with a relationship to the debtor.

9. ___ The Bankruptcy Code allows the court to void fraudulent transfers of property if the transfers occurred within one year of the filing of the petition in bankruptcy.

10. ___ Once the property is distributed to satisfy any allowed claims, any existing unpaid claims will not be discharged and the debtor is still responsible for them.

11. ___ Wilson files for a Chapter 7 bankruptcy and has several unsecured creditors, with the Handy Dandy Tool Co. being one of them. Wilson owes Handy Dandy $1,500, but his Bankruptcy estate has only enough to pay all of his unsecured creditors .05 on the dollar. Handy Dandy will receive $75.00 from Wilson's estate and may thereafter collect the unpaid balance from Wilson in a separate lawsuit.

12. ___ A creditor such as one who is owed alimony may not participate in the distribution of the bankruptcy estate.

13. ___ A party who has no interest may file an objection to the discharge of a debt.

14. ___ A bankruptcy may be revoked if discharge is obtained through the fraud of the debtor.

15. ___ Creditors may file an involuntary petition under Chapter 11 or the debtor may voluntarily file the petition him/herself.

## Multiple Choice

16. A voluntary petition for bankruptcy must include which of the following?
    a. A list of secured and unsecured creditors
    b. A list of the property owned by the debtor, including exempt property
    c. A statement of the debtor's financial affairs, and the debtor's income and expenses
    d. All of the above.

17. A permanent trustee is
    a. required to set aside exempt property.
    b. required to separate secured and unsecured property.
    c. required to take immediate possession of the debtor's property.
    d. elected at the first meeting of the creditors

18. If a debtor's equity in property exceeds the exemption limits, a trustee may
    a. liquidate the property to realize the excess value for the bankruptcy estate.
    b. sell the home and not distribute the excess to the debtor's creditors.
    c. require the debtor to file a declaration of Homestead after the bankruptcy.
    d. none of the above.

19. Since a secured creditor's claim takes priority over unsecured creditor's claims, what may the secured creditor do with regard to the debt that is owed?
    a. Foreclose on the collateral and use the proceeds to satisfy the debt.
    b. Let the trustee keep the collateral, dispose of it at sale and giveproceeds to him or her.
    c. Accept the collateral in full satisfaction of the debt.
    d. All of the above.

20. Once a plan of reorganization is completed, the debtor is
    a. granted a discharge of all claims not included in the plan.
    b. not granted a discharge of all claims not included in the plan.
    c. not considered bankrupt.
    d. free to incur more debt using his or her same creditors.

21. Which of the following tests are included in the acceptance method with regard to a Chapter 11 bankruptcy?
    a. The plan must be in the best interests of each class of claims and interests.
    b. The plan must be feasible in terms of the debtor surviving as an ongoing concern.
    c. At least each class of claims must vote to accept the plan.
    d. all of the above.

22. A Chapter 13 petition for bankruptcy is also referred to as what?
    a. a corporation's easy way out
    b. The Debtor's Reform Act
    c. consumer debt adjustment
    d. the discharge of all claims

23. What is an advantage of filing under Chapter 13?
    a. It avoids the stigma of Chapter 7 liquidation.
    b. It is less expensive than a Chapter 7 proceeding.
    c. More property may be retained than is exempt under Chapter 7
    d. All of the above

24. When filing a Chapter 13 petition, what is meant when the debtor states that he or she desires a composition?
    a. That the debtor wants a longer period of time to pay whatever debts are owed.
    b. It means that that the debtor wants a provision for a reduction of debts.
    c. It means that the debtor wants to provide an explanation via a writing so that the court will exonerate him or her from any and all debts.
    d. None of the above.

25. What is meant by the term hardship discharge?
    a. A discharge given to the debtor even if he or she does not complete the payments called for in the plan.
    b. A discharge given to "family farmers."
    c. A discharge granted for foreseeable circumstances that were the fault of the debtor.
    d. A discharge from all paid debts that weren't covered by the plan.

## Short Answer

26. To what does the term, "a fresh start" refer in terms of the debtor?

27. What is the most familiar type of bankruptcy?

28. What does Chapter 7 Bankruptcy involve?

29. What is a petition as it applies to bankruptcy?

30. How many creditors must sign an involuntary petition if a debtor has 12 or more creditors?

31. Which bankruptcy meeting is the judge prohibited from attending?

32. What may a secured creditor whose claims exceed the value of the debtor's collateral do?

33. List three examples of property that is exempt from bankruptcy.

34. Give examples of noncore proceedings involving the debtor.

35. What does filing of a voluntary petition or an unchallenged involuntary petition designate?

   _____

36. What is the next step of the court after an order for relief is granted?

   _____

37. When is a permanent trustee elected?

   _____

38. What must unsecured creditors file that states the amount of their claims against the debtor?

   _____

39. What is a relief from stay?

   _____

40. What is a reaffirmation agreement?

   _____

# Answers to Refresh Your Memory

1. fresh start  [p 632]
2. straight bankruptcy  [p 644]
3. discharged  [p 644]
4. petition  [p 634]
5. involuntary petition  [p 634]
6. core proceedings  [p 633]
7. non-core proceedings  [p 633]
8. meeting of the creditors  [p 636]
9. proof of claim  [p 636]
10. automatic stay  [p 637]
11. discharge  [p 638]
12. Homestead exemption  [p 642]
13. statutory priority  [p 648]
14. modified  [p 655]
15. debtor-in-possession  [p 656]

# Critical Thought Exercise Model Answer

   The restriction against discharge of student loans was meant to remedy an abuse by students who, immediately upon graduation, would file bankruptcy to discharge educational loans. These students often had no other indebtedness and could pay their debts out of future wages.

   Mills has truly fallen on hard times. Her monthly income does not meet her usual expenses. The combination of no support from her husband, four in-home dependents, and no prospects for increased income, give rise to a situation where a court could easily find that repayment of the educations loans would create undue hardship. The restriction against discharge of educational loans was passed by Congress to stop an abuse. The restriction was never intended to prevent a deserving petitioner from getting protection and a fresh start from the bankruptcy court. Mills should be allowed to have all of her debts discharged in bankruptcy to avoid undue hardship.

# Answers to Practice Quiz

## True/False

1.  False   The main goal of federal bankruptcy law is to discharge the debtor from burdensome debts. [p 632]
2.  True    The proof of claim must be filed in a timely manner which is usually interpreted to mean within six months of the first meeting of creditors. [p 636]
3.  True    A bankruptcy estate is created upon the start of a Chapter 7 proceeding. [p 639]
4.  True    Property obtained after petition does not become part of the bankruptcy estate.[p 639]
5.  False   Earnings from property of the estate such as these are property of the estate. [p 639]
6.  False   A Declaration of Homestead must be filed by the debtor prior to bankruptcy. [p 642]
7.  True    Debtors who favor certain unsecured creditors often given them a secured interest in property by giving them a preferential lien. [p 643]
8.  True    Preferential liens may be voided by the court. [p 643]
9.  True    The Bankruptcy Code gives the court the authority to avoid fraudulent transfers of property that happen within one year of filing of the petition in Bankruptcy. [p 644]
10. False   The debtor is no longer legally responsible for remaining unpaid claims once property has been distributed to satisfy the allowed claims. [p 638]
11. False   The Handy Dandy Tool Co. cannot collect the remaining balance and must write it off as a bad debt as per the provisions stated in Chapter 7. [p 650]
12. False   Creditors who have non-dischargeable debts such as alimony against the debtor may participate in the distribution of the bankruptcy estate. [p 638]
13. False   Any party of interest is allowed to file an objection to discharge of a debt. [p 652]
14. True    If the discharge is procured through the fraud of the debtor, a party of interest is allowed to bring a motion for revocation of the bankruptcy. [p 652]
15. True    A petition under Chapter 11 may be filed voluntarily by the debtor or creditors may file an involuntary petition. [p 656]

## Multiple Choice

16. D   Answer D is the correct answer, as answers A, B, and C all state what must be contained in a voluntary petition for bankruptcy. [p 634]
17. D   Answer D is the correct answer, as an appointed trustee may only employ disinterested professionals not interested professionals in the estate's administration. Answers A, B, and C are all incorrect as these state the things that an appointed trustee must do. [p 645]
18. A   Answer A is the correct answer, as it properly states what the trustee may do in the situation where the debtor's equity in property exceeds the exemption limits. Answer B is incorrect, as the trustee may be able to sell a debtor's home, pay off the mortgage and use the remaining proceeds to pay off the debtor's creditors. Answer C is incorrect, as Declarations of Homestead are usually filed prior to bankruptcy under most state laws. Answer D is incorrect for the reasons given above. [p 642]
19. D   Answer D is the correct answer, as answers A, B, and C all state options that a secured creditor has with respect to the claims that may be made on a debtor's property. [p 649]
20. A   Answer A is the correct answer, as the debtor is granted a discharge of all claims not included in the completed plan of reorganization. Answer B is incorrect, as it is not a true

statement. Answer C is incorrect because the debtor is bankrupt if he or she has filed a plan of reorganization. Answer D is incorrect based on its absurdity. [p 660]

21. D   Answer D is correct , as answers A, B, and C all state the tests that the court considers before confirming a plan of reorganization under a Chapter 11 bankruptcy. [p 660]

22. C   Answer C is correct, as Chapter 13 is also called consumer debt adjustment, which is a rehabilitation form of bankruptcy for natural persons. Answer A is incorrect, as Chapter 13 applies to natural persons, not corporations. Answer B is incorrect, as there is no such thing. Answer D is incorrect, as all debts are not discharged under Chapter 13, rather the court supervises the debtor's plan for payment of unpaid debts by installments. [p 652]

23. D   Answer D is the correct answer, as answers A, B, and C all state the advantages that the debtor has under Chapter 13. [p 652]

24. B   Answer B is the correct answer, as it properly defines the meaning of composition as applied to a Chapter 13 petition. Answer A is incorrect, as this defines what an extension is with regard to a Chapter 13 petition. Answer C is incorrect, as it makes no sense. Answer D is incorrect for the reasons given above. [p 653]

25. A   Answer A is the correct answer, as it describes what a hardship discharge is. Answer B is incorrect, as Chapter 12 of the Bankruptcy Code gives family farmers a special type of bankruptcy protection. It allows them to reorganize financially. Answer C is incorrect, as it improperly states a situation that would not allow a debtor to have a hardship discharge. Answer D is incorrect as an order for discharge applies to unpaid debts covered by the plan not paid debts that were not covered by the plan. [p 652]

## Short Answer

26.   The term fresh start refers to giving a debtor a relief from legal duty for past debts. [p 632]
27.   Chapter 7 liquidation bankruptcy is the most familiar type of bankruptcy. [p 644]
28.   The debtor's nonexempt property is sold for cash and then the cash is distributed to the debtor's creditors. Thereafter any unpaid debts are discharged. [p 644]
29.   A petition is filed with the bankruptcy court to begin the bankruptcy proceeding. [p 634]
30.   Petition must be signed by at least three creditors if debtor has more than 12. [p 634]
31.   The first meeting of creditors. [p 636]
32.   The secured creditor may submit a proof of claim and become an unsecured claimant as to the difference. [p 649]
33.   Answers will vary. Interest up to $2,950 in one motor vehicle, interest in jewelry up to $1,225 that is held for personal use, interest up to $1,850 in value in implements, tools, or professional books used in the debtor's trade. [p 639]
34.   Decisions on personal injury, civil proceedings and divorce proceedings. [p 633]
35.   It constitutes an order for relief. [p 636]
36.   The court calls a first meeting of creditors. [p 636]
37.   At the first meeting of creditors. [p 645]
38.   Unsecured creditors must file a proof of claim. [p 636]
39.   A secured creditor may petition the court for a relief from stay in situations when the creditor is not adequately protected during the bankruptcy proceeding. [p 637]
40.   This is an agreement entered into by the debtor with a creditor prior to discharge where the debtor agrees to pay the creditor a debt that would otherwise be discharged. [p 638]

# Chapter 25
# AGENCY RELATIONSHIPS

## Chapter Overview

Agency allows one person to act on behalf of another, increasing the ability of businesspeople to conduct business activities and making the operation of partnerships and corporations possible. Principals and agents owe each other certain duties and are liable for breaching these duties. Rules have developed that hold principals, agents, and independent contractors liable to third persons for contracts and tortious behavior. Agency is governed by agency law, developed through common law. This chapter looks at the formation and termination of agencies, and the liability of principals, agents, and independent contractors too each other and to third persons.

## Objectives

Upon completion of the exercises contained in this chapter, you should be able to:

1. Discuss the creation of an agency and distinguish between an express and implied agency.
2. Recognize and define a principal-independent contractor relationship.
3. Discuss the duties that the principal owes to the agent and the agent owes to the principal.
4. Discuss the various ways an agency may be terminated by law and the acts of the parties.
5. Define the doctrine of apparent agency.

## Practical Application

You should be able to understand how agencies are created and terminated. You should be able to recognize an irrevocable agency and if there has been a wrongful termination. You should be able to distinguish between the types of employment relationships and the liabilities of each. This chapter will be useful because agencies are an essential part of any successful business.

## Helpful Hints

This chapter is very easy to apply to either past employment experiences or future endeavors. This chapter easier to learn if you place yourself in the situation you are trying to learn about. Becoming familiar with basic terminology given will help make the concepts clearer.

## Study Tips

### Vocabulary

- **Agency by Ratification**. An agency that is created by a principal ratifying an agency that is created by an unauthorized act such as the misrepresentation of oneself as another's agent when in fact he or she is not an agent at all.

- **Agency**. Restatement Second of Agency defines agency as "a fiduciary relationship which results from the manifestation of consent by one person to another that the other shall act in his behalf and subject to his control, and consent by the other so to act."
- **Agent**. A party who agrees to act on behalf of another.
- **Apparent Agency**. An agency that the principal creates that appears to exist but really does not exist.
- **At-will employee**. An employee without an employment contract.
- **Employer-employee relationship**. An association that results when an employer hires an employee to perform some type of physical service.
- **Exclusive agency contract**. A distinct contract between the principal and agent whereby the principal agrees not to employ any agent other than the exclusive agent.
- **Express Agency**. An express agreement between a principal and agent thereby agreeing to enter into an agency agreement with one another.
- **Implied Agency**. An agency that is inferred from the parties' conduct and where there has not been an express creation of an agency between the principal and the agent.
- **Independent contractor**. A person or business who is not an employee but who is hired by a principal to perform a task on his behalf. This person is not controlled by the principal as to performance of the task that he or she is employed to do.
- **Power of Attorney**. An agency agreement that expressly gives an agent authority to sign legal documents on principal's behalf. The agent is known as an Attorney-in-fact.
- **Principal**. A party who employs another individual to act on his or her behalf.
- **Principal-agent relationship**. A relationship whereby an employee is hired and given the authority to act and enter into contracts on the employer's behalf.
- **Renunciation of Authority**. The termination of an agency contract by an agent.
- **Revocation of Authority**. The termination of an agency contract by a principal.
- **Strategic Alliance**. An agreement between two or more businesses from different countries to accomplish a certain purpose or function.
- **Wrongful Termination**. A violation of the terms of the agency contract thereby resulting in the termination of the agency contract.

## Agency

The principal and agent form an agency relationship by mutual consent. The relationship is fiduciary and the agent works for and under the control of the principal.

- The principal employs the agent to act on his or her behalf.
- The agent agrees to act on behalf of the principal.

**Persons Who Can Initiate an Agency Relationship.** If an individual has the capacity to enter into a contract, then he or she can appoint an agent to act on his or her behalf.

**Principal-Agent Relationship.** Where an employer hires an employee and gives the employee power to act and enter into contracts on his or her behalf.

**Employer-Employee Relationship.** Where an employer hires an employee to perform some sort of physical service. An employee is not an agent unless specifically empowered.

**Principal-Independent Contractor Relationship.** Persons and businesses hired to perform certain tasks on behalf of the principal.

- The degree of control that an employer has over an agent is the determining factor on whether one is an employee or an independent contractor.

## Formation of an Agency

The four ways an agency may be formed are expressly, impliedly, apparently, by ratification.

**Express Agency.** This is the most common type of agency wherein an agent and a principal expressly agree to enter into an agency agreement with one another.
- It may be oral or in writing; agreements must adhere to the Statute of Frauds.
- An exclusive agency contract states that the principal cannot employ any other agent than the exclusive agent.
- With multiple agents, the agencies terminate when the purpose is accomplished.

*Power of Attorney.* This is a formal express agency agreement used to give an agent, the attorney-in-fact, the power to sign legal documents on behalf of the principal.
- It may be general, giving broad powers to the agent to act in any matters on the principal's behalf.
- It may be special, giving limited powers as provided for in the parties' agreement.
- It must be written and usually must be notarized.

**Implied Agency.** An agency that is created by the parties' conduct.
- The implied authority of the agent may be given by custom in the industry, the agent's position or the prior dealing between the parties.
- There cannot be a conflict between the express and implied authority.

*Incidental Authority.* This is implied authority to act in emergency situations and other contingent circumstances in order to protect the principal's property and rights.

**Apparent Agency.** An agency by estoppel, or apparent agency, is created when a principal gives the appearance of an agency that in reality does not exist.
- The principal is bound to a contract entered into by the apparent agent while acting within the parameters of the apparent agency.

**Agency by Ratification.** An agency that results from a principal ratifying an unauthorized act by another who claims to be an agent when in reality he or she is not the principal's agent.

## Duties of the Principal

The principal's duties may also be stated in the parties' contract or implied by law.
An easy mnemonic to remember the principal's duties is: **C**onnie **R**emembers the **In**dian **C**oin.

> **C**ompensation – The principal has a duty to compensate an agent for services provided.
> **R**eimbursement – The principal has a duty to reimburse the agent for all expenses.
> **I**ndemnification – The principal has a duty to indemnify the agent for losses.
> **C**ooperation – The principal has a duty to cooperate with and help the agent.

**Principal's Duty of Compensation.** The principal owes a duty to compensate an agent for the services he or she has provided.

**Principal's Duty of Reimbursement and Indemnification.** The principal has a duty to reimburse the agent for all expenses the agent has expended from his or her own money if the expenses were authorized and within the scope of the agency and necessary to discharge the agent's duties in carrying out the agency.

- The principal has a duty to indemnify the agent for losses that the agent may suffer due to the principal's misconduct.

**Principal's Duty of Cooperation.** The principal has a duty to cooperate with and help the agent in the performance of the agent's duties and the goal of the agency.

## The Agent's Duties

The agent's duties are presented in the parties' agency agreement or implied by law.
An easy mnemonic to remember the agent's duties is: <u>L</u>oyal <u>P</u>ercy's <u>A</u>ccounting is <u>N</u>oteworthy.

<u>L</u>oyalty – The agent has a duty to be faithful to the principal.
<u>P</u>erformance – The agent has a duty to perform the lawful duties stated in the contract.
<u>A</u>ccountability – The agent has a duty to keep an accurate accounting of all transactions.
<u>N</u>otification – The agent has a duty of notification to principal of important information.

**Agent's Duty of Performance.** Agent must perform lawful duties stated in the parties' contract.

- Agent must meet degree of reasonable care, skill and diligence implied in all contracts.
- An agent that presents himself or herself as having higher than average skills will be held to a higher standard of performance.

**Agent's Duty of Notification.** The agent owes a duty of notification to the principal if the agent learns information that is important to the principal.

*Imputed Knowledge.* It is assumed that the principal knows the information that the agent knows.

**Agent's Duty of Accountability.** The agent owes a duty to keep an accurate accounting of all transactions performed on behalf of the principal.

- The agent must keep records of all money that has been spent and all money that has been received during the duration of the agency.
- The principal's separate account must be maintained by the agent and the principal's property must be used in an authorized manner.

**Agent's Duty of Loyalty to the Principal.** The agent owes a duty to be faithful to the principal.

- Self-Dealing. An agent is prohibited from undisclosed self-dealing with the principal.
- Usurping an Opportunity. An agent may not usurp an opportunity that belongs to the principal unless upon consideration the principal has rejected it.
- Competing with the Principal. An agent may not compete with the principal.
- Misuse of Confidential Information. An agent may not misuse confidential information regarding the principal' affairs.
- Dual Agency. An agent may not act for two or more different principals in the same transaction as this is a dual agency. The parties may agree to it though.

## Tort Liability to Third Parties

The principal and agent are personally responsible for their own tortious conduct.

- The principal is liable for the agent's conduct if acting within the scope of authority.
- The agent is only liable for the torts of the principal if he or she directly or indirectly participates in or abets and aids the conduct of the principal.
- The factors that determine whether an agent's conduct was within the scope of his or her employment include:
  o Did the principal request or authorize the agent's act?
  o Was the principal's purpose being advanced by the agent when the act occurred?
  o Was the agent employed to perform the act that he or she completed?
  o Was the act accomplished during the time that the time of employment authorized by the principal.

**Negligence.** Liability for negligence is based on the doctrine of *respondeat superior* which assesses liability based on the employment relationship between the principal and agent not on any fault of the principal.

*Frolic and Detour.* An agent performs a personal errand while performing a job for the principal.
- The court will examine if the detour is minor or substantial.

*The Coming and Going Rule.* Under common law, a principal is not held liable for injuries caused by employees and agents who are on their way to or from work.
- This rule holds true regardless if the principal provided the transportation.

*Dual-Purpose Mission.* When agent is doing something for him or herself and for the principal.
- The majority rule holds that both the principal and agent are liable if an injury occurs while the agent is on this sort of mission.

**Intentional Torts.** If the intentional tort occurs outside of the principal's scope of business, the principal is not liable.
- The doctrine of vicarious liability applies in the situation where the agent or employee commits an intentional tort in the scope of his or her employment.
- The Motivation Test and the Work-Related Test are applied to determine if the torts were committed within the scope of the agent's employment.
  o The Motivation Test states if motivation in causing the intentional tort was the principal's business, then the principal is liable for any injury caused by the tort.
  o The Work-Related Test states that if the intentional tort was performed during a work-related time or space, the principle is liable for any injuries caused by the intentional torts. The motivation of the agent is not considered.

**Misrepresentation.** The tort of intentional misrepresentation is also known as fraud or deceit.
- The principal is liable for the misrepresentation of the agent if it is made during the scope of his or her employment.
- The third party may rescind the contract with the principal and recover any consideration paid or affirm the contract and recover damages.

## Contract Liability to Third Parties

If an agent is authorized by the principal to enter into a contract with a third party, then the principal is liable on the contract. The class of the agency must be studied to determine extent of liability for the principal and agent.

- There are three types of agency classifications: the fully disclosed agency, the partially disclosed agency and the undisclosed agency.

**Fully Disclosed Agency.** The third party knows on whose behalf the agent is acting.
- The agent's signature clearly indicates the agency and the principal.
- The principal is liable in a fully disclosed agency situation.
- The agent is not liable, as the third party relied on credit and reputation of the principal.

**Partially Disclosed Agency.** Agent's status is disclosed but principal's identity is undisclosed.
- The agent's signature clearly indicates the agency, though not the principal.
- Both the principal and agent are liable on a third-party contract.
- If the agent is made to pay, he or she may seek indemnification from the principal.

**Undisclosed Agency.** A third party does not know about the agency or the principal's identity.
- The signature of the agent does not indicate the agency or the principal.
- The principal and the agent are liable on a contract with a third party, as the agent's nondisclosure makes him a principal to the contract.
- The agent may seek indemnification from the principal if made to pay on the contract.

**Agent Exceeding the Scope of Authority.** An agent who enters into a contract with a third party has given an implied warranty of authority that he or she has the authority to do so.
- The principal will not be liable on the contract where the agent has exceeded his or her authority on the contract unless the principal ratifies the contract.
- The agent is liable for breaching the implied warranty of authority.

# Independent Contractor

Persons and businesses who are not employees but are retained by principals to perform certain tasks, are called independent contractors.

**Factors for Determining Independent Contractor Status.** The degree of control that an employer has over an agent is the most important factor in determining whether someone is an employee or an independent contractor.
- If the principal asserts little control, the person is an independent contractor.
- If the principal exerts substantial control, the person is an employee.
- The label of independent contractor is not enough, other factors are considered:
  o Whether the worker is in a distinct occupation or an independent business.
  o The length and amount of time the agent has worked for the principal.
  o Whether the principal or agent supplies the tools and equipment for the job.
  o The degree of skill necessary.
  o Whether the worker hires employees to assist.
  o Whether payment is made by time or by job.
  o Whether employee has control of the manner and means of acquiring results.

**Liability for Independent Contractor Contracts.** A principal can authorize an independent contractor to enter into contracts and will be bound by these contracts.

**Liability for Independent Contractor Torts.** The general rule is that a principal is not liable for the torts of its independent contractors, as they do not control the means used to complete the job.

**Exceptions in Which a Principal is Liable for the Torts of an Independent Contractor.**
There are exceptions where principal will be liable for torts of an independent contractor.

*Inherently Dangerous Activities.* Principals may not avoid strict liability for dangerous activities.

*Negligence in the Selection of an Independent Contractor.* Principals may not avoid liability for hiring an unqualified or knowingly dangerous person who injures someone while on the job.

*Non-Delegable Duties.* A principal may not avoid liability by delegating non-delegable duties.

## Termination of an Agency

An agency contract may be terminated by an act of the parties or by operation of law.
- The agent can no longer represent the principal or bind the principal to contracts.

**Termination by Acts of the Parties.** Parties can terminate the agency by agreement or by their actions. There are four ways to terminate an agency relationship by the actions of the parties: Mutual Agreement, Lapse of Time, Purpose Achieved, Occurrence of a Specified Event.

*Notification Required at the Termination of an Agency.* Principal must give notice to third parties
- If the principal fails to give notice, the agent has apparent authority.
- The notification requirements that must be met are:
  o Parties who dealt with the agent must be given direct notice, written or verbal.
  o Parties with knowledge of the agency must be given direct or constructive notice
  o Parties who have no knowledge of the agency must be given no notice.
- Principal should recover any written authority given to agent.

**Agencies Coupled with an Interest.** These irrevocable agencies do not end with the death or incapacity of either party and only terminates upon performance of the agent's obligations.

**Termination by Operation of Law.** There are six ways to terminate an agency relationship by operation of law.
- Death. The death of either the agent or principal ends the agency relationship.
- Insanity. Insanity of either party ends the agency relationship.
- Bankruptcy. If the principal is found bankrupt, the agency is terminated.
- Changed circumstances. – If circumstances lead the agent to determine that the original instructions received from the principal no longer apply, then the agency will end.
- War. War between the agent and principal's countries terminates the agency.

*Termination by Impossibility.* The agency ends if circumstances make the agency impossible.
- Loss or destruction of the subject matter of the agency.
- Loss of a required qualification.
- A change in the law. If agency has a provision that becomes illegal, the agency ends.

**Wrongful Termination of an Agency or Employment Contract**. Agency and employment contracts that do not specify a definite end time can be terminated at will without liability.
- A revocation of authority happens when a principal ends an agency agreement.
- A renunciation of authority happens when an agent ends an agency agreement.
- If the principal's or agent's termination of an agency contract breaches the agency contract, then the termination may be considered to be wrongful.

# Refresh Your Memory

The following exercises will help to test your memory regarding the principles given in this chapter. Read each question twice, then place your answer in the blank provided for each question. Review the chapter material for any questions you are unable to answer or remember.

1.   A(n) _____ is a party who employs another individual to act on his or her behalf.

2.   A(n) _____ is an individual who agrees to act on behalf of another.

3.   A(n) _____ _____ is the most common type of agency.

4.   A(n) _____ _____ _____ is a formal type of agency agreement that is used to empower an agent to sign legal documents.

5.   If the _____ is declared bankrupt, the agency relationship is ended.

6.   Agency agreements formed for illegal purposes are void and against _____ _____.

7.   In a(n) _____ _____ the relationship is inferred from the conduct of the parties.

8.   A(n) _____ _____ _____ occurs when a person misrepresents him-or herself as another's agent when he or she is not and the purported principal accepts the act.

9.   A principal is liable for the _____ conduct of an agent who is acting within the _____ of his or her authority.

10.   In a(n) _____ _____ agency, their third party knows that the agent is acting for a principal, but not the identity of the principal.

11.   In a(n) _____ agency, the third party does not know an agent is acting for a principal.

12.   If an agency is terminated by _____ _____ _____, the stipulated time of the agency has expired.

13.   When an agency is terminated by agreement, the principal must give parties who dealt with the agency _____ notice.

14.   An agency coupled with an interest is a type of agency that is _____ by the principal.

15.   If an agency is for a specific term or purpose, the _____ _____ of the agency contract by either the principal or the agent is a _____ _____ of the agency.

# Critical Thought Exercise

Dave Polk was a self-employed handyman, doing business under the name Polk Speedy-Fix. From 1994-2001, Polk performed maintenance and repair work for numerous people in Sun City

West, Arizona, including Frank and Martha Hamilton. Polk did landscape maintenance, cactus trimming, painting, plumbing, and carpentry. Polk completed a job in May 2001 for the Hamilton's wherein he replaced a toilet and vanity. Polk was then hired to trim a 30-foot tall palm tree in the Hamilton's side yard. Polk was paid $20 per hour for his previous jobs by the Hamiltons. Polk was to receive the same rate of pay for trimming the palm tree.

When Polk arrived to trim the palm tree, Mr. Hamilton told him he wanted it trimmed to a height that was approximately the same as the house, along with trimming back the fronds so that they were at least five feet from the homes of both the Hamiltons and their neighbors. Polk took out several saws and two ladders from his repair van. Polk also borrowed a tree trimming saw and a rope from the Hamiltons. When his ladder was unable to reach the top areas of the tree, Polk climbed the tree. Polk fell from the palm tree when the rope broke and he received severe injuries to his back, pelvis, and internal organs. At age 32, he was totally unable to work.

Polk sued the Hamiltons to recover for his injuries, claiming that he was working as an employee at the time of his injuries and was therefore entitled to workers' compensation protection from the Hamiltons. The Hamiltons argued that Polk was an independent contractor.

Was Polk an employee of the Hamiltons or an independent contractor?

*Please compose your answer on a separate sheet of paper or on your computer.*

# Practice Quiz

## True/False

1. ___ The principal is the party who is hired by another person to act on his or her behalf.

2. ___ Insane persons and minors generally may not appoint agents.

3. ___ An employer-employee relationship exists when an employer hires an employee to perform some form of physical service.

4. ___ A beanie baby assembly person is an employee of the Ty corporation because he or she performs a mental task.

5. ___ A principal may not give an independent contractor the authority to enter into contracts.

6. ___ Express agency contracts can be either oral or written.

7. ___ Another name for an apparent agency is an agency by estoppel.

8. ___ A principal is not prevented from denying the agency relationship exist when the apparent agency is established.

9. ___ Parties to an agency contract may agree to terminate their agreement.

10. ___ Changed circumstances are enough to terminate an agency.

11. ___ The death of either the agent or the principal will not end the agency relationship.

12. ___ The agency relationship is terminated if the agent is found to be bankrupt.

13. ___ When an agent terminates an agency, it is called a renunciation of authority.

14. ___ An agency can only be formed to accomplish a lawful purpose.

15. ___ When an employer employs an employee and gives that employee the authority to act and enter into contracts on his or her behalf, it is a principal-agent relationship.

## Multiple Choice

16. A party who employs another individual to act on his or her behalf is called a(n)
    a. agent.
    b. independent contractor.
    c. principal.
    d. vice-principal.

17. A principal-agent relationship is formed when
    a. a person or business who is not an employee is hired to perform a certain task on the principal's behalf.
    b. an employer hires an employee and grants that employee authority to act and enter into contracts on his or her behalf.
    c. a principal authorizes an independent contractor to enter into contracts.
    d. the principal exerts a large degree of control over the employee.

18. What is the most significant factor in determining whether someone is an employee or an independent contractor?
    a. Whether the employee can act and enter into contracts on behalf of the principal.
    b. Whether the president of a corporation has the authority to enter into major contracts on the corporation's behalf.
    c. Whether the principal and agent expressly agree to enter into an agency agreement with one another.
    d. The degree of control that the employer has over the agent.

19. What is required of the signature of the agent in a fully disclosed agency?
    a. The signature of the agent does not indicate the agency or identify the principal.
    b. The signature of the agent clearly indicates the agency, not the identity of the principal.
    c. The signature of the agent clearly indicates the agency and the identity of the principal.
    d. None of the above.

20. Authority that is derived from the conduct of the parties, custom and usage of trade, or act that is incidental to carrying out the agent's duties is
    a. express authority.
    b. retroactive authority.
    c. obvious authority.
    d. implied authority.

21. Which of the following is true with regard to an apparent agency?
    a. The principal creates the appearance of a non-existing agency.
    b. The principal is estopped from denying the agency relationship.
    c. The principal's actions, not the agent's actions create an apparent agency.
    d. all of the above

22. An agency by ratification occurs when
    a. The principal creates the appearance of an agency that in actuality does not exist.
    b. The principal and agent enter into an expressly stated agency agreement.
    c. A person misrepresents himself or herself as another's agent when he or she is not and the person accepts the unauthorized act.
    d. none of the above

23. Which of the following is considered part of an agent's duty of performance?
    a. The agent is to perform the lawful duties as set forth in the contract.
    b. The agent is to meet the standards of reasonable care in all contracts.
    c. The agent is to meet the standards of skill and diligence implicit in all contracts.
    d. all of the above

24. Which of the following is false with regard to an agent's misuse of confidential information?
    a. The agent must not disclose any confidential information about the principal's affairs.
    b. The agent is prohibited from using general information, knowledge, or experience acquired during the course of the agency.
    c. The agent may not misuse business plans, technological innovations, customer lists or trade secrets.
    d. All of the above statements are false.

25. What may the court consider in determining whether an agent's conduct occurred within the scope of his or her employment?
    a. Was it the kind of act that the agent was employed to perform?
    b. Was the agent advancing the principal's purpose when the act occurred?
    c. Did the act occur substantially within the location of employment authorized by the employer?
    d. All of the above

## Short Answer

26. When does the employer-employee relationship exist?

    _____

27. A great deal of control over and individual may indicate what type of relationship exists?

    _____

28. Whose actions create an apparent agency?

    _____

29. Give three ways that the parties may terminate an agency relationship.

    _____

30. Give two ways that an agency relationship may terminate where a situation presents itself and thereby makes its fulfillment impossible.

    _____

31. When an agent terminates an agency, it is referred to as what?

    _____

32.. When will a principal be liable for the tortuous conduct of an independent contractor?

_____

_____

33. What effect do the agent's actions after the principal dies have on the principal's estate?

_____

34. Of what does constructive notice of the termination of an agency usually consist?

_____

35. List the three types of employment relationships?

_____

36. What are some of the characteristics of an independent contractor?

_____

37. What is an apparent agency?

_____

38. If no termination date is stated, when does an agency terminate?

_____

39. Give three ways to terminate an agency by operation of law.

_____

40. What does the agent's duty of accountability require?

_____

## Answers to Refresh Your Memory

1. principal [p 677]
2. agent [p 677]
3. express agency [p 670]
4. power of attorney [p 681]
5. principal [p 703]
6. public policy [p 678]
7. implied agency [p 681]
8. agency by ratification [p 684]
9. negligent, scope [p 687]
10. partially disclosed [p 696]
11. undisclosed [p 696]
12. lapse of time [p 702]
13. direct [p 702]
14. irrevocable [p 682]
15. unilateral termination, wrongful termination [p 704]

# Critical Thought Exercise Model Answer

A court would have to determine Polk's status as to employee versus independent contractor based upon answering several questions.

*Did the Hamiltons exercise control over the details of Polk's work?* Polk was instructed to trim the tree to an approximate size. The Hamiltons gave no other instructions concerning how the task was to be accomplished.

*Was Polk engaged in an occupation or business distinct from that of the Hamiltons?* Polk had an ongoing handyman business and accepted work from numerous people. The Hamiltons were not in the home repair or landscape maintenance business.

*Is the type of work usually done under the employer's direction or by a specialist without supervision?* Tree trimming is a job that requires skill and training. It is not the type of job a homeowner would supervise. The Hamiltons did not supervise Polk.

*Does the employer supply the tools at the place of work?* Polk had his own van with tools for his jobs. In this case, Polk did borrow a saw and a piece of rope, but this does not appear to be the usual way that Polk accomplishes his tasks.

*For how long was Polk employed?* Polk was only hired for a limited time until a specific job was completed. He was hired separately for the bathroom work and the tree trimming.

*What was the method of payment—periodic or upon completion of the job?* Polk was paid an hourly wage, but he was paid by the job instead of receiving a paycheck every week or month.

*What degree of skill is required of the worker?* Each of the jobs performed by Polk required skill and specialized knowledge. The average homeowner does not have the skill or ability to trim a large tree. A tree trimming service usually performs the cutting back of a large tree.

Polk's status as an independent contractor is borne out by the above analysis. Polk had his own handyman business with his own tools and possessed special skills for accomplishing tasks that are often handled by trades people and specialists. The fact that he was hired for more than one job does not change the fact that he acted as an independent contractor on each job. Thus, the Hamiltons were under no obligation to purchase workers' compensation insurance for Polk.

# Answers to Practice Quiz

## True/False

1. False    The party who hires another individual to act on his or her behalf is called the principal. [p 677]
2. True    Individuals such as insane persons and minors lack contractual capacity and therefore may not appoint an agent. [p 678]
3. True    An employer-employee relationship exists when an employer hires and employee to perform some sort of physical service not mental service. [p 678]
4. False    An employer-employee relationship would be present in the beanie baby example as assembly of the beanie babies is a physical task. [p 678]
5. False    Independent contractors may receive authorization from a principal to enter into contracts. [p 679]
6. True    Express agency contracts can be either written or oral. [p 679]
7. True    An apparent agency is also known as an agency by estoppel as the principal is estopped from denying the agency relationship and is bound to contracts entered into by the apparent agent while acting within the scope of the apparent agency. [p 682]

8. False   When an apparent agent is acting with in the scope of the apparent agency, the principal is estopped from denying the agency relationship and is bound to contracts entered into by the agent. [p 682]

9. True   The parties to an agency contract may mutually agree to end their agreement. [p 702]

10. True   An unusual change in circumstances that would cause an agent to believe that the principal's original instructions are no longer valid is sufficient to terminate the agency. [p 703]

11. False   The death of either party in an agency relationship will terminate the agency relationship. [p 703]

12. False   The bankruptcy of the principal will terminate the agency. The bankruptcy of the agent in most cases will not terminate the agency. [p 703]

13. True   An agent's termination of the agency is called a renunciation of authority whereas a principal's termination of the agency is called a revocation of authority. [p 704]

14. True   Agency contracts may not violate public policy and must be created to attain a lawful purpose. [p 678]

15. True   When an employer hires an employee and grants that employee the power to act and enter into contracts on his or her behalf, a principal-agent relationship exists. [p 678]

## Multiple Choice

16. C   Answer C is correct, as a principal is an individual who hires another party to act on his her behalf. Answer A is incorrect, as an agent is the party who agrees to act on behalf of another not one who hires another to act on his or her behalf. Answer B is incorrect, as an independent contractor is a party who is hired by a principal to perform a certain task on his or her behalf. Answer D is incorrect, as there is no such terminology with regard to agency law. [p 677]

17. B   Answer B is the correct answer, as it states when a principal-agent relationship is formed. Answer A is incorrect, as this states the definition of an independent contractor. Answer C is incorrect because, even though a principal may authorize an independent contractor to enter into contracts on his or her behalf, the independent contractor is not an employee as is the requirement for a true principal-agent relationship to exist. Answer D is incorrect, as the mere exertion of a large degree of control over the employee would only substantiate an argument that an individual is an employee verses and independent contractor. Further, there would also need to be an assertion that the employee had the authority to enter into contracts on the employer's behalf thereby elevating his or her status to that of an agent. [p 678]

18. D   Answer D is the correct answer, as the degree of control that an employer has over the individual in determining whether someone is an employee or independent contractor. Answer A is incorrect, as determining whether an individual could enter into contracts on another's behalf would be helpful in demonstrating whether or not someone was an agent, not an employee or independent contractor. Answer B is incorrect as, the answer lends itself toward determining whether the president is an agent or an employee. Answer C is incorrect, as an agreement between principal and agent would not necessarily determine whether someone was an employee or an independent contractor as both an employee and independent contractor may be agents. [p 699]

19. C   Answer C is the correct answer, as the signature of the agent must clearly indicate the agency and the identity of the principal in a fully disclosed agency. Answer A is incorrect, as the signature of the agent does not indicate the agency or identify the principal in an undisclosed agency. Answer B is incorrect, as the signature of the agent clearly indicates the agency, not the identity of the principal in a partially disclosed agency. Answer D is incorrect, for the reasons stated above. [p 695-696]

20. D   Answer D is the correct answer, as implied authority can be inferred from the parties' conduct, custom and usage of the trade.  Answer A is incorrect, as express authority is given to the agent by the principal without having to draw inferences from the parties' conduct.  Answer B is incorrect, as there is no legal basis entitled retroactive authority.  Answer C is incorrect, as there is also no legal basis entitled obvious authority.  [p 681]

21. D   Answer D is the correct answer, as answers A,B, and C are all true statements concerning an apparent agency.  [p 682]

22. C   Answer C is the correct answer, as it correctly describes when an agency by ratification occurs.  Answer A is incorrect, as this describes an apparent agency.  Answer B is incorrect, as this describes an express agency.  Answer D is incorrect, based on the reasoning given above.  [p 684]

23. D   Answer D is correct, as answers A, B and C are all considered part of an agent's duty of performance.  [p 685]

24. B   Answer B is correct, as the agent is not prohibited from using general information, knowledge, or experience acquired during the course of the agency.  Answers A and C are incorrect, as these statements are true with regard to an agent's misuse of confidential information.  Answer D is incorrect, based on the reasoning given above.  [p 686]

25. D   Answer D is correct, as answers A, B, and C all state what the court may consider in deciding whether an agent's contract occurred within the scope of employment.  [p 687]

## Short Answer

26.   When an employer employs an employee to perform some form of physical service. [p 678]
27.   It may indicate that an employee-employer relationship exists. [p 699]
28.   The principal's actions create an apparent agency. [p 682]
29.   Lapse of time, mutual agreement and purpose achieved are three ways that the parties may terminate an agency relationship. [p 702]
30.   The loss or destruction of the subject matter of the agency and loss of a required qualification are two ways that an agency relationship may terminate if a situation presents itself that makes the agency purpose impossible to fulfill. [p 704]
31.   Renunciation of authority. [p 704]
32.   Liability will be imposed on a principal for tortuous conduct of an independent contractor that he or she has hired for inherently dangerous activities assigned to the independent contractor as well as for the negligent selection of an independent contractor. [p 701]
33.   The agent's actions after the principal's death do not bind the principal's estate. [p 703]
34.   Constructive notice involves placing a notice of the termination of the agency in a newspaper that is distributed throughout the community. [p 702]
35.   Employer-employee, principal-agent, and principal-independent contractor relationship. [p 678-679]
36.   Some of the characteristics include but are not limited to whether the principal supplies the tools and equipment used in the work, the method of payment, whether it is by time or by the job, and the degree of skill necessary to complete the task. [p 699]
37.   An apparent agency is one that arises when a principal creates the appearance of an agency that in actuality does not exist. [p 682]
38.   Where no termination date has been stated, the agency terminates after a reasonable time has passed.  [p 702]
39.   Death, insanity and bankruptcy are three ways an agency contract may be terminated by operation of law. [p 703]
40.   That the agent maintain an accurate accounting of all transactions undertaken on the principal's behalf.  The principal can demand and accounting at any time. [p 686]

# Chapter 26
# SOLE PROPRIETORSHIPS AND
# GENERAL AND LIMITED PARTNERSHIPS

## Chapter Overview

When starting a business, one must decide under which form of business organization the business will operate. This decision depends on many factors, including the ease and cost of formation, capital requirements of the business, flexibility of management decisions, government restrictions, the extent of personal liability, and tax considerations. This chapter introduces entrepreneurship, sole proprietorships, general partnerships, and limited partnerships.

## Objectives

Upon completion of the exercises in this chapter, you should be able to:

1.  Discuss the different entrepreneurial forms of business.
2.  Compare and explain the advantages and disadvantages of forming and operating a business as a sole proprietorship.
3.  Discuss the formation of general and limited partnerships.
4.  Distinguish between liability of a sole proprietorship, and general and limited partnerships.

## Practical Application

You will be able to understand the positive and negative aspects of operating a business as a sole proprietorship. You will be able to identify the differences between a sole proprietorship and partnerships, and between general and limited partnerships. You will be able to recognize the varying magnitude of liability associated with conducting business in these forms.

## Helpful Hints

You should commit the definition of an entrepreneur to memory and be familiar with the fact that there are various choices in which to operate an entrepreneur's business organization. You should become familiar with the pros and cons of operating a business as a sole proprietorship, as a general partnership, and as a limited partnership.

## Study Tips

### Entrepreneurship

An entrepreneur is an individual who creates and operates a new business.

**Entrepreneurial Forms of Conducting Business.** There are many options when choosing the legal form in which to conduct a business, each of which has advantages and disadvantages.

- Sole proprietorship
- General partnership
- Limited partnership
- Corporation
- Limited liability company
- Franchise
- Joint venture

## Sole Proprietorship

The sole proprietorships is the simplest, most common business organization form in the U.S.

- The sole proprietor is the owner of the business, and *is* the business.
- A sole proprietorship is not a distinct legal entity.

*Advantages of a Sole Proprietorship.* There are several advantages to this type of business form.

- Easy to form and relatively inexpensive.
- The owner can make all management decisions, including hiring and firing.
- The owner has the right to all profits of the business.
- It is easily transferred or sold without anyone else's approval.

*Disadvantages of a Sole Proprietorship.* There are several disadvantages to this business form.

- Access to capital is limited to personal funds plus any loans the proprietor can obtain.
- The sole proprietor is held responsible for the business's contracts and torts he/she or any of his or her employees commit in the course of employment.

**Creation of a Sole Proprietorship.** There are no state or federal formalities, so is easy to create.

- Some local governments may require a license to do business within the city.
- A business is a sole proprietorship by default if not other form is chosen.

**d.b.a. – "Doing Business As".** A sole proprietorship may conduct itself under the name of the sole proprietor or a trade name, commonly referred to as d.b.a. (doing business as).

- If a d.b.a. is used, most states require the filing of a fictitious business name statement.
  - o This statement gives the name and address of the applicant, address of the business and the trade name.
  - o Publication of the notice of the trade name is often required.

**Personal Liability of Sole Proprietors.** A sole proprietorship involves great risk of liability.

- If the sole proprietorship fails, the owner will lose his/her entire capital contribution.
- The sole proprietor has unlimited personal liability, thereby subjecting his or her personal assets to creditors claims.

## General Partnership

A general partnership, or partnership, is a voluntary association of two or more persons for carrying on a business as co-owners for profit.

- Its formation creates certain rights and duties among partners and with third parties, which are established in the partnership agreement and in law.

- General partners are personally liable for the debts and obligations of the partnership.

**Uniform Partnership Act (UPA).** The Uniform Partnership Act details laws concerning formation, operation and dissolution of basic partnerships.

- It adopted the entity theory of partnership, where partnerships are seen as separate legal entitles which can hold title to property, and transact business in the partnership name.

**General Partnership Name.** An ordinary partnership may operate under the names of any one or more of the partners or under a fictitious business name.

- It must file a fictitious business name statement if it operates under a fictitious name.
- It cannot indicate that the partnership is a corporation.
- It cannot be similar to a name used by any existing business entity.

**Formation of a General Partnership.** A general partnership may be formed with little formality. The most important factor in showing coownerhsip is whether the parties share the profits and management of the business. There are four requirements that must be met to be considered a general partnership.

- It must be an association of two or more persons.
  o All partners must be in agreement of each participating co-partner.
  o Person includes natural persons, partnerships, associations and corporations.
- These persons must be carrying on a business.
  o Co-ownership such as joint tenancy, tenancy by the entireties, and tenancy in common qualify.
  o A series of transactions conducted over a period of time.
- These individuals must be operating as co-owners.
  o Essential to form a partnership.
  o Co-ownership is evaluated based on the sharing of business profits and management responsibility.
- The business must be for profit or have a profit motive.

**The General Partnership Agreement.** An agreement to form a partnership may be verbal, written, implied, or can be created inadvertently.

- A written agreement is called a partnership agreement or articles of partnership.
  o A written document is good evidence of the terms of the agreement in a dispute.
  o Where the document does not address a contingency, the UPA will control.
- Some states require that certificates of partnership be filed with the state.

**Right to Participate in Management.** All partners have equal rights in the conduct and management of the partnership, unless otherwise agreed.

**General Partners' Rights to Share in Profits.** A partner has the right to an equal share in the partnership's profits and losses, unless otherwise agreed.

- Agreements often allocate profits and losses in proportion to capital contributions.
- If the agreement provides for the sharing of profits but is silent on how losses will be shared, losses are shared in the same proportion as profits.
- If the agreement provides for the sharing of losses but is silent on how profits will be shared, profits are shared equally.

**Right to Compensation and Reimbursement.** A partner is entitled to indemnification for expenditures incurred in the ordinary and property conduct of the business.

- No partner is entitled to payment for his or her performance in the business, unless otherwise agreed.
- Income earned by partners from providing services elsewhere belongs to the partnership, unless otherwise agreed.

**Right to Return of Loans and Capital.** .
- A partner who makes a loan to the business becomes a creditor of the partnership with the right to repayment of the loan.
  - o This right is subordinated to creditor claims of nonpartners.
  - o The loan is subject to interest from the date of the loan.
- The partners are entitled to the return of their capital contributions on termination of the partnership.
  - o This right is subordinated to the rights of creditors.

**Right to Information.** Each partner has the right to demand full and accurate information from any other partner regarding the partnership.
- Each partner has the duty to provide such information upon demand.

**Duties of Partners.** Partners owe certain duties to the partnership and their partners.

*Duty of Loyalty.* Partners are in a fiduciary relationship with one another where they owe each other a duty of loyalty that cannot be waived. If there is a conflict between partnership and personal interests, the partner must choose the interest of the partnership.
- Self-Dealing. This happens when a partner deals personally with the partnership in such activities as buying or selling goods or property to the partnership.
  - o Full disclosure must be made and consent from others partners obtained.
- Usurping a Partnership Opportunity. If a third party offers an opportunity to a partner as a partner, he or she cannot take it before offering it to the partnership.
- Competing with the Partnership. A partner cannot compete with the partnership without the consent of the other partners.
- Secret Profits. Partners may not make secret profits from partnership business.
- Breach of Confidentiality. There is a duty to keep partnership information confidential.
- Misuse of Property. There is a duty not to use partnership property for personal uses.

*Duty of Care.* This duty requires that partners use the same degree of care and skill that a reasonable business manager would use in the same circumstances.
- Breach of this duty is negligence.

*Duty to Inform.* Partners owe a duty to their co-partners to inform them of all information relevant to the partnership.
- Partners are imputed with knowledge of all notices relating to the partnership.

*Duty of Obedience.* This duty requires that the partners adhere to the provisions of the partnership agreement and partnership decisions.

**Right to an Accounting.** Instead of being allowed to sue one another, partners may bring an action for an accounting against the other partners.
- This allows the court to review the partnership transactions and award each partner his or her share of the assets.

## Liability of General Partners

General partners are personally liable for the contracts and torts of the partnership.

**Tort Liability.** The partnership is liable for tortious conduct of a partner or employee committed while the person is acting within the ordinary course of partnership business or with the authority of his or her co-partners.
- Partners are jointly and severally liable for torts and breaches of trust.
    o A third party can sue one or more of the partners separately.
    o Judgment is collected against the partners who are sued.
- The partners and partnership who are made to pay may seek indemnification from the partner who committed the wrongful act.
- A release of one partner does not discharge the other partners.

**Contract Liability.** A partnership must act through its agents, or partners, and is liable for contracts entered into on its behalf.
- Partners are jointly liable for the contracts and debts of the partnership.
    o A third party must name all partners in the lawsuit.
    o Judgment is collected against any or all of the partners.
- A release of one partner releases all partners.
- A partner who is made to pay more than a proportionate share may seek indemnification from the partnership and the partners who did not pay their share.

**Liability of Incoming Partners.** A new partner is liable for the existing debts and obligations of the partnership to the extent of his or her capital contribution.
- The new partner is personally liable for debts and obligations incurred after joining.

## Dissolution of a General Partnership

The dissolution of a partnership is the change in relation of the partners caused by a partner ceasing to part of the business.
- A partnership for a term dissolves automatically when the term expires.
- A partnership for a particular purpose dissolves when the purpose is accomplished.
- A partner in a partnership at will may withdraw and dissolve it at any time.
- A winding up of the partnership follows its dissolution.
    o This is the liquidation of partnership assets and the distribution of proceeds.

**Wrongful Dissolution.** A partner who withdraws from a partnership for a term before the term expires does not have that right and causes a wrongful dissolution for which there is liability.

**Notice of Dissolution.** The dissolution of a partnership terminates the authority of partners to act on behalf of the business and notice must be given to certain third parties.
- Third parties who have actually dealt with the partnership must be given actual notice.
- Third parties who have not dealt with the partnership but have knowledge of it must be given either actual or constructive notice.
- Third parties who have not dealt with the partnership and do not have knowledge of it do not have to be given notice.
- If notice is not given and a partner enters into a contract, liability may arise from apparent authority.

**Distribution of Assets.** Proceeds from liquidation are distributed to satisfy claims against the partnership.
- If creditors' claims cannot be satisfied from the proceeds, the partners are personally liable for the partnership debts and obligations.
- After distribution, the partnership automatically terminates.
  - The legal existence of the partnership ends.

**Continuation of a General Partnership After Dissolution.** When a partnership is continued, the old partnership is dissolved and a new partnership is created.
- The new partnership consists of the remaining partners and any new ones.
- The creditors of the old partnership become creditors of the new partnership.
- A continuation agreement sets forth the events that allow continuation, the amount to be paid outgoing partners, and other details.

**Liability of Outgoing Partners.** Dissolution of a partnership does not discharge the liability of outgoing partners for existing partnership debts and obligations.

**Right of Survivorship.** Each partner is a co-owner in the partnership as a tenant in partnership, with rights of survivorship.
- A deceased partner's rights to partnership property pass to the remaining partner(s), not to his or her heirs.
  - The value of the partner's interest passes to his or her beneficiaries.
- The death of the last surviving partner causes the rights in partnership property to vest in the deceased partner's legal representative.

## Limited Partnership

A limited partnership has two types of partners, general partners and limited partners, and must have at least one of each.
- General partners invest capital and have unlimited personal liability.
- Limited partners invest capital, do not participate in management, and have personal liability only to the extent of their capital contribution.
- A person may be both a general and a limited partner in the same limited partnership.
- A corporation can be the sole general partner, with liability to the extent of its assets.

**The Revised Uniform Limited Partnership Act (ULPA).** This Act is a comprehensive, modern, uniform set of rules for the formation, operation, and dissolution of limited partnerships.

**Certificate of Limited Partnership.** Formation is formal and requires public disclosure.
- Two or more persons must execute and sign a certificate of limited partnership, which must then be filed with the appropriate state entities.
  - The limited partnership is formed upon filing of this certificate.

**Amendments to the Certificate of Limited Partnership.** A certificate of amendment must be filed with the same state offices as the original certificate to keep information on the limited partnership current.

**Name of the Limited Partnership.** Generally, the name cannot include the surname of a limited partner or a name similar to those of corporations or limited partnerships, but must include the words "limited partnership."

**Capital Contributions.** Capital contributions of general and limited partners can be cash, property, services, promissory notes, or other obligations.

**Defective Formation.** Defective formation happens when a certificate of limited partnership is not properly filed or there are defects in the certificate or another statutory requirement is not met.
- Limited partners can find themselves liable as general partners.
- Defects can be cured, but the limited partners will be liable to third parties who believe them to be general partners.

**Limited Partnership Agreement.** A limited partnership agreement, or articles of limited partnership, specifies the rights and duties of the general and limited partners, and the terms and conditions of operation, termination, and dissolution of the partnership.

**Share of Profits and Losses.** The agreement can specify how profits and losses from the business are to be allocated.
- Without an agreement, profits and losses are shared according to the value of the partner's capital contribution.
  - A limited partner is liable for losses only to the extent of his or her capital contribution.

**Right to Information.** Each limited partner has the right to information regarding the business.

**Admission of New Partners.** A new limited partner can be added only with written consent of all partners.
- A new general partner can be admitted only with written consent of each partner.

**Foreign Limited Partnerships.** A limited partnership is a domestic limited partnership in the state in which it is organized, and a foreign limited partnership in all other states.
- A certificate of registration in each state is necessary for the foreign limited partnership to conduct business.

## Liability of General and Limited Partners

General partners have unlimited personal liability for the debts and obligations of the limited partnerships.
- Limited partners are only liable for debts and obligations of the limited partnership to the extent of their capital contributions.

**Participation in Management.** General partners have the right to manage the limited partnership, whereas limited partners do not have the right to participate in management.
- If a limited partner participates in management of the limited partnership, he or she can be liable the same as a general partner.

**Permissible Activities of Limited Partners.** There are several types of activities that a limited partner may engage in without losing their limited liability.
- They can be an agent, employee, or a contractor of the partnership; a consultant or advisor to a partner; a surety for the partnership; approve or disapprove amendments to the partnership agreement.

- They can vote on matters such as the dissolution and winding up of the partnership; the sale, transfer, exchange, lease, or mortgage of substantially all assets of the partnership; the incurrence of extraordinary indebtedness of the partnership; a change in the nature of the business; the removal of a general partner.

**Liability on Personal Guarantee.** If a limited partner personally guarantees a loan made by a creditor to the limited partnership, the creditor can enforce the guarantee against the limited partner in the event of default by the partnership.

## Dissolution of a Limited Partnership

A limited partnership can be dissolved and would up the same as a general partnership.
- At dissolution and start of winding up, a certificate of cancellation must be filed with the appropriate state entity.

**Causes of Dissolution.** Four events cause the dissolution of a limited partnership.
- The end of the life of the partnership: the end of a set time or completion of a project.
- The written consent of all general and limited partners.
- The withdrawal of a general partner.
  - Unless the certificate of limited partnership provides otherwise.
  - Unless all partners agree to continue the business.
- The entry of a decree of judicial dissolution.

**Winding Up.** A limited partnership must wind up its affairs upon dissolution in the same way that a general partnership must.

**Distribution of Assets.** After liquidation of the assets, the proceeds must be distributed according to a statutory priority that pays creditors first and partners last.

# Refresh Your Memory

The following exercises will help to test your memory regarding the principles given in this chapter. Read each question twice, then place your answer in the blank provided for each question. Review the chapter material for any questions you are unable to answer or remember.

1.  A(n) _____ is a person who forms and operates a new business.

2.  A(n) _____ is the most basic form of business organization.

3.  In a sole proprietorship the _____ _____ bears the risk of loss.

4.  The sole proprietor has _____ personal liability.

5.  A sole proprietorship is not a separate legal _____ from the person who owns it.

6.  Operating under a(n) _____ _____ is commonly designated as d.b.a.

7.  A(n) _____ _____ is an association of two or more persons to carry on as co-owners of a business for profit.

8.  The _____ _____ of partnerships holds that they are separate _____ _____ that can hold title to property, and transact business.

9.  Partners have _____ _____ _____ liability for torts committed by partners acting on partnership business.

10. _____ _____ occurs when a partner withdraws from a partnership without the right to do so.

11. _____ of dissolution must be given to all partners.

12. _____ _____ of dissolution must be given to third parties who have not dealt with the partnership but have knowledge of it.

13. Unless otherwise agreed, the profits and losses of a limited partnership are shared on the basis of the value of the partners' _____ _____.

14. A(n) _____ partner is liable only for the debts and obligations of the limited partnership up to their capital contribution.

15. A(n) _____ partner is liable as a(n) _____ partner if his or her participation in the control of the business is substantially the same as that of a(n) _____ partner.

## Critical Thought Exercise

Larry and Diane Ortiz own and operate Maria's Restaurant in Houston, Texas. As husband and wife, they operate the restaurant as a sole proprietorship. As part of the advertising plan for Maria's, they participate in several 2-for-1 dinner coupon books and school fundraiser sticker books. An average of 15 2-for-1 coupons are redeemed each week. After Larry Ortiz is struck with a serious illness, the restaurant is sold to Bob Nelson. Nelson files the proper fictitious business name statement with the county and city clerk. The sale of the restaurant did not include the assignment of any contracts entered into prior to the sale by Larry and Diane Ortiz.

After Nelson remodels the restaurant, he reopens it with a Grand Reopening advertising campaign. Signs stating, "New Owners" are posted at the restaurant and the same notice is in each advertisement. When Nelson refuses to honor the 2-for-1 coupons, 24 plaintiffs file suit against Maria's Restaurant and Bob Nelson for breach of contract and fraud.

Is Bob Nelson liable because he failed to honor coupons for Maria's Restaurant?

*Please compose your answer on a separate sheet of paper or on your computer.*

## Practice Quiz

## True/False

1.  ____ An entrepreneur may operate a new business only by himself.

2.  ____ One of the major forms of business organization is a limited liability company.

3. ___ The extent of an individual's personal liability should be a factor in determining which form of business organization is best.

4. ___ In a sole proprietorship, there is a separate entity.

5. ___ One of the disadvantages to operating a business as a sole proprietorship is the legal responsibility for the contracts and torts of the business.

6. ___ The sole proprietor is responsible for the torts that he or she or any of his or her employees commit during the course of employment.

7. ___ The least common form of business organization in the United States is the sole proprietorship.

8. ___ The initials d.b.a. stand for doing business as.

9. ___ It is not necessary to procure a license to operate a sole proprietorship within the city.

10. ___ If a form of business organization has not been chosen, then it will operate by default as a corporation.

11. ___ A sole proprietorship may not operate under a trade name or under the name of the sole proprietor.

12. ___ A fictitious business name statement needs to contain the name of the applicant, as the trade name is insufficient for identification of the business.

13. ___ The rights and duties in a partnership are established in the partnership agreement and by law.

14. ___ An agreement to share losses of a business indicates that the business may be a partnership

15. ___ A partner may be held liable for torts as well as breaches of trust even if he or she did not participate in the commission of the act.

## Multiple Choice

16. What is the general rule regarding the individual liability of limited partners for the obligations or conduct of the partnership?
    a. The limited partners are not liable beyond the amount of their capital contribution.
    b. The limited partners are liable regardless of their capital contribution.
    c. The limited partners are liable up to one third of their initial capital contribution.
    d. The limited partners are not liable regardless of their capital contribution.

17. If a partnership agreement provides for the sharing of losses but is silent on sharing profits
    a. Profits are shared proportionally to capital contributions.
    b. A court must decide how the profits will be shared.
    c. Profits are shared equally.
    d. None of the above.

18. Which of the following is true with regard to the dissolution of a partnership?
    a. A partner has the power to withdraw and dissolve the partnership at any time.
    b. Notice of dissolution must be given to certain third parties.
    c. A partner is liable for damages caused by a wrongful dissolution of the partnership.
    d. all of the above

19. The term tenant in partnership refers to what as it pertains to the death of a partner?
    a. It refers to the remaining tenant's position on their joint office space.
    b. It refers to the vestment of deceased partner's right in specific partnership property in the remaining partner or partners.
    c. It refers to the limited use of the partnership for business ventures.
    d. It doesn't refer to anything specific other than the capacity to be in a partnership.

20. Which of the following does the Revised Uniform Limited Partnership Act (RULPA) allow?
    a. It permits a corporation to be the sole general partner of a limited partnership.
    b. It requires a limited partnership to have one or more general partners and one or more limited partners.
    c. There are no upper limits on the number of general or limited partners allowed in a limited partnership.
    d. All of the above

21. In which situation would limited partners be individually liable for the debts, obligations and tortuous acts of the partnership?
    a. When a limited partner participated in the management and control of the partnership.
    b. When there has been substantial compliance in good faith with the statutory requirements to create a limited partnership.
    c. Where the limited partner has not signed an enforceable personal guarantee that guarantees the performance of the limited partnership.
    d. None of the above

22. Which of the following is true with respect to a Limited Liability Partnership?
    a. Articles of partnership need not be filed.
    b. The Limited Liability Partnership law of the United States govern the operation of the LLP regardless of where it is organized.
    c. The LLP is a domestic LLP in the state in which it is organized.
    d. An LLP may not do business in other states.

23. What type of action do partners of a partnership have the right to bring against the other partners?
    a. The partners may bring an action in law against the other partners.
    b. The partners may bring an action for an accounting against the other partners.
    c. The partners may bring an action for the right to vote against the other partners.
    d. The partners may bring an action for profit sharing against the other partners.

24. A partner who is made to pay more than his or her proportionate share of contract liability may seek what remedy from the partnership and from those partners who have not paid their share of the loss?
    a. an injunction
    b. an order for specific performance

c. a retrial

d. indemnification

25. What is the trade-off in being classified as a limited partner?

    a. The limited partner is only liable for the debts and obligations of the limited partnership up to his or her capital contribution.

    b. The limited partner gives up his or her right to participate in the control and management of the limited partnership.

    c. The limited partner is liable the same as a general partner would be.

    d. The limited partner can participate in management as compared to a general partner who can not.

## Short Answer

26. An individual's choice of the type of business organization that he or she wants to operate as depends on several factors. Give at least two of these factors.

_____

27. Sandy Simpkins wants to open her own craft store. She asks for your input regarding the formalities in forming a sole proprietorship. What will you tell her?

_____

28. If Ben Barnes conducts a business called Barnes Bikes, which of these two names is the trade name?

_____

29. What is another name for a fictitious business name statement?

_____

30. What is the right of survivorship in regards to partnerships?

_____

31. What do the initials UPA stand for?

_____

32. What was the goal of the UPA?

_____

33. Explain the term entrepreneur?

_____

34. What are three major forms of business organization?

_____

35. Give at least two advantages of operating a business as a sole proprietorship.

_____

36. What is one disadvantage of operating a sole proprietorship?

_____

37. What are the formalities required to create a sole proprietorship?

   _____

38. What do the initials d.b.a. stand for?

   _____

39. If a business is operating under a fictitious business name, what must it file?

   _____

40. From where may creditors satisfy the claims they have against a sole proprietor?

   _____

## Answers to Refresh Your Memory

1. entrepreneur [p 714]
2. sole proprietorship [p 715]
3. sole proprietor [p 716]
4. unlimited [p 716]
5. entity [p 715]
6. trade name [p 716]
7. general partnership [p 718]
8. entity theory, legal entities [p 719]
9. joint and several [p 724]
10. Wrongful dissolution [p 727]
11. Notice [p 741]
12. Constructive notice [p 727]
13. capital contributions [p 731]
14. limited [p 735]
15. limited, general, general [p 735]

## Critical Thought Exercise Model Answer

A sole proprietorship has no legal identity separate from that of the individual who owns it. In this case, the 2-for-1 offers were made by Larry and Diane Ortiz. Only Larry and Diane Ortiz can be held liable for not honoring the coupons and fundraiser stickers, unless Nelson assumes the liability as part of an assignment and delegation. Bob Nelson did not assume any of the liabilities or any of the contracts that had been made with Maria's Restaurant when it was owned by Larry and Diane Ortiz. Bob Nelson did not assume liability for the coupons simply because he chose to use the same name for his restaurant. The sole proprietor who does business under one or several names remains one person. There is no continuity of existence for Maria's Restaurant because upon the sale of the restaurant, the sole proprietorship of Larry and Diane Ortiz ended.

In this case, "Maria's Restaurant" has no legal existence. Bob Nelson did not continue the previous sole proprietorship. He began a new sole proprietorship, that of Bob Nelson, doing business as Maria's Restaurant.

# Answers to Practice Quiz

## True/False

1. False   An entrepreneur may conduct a business alone or with others. [p 714]
2. True   A limited liability company is one of the many different forms of business organizations. [p 714]
3. True   The extent of an individual's personal liability is one of many factors that will   be part of the decision making process with regard to the type of business organization that would be best suited to the individual. [p 714]
4. False   The owner is the business in a sole proprietorship. [p 715]
5. True   Liability for the torts and contracts of the business is a disadvantage of operating as a sole proprietorship. [p 716]
6. True   The sole proprietor is responsible for the torts that he or she or any of his or her employees commit during the course of employment. [p 716]
7. False   In the United States, the most common form of business organization is the sole proprietorship. [p 715]
8. True   The initials d.b.a. stand for doing business as. [p 716]
9. False   In order to do business within the city, many local governments require the business to obtain a license for the same.  This includes sole proprietorships. [p 716]
10. False   A business will operate as a sole proprietorship where no form of business organization has been chosen. [p 716]
11. False   Since a sole proprietor and a sole proprietorship are one and the same, a business may operate under the name of the sole proprietor or under a trade name.  [p 716]
12. True   The fictitious business name statement must contain the name of the applicant, the applicant's address, trade name and business address. [p 716]
13. True   The rights and duties in a partnership are established by law and in the partnership agreement. [p 718]
14. True   Strong evidence of a partnership agreement is present when an agreement to share losses of a business is in place. [p 719]
15. True   Under the UPA, partners are jointly and severally liable for torts and breaches of trust regardless of their participation in the commission of the act. [p 724]

## Multiple Choice

16. A   Answer A is the correct answer, as it states the general rule with regard to individual liability of limited partners for the obligations or conduct of the partnership.  Answers B, C and D are all incorrect statements of law and are therefore the wrong answers. [p 729]
17. C   Answer C is correct, as the partners share profits equally this instance.  Answers A, and B are incorrect, as they do not properly state how profits will be shared in this instance.  Answer D is incorrect for the above reasons. [p 721]
18. D   Answer D is the correct answer, as answers A, B, and C are all true statements with regard to the dissolution of a partnership. [p 726]
19. B   Answer B is the correct answer, as it properly states what the term tenant in partnership refers to, hence the vestment of the deceased partner's right in specific partnership property in the remaining partner or partners.  Answer A is incorrect, as it makes no sense.  Answer C is incorrect, as it is a misstatement of law.  Answer D is also incorrect, as it is a false statement.  [p 728]
20. D   Answer D is the correct answer, as answers A, B, and C are all permissible under the Revised Uniform Limited Partnership Act (RULPA).  [p 729]

21. A  Answer A is the correct answer, as it states a situation where the limited partner would be individually liable for the debts, obligations and tortuous acts of the partnership. Answers B and C are not correct as, they do not state situations in which liability would be imposed. Answer D is incorrect based on the reasoning given above. [p 735]

22. C  Answer C is the correct answer, as it is the only true statement regarding a Limited Liability Partnership. Answer A is incorrect, as the statement is false. Answer B is a misstatement of law, as it is supposed to be of the state in which the LLP is organized, not the United States. Answer D is incorrect, as an LLP may do business in other states. [p 734]

23. B  Answer B is the correct answer, as it is the only answer that correctly states the type of action partners in a partnership have a right to bring against the other partners. Answer A is incorrect, as the partners generally may not bring an action in law against the other partners. Answers C and D are incorrect, as they are incorrect statements of law. [p 723]

24. D  Answer D is the correct answer, as indemnification is the proper remedy that a partner may seek when a partner pays more than his or her proportionate share of contract liability. That partner may seek the excess from those partners who have not paid their share of the loss. Answers A, B and C are all incorrect, as they do not apply in this situation. [p 725]

25. B  Answer B is the correct answer, as it correctly states the trade-off of being classified as a limited partner. Answer A is incorrect, as it is a statement of fact, not a trade-off. Answer C is incorrect, as it is a misstatement of law. A limited partner is not liable to the same extent as a general partner. Answer D is incorrect, as a general partner can participate in management, whereas a limited partner cannot. [p 735]

## Short Answer

26. Answers will vary. The ease and cost of formation and the extent of personal liability. [p 714]

27. Sandy Simpkins should be told that there are no formalities in forming a sole proprietorship. [p 716]

28. Barnes Bikes is the trade name as that is the name of the business under which Ben Barnes, the individual, is operating his business. [p 716]

29. Another name for a fictitious business name statement is a certificate of trade name. [p 716]

30. A deceased partner's right in specific partnership property vests in the remaining partner or partners, rather than in his or her heirs. [p 728]

31. UPA stands for the Uniform Partnership Act. [p 718]

32. The goal of the UPA was to establish consistent partnership law that was uniform throughout the United States. [p 718]

33. An individual who forms and operates a new business. [p 714]

34. Answers will vary. Sole proprietorship, general partnership, corporation. [p 714]

35. Answers will vary. The owner has the right to make all management decisions with regard to the business. The owner has the right to receive all of the profits made by the business. [p 715]

36. The sole proprietor's access to capital is limited to personal funds in addition to any loans that he or she may obtain. [p 716]

37. There are no formalities that are required to create a sole proprietorship. [p 716]

38. Doing business as. [p 716]

39. A business must file a fictitious business name statement. [p 716]

40. Creditors may satisfy their claims against the business from the personal assets of a sole proprietor. [p 716]

# Chapter 27
# CORPORATE FORMATION
# AND FINANCING

## Chapter Overview

Corporations were first formed in medieval Europe, with Great Britain granting corporate charters from the 1500s. The English law of corporations applied to the U.S. states until the U.S. developed its own corporate law, which had state legislatures granting corporate charters. States began enacting general corporation statutes that did not require approval of the legislature to form each corporation. Thus, most corporations today are formed through general corporation laws of the states. This chapter introduces the formation and financing of corporations.

## Objectives

Upon completion of the exercises in this chapter, you should be able to:

1.  Discuss the meaning, major characteristics, and formation of a corporation.
2.  Distinguish between common stock preferred stock.
3.  Discuss the preferences that are connected with preferred stock.
4.  Differentiate between authorized, issued, treasury, and outstanding shares of stock.
5.  Explain the organization and operation of multinational corporations.

## Practical Application

You should be able to understand how a corporation is formed and operates. You should be able to recognize the benefits and concerns with operating a business as a corporation. You should have an appreciation of the impact corporations have on the world and our every day lives.

## Helpful Hints

Organization is the key to learning the topics introduced in this chapter. A corporation starts out small and eventually grows into a fully functioning entity. If you keep in mind that the different aspects of operating a business as a corporation all depend on one another, you will begin to see how the entire picture fits together.

## Study Tips

### Nature of the Corporation

Corporations are created according to the laws of the state in which it is incorporated, which regulate the formation, operation and dissolution of corporations.

**The Corporation as a Legal "Person".** A corporation is considered to be a separate and distinct legal person or legal entity.
- It is an artificial person that is state created that can bring a lawsuit or be sued.
- It may enter into and enforce contracts, hold title to and transfer property.
- It may be found civilly and criminally liable, have fines assessed or its license revoked.

*Limited Liability of Shareholders.* The shareholders have limited liability, only to the extent of their capital contributions.

*Free Transferability of Shares.* Corporate shares are freely transferable by the shareholder.

*Perpetual Existence.* Corporations have a perpetual existence if there is no duration stated in the corporation's articles of incorporation.
- Shareholders may voluntarily terminate the corporation's existence.
- Death, insanity or bankruptcy of a shareholder has no affect on its existence.

*Centralized Management.* The shareholders elect the directors, who in turn appoint corporate officers to conduct the corporation's daily business.

**Public and Private Corporations.** Government-owned (or public) corporations are formed with a governmental or political reason in mind.
- Private corporations are created to carry on a privately owned business.

**Profit and Nonprofit Corporations.** Private corporations may be for profit or non-profit.
- Profit corporations conduct business for profit.
  o These can distribute profits to shareholders.
- Non-profit are created for charitable, educational, scientific or religious reasons.
  o These may not distribute any profit to their members, directors, or officers.
  o The Model Nonprofit Corporation Act governs nonprofit corporations.

**Publicly Held and Closely Held Corporations.** Publicly held corporations are generally large corporations with hundreds, even thousands, of shareholders with shares traded on organized securities markets. Shareholders seldom participate in this type of corporation's management.
- Closely held corporations are relatively small corporations whose shares are held by a few shareholders, mostly comprised of family, friends and relatives.
  o The shareholders do participate in a closely held corporation's management.
  o Sometimes the shareholders try to prevent outsiders from becoming shareholders.

**Professional Corporations.** These are formed by professionals, such as dentists, doctors, lawyers, and accountants.
- This type of corporation is formed like other corporations.
  o Its professional members are generally not liable for the torts committed by its agents or employees.
- The initials indicate it is a professional corporation.
  o The initials P.C. for Professional Corporation or S.C. for service corporation.

**Domestic, Foreign, and Alien Corporations.** A domestic corporation is a corporation in the state in which it was formed.
- A foreign corporation is a corporation in any state or jurisdiction other than the one in which it was formed.

- An alien corporation is a corporation that is incorporated in another country.

## Incorporation Procedures

Corporations are creations of statutes and organizers must comply with the state's corporations code in forming a corporation.

**Selecting a State for Incorporating a Corporation.** A corporation can be incorporated in only one state, though it can do business in other states.
- Small corporations look to the convenience where it will do most of its business.
- Large corporations look to the state where laws will be most favorable to operations.

**Selecting a Corporate Name.** Organizers must choose a name for the corporation.
- The name must contain the words corporation, company, incorporated, limited or an abbreviation of any one of these
- The name cannot contain a word or phrase that states or implies that the corporation is organized for a purpose different than that in the articles of incorporation
- A trademark search should be conducted to make sure that the name is available for use
- A domain name search for purposes of Internet use should also be performed

**Incorporators.** An incorporator is the person or persons, partnerships or corporations that are responsible for the incorporation of the corporation.

**Promotor's Liablity.** A promoter is an individual or individuals who organizes and starts the corporations, who may enter into contracts before the corporation is formed, find investors and sometimes subject themselves to liability as a result of all that is done.
- If the corporation never comes into existence, then the promoter is solely liable on the contract unless the third party exempts the promoter.
- If the corporation is formed, it is liable on the promoter's contract if it agrees to be bound to the contract as per a board of director's resolution.
- The promoter remains liable on the contract unless a novation is entered into.
  - A novation is a three-party agreement wherein the corporation assumes the promoter's contract liability with the third party's consent.
  - A novation has the effect of leaving the corporation solely liable on the promoter's contract.

**Articles of Incorporation.** This corporate charter is the basic document that must be filed with and approved by the state in order to be officially incorporated. The articles must contain:
- the name of the corporation
- number of shares the corporation is authorized to issue
- address of the corporation's registered office
- agent for the corporation
- name and address of each incorporator
- duration, regulation of powers and corporate affairs
- the corporate purpose

*Amending the Articles of Incorporation.* Amendments to the articles of incorporation must be filed with the secretary of state after the shareholders approve them.

**Corporate Status.** This begins when the articles of incorporation are filed. Upon the secretary of state's filing of the articles of incorporation, it is conclusive proof that the incorporators have satisfied all conditions of the incorporation.
- Failure to file articles of incorporation is definite proof the corporation does not exist

**Purpose of a Corporation.** A general purpose clause, which allows the corporation to engage in any lawful activity, should be in a corporation's articles.

**Registered Agent.** A registered agent must be identified along with a registered office.
- The purpose of the agent is to accept service of process on behalf of the corporation.

**Corporate Bylaws.** Corporate bylaws are a more exacting set of rules adopted by the directors.
- They contain provisions for managing the business and the affairs of the corporation.
- They may also be amended.

**Corporate Seal.** A corporate seal is a design affixed by a metal stamp containing the name and date of incorporation.

**Organizational Meeting.** An organizational meeting of the first corporate directors must be held upon the filing of the articles of incorporation.
- The bylaws are adopted, officers elected and other business transacted.
- Additional matters such as ratification of promoter's contracts, approving the form of stock certificates, etc are also discussed.

**S Corporations.** S Corporation has been defined as those which elect to be taxed under Chapter S thereby avoiding double taxation. Note C corporations are all other corporations.

*Electing to be an S Corporation.* Corporations meeting specific criteria may elect to be an S Corporation.
- Shareholders who collectively hold at least a majority of shares can vote to rescind this election at any time

## Financing the Corporation

The sale of equity and debt securities is the most common way to finance the operation of a corporation.
- Equity securities are stocks which represent the ownership rights in the corporation in the form of common stock or preferred stock.

**Common Stock.** This is a kind of equity security that represents the residual value of the corporation. Holders are issued common stock certificates and are called common shareholders.
- It has no preferences, so creditors and preferred shareholders receive their interest first.
- There is no fixed maturity date.
- Common stockholders may vote on mergers, elect directors and receive dividends.
- Common stockholders receive dividends.

*Par Value and No Par Shares.* This refers to a value assigned to common shares.
- Par value is the lowest price that the shares may be issued.
- Most shares are no-par shares where no value is assigned to them.

**Preferred Stock.** This is a kind of equity security that is given preferences and rights over common stock. Holders of this type of stock are issued preferred stock certificates.
- The general rule with regard to voting is that this class of stock may not do so, unless there has been a merger or there has been a failure to pay a dividend.

*Dividend Preference.* This is the right to receive a fixed dividend during the year.

*Liquidation Preference.* This is the right to be paid before common stockholders if the corporation is dissolved and liquidated.

*Cumulative Dividend Right.* This right provides that any missed dividend payments, arrearages, must be paid to preferred stockholders before the common shareholders can receive dividends.

*Right to Participate in Profits.* This right allows the preferred stockholder to participate in profits of the corporation with the common stockholders, in addition to the fixed dividend.

*Conversion Right.* This right permits the stockholder to convert their shares into common stock.

**Redeemable Preferred Stock.** Redeemable preferred stock (also termed callable preferred **stock)** allows the corporation to buy back the preferred stock at a future date.

**Authorized, Issued and Outstanding Shares.**
- Authorized shares are the number of shares provided for in the articles of incorporation
- Authorized shares that have been sold are called issued shares.
- Repurchased shares are called treasury shares.
- Shares of stock that are in the shareholder hands are called outstanding shares.

**Consideration to Be Paid for Shares.** This may include any property or benefit to the corporation as determined by the board of directors.

**Stock Options and Stock Warrants.** A corporation can grant stock options and warrants that allow parties to purchase common or preferred shares at a certain price for a specific time.
- A stock option is the nontransferable right to purchase corporate stock at a set price during an option period.
  - This is generally given to top-level managers.
- A stock warrant is an option demonstrated by a certificate whereby the holder can exercise the warrant and buy common stock at a stated price during the warrant period.
  - Warrants are both transferable and nontransferable.

**Debt Securities.** These fixed income securities establish a debtor-creditor relationship where the corporation (debtor) borrows money from the investor (creditor) to whom the security is issued.
- A debenture is a long-term unsecured debt instrument that is based on the corporation's general credit standing.
- A bond is a long-term debt security that is secured by some form of collateral.
- A note is a debt security with a maturity of five years or less.

*Indenture Agreement.* An indenture is a contract between the corporation and the holder that contains the terms of the debt security.

## Corporate Powers

A corporation has both the express and implied powers to perform acts and enter into contracts that a physical person has.

**Express Powers.** Express powers may be found in the U.S. Constitution, state constitutions, federal statutes, articles of incorporations, bylaws and resolutions by the board of directors.
- Corporations may purchase, own, and lease real as well as personal property.
- They may borrow money, incur liability, make donations and perform various other financial functions.

**Implied Powers.** The implied powers of a corporation are those that go beyond the express powers and that allow a corporation to accomplish its corporate purpose.

**Ultra Vires Act.** This refers to a corporate act that goes beyond its express and implied powers.
- An injunction as well as damages and an action to enjoin the act or dissolve the corporation are the remedies available for the commission of an ultra vires act.

## Dissolution and Termination of Corporations

The life of a corporation may be ended voluntarily or involuntarily.

**Voluntary Dissolution.** This occurs upon recommendation of the board of directors and a majority vote of the shares entitled to vote.

**Administrative Dissolution.** This is an involuntary dissolution of a corporation that is ordered by the secretary of state to comply with certain procedures required by law.

**Judicial Dissolution.** A corporation is dissolved by a court proceeding initiated by the state.

**Winding-Up, Liquidation and Termination.** The corporate existence continues after dissolution to the extent that it must wind up and liquidate the business affairs.

*Winding-up and Liquidation.* This refers to the method in which a dissolved corporation's assets are gathered, liquidated and then distributed to creditors, shareholders and other claimants.

*Termination.* This is the ending of the corporation that happens only after the winding-up of the corporate affairs, the liquidation of its assets and the distribution of the proceeds to the claimants.

# Refresh Your Memory

The following exercises will help to test your memory regarding the principles given in this chapter. Read each question twice, then place your answer in the blank provided for each question. Review the chapter material for any questions you are unable to answer or remember.

1. The _____ is the person responsible for organizing and starting the corporation.

2. Private corporations are classified as either _____ or _____.

3.    Local government corporations are called _____ _____.

4.    Individuals, such as doctors and lawyers, form _____ corporations.

5.    A(n) _____ corporation is a corporation in the state in which it was formed

6.    A(n) _____ corporation is a corporation in any state or jurisdiction than the one in which it is formed.

7.    A(n) _____ corporation is a corporation that is incorporated in another country.

8.    A(n) _____ _____ is an individual or corporation that has the authority to accept service of process on behalf of the corporation.

9.    A(n) _____ _____ is a person who owns common stock.

10.   The failure to file _____ _____ _____ is conclusive proof of the nonexistence of the corporation

11.   Shareholders are liable for the debts and obligations of the corporation only to the extent of their _____ _____.

12.   Shares of a corporation are freely _____ by shareholders.

13.   Corporations exist in _____ unless a specific duration is stated in the articles of incorporation.

14.   The _____ and the _____ form the corporation's management.

15.   A corporation may be formed for "any _____ _____."

# Critical Thought Exercise

Gus Hill runs a successful sole proprietorship under the name "Custom Rides." Hill makes custom motorcycles that often sell for over $40,000 each. Hill decides to expand the business and make motorcycles that are more of a standard production. In order to do this, Hill decides to form a corporation and solicit investors through the sale of company stock. Hill contacts an attorney and requests that all of the paperwork necessary for the incorporation be prepared. To prepare for the expanded business that will be done by the corporation, Hill leases a large manufacturing building from LandCo for one year at $12,000 per month. Hill also signs a $175,000 contract with VanTolker Tool Co. for the purchase of equipment and an employment contract with Dirk Dodds, who was hired to serve as plant manager and chief financial officer. Dodds' contract stated that he understood that his $130,000 yearly salary would come from corporate income and that Hill had no ability to pay his salary.

The corporation is formed and all legal filings are complete. Custom Rides immediately begins making payments on all three contracts. Custom Rides, Inc. operates for eight months before poor sales make it unable to meet its financial obligations. Landco, Dodds, and VanTolker all file suit against Custom Rides, Inc. and Gus Hill personally to recover their contract damages.

Is Gus Hill personally liable for the contracts he signed on behalf of Custom Rides, Inc.?

*Please compose your answer on a separate sheet of paper or on your computer.*

# Practice Quiz

## True/False

1. ___ There is not a general federal corporation law governing the formation and operation of private corporations.

2. ___ Members of a professional corporation are not liable for the torts committed by its employees or agents.

3. ___ Most corporations are publicaly owned.

4. ___ A domestic corporation is in the state in which it does business.

5. ___ An alien corporation is a corporation that is incorporated in another country.

6. ___ The articles of incorporation must be prepared and filed as well as approved by the state before the corporation can be officially incorporated.

7. ___ A corporation may be formed for any unlawful purpose.

8. ___ An organizational meeting of the initial corporate directors is required.

9. ___ One of the major advantages of doing business as an S corporation is that there is double taxation.

10. ___ The secretary of state's filing of the articles of incorporation is conclusive proof of the existence of the corporation.

11. ___ One class of preferred stock may not be given preferences over another class of preferred stock.

12. ___ Stock options are often issued to attract executive talent to work for the corporation.

13. ___ Stock Options are transferable.

14. ___ A "C" Corporation must pay federal income tax at the corporate level.

15. ___ There are not any requirements in becoming an S corporation.

## Multiple Choice

16. What corporation type is formed for educational, scientific, charitable or religious purpose?
    a. An S Corporation
    b. A public corporation
    c. A nonprofit corporation
    d. A publicly held corporation

17. Shares that are referred to as being authorized are
    a. shares of stock that are in shareholder hands.
    b. the number of shares provided for in the articles of incorporation.
    c. shares of stock repurchased by the company itself.
    d. stock that permits the corporation to redeem the preferred stock at some future date.

18. An administrative dissolution of a corporation is
    a. a dissolution recommended by the board of directors.
    b. an involuntary dissolution by a judicial proceeding.
    c. an involuntary dissolution that is ordered by the secretary of state.
    d. all of the above.

19. The ending of a corporation that happens after the winding-up of the corporation's affairs is known as
    a. winding-up.
    b. judicial dissolution.
    c. voluntary dissolution.
    d. termination.

20. A corporation in the state in which it is formed is a(n)
    a. domestic corporation.
    b. alien corporation.
    c. foreign corporation.
    d. promoter's corporation.

21. A corporation whose shares are owned by a few shareholders would most likely be
    a. a closely held corporation.
    b. a publicly held corporation.
    c. a government-owned corporation
    d. All of the above

22. As a general rule, shareholders are liable
    a. only to the extent of the debts of the corporation.
    b. only to the extent of their capital contributions.
    c. only to the extent of the assessments of fines or other sanctions.
    d. none of the above.

23. What are the most dominant form of business organization in the United States?
    a. partnerships
    b. sole proprietorships
    c. joint ventures
    d. corporations

24. Who make policy decisions concerning the operation of the corporation?
    a. the shareholders
    b. the consumers
    c. the board of directors
    d. all of the above

25. Which of the following is true with respect to common stock holders?
    a. They have a right to elect directors.
    b. They have a right to vote on mergers.
    c. They receive dividends declared by the board of directors.
    d. All of the above

## Short Answer

26. Who is the person or persons who organizes and starts the corporation?

27. List three things that the articles of incorporation must include.

28. What is a domestic corporation?

29. What must be filed upon approval of an amendment of the articles of incorporation by the shareholders?

30. What is a registered agent?

31. What does the failure to file articles of incorporation conclusively prove?

32. What do the initials S.C. stand for when identifying a corporation?

33. What is a person who owns common stock called?

34. To what does the term liquidation preference refer?

35. What are repurchased shares often called?

36. What is a note?

37. What is an alien corporation?

38. What is a stock warrant?

39. Give three characteristics of a corporation.

40. What is a foreign corporation?

## Answers to Refresh Your Memory

1.  Promoter  [p 756]
2.  profit, non-profit.  [p 752]
3.  municipal corporations.  [p 752]
4.  professional  [p 753]
5.  domestic  [p 753]
6.  foreign  [p 753]
7.  alien  [p 753]
8.  registered agent  [p 758]
9.  common stockholder  [p 762]
10. articles of incorporation  [p 758]
11. capital contributions  [p 751]
12. transferable  [p 751]
13. perpetuity  [p 751]
14. directors, officers  [p 751]
15. lawful purpose  [p 758]

## Critical Thought Exercise Model Answer

Before a corporation is formed, a promoter takes the preliminary steps in organizing the corporation.  The promoter makes contracts with investors and third parties.  A promoter may purchase or lease property and goods with the intent that it will be sold or transferred to the corporation when the corporation is formed.  The promoter may also enter into contracts with professionals whose services are needed.  As a general rule, a promoter is held personally liable on preincorporation contracts.  A promoter is not an agent when the corporation does not yet exist.  If, however, the promoter secures a contracting party's agreement to only hold the corporation liable, then the promoter will not be held liable for any breach.  Additionally, the promoter's personal liability continues even after the corporation is formed unless the promoter gains a release of liability from the third party.  It does not matter whether or not the contract was made in the name of, or on behalf of, the named corporation.

Hill was acting as a promoter when he entered into contracts with LandCo, VanTolker, and Dodds.  The fact that he signed the contracts as a purported agent of Custom Rides, Inc. will have no effect because the corporation had yet to be incorporated.  The employment with Dodds is different than the others because Dodds agreed to seek payment only from Custom Rides, Inc., effectively releasing Hill from any personal liability.  Even though Custom Rides, Inc. adopted the contracts executed with LandCo and VanTolker, the lack of a formal novation meant that Hill remained personally liable after incorporation.  There could not have been a ratification of the preincorporation contracts because there was no principal to ratify the agent's acts at the time the contract was executed.  Therefore, Hill will be personally liable to both LandCo and VanTolker.

## Answers to Practice Quiz

# True/False

1. True    There is no federal corporation law that governs the formation and operation of private corporations. [p 752]
2. True    Members of professional corporations are not liable for the torts committed by its employees or agents. [p 753]
3. False    Privately owned corporations comprise a large sector of the corporate world. [p 752]
4. False    A corporation in the state in which it was formed is a domestic corporation. [p 753]
5. True    An alien corporation is one that is incorporated in another country. [p 753]
6. True    Corporations are formed only if the state's statutory formalities are followed. [p 756]
7. False    A corporation may not be formed for an unlawful purpose, but, it may be formed for a lawful purpose. [p 758]
8. True    The initial organizational meeting of the corporation's directors is mandatory not optional. [p 759]
9. False    Shareholders and corporations avoid double taxation by doing business as an S Corporation. [p 760]
10. False    The filing of the articles of incorporation by the secretary of state is conclusive proof that all conditions of incorporation have been satisfied by the incorporators. [p 758]
11. False    Preferred stock may have preferences over various classes of preferred stock. [p 762]
12. True    Stock options are often issued to attract executives to work for a corporation. [p 764]
13. False    Stock options that are granted are usually nontransferable. [p 764]
14. True    "C" Corporations must pay federal income tax at the corporate level. [p 760]
15. False    Corporations must meet specific requirements in order to elect to be an S Corporation. [p 760]

# Multiple Choice

16. C.    Answer C is the correct answer, as nonprofit corporations are formed for educational, scientific or religious purposes. Answer A is incorrect, as the reasons given for formation are not the reasons individuals would form an S Corporation. S Corporations are formed for a variety of reasons, with a primary one being to avoid double taxation. Answer B is incorrect, as public corporations are formed to meet specific governmental or political purposes. Answer D is incorrect as a publicly held Corporation is one with many shareholders whose securities are often traded on a national stock exchange. [p 752]
17. B.    Answer B is the correct answer, as authorized shares are the number of shares provided for in the articles of incorporation. Answer A is incorrect, as this answer gives the definition for outstanding shares, not authorized shares. Answer C is incorrect, as this provides the definition for treasure shares. Answer D is incorrect, as it gives the definition for redeemable stock. [p 763]
18. C.    Answer C is the correct answer, as an involuntary dissolution ordered by the secretary of state is an administrative dissolution. Answer A is incorrect, as dissolutions that are recommended by the board of directors are usually voluntary in nature. Answer B is incorrect, as involuntary dissolutions by judicial proceedings are judicial dissolutions. Answer D is incorrect based on the reasons given above. [p 766]
19. D.    Answer D is the correct answer, as termination with respect to corporations is the ending that results from winding-up the corporation's affairs. Answer A is incorrect, as winding-up involves liquidating the corporate assets and it precedes termination. Answer B is incorrect, as a judicial dissolution is involuntary and initiated by a judicial proceeding. Answer C is incorrect, as a voluntary dissolution is a step toward

ending a corporation, but is not the ending itself of the corporation. [p 767]

20. A. Answer A is the correct answer, as a domestic corporation is one in the state in which it is formed. Answer B is incorrect, as an alien corporation is one that is incorporated in another country. Answer C is incorrect, as a foreign corporation is one in any state or jurisdiction other than the one in which it was formed. Answer D is incorrect, as there is no such thing as a promoter's corporation. [p 753]

21. A Answer A is the correct answer, as a closely held corporation is one in which its shares are owned by a few shareholders. Answer B is incorrect, as publicly held corporations have many shareholders and are traded on organized securities markets. Answer C is incorrect, as government-owned corporations are formed to meet specific governmental or political purpose. Answer D is incorrect based on the reasoning above. [p 752]

22. B Answer B is the correct answer, as shareholders liability is limited only to the extent of their capital contributions. Answer A is incorrect, as it does not make any sense. Answer C is incorrect for the same reason, in that it does not make any sense. Answer D is incorrect based on the reasoning given above. [p 751]

23. D Answer D is the correct answer, as corporations are the most dominant form of business organization in the United States. Answers A, B and C are all incorrect as none of these are the dominant form of business organization in the United States. [p 750]

24. C Answer C is the correct answer, as the board of directors makes policy decisions concerning the operation of the corporation. Answers A, B and D are all incorrect, as none of these answer choices make policy decisions concerning the operation of the corporation. [p 751]

25. D Answer D is the correct answer, as answers A, B, and C all are true with respect to common stock holders. [p 762]

## Short Answer

26. Promoter [p 756]
27. name of the corporation, the number of shares the corporation is authorized to issue and the name and address of each incorporator (answers will vary) [p 756]
28. A domestic corporation is a corporation in the state in which it was formed. [p 753]
29. The articles of amendment must be filed. [p 757]
30. An individual or corporation that has the authority to accept service of process on behalf of the corporation. [p 758]
31. Nonexistence of the corporation. [p 758]
32. The initials S.C. stand for service corporation. [p 753]
33. Common stockholder [p 762]
34. The right to be paid prior to common stockholders if the corporation is dissolved and liquidated is a liquidation preference. [p 762]
35. Treasury shares. [p 763]
36. A debt security with a maturity of five years or less. [p 764]
37. An alien corporation is a corporation that is incorporated in another country. [p 753]
38. A stock warrant is a stock option that is evidenced by a certificate. [p 764]
39. Answers will vary. The corporate shares are freely transferable, shareholders generally have limited liability, and a corporation can exist in perpetual existence unless the duration is stated otherwise in the articles of incorporation. [p 751]
40. A foreign corporation is a corporation in any state or jurisdiction other than the one in which it is formed. [p 753]

# Chapter 28
# CORPORATE GOVERNANCE
# AND THE SARBANES-OXLEY ACT

## Chapter Overview

In managing a corporation, the shareholders, directors, and officers each have different roles. As a legal entity, the corporation is liable for the actions taken by its directors and officers, and for contracts entered into on its behalf. The directors and officers each have rights and duties to the corporation and its shareholders. The rights, duties and liability of corporate shareholders, directors, and officers are examined in this chapter.

## Objectives

Upon completion of the exercises in this chapter, you should be able to:

1. Discuss the function of shareholder, directors, and officers in corporate management.
2. Discuss a director's and officer's duty of care and the business judgment rule.
3. Explain the director's duty of loyalty and how it can be breached.
4. Explain what is meant by the corporate veil or alter ego doctrine.
5. Discuss the effect of the Sarbanes-Oxley Act on corporate governance.

## Practical Application

Whether you are a shareholder, a director, officer or a corporate observer, this chapter will provide you with practical information regarding the internal management structure and its direct impact on one another. This knowledge will provide you with the ability to make educated decisions as may pertain to the basic decisions associated with the management of corporations.

## Helpful Hints

If you view the corporation as a pyramid with the shareholders, directors and officers each representing a tier of that pyramid and each tier having different responsibilities that impact the other tiers, you will begin to better understand their importance in keeping the pyramid in tact in order to avoid corporate collapse.

## Study Tips

### Shareholders

The shareholders are the owners of the corporation. They vote on the directors and other important actions to be taken by the corporation, but cannot bind the corporation to any contract.

**Shareholders' Meetings.** Annual shareholder meetings are held in accordance with the bylaws to take actions such as the election of directors and independent auditors.

- Special shareholder meetings may be conducted to evaluate and vote on significant or emergency issues.

*Notice of Meetings.* Shareholders must be given written notice of annual and special meetings.

**Proxies.** Attendance at a shareholder meeting may be by a proxy, which is another person who acts as an agent of the shareholder.

**Voting Requirements.** A corporation must have at least one class of stock with voting rights.

- Only shareholders who own stock as of the record date may vote at a meeting.

**Quorum and Vote Required.** As long as a majority of the shares entitled to vote are present, there will be a quorum to hold the meeting.

- An affirmative vote for elections other than the board of directors is required.

**Straight (Non-cumulative) Voting.** In this method, used if the articles do not specify another method, each shareholder votes the number of shares he or she owns on candidates for the directors positions that are open.

- A majority shareholder can elect the entire board of directors.

**Cumulative Voting.** This method entails a shareholder accumulating all of his or her votes and voting them all for one candidate or dividing his or her votes among many candidates.

- A shareholder may multiply the number of shares he or she owns by the number of directors to be elected and then vote the entire amount on a single candidate or apportion the product among contenders.
- This method is good for minority shareholders.

**Supramajority Voting Requirement.** The articles of incorporation can require a greater than majority of shares to comprise a quorum or the shareholders' vote.

**Voting Trusts.** The shareholders transfer their stock certificates to a trustee who is given the authority to vote the shares.

**Shareholder Voting Agreements.** Two or more shareholders agree on how shares will be voted.

**Right of First Refusal.** The right of first refusal is an agreement that shareholders enter into which grants one another the right of first refusal to purchase shares they are going to sell.

**Buy-and-Sell Agreement.** A buy-and sell agreement is where the shareholders are required to sell their shares to the other shareholders or the corporation at a price set in the agreement.

**Preemptive Rights.** Preemptive rights give existing shareholders the option buying new shares being issued in proportion to their current ownership interest, preventing dilution of their interest.

**Right to Receive Information and Inspect Books and Records.** Shareholders have a right to be current on financial affairs of the corporation and must be given an annual financial statement.

- Shareholders have an absolute right to inspect the articles of incorporation, bylaws, minutes, and so on within the past three years.

**Dividends.** When a corporation declares a dividend, shareholders on the record date are entitled to receive the dividend. Dividends are declared at the discretion of the board of directors.

*Stock Dividends.* Shares of stock paid in proportion to existing owner interests may be a dividend

**Derivative Lawsuits.** When the corporation is harmed, the directors are empowered to bring an action on behalf of the corporation.
- If the corporation does not bring a lawsuit, the shareholders have the right to bring it on the corporation's behalf.

**Piercing the Corporate Veil.** Piercing the veil occurs when a corporation has not been formed with sufficient capital, commingling of personal with corporate funds has transpired or there's been a failure to maintain books and hold meetings.
- If a corporation is used for improper purposes by a shareholder or many shareholders, the shareholder(s) may be personally liable for obligations and debts of the corporation

**Controlling Shareholder's Breach of Fiduciary Duty.** Courts have held that a controlling shareholder owes a fiduciary duty to minority shareholders.
- A controlling shareholder owns enough shares to effectively control the corporation.

# Board of Directors

The board of directors makes policy decisions and employs the major officers for the corporation. They also make suggestions concerning actions to be implemented by shareholders.

**Compensating Directors.** Directors may set their own compensation fee and are often paid an annual retainer and an attendance fee for each meeting attended.
- Directors are required to have access to the books, records, facilities, premises as well as any other information concerning the corporation's formation.

**Selecting Directors.** There are two types of directors, an inside director and an outside director.
- An inside director is a director who is also an officer of the corporation.
- An outside director is a director who is not an officer of the corporation.
- The number of directors is stated in the articles of incorporation.

**Term of Office.** A director's term expires at the next annual shareholders' meeting following his or her election.
- Terms may be staggered so that only a part of the board is up for election each year.

**Meetings of the Board of Directors.** Directors can act only as a board, not individually. Each director has the right to participate in meetings and has one vote. They cannot vote by proxy.
- Regular meetings are held according to the bylaws.
- Special meetings can be convened with notice for business such as issuing new shares, considering mergers, and defense against takeover attempts.

**Quorum and Voting Requirement.** A quorum is the number of directors required to hold a board of directors' meeting or conduct business of the board.

**Committees of the Board of Directors.** Directors may create committees of the board and give certain powers to those committees.

- The board may not delegate the power to declare dividends, initiate actions the require shareholders' approval, appoint members to fill openings on the board, amend the bylaws, approve a merger plan that does not require shareholder approval or authorize the issuance of shares.

*Sarbanes-Oxley Act Imposes Duties on Audit Committee.* This Act requires that public companies have audit committees.

- Members must be outside members of the board.
  - o One member must be a financial expert.
- The committee is responsible for the appointment, payment, and oversight of public accounting firms employed to audit the company.
- Public companies must establish, maintain, and assess adequate internal controls and procedures for financial reporting.

# Corporate Officers

Corporate officers are appointed by the board of directors. They have the responsibility of managing the day-to-day operation of the corporation. Typically, corporations have a president, one or more vice-presidents, a secretary and a treasurer.

- The board of directors may remove any officer unless there is an employment contract to the contrary.

**Agency Authority of Officers.** Officers have the express, implied and apparent authority to bind the corporation to contract. The corporation can ratify an unauthorized act of an officer or agent.

# Liability of Corporate Directors and Officers

Directors and officers owe the fiduciary duties of obedience, care and loyalty.

**Duty of Obedience.** A director or officer must not intentionally or negligently act outside of their authority.

- A director who breaches this duty is personally responsible for any resulting damages caused to the corporation or its shareholders.

**Duty of Care.** The duty of due care involves an officer's or director's obligation to discharge his or her duties in good faith and with the care of an ordinary prudent person in a like position would use, and in a manner that is in the best interests of the corporation.

- A director who breaches this duty is personally responsible, usually for negligence, for any resulting damages caused to the corporation or its shareholders.

*The Business Judgment Rule.* A director or officer's duty of care is measured as of the time that he or she makes a decision.

- Honest mistakes of judgment do not render the director or officer liable.

*Reliance on Others.* A director is not liable if information he or she relied upon is false, misleading or unreliable unless the director or officer has knowledge that would cause his or her reliance to be unwarranted.

- An officer's reliance is more limited because they are more familiar with operations.

*Dissent to Directors' Action.* If an individual director dissents to an action taken by a majority of the board of directors, to avoid liability he or she must either resign or register this dissent.
- By placing it in the meeting's minutes,
- By filing a written dissent to the secretary or
- By forwarding the dissent by registered mail to the secretary right after the meeting.

**Duty of Loyalty.** Officers and directors are to place their personal interest below that of the corporation and its shareholders.

*Usurping a Corporate Opportunity.* Directors and officers may not steal a corporate opportunity for themselves.

*Self-Dealing.* Officers and directors may not enter into contracts with the corporation that will benefit themselves without first disclosing their interest and having the disinterested directors or the shareholders approve the transaction.

*Competing with the Corporation.* Directors and officers cannot engage in activities that compete with the corporation without first disclosing the activity and having the disinterested directors or the shareholders approve the activity.

*Making a Secret Profit.* If a director or officer breaches the duty of loyalty and makes a secret profit from a transaction, the corporation can sue to recover the secret profit.

**State Constituency Statutes.** Many states have enacted these statutes that allow directors to consider constituents other than shareholders when making decisions.

## Criminal Liability

Officers, directors, employees and agents are personally liable for crimes that are committed while acting on behalf of the corporation. Punishment includes fines and imprisonment.
- Since corporations cannot be imprisoned, penalties are often fines or loss of privilege.

## Sarbanes-Oxley Act

The Sarbanes-Oxley Act was enacted to improve corporate governance rules, eliminate conflicts of interest, and instill confidence in investors and the public about management.

**Sarbanes-Oxley Act Improves Corporate Governance.** This Act has changed the rules of corporate governance.

*CEO and CFO Certification.* The CEO and CFO of a public company must file a statement with each annual and quarterly report certifying that the signing officer has reviewed the report and that the report does not contain false statements or material omissions and that the financial statements fairly present the operation and financial condition of the company.

*Reimbursement of Bonuses and Incentive Pay.* If the company is required to restate the financial statements because of material noncompliance with financial reporting requirements, the CEO and CFO must reimburse the company for any bonuses, incentives, or securities trading profits made because of the noncompliance.

*Prohibition on Personal Loans.* Personal loans to directors or executive officers are prohibited.

*Tampering with Evidence.* Tampering with evidence is criminalized under the Act.

*Bar from Acting as an Officer or a Director.* Any person who has committed securities fraud may be prohibited from acting as an officer or a director of a public company.

# Refresh Your Memory

The following exercises will help to test your memory regarding the principles given in this chapter. Read each question twice, then place your answer in the blank provided for each question. Review the chapter material for any questions you are unable to answer or remember.

1. A written document a shareholder signs authorizing another person to vote his or her shares at the shareholders' meetings in the event of a shareholder's absence is a(n) _____.

2. A(n) _____ _____ is an exact date in the corporate bylaws that decides whether a shareholder may vote at a shareholder meeting.

3. If a majority of shares entitled to vote are represented at a meeting either by proxy or in person, there is a(n) _____ to hold the meeting.

4. _____ _____ give existing shareholders the option of subscribing to new shares being issued in proportion to their current ownership interest.

5. Shareholders have the _____ _____ _____ with respect to the books and records of the corporation.

6. A(n) _____ _____ is a director who is also an officer of the corporation.

7. A meeting brought by the board of directors to discuss new shares, merger proposals, hostile takeover attempts is a(n) _____ meeting.

8. _____ is when an individual director opposes action taken by a majority of the board.

9. _____ are employees of the corporation who are appointed by the directors to manage the day-to-day operations of the corporation.

10. A(n) _____ _____ meeting must be held annually to elect directors and vote on other matters.

11. The affirmative vote of the _____ of the voting shares represented at a shareholders' meeting constitutes an act of the shareholders for actions other than the election of directors.

12. Shareholders have the right to _____ their shares.

13. Under _____ voting, a shareholder is entitled to multiply the number of shares he or she owns by the number of directors to be elected and cast the product for a single candidate or distribute the product among two or more candidates.

14. Under _____ voting, each shareholder votes the number of shares he or she owns on candidates for each of the positions open for election.

15. Directors have the _____ to pay dividends to shareholders.

## Critical Thought Exercise

Ned West was the sole shareholder and president of Westward Co., a corporation that ran truck stops along interstate highways. The corporation did not have its own bank accounts. All business was conducted through West's personal account. All supplies, payroll, debts, and purchases were handled through this one checking account. West paid all of his personal expenses out of this account. All receipts from the truck stops were deposited into the same account. While the corporation was in business, no directors meetings were ever held. All decisions for the corporation were made solely by West.

For a four-year period, Westward Co. accumulated $187,455 in federal tax liabilities. The government is now seeking to collect the overdue tax payments directly from West. West argues that the government is ignoring his corporate entity.

Can the government pierce the corporate veil in this case and force West to incur personal liability for the taxes owed by Westward Co.?

*Please compose your answer on a separate sheet of paper or on your computer.*

## Practice Quiz

### True/False

1. ____ The rights of shareholders, directors and officers do not differ from one another.

2. ____ A corporation can be held liable for acts of its directors and officers as a legal entity.

3. ____ A corporation's shareholders are not agents of the corporation and as such may not bind the corporation to any contracts.

4. ____ It is not necessary for any class of shares of the corporation to have voting rights.

5. ____ A shareholder can accumulate all of his/her votes and vote them all for one candidate.

6. ____ The supramajority voting requirement is one in which the corporation's bylaws requires a lesser number of shares to constitute a quorum.

7. ____ The board of directors of a corporation are responsible for formulating policy decisions affecting the management, supervision and control of the operation of the corporation.

8. ___ An outside director is a member of the board of directors, but who is not an officer of the corporation.

9. ___ An individual must have special qualifications to be elected a director of a corporation.

10. ___ The articles of incorporation cannot require a greater than majority of directors to compose a quorum of the vote of the board.

11. ___ Dividends are not automatically paid to shareholders.

12. ___ A director or officer who breaches the duty of care is personally liable to the corporation and its shareholders for any damages caused by the breach.

13. ___ Officers and directors are entitled to rely on information, statements and opinions presented by officers and employees of the corporation as they generally are not able to investigate every corporate matter.

14. ___ Usurping a corporate opportunity is a violation of an officer's or director's duty of care.

15. ___ Officers and directors can engage in activities that compete with the corporation regardless if full disclosure is made and a majority of the disinterested directors or shareholders endorse the activity.

## Multiple Choice

16. Alice and Harvey are on the Board of Directors of the Whizo Corporation. They want to create committees of the board and delegate certain powers to those committees. Which of the following would be the type of committee that Alice and Harvey may create?
    a. The Compensation Committee
    b. The Regular Meeting Committee
    c. The Crime Committee
    d. None of the above

17. What officers do most corporations have?
    a. President, vice-president, coordinator
    b. President, one or more vice presidents, secretary and treasurer
    c. President, vice-president, human resource director, treasurer
    d. President, vice-president, secretary and an agent

18. Which of the following expresses the duties that the officers and directors owe to the corporation and its shareholders?
    a. Duty of obedience, duty to spend, duty of care
    b. Duty of loyalty, duty of care, duty to account properly
    c. Duty of loyalty, duty of care, duty of obedience
    d. Duty of loyalty, duty to make decisions, fiduciary duty

19. Under the business judgment rule, directors or officers not liable for
    a. Usurping a corporate opportunity
    b. Self-dealing
    c. Honest mistakes of judgment
    d. Lending trade secrets to corporate competitors

20. Which situation best describes when the court will pierce the corporate veil?
    a. When the corporation has been formed with thin capitalization.
    b. When there has been a commingling of personal and corporate assets.
    c. When there has been a failure to maintain corporate books and records.
    d. All of the above.

21. What must be in a corporation's written notice to its shareholders of the annual meeting?
    a. place
    b. day
    c. time
    d. all of the above

22. Which of the following is not true with respect to preemptive rights?
    a. These rights give existing shareholders the option of subscribing to new shares being issued in proportion to their current ownership interests.
    b. The purchase of shares based on preemptive rights can prevent a shareholder's interest from being diluted.
    c. Shareholders who do not exercise their preemptive rights may accumulate rights for the future when new shares become available for purchase.
    d. Shareholders are given a reasonable period of time to exercise their preemptive rights.

23. When may a shareholder bring a derivative lawsuit?
    a. If the shareholder fairly and adequately represents the interests of the corporation.
    b. If the shareholder made a written demand on the corporation to take suitable actions.
    c. If the shareholder was a shareholder of the corporation at the time of the act complained of.
    e. All of the above

24. Which of the following is true with respect to constituency statutes?
    a. Constituency statutes apply the strict principle that shareholders are the only "owners" of the corporation.
    b. Constituency statutes acknowledge the rights of a variety of participants, including lender, suppliers, and distributors.
    c. Constituency statutes allow directors to consider only the shareholders when making decisions.
    d. None of the above

25. Which of the following powers must be exercised by the board itself?
    a. amending the bylaws
    b. recommend independent public accountants and supervise the audit of the corporation's financial records by the accountant
    c. invest and reinvest the funds of the corporation
    d. review and decide whether to pursue requests by shareholders for the corporation to sue persons who have allegedly harmed the corporation

## Short Answer

26. At what type of meetings are directors elected?

27.  What is the right of first refusal as it pertains to stock?

_____

28.  What is included in the annual financial statement provided to a corporation's shareholders?

_____

29.  In order to reflect technology, what does the Revised Model Corporations Act provide with respect to directors' meetings?

_____

30.  What is a stock dividend?

_____

31.  Define the meaning of fiduciary duty.

_____

_____

32.  Tell what D &O insurance is and what its main purpose is.

_____

_____

33.  What does indemnification mean as it applies to the corporation?

_____

_____

34.  What is a voting trust?

_____

35.  When can an act that can be taken at a shareholders' meeting be taken without a meeting?

_____

36.  What is the main responsibility of the corporations' officers?

_____

37.  What is the straight voting method?

_____

38.  What is the cumulative voting method?

_____

_____

39.  What is a buy-and-sell agreement?

_____

40.  What is a derivative suit?

_____

## Answers to Refresh Your Memory

1.   proxy  [p 778]
2.   record date  [p 778]
3.   quorum  [p 778]
4.   preemptive rights  [p 780]
5.   right of inspection  [p 781]
6.   inside director  [p 786]
7.   special  [p 787]
8.   Dissension  [p 792]
9.   Officers  [p 777]
10.  annual shareholders'  [p 777]
11.  majority  [p 778]
12.  transfer  [p 780]
13.  cumulative  [p 779]
14.  straight  [p 778-779]
15.  discretion  [p 781]

## Critical Thought Exercise Model Answer

In corporate law, if personal and company interests are commingled to the extent that the corporation has no separate identity, a court may "pierce the corporate veil" and expose the shareholders to personal liability.  West mixed all aspects of his personal business with corporate business.  All purchases and payroll checks were made from his personal account.  There is no way to separate corporate receipts from West's personal funds.  In order to prevent a creditor from "piercing the corporate veil" a sole stockholder needs to careful to preserve the corporate identity.  Maintaining separate accounts and detailed records are imperative if corporate identity is to be preserved.  West did not attempt to preserve the identity of Westward Co.

Another key factor that favors the government in this case is the failure of Westward Co to hold directors meetings.  The failure of the sole shareholder to comply with statutory corporate formalities demonstrates that the corporate form may be a sham.  West never consulted with his directors and made all decisions for Westward Co. by himself.  When the corporate business is treated in such a careless and flippant manner, the corporation and the shareholder in control are no longer separate entities, requiring the sole shareholder to assume personal liability to creditors of the corporation.  West totally ignored the corporate identity and now the government will be allowed to "pierce the corporate veil." West will be personally liable for the corporation tax debt.

## Answers to Practice Quiz

### True/False

1.   False   Shareholders, directors and officers all have different rights in managing the corporation.  [p 777]
2.   True    A corporation can be held liable for the acts of its directors and officers because it is a legal entity.  [p 777]
3.   True    Shareholders are not agents of a corporation and cannot bind it to contracts. [p 777]
4.   False   At least one class of shares of the corporation must have voting rights.  [p 778]
5.   True    A shareholder can gather all of his or her votes and vote them all for one candidate

under the cumulative voting method. [p 779]

6.  False   A requirement that a greater than majority of shares constitutes a quorum of the vote of shareholders is a supramajority voting requirement. [p 780]

7.  True    The board of directors, not shareholders, is responsible for formulating policy decisions affecting management, supervision and the operation of the corporation. [p 785]

8.  True    An outside director is a person who sits on the corporation's board of directors but is not an officer of the corporation. [p 786]

9.  False   A person need not have any special qualifications to be elected as a director of a corporation. [p 786]

10. False   A greater majority of directors can be required in order to constitute a quorum for the vote of the board of directors. [p 787]

11. True    Shareholders are not automatically paid dividends. Dividends are paid at the discretion of the board of directors. [p 781]

12. False   An officer or director who breaches the duty of care is personally liable to the corporation and its shareholders for any damages caused by the breach. [p 790]

13. True    Officers and directors are entitled to rely on information, statements and opinions presented by officers and employees of the corporation as they generally are not able to investigate every corporate matter. [p 791]

14. False   Usurping a corporate opportunity is a breach of the duty of loyalty not a breach of the duty of care. [p 794]

15. False   Directors and officers cannot engage in activities that compete with the corporation unless full disclosure of the activity is made and there is director or shareholder approval. [p 795]

## Multiple Choice

16. A   Answer A is the correct answer, as Alice and Harvey as members of the Board of Directors may create a Compensation Committee provided all of the other board Members ratify it. A compensation committee approves management Compensation, including bonuses, salaries, stock plans, fringe benefits, etc. Answers B, and C are incorrect, as these type of committees that are usually Created by Board of Directors. Answer D is incorrect based on the reasons given above. [p 787-788]

17. B   Answer B is correct, as it properly states the officers that most corporations have. Answer A is incorrect, as a coordinator is not an officer. Answer C is incorrect, as the human resource director is a member of personnel, not an officer. Answer D is incorrect, as an agent is not usually an officer of a corporation. [p 788]

18. C   Answer C is the correct answer, as it properly states the duties that officers and directors owe to the corporation and its shareholders. Answer A is incorrect, as the officers and directors do not owe a duty to spend. Answer B is incorrect, as the officers and directors do not owe a duty to account. Answer D is incorrect, as the duty to make decisions may be implied, however, this is too broad of a statement to encompass it in the directors' and officers' duties. [p 790]

19. C   Answer C is correct, as the business judgment rule states that the directors or officers are not liable for honest mistakes in judgment. Answers A, B and D are all incorrect, as they all are activities for which the directors and officers would be held liable for participating in. [p 791]

20. D   Answer D is correct, as answers A, B, and C all are situations that describe when the court will pierce the corporate veil and hold the shareholder personally liable for the debts and obligations of the corporation. [p 783]

21.    D      Answer D is correct, as a corporation's written notice to its shareholders when calling the annual meeting must state the place, day and time. Therefore, answers A, B, and C are all correct which in turn makes D the right answer. [p 778]

22.    C      Answer C is correct, as it is the only statement that is not true with respect to preemptive rights. If a shareholder does not exercise his or her preemptive rights within a reasonable time (usually 30 days), then the shares may be sold to anyone. Answers A, B and D are all incorrect, as they all are true statements with respect to preemptive rights. [p 780-781]

23.    D      Answer D is correct, as all of the statements in answers A, B, and C indicate what a shareholder must do in order to bring a derivative suit. [p 781-782]

24.    B      Answer B is correct, as constituency statutes acknowledge the rights of a variety of participants other than the shareholders themselves. Answers A, and B are not correct statements with regard to constituency statutes. Answer D is incorrect based on the reasoning given above. [p 796]

25.    A      Answer A is correct, as the board of directors must amend the bylaws and cannot appoint a committee to do so. Answers B, C, and D are incorrect as each of these actions are things that committees appointed by the board may do. [p 788]

## Short Answer

26. Annual shareholders' meetings. [p 777]
27. An agreement entered into by shareholders that grant one another the right of first refusal to purchase shares that they are going to sell. [p 780]
28. Balance sheets, income statements and a statement of changes in shareholder equity are the types of information found in an annual financial statement. [p 781]
29. It permits the board of directors' meetings to be held by way of a conference call. [p 787]
30. A stock dividend is additional shares of stock paid as a dividend. [p 781]
31. The duty of loyalty, integrity, honesty, trust and confidence owed by directors and officers to their corporate employers is what is known as their fiduciary duty. [p 790]
32. D & O insurance is directors' and officers' liability insurance a corporation may purchase to defend an officer or director who has been sued in his or her corporate capacity. [p 789]
33. Indemnification in the corporate sense means that the corporation as opposed to the officer or director is liable and pays the costs associated with litigation as well as judgments or settlements associated with the lawsuit. [p 790]
34. It is a situation where the shareholders transfer their stock certificates to a trustee who is authorized to vote their shares. [p 780]
35. If all of the corporate shareholders sign a written consent approving of the action. [p 778]
36. The main responsibility of the corporations' officers is to manage the day-to-day operations of the corporation. [p 789]
37. Under straight voting, each shareholder votes the number of shares he or she owns on candidates for each of the positions open for election. [p 778]
38. Under cumulative voting, a shareholder is entitled to multiply the number of shares he or she owns by the number of directors to be elected and cast the product for a single candidate or distribute the product among two or more candidates. [p 779]
39. An agreement that requires selling shareholders to sell their shares to the other shareholders or to the corporation at the price specified in the agreement. [p 780]
40. When the corporation is harmed, the directors are empowered to bring an action on behalf of the corporation. If they do not, the shareholders have the right to bring it on the corporation's behalf. [p 781]

# Chapter 29
# CORPORATE ACQUISITIONS AND MULTINATIONAL CORPORATIONS

## Chapter Overview

Corporations must seek shareholder approval for fundamental changes, which requires the solicitation of votes from shareholders. Corporations may acquire other entities through merger, consolidation, or by hostile tender offer, against which the entity facing acquisition may erect barriers or impediments. Multinational corporations, through a variety of arrangement, conduct business around the world. This chapter discusses fundamental corporate changes, acquisitions and defensive maneuvers, and the role of multinational corporations in international business.

## Objectives

Upon completion of the exercises in this chapter, you should be able to:

1. Explain the process of soliciting proxies.
2. Understand when a shareholder can insert a proposal in proxy materials.
3. Explain the process involved in approving a merger or share exchange.
4. Define tender offer and describe defensive maneuvers to prevent hostile takeover.
5. Discuss the use of multinational corporations in conducting international business.

## Practical Application

For those businesspersons that obtain ownership interests in corporations or choose the corporation as their business form, obtaining or maintaining control of the company is often imperative. It is wise to understand how control of the company may be lost and what efforts can lawfully be made to thwart a proxy battle or hostile takeover.

## Helpful Hints

Mergers, acquisitions, proxy fights, and tender offers are realties that are realized by following laws regulating these processes and changes. Individuals have a greater ability to control their financial stake in a corporation if they understand their rights and duties under these laws. The following exercises will help you to better understand this area of corporate law.

## Study Tips

### Proxy Solicitation and Proxy Contests

Shareholders can exercise their right to vote in person or by proxy.

- A proxy is a means by which a shareholder authorizes another person to represent him or her and vote his or her shares at a shareholders' meeting.
- A proxy card is a written document signed by a shareholder that authorizes another person to vote the shareholder's shares.

**Federal Proxy Rules.** Section 14(a) of the Securities Exchange Act of 1934 gives the SEC the authority to regulate the solicitation of proxies.

- A proxy statement must fully describe the matter for which the proxy is being solicited, who is soliciting the proxy, and any other pertinent information.

**Antifraud Provision.** Section 14(a) prohibits misrepresentations or omissions of a material fact in proxy materials.

**Proxy Contests.** When shareholders oppose the actions of incumbent directors and management, they may challenge the management in a proxy contest in which both sides solicit proxies.

*Reimbursement of Expenses.* The incumbent management can obtain reimbursement from the corporation if the proxy contest concerns an issue of corporate policy.

- The dissenting group can get reimbursed only if it wins the proxy contest.

**SEC Proxy Rules.** Shareholders who own less than $5 million in stock of a company may communicate with other shareholders without filing proxy solicitation materials with the SEC.

- Companies must unbundle propositions so shareholders can vote on each issue.
- Performance charts must be included in annual reports.
- Annual reports must provide tables that summarize executive compensation.

## Shareholder Resolutions

The SEC lets a shareholder submit a resolution to be considered by other shareholders if the shareholder owned at least 1,000 shares for two years, the resolution is not more than 550 words.

- If management does not oppose the resolution it may be included in proxy materials.
- If management does not support the resolution, it may be included in proxy materials by the corporation if it relates to the corporation's business, concerns a policy issue, and does not concern payment of dividends.

## Mergers and Acquisitions

Mergers, consolidations, share exchanges, and sale of assets are friendly in nature, as both corporations have agreed to the combination of corporations or acquisition of assets.

**Mergers.** This occurs when a corporation is absorbed in another corporation and ceases to exist.

- The corporation that continues is the surviving corporation.
- The other is the merged corporation.
- Shareholders of the merged corporation receive stock or securities of the surviving one.

**Consolidations.** When two or more corporations combine to form an entirely new corporation.

- The two consolidated corporations are called merged corporations and cease to exist.
- The new corporation is the consolidated corporation.

**Share Exchanges.** This occurs when one corporation (parent) acquires all the shares of another corporation (subsidiary) and both corporations retain their separate legal existence.

**Required Approvals for a Merger or Share Exchange.** An ordinary merger or share exchange requires the recommendation of the board of directors of each corporation and an affirmative vote of the majority of shares of each corporation that is entitled to vote.
- The articles of merger or share exchange must be filed with the secretary of state.
- The secretary of state will issue a certificate of merger or share exchange.

**Short-Form Mergers.** If the parent corporation owns 90 percent of the subsidiary corporation, a short-form merger procedure may be followed.
- Approval of shareholders of neither corporation is required for short-form merger.
- All that is required is approval of the board of directors of the parent corporation.

**Sale or Lease of Assets.** A corporation may sell, lease, or otherwise dispose of all or substantially all of its property.
- Such a sale requires the recommendation of the board of directors and an affirmative vote of the majority of the shares of the selling corporation that is entitled to vote.

**Dissenting Shareholder Appraisal Rights.** Shareholders who object to a proposed merger, share exchange, or sale or lease of all or substantially all of the property of a corporation have a right to have their shares valued by a court and receive cash payment from the corporation.

## Tender Offers

A tender offer, often called a hostile tender offer, is an offer that an acquirer (tender offeror) makes directly to a target corporation's shareholders in an effort to acquire the target corporation.
- Shareholders of the target make their own decision about selling to the tender offeror.

**The Williams Act.** This Act regulates tender offers, whether made with cash, securities, or other consideration, and gives disclosure requirements and antifraud provisions.

**Tender Offer Rules.** The Williams Act does not require that the management of the target company or the SEC be notified until the offer is made.
- The offer cannot be closed before 20 days after the commencement of the tender offer.
- The offer must be extended for 10 days if the tender offer increases the number of shares that it will take or the price it will pay.
- The fair price rule stipulates that any increase in price paid for shares must be offered to all shareholders, even those who have already tendered their shares.
- The pro rata rule requires that shares must be purchased on a pro rata basis if too many shares are tendered.

**Antifraud Provision.** Section 14(e) of the Williams Act prohibits fraudulent, deceptive, or manipulative practices in connection with tender offers.

**Leveraged Buyout.** Many tender offerors do not have the funds to purchase the stock from shareholders of the target corporation and rely on raising money from creditors.
- Tender offeror uses loans to purchase stock from stockholders of the target corporation.
  - These bridge loans are paid back after assets of the target corporation are sold.
- Tender offeror sells junk bonds, risky corporate bonds that pay a higher rate of interest.

- After the tender offer is completed, the acquiring company is saddled with huge debts.
  - ○ When it merges with the target corporation the resulting company's capital structure consists of a low amount of equity and huge amounts of debt.

**Fighting a Tender Offer.** The incumbent management of a target corporation may desire to oppose a tender offer, and may use a variety of activities to impede or defeat the tender offer.
- Persuasion of shareholders, media campaigns used to oppose the tender offer
- Delaying lawsuits, suits filed alleging antitrust or securities violations to buy time
- Selling a crown jewel, selling an asset that makes the target corporation less attractive
- White knight merger, merger with friendly party that will leave target intact
- Pac-Man tender offer, target makes tender offer for the tender offeror
- Adopting a poison pill, strategy built into articles of incorporation, bylaws, contracts, or leases whereby large payouts or termination of contracts become effective if the corporation changes hands
- Issuing additional stock, issuing more stock makes tender offeror buy more shares
- Creating Employee Stock Ownership Plan (ESOP), block of stock owned by employees is used to oppose acquirer in proxy fight
- Flip-over and flip-in rights plans, allows stockholders to buy twice the value in stock to make company too expensive to buy
- Greenmail and standstill agreements, target pays premium to get back shares from tender offeror

**Business Judgment Rule.** The directors of a corporation owe a fiduciary duty to act carefully and honestly when acting on behalf of the corporation.
- The Business judgment rule protects the decisions of the board of directors, who act on an informed basis, in good faith, and in the honest belief that the action taken was in the best interests of the corporation and its shareholders.

## State Antitakeover Statutes

These statutes are enacted by states to protect corporations incorporated in or doing business in the state from hostile takeovers. They are often challenged as unconstitutional because they violate the Williams Act and the Commerce and Supremacy Clauses of the U.S. Constitution.

**Exon-Florio Law.** The Exon-Florio Law of 1988, as amended by the Byrd-Exon Amendment of 1992 mandates the President of the United States to suspend, prohibit, or dismantle the acquisition of U.S. businesses by foreign investors if there is credible evidence that the foreign investor might take action that threatens to impair the national security.

## Multinational Corporations

International networks, or multinational enterprises, are made up of companies of different nationalities that constitute a single economic unit connected by shareholding, managerial control, or contractual agreement.
- Subcontracts with independent firms in a host country is the simplest international operating structure.
- National multinational firms create wholly owned branches and subsidiaries overseas.
- International multinational firms are made up of two or more parents from different countries that co-own operating businesses in two or more countries.

**International Branch Office.** An office of the corporation that is not a separate legal entity.

- The corporation is liable for the contracts and the torts committed by personnel.

**International Subsidiary Corporation.** A separate legal entity where the parent company usually owns all or the majority of the subsidiary corporation.

- It is organized under the laws of the foreign country.
- The parent corporation is not liable for the contracts or torts committed.

# Refresh Your Memory

The following exercises will help to test your memory regarding the principles given in this chapter. Read each question twice, then place your answer in the blank provided for each question. Review the chapter material for any questions you are unable to answer or remember.

1. A(n) _____ _____ is a written document signed by a shareholder that authorizes another person to vote the shareholder's shares.

2. Section 14(a) of the Securities Exchange Act of 1934 gives the SEC the authority to regulate the _____ _____ _____ .

3. When shareholders oppose the actions of incumbent directors and _____ , they may challenge the management in a(n) _____ contest.

4. A(n) _____ corporation is one that continues after a merger.

5. When two or more corporations combine to form an entirely new corporation, a(n) _____ occurs.

6. A share exchange occurs when a(n) _____ corporation acquires all the shares of the _____ corporation and both corporations retain their separate legal existence.

7. _____ of merger or share exchange must be filed with the Secretary of State.

8. If the parent corporation owns 90 percent of the subsidiary corporation, a(n) _____ _____ _____ procedure may be followed.

9. The Williams Act regulates _____ _____ .

10. The _____ _____ rule stipulates that any increase in price paid for shares under a tender offer must be offered to all shareholders, even those who have already tendered their shares.

11. The _____ _____ rule provides that shares must be purchased on a(n) _____ _____ basis if too many shares are tendered.

12. Shareholders who tender their shares have an absolute right to _____ them at any time prior to the closing of the tender offer.

13. One defense to a hostile tender offer is to sell the _____ _____, or sell a valuable asset that the tender offeror is particularly interested in acquiring.

14. A(n) _____ _____ is an office of the corporation, not a separate legal entity.

15. A(n) _____ _____ is organized under the laws of the foreign country and is a separate legal entity.

## Critical Thought Exercise

Blue Cab Co. was merged into Atlantic Cab Corp., with Atlantic being the surviving corporation in the merger. Atlantic did not take over any of the cabs owned by Blue because they were old and in disrepair. Blue Cab was poorly run and owed over $600,000 to Valley Bank for cab purchases. Blue Cab also owed over $60,700 to Fleet Gas Co for fuel purchased by its employees. Blue Cab is owed $43,000 by Broadway Actors Transportation, Inc. (BAT) for limousine services rendered pursuant to a contract. Blue Cab has already commenced suit against BAT for breach of contract. Valley Bank and Fleet Gas brought a suit against Atlantic for payment of the debts. The board of directors of Atlantic refused to honor the debts of Blue Cab because the purpose in taking over Blue Cab was to eliminate a competitor. Atlantic had no desire to acquire the assets of Blue Cab. Co. Atlantic argued that it had never agreed to assume any debt owed by Blue Cab.

What is the effect of the merger and will Valley Bank and Fleet Gas be able to recover breach of contract damages from Atlantic? Can Atlantic maintain the suit against BAT?

*Please compose your answer on a separate sheet of paper or on your computer.*

## Practice Quiz

### True/False

1. ___ A proxy is a way for a shareholder to vote his/her shares at a shareholders' meeting.

2. ___ In order to act as a proxy, you must be an officer or director of the corporation.

3. ___ The Securities Act of 1934 authorized the SEC to regulate the solicitation of proxies.

4. ___ A proxy statement must contain information about who is soliciting the proxy and the number of proxies already solicited on the matter.

5. ___ The dissenting group is not entitled to recover its proxy contest costs for all policy issue contests unless it wins.

6. ___ A merger combines two corporations, with both of the original corporations surviving.

7. ___ In a share exchange, both corporations retain their separate legal existence.

8. \_\_\_ In an ordinary merger, approval is needed by votes of both board of directors, as well as by the shareholders.

9. \_\_\_ Shareholder appraisal rights may be exercised in mergers, consolidations, short-form mergers, and sales of substantially all the corporate assets not in the ordinary course of business.

10. \_\_\_ Placing additional stock on the market increases the number of outstanding shares that the tender offeror must purchase in order to gain control of the target corporation.

11. \_\_\_ Mergers with friendly parties that promise to leave the target corporation and/or its management in tact are known as white knight mergers.

12. \_\_\_ Large severance payments received by top executives upon their departure from their employment at the corporation are known as a golden parachute.

13. \_\_\_ State takeover statutes are aimed at permitting takeovers by hostile takeovers.

14. \_\_\_ The pro rata rule stipulates that any increase in price paid for shares tendered must be offered to all shareholders, even those who have previously tendered their shares.

15. \_\_\_ The fair price rule holds that the shares must be purchased on a pro rata basis if too many shares are tendered.

## Multiple Choice

16. Proxy solicitations are regulated by the Securities and Exchange Act of 1934 under
    a. Section 10(b).
    b. Section 14(a).
    c. Section 14(e).
    d. Section 16(a).

18. A shareholder's proxy can be granted to
    a. only another shareholder.
    b. officers only.
    c. officers or directors only.
    d. anyone.

18. What is required in order for a merger to use the short-form procedure?
    a. There must be agreement by both boards of directors to use the short-form procedure.
    b. There must be an increase of less than 20 percent in the number of shares of voting stock of the surviving corporation.
    c. There must be ownership by the parent corporation of at least 90 percent of the shares of the subsidiary corporation before the merger.
    d. The SEC must approve the use of the short-form procedure.

19. Typically, a shareholder is allowed to exercise a right of appraisal in conjunction with
    a. regular mergers.
    b. short-form mergers.
    c. sale or lease of substantially all of the corporate assets.
    d. all of the above.

20. Jungle Corporation purchases a large bloc of shares in Harvest Corporation as its first step in an attempt to take over Harvest. The management of Harvest immediately purchases a similar size bloc of shares in Jungle and notifies it of Harvest's intent to take over Jungle. This defensive tactic is an example of
   a. a flip-over plan.
   b. selling a crown jewel.
   c. adopting a poison pill.
   d. a Pac-Man tender offer.

21. Which rule protects the decisions of a board of directors that acts on an informed basis, in good faith, and in the honest belief that the action taken was in the best interests of the corporation and its shareholders?
   a. the business judgment rule
   b. the fiduciary duty rule
   c. the duty of due care rule
   d. the employee stock ownership rule

22. What is meant by the term greenmail?
   a. mail that is placed in a green envelope
   b. tactic that make the target corporation more expensive to the tender offeror
   c. Where the tender offor will agree to give up its tender offer and agree not to purchase any further shares if the target corporation agrees to buy back the stock at a premium over fair market value.
   d. none of the above.

23. An offer than an acquirer makes directly to a target corporation's shareholders in an attempt to acquire the target corporation or control of the target corporation is known as a
   a. target offer
   b. tender offer
   c. fair value offer
   d. regular course of business offer

24. Which act regulates all tender offers, whether they are made with securities, cash, or other consideration?
   a. The Tender Offer Act.
   b. The SEC Act
   c. The Target Corporation Act
   d. The Williams Act

25. An ordinary merger or share exchange requires
   a. the recommendation of the board of directors of each corporation.
   b. an affirmative vote of the majority of shares of each corporation that is entitled to vote.
   c. compliance with RMBCA Section 11.03.
   d. all of the above

## Short Answer

26. What must a proxy statement contain?

_____

_____

27. What does Section 14(a) of the Securities Exchange Act of 1934 prohibit?

28. When may a dissenting group get reimbursed for expenses associated with a proxy contest?

29. Explain the term merger.

30. Explain the concept of a share exchange.

31. What approvals are required for a regular merger?

32. When can corporations use the short-form merger procedure?

33. What is a tender offer?

34. What is required by the fair price rule?

35. What is required by the pro rata rule?

36. What are withdrawal rights?

37. What is meant by a poison pill?

38. What effect does issuing additional stock have on a tender offer?

39. What is the liability of a branch office for contracts and torts of personnel?

40. What is the liability of a subsidiary corporation for contracts and torts of personnel?

# Answers to Refresh Your Memory

1.  proxy card  [p 808]
2.  solicitation of proxies  [p 808]
3.  management, proxy  [p 809]
4.  surviving  [p 812]
5.  consolidation  [p 812]
6.  parent, subsidiary  [p 813]
7.  Articles  [p 814]
8.  short form merger  [p 814]
9.  tender offers  [p 817]
10. fair price  [p 817]
11. pro rata, pro rata  [p 817]
12. withdraw  [p 817]
13. crown jewel  [p 817]
14. branch office  [p 823]
15. subsidiary corporation  [p 824]

# Critical Thought Exercise Model Answer

A merger involves the legal combination of two or more corporations in a manner that only one of the corporations continues to exist. When Blue Cab merged into Atlantic, Atlantic continued as the surviving corporation while Blue Moon ceased to exist as an entity. After the merger, Atlantic would be recognized as a single corporation, possessing all the rights, privileges, and powers of itself and Blue Cab Co. Atlantic automatically acquired all the assets and property of Blue Cab without the necessity of formality or deeds. The shareholders of Blue Cab receive stock or securities of Atlantic or other consideration as provided in the plan of merger. Atlantic becomes liable for all of Blue Cab's debts and obligations. Atlantic's articles of incorporation are deemed amended to include any changes that are stated in the articles of merger.

In a merger, the surviving corporation obtains the absorbed corporation's preexisting obligations and legal rights. If the merging corporation had a right of action against a third party, the surviving corporation can bring or maintain a suit after the merger to recover the merging corporation's damages. Atlantic will inherit Blue Cab's right to sue BAT and will be entitled to recover whatever damages Blue Cab was entitled to collect.

# Answers to Practice Quiz

## True/False

1.  True   A shareholder may exercise his or her right to vote at a shareholders' meeting by proxy, which authorizes another person to vote the shares. [p 808]
2.  False  The proxy need not be a director or officer. [p 808]
3.  True   This is authorized by Section 14(a) of the act. [p 808]
4.  False  The materials must contain information about who is soliciting the proxy and the matter for which the proxy is being solicited. [p 809]
5.  True   The dissenting group must win to get reimbursed. [p 810]

6. False   In a merger, one corporation is absorbed into another corporation and the first ceases to exist. [p 812]

7. True   Both the parent and subsidiary corporations continue to exist. [p 813]

8. True   The approval needed is recommendation by both boards of directors and votes of the shareholders of each corporation. [p 813]

9. True   If the dissenter is not satisfied with the value placed on shares by the corporation, he or she may petition the court to determine the fair value of the shares. [p 814]

10. True   When issuing additional stock, the placing of additional stock on the market increases the number of outstanding shares that the tender offeror must purchase in order to gain control of the target corporation. [p 818]

11. True   A white knight merger involves friendly parties that promise to leave the target corporation and/or its management in tact. [p 818]

12. True   A golden parachute describes the large severance payments received by top executives when they leave their employment at a corporation. [p 815]

13. False   There is no such thing as a state takeover statute that permits corporation to be taken via a hostile takeover. Rather, there are antitakeover statutes that are geared toward protecting corporations that are either incorporated in or do business within the state from hostile takeovers. [p 821]

14. False   This states the fair price rule, not the pro rata rule. The pro rata rule states that the shares must be purchased on a pro rata basis if too many shares are tendered. [p 817]

15. False   This states the pro rata rule, not the fair price rule. The fair price rule holds that any increase in price paid for shares tendered must be offered to all shareholders, even those who have previously tendered their shares. [p 817]

## Multiple Choice

16. B   This section promotes full disclosure during the proxy solicitation process. Choice A is a section relating to insider trading. Choice C is the section prohibiting fraud in the proxy solicitation process. Choice D relates to a section that prohibits short-swing profits in the sale of securities by insiders. [p 808]

17. D   Any person may be authorized to act as a proxy. Choices A, B, and C state choices that may be selected by a shareholder, but they are too restrictive because anyone can be chosen. [p 808]

18. C   All that is required is the approval of the board of supervisors of the parent company as long as the 90 percent condition is met. Choice A is incorrect because no approval is needed from the board of the subsidiary. Choice B is incorrect because this is a condition that negates the need for surviving shareholder approval in a regular merger situation. Choice D is not correct because SEC approval is not needed. [p 814]

19. D   Appraisal rights apply to mergers, a share exchange, or sale or lease of all or substantially all of the property of the corporation. Objecting shareholders are provided a statutory right to dissent and obtain payment of the fair value of their shares. Choices A, B, and C are correct, but D is the correct answer because all choices are correct. [p 814]

20. D   In a Pac-Man or reverse tender offer, the target makes a tender offer for the tender offeror. A is not correct because a flip-over allows stockholders to buy twice the value in stock to make the company too expensive to buy. B is not correct because there has been no sale of a valuable asset by Harvest. C is not correct because this was an act by Harvest management, not a strategy built into the articles of incorporation, bylaws, or contracts of Harvest. [p 818]

21. A   Answer A is correct, as the business judgment rule protects the decisions of a board of directors that acts on an informed basis, in good faith, and in the honest belief that the action taken was in the best interests of the corporation and its shareholders. Answers

B, C, and D are all incorrect, as there are no such rules. [p 818]

22. C   Answer C is correct, as it adequately defines the term greenmail. Answer A is incorrect, as it is absurd. Answer B is incorrect, as it is opposite of the true meaning of greenmail. Answer D incorrect based on the reasoning given above. [p 818]

23. B   Answer B is correct, as the question defines a tender offer. Answer A is incorrect, as there is no such thing as a target offer. Answers C and D are also incorrect, as these types of offers do not exist as well. [p 816]

24. D   Answer D is correct, as the Williams Act regulates all tender offers, regardless of what they are made with. Answers A, B, and C are incorrect, as there are no such acts. [p 817]

25. D   Answer D is correct, as an ordinary merger or share exchange requires all of the things mentioned in answers A, B, and C. [p 813]

## Short Answer

26.   The proxy statement must fully describe (1) the matter for which the proxy is being solicited, (2) who is soliciting the proxy, and (3) any other pertinent information. [p 809]

27.   Section 14(a) prohibits misrepresentations or omissions of a material fact in proxy materials. [p 809]

28.   The expenses of the dissenting group are reimbursed only if it wins the proxy contest. If the proxy contest concerns a personal matter, neither side may recover its expenses. [p 810]

29.   A merger occurs when one corporation is absorbed into another corporation and ceases to exist. Title to all assets of the merged corporation passes to the surviving corporation without formality or deeds. [p 812]

30.   In a share exchange, both corporations retain their separate legal existence. The parent corporation owns all the shares of the subsidiary corporation. [p 813]

31.   A merger requires (1) the recommendation of the board of directors of each corporation and (2) an affirmative vote of the majority of shares of each corporation that is entitled to vote. [p 813]

32.   The short-form procedure can be used if the parent corporation owns 90 percent or more of the outstanding stock of the subsidiary corporation. [p 814]

33.   A tender offer is an offer that an acquirer makes during a hostile takeover directly to a target corporation's shareholders in an effort to acquire the target corporation. The shareholders each make an individual decision about whether to sell their shares to the tender offeror. [p 816

34.   The fair price rule states that any increases in price paid by the tender offeror for shares must be offered to all shareholders, even those who have already tendered shares. [p 817]

35.   The pro rata rule requires that shares must be purchased on a pro rata basis if too many shares are tendered. [p 817]

36.   Shareholders who tender their shares have an absolute right to withdraw them at any time prior to the closing of the tender offer. [p 817]

37.   A poison pill is a defense to a hostile takeover bid where the target company has provisions in contracts and leases that have them expire if ownership of the corporation changes hands. [p 818]

38.   It increases the number of shares that a tender offeror must purchase to gain control of the target corporation. [p 818]

39.   A branch office is an office of the corporation, not a separate legal entity, so has no legal liability separate from the corporation. [p 823]

40.   A subsidiary corporation is a separate legal entity, wholly or substantially owned by the parent company. As a separate entity, it is liable for its own contracts and torts committed by personnel. [p 824]

## Chapter 30
# LIMITED LIABILITY COMPANIES
# AND LIMITED LIABLITY PARTNERSHIPS

## Chapter Overview

Owners may operate a business as a limited liability company (LLC), an unincorporated business entity that combines the most favorable features of general partnerships, limited partnerships, and corporations. The owners of an LLC can manage the business and enjoy limited liability, and can choose to be taxed as a partnership. Most states allow certain types of professionals, such as accountants and lawyers, to operate as a limited liability partnership (LLP), which allows the owners to have limited liability. This chapter introduces the formation and operation of LLCs and LLPs, and the liability of their owners.

## Objectives

Upon completion of the exercises in this chapter, you should be able to:

1. Characterize a limited liability company (LLC) and a limited liability partnership (LLP).
2. Explain the procedure for organizing a LLC and a LLP.
3. Explain the limited liability shield provided by a LLC and a LLP.
4. Differentiate between a member-managed LLC and a manager-managed LLC.
5. Discuss when members and managers owe fiduciary duties of loyalty and care to the LLC.

## Practical Application

You should be able to recognize the benefits of conducting a newly organized business as a limited liability company. You should be able to identify the choices available and why a company may choose this form from a tax, liability and management perspective.

## Helpful Hints

Review the advantages and disadvantages of sole proprietorships, partnerships, limited partnerships and corporations. Compare these advantages and disadvantages to those of limited liability companies and limited liability partnerships. Apply these comparisons to hypothetical situations to analyze what business form is best for specific circumstances and needs.

## Study Tips

### Limited Liability Company (LLC)

Limited liability companies, known as LLCs, are created by state law.

- An LLC is a separate legal entity separate from its members.
  o It can sue or be sued, enter into or enforce contracts, transfer and hold title to property and be civilly and criminally liable under the law.

**The Uniform Limited Liability Company Act (ULLCA).** This Act codifies limited liability company law, with its primary goal to establish a comprehensive limited liability company law that is uniform throughout the United States.
- Many states have adopted the ULLCA, which sets forth the laws concerning formation, operation and termination of the LCC.

**Taxation of LLCs.** An LLC is taxed as a partnership unless it elects to be taxed as a corporation.
- This avoids double taxation, as the income or losses "flow through" to the members.

**Powers of an LLC.** An LLC has the same powers as an individual to carry on its business.
- It can own and transfer property, make contracts, borrow and lend money, etc.

## LLC Members' Limited Liability

Debts and obligations of the LLC are entirely those of the LLC.
- Owners are called members.
  o They have limited liability, as they are usually not personally liable to third parties for debts, obligations and liabilities beyond their capital contribution.
  o Failure of an LLC to follow usual company formalities will not expose members to personal liability.

**Liability of an LLC.** Liability for loss or injury caused by a wrongful act or omission by a member, agent, etc within the ordinary course of business of the LLC will attach to the LLC.

**Liability of Managers.** Managers of an LLC are not personally liable for the debts, obligations, and liabilities of the LLC they manage.

**Liability of Tortfeasors.** A tortfeasor, one who intentionally or unintentionally causes injury of death to another, is personally liable to those he or she injures and the heirs of those he or she kills through wrongful conduct.
- This rule applies to members and managers.

## Formation of an LLC

A limited liability company may be organized for any lawful purpose. A LLC cannot operate the practice of certain professions, such as doctors or lawyers, but these professionals can conduct business as a limited liability partnership.
- A LLC can conduct business in all states, but may only be registered in one.
  o It is usually organized in the state that it will be transacting most of its business.
- The name must have the words "limited liability company" or limited company or the abbreviations L.L.C. or LLC or LC.

**Articles of Organization.** Articles of organization must be delivered to the secretary of state's office for filing.
- The existence of the LLC begins when the articles are filed.
- The articles must contain

- o   the name and address of the initial LLC office,
- o   the name and address of the initial agent for service of process,
- o   the name and address of each organizer
- o   whether the LLC is a term LLC
  - ▪   if yes, then the specifics of the term must be stated.
- o   whether the LLC is to be manager-managed
  - ▪   the identity and address(es) of the manager(s).
- o   whether members will be personally liable for debts and obligations of the LLC

**Duration of an LLC.**  An LLC is either an at-will LLC or a term LLC.
- •   The term LLC states how long the LLC will exist.
- •   An at-will LLC does not state a term of duration.

**Capital Contribution to an LLC.**  A member's capital may consist of money, real property, personal property, intangible property, services performed, and so on.
- •   A member's death will not excuse a member's obligation to contribute, nor will disability or the inability to perform.

**Certificate of Interest.**  This, like a stock certificate, indicates a member's ownership interest in the LLC.

**Operating Agreement.**  Members of an LLC may enter into an operating agreement to regulate the affairs of the company and the conduct of its business.

**Conversion of an Existing Business to an LLC.**  Many businesses convert to operate as a limited liability company to obtain tax benefits and utilize the limited liability benefit.
- •   In order to convert, ULLCA at section 902 requires
  - o   that there be a statement of terms contained in an agreement of conversion,
  - o   that the agreement be approved by all parties and owners concerned, and
  - o   that the articles of organization be filed with the secretary of state indicating the prior business name and form of operation.

**Dividing an LLC's Profits and Losses.**  A member has the right to an equal share in the profits of an LLC, unless otherwise agreed.
- •   Losses are shared equally, unless otherwise agreed.
- •   Profits and losses do not have to be distributed in the same proportion.

**Distributional Interest.**  The ownership share of a member is called the distributional interest.
- •   A member's interest may be transferred.

## Why Operate a Business as a Limited Liability Company (LLC)?

There are several reasons why an LLC should be used, rather than an S Corporation, a partnership, or a limited partnership.
- •   S Corporations have several undesirable restrictions concerning who can be shareholders, how many shareholders and the percentage of stock that may be owned, whereas the LLC has none of these limitations.
- •   Members of the LLC have limited liability instead of personal liability for the obligations of the general partnership.

- The LLC allows all members to take part in management of the business with limited liability to its members. The limited partnership requires at least one general partner who is personally liable for the partnership's obligations. Limited partners may not take part in the management of the business.

## Management of an LLC

An LLC is considered member-managed unless it is deemed manager-managed in the articles of organization.
- In a member-managed LLC, the members have the right to manage the LLC.
- In a manger-managed LLC, the members designate a manager or managers, delegating their rights to manage the LLC.
  - A manager may be a member or a nonmember.

**Member-Managed LLC.** In a member-managed LLC, each member has equal rights in the management of the business.
- Matters relating to LLC business are decided by a majority vote of the members.

**Manager-Managed LLC.** In a manger-managed LLC, only designated managers control management of the LLC.
- Each manager has equal rights in the management of the business.
- Member who are not managers have no rights to manage the LLC.
- Matters relating to LLC business are decided by a majority vote of the managers.

**Compensation and Reimbursement.** A nonmanager member is not entitled to remuneration for services performed for the LLC; managers are compensated according to employment contracts.
- An LLC is required to reimburse members and managers for payments made on behalf of the LLC and to indemnify managers and members for liabilities incurred.

**Agency Authority to Bind an LLC to Contracts.** In a member-managed LLC, all members have agency authority to bind the LLC to contracts.
- In a manager-managed LLC, the managers have authority to bind the LLC to contracts, but nonmanager members do not.

**Duty of Loyalty Owed to an LLC.** Regardless if a person is a member or a manager of a LLC, the duty of loyalty is a fiduciary duty owed to the LLC.
- This means that the parties must act honestly with no usurping of LLC opportunities, no self-dealing, no competition with the LLC, and no making of secret profits.

**Limited Duty of Care Owed to an LLC.** There is a limited duty of care owed to the LLC.
- This means that a manger or member must not engage in a known violation of the law, intentional conduct, grossly negligent conduct, or reckless conduct.
- Liability for ordinary negligence will not be assessed against a member or manager.

**No Fiduciary Duty Owed by a Nonmanager Member.** A member of a manager-managed LLC who is not a manager owes no fiduciary duty of loyalty or care to the LLC.

## Dissolution of an LLC

A member may disassociate from an LLC by withdrawing from a term or an at-will LLC.

- Wrongful disassociation from an at-will LLC occurs if the power to withdraw is absent from the operating agreement.
- Once a member is disassociated, he or she may not participate in the management of the LLC.
  - The member's duties of loyalty and care to the LLC end upon disassociation.

**Payment of Distributional Interest.** Rightful disassociation requires the LLC's purchase of the disassociated member's distributional interest.

**Notice of Disassociation.** For two years after disassociation, a member has apparent authoroity to bind the LLC except to those who know of the disassociation or have been given notice.
- An LLC may give constructive notice of a disassociating member by filing a statement of disassociation with the secretary of state.

**Continuation of an LLC.** A term LLC may be continued in two instances.
- The members unanimously vote prior to the expiration of the current LLC.
- The a simple majority vote of the members can contue the LLC as an at-will LLC.

**Winding Up an LLC's Business.** Winding up is "the process of preserving and selling the assets of the LLC and distributing the money and property to creditors and members."
- Assets of the LLC must be used to pay the **creditors first**, followed by any surplus left over to be distributed to the members in equal shares unless the operating agreement provides otherwise.
- After dissolution and winding up, articles of termination may be filed with the secretary of state.

## Limited Liability Partnership (LLP)

In a limited liability partnership (LLP), there does not have to be a general partner with unlimited personal liability for the debts and obligations of the partnership.
- All partners are limited partners with liability only up to their capital contribution.
- Most states restrict an LLP to certain professions.
- LLPs enjoy the "flow through" tax benefits of most partnerships.

**Articles of Partnership.** LLPs must be created formally by filing articles of partnership with the secretary of state.
- The LLP is a domestic LLP in the state in which it is organized.
- The LLP is a foreign LLP in every other state.

**LLP Liability Insurance.** Many states require LLPs to carry a minimum of $1 million in liability insurance that covers negligence, wrongful acts, and misconduct.

## Refresh Your Memory

The following exercises will help to test your memory regarding the principles given in this chapter. Read each question twice, then place your answer in the blank provided for each question. Review the chapter material for any questions you are unable to answer or remember.

1.  Limited liability companies are created by _____ law.

2.  A limited liability company is a separate legal _____.

3.  Owners of the Limited Liability Company are usually called _____.

4.  The main objective of the _____ _____ _____ Act is to establish a uniform comprehensive Limited Liability Company law throughout the United States.

5.  Members of a Limited Liability Company have _____ liability.

6.  A(n) _____ is a person who intentionally or unintentionally causes injury or death to another person.

7.  The _____ _____ _____ must be filed with the secretary of state to form a Limited Liability Company.

8.  A(n) _____ _____ Limited Liability Company is one that has no specified term of duration

9.  A member's _____ _____ may take the form of personal or real property, money, tangible or intangible property.

10. A(n) _____ _____ _____ evidences a member's ownership interest in a Limited Liability Company.

11. In a(n) _____ managed LLC, the members have designated certain members or nonmembers to manage the LLC.

12. A member of a manager-managed LLC who is not a manager owes _____ _____ duty of loyalty or care to the LLC.

13. The _____ of a member from a term LLC before the expiration of the specified term is wrongful.

14. In an LLP, all partners are _____ partners and stand to lose only their capital contribution if the partnership fails.

15. The _____ _____ _____ must be filed with the secretary of state to form an LLP.

# Critical Thought Exercise

Hal, Mike, Sue, and Gail are college friends and have talents in the areas of e-commerce, marketing, product development, and business management. The four meet with a fifth friend, Karl, who is a second–year law student. They explain to Karl their idea for an Internet business that sends local cuisine from participating restaurants and caterers to students and military personnel who are away from home and miss their favorite food. Karl draws up the articles of organization as his contribution to being brought in as a member of the new limited liability company, "GoodGrub.com, LLC." Karl then decides that he does not have the time or energy to devote to the business. Karl declines the offer to join the LLC. Sue files the articles of organization with the secretary of state, but there is no mention of whether GoodGrub.com will be a manager-managed or member managed LLC. It was originally anticipated that Hal would be the manager of the LLC but all four members begin to manage Good Grub.com and it is very successful. To keep up with demand and to expand their business into new markets, Hal and Gail secure a $200,000 loan from Jefferson Bank. When Hal is dividing up yearly profits, he gives each member 15% of the profits and invests the other 40% in the expansion efforts.

The resulting dispute over profits and quick expansion of the business leads to turmoil. GoodGrub.com is unable to meet its financial obligations. Mike, Sue, and Gail sue Hal for a full distribution of profits. Jefferson bank sues GoodGrub.com, Hal, Mike, Sue, and Gail to recover the $200,000 loan.

Did Hal have authority to withhold distribution of profits? Who is liable to Jefferson Bank?

*Please compose your answer on a separate sheet of paper or on your computer.*

# Practice Quiz

## True/False

1. \_\_\_\_  Owners of an LLC are called legal entities.

2. \_\_\_\_  If a member or manager of an LLC negligently injures another person, he or she is not personally liable to the injured person.

3. \_\_\_\_  LLC's are often utilized for businesses of professional associations.

4. \_\_\_\_  The mere filing of the articles of organization by the secretary of state is conclusive proof that the organizers have fulfilled all conditions required to create an LLC.

5. \_\_\_\_  An LLC without a specified term of duration is called an at-will LLC.

6. \_\_\_\_  A term LLC is another name for an at-will LLC.

7. \_\_\_\_  A general partnership may not be converted to a LLC.

8. \_\_\_\_  An LLC may own and transfer personal property.

9. \_\_\_\_  The operating agreement of an LLC may only be oral.

10. \_\_\_\_  An LLC is a member-managed LLC unless it is designated as a manager-managed LLC in the articles of organization.

11. \_\_\_\_  If Henrietta as a member of an LLC disassociates herself from a term LLC before the expiration of a specified term, her action will not be considered wrongful.

12. \_\_\_\_  One way for the Tiny Toy Company to give notice of a member's disassociation is by filing a statement of disassociation with the secretary of state.

13. ___ A member does have the right to an equal share in the LLC's profits.

14. ___ All members, including those who have wrongfully disassociated from the LLC may participate in the winding-up of the LLC's business.

15. ___ Certain formalities including statutory requirements must be met when forming a LLC.

## Multiple Choice

16. Which of the following does not need to be placed in the articles of organization of a LLC?
    a. The name and address of the initial agent for service of process
    b. The name and address of each organizer
    c. The name and address where the limited partnership will be primarily operating
    d. Whether the LLC is a term LLC and if so, the term specified

17. If an LLC is debating on which state to organize itself in, and cannot decide which one to choose between Maine and Vermont, what should it consider?
    a. It should try to be an LLC as to both states.
    b. It should consider organizing in a state that it feels most comfortable with.
    c. It should consider the codes of the state as well as the state in which it will be doing most of its business.
    d. It should consider the government of the state in which it wants to operate.

18. Before Edward decides upon the way he wants to operate a business, he comes to you and asks about the powers an LLC has. Which of the following best describes these powers?
    a. An LLC has the power to waive the distribution of assets upon winding-up the LLC.
    b. An LLC has the power to own and transfer personal property.
    c. An LLC has the power to refuse reimbursement to members and managers for payments made on behalf of the LLC for business expenses.
    d. All of the above.

19. What does the duty of care impose upon a member of the member-managed LLC in discharging his or her duties to the LLC and its other members?
    a. The members of a member-managed LLC are held to the express terms of the articles of organization and operating agreement and are required to act in "good faith" and deal fairly in all regards in achieving the objectives of the LLC.
    b. The members of a member-managed LLC are held to the express terms of the articles of organization, however, a member is not held to achieving the objectives of the LLC when discharging his or her duties to the LLC and its other members.
    c. The members must not usurp an LLC business opportunity.
    d. None of the above.

20. If Brenda wants to operate an LLC under the name of Brenda's Beautiful Babes, which of the following must she be aware of?
    a. She must be aware that LLC's have no restrictions on shareholders.
    b. She must be aware that the name she has chosen must contain the words limited liability company or an acceptable abbreviation as per the ULLCA code.
    c. She must be aware that the name she has chosen may not make a profit for her.
    d. She must be aware that trademark issues are not applicable to her.

21. If a member of an LLC cannot make the required contribution of property or services, he or she is obligated to
    a. pay creditors who relied on his or he statements.
    b. contribute money equal to the value of the promised contribution.
    c. contribute money less than the value of the promised contribution.
    d. do nothing and is excused at least once from his or her obligation.

22. If an LLC is formed between two people but they do not have an agreement as to how profits are to be shared, the most probable outcome under the ULLCA would be
    a. that each member has the right to an equal share in the LLC's profits.
    b. that each member has no right to any share in the LLC's profits.
    c. that the two members must dissolve their LLC and reform it with an agreement as to profit distribution.
    d. all of the above

23. What do an LLC's income or losses flow through?
    a. a trust account
    b. the entity level
    c. the members' individual income tax returns
    d. at an entrepreneurial level

24. If a member or a manager of an LLC negligently causes injury or death to another person, he or she is
    a. not personally liable as the corporate veil of the LLC shields the member or manager from liability.
    b. personally liable if it is a member only who is negligent.
    c. personally liable if it is a manager only who is negligent.
    d. personally liable to the injured person or the heirs of a deceased person.

25. An LLC is often used instead of an S corporation because
    a. an S corporation cannot have any more than 75 shareholders and one class of stock
    b. the members of an LLC have limited liability
    c. an LLC's provides limited liability to all members regardless of their participation in management of the business.
    d. all of the above

## Short Answer

26. How many persons may organize an LLC?

    _____

27. In a member-managed LLC, who has the authority to bind the LLC to contracts?

    _____

28. In a manager-managed LLC, who has the authority to bind the LLC to contracts?

    _____

29. When is an LLC bound to contracts?

    _____

30. What effect does a member's disassociation from an LLC have on the member with respect to the LLC?

_____

_____

31. How may an LLC terminate its existence after it has dissolved or wound-up its operations?

_____

32. When does the existence of an LLC begin?

_____

33. How may the articles of organization be amended in an LLC?

_____

34. As it pertains to member-managed LLC's and manager-managed LLC's, what does the duty of loyalty include?

_____

_____

35. When selecting a name for a new LLC, what words must be contained in the name?

_____

36. What is the main benefit of opting for an LLC instead of a general partnership for conducting business?

_____

37. What is the primary advantage of an LLC as opposed to a limited partnership?

_____

_____

38. What is an at-will Limited Liability Company?

_____

39. What form may a member's capital contribution be to an LLC?

_____

40. What document evidences a member's ownership interest in an LLC?

_____

# Answers to Refresh Your Memory

1. State [p 833]
2. entity [p 833]
3. members [p 835]
4. Uniform Limited Liability [p 834]
5. limited [p 835]
6. tortfeasor [p 837]
7. Articles of Organization [p 838]
8. at-will [p 838]

9.   capital contribution [p 839]
10.  certificate of interest [p 839]
11.  manager [p 841]
12.  no fiduciary [p 844]
13.  disassociation [p 844]
14.  limited [p 845-846]
15.  Articles of Partnership [p 846]

# Critical Thought Exercise Model Answer

GoodGrub.com could be either a member-managed or manager-managed LLC depending upon the wishes of its members. An LLC is a member-manages LLC unless it is designated as a manager-managed LLC in its articles of organization. The articles of organization do not specify whether the members named any member as a manager. Therefore, GoodGrub.com will be deemed a member-managed LLC. As a member-managed LLC, all members have agency authority to bind the LLC to contractual obligations. An LLC is only bound to contracts that are in the ordinary course of business or that have been authorized. As members, Hal and Gail have full authority to enter into the loan agreement with Jefferson Bank. Their action will legally obligate GoodGrub.com to repay the loan from GoodGrub.com assets.

The failure of GoodGrub.com to observe company formalities does not create personal liability for the members for the debts of the LLC. There is not mention of how the four members were running the company, but nothing in the facts would allow Jefferson Bank to seek repayment of the loan from the individual members.

Though an LLC will usually have a written operating agreement to regulate the affairs of the company and how the members will run the company, the agreement may be oral. Though Hal was the anticipated manager of GoodGrub.com, all four members assumed a management role and the articles of organization did not specify a manager-managed LLC. All four members have the right to determine how the profits will be divided or reinvested. Any matter relating to the business of the LLC is decided by a majority vote of the members. Hal is obligated to acquiesce in the desires of the other three members as to how the profits should be divided.

# Answers to Practice Quiz

## True/False

1.  False   Members are what the owners of the LLC are generally called. [p 835]
2.  False   A member or manager of an LLC who negligently injures another person is personally liable to the injured person. [p 838]
3.  False   LLCs cannot conduct the practices of accountants, doctors and lawyers. [p 838]
4.  True    According to ULLCA Section 202, the filing of the articles of organization by the secretary of state is conclusive proof that the organizers have satisfied all conditions required to create an LLC. [p 838]
5.  True    An at-will LCC is one in which there is no specified term or duration. [p 838]
6.  False   These are two different terms with different meanings. An at-will LCC has no specified term or duration whereas a term LLC has a specified term or duration. [p 838]
7.  False   A general partnership may be converted to a LLC. [p 840]
8.  True    An LLC may own and transfer personal property. [p 834]

9. False Oral or written operating agreements and amendments are acceptable. [p 839]

10. True An LLC is a member managed LLC unless it is designated as a manger-managed LLC. [p 841]

11. False Disassociation from an LLC by a member prior to the expiration of the specified term is considered wrongful. [p 844]

12. True Constructive notice of a member's disassociation from an LLC is accomplished by filing a statement of disassociation with the secretary of state. [p 844]

13. True A member does have the right to an equal share in the LLC's profits. [p 840]

14. False Members who have not wrongfully disassociated themselves from the LLC may take part in the winding-up of the LLC. [p 844]

15. True Since LLC's are created by statute, certain statutory requirements and formalities must be adhered to at formation. [p 846]

## Multiple Choice

16. C Answer C is the correct answer, as the name and address of where a limited partnership will be operating is not relevant to the information that must be contained in the articles of organization of an LLC. Answers A, B, and D all provide information that does need to be placed in the articles of organization and therefore are all incorrect answers as per the question. [p 838]

17. D Answer D is the correct answer, as the company is termed a domestic LLC in the state in which it is organized (here Maine) and is termed a foreign LLC in any state other than the one it was organized (here Vermont). Answers A, B, and C are all incorrect, as none of them properly identify the type of LLC each is within any given answer. [p 838]

18. B Answer B is the correct answer, as it properly states one of the powers that Edward's LLC would have should he choose that form of business to operate under. Answer A is incorrect, as it is a false statement. Answer C is incorrect, as an LLC does not have the power to refuse reimbursement for expenses on behalf of the LLC. Answer D is incorrect based on the reasoning given above. [p 834]

19. D Answer D is the correct answer, as answers A, B, and C have nothing to do with the duty of care imposed on a member of an LLC. [p 843]

20. B Answer B is the correct answer, as under ULLCA Section 105 (a), Brenda must make sure that the proper words or abbreviations are included in the name that she has chosen. Answer A is inapplicable to Brenda's operation and concern for the name she has chosen. Answer C is incorrect, as it is not relevant in terms of the name she has chosen for her LLC. Answer D is incorrect, as trademark issues are applicable and important to her, especially when choosing a name for an LLC. [p 838]

21. B Answer B is the correct answer, as a member's capital contribution to an LLC may be in the form of money, personal property, real property, other tangible property, intangible property, and the like. Further, if a member cannot make the required contribution of property or services, he or she is obligated to contribute money equal to the value of the promised contribution. Answer A is incorrect, as it has no relevance toward making the required contribution of property. Answer C is incorrect, as contributing less than the value of the promised contribution would not fulfill the members obligation to contribute money equal to the value of the promised contribution. Answer D is incorrect, as doing nothing does not satisfy the obligation of a member's capital contribution obligation. Further, there is nothing in the ULLCA code to indicate a member's obligation is excused once or for any reason for that matter. [p 839]

22. A Answer A is the correct answer, as the ULLCA at Section 405(a) mandates that a member has the right to an equal share in the LLC's profits. Answer B is incorrect, as it is not a correct statement of law. Answer C is incorrect, as the ULLCA does not make

dissolution and reformation a requirement toward deciding how profits are to be shared among members of an LLC. Answer D is incorrect for the reasons stated above. [p 840]

23. C   Answer C is the correct answer, as an LLC's income or losses flow through the member's individual income tax returns in order to avoid double taxation. Answer A is an incorrect statement of law. Answer B is incorrect, as an LLC is not taxed at an entity level. Answer D is incorrect, as it is not applicable to LLC's and the income or losses of the same. [p 834]

24. D   Answer D is the correct answer, as a member or manager of an LLC who negligently causes injury or death to another person is personally liable to the injured person or the heirs of a deceased person. Answer A is incorrect, as the corporate veil of the LLC does not shield the member or manager from liability. Answers B and C are incorrect, as liability attaches to members or managers if either are negligent. Liability is not exclusive to one or the other. [p 837]

25. D   Answer D is the correct answer, as answers A,B, and C all reflect why an LLC is often used instead of an S corporation, with the main reason being that the S corporations are subject to many restrictions and unfavorable consequences that do not exist with an LLC. [p 841]

## Short Answer

26. One or more persons may organize an LLC. [p 838]
27. All members have agency authority to bind the LLC to contracts in a member-managed LLC. [p 842]
28. Only the designated managers have authority to bind the LLC to contracts in a manger-managed LLC. [p 843]
29. An LLC is bound to contract that are in the ordinary course of business or that the LLC has authorized. [p 843]
30. A member's disassociation terminates that member's right to take part in the management of the LLC or act as an agent of the LLC, or conduct any of the LLC's business. [p 844]
31. It may terminate its existence by filing articles of termination with the secretary of state. [p 845]
32. It begins when the articles of organization are filed. [p 838]
33. The articles may be amended by filing articles of amendment with the secretary of state. [p 838]
34. The duty of loyalty includes the duty not to usurp the LLC's opportunities, make profits, secretly deal with the LLC, secretly compete with the LLC, or represent any interests adverse to those of the LLC [ULLCA Section 409(b)]. [p 843]
35. The words "limited liability company" or "limited company" or an acceptable abbreviation under ULLCA Section 105(a) must be contained in the name. [p 838]
36. Members of an LLC have limited liability as compared to a general partnership where the partners are personally liable for the obligations of the partnership. [p 841]
37. An LLC gives limited liability to all members regardless of their participation in the management of the business whereas a limited partnership requires that at least one general partner must be personally liable for the obligations of the partnership. [p 841]
38. An at-will LLC is one that has no specified term of duration. [p 838]
39. A member's capital contribution may take the form of personal or real property, money, tangible or intangible property, etc. (Answers will vary.) [p 839]
40. A certificate of interest. [p 839]

# Chapter 31

# FRANCHISES AND
# SPECIAL FORMS OF BUSINESS

## Chapter Overview

Franchising has become an important method of distributing goods and services. Franchises account for 25 percent of retail sales and 15 percent of the gross domestic product. Special forms of business are used in international and domestic commerce. Licensing lets one business use another's intellectual property. Joint ventures let businesses combine their resources. Strategic alliances are used to enter foreign markets. This chapter introduces franchising, licensing, joint ventures, and strategic alliances.

## Objectives

Upon completion of the exercises in this chapter, you should be able to:

1. Describe a franchise and distinguish between the various forms of franchises.
2. Discuss the rights and duties of the parties to a franchise agreement.
3. Explain the contract and tort liability of franchisors and franchisees.
4. Define licensing and describe how trademarks and intellectual property are licensed.
5. Discuss international franchise formation, partnering and strategic alliances.

## Practical Application

You should be able to identify issues in franchise formation by applying contract law principles to a franchise arrangement. You should be able to follow the rights and liabilities linked with use of trademarks, service marks, patents, copyrights, trade names, and trade dress as they apply to franchises and licenses. You should be able to discuss contract and tort liability of the parties to franchises. You should be able to identify the reasons for using franchising, partnering, and strategic alliances.

## Helpful Hints

The biggest problem areas concerning franchises are in the areas of genuineness of assent, discharge, remedies, and intellectual property. It will be very helpful to review the pertinent chapters presented earlier in this text as part of the overall understanding of franchises.

## Study Tips

### Franchise

A franchise is established when one party licenses another party to use the franchisor's trade name, trademarks, patents, copyrights, and other property in the distribution and selling of goods and services.

- The franchisor is the party who does the licensing in a franchise arrangement.
- The franchisee is the party who is licensed by the franchisor in a franchise arrangement.
- A franchise is both the agreement and the franchise outlet.
- The advantages to franchising:
  - o The franchisor can reach new markets.
  - o The franchisee has access to the franchisor's knowledge and resources.
  - o Consumers are assured of uniform quality.

**Types of Franchises.** There are four types of franchises: distributorship, processing plant, chain-style, and area franchises.

*Distributorship Franchise.* The franchisor manufactures a product and licenses a retail franchisee to distribute the product to the public.

*Processing Plant Franchise.* The franchisor provides a secret formula or process to the franchisee, and the franchisee manufactures the product and distributes it to retail dealers.

*Chain-Style Franchise.* The franchisor licenses the franchisee to make and sell its products or distribute services to the public from a retail outlet serving an exclusive territory.

*Area Franchise.* The franchisor grants the franchisee a franchise for an agreed-upon geographical area within which the franchisee may sell franchises on behalf of the franchisor.
- The area franchisee is called a subfranchisor.

**State Disclosure Laws.** These laws require franchisors to register and deliver disclosure documents to prospective franchisees.
- The Uniform Franchise Offering Circular (UFOC) is a uniform disclosure document that requires the franchisor to make specific presale disclosures to prospective franchisees.

**FTC Franchise Rule.** A rule set out by the FTC that requires franchisors to make full presale disclosures to prospective franchisees.

*Disclosure of Sales or Earnings Projections Based on Actual Data.* If sales or earnings projections for a franchise are based on actual figures, the franchisor must disclose how many franchises have had such results and must include a cautionary statement there is no assurance that these results will be obtained.

*Disclosure of Sales or Earnings Projections Based on Hypothetical Data.* If sales or earnings projections for a franchise are based on hypothetical figures, the franchisor must disclose the underlying assumptions, the number of franchises with such results, and a cautionary statement the results may not be obtained.

**Trademarks.** Success for a franchisor is the ability to keep a positive public perception of the quality of goods and services linked with its trade name, trademarks, and service marks.
- Franchisors license the use of their trade names, trademarks, and service marks, and prohibit the franchisee from misusing these marks.

**Trade Secrets.** Franchisors license and disclose trade secrets to franchisees.
- Misappropriation of trade secrets is unfair competition and is grounds for a lawsuit and damages from the franchisee.

**The Franchise Agreement.** Once the application from a prospective franchisee is accepted by the franchisor, the parties enter into an agreement which specifies the terms and conditions of the franchise.

- Quality Control Standards are standards for performance and product quality that preserve the franchisor's market name and reputation.
- Training requirements are employee standards that meet the franchisor's specifications.
- Covenant not to compete is an agreement by the franchisee to not compete with the franchisor for a period of time in a specified area after the termination of the franchise.
- An arbitration clause provides that disputes are subject to arbitration.
- Other terms and conditions, such as capital requirements, restrictions on use of franchisor property, standards of operation, duration, conditions for termination, etc.

**Franchise Fees.** These are fees payable by the franchisee as set forth in the franchise agreement.
- Initial License Fee is a lump-sum payment to obtain a franchise.
- Royalty Fee is a fee for use of franchisor's trade name, property, and assistance that is computed as a percentage of the franchisee's gross sales.
- Assessment Fee is fee for advertising and administrative costs.
- Lease Fee is a payment for land or equipment leased from the franchisor.
- Cost of Supplies is a payment for supplies purchased from the franchisor.

**Termination of a Franchise.** The franchise agreement usually states reasons or conditions that allow the franchisor or franchisee to terminate the franchise agreement.
- Termination "For Cause" is a termination of franchise agreement for failure to fulfill the duties imposed by the agreement.
- Termination-At-Will Clauses are generally void as unconscionable.
- Wrongful Termination is a termination of the franchise agreement without cause.

**Breach of the Franchise Agreement.** The aggrieved party can sue the breaching party for rescission of the agreement, restitution, and damages.

**International Franchising.** The international market currently offers much opportunity for franchisors.
- Franchising provides international expansion without the capital investment of company-owned stores in these new markets.
  o The foreign franchise knows the market, culture, and business traditions.
- International franchising provides challenges of different laws, dispute settlement, and culture.

## Liability of Franchisor and Franchisee

When properly organized, the franchisee and franchisor are separate legal entities and the franchisor deals with the franchisee as an independent contractor.
- If the franchisee is an independent contractor, the franchisor is not liable for the franchisee's torts and contracts.
- Franchisors and franchisees are liable for their own torts.

**Apparent Agency.** This type of agency that arises when a franchisor creates the appearance that a franchisee is its agent when in fact an actual agency does not exist.
- The franchisor is responsible for the torts and contracts the franchisee committed or entered into within the scope of the agency.

## Licensing

Licensing occurs when one business that owns trademarks, service marks, trade names, and other intellectual property allows another business to use this property in the distribution of goods and services.

- The licensor is the party who grants the license.
- The licensee is the party to whom the license is granted.

## Joint Venture

A joint venture is an arrangement where two or more businesses combine their resources in pursuit of a single project or transaction.

- The parties to a joint venture are called joint venturers.
- Joint venturers have equal rights to manage the joint venture.
- Joint venturers owe fiduciary duties of loyalty and care.

**Joint Venture Partnership.** This is a joint venture that is operated as a partnership.

- Each joint venturer is considered to be a partner.
- Each joint venturer is liable for the debts and obligations of the joint venture partnership.

**Joint Venture Corporation.** This is a separate corporation that operates the joint venture.

- The joint venturers are shareholders of the joint venture corporation.
- The joint venture corporation is liable for its own debts and oblgations.
  - o The joint venturers are only liable for corporate debts and obligations up to the amount of their capital contributions.

**Strategic Alliance.** This is an arrangement between two or more companies in the same industry where they agree to ally themselves to accomplish a specific objective.

- The alliance lets them reduce risks, share costs, combine technologies, and extend markets.
- Alliances do not give the same protection as mergers, joint ventures, or franchises.

# Refresh Your Memory

The following exercises will help to test your memory regarding the principles given in this chapter. Read each question twice, then place your answer in the blank provided for each question. Review the chapter material for any questions you are unable to answer or remember.

1. When one party _____ another party to use the franchisor's name, trademarks, patents, copyrights, and other property, a franchise is formed.

2. In a distributorship franchise, the franchisor _____ a product and licenses a retail franchisee for _____ .

3. In a(n) _____ _____ franchise, the franchisor provides a secret formula or process to the franchisee, and the franchisee manufactures the product and distributes it to retailers.

4. In a(n) _____ _____ franchise, the franchisor licenses the franchisee to make and sell its products or distribute services to the public from a retail outlet serving a(n) _____ territory.

5. The Uniform Franchise Offering Circular is a uniform _____ document.

6. The FTC franchise rule requires franchisors to make full _____ disclosures to prospective franchisees.

7.   The _____ license fee is a lump-sum payment to obtain a franchise.

8.   A(n) _____ fee is assessed for use of the franchisor's name, property and _____.

9.   An assessment fee is for _____ and administrative costs.

10.  A(n) _____ is a distinctive mark, symbol, name, _____, _____, or device that identifies the goods or products of the owner.

11.  Anyone who steals and uses a franchisor's trade secret is liable for _____ of a trade secret.

12.  A(n) _____ _____ arises when a franchisor creates the appearance that a franchisee is its agent, when in fact an actual agency does not exist.

13.  A(n) _____ _____ _____ is a joint venture that is operated as a partnership.

14.  A(n) _____ _____ _____ is a separate corporation that operates the joint venture.

15.  A(n) _____ _____ is an arrangement between two companies in the same industry to combine their resources to pursue a project.

## Critical Thought Exercise

Federal Foods, Inc. runs company stores and sells franchises for its restaurants, known as Yum-Me's. Under the franchise agreement with Federal, each franchisee agrees to hire and train all employees and staff in strict compliance with Yum-Me's standards and policies. Federal employs area supervisors who are responsible for reviewing and approving all personnel actions at any restaurant within the four restaurant chains owned by Federal. This includes comprehensive policies relating to employee hiring, training, discipline, and work performance. As part of the franchise agreement, Federal retains the right to terminate any franchise that violates the rules or policies of the franchisor. In practice, the area managers approve the hiring of whatever employees the franchisee desire and the policies that the franchisee desires to create and implement. The area managers inspect each franchise, dictate the food production method, and enforce customer relations policies that were created by Federal.

Ned, a crew leader at a Yum-Me's restaurant, has repeatedly harassed female employees and customers by making rude and explicit sexual remarks. The franchisee and the on-site manager have done nothing to correct Ned's behavior. Two female employees and three customers have filed suit in federal court against Federal based upon Ned's acts. Federal argues that a franchisor cannot be held liable for harassment by franchise employees. Who should prevail?

*Please compose your answer on a separate sheet of paper or on your computer.*

## Practice Quiz

### True/False

1.   ___   A franchisor and franchisee are established as separate corporations.

2. ___ A franchise is any arrangement other than one in which the owner of a trademark, a trade name, or a copyright has licensed a franchisee to use it in selling goods or services.

3. ___ An automobile dealership is not an example of a distributorship type of franchise.

4. ___ The party who is granted a franchise is a franchisor.

5. ___ A Coca-Cola bottling franchise is an example of a processing plant franchise.

6. ___ Burger King is an area style franchise.

7. ___ Area franchises are a useful business arrangement for expanding into foreign markets.

8. ___ A Uniform Franchise Offering Circular requires the franchisor to make specific disclosures to prospective franchisees.

9. ___ Only one state, California, has enacted statutes that require franchisors to make specific presale disclosures to prospective franchisees.

10. ___ The FTC franchise rule requires the same disclosures to be made by franchisors in all states.

11. ___ The least important assets of a franchisor are its name and reputation.

12. ___ The franchisee's use of the franchisor's name and reputation are still subject to control by the franchisor with respect to the quality of the franchisee's goods or services.

13. ___ Franchisees and their personnel are not required to attend training programs.

14. ___ A franchisor cannot protect itself from a franchisee that opens a competing business in the same area after termination of the franchise.

15. ___ Franchisees ordinarily make payments for a franchise license and separate fees for other products and services obtained from the franchisor.

## Multiple Choice

16. An automobile dealership is
    a. a chain-style franchise.
    b. a distributorship franchise.
    c. a processing plant franchise.
    d. an area franchise.

17. The party to whom a franchise is granted is the
    a. franchisor.
    b. franchisee.
    c. principal.
    d. agent.

18. Bogart enters into an agreement whereby he receives an exclusive territory covering four states in which he is authorized to establish a plant to manufacture Fizzy Beer. After receiving Fizzy's secret formula, Bogart begins making beer. This is a
    a. processing plant franchise.
    b. chain-style franchise.
    c. distributorship.
    d. none of the above.

19. For which type of franchise does the franchisee have the right to grant franchises to others within a geographical area?
    a. Processing plant franchise
    b. Chain-style franchise
    c. Area franchise
    d. Distributorship franchise

20. The FTC franchise rule requires franchisors to
    a. share profits with franchisees.
    b. supply advertising and administrative services to the franchisee.
    c. supply trademarks and secret formulas to the franchisee.
    d. make presale disclosures to prospective franchisees.

21. A payment for any land equipment obtained from the franchisor, that is billed either as a flat monthly or annual fee or as a percentage of gross sales or another agreed-upon amount is known as
    a. cost of supplies fee
    b. lease fees
    c. royalty fees
    d. none of the above

22. A fee that is for the continued use of the franchisor's trade name, property, and assistance that is often computed as a percentage of the franchisee's gross sales is a
    a. covenant not to compete fee
    b. arbitration fee
    c. royalty fee
    d. supply fee

23. A clause that provides that any claim or controversy arising from the franchise agreement or an alleged breach thereof would most likely be a(n)
    a. arbitration clause
    b. training requirement
    c. capital requirement
    d. quality control clause

24. Since the franchisor and franchisee are separate legal entities, the franchisor deals with the franchisee as
    a. a banker
    b. an employee
    c. an agent
    d. an independent contractor

25. If a franchise is terminated without just cause, the franchisee can sue the franchisor for
    a. assault
    b. breach of covenant not to compete

c. general liability
d. wrongful termination

## Short Answer

26. What is a processing plant franchise?

_____

27. Why is Mc Donald's not a processing plant franchise?

_____

_____

28. Why are quality control standards important to the franchisor?

_____

29. Give five examples of a type of franchise fee.

_____

30. What is the purpose of an assessment fee and what does it cover?

_____

31. What may an aggrieved party recover in a suit for breach of a franchise agreement?

_____

32. What is a strategic alliance?

_____

33. What is a joint venture?

_____

34. What is an apparent agency?

_____

35. What is wrongful termination of a franchise agreement?

_____

36. What role does a franchisor play in a franchise?

_____

37. Why is the independent contractor status of a franchisee important to a franchisor?

_____

_____

38. What is termination for cause of a franchise agreement?

_____

39. Why is a termination-at-will clause in a franchise agreement generally considered void?

_____

40. What award can the aggrieved party receive for misappropriation of a trade secret?

_____

# Answers to Refresh Your Memory

1. licenses  [p 854]
2. manufactures, distribution  [p 855]
3. processing plant  [p 855]
4. chain-style, exclusive  [p 855]
5. disclosure  [p 855]
6. presale  [p 856]
7. initial  [p 859]
8. royalty, assistance  [p 859]
9. advertising  [p 859]
10. trademark, word, motto  [p 872]
11. misappropriation  [p 858]
12. apparent agency  [p 866]
13. Joint Venture Partnership  [p 869]
14. Joint Venture Corporation  [p 869]
15. Strategic alliance  [p 870]

# Critical Thought Exercise Model Answer

Liability for Ned's acts may be imputed to Federal because of an agency relationship that exists between Federal and the employees of the franchisee. An agency results from the manifestation of consent by one person to another so that the other will act on his or her behalf and subject to the control of the principal, and consent by the agent to so act. An agency agreement may be evidenced by an express agreement between the parties, or it may be implied from the circumstances and conduct of the parties. The principal's consent and right to control the agent are the essential elements of an agency relationship.

The franchise agreement in this case required adherence to comprehensive policies and rules for the operation of the restaurant. Federal enforces these rules and policies by sending area managers to inspect each franchisee. The area managers also approve the hiring and training of each employee. Federal controls the franchisee and the employee's of Yum-Me Restaurant by retaining the right to terminate the franchise agreement. Most importantly, the franchise agreement gave Federal the right to control the franchisees in the very parts of the franchisee's business that resulted in the injuries to the plaintiffs, these parts being the areas of employee training and discipline. Federal, the franchisor, may be held liable under an agency theory for the intentional acts of sexual discrimination by the employee of its franchisee.

# Answers to Practice Quiz

## True/False

1. True  They are separate business entities.  [p 854]
2. False  A franchise is any arrangement in which the owner of a trademark, a trade name, or a copyright or other intellectual property has licensed a franchisee to use it in selling goods or services.  [p 854]
3. False  This is a distributorship franchise, where the franchisee serves as a distributor for goods manufactured by the franchisor.  [p 855]
4. False  The party who is granted a franchise is a franchisee.  [p 854]

5. True This is a processing plant franchise, where the franchisee is given a secret formula from which it manufactures the product and then distributes it to retailers. [p 855]

6. False This is a chain-style franchise, where the franchisee makes and sells the licensed product from a retail outlet. [p 855]

7. True It allows expansion that overcomes government regulation and takes advantage of the franchisee's cultural knowledge. [p 855]

8. True The disclosures are to prospective franchisees. [p 855]

9. False Many states have enacted statutes that require franchisors to make specific presale disclosures to prospective franchisees. [p 855]

10. True The FTC franchise rule requires the same disclosures to be made by franchisors in all states. [p 856]

11. False The most important assets of a franchisor are its name and reputation. [p 859]

12. True The quality control standards in the franchise agreement provide protection. [p 859]

13. False These training requirements can be part of the franchise agreement. [p 859]

14. False A covenant not to compete can be inserted into the franchise agreement. [p 859]

15. False This is called the initial license fee. [p 859

## Multiple Choice

29. B B is correct because in a distributorship franchise, the franchisor manufactures the product and the franchisee distributes the product within a geographical area. This is how automobiles are distributed. A is not correct because the franchisee makes the product in a chain-style and sells it at an outlet. C is not correct because the automobile dealer is not given a secret formula from which to produce cars. D is not correct because the dealership does not set up multiple dealerships within a geographical area as part of the franchise. [p 855]

17. B The franchisee receives the license from the franchisor. A is not correct because the franchisor grants the franchise. C and D are not correct because a franchise is not an agency relationship.

18. A The processing plant franchise involves licensing a formula to allow the franchisee to manufacture and distribute a product to the franchisor's specifications. B is not correct, as a chain-style franchise makes and sells products from a retail outlet. C is incorrect because a distributor does not make the product. D is incorrect because A is correct. [p 854]

19. C The area franchise gives the franchisee the rights to select the placement and number of franchises within its geographical area. A, B, and D are incorrect because the franchisee in these franchises has no authority to grant an additional franchise to another. [p 855]

20. D The full disclosures must have cautionary language concerning risk and facts concerning anticipated profits. A, B and C are not requirements of the FTC rule, but may be part of the duties of a franchisor under specific franchise agreement. [p 855]

21. B Answer B is correct, as this describes a lease fee. Answer A is incorrect, as cost of supplies involves payment for supplies purchased from the franchisor. Answer C is incorrect, as a royalty fee is a fee for the continued use of the franchisor's trade name, property, and assistance that is often computed as a percentage of the franchisee's gross sales. Answer D is incorrect based on the reasoning given above. [p 856]

22. C Answer C is correct, as this describes a royalty fee. Answer A is incorrect, as there is no such thing as a covenant not to compete fee. Answer B is incorrect, as this does not describe anything associated with the fees of an arbiter. Answer D is incorrect, as there is no such thing as a supply fee per se. [p 859]

23. A Answer A is correct, as it appropriately describes an arbitration clause. Answers B, C, and D are all incorrect, as none of these things exist in terms of franchise agreements and the breach of the same. [p 859]

24. D Answer D is correct, as the franchisee is dealt with by the franchisor as an independent contractor.

Answer A is incorrect, as it makes no sense. Answer B is incorrect, as the relationship between the franchisor and franchisee is not one of employment. Answer C is incorrect, as an agent also indicates that there is some sort of employment relationship which once again is not the case between a franchisee and franchisor. [p 864]

25. D  Answer D is correct, as this describes wrongful termination. Answer A is incorrect, as there is nothing to indicate an assault, and further assault deals with the area of intentional torts to the person not franchises. Answer B is incorrect, as a breach of a covenant not to compete has no relationship to the termination of a franchise without cause. Answer D is incorrect, as the answer is phrased in terms of a remedy verses a cause of action that a suit may be based upon. [p 861]

## Short Answer

26. A processing plant franchise provides a secret formula or process to the franchisee, and the franchisee manufactures the product and distributes it to retail dealers. [p 855]
27. A processing plant franchise does not sell the product out of a retail outlet after making it. McDonald's not only makes the product, but also serves as the retailer. Therefore, a McDonald's franchise is a chain-style franchise. [p 855]
28. The franchisor's most important assets are its name and reputation. The quality control standards set out in a franchise agreement are intended to protect those assets. [p 859]
29. initial license fee, royalty fee, assessment fee, lease fees payment, cost of supplies payment. [p 859]
30. An assessment fee pays for advertising and promotional campaigns and administrative costs. It is billed either as a flat monthly fee or a percentage of gross sales. [p 859]
31. The aggrieved party may sue for rescission, restitution, and damages. [p 861]
32. An arrangement between two or more companies in the same industry whereby they agree to ally themselves to accomplish a designated objective. [p 870]
33. Whereby two or more business entities combine their resources to pursue a single project or transaction. [p 869]
34. Agency that results when a franchisor creates the appearance that a franchisee is its agent when in fact an actual agency does not exist. [p 866]
35. Wrongful termination occurs if a franchise agreement is terminated without just cause. [p 861]
36. The franchisor is the owner of a mark or intellectual property who licenses that property to another party to use in the selling of goods or services. [p 854]
37. An independent contractor is a separately organized and operated business that is not the agent of another party with whom it does business, thus relieving the franchisor of liability in the business of the franchisee. [p 864]
38. Termination "For Cause" is a termination of franchise agreement for failure to fulfill the duties imposed by the agreement. [p 859]
39. This clause is considered unconscionable because the franchisee has spent time, money, and effort developing the franchise. [p 861]
40. Damages and an injunction prohibiting further unauthorized use of the trade secret. [p 858]

# Chapter 32

# INVESTOR PROTECTION AND ONLINE SECURITIES TRANSACTIONS

## Chapter Overview

Before the 1929 stock market crash, fraud and dealing on inside information was rampant. The crash motivated Congress to address investor security and it passed two key pieces of legislation to try to remedy the problem. The Securities Act of 1933 requires public disclosure of material information by those who issue securities to the public. The Securities Exchange Act of 1934 seeks to prevent fraud in the trading of securities, especially insider trading the recent regulation of the online sale of securities. States have passed additional protective statutes. This chapter examines investor protections.

## Chapter Objectives

Upon Completion of the exercises in this chapter, you should be able to:

1. Describe public offerings of securities and registration of those securities with the SEC.
2. Describe the exemptions from registration.
3. Define insider trading violations of Section 10(b) of the Securities Exchange Act of 1934.
4. Explain how tippers and tippees become liable for insider trading.
5. Explain the meaning of short-swing profits that violate Section 16(b) of the SEC Act of 1934.

## Practical Application

An investor should know the protections available under federal and state law that prevent fraudulent loss of their investment. Those persons and businesses that issue securities, and the people who work for them, should know the standards to which the federal government will hold them. The unsuspecting investor should know what acts may make them part of a fraudulent or criminal transaction so that liability can be avoided. Unless each person familiarizes himself with federal securities law, there is an increased risk of financial loss, damage to their business, and exposure to criminal prosecution.

## Helpful Hints

The securities laws regulate transactions involving the issuance and trading of securities. Focus on the individual transaction or related transactions and the information exchanged or withheld as to the particular transaction. It is the improper release or suppression of material information and trading upon that information that triggers the application of the securities laws. You should develop a working knowledge of key terms and pay attention to how they are applied by the courts.

# Study Tips

## Definition of a Security

Federal securities laws define what makes a security.
- An interest or instrument that is common stock, preferred stock, bond, debenture, or warrant,
- An interest or instrument that is expressly mentioned in securities acts, and
- An investment contract.

**The Securities and Exchange Commission (SEC).** A federal administrative agency that is empowered to administer federal securities laws.
- It can adopt rules and regulations to interpret and implement federal securities laws.
- It can investigate alleged securities violations and bring enforcement actions.
- It can regulate the activities of brokers and advisors.

## Securities Act of 1933 – Going Public

The Securities Act of 1933 is a federal statute that primarily regulates the issuance of securities by a corporation, a general or limited partnership, an unincorporated association, or an individual.
- The issuer is the business or party selling the securities to the public.
- An IPO is an initial public offering.
- Investment bankers are independent securities companies.

**Registration Statement.** A document that an issuer of securities files with the SEC that contains required information about the issuer, the securities to be issued, and other relevant information.
- The SEC does not evaluate the merits of the offering, merely that disclosure has been met.

**Prospectus.** A written disclosure document that must be submitted to the SEC along with the registration statement and given to prospective purchasers of the securities.

**Limitations on Activities During the Registration Process.** There are limits to the types of activities that an issuer, an underwriter, and a dealer may engage in during the registration process.

*Prefiling Period.* A period of time that begins when the issuer first contemplates issuing securities and ends when the registration statement is filed.
- The issuer cannot sell or offer to sell the securities.
- The issuer may not condition the market by engaging in a public relations campaign.

*Waiting Period.* A period of time that begins when the registration statement is filed with the SEC and continues until the registration statement is declared effective.
- The issuer is encouraged to condition the market during this time.
- Unapproved writings and actual sales are prohibited.

*Posteffective Period.* The period that begins when the registration statement becomes effective and runs until the issuer either sells all of the offered securities or withdraws them from sale.
- The issuer, its underwriter, and dealers may close the offers received prior to the effective date and solicit new offers and sales.
- A final prospectus must be delivered by the issuer to the investor prior to or at the time of confirming a sale or sending a security to a purchaser.

**Going Public Over the Internet.** Companies are permitted to issue securities over the Internet.
- Federal securities laws that regulate traditional issuance of securities apply.

**Sale of Unregistered Securities.** The sale of securities that should have been registered but were not violates the Securities Act and investors can rescind their purchase and recover damages.

**Regulation A Offerings.** This regulation permits issuers to sell up to $5 million in securities during a 12-month period under a simplified registration process.
- Offerings over $100,000 must file an offering statement, which has less disclosure than a registration statement.

**Small Corporate Offering Registration Form (SCOR).** This registration form can be used for the sale of securities not exceeding $1 million during a 12-month period.
- A question-and-answer form that can be completed without assistance of a securities lawyer.

**Private Actions.** Private parties injured by violations of the Securities Act have recourse against the violator.
- Section 12 of the 1933 act imposes civil liability on those who violates Section 5 of the act.
  - Under Section 12, a purchaser may rescind the purchase or sue for damages.
- Section 11 of the Securities Act of 1933 imposes civil liability on persons who intentionally defraud investors by making misrepresentations or omissions of material facts in the registration statement or who are negligent for not discovering the fraud.
  - All defendants but the issuer may assert a due diligence defense.

**SEC Actions.** For violations of the 1933 Act, the SEC may issue a consent order, bring an action seeking an injunction, or request disgorgement of profits by the court.

**Criminal Liability.** Section 24 of the Securities Act of 1933 imposes criminal liability of up to five years prison for violating the act or the rules and regulations adopted thereunder.

**Sarbanes-Oxley Act Erects a Wall Between Investment Bankers and Security Analysis.** The Sarbanes-Oxley Act establishes rules for separating the investment banking and securities advice functions of securities firms, eliminating many conflicts of interest.
- Securities firms must create structural and institutional "walls" between their investment banking and securities analysis areas.
- Securities analysts must disclose any conflicts of interest.

## Private Transactions Exempt From Registration

Certain transactions are exempt from registration, but must still comply with antifraud provisions of the federal securities laws. The issuer is required to provide investors with adequate information.

**Non-issuer Exemption.** An exemption from registration that permits average investors from registering the resale of their securities because they are not the issuer, an underwriter, or a dealer in securities.

**Intrastate Offerings.** An exemption from registration that permits local businesses to raise capital from local investors to be used in the local economy without the need to register with the SEC.
- The issuer must be a resident of the state for which the exemption is claimed.
- The issuer must be doing business in that state.
- The purchasers of all securities must be residents of that state.

**Private Placements.**  An exemption from registration that permits issuers to raise capital from an unlimited number of accredited investors and no more than 35 nonaccredited investors without having to register the offering with the SEC.

- An accredited investor may be:
  - o  Any person with a net worth of at least $1 million.
  - o  Any person who has had an annual income of $200,000 for the previous two years and expects to make $200,000 in the current year.
  - o  Any corporation, partnership, or business trust with assets of $5 million.
  - o  Insiders of the issuers, such as officers and directors of corporate issuers and general partners of partnership issuers.
  - o  Institutional investors such as registered investment companies, pension plans, and colleges and universities.

**Small Offerings.**  Rule 504 exempts from registration offerings that do not exceed $1 million during a 12-month period.

**Rule 144A "Qualified Institutional Investors"**  This SEC rule permits qualified institutional investors to buy unregistered securities without being subject to the holding periods of Rule 144.

**Resale Restrictions.**  Securities that were issued for investment purposes pursuant to the intrastate private placement, or small offering exemption are restricted securities, as they cannot be resold for a limited period of time after their initial issue.

- Rule 147 stipulates that securities sold pursuant to an intrastate offering exemption cannot be sold to nonresidents for a period of nine months.
- Rule 144 provides securities sold pursuant to private placement or small offering exemptions must be held for one year from the date when the securities are last sold by the issuer.

**Preventing Transfer of Restricted Securities**.  To protect the nontransferability of restricted shares, the issuer must:

- Require investors to sign an affidavit promising not to transfer them in violation of restriction.
- Place a legend on the stock certificate describing the restriction.
- Notify the transfer agent not to record a transfer that would violate the restriction.

## Securities Exchange Act of 1934 – Trading In Securities

The Securities Exchange Act of 1934 primarily regulates the trading of securities.
- It provides for the registration of certain companies, the filing of periodic reports, and the regulation of securities exchanges, brokers, and dealers.

**Section 10(b) and Rule 10b-5.**  This provision of the Securities Exchange Act of 1934 prohibits the use of manipulative and deceptive devices in the purchase or sale of securities in contravention of the rules and regulations prescribed by the SEC.

- Rule 10b-5 is a rule adopted by the SEC to clarify the reach of Section 10(b) against deceptive and fraudulent activities in the purchase and sale of securities.
- Only conduct involving scienter, or intentional conduct, violates this section and rule.

**Insider Trading.**  When an insider makes a profit by personally purchasing shares of the corporation prior to public release of favorable information or by selling shares of the corporation prior to the public disclosure of unfavorable information.

**Insiders.** Insiders are defined by Section 10(b) and Rule 10b-5.
- Officers, directors and employees at all levels of the company,
- Lawyers, accountants, consultants, and other agents hired by the company to provide services or work to the company,
- Others who owe a fiduciary duty to the company.

**Misappropriation Theory.** Sometimes the person who possesses inside information is an outsider who has misappropriated the information in violation of his or her fiduciary duty.
- Such behavior violates insider trading regulations.

**Tipper-Tippee Liability.** A tipper is a person who discloses material nonpublic information to another person, and a tippee is the person who receives material nonpublic information from a tipper.
- A tippee is liable for acting on material information that he or she knew or should have known was not public.
- The tipper is liable for the profits made by the tippee.

**Private Actions.** Section 10(b) and Rule 10b-5 do not expressly provide for private recourse against the violator, but courts have implied this right.
- A private plaintiff may rescind the securities contract or sue for damages.

**SEC Actions.** For violations of the Securities Exchange Act of 1934, the SEC may issue a consent order, bring an action seeking an injunction, or request disgorgement of profits by the court.
- The Insider Trading Sanctions Act permits SEC to obtain civil penalty of up to three times the illegal profits gained or losses avoided by insider trading.

**Criminal Liability.** Makes it a criminal offense to willfully violate the 1934 act or the rules or regulations adopted thereunder.

**Sarbanes-Oxley Act.** The SEC may prohibit a person who has committed securities frauds from acting as an officer or director of a public company.

**Fair Disclosure to All.** The Regulation Fair Disclosure prohibits companies from leaking important information to securities professionals before the information is disclosed to the public.

## Short-Swing Profits

**Section 16(a).** This section of the Securities Exchange Act of 1934 defines any person who is an executive officer, a director, or a 10 percent shareholder or an equity security of a reporting company as a statutory insider for Section 16 purposes.
- Such insiders must file reports with the SEC disclosing their ownership and trading in the company's securities.

**Section 16(b).** This section of the Securities Exchange Act of 1934 requires that any profits made by a statutory insider on transactions involving short-swing profits belong to the corporation.
- This provision has strict liability and defenses are generally not recognized.
- Neither intent nor possession of inside information need be shown.

**SEC Section 16 Rules.** Certain rules have been adopted concerning this section.
- Clarify definition of officer to only executive officers who perform policy-making functions.
- Relieve insiders of liability for transactions occuring within six months after becoming insider.

- Continue the rule that insiders are liable for transactions that occur within six months of the last transaction engaged in while an insider.

## State Securities Laws

Most states have enacted securities laws which generally require the registration of securities, provide exemptions from registration, and contain broad antifraud provisions.
- The Uniform Securities Act, adopted by many states, coordinates state laws with federal laws.

## Commodities Regulation

Commodities include grains, animals, animal products, foods, metals, and oil.
- A commodities futures contract is an agreement to busy or sell a specific amount and type of commodity as some future date at a price established at the time of contracting.
  - Standardized terms are established.
  - Contracts can be bought and sold on commodities exchanges.
- Commodity Exchange Act (CEA) of 1936 regulates trading of commodity futures contracts.
- Commodity Futures Trading Commission regulates trading in commodities futures contracts.

# Refresh Your Memory

The following exercises will help to test your memory regarding the principles given in this chapter. Read each question twice, then place your answer in the blank provided for each question. Review the chapter material for any questions you are unable to answer or remember.

1.   The _____ _____ _____ _____ is the federal agency that is empowered to administer federal securities laws.

2.   An issuer of securities files with the SEC a(n) _____ _____ that contains required information about the issuer, the securities to be issued, and other relevant information.

3.   A(n) _____ is a written disclosure document that must be submitted to the SEC along with the registration statement and given to prospective purchasers of the securities.

4.   The _____ _____ is a period of time that begins when the registration statement is filed with the SEC and continues until the registration statement is declared effective.

5.   An exemption from registration that exempts average investors from registering the resale of their securities is a(n) _____ exemption.

6.   The _____ _____ exemption from registration permits local business to raise capital from local investors to be used in the local economy without the need to register with the SEC.

7.   _____ securities are securities that were issued for investment purposes pursuant to an exemption; they cannot be resold for a limited period of time after their initial issue.

8.   _____ _____ provides that securities sold pursuant to the private placement or small offering exemptions must be held for one year from date when the securities are last sold by issuer.

9. Section 24 of the Securities Act of 1933 imposes criminal liability of up to _____ years per violation of the act.

10. _____ means intentional conduct.

11. The SEC may request the court to order the defendant to _____ illegally gained profits.

12. Section 16(b) of the Securities Exchange Act of 1934 requires that any profits made by a(n) _____ _____ on transactions involving short-swing profits belong to the corporation.

13. The _____ _____ _____ prohibits companies from leaking important information to securities professionals before the information is disclosed to the public.

14. _____ include grains, animals, animal products, foods, metals, and oil.

15. A(n) _____ _____ _____ is an agreement to busy or sell a specific amount and type of commodity as some future date at a price established at the time of contracting

## Critical Thought Exercise

Jerry Dallas is a corporate officer for CompuGames (CG), the leading manufacturer of hand-held computer games. The profit margin of CG is greatly impacted by the cost of the microprocessor it purchases for its games from Mini-Micro. Dallas tells his girlfriend, Julie Profit, that she should watch for any announcement of a price increase of 20% or more by Mini-Micro and sell her stock in CG if there is such a large price increase. Profit has a friend, Louis Nooze, who works in the public relations department at Mini-Micro. She asks Nooze to tell her if he hears of an announcement of price increases by Mini-Micro. Two days before a 33% price increase is to be announced by Mini-Micro, Nooze gives the news to Profit. Profit calls her stockbroker and sells all her stock in CG. When the price increase is announced, CG stock falls from $38 per share to $22 per share. By selling her stock before the announcement by Mini-Micro, Profit realizes a profit of $800,000.

If a stockholder initiates a suit against Dallas, Profit, and Nooze, will any of these people be liable for realizing illegal profits based upon insider trading or misappropriation?

*Please compose your answer on a separate sheet of paper or on your computer.*

## Practice Quiz

### True/False

1. ___ A security may not consist of an investment contract.

2. ___ The Securities Act of 1934 is a federal statute that primarily regulates the trading in securities.

3. ___ The Securities and Exchange Commission cannot adopt rules and regulations to interpret and implement federal securities laws.

4. ___ A registration statement must be filed, and specific contents are mandatory.

5. ___ A prospectus is a written disclosure document that is filed with the SEC and provided to prospective investors.

6. ___ The registration period for securities offerings is divided into three time periods.

7. ___ The prefiling period ends before the registration statement is filed.

8. ___ The issuer is discouraged from conditioning the market during the waiting period.

9. ___ The posteffective period begins when the registration statement becomes effective.

10. ___ The issuer must deliver a final prospectus prior to or at the time of confirming a sale.

11. ___ Securities issued by the government and common carriers are exempt from registration requirements.

12. ___ The Securities Act of 1933 exempts securities transactions not made by an issuer, an underwriter, or a dealer from registration.

13. ___ The intrastate offerings exemption requires that the issuer be a resident of the state for which the exemption is claimed, and the purchasers of the securities must be residents of that state.

14. ___ An accredited investor may under the private placement exemption include any person with a net worth of at least $1 million.

15. ___ Restricted securities can be resold for a limited period of time after their initial issue.

## Multiple Choice

16. The securities Act of 1933 primarily regulates
    a. short-swing profits.
    b. issuance of securities.
    c. insider trading.
    d. none of the above.

17. Which of the following descriptions does not need to be contained in a registration statement?
    a. The securities being offered for sale
    b. The registrant's business
    c. The degree of competition in the industry
    d. The SEC's opinion as to the merits of the securities offered

18. The written disclosure document that must be submitted to the SEC and is given to all prospective investors to enable them to evaluate the financial risk of the investments is called a(n)
    a. registration statement.
    b. prospectus.
    c. tombstone advertisement.
    d. offering statement.

19. The time period of the registration process during which the issuer cannot tout the prospectus to potential purchasers is the
    a. prefiling period.
    b. waiting period.

c.  posteffective period.
d.  all of the above.

20. Lansing & Bismarck is a consulting firm that specializes in corporate reorganizations. Toji Bismarck learns that Superior Corp., a pharmaceutical company for whom he is doing temporary work, is about to announce that its scientists have developed a totally effective drug that will both prevent and cure lung cancer. Bismarck tells his wife, Sue, to buy the stock. Sue purchases $10 worth of Superior stock. Sue calls her brother, Ned, the next day. Ned purchases $50,000 worth of Superior stock that immediately climbs to $2.5 million when the drug discovery is announced. Sue's stock climbs to $500. Toji is liable for
    a.  only the $490 profit made by Sue.
    b.  all the profit made by both Sue and Ned, if Ned knew the tip was material inside information.
    c.  all the profit made on both Sue's and Ned's trades, regardless of the tippees knowledge.
    d.  none of the profits made on the trades because Toji lacked scienter.

21. Section 24 of the Securities Act of 1933 imposes which of the following on individuals who willfully violate either the act or the rules and regulations imposed within it?
    a.  fined up to $10,000
    b.  imprisoned up to five years
    c.  both a and c
    d.  none of the above

22. Which of the following prohibits the use of manipulative and deceptive devices in contravention of the rules and regulations prescribed by the SEC?
    a.  Rule 504
    b.  Section 10 (b)
    c.  Section 16 (b)
    d.  All of the above

23. A security is defined as
    a.  Common securities.
    b.  Statutorily defined securities.
    c.  Investment contracts.
    d.  All of the above.

24. Limits on the types of activities that an issuer, an underwriter, and a dealer may engage in during the registration process are divided into three time periods:
    a.  Prefiling period, waiting period, and postfiling periods.
    b.  Preeffective period, waiting period, and posteffective periods.
    c.  Preeffective period, waiting period, and postfiling periods.
    d.  Prefiling period, waiting period, and posteffective periods.

25. Certain transactions in securities are exempt from registration. Which of the following identifies such an exemption?
    a.  Nonuser exemption.
    b.  Interstate Offerings exemption.
    c.  Small Offerings exemption.
    d.  Privity Placements exemption.

## Short Answer

26. What is a security?

_____

_____

27. If your lawyer was preparing a registration statement, what must be contained within it?

_____

_____

28. What is the "plain English" rule adopted by the SEC for securities offerings?

_____

_____

29. What are the three time periods during the registrations process?

_____

30. What is a Regulation A offering?

_____

_____

31. What is a nonissuer exemption from registration?

_____

_____

32. What are restricted securities?

_____

33. What is prohibited by Section 10(b) of the Securities Exchange Act of 1934?

_____

_____

34. What does Regulation Fair Disclosure (Reg FD) prohibit?

_____

35. What is required by Section 16(b) of the Securities Exchange Act of 1934?

_____

36. What defense may be asserted against the imposition of a Section 11 liability action?

_____

37. What is a consent order?

_____

38. What is insider trading?

_____

_____

39. What is the tipper's liability for insider trading?

_____

40.  What is a commodities futures contract?

_____

_____

## Answers to Refresh Your Memory

1.  Securities and Exchange Commission  [p 881]
2.  registration statement  [p 882]
3.  prospectus  [p 882]
4.  waiting period  [p 885]
5.  non-issuer  [p 890]
6.  intrastate offerings  [p 890]
7.  Restricted  [p 891]
8.  Rule 144  [p 892]
9.  five  [p 888]
10.  Scienter  [p 893]
11.  disgorge  [p 898]
12.  statutory insider  [p 898]
13.  Regulation Fair Disclosure  [p 898]
14.  Commodities  [p 901]
15.  commodities futures contract  [p 901]

## Critical Thought Exercise Model Answer

Under section 10(b) of the Securities Exchange Act of 1934 and SEC Rule 10b-5, persons may be sued and prosecuted for the commission of fraud in connection with the sale or purchase of any security.

The 1934 Act prohibits officers and directors from taking advantage of inside information they obtain as a result of their position to gain a trading advantage over the general public.  Section 10(b) and Rule 10b-5 cover not only corporate officers, directors, and majority shareholders but also any persons having access to or receiving information of a nonpublic nature on which trading is based.  The key to liability under Section 10(b) and Rule 10b-5 is whether the insider's information is material.  A significant change in a company's financial condition would be material information.  The cost of an essential part from a supplier would create that significant change.

Jerry Dallas did not act upon inside information in this case, nor did he act as a tipper.  The information he gave was general advice as to the strength of his company and the market factors that affected the price of its main product.  All he did was advise Profit to watch for any announcements of a price increase from Mini-Micro.  He did not provide any insider information regarding CG.  Therefore, Dallas will not be liable for the profit realized by Profit.

To find liability for Nooze, his level of knowledge must be established.  Though it appears that he is acting as a tipper, the information that he provided is not being used to trade on Mini-Micro stock.  There is no information as to whether Profit told him the purpose of wanting to know when a price increase would occur.  Under the tipper theory, however, liability is established when the inside information is obtained as a result of someone's breach of a fiduciary duty to the corporation whose shares are involved in the trading.  In this case, Nooze owes no fiduciary duty to CG.  There is no proof that his information leak hurt Mini-Micro in any way.

Under a theory of misappropriation, both Nooze and Profit may be liable.  The misappropriation theory holds that if an individual wrongfully obtains inside information and trades on it for his or her own personal gain, then the person should be held liable because the individual stole information rightfully belonging to another.  Profit and Nooze both knew that they were taking information that was material and belonged to Mini-Micro.  Liability should be imposed upon Profit because she traded upon this stolen information. Though Nooze also misappropriated the information, there is a lack of evidence as to his knowledge that it would be used for making a trade of CG stock.

# Answers To Practice Quiz

## True/False

1. False   A security may not consist of an investment contract, as well as the typical stock, bond, debenture, or warrant. [p 879]
2. True    The Securities Exchange Act of 1934 regulates the trading in securities. [p 892]
3. False   The Securities and Exchange Commission can adopt rules and regulations to interpret and implement federal securities laws. [p 881]
4. True    The registration statement must contain information about the issuer, the securities to be issued, and other relevant information. [p 882]
5. True    The prospectus must be given to prospective purchasers of the securities and filed with the SEC. [p 882]
6. True    It is divided into three time periods: prefiling, waiting, and posteffective. [p 883]
7. False   The prefiling period ends when the registration statement is filed. [p 883]
8. False   The issuer is encouraged to condition the market during the waiting period. [p 883]
9. True    The posteffective period begins when the registration statement becomes effective. [p 886]
10. True   The final prospectus must be delivered prior to or at the time of confirming a sale. [p 887]
11. True   These securities are exempt from registration. [p 892]
12. True   Nonissuers, such as average investors, do not have to file a registration statement. [p 890]
13. True   The purchaser must reside in the same state as the issuer. [p 890]
14. True   An accredited investor may under the private placement exemption include any person with a net worth of at least $1 million. [p 891]
15. False  Rule 144 provides that securities sold pursuant to the private placement or small offering exemption must be held for one year. [p 891]

## Multiple Choice

16. B   Requirements that must be followed by issuers of securities are set forth in this act, such as registration requirements. A is incorrect because short-swing profits are covered by Section 16(b) of the 1934 act. C is incorrect because Section 10(b) of the 1934 act covers inside trading. Choice D is incorrect because choice B is available. [p 881]
17. D   The SEC does not pass upon the merits of the securities offered. Choices A, B, and C must be described in the registration statement. [p 882]
18. B   The prospectus discloses much of the contents of the registration statement and must have some parts written in plain English. A is incorrect because it is a filing with the SEC that does not require the plain English clarity of a prospectus. C is incorrect because it is only an advertisement telling potential investors where they can obtain a prospectus. Choice D relates to Regulation A offerings and requires much less disclosure. [p 882]
19. A   The issuer cannot condition the market and run a public relations campaign during this period. Choices B and C are incorrect because the issuer is expected or required to provide a prospectus during these periods. Choice D is incorrect because B and C are incorrect. [p 883]
20. C   Toji is liable as the tipper for all profits made by any tippee or remote tippee. Toji's liability is not dependant upon Ned's knowledge of the nature or source of the tip. A is not correct because Toji is liable for the profits of remote tippees. B is not correct because Ned's knowledge is not relevant to Toji's liability. D is not correct because Toji should have known that his tip would be acted upon. [p 896]

21. C  Answer C is the correct answer (which encompasses both answers A and B), as a violator who willfully violates either the act or rules and regulations adopted thereunder may be fined up to $10,000 or imprisoned up to five years, or both.  Answer D is incorrect for the reasons stated above.  [p 888]
22. B  Answer B is the correct answer, as Section 10(b) of the Securities and Exchange Act of 1934 prohibits the use of manipulative and deceptive devices in contravention of the rules and regulations prescribed by the SEC.  Answer A is incorrect, as Rule 504 applies to exemptions of registration of securities that do not exceed a certain dollar amount.  Answer C is incorrect, as Section 16 (b) pertains to the requirements regarding any profits made by a statutory insider on transactions involving short-swing profits.  Answer D is incorrect based on the reasons given above.  [p 893]
23  D  Answer D is correct, as all Answers A, B, and C are correct answers.  [p 879]
24. D  Answer D is correct, as Answers A, B, and C are incorrect statements of time periods.  [p 883]
25. C  Answer C is correct, as an exemption for small offerings is provided by Rule 504.  Answer A is incorrect, as the exemption is a nonissuer exemption.  Answer B is incorrect, as the exemption is the intrastate offerings exemption.  Answer D is incorrect, as the exemption is the private placements exemption.  [p 890-891]

## Short Answer

26. A security is an interest or instrument that is common stock, preferred stock, a bond, a debenture, or a warrant; an interest or instrument that is expressly mentioned in securities acts; and an investment contract.  [p 879]
27. A registration statement must contain descriptions of the securities being offered for sale, the registrant's business, the management of the registrant, pending litigation, how the proceeds will be used, government regulation, the degree of competition, and any special risk factors.  [p 882]
28. Instead of arcane legal language, issuers of securities must use plain English language on the cover page, in the summary, and in the risk factor sections of their prospectuses.  [p 882-883]
29. Prefiling period, waiting period, and posteffective period.  [p 883]
30. Regulation A permits an issuer to sell up to $5 million of securities during a 12-month period pursuant to a simplified registration process.  Such offerings may have an unlimited number or purchasers who do not have to be sophisticated investors.  [p 887]
31. Nonissuers, such as average investors, do not have to file a registration statement prior to reselling securities they have purchased.  This is because the Securities Act of 1933 exempts securities transactions not made by an issuer, an underwriter, or a dealer from registration.  [p 890]
32. Securities that were issued for investment purposes pursuant to the intrastate, private placement, or small offering exemption.  [p 891]
33. Section 10(b) prohibits the use of manipulative and deceptive devices in the purchase or sale of securities in contravention of the rules and regulation prescribed by the SEC.  [p 893]
34. Reg FD prohibits companies from leaking important information to securities professionals before the information is disclosed to the public.  [p 898]
35. Section 16(b) requires that any profits made by a statutory insider on transactions involving short-swing profits belong to the corporation.  [p 898]
36. Due diligence.  [p 888]
37. Where a defendant agrees not to violate securities laws in the future but does not admit to violating securities laws in the past.  [p 888]
38. It occurs when an insider makes a profit by purchasing shares of the commodity prior to public release of favorable information or selling shares of the corporation prior to public disclosure of unfavorable information.  [p 893]
39. The tipper is liable for his or her own profits and the profits made by the tippee.  [p 896]
40. A commodities futures contract is an agreement to busy or sell a specific amount and type of commodity as some future date at a price established at the time of contracting.  [p 901]

# Chapter 33

# ANTITRUST LAW

## Chapter Overview

After the Civil War, America changed from an agricultural to an industrialized nation. Freedom of competition suffered with the formation of powerful business trusts that monopolized large segments of the country's economy. The anticompetitive practices of these large corporate enterprises resulted in monopolies in the oil, gas, sugar, cotton, and whiskey industries. Congress passed antitrust laws to limit the anticompetitive behavior of powerful trusts. This chapter examines antitrust laws.

## Objectives

Upon completion of the exercises in this chapter you should be able to:

1.  Explain the purpose of antitrust laws and describe the federal antitrust statutes.
2.  Describe horizontal and vertical trade restraints that violate Section 1 of the Sherman Antitrust Act.
3.  Explain acts of monopolization that violate Section 2 of the Sherman Antitrust Act.
4.  Describe the scope of Section 7 of the Clayton Act as it relates to mergers.
5.  Apply Section 5 of the Federal Trade Commission Act to antitrust cases.

## Practical Application

As seen in the application of antitrust laws in the case of *United States v Microsoft Corp.*, antitrust laws remain a vital part of the federal government's enforcement of freedom of competition. Whether it is the small investor, consumer, or business partners of large corporations, anticompetitive behavior can still damage many economic interests. When corporations are allowed to dominate large segments of the economy, their failure is more devastating because there is a void that is unfilled by an able competitor. The government will continue to examine each merger, acquisition, and anti-competitive contract through the scope of the federal antitrust laws. Our economy depends upon their existence and enforcement.

## Helpful Hints

It is important to understand the mandates of the major federal antitrust laws and the activities that trigger their application to the conduct of an individual, small business, or corporation. Examine each act individually for the type of conduct it prohibits. Focus on activities that have started federal intervention in the past. You should be better able to predict behavior that will be called into question in the future.

## Study Tips

### Federal Antitrust Laws

Congress has passed several laws that limit anticompetitive behavior in business.

- The Sherman Act makes some kinds of restraints of trade illegal.
- The Clayton Act regulates mergers and prohibits some exclusive dealing arrangements.
- The Federal Trade Commission Act prohibits unfair methods of competition.
- The Robinson-Patman Act prohibits price discrimination.

**Antitrust Enforcement.** Federal antitrust statutes are broadly written to allow the government to respond to economic, business, and technological changes.

**Government Actions**. Enforcement of antitrust laws is divided between the Antitrust Division of the Justice Department and the Bureau of Competition of the Federal Trade Commission (FTC).
- The Sherman Act is the only major act with criminal sanctions.
- The government may seek civil damages, including treble damages for antitrust violations.
- The courts can also order divestiture of assets, cancellation of contracts, liquidation of businesses, any other reasonable remedy that will effectuate freedom of competition.

**Private Actions**. Section 4 of the Clayton Act allows any private person who suffers antitrust injury to his or her business or property to bring a private civil action against the offenders.
- They may recover treble damages, costs of suit, and attorneys' fees.

**Effect of a Government Judgment**. A government judgment against a defendant for an antitrust violation may be used as prima facie evidence of liability in a private civil action.
- Defendants often settle government actions without admitting guilt or liability.
- Section 16 of the Clayton Act lets the government or a private plaintiff obtain an injunction against anticompetitive behavior.

# Restraints of Trade: Section 1 of the Sherman Act

Section 1 outlaws anticompetitive behavior, specifically contracts, combinations, and conspiracies in restraint of trade. To determine if a restraint is lawful, a court applies the rule of reason and *per se* rule.

**Rule of Reason**. The Supreme Court held that only unreasonable restraints of trade violate Section 1. The courts examine the following factor when trying to apply the rule of reason:
- The pro- and anticompetitive effects of the challenged restraint.
- The competitive structure of the industry.
- The firm's market share and power.
- The history and duration of the restraint.
- Other relevant factors.

*Per Se* **Rule**. Some restraints are automatically a violation of Section 1 and no balancing of pro- and anticompetitive effects is necessary.
- Once a restraint is characterized as a per se violation, there is no defense or justification for it.
- If a restraint is a not per se violation, it is examined under the rule of reason.

**Horizontal Restraints of Trade**. A horizontal restraint of trade occurs when two or more competitors at the same level of distribution enter into a contract, combination, or conspiracy to restrain trade.

*Price-Fixing*. This occurs when competitors in the same line of business agree to set the price of goods or services they sell: raising, depressing, fixing, pegging, or stabilizing the price of a commodity or service.
- Price-fixing is a per se violation.

*Division of Markets.* This occurs when competitors agree that each will serve only a designated portion of the market. It is a per se violation to enter into a market-sharing arrangement that divides customers, geographical area, or products.

- Division of markets is a per se violation.

*Group Boycotts.* This occurs when two or more competitors at one level of distribution agree not to deal with others at another level of distribution.

- Most, but not all, group boycotts are per se violations.

*Other Horizontal Agreements.* Some agreements at the same level are lawful, such as trade association rules, exchanging non-price information, and participating in joint ventures.

- These horizontal restraints are examined using the rule of reason.

**Vertical Restraints of Trade.** A vertical restraint of trade occurs when two or more parties on different levels of distribution enter into a contract, combination, or conspiracy to restrain trade.

- The Supreme Court has applied both the per se rule and the rule of reason in determining the legality of vertical restraints of trade under Section 1.

*Resale Price Maintenance.* This occurs when a party at one level of distribution enters into an agreement with a party at another level to adhere to a price schedule that either sets or stabilizes prices.

- Setting minimum resale prices is a per se violation.

*Nonprice Vertical Restraints.* These occur when a manufacturer assigns exclusive territories to retail dealers or limits the number of dealers in a geographical area.

- They are unlawful if their anticompetitive effects outweigh their procompetitive effects.
- These restraints are examined using the rule of reason.

**Defenses to Section 1 of the Sherman Act.** The courts have recognized several defenses to alleged violations of Section 1 of the Sherman Act.

*Unilateral Refusal to Deal.* A unilateral choice by one party to refuse to deal with another party does not violate Section 1, as there is no action by two or more parties in concert; known as the *Colgate* doctrine.

*Conscious Parallelism.* A defense if two or more firms act the same but no concerted action is shown.

*Noerr Doctrine.* Under this doctrine two or more persons may petition the executive, legislative, or judicial branch of the government or administrative agencies to enact laws or take other action without violating antitrust laws.

- Under the "sham" exception, petitioners are not protected if the petition is baseless.

## Monopolization: Section 2 of the Sherman Act

Section 2 prohibits the act of monopolization and attempts or conspiracies to monopolize trade.

- To prove violation of Section 2, requires showing defendant possesses monopoly power in the relevant market and is engaged in a willful act of monopolization to acquire or maintain power.

**Defining the Relevant Market.** Requires defining relevant product or service and geographical market.

- The relevant product market generally includes substitute products or services that are reasonably interchangeable with the defendant's products or services.
- The relevant geographical market is defined as the area in which the defendant and its competitors sell the product or service.

**Monopoly Power**. This is the power to control prices or exclude competition measured by the market share the defendant possesses in the relevant market.

- Market share above 70 percent is monopoly.
- Market share under 20 percent is not monopoly.

**Willful Act of Monopolizing**. This requires an act of monopolizing for there to be a violation.

- Possession of monopoly power without such act does not violate Section 2.

**Defenses to Monopolization**. Only two defenses to a charge of monopolization have been recognized.

- Innocent acquisition. Acquisition from superior business acumen, skill, foresight, or industry.
- Natural monopoly. A small market that can only support one competitor.

**Attempts and Conspiracies to Monopolize**. Firms that attempt or conspire to monopolize mayb e found liable under Section 2.

- A single firm may attempt to monopolize.
- Two or more firms are required for a conspiracy to monopolize.

# Mergers: Section 7 of the Clayton Act

Section 7 provides that it is unlawful for a person or business to acquire stock or assets of another where in any line of commerce or in any activity affecting commerce in any section of the country, the effect of such acquisition may be substantially to lessen competition or to tend to create a monopoly.

**Line of Commerce**. Determining the line of commerce that will be affected by the merger involves defining the relevant product or service market.

- It includes products or services that consumers use as substitutes.
    - If an increase in the price of one product or service leads consumers to purchase another product or service, the two products are substitutes for each other.
    - The two products are part of the same line of commerce, as they are interchangeable.

**Section of the Country**. Defining the relevant section of the country consists of defining the relevant geographical market that will feel the direct and immediate effects of the merger.

**Probability of a Substantial Lessening of Competition**. If there is a probability that a merger will substantially lessen competition or create a monopoly, the court may prevent the merger under Section 7.

**Types of Mergers.** In applying Section 7, mergers are generally classified as bengi horizontal, vertical, market extension, or conglomerate mergers.

*Horizontal Mergers.* A merger between two or more companies that compete in the same business and geographical market.

- The court uses the presumptive illegality test for determining the lawfulness of horizontal mergers. Under this test the merger is illegal under Section 7 if:
    - Merged firm would have a 30 percent or more market share in the relevant market and
    - Merger would cause increase in concentration of 33 percent or more in relevant market.
- Other factors to consider are the past history of the firms involved, the aggressiveness of the merged firms, the economic efficiency of the proposed merger, and consumer welfare.

*Vertical Mergers.* A vertical merger is a merger that integrates the operations of a supplier and customer.

- In a backward vertical merger, the customer acquires the supplier.

- In a forward vertical merger, the supplier acquires the customer.
- Vertical mergers do not increase market share but may cause anticompetitive effects.

*Market Extension Mergers.* Merger between two companies in similar fields whose sales do not overlap.
- A merger between two regional businesses is called a geographical market extension merger.
- A merger between seller of similar products is called a product market extension merger.

*Conglomerate Mergers.* Are mergers between firms in totally unrelated businesses. Section 7 examines the lawfulness of such mergers under the following theories:
- The Unfair Advantage Theory holds that a merger may not give the acquiring firm an unfair advantage over its competitors in finance, marketing, or expertise.

**Defenses to Section 7 Actions.** There are two primary defenses to these actions.
- The Failing Company Doctrine, where a competitor may merge with a failing company if:
  o There is no other reasonable alternative for the failing company.
  o No other purchaser is available.
  o Assets of the failing company would disappear from the market if merger did not proceed.
- The Small Company Doctrine, where two small companies are permitted to merge if it would make them more competitive with a large company.

**Premerger Notification.** The Hart-Scott-Rodino Antitrust Improvement Act requires certain firms to notify the FTC and the Justice Department in advance of a proposed merger.

## Tying Arrangements: Section 3 of the Clayton Act

Section 3 prohibits tying arrangements involving sales and leases of goods.
- Tying arrangements are vertical restraints where a seller refuses to sell one product to a customer unless the customer agrees to purchase a second product from the seller.
- The defendant must be shown to have sufficient economic power in the tying product market to restrain competition.
- A tying arrangement is lawful if there is a justifiable reason for it.

## Price Discrimination: Section 2 of the Clayton Act

Section 2(a) prohibits direct and indirect price discrimination by sellers or a commodity of a like grade and quality where the effect of such discrimination may be to substantially lessen competition or to tend to create a monopoly in any line of commerce.

**Direct Price Discrimination.** To prove a violation of Section 2(a), the plaintiff must show sales to two or more purchasers involving goods of like grade and quality that results in actual injury.

**Indirect Price Discrimination**. This is a form of price discrimination, like favorable credit terms and reduced shipping charges, that is less readily apparent than direct forms of price discrimination.

**Defenses to Section 2(a) Actions**. There are three statutory defenses:

*Cost Justification.* A seller's price discrimination is not unlawful if the price differential is due to "differences in the cost of manufacture, sale, or delivery" of the product.
- Quantity or volume discounts are lawful to the extent they are supported by cost savings.

*Changing* Conditions. Price discrimination is not unlawful if it is in response to "changing conditions in the market for or the marketability of the goods."

*Meeting the Competition.* A seller may engage in price discrimination to meet a competitor's price.

## Unfair Methods of Competition: Section 5 of the Federal Trade Commission Act

Section 5 prohibits unfair methods of competition and unfair or deceptive acts or practices in or affecting commerce. Section 5 covers conduct that
- violates any provision of the Sherman Act of the Clayton Act,
- violates the spirit of those acts,
- fills the gaps of those acts, and
- offends public policy, or is immoral, oppressive, unscrupulous, or unethical, or causes substantial injury to competition or consumers.

## Exemptions From Antitrust Laws

Some industries and businesses are exempt from federal antitrust laws, under three exemptions.

**Statutory Exemptions.** These include labor unions, agricultural cooperatives, export activities of American companies, and insurance business that is regulated by a state.
- Other statutes exempt railroad, shipping, utility, and securities industries from most of the reach of antitrust law.

**Implied Exemptions.** These are given by federal court decision.
- Two such exemptions include professional baseball and the airline industry.

**State Action Exemptions.** These are economic regulations, such as utility rates, mandated by state law.
- This is a form or price-fixing, but states and utilities are not liable for anti-trust violations.

## State Antitrust Laws

Most states have enacted antitrust statutes, which are generally patterned after federal statutes.

# Refresh Your Memory

The following exercises will help to test your memory regarding the principles given in this chapter. Read each question twice, then place your answer in the blank provided for each question. Review the chapter material for any questions you are unable to answer or remember.

1.  The Sherman Act is the only major antitrust act with _____ sanctions.

2.  Section 1, Sherman Act, prohibits contracts, combinations, and conspiracies in _____ of trade.

3.  The rule of _____ holds that only _____ restraints of trade violate Section 1 of the Sherman Act.

4.  Horizontal _____ _____ occurs when the competitors in the same line of business agree to set the price of goods or services they sell.

5.  The _____ _____ _____, where competitors agree that each will serve only a designated portion of a market, is a per se violation of the Sherman Act.

6.  When a party at one level of distribution requires a party at another level of distribution to sell a good or service at a designated price, that is _____ _____ _____.

7.  Section 2 of the Sherman Act prohibits the act of _____ and attempts or _____ to monopolize trade.

8.  A merger is illegal if it will lessen the competition in any _____ of commerce.

9.  A defense of _____ _____ _____, which alleges that the monopoly was acquired by superior skill, foresight, or industry, may be raised against an alleged violation of Section 2 of the Sherman Act.

10. A(n) _____ merger is one between two or more firms that compete in the same business and geographical market.

11. A(n) _____ merger is one between firms at different levels of distribution that integrates the operations of a supplier and a customer.

12. A(n) _____ _____ merger is a merger between two companies in similar fields whose sales do not overlap.

13. The _____ _____ _____ is a defense to a Section 7 violation under the Clayton Act that allows two or more _____ companies to merge without liability if the merger allows them to compete more effectively with a large company.

14. The Robinson-Patman Act prohibits price _____ in the sale of goods.

15. Quantity or volume discounts are lawful under Section 2 of the Clayton Act because of the _____ _____ defense.

# Critical Thought Exercise

When the partners of The Four Brothers Pizza Shoppe terminated the partnership, they divided the greater Chicago area into four parts and agreed to restrict the geographical area within which each would advertise and deliver pizzas. Two years later one partner filed suit against the other three alleging in part that the restriction on advertising and delivery area was a per se violation of the Sherman Act. Was the agreement made as part of a breakup of a partnership that divided a city into geographical areas for advertising and delivery a violation of antitrust law?

*Please compose your answer on a separate sheet of paper or on your computer.*

# Practice Quiz

## True/False

1.  ____ The rule of reason holds that any unreasonable restraints of trade violate the Sherman Act.

2. ___ A horizontal restraint of trade occurs when two companies at the same levels of distribution enter into an agreement to restrain trade.

3. ___ Price-fixing agreements occur between sellers. Agreements between buyers are not price-fixing restraints of trade under the Sherman Act.

4. ___ Division of markets is a per se violation of Section 1.

5. ___ A group boycott would occur if a group of television manufacturers agreed not to sell their products to certain discount retailers.

6. ___ A vertical restraint of trade occurs when two or more parties on different levels of distribution enter into an agreement to restrain trade.

7. ___ Trade associations can help avoid antitrust liability by discussing or exchanging price information about current or future sales to customers.

8. ___ Conscious parallelism is when two or more firms act the same but no concerted action is shown.

9. ___ As part of its burden of proof regarding violation of Section 2 of the Sherman Act, the government needs to prove that a defendant possesses monopoly power in the relevant market.

10. ___ The relevant geographical market, for Section 2 analysis, is defined as the area in which the defendant and its competitors sell the product or service.

11. ___ For an antitrust action to be sustained, the defendant must not possess monopoly power in the relevant market.

12. ___ There are only two defenses to a charge of monopolizing: innocent acquisition and natural monopoly.

13. ___ Section 7 of the Clayton Act applies to all methods of external expansion.

14. ___ If ABC Beer, a beer that is sold nationally, desires to merge with Little Beer, which is sold in Ohio, Indiana, and Michigan, the relevant geographical market for this merger will be the direct and immediate effects of the merger which would be in the area of the three states.

15. ___ The test for determining the lawfulness of horizontal mergers is the presumptive illegality test.

## Multiple Choice

16. Section 1 of the Sherman Act outlaws certain
    a. restraints of trade.
    b. monopolization.
    c. mergers.
    d. tying arrangements.

443

Chapter 33

17. Which of the following is a defense to a Section 1 violation?
    a. Innocent acquisition
    b. Unilateral refusal to deal
    c. The failing company doctrine
    d. Meeting the competition

18. Section 2 of the Sherman Act prohibits
    a. restraint of trade.
    b. mergers.
    c. monopolization.
    d. tying arrangements.

19. The power to control prices or exclude competition measured by the market share the defendant possesses in the relevant market is
    a. price-fixing.
    b. a tying arrangement.
    c. the unfair advantage theory.
    d. monopoly power.

20. The protection of quality control coupled with a trade secret may save a
    a. tie-in arrangement.
    b. price-fixing arrangement.
    c. division of markets arrangement.
    d. resale price maintenance arrangement.

21. When a party at one level of distribution enters into an agreement with a party at another level to adhere to a price schedule that either sets or stabilizes prices, this is known as
    a. resale pricing maintenance.
    b. the Colgate doctrine.
    c. a unilateral refusal to deal.
    d. none of the above

22. Which of the following holds that two or more persons may petition the executive, legislative, or judicial branch of the government or administrative agencies to enact or to take other action without violating the antitrust laws?
    a. Section 2 of the Sherman Act
    b. conscious parallelism
    c. The Noerr doctrine
    d. The Online Commerce and Internet Law Doctrine

23. Mergers between firms in unrelated businesses are often termed
    a. market extension mergers
    b. horizontal mergers
    c. vertical mergers
    d. conglomerate mergers

24. The failing company doctrine is
    a. a defense whereby a competitor may merge with a failing company.
    b. used if there is no other reasonable alternative for a failing company.
    c. available if the assets of the failing company would completely disappear from the market if the anticompetitive merger were not allowed to go through.
    d. all of the above

25. Which of the following best describes when price discrimination is not unlawful?
    a. When the price of goods is raised to reflect deterioration of goods.
    b. When the price of goods is raised to make a profit.
    c. If it is in response to changing conditions in the market for or the marketability of goods.
    d. None of the above

## Short Answer

26. What is price-fixing?

27. What is the doctrine of conscious parallelism?

28. Name two defenses to a monopolization charge and give an example of each.

29. What test does the court apply to determine the relevant product or service market in Section 7 analysis under the Clayton Act?

30. Explain the difference between a forward vertical merger and a backward vertical merger.

31. What is a conglomerate merger?

32. If two companies are proposing a merger, what must they do to comply with the Hart-Scott-Rodino Antitrust Improvement Act?

33. If a doctor charges one patient $200 for the same procedure as she charged another patient only $55, is this price discrimination a violation of the Robinson-Patman Act?

34. What are the three elements necessary to prove a violation of Section 7 of the Clayton Act?

35. What are the four types of mergers?

36. What is a tying arrangement?

37. What other name is used to refer to Section 2 of the Clayton Act?

38. What are the three types of price discrimination that are not unlawful?

_____

39. What type of conduct does Section 5 of the Federal Trade Commission Act cover?

_____

_____

40. The courts have held that certain industries are implicitly exempt from federal antitrust laws. Name two of these industries.

_____

## Answers to Refresh Your Memory

1. criminal [p 914]
2. restraint [p 915]
3. reason, unreasonable [p 915]
4. price-fixing [p 916]
5. division of markets [p 918]
6. resale price maintenance [p 921]
7. monopolization, conspiracies [p 928]
8. line [p 929]
9. superior business acumen [p 927]
10. horizontal [p 930]
11. vertical [p 931]
12. market extension [p 931]
13. small company doctrine, small [p 931]
14. discrimination [p 932]
15. cost-justification [p 933]

## Critical Thought Exercise Model Answer

Society's welfare is harmed if rival businesses are permitted to join in an agreement that consolidates their market power or otherwise restrains competition. The types of trade restraints that Section 1 of the Sherman Act prohibits are generally divided into horizontal and vertical restraints. A horizontal restraint is any agreement that in some way restrains competition between rival businesses competing in the same market. These agreements include price fixing, group boycotts, and horizontal market division. It is a per se violation of Section 1 of the Sherman Act for competitors to divide up territories or customers. The effect of the agreement between the four former partners is to say, "That will be your market and this will be mine." The agreement to limit advertising and delivery to different geographical areas was intended to be, and was in practice, an agreement to allocate markets so that the per se rule of illegality applies.

## Answers to Practice Quiz

### True/False

1. True   Only unreasonable restraints of trade violate Section 1 of the Sherman Act. [p 915]
2. True   The two companies must be on the same level of distribution. [p 916]

3.  False   While most price-fixing occurs between sellers, an agreement among buyers to set the price they will pay for goods of services is also price-fixing. [p 916]
4.  True    Division of markets is a per se violation of Section 1. [p 918]
5.  True    This would be two or more competitors at one level of distribution agreeing not to deal with others at a different level of distribution. [p 919]
6.  True    They would be on different levels of distribution in a vertical restraint of trade. [p 921]
7.  False   They can avoid liability by not agreeing to share or split customers or geographical areas or operate only during agree-upon hours. [p 924-925]
8.  True    There is no Section 1 violation because each firm is acting on its own. [p 923]
9.  True    The government needs to prove that a defendant possesses monopoly power in the relevant market. [p 925]
10. True    The relevant geographical market is defined as the area in which the defendant and its competitors sell the product or service. [p 925]
11. False   For an antitrust action to be sustained, the defendant must possess monopoly power in the relevant market. [p 925]
12. True    While innocent acquisition due to superior business acumen is a defense, the only other defense is that of natural monopoly, caused by the market only being able to support one competitor. [p 927]
13. True    Section 7 applies to all methods of external expansion, including technical mergers, consolidations, purchases of assets, subsidiary operations, and joint ventures. [p 929]
14. True    The relevant geographical market is the area that will feel the direct and immediate effects of the merger. The area of the three states is the geographical market. [p 925]
15. True    The presumptive illegality test is applied to horizontal mergers. [p 930]

## Multiple Choice

16. A   A is correct, as Section 1 prohibits different types of horizontal or vertical restraints of trade. Choice B is prohibited by Section 2. Choice C is prohibited by Section 7 of the Clayton Act. Choice D is prohibited by Section 3 of the Clayton Act. [p915]
17. B   It is a defense because it does not involve a concerted action between two or more parties. Choice A is a defense to a Section 2 monopolization charge. Choice C is a defense to a charge under Section 7 or the Clayton Act. Choice D is a defense to a price discrimination charge under Section 2 of the Clayton Act. [p 922]
18. C   Section 2 prohibits the act of monopolization and attempts or conspiracies to monopolize. Choice A is prohibited by Section 1 of the Sherman Act. Choice B is prohibited by Section 7 of the Clayton Act. Choice D is prohibited by Section 3 of the Clayton Act. [p 925]
19. D   Choice D is correct because monopolization power is controlling the two key aspects of the market: prices and competition. Choice A is a restraint of trade, not a part of analyzing a monopoly. Choice B relates to a violation of the Clayton Act, not Section 2 of the Sherman Act. Choice C is relates to conglomerate mergers. [p 926]
20. A   This is lawful in situations where there is a legitimate reason for the tying arrangement. Choices B, C, and D are per se violations for which no justifications are allowed. [p 932]
21. A   Answer A is correct, as resale pricing (or vertical price-fixing) happens when a party at one level of distribution enters into an agreement with a party at another level to stick to a price schedule that either sets or stabilizes prices. Answer B is incorrect, as the "Colgate doctrine" applies to a unilateral refusal to deal, not to agreements regarding price scheduling, and the like. Answer C is incorrect, as a unilateral refusal to deal concerns the Colgate doctrine which as previously discussed does not apply to agreements regarding price scheduling. Answer D is incorrect based on the reasons given above. [p 921]
22. C   Answer C is the correct answer, as the Noer doctrine states that two or more persons may petition the executive, legislative, or judicial branch of the government or administrative agencies to enact laws or take other action without violating antitrust laws. Answer A is incorrect, as Section 2 of

the Sherman Act was promulgated in response to growing concern about the power generated by anticompetitive activity. Answer B is incorrect, as conscious parallelism is where two or more firms act the same, however no concerted action is show. Answer D is incorrect, as there is no such doctrine. [p 923]

23. D Answer D is correct, as conglomerate mergers are ones that are between firms in unrelated businesses. Answer A is incorrect, as a market extension merger is one between two companies in similar fields whose sales do not overlap. Answer B is incorrect, as a horizontal merger is one between two or more companies that compete in the same business and geographical market. Answer C is incorrect, as a vertical merger is one that integrates the operations of a supplier and a customer. [p 931]

24. D Answer D is correct, as answers A,B, and C all describe what the failing company doctrine entails. [p 931]

25. C Answer C is correct, as it appropriately describes when price discrimination is not unlawful which of course would be if it is in response to changing conditions in the market for or the marketability of goods. Answers A and B are both incorrect, as they makes no sense in light of the question being asked. Answer D is incorrect based on the reasoning given above. [p 933]

## Short Answer

26. Price fixing occurs when competitors in the same line of business agree to set the price of the goods or services they sell. It is accomplished by raising, depressing, fixing, pegging, or stabilizing the price of a commodity or service. [p 916]

27. If two competing manufacturers of a similar product both separately reach an independent decision not to deal with a retailer. There is not violation of Section 1 because each of the manufacturers acted on its own. [p 923]

28. (1) innocent acquisition (for example, acquisition because of superior business acumen, skill, foresight, or industry), (2) natural monopoly (for example, a small market that can only support one competitor, such as a small-town newspaper). [p 927]

29. The courts apply the functional interchangeability test. Under this test, the relevant line of commerce includes products or services that consumers use as substitutes. If two products are substitutes for each other, they are considered as part of the same line of commerce. [p 929]

30. In a backward vertical merger the customer acquires the supplier, while in a forward vertical merger the supplier acquires the customer. [p 931]

31. It is a merger that does not fir in the other categories of mergers and involves a merger between firms in totally unrelated businesses. [p 931]

32. They are required to notify the FTC and the Justice Department in advance of a proposed merger. [p 932]

33. No, because Section 2 of the Clayton Act does not apply to the sale of services. [p 932]

34. Line of commerce, section of the country, and probability of a substantial lessening of competition. [p 929]

35. Horizontal, Vertical, Market Extension, and Conglomerate Mergers. [p 930]

36. It is an arrangement where a seller refuses to sell a product to a customer unless the customer purchases a second product. [p 932]

37. The Robinson-Patman Act. [p 932]

38. Differences due to cost justification, changing conditions, and meeting the competition. [p 933]

39. Section 5 covers conduct that violates any provision of the Sherman Act or the Clayton Act, violates the "spirit" of those acts, fills the gaps of those acts, and causes substantial injury to competitors or consumers. [p 934]

40. Professional baseball and airlines. [p 935]

# Chapter 34

# CONSUMER PROTECTION
# AND ENVIRONMENTAL LAW

## Chapter Overview

Both federal and state governments have enacted consumer protection laws that promote product safety and prohibit abusive, unfair, and deceptive selling practices. This was a drastic change from the principle of *caveat emptor*, or "let the buyer beware." In an effort to curtail the damaging effects of pollution, the federal government and states have created environmental protection laws. This chapter examines both consumer protection laws and environmental protection laws.

## Objectives

Upon completion of the exercises in this chapter, you should be able to:

1.  Discuss the regulation of drugs, cosmetics, and medical devices.
2.  Explain the regulation of packaging, labeling, and poison prevention labeling.
3.  Identify the key elements of consumer protection statutes.
4.  Describe the mandates of the Clean Air Act, the Clean Water Act, and other similar laws.
5.  Discuss how the Endangered Species Act protects endangered and threatened species.

## Practical Application

You should be able to understand the duties, obligations, and requirements placed upon businesses when they deal in the manufacture, sale, or distribution of consumer goods or services. You should be able to understand the duties, obligations and requirements placed on businesses when their actions have an effect on the environment. You should be able to determine your specific rights and obligations whether you are a business that must comply with the law or a consumer who is seeking to enforce a protected right.

## Helpful Hints

Your analysis of consumer protection should begin with basic definitions and requirements of the statute. Your focus then should turn to the act or nature of the product. By determining where the act or product fits in the legislative scheme of consumer protection, you can alleviate the illegality or enforce the mandates contained in a consumer law.

With all of the different regulations that have been enacted to curtail pollution and its effects upon the environment, you should organize your analysis of a situation according to the type of damage done or the segment of the environment that is at risk. This will lead you to the correct statute or regulation for guidance as to how the situation will be handled by the appropriate agency or the courts.

# Study Tips

## Food, Drug, and Cosmetic Safety

The Food, Drug, and Cosmetic Act (FDCA) regulates much of the testing, manufacture, distribution, and sale of foods, drugs, cosmetics, and medical products and devices in the United States.
- The Food and Drug Administration (FDA) administers the act.

**Regulation of Food**. The FDCA prohibits the shipment, distribution, or sale of adulterated food, which is any food that consists in whole or in part of any "filthy, putrid, or decomposed substance" that is unfit for consumption.
- The FDCA prohibits false and misleading labeling of food products.
- It mandates affirmative disclosure of information on food labels.

**Food Labeling.** The Nutritional Labeling and Education Act requires food manufacturers and processors to provide more nutritional information on virtually all foods and forbids them from making scientifically unsubstantiated heath claims.
- The law requires labels on food items with information on calories, fat, fiber, cholesterol, etc.

**Regulation of Drugs.** The FDA regulates drug testing, licensing, manufacturing, distribution, and sale.
- Users of drugs must be provided with a copy of detailed directions that include any warnings and list possible side effects.

**Regulation of Cosmetics**. The FDA regulations require cosmetics to be labeled, to disclose ingredients, and to contain warnings as to any carcinogenic ingredients.
- The FDA may remove from the market any product that makes a false claim of preserving youth, increasing virility, or growing hair.

**Regulation of Medicinal Devices**. The FDA has authority under the Medicinal Device Amendment to the FDCA to regulate medicinal devices, such as heart pacemakers, surgical equipment, and other diagnostic, therapeutic, and health devices.
- The FDA is empowered to remove quack devices from the market.

## United Nations Biosafety Protocol for Genetically Altered Foods

The Biosafety Protocol was passed to resolve a dispute between exporters of genetically modified agricultural products and countries that desired to keep the products out of their country.
- As a compromise, the 138 countries that signed the protocol agreed to allow the importation of genetically engineered foods as long as they were clearly labeled with the phrase "May contain living modified organisms."
  - This allows consumers to decide themselves whether to purchase altered food products.

## Product Safety

The Consumer Product Safety Act regulates potentially dangerous consumer products and created the Consumer Product Safety Commission (CPSC).
- The CPSC is an independent federal agency that interprets the CPSA, conducts research on the safety of products, and collects data and regarding injuries caused by products.
- The CPSC sets safety standards for consumer products and has the power to compel a manufacturer to recall, repair, or replace a hazardous product.

o The CPSC can seek injunctions and seize hazardous products.

o It can also seek civil and criminal penalties.

## Unfair and Deceptive Practices

When sellers engage in unfair, deceptive, or abusive techniques, the Federal Trade Commission (FTC), under the authority of the Federal Trade Commission Act (FTC Act), is authorized to bring an administrative proceeding to attack the unfair or deceptive practice.

- If the FTC finds a violation under Section 5 of the FTC Act, it may order a cease-and-desist order, an affirmative disclosure to consumers, or corrective advertising.
- The FTC may sue for damages on behalf of consumers in either state or federal court.

**False and Deceptive Advertising**. This is prohibited under Section 5, and occurs when advertising contains misinformation or omits important information that is likely to mislead a "reasonable consumer" or makes an unsubstantiated claim.

*Bait and Switch*. This occurs when a seller advertises the availability of a low-cost discounted item but then pressures the buyer into purchasing more expensive merchandise. Bait and switch occurs when

- The seller refuses to show consumers the advertised merchandise.
- The seller discourages employees from selling the advertised merchandise or
- The seller fails to have adequate quantities of the merchandise available.

**Door-to Door Sales**. These may entail overaggressive or abusive practices.

- These tactics are handled on a state level where laws give consumers a certain number of days to rescind door-to-door sales, usually three.

## Environmental Protection

Federal and state governments have enacted statutes to protect air and water from pollution, to regulate hazardous wastes, and to protect wildlife.

**Environmental Protection Agency (EPA).** The EPA coordinates the implementation and enforcement of federal environmental protection laws.

**Environmental Impact Statement.** The National Environmental Policy Act (NEPA) mandates that the "adverse impact" of proposed legislation, rule making, or other federal government action on the environment be considered before the action is implemented.

- NEPA requires an Environmental Impact Statement (EIS) be prepared for any proposed legislation or major federal action that significantly affects quality of the human environment.
- The EIS must describe the affected environment and the impact of the proposed action, identify and discuss alternatives, list resources committed, and contain a cost-benefit analysis.

## Air Pollution

The *Clean Air Act* provides comprehensive regulation of air quality in the United States.

**Sources of Air Pollution.** The Clean Air Act regulates both stationary (manufacturing plants) and mobile (automobiles) sources.

- It requires states to identify major stationary sources of air pollution and develop plans to reduce air pollution from these sources.
- Motor vehicles are required to have emissions controls.

**National Ambient Air Quality Standards.** The Clean Air Act directs the EPA to establish national ambient air quality standards (NAAQS) for certain pollutants.
- Primary levels protect humans.
- Secondary levels protect vegetation, climate, visibility, and economic values.
- The states are responsible for enforcing these levels.

**Nonattainment Areas.** These are regions that do not meet air quality standards and are classified into five categories: marginal, moderate, serious, severe, and extreme.
- Deadlines are established for areas to meet attainment levels and states must submit compliance plans that
  - identify major sources of air pollution and require them to install pollution control equipment
  - institute permit systems for new stationary courses
  - implement inspection programs to monitor mobile sources
- States that fail to develop and implement a plan are subject to the following sanctions:
  - loss of federal highway finds
  - limitations on new sources of emissions

**Smog Swapping.** The Clean Air Act Amendment of 1990 allows companies to trade sulfur dioxide emissions (the pollutant that causes acid rain).
- Companies still face strict quotas, but they are free to satisfy their limits by buying pollution credits from other companies.
- These credits are actually traded on the Chicago futures market.

## Water Pollution

Pursuant to the Clean Water Act, the EPA has established water quality standards that define which bodies of water can be use drinking water, recreation, wildlife, and agricultural and industrial uses.

**Point Sources of Water Pollution.** The Clean Water Act authorizes the EPA to establish water pollution standards for point sources of water pollution, which are stationary sources of pollution such as paper mills, manufacturing plants, electric utility plants, and sewage plants.
- The EPA sets standards for technology that must be used
- The EPA requires dischargers of pollution to keep records, maintain monitoring equipment, and keep samples of discharges.

**Thermal Pollution.** The Clean Water Act prohibits thermal pollution because it damages the ecological balance and decreases oxygen in a waterway.

**Wetlands.** The Clean Water Act forbids the filling or dredging of wetlands unless a permit has been obtained from the Army Corps of Engineers.
- Wetlands include swamps, bogs, marshes, and similar areas that support birds, animals, and vegetative life.

**Safe Drinking Water Act.** The Safe Drinking Water Act authorizes the EPA to establish national primary drinking water standards and prohibits dumping of waste into wells.

**Ocean Protection.** The Marine Protection, Research, and Sanctuaries Act requires a permit for dumping waste and foreign material into ocean waters and establishes marine sanctuaries as far seaward as the Continental Shelf and in the Great Lakes and their connecting waters.

- The Clean Water Act authorizes the U.S. government to clean up **oil spills** within 12 miles of shore and on the Continental Shelf and to recover the cleanup costs from responsible parties.
- The *Oil Pollution Act of 1990*, which is administered by the Coast Guard, requires the oil industry to adopt procedures that can more readily respond to oil spills.

## Toxic Substances and Hazardous Waste

Many of the chemicals used for agriculture, mining, and industry contain toxic substances that cause birth defects, cancer, and other health-related problems.
- Wastes, which contain hazardous substances that can harm the environment or pose a danger to human health, are generated by agriculture, mining, industry, other businesses, and households.

**Toxic Substances Control.** The Toxic Substances Control Act requires manufacturers and processors to test new chemicals to determine their effect on human health and the environment before the EPA will allow them to be marketed.
- The EPA requires special labeling for toxic substances and may limit or prohibit their manufacture and sale.
- A toxic substance that poses an imminent hazard may be removed from commerce.

**Insecticides, Fungicides, and Rodenticides.** The Insecticide, Fungicide, and Rodenticide Act requires pesticides, herbicides, fungicides, and rodenticides to be registered with the EPA.
- The EPA may deny, suspend, or cancel the registration if it finds that the chemical poses an imminent danger.
- The EPA sets standards for the amount of residue that is permitted on crops sold for human and animal consumption.

**Hazardous Waste.** Congress enacted the Resource Conservation and Recovery Act to regulate the disposal of new hazardous waste.
- The act authorizes the EPA to regulate facilities that generate, treat, store, transport, and dispose of hazardous wastes.
  - Any substance that is toxic, radioactive, or corrosive or can ignite is a hazardous material.
- Hazardous wastes are tracked and regulated from the moment they are created to the time of their final disposal or storage.

**Superfund.** The Comprehensive Environmental Response, Compensation, and Liability Act gave the federal government a mandate to deal with years of abuse and neglect in the disposal of hazardous waste.
- The EPA is required by the Superfund to identify sites in the United States where hazardous wastes have been disposed, stored, abandoned, or spilled, and rank these sites regarding the severity of the risk they pose.
- Sites with highest ranking are put on National Priority List and receive first priority for cleanup
- The Superfund provides for the creation of a fund to finance the cleanup of sites.
- The EPA can order a responsible party to clean up a hazardous waste site.
  - If the party fails to do so, the EPA can clean up the site and recover the cost from any responsible party under a theory of strict liability.
- The Superfund contains a right to know provision that requires businesses to disclose the presence of certain listed chemicals to the community, annually disclose emissions of chemical substances released into the environment , and immediately notify the government of spills, accidents, and other emergencies involving hazardous substances.

**Nuclear Waste.** Nuclear power plants create radioactive waste that maintains high radioactivity for a very long period of time. Two federal agencies monitor and regulate nuclear energy in the United States.

- The Nuclear Regulatory Commission (NRC) regulates the construction and opening of commercial nuclear power plants.
  - The NRC monitors the plants and may close an unsafe plant.
- The EPA sets standards for allowable levels of radioactivity in the environment and regulates the disposal of radioactive waste.
  - The EPA also regulates thermal pollution caused by the nuclear power plants and emissions and uranium production.
- The Nuclear Waste Policy Act of 1982 mandates that the federal government select and develop a permanent site for the disposal of nuclear waste.

## Endangered Species

The Endangered Species Act protects endangered species and threatened species of animals.
- The EPA and the Department of Commerce designate critical habitats for each endangered and threatened species.
- Real estate or other development in these habitats is prohibited or severely limited.
- In addition to the Endangered Species Act, there are numerous other acts that protect migratory birds, eagles, horses, burros, marine mammals, and fish.

## State Environmental Protection Laws

Many state and local governments have created laws to protect the environment.
- Some states have created special statutes to protect unique areas within their boundaries.

# Refresh Your Memory

The following exercises will help to test your memory regarding the principles given in this chapter. Read each question twice, then place your answer in the blank provided for each question. Review the chapter material for any questions you are unable to answer or remember.

1.  The FDCA regulates the testing, _____, distribution, and _____ of food, drugs, _____, and medicinal products and devices in the United States.

2.  The FDCA prohibits the shipment, distribution, or sale of _____ food.

3.  The FDA is empowered to remove "_____" medicinal devices from the market.

4.  As part of its powers under the Consumer Product Safety Act, the CPSA is authorized to collect data regarding _____ caused by consumer products.

5.  If a consumer product is found to be imminently hazardous, the manufacturer can be required to _____, repair, or _____ the product.

6.  The _____ _____ _____ coordinates the implementation and enforcement of the federal environmental protection laws.

7.  The National Environmental Policy Act requires that a(n) _____ _____ _____ be prepared for all proposed legislation and major federal action that significantly affects the quality of the human environment.

8. The _____ _____ _____ was enacted to assist states in dealing with air pollution.

9. The Clean Air Act directs the EPA to establish national _____ _____ _____ standards for certain pollutants at two different levels: primary and secondary.

10. Industrial plants, oil refineries, and public utilities are _____ sources of air pollution.

11. The _____ _____ _____ _____ Act requires food manufacturers and processors to provide nutritional information on food products and prohibits the making of scientifically unsubstantiated health claims.

12. The _____ _____ _____ Act authorized the EPA to establish national minimum quality of water standards for human consumption.

13. The Clean Water Act authorizes the US government to clean up _____ _____ and spills of other _____ _____ in ocean waters within 12 miles of the shore and on the Continental Shelf.

14. The Comprehensive Environmental Response, Compensation, and Liability Act, commonly known as _____, gives the federal government a mandate to deal with hazardous wastes that have been spilled, stored, or abandoned.

15. The _____ _____ _____ is a federal agency that licenses the construction and opening of commercial nuclear power plants.

# Critical Thought Exercise

Sarah is a biology student at Evermore University. One of her professors has given an assignment for each student to bring in a commercially prepared food item to class. Sarah brings in a 4 ounce box of golden raisins and proceeds to follow the professor's instructions to identify all foreign materials in her food item. She carefully looks at the raisins under the microscope and identifies a total of 35 fly eggs from her 4 ounces of raisins. Sarah is sickened and appalled to find fly eggs in her raisins, as she has always loved eating golden raisins.

Sarah would like to complain about finding fly eggs in her commercially packaged raisins. To whom should she complain and does she have a legitimate complaint?

*Please compose your answer on a separate sheet of paper or on your computer.*

# Practice Quiz

## True/False

1. ____ The FDCA prohibits the sale of adulterated food, and regulates the misleading labeling of food.

2. ____ Testing of cosmetics is not done by the Food and Drug Administration.

3. ____ The FDA can obtain orders for the seizure, recall, and condemnation of adulterated food.

4. ____ The FDA does not allow defects or contaminants to be in food without the food being deemed adulterated.

5. ___ Terms such as *low fat*, *light*, and *natural* have standards that can be enforced by the FDA.

6. ___ Before a new miracle drug can be sold to needy patients, the drug manufacturer must go through a brief licensing process by the FDA.

7. ___ Manufacturers are prohibited from touting the medical benefits of charms and bracelets.

8. ___ Motor Vehicles, boats, aircraft and firearms are regulated by the Consumer Product Safety Commission.

9. ___ The FTC may not force a company to purchase corrective advertising to remedy an unfair or deceptive practice.

10. ___ The FTC may sue for damages on behalf of an individual consumer for false advertising.

11. ___ If a business makes an unsubstantiated claim, such as "Our juice is 20% more nutritional than XYZ Juice," the FTC may pursue a violation of Section 5 of the FTC Act.

12. ___ The purpose of an environmental impact statement is to provide enough information about the environment to enable the federal government to determine the feasibility of a project.

13. ___ Although the EPA establishes air quality standards, the states are not responsible for their enforcement.

14. ___ Automobile and other vehicle emissions are not considered mobile sources of air pollution under the Clean Air Act.

15. ___ The Clean Water Act forbids the filling or dredging of wetlands unless a permit is obtained from the Army Corps of Engineers.

## Multiple Choice

16. False and misleading labeling of food products is prohibited by the
    a. Consumer Product Safety Act.
    b. Fair Packaging and Labeling Act.
    c. Poison Prevention Packaging Act.
    d. Food, Drug, and Cosmetic Act.

17. Food is deemed adulterated if it consists in whole or in part of any
    a. filthy, putrid, or decomposed substance.
    b. food that is improperly labeled.
    c. food that does not contain the correct amount in the container.
    d. incorrectly colored or misshaped food.

18. Tolerances for pesticides used on agricultural products are regulated by the
    a. Federal Trade Commission.
    b. Food and Drug Administration.
    c. Consumer Product Safety Commission.
    d. Department of Justice.

19. Because the CPSC regulates potentially dangerous consumer products, it
    a.  seeks injunctions to stop anyone from making products.
    b.  seeks criminal penalties for the manufacture of potentially dangerous products.
    c.  issues product safety standards for consumer products that pose an unreasonable risk of injury.
    d.  makes private parties file all suits and requests for injunctions.

20. Under the Clean Air Act, the EPA establishes primary and secondary levels of allowable pollution. These standards are called
    a.  adverse impact.
    b.  national ambient air quality standards.
    c.  pollution credits.
    d.  the National Pollutant Discharge Elimination System.

21. The trading of pollution credits is allowed under the
    a.  Clean Air Act Amendments of 1990.
    b.  Clean Water Act.
    c.  River and Harbor Act.
    d.  Safe Drinking Water Act.

22. Under the Clean Water Act, dischargers of pollution are not required to
    a.  pay a "use fee" each time they discharge pollutants.
    b.  keep records.
    c.  maintain monitoring equipment.
    d.  keep samples of discharges

23. The Clean Water Act does not regulate
    a.  thermal pollution.
    b.  national primary drinking water standards.
    c.  wetlands.
    d.  oil spills.

24. The operator of a hazardous waste disposal site will have to clean up contamination caused by improper dumping of hazardous waste over 30 years ago by a previous owner of the waste site pursuant to the
    a.  Toxic Substances Control Act.
    b.  Insecticide, Fungicide, and Rodenticide Act.
    c.  Resource Conservation and Recovery Act.
    d.  Comprehensive Environmental Response, Compensation, and Liability Act.

25. Under the Endangered Species Act, a wildlife form may be declared threatened or endangered by
    a.  the EPA.
    b.  the Department of Commerce.
    c.  the secretary of the interior.
    d.  the Endangered Species Commission.

## Short Answer

26. Explain the meaning of adulterated food.

_____

_____

27. Which Act regulates food, food additives, drugs, cosmetics, and medicinal devices?

_____

28. What is required of food manufacturers and processors in the Nutrition Labeling and Education Act?

_____

_____

29. List three examples of "action levels."

_____

30. Name three of the FDA requirements for cosmetics.

_____

31. List four types of medicinal devices controlled by the FDCA.

_____

32. Explain why the United States felt that trade barriers were being used against genetically modified foods and what the United States had to concede to get its exports into foreign countries.

_____

_____

_____

33. What are three things that the Consumer Product Safety Commission is empowered to do?

_____

_____

34. What is false and deceptive advertising under Section 5 of the FTC Act?

_____

_____

35. What does the National Environmental Policy Act mandate?

_____

36. What is a nonattainment area?

_____

37. What is thermal pollution?

_____

38. What are toxic substances?

_____

39. What is hazardous waste?

_____

_____

40. Which legislative act authorizes the US government to clean up oil spills in the oceans within 12 miles of shore?

_____

# Answers to Refresh Your Memory

1. manufacture, sale, cosmetics  [p 947]
2. adulterated  [p 948]
3. quack  [p 952]
4. injuries  [p 954]
5. recall, replace  [p 954]
6. Environmental Protection Agency  [p 957]
7. environmental impact statement  [p 957]
8. Clean Air Act  [p 958]
9. ambient air quality  [p 958]
10. stationary  [p 958]
11. Nutrition Labeling and Education  [p 950]
12. Safe Drinking Water  [p 961]
13. oil spills, hazardous substances  [p 963]
14. Superfund  [p 965]
15. Nuclear Regulatory Commission  [p 965]

# Critical Thought Exercise Model Answer

Sarah should file her complaint with the Food and Drug Administration (FDA), as it is responsible for enforcing the Food, Drug, and Cosmetic Act (FDCA), which regulates the testing, manufacture, distribution, and sale of foods, drugs, cosmetics, and medicinal products and devices in the US. Under this Act, the shipment, distribution, or sale of adulterated food is prohibited. Food is deemed adulterated if it consists in whole or in part of any "filthy, putrid, or decomposed substance" or if it is otherwise "unfit for food."

However, food may contain contaminants and still be lawfully distributed or sold, it just has to be unadulterated. The FDA has set ceilings, or "action levels," for contaminants for various foods. The courts have upheld the presence of some contamination in food as lawful. The FDA can mount inspections and raids to enforce its action levels. If it finds that the federal tolerance system has been violated, it can seize the offending food and destroy it at the owner's expense.

Under the FDA guidelines, golden raisins can contain up to 35 fly eggs per 8 ounces before they are sufficiently defective to warrant FDA investigation. Sarah found 35 fly eggs in her sample of 4 ounces of golden raisins. This would seem to indicate that the golden raisins were adulterated, as they contained the entire allowable level of fly eggs in 4 ounces, rather than in the FDA standard of 8 ounces.

# Answers to Practice Quiz

## True/False

1. True    The FDCA prohibits the sale of adulterated food or the use of false or misleading labels on food products. [p 948]
2. False   Under the FDCA, the FDA tests food, drugs, cosmetics, and medicinal devices. [p 952]
3. True    This authority also extends to drugs, cosmetics and medicinal devices. [p 947]
4. False   Until the amount of a contaminant reaches an "action level," the food is still considered safe for human consumption. [p 949]
5. True    The Nutritional Labeling and Education Act lead to regulations that were adopted by the FDA that set standard definitions for these terms. [p 950]

459

6. False    The licensing process of the FDA for new drugs requires and application, hearing, and an investigation, which can take many years. [p 950]
7. True    The FDA may remove quack medicinal devices from the market. [p 952]
8. False    These products are regulated by other government agencies. [p 954]
9. False    This is one of the remedies that include issuing a cease-and-desist order or requiring an affirmative disclosure to consumers. [p 955]
10. True    The FTC may sue in state or federal court to obtain compensation for consumer for any deceptive practice, including false advertising. [p 955]
11. True    The FTC may seek to halt any false advertising that makes an unsubstantiated claim. [p 955]
12. True    The EIS is also used as evidence in court whenever a project is challenged as violating the NEPA. [p 957]
13. False    Although the EPA establishes air quality standards, the states are responsible for their enforcement. The federal government does have the right to enforce the standards if the states fail to do so. [p 958]
14. False    Automobile and other vehicle emissions are considered mobile sources of air pollution under the Clean Air Act. [p 958]
15. True    The Clean Water Act forbids the dredging or filling of wetlands without a permit from the Army Corps of Engineers. [p 961]

## Multiple Choice

16. D    D is correct because the truthful content of food labels is controlled by the FDCA. Choice A is not correct because it relates to standards for production and distribution of safe consumer goods. Choice B is incorrect because it relates to information required on labels attached to consumer goods. Choice C is wrong because it relates to the requirement of childproof packaging. [p 948]
17. A    A is correct because it sets forth a type of substance that is unfit for human consumption. B and C are incorrect because they do not relate to the quality of food. D is incorrect because it involves defects that do not prevent the food from being fit for human consumption. [p 948]
18. B    B is correct because the FDA regulates numerous products under the FDCA, including pesticides under the Pesticide Amendment of 1954. Choice A is incorrect because it does not create regulations for use of products, but is usually restricted to deceptive and unfair practices. Choice C is incorrect because the CPSC is concerned with the creation of safe products, not the regulation of their use. Choice D is incorrect because the Department of Justice is concerned with criminal violations, not the regulation of product use. [p 947]
19. C    C is correct because the CPSC has the responsibility to make sure that potentially dangerous products are made in a safe way so that consumers will not be hurt by products that don't meet minimum safety standards. Choices A and B are incorrect because they are remedies for violations, not a method for dealing with potentially dangerous products. Choice D is incorrect because the CPSC takes action on behalf of consumers. [p 954]
20. B    B is correct because ambient levels set the amount that exists overall that is unhealthy for humans, vegetation, etc. Choice A is incorrect because adverse impact relates to an environmental impact statement which is not a standard, but an individual report. Choice C is not correct because pollution credits refer to the amount of pollution that a business can use or trade. Choice D is incorrect because NPDES refers to water pollution, not air pollution. [p 958]
21. A    A is correct because the Clean Air Act Amendments of 1990 allow the trading of pollution credits. Choices B, C, and D are incorrect because they are legislative acts for the protection of the environment that do not address the trading of pollution credits. [p 968]
22. A    A is correct because a use fee is not part of the legislative scheme. Choices B, C, and D are incorrect because they are all requirements under the Clean Water Act. [p 960]
23 B    B is correct because national primary drinking standards are regulated by the Safe Drinking Water Act, not the Clean Water Act. Choices A, C, and D are not correct because they are all areas regulated by the Clean Water Act. [p 961]

24. D   Choice D created the Superfund, which requires the current operator to pay cleanup costs for past improper dumping. Choices A, B, and C do not pertain to the cleanup of hazardous waste sites. [p 965]

25. C   Choice C is empowered to declare a species either endangered or threatened. Choices A and B are required to designate critical habitats once a species is put on the endangered or threatened list, but the list is created by the secretary of the interior. Choice D does not exist. [p 966]

## Short Answer

26.   Food is adulterated if it consists in whole or in part of any filthy, putrid, or decomposed substance. Some quantity of contaminants are allowed in food as long as the amount of contaminants does not exceed action limits set by the FDA. [p 948]

27.   Federal Food, Drug, and Cosmetic Act (FDCA). [p 947]

28.   They are required to provide nutritional information on virtually all food. This includes the number of calories derived from fat, amount of dietary fiber, saturated fat, cholesterol, and a variety of other substances. [p 950]

29.   Answers will vary: 35 fly eggs per 8 ounces of golden raisins, two rodent hairs per pound of popcorn, 20 insects per 100 pounds of shelled peanuts, 20 maggots per 3 ½ ounces of canned mushrooms, 10 fly eggs per 3 ½ ounces of tomato juice. [p 949]

30.   Cosmetics must be labeled, ingredients in cosmetics must be disclosed, and cosmetics must contain warnings if they are carcinogenic. [p 952]

31.   Heart pacemakers, kidney dialysis machines, defibrillators, and surgical equipment. [p 952]

32.   There was no evidence that the genetically altered foods were unsafe, but foreign countries were prohibiting the importation of these foods into their countries. The United States had to sign the Biosafety Protocol and agree that all genetically engineered foods would be clearly labeled with the phrase "May contain living modified organisms." [p 953]

33.   The CPSC is empowered to adopt rules and regulations to interpret and enforce the CPSA, conduct research on the safety of consumer products, and collect data regarding injuries caused by consumer products. [p 954]

34.   It is advertising that contains misinformation or omits important information that is likely to mislead a "reasonable consumer" or makes an unsubstantiated claim. [p 955]

35.   That the federal government consider the adverse impact a federal government action would have on the environment before the action is implemented. [p 957]

36.   It is a region that does not meet federal air quality standards. [p 958]

37.   Thermal pollution involves heated water or material being discharged into waterways and upsetting the ecological balance and decreases the oxygen content. [p 961]

38.   Toxic substances are chemicals used for agricultural, industrial, and mining uses that cause injury to humans, birds, animals, fish, and vegetation. [p 964]

39.   Hazardous waste is solid waste that may cause or significantly contribute to an increase in mortality or serious illness, or pose a hazard to human health or the environment, if improperly managed. [p 964]

40.   The Clean Water Act. [p 963]

## Chapter 35

# EMPLOYMENT, WORKER PROTECTION, AND LABOR LAW

## Chapter Overview

Prior to the Industrial Revolution, employment was subject to the common law of contracts and agency law, giving employees and employers equal bargaining power. With industrialization came large corporate employers with much stronger bargaining power than the employees, and employees were subjected to unsafe working conditions, long hours and low pay. Federal and state laws were created to protect the rights of workers, with more legislation giving workers the right to form and join labor unions. Unions, by negotiation with employers, received better working conditions, higher wages, and greater benefits for their members. Labor unions and labor relations law are introduced in this chapter.

## Objectives

Upon completion of the exercises in this chapter, you should be able to:

1.  Describe how state workers' compensation laws function and the benefits that are available.
2.  Explain employer's obligation under OSHA to provide and maintain safe work conditions.
3.  Describe the minimum wage and overtime pay rules of the Fair Labor Standards Act.
4.  Discuss how a union is organized and the process of collective bargaining.
5.  Describe the right to strike and picket and the limitations placed on these rights.

## Practical Applications

You should be able to understand when conduct involved in a particular labor relationship is legal or illegal. You should be able to identify the general legal principle that applies to a dispute and understand the likely outcome. You should be able to recognize the situations where employee rights and protection are applicable and the specific laws that cover a dispute or loss of income. You should be able to identify the limits of protections and the requirements that must be met to gain protection under various statutes.

## Helpful Hints

Both state and federal governments and the courts have created a large body of statutory and case law that will dictate the proper conduct of the parties and the consequences of illegal activity. Examine each statute and case closely for the precise conduct that was either condoned or forbidden. By understanding what conduct triggers which rule of law, you will be more effective in your labor relationships. Both employee and employer benefit by a clear understanding of how the various employment protection statutes function. The requirements of some laws apply only to specific employers. Employees often have requirements of notice and cooperation to gain enforcement of their rights. Employers must understand and adhere to the requirements imposed by government regulation in the workplace or they subject themselves to the high costs of law suits and lost production in the workplace.

# Study Tips

## Workers' Compensation

These acts seek to compensate employees for injuries that occurred on the job regardless of fault.
- The amount of compensation payable to the employee is set by statute.

**Workers' Compensation Insurance.** Most states require Employers to have insurance from private insurance companies or state funds to cover workers' compensation claims.
- Some states allow employers to self-insure if they can demonstrate the ability to pay claims.

**Employment-Related Injury.** The injury must have arisen out of and in the course of employment.

**Exclusive Remedy.** Payment under the workers' compensation statute is the employee's exclusive remedy, meaning that an employee cannot sue their employee when they are injured on the job.
- Exception: An employer intentionally injures a worker, the worker can also sue the employer.

## Occupational Safety

The Occupational Safety and Health Act was enacted to promote safety in the workplace.
- It imposes recordkeeping and reporting requirements upon the employer.
- It requires that employers post notices informing employees of their rights under the Act.
- The enforcement arm is the Occupational Safety and Health Administration (OSHA).

**Specific Duty Standards.** OSHA standards address safety requirements for equipment, set maximum exposure levels for hazardous substances, regulate machinery location, and establish safety procedures.

**General Duty Standards.** The Act imposes a general duty to provide a work environment free from recognized hazards that are causing or are likely to cause death or serious physical harm to employees.
- OSHA has adopted regulations to enforce the safety standards created by the act.
- OSHA may inspect places of employment and cite the employer for violations.
- OSHA violations carry both civil and criminal penalties.

## Fair Labor Standards Act (FLSA)

The FSLA prohibits child labor and establishes minimum wage and overtime pay requirements.
- The United States Department of Labor is the enforcement arm for this Act.
- Managerial, administrative, and professional employees are exempt from wage and hour rules.

**Child Labor.** The FLSA forbids the use of oppressive child labor and makes it unlawful to ship goods produced by the use of oppressive child labor.
- Children under 14 cannot work, except as newspaper deliverers.
- Children 14 and 15 may work limited hours in nonhazardous jobs.
- Children 16 and 17 may work unlimited hours in nonhazardous jobs.
- Children working in agriculture and child actors and performers are exempt.

**Minimum Wage.** The FLSA institutes minimum wage requirements for workers.
- The minimum wage is set by Congress and can be changed.
- Employers are permitted to pay less to students and apprentices.

- Some states have set minimum wage laws at a higher rate.

**Overtime Pay.** The FLSA institutes overtime pay requirements for workers.
- An employer cannot require nonexempt employees to work more than 40 hours per week
  - Unless they are paid 1-1/2 time their regular pay for each hour of overtime.

## Other Worker Protection Laws

The federal government has enacted other statutes that regulate the employment relationship.

**Consolidated Omnibus Budget Reconciliation Act (COBRA).** Provides that employee or his beneficiaries must have the opportunity to maintain group health coverage upon dismissal or death.
- Government employees are covered by the Public Health Service Act.

**Family and Medical Leave Act.** The act guarantees workers unpaid time off for medical emergencies.
- Applies to employers with 50 or more employees.
- Covers time off for birth or care of child, serious health condition, and care for spouse, parent, or child with a serious health problem.
- Employee must be restored to their same or a similar position upon their return.

**Employee Retirement Income Security Act (ERISA).** ERISA is designed to prevent fraud and abuses associated with private pension funds.
- Requires that the pension plan be in writing and name a pension fund manager.
- Dictates how pension funds can be invested, sets time limits for when pension rights must vest

**Immigration Laws.** The Immigration Reform and Control Act and the Immigration Act make it unlawful for employers to hire illegal immigrants.
- Employer must examine documents to determine employee's right to work in the country
- Employer must maintain records for compliance.
- These Acts are administered by the U.S. Immigration and Customs Enforcement.

## Government Programs

The federal government has created programs that provide benefits to workers and their dependents.

**Unemployment Compensation.** Under the Federal Unemployment Tax Act (FUTA) and state laws, employers must pay unemployment taxes to compensate employees during periods of unemployment.
- Employee does not receive benefits if they are discharged for misconduct or quit without cause

**Social Security.** Under the Federal Insurance Contributions Act (FICA), employees and employers make matching contributions to the Social Security Fund.
- The funds are used to pay current recipients of Social Security.
- The Self-Employment Contributions Act requires self-employed individuals to contribute an amount equal to the combined employer and employee amount.

## Labor Law

Few laws protected workers from abuses in the 1880s and workers organized unions for bargaining strength. By the early 1900s employers were using violence to fight unions, and courts were on their side

- American Federation of Labor (AFL), formed in 1886 for skilled craft works and artisans.
- Congress of Industrial Organizaitons (CIO), formed in 1935 for semi- and un-skilled workers.
- In 1955, the AFL and CIO were combined into the AFL-CIO.
- Approximately 10 percent of private-sector employees belong to unions today

**Federal Labor Union Statutes.** Congress passed laws to protect workers and the right to organize unions in the early 1900s; other statutes were enacted in the 1930s to give workers rights and protections.
- Norris-LaGuardia Act was enacted in 1932 and made it legal for employees to organize.
- National Labor Relations Act (NLRA), or Wagner Act, was enacted in 1935 and established the right of employees to form, join, and participate in unions. It placed a duty on employers to bargain and deal in good faith with unions.
- Labor-Management Relations Act, or Taft-Hartley Act, was enacted in 1947 and expanded the activities that union were allowed to engage in, gave employers the right to speak out against the unions, and gave the President the right to enjoin a strike for up to 80 days if the strike would create a national emergency.
- Labor-Management Reporting and Disclosure Act, or Landrum-Griffin Act, was enacted in 1959 and regulates internal union affairs and establishes the rights of members.
  o Title I, labor's "bill of rights", was enacted in 1959 and gave each member equal rights and privileges to nominate candidates, vote, and participate in meetings.
- Railway Labor Act was enacted in 1926 and allows railroad and airline employees to organize and created a mechanism for the adjudication of grievances.

**National Labor Relations Board (NLRB).** The NLRA created the NLRB, which is the administrative body comprised of five members appointed by the president.
- It oversees union elections, prevents unfair labor practices, and enforces federal labor laws.

# Organizing a Union

Section 7 of the NLRA grants employees the right to form a union.
- The group that the union is seeking to represent, the appropriate bargaining unit, must be defined before it can petition for an election.
- Managers and professional employees may not belong to unions formed by employees whom they manage.

**Types of Union Elections.** If 30 percent of the employees in the bargaining unit are interested in joining or forming a union, the NLRB can petitioned to investigate and set an election date.
- A contested election is one that the employer contests and constitutes most elections.
  o The NLRB must supervise these elections
  o A simple majority wins the election.
- A consent election is one that the employer does not contest.
  o It may be held without NLRB supervision.
- A decertification election is one where employees no longer want union representation.
  o It must be supervised by the NLRB.

**Union Solicitation on Company Property.** If union solicitation is being conducted by employees, the employer may restrict activities to employees' free time.
- Activities may be limited to nonworking areas.
- Off duty employees may be barred from soliciting on company premises.
- Non-employees can be prohibited from soliciting anywhere on company property.

- Employers can dismiss employees who violate these rules.
- The inaccessibility exception applies where the location of the business and living quarters of employees place them beyond the reach of reasonable union efforts to communicate with them

**Illegal Interference with an Election.**  Section 8(a) of the NLRA makes it an unfair labor practice for the employer to interfere with, coerce, or restrain employees from their right to for and join unions.

- Section 8(b) of the NLRA prohibits unions from engaging in unfair labor practices that interfere with a union election.

**Collective Bargaining.**  This is the act of negotiation, done in good faith, between the union and the employer to obtain a collective bargaining agreement.

- Compulsory subjects, which must be negotiated, include wages, hours, and other terms and conditions of employment.
- Illegal subjects, which may not be negotiated, include closed shops and discrimination.
- Permissive subjects, why may be negotiated, include issues like the size and composition of the supervisory force, location of plants, and corporate reorganizations.

**Union Security Agreements.**  Elected unions may have a union security agreement to ensure its power.

- In a union shop, an employee must join the union within a certain time after being hired.
  - o Employees who do not join must be discharged by the employer.
  - o Union shops are legal.
- In an agency shop, employees do not have to become union members, but they do have to pay an agency fee to the union.

**State Right-to-Work Laws.**  States are free to enact laws that outlaw union and agency shops.  Today, there are 22 states that have enacted right-to-work laws.

## Strikes and Picketing

The NLRA allows union management to recommend that the union call a strike if a collective bargaining agreement cannot be reached.  A majority vote of the members must agree to the strike.

**Picketing.**  This usually involves the striking employees and union representatives walking in front of the employer's premises carrying signs announcing their strike.

- Picketing is lawful unless it involves violence, obstructs customers, prevents nonstriking employees from entering, or prevents pickups and deliveries.

**Secondary Boycott Picketing.**  This is union action by the union to bring pressure on the employer by picketing suppliers or customers.

- It is illegal if directed against the neutral employer instead of the struck employer's product.

**Illegal Strikes.**  Several types of strikes are illegal and are not protected by federal labor law.  Illegal strikers may be discharged by the employer with no rights to reinstatement.

- Violent strikes where employees cause substantial damage to property.
- Sit-down strikes where employees continue to occupy the employer's premises.
- Partial or intermittent strikes where employees strike some of the day or workweek and work the rest of the time.
- Wildcat strikes where individual members go on strike without proper authorization from the union, though these can become lawful if ratified by the union.

- Strikes during the 60-day cooling-off period where the strike begins during the mandatory cooling off period designed to give the employer and union time to negotiate a settlement.
- Strikes in violation of a no-strike clause.

**Crossover and Replacement Workers.** Individual members of a union do not have to honor a strike.
- Employees who choose not to strike or return to work after joining the strikers for a time are crossover workers.
- The employer may continue operations by using management and hiring replacement workers.

**Employer Lockout.** This occurs when an employer reasonably anticipates a strike by some employees and it chooses to prevent those employees from entering the premises.

**Plant Closing Act.** The Worker Adjustment and Retraining Notification (WARN) Act requires employers to give their employees 60 days' notice before engaging in certain plant closings or layoffs.
- A plant closing is a permanent or temporary shutdown of a single site that results in a loss of employment of 50 or more employees during any 30-day period.
- A mass layoff is a reduction of 33 percent of the employees or at least 50 employees during any 30-day period.
- Employers are exempted from notice if the closing or layoff is caused by unforeseeable business circumstances or the business was actively seeking capital or business that would have avoided or postponed the shutdown.

# Refresh Your Memory

The following exercises will help to test your memory regarding the principles given in this chapter. Read each question twice, then place your answer in the blank provided for each question. Review the chapter material for any questions you are unable to answer or remember.

1. The relationship between employers and employees changed dramatically when the United States became _____ in the late 1880s.

2. As a reaction to employment abuses, workers organized unions to gain _____ strength.

3. Approximately _____ percent of private-sector workers belong to labor unions.

4. In 1932, the _____ _____ Act created the right of workers to organize.

5. The NLRA, also known as the _____ Act, placed an affirmative duty on employers to bargain and deal in good faith.

6. To recover under workers' compensation, the workers' injuries must have been _____ related.

7. In the interest of promoting _____ in the workplace, Congress, in 1970, enacted the Occupational Safety and Health Act.

8. The Fair Labor Standards Act forbids the use of _____ _____ _____ and makes it unlawful to ship goods produced by businesses that use _____ _____ _____.

9. The FSLA establishes _____ wage and _____ pay requirement for workers.

10. COBRA provides that an employee of a private employer or the employee's _____ must be offered the opportunity to continue his or her group _____ insurance after the dismissal or death of the employee or the loss of coverage due to certain qualifying events.

11. Wages, hours, and other terms and conditions of employment are examples of _____ subject for collective bargaining.

12. A(n) _____ shop is an establishment where an employee must join a union within a certain number of days after being hired.

13. _____ is illegal if it is accompanied by violence or obstructions customers, nonstriking workers, or suppliers from entering the employer's premises.

14. Violent strikes and sit-down strikes are examples of _____ strikes.

15. A(n) _____ worker is an employee who does not honor a strike who either chooses not to strike or returns to work after joining strikers for a time.

# Critical Thought Exercise

Sid Frost worked as a merchandising supervisor for Global-Mart, Inc., a large discount store employing over 26,000 people. When Frost suffered his third stroke in April 1999, he took leave from work, which was covered by the Family and Medical Leave Act (FMLA) of 1993. The Vice-President of Personnel for Global-Mart approved the leave. Mike Allen, who had been hired only two months after Frost in 1984, temporarily filled Frost's position. When Frost returned to work, he discovered that Allen had been promoted to senior supervisor and given a $7,000 raise. The senior supervisor position is filled from the supervisor classification based upon seniority. Global-Mart refused to allow Frost to return to his position as a supervisor and demoted him to a senior salesman position that required travel away from home on a weekly basis. Six weeks later Global-Mart fired Frost because he was unable to keep up the schedule required by his position and because his expense account was not timely filed by month's end.

Frost sues Global-Mart for violation of the FMLA based upon Global-Mart's failure to promote him to senior supervisor or return him to his prior position. Did Global-Mart violate the FMLA?

*Please compose your answer on a separate sheet of paper or on your computer.*

# Practice Quiz

## True/False

1. ___ Accidents that occur at a company cafeteria or while on a business lunch for an employer are not covered by workers' compensation.

2. ___ If an employer intentionally injures a worker during work hours, the employee's remedy is not limited to workers' compensation benefits.

3. ___ Federal, State and local governments do not have to comply with the Occupational Safety and Health Act.

4. \_\_\_ OSHA is empowered to enter a business of the employer to inspect for health hazards and safety violations.

5. \_\_\_ Under the Fair Labor Standards Act, children ages 14 and 15 may work unlimited hours but only in hazardous jobs.

6. \_\_\_ If an employee works 50 hours one week he or she is entitled to any overtime pay because they worked over 40 hours per week.

7. \_\_\_ The Family Medical Leave Act applies to private employers with 50 or more employees, as well as to federal, state, and local governments.

8. \_\_\_ Employees covered by the Family and Medical Leave Act are entitled receive up to 16 weeks of unpaid leave during any 12-month period.

9. \_\_\_ Only semiskilled and unskilled worker were permitted to join the American Federation of Labor (AFL).

10. \_\_\_ During the Great Depression of the 1930s, several federal statutes were enacted giving workers certain rights and protections.

11. \_\_\_ The right to bargain collectively with employers was granted by the Norris-LaGuardia Act.

12. \_\_\_ The NLRB oversees union elections.

13. \_\_\_ If at least 30 percent of the employees in the bargaining unit are interested in forming a union, the NLRB can be petitioned to investigate and set an election date.

14. \_\_\_ Illegal strikers may not be discharged by the employer with no rights to reinstatement.

15. \_\_\_ Unions may not adopt internal rules to regulate the union.

## Multiple Choice

16. OSHA standards establish rules pertaining to
    a. minimum wage.
    b. amounts of compensation after a work-related injury.
    c. maximum levels for exposure to hazardous chemicals.
    d. age requirements for use of child labor.

17. Employers who establish pension plans for their employees are subject to the recordkeeping, disclosure, and other requirements of
    a. COBRA.
    b. ERISA.
    c. FUTA.
    d. FICA.

18. The Family and Medical Leave Act requires an eligible employee who takes leave to on their return
    a. accept whatever position is open at the tine.
    b. accept a reduction in pay if someone else has been promoted.
    c. forfeit benefits equal to the value of the leave.
    d. be restored to either the same or an equivalent position with equivalent employment benefits and pay.

19. Social Security benefits include
    a. survivors' benefits to family members of deceased workers.
    b. the right to continue group health insurance provided by the employer.
    c. the right to take time off for the birth of a child.
    d. payments for a period of time when the employee is temporarily unemployed.

20. The act that placed a duty on employers to bargain and deal in good faith with unions was the
    a. Norris-LaGuardia Act.
    b. National Labor Relations Act.
    c. The Railway Labor Act.
    d. none of the Above.

21. The Landrum-Griffin Act includes a rule that
    a. gives employees the right to form unions.
    b. allows an injunction to be issued to stop unfair labor practices.
    c. makes union officials accountable for union funds and property.
    d. requires a 60-day notice for certain plant closures.

22. The administrative agency created to enforce the Wagner Act (NLRA) is the
    a. NLRB.
    b. AFL.
    c. CIO.
    d. Labor Board of Conciliation and Arbitration.

23. The act of negotiating by a union with an employer is called
    a. collective bargaining.
    b. picketing.
    c. a wildcat action.
    d. a secondary boycott.

24. A wildcat strike takes place when
    a. striking employees continue to occupy the premises of the employer.
    b. individual union members go out on strike without proper authorization from the union.
    c. employees strike part of the day and work part of the day.
    d. striking employees cause substantial damage to the property of the employer.

25. Picketing is lawful unless
    a. it is accompanied by violence.
    b. obstructs customers from entering the employer's place of business or prevents nonstriking employees from entering the premises.
    c. prevents pickups and deliveries at the employer's of business.
    d. all of the above.

## Short Answer

26. Why were workers' compensation laws created?

27. Describe four examples of specific duty standards created by OSHA.

28. What can OSHA do upon finding a safety violation after an inspection of a place of employment?

29. According to the Fair Labor Standards Act, what type or work can a child under 14 accept?

30. If children cannot work in hazardous jobs, who determines what job is hazardous?

31. To whom may an employer pay less than minimum wage?

32. What is the prerequisite for an employee to be covered by the Family and Medical Leave Act?

33. Under the Immigration Reform and Control Act of 1986, an employer must attest to what facts before an employee may be hired?

34. How much must a self-employed person contribute to Social Security?

35. Which Act helped to implement a program whereby employers are now required to pay unemployment taxes?

36. What does the Consolidated Omnibus Budget Reconciliation Act (COBRA) provide?

37. Which industries does the Railway Labor Act cover?

38. What is the rule for union solicitation by nonemployee union representatives on company property?

39. What is the difference between a union shop and an agency shop?

_____

_____

40. What is a strike?

_____

## Answers To Refresh Your Memory

1. industrialized [p 979]
2. bargaining [p 992]
3. 10 [p 992]
4. Norris-LaGuardia [p 992]
5. Wagner [p 992]
6. employment [p 980]
7. safety [p 984]
8. oppressive child labor, oppressive child labor [p 986]
9. minimum, overtime [p 986]
10. beneficiaries, health [p 988]
11. compulsory [p 996]
12. union [p 996]
13. Picketing [p 998]
14. illegal [p 1000]
15. crossover [p 1000]

## Critical Thought Exercise Model Answer

The FMLA guarantees workers unpaid time off work for medical emergencies. There is little doubt that a stroke is a medical emergency and Global-Mart had approved the leave for Frost. The FMLA will apply to Global-Mart because it has over 50 employees. Under the FMLA, the employer must guarantee employment in the same position or a comparable position when the employee returns to work. Employers who violate the FMLA may be held liable for damages to compensate employees for unpaid wages, lost benefits, denied compensation and actual monetary losses up to an amount equivalent to the employee's wages for twelve weeks. The employer may also be required to grant a promotion that has been denied. The restored employee is not entitled to the accrual of seniority during the leave period, however. Frost was not returned to his former position when he returned. He was forced to take a demotion, which required travel. Global-Mart violated the FMLA by demoting Frost. The failure to promote Frost may not be a violation because the promotion was based upon seniority and Frost had less seniority than Allen at the time of the promotion. Therefore, Global-Mart should be ordered to return Frost to his prior supervisor position but will not be required to promote him to senior supervisor. Global-Mart will also be required to pay damages for lost wages during the time Frost was not working due to his firing.

## Answers to Practice Quiz

## True/False

1. False    These activities are considered to have been done in the course of his or her employment and would be entitled to workers' compensation coverage. [p 980]
2. True    The employee can collect workers' compensation benefits *and* sue the employer. [p 980]
3. . True    The act applies only to private employers. [p 984]
4. True    OSHA is empowered to inspect places of employment for health hazards and safety violations. [p 985]
5. False    Children ages 14 and 15 may work limited hours in nonhazardous jobs that are approved by the Department of Labor. [p 986]
6. True    The employee is entitled to overtime pay for each hour worked in excess of 40 hours in a week. Each week is treated separately. [p 986]
7. True    Unlike other employee statutes discussed in this chapter, the Family and Medical Leave Act applies to all government employees. [p 989]
8. False    This 12 weeks of leave can be used for the birth of a child, family illness, or several other reasons set forth in the statute. [p 989]
9. False    Only skilled craft workers were permitted to join the AFL. [p 992]
10. True    During the Great Depression of the 1930s, several federal statutes were enacted giving workers certain rights and protections. [p 992]
11. False    This right was created by the National Labor Relations Act. [p 992]
12. True    The National Labor Relations Act created the NLRB and gave it the responsibility of overseeing all union elections. [p 992]
13. True    Only 30% approval within the bargaining unit is needed to petition for an election. [p 993]
14. False    Illegal strikers are not protected by federal labor laws. [p 1000]
15. False    Unions may adopt internal union rules to regulate the operation of the union. [p 993]

## Multiple Choice

16. C    C is correct because it states one type of safety standard set by OSHA. A is incorrect because minimum wage is set by the Fair Labor Standards Act. B is incorrect because workers' compensation is set by state workers' compensation acts. D is incorrect because child labor laws are set forth in the Fair Labor Standards Act. [p 984]
17. B    B is correct because the Employee Retirement Income Security Act controls all aspects of private pensions created by employers for their employees. A is incorrect because COBRA deals with maintaining group health insurance. C is incorrect because FUTA deals with unemployment compensation. D is incorrect because FICA deals with contributions to Social Security. [p 989]
18. D    D is correct be cause it is the full statement of what is required when an employee returns from leave under the FMLA. Choice A is incorrect because an employee must be returned to the same or an equivalent position. Answer B is not correct because the employee must be returned to the same level of pay after a leave. C is incorrect because there can be no loss of benefits to an employee who takes a leave under the FMLA. [p 989]
19. A    Answer A is correct because survivor's rights are part of the compensation plan built into Social Security to help the family of a deceased worker. B is incorrect because continued group health insurance is covered by COBRA, not Social Security. Answer C is incorrect because leave for the birth of a child is covered by the Family and Medical Leave Act. D is incorrect because unemployment compensation is covered by FUTA. [p 990-991]
20. B    Choice B is correct as the NLRA was the act that created the duty of good faith bargaining. Choices A, C, and D are labor acts, but they did not address the duty to bargain and deal in good faith. [p 992]

21. C  C is one of the duties imposed by the Landrum-Griffin Act. Choice A is incorrect because that right is contained in the NLRA. Choice B is incorrect because that rule is also contained in the NRLA. Choice D is incorrect because that rule is contained in the Plant Closing Act. [p 992]

22. A  A is correct because the NLRB is the administrative body appointed by the president to enforce the NRLA. Choices B and C are incorrect because they are labor unions. Choice D is incorrect because it is a Mexican labor agency. [p 992]

23. A  A is correct because the act of negotiating a contract or collective bargaining agreement is also called collective bargaining. Choices B, C, and D are incorrect because they all relate to strikes and picketing as part of a strike. [p 996]

24. B  Answer B correctly defines a wildcat strike. Choice A is incorrect because it defines a sit-down strike. Choice C is incorrect because it defines a partial strike. Choice D is incorrect because it defines a violent strike. [p 1000]

25. D  D is correct because choices A, B, and C all state correct examples of illegal picketing. [p 998]

## Short Answer

26. Workers' compensation laws were created because workers and their families were being left uncompensated after the employee was injured or killed on the job. The employee had to sue his employer for negligence and if the employer successfully defended against the suit, the employee received nothing. Workers' compensation gives compensation without regard to fault. [p 979]

27. Safety requirements for equipment, such as guards on drills and saws. Setting the maximum exposure levels to hazardous chemicals. Regulate the location of machinery and clearance around machinery. Establish safety procedures. [p 984]

28. If a violation is found, OSHA can issue a written citation that requires the employer to abate or correct the situation. [p 985]

29. Children under 14 cannot work except as newspaper deliverers. [p 986]

30. The Department of Labor determines which occupations are hazardous (e.g., mining, roofing, working with explosives, working with caustic chemicals). [p 986]

31. The Department of Labor permits employers to pay less than the minimum wage to students and apprentices. [p 986]

32. To be covered, the employee must have worked for the employer for at least one year and have performed more than 1,250 hours of service during the previous 12-month period. [p 989]

33. The employer must fill out INS Form I-9, which attests that the employer has inspected documents of the employee and has determined that he or she is either a U.S. citizen or is otherwise qualified to work in the country. [p 989]

34. Under the Self-Employment Contribution Act the self-employed individual must contribute an amount to Social Security that is equal to the combined amount contributed by the employer and employee under FICA. [p 991]

35. Federal Unemployment Tax Act (FUTA) [p 990]

36. It provides that an employer must offer an employee or the employee's beneficiaries the opportunity to continue health benefits, upon payment of premium, after termination of employment due to dismissal or death. [p 988]

37. The railroads and airlines. [p 992]

38. An employer may prohibit solicitation on company property unless the employees cannot otherwise be contacted. [p 994]

39. A union shop is where an employee must join a union within a certain number of days after being hired. An agency shop is where employees do not have to join the union but must pay an agency fee equal to union dues. [p 996-997]

40. A strike is a cessation of work by union members in order to obtain economic benefits, to correct an unfair labor practice, or to preserve their work. [p 1004]

# Chapter 36

# EQUAL OPPORTUNITY IN EMPLOYMENT

## Chapter Overview

Employees were subject to termination at any time for any reason and employers were free to hire and promote any one they chose under the common law. This tended to foster employment barriers to minority classes and created a difficult environment for employees. Congress created comprehensive federal laws, beginning in the 1960's, that guaranteed equal employment opportunity and worked to overcome employment discrimination. This chapter introduces equal opportunity in employment laws.

## Objectives

Upon completion of the exercises in this chapter, you should be able to:

1. Describe the protection provided by Title VII of the Civil Rights Act of 1964.
2. Identify examples of discrimination based upon race, color, and national origin.
3. Describe conduct that creates sex discrimination, including sexual harassment.
4. Discuss the important protections contained in the Equal Pay Act of 1963.
5. Explain the protections provided by the Age Discrimination in employment Act.
6. Describe the scope and protections of the Americans with Disabilities Act.

## Practical Application

Antidiscrimination laws set forth mandates for employers and protections for employees that alter the course of conduct of people in the business environment. You should be able to recognize the situations where discrimination is unlawful and instances where a defense to discrimination may apply. This will allow you to make decisions that stay within the requirements set forth by the federal laws.

## Helpful Hints

It is beneficial to know the basic definition or content of each antidiscrimination law and understand the examples of how they are applied. You should focus on the type of conduct involved in a real-life or hypothetical situation to determine which area of law is applicable and what actions must be taken to correct the action.

## Study Tips

### Title VII of the Civil Rights Act of 1964

Title VII of the Civil Rights of 1964, otherwise known as the Fair Employment Practices Act, was meant to eliminate job discrimination based upon a person's race, color, religion, sex, or national origin.

**Scope of Coverage of Title VII.**
- Title VII applies to:
  - employers with 15 or more employees
  - employment agencies
  - labor unions with 15 or more employees
  - state and local governments
  - most federal employees
- Title VII does not apply to Indian tribes or tax-exempt private clubs
- Title VII prohibits discrimination in
  - Hiring
  - Promotion or demotion
  - Compensation and fringe benefits
  - Job training opportunities
  - Referrals
  - Dismissal
  - Terms of employment
  - Work rules
- Title VII addresses two types of discrimination: disparate treatment and disparate impact.

*Disparate-Treatment Discrimination.* This occurs when an employer treats a specific individual less favorably than others because of that person's race, color, religion, sex, or national origin.

*Disparate-Impact Discrimination.* This occurs when an employer discriminates against an entire protected class, with a causal link between the challenged practice and the statistical imbalance.

*Intentional Discrimination.* In these cases, the aggrieved party can recover compensatory damages, as well as punitive damages when there is a showing of malice or reckless indifference to protected rights.

**Equal Employment Opportunity Commission (EEOC).** The Equal Employment Opportunity Commission (EEOC) is appointed by the President and is responsible for enforcing the provisions of all the federal laws that address areas of discrimination in the workplace.
- The EEOC is empowered to investigate, issue opinions and directives to offending employers, bring suit against the violator, and seek injunctive relief to stop the conduct that violated a law.
- An employee can file suit directly against the employer if the EEOC issues a right to sue letter.

**Remedies for Violations of Title VII.** A successful plaintiff can recover back pay and reasonable attorneys' fees, and may be awarded equitable remedies.
- Court may order reinstatement, with seniority rights, or issue injunctions to induce compliance.

**Race, Color, and National Origin Discrimination.** Title VII prohibits employment discrimination on:
- Race, which refers to broad categories like African American, Caucasian, Asian, etc.
- Color, which refers to the color of a person's skin.
- National origin, which refers to the country of ancestry or cultural characteristics.

**Sex Discrimination.** Discrimination based on sex is prohibited and applied equally to males and females. The Pregnancy Discrimination Act forbids bias against pregnancy, birth, or allied medical conditions.

**Sexual Harassment.** Requesting that an employee have sex with the employer to get hired, receive a promotion, or prevent discharge, are all forms of sexual harassment prohibited by Title VII.
- Lewd remarks, touching, intimidation, posting pinups, and other verbal or physical conduct of a sexual nature that occurs on the job are sexual harassment and violate Title VII.

**Same Sex Discrimination.** The 1998 case of *Omcale v. Sundowner Offshore Services, Incorporated*, held that same-sex discrimination and harassment violated Title VII.

**Employer's Defense to a Charge of Sexual Harassment.** An employer may raise an affirmative defense against liability or damages for sexual harassment by proving that:
- The employer exercised reasonable care to prevent and correct promptly any sexually-harassing behavior, and
- The plaintiff employee unreasonably failed to take advantage of any preventive or corrective opportunities by the employer or to otherwise avoid harm.

**Religious Discrimination.** Under Title VII, the employer has a duty to reasonably accommodate the religious observances, practices, or beliefs of employees if it does not cause undue hardship to employer.

**Defenses to a Title VII Action.** Title VII and pertinent case law recognize several defenses to a charge of discrimination.

*Merit.* Employers can select or promote employees based on merit.
- A promotion can lawfully be based upon experience, skill, education, and ability tests.

*Seniority.* An employer may maintain a seniority system that rewards long-term employees.
- The system is lawful unless persons in a position of seniority achieved their position through intentional discrimination in the past.

*Bona Fide Occupational Qualification.* Employment discrimination based on a protect class (such as sex, but other than race or color), is lawful if it is job related and a business necessity.

## Civil Rights Act of 1866

Section 1981 of this act gives all persons equal contract rights, and prohibits racial discrimination and discrimination based upon national origin.
- Private plaintiff can bring action without going through technical requirements of Title VII, and
- There is no limitation period on the recovery of back pay (claimant can only go back two years under Title VII) and no cap on the recovery of compensatory or punitive damages.

## Equal Pay Act

The Equal Pay Act of 1963 protects both sexes from pay discrimination based on sex.
- The act prohibits disparity in pay for jobs that require equal skill, equal effort, equal responsibility, or similar working conditions.
  - o If two jobs are determined to be equal and similar, an employer cannot pay disparate wages to members of different sexes.

**Criteria That Justify a Differential in Wages.** Disparate pay is allowed if based upon seniority, merit, quantity or quality of product (commission), or one based on a factor other than sex (shift differential),

## Age Discrimination in Employment Act (ADEA)

The Age Discrimination in Employment Act of 1967 prohibits age discrimination in all employment decisions, including hiring, promotions, compensation, and other terms and conditions of employment.
- The Older Worker Benefit Protection Act prohibits age discrimination for employee benefits.

**Protected Age Categories.** Originally, the ADEA protected persons between the ages of 40 and 65. It was amended to protect persons up to age 70, and further amended to protect all employees over age 40.

## Americans With Disabilities Act (ADA)

The Americans with Disabilities Act obligates employers and providers of public transportation, telecommunications, and public accommodations to accommodate individuals with disabilities.
- Title I prohibits employment discrimination against qualified individuals with disabilities in job application procedures, hiring, compensation, training, promotion, and termination.
- Title I requires an employer to make reasonable accommodations to individuals with disabilities that do not cause hardship to the employer.

**Qualified Individual with a Disability.** Such an individual is a person who, with or without reasonable accommodation, can perform the essential functions of the job that person desires or holds.
- A disabled person is one who has a physical or mental impairment that substantially limits one or more major life activities, has a record of an impairment, or is seen as having an impairment.

**Forbidden Conduct.** Employers may not inquire into the existence, nature, or severity of a disability during the application process.

**Procedure and Remedies.** An aggrieved individual must file a charge with the EEOC, which can take action against the employer or allow the individual to sue privately.
- Relief: injunction, hiring or reinstatement, attorneys' fees, compensatory and punitive damages.

## Affirmative Action

This is a policy that provides that certain job preferences will be given to minority or other protected class applicants when an employer makes an employment decision.
- Affirmative action plans must be narrowly tailored to achieve some compelling interest.
- Affirmative action plans will not be upheld when they discriminate against a majority after past discriminatory practices have already been rectified.
- The courts will not allow employers to give a preference to a minority when another employee is far better qualified for a position.

**Reverse Discrimination.** Title VII protects members of majority classes from discrimination.
- Plans with preestablished numbers or percentage quotas of minority applicants are illegal.

## State and Local Government Antidiscrimination Laws

Many state and local governments have enacted laws to prevent employment discrimination.
- Classes protected by federal laws are included, as well as classes not under federal protection.

## United Nations Treaty to Protect the Rights of the Disabled

The United Nations Convention on Rights of Persons with Disabilities requires countries to keep disabled people from exploitation and abuse and to protect their rights in education, work, and healthcare.
- It advocates keeping the disabled in their communities rather than segregating them.

# Refresh Your Memory

The following exercises will help to test your memory regarding the principles given in this chapter. Read each question twice, then place your answer in the blank provided for each question. Review the chapter material for any questions you are unable to answer or remember.

1.  Title _____ of the _____ _____ _____ of 1964 was intended to eliminate job discrimination based on five protected classes.

2.  Title VII applies to employers with _____ or more employees.

3.  _____ _____ discrimination occurs when an employer treats a specific individual less favorably because of their membership in a protected class.

4.  A(n) _____ _____ _____ letter is issued if the EEOC chooses not to file suit on behalf of a claimant.

5.  _____ _____ refers to the country of a person's ancestors or cultural characteristics.

6.  The Pregnancy Discrimination Act forbids employment discrimination because of pregnancy, _____, or related _____ conditions.

7.  Refusing to hire someone unless they have sex with the manager is _____ _____.

8.  The frequency and severity of sexual harassment are two factors considered in determining whether the employee is being subjected to a(n) _____ _____ _____.

9.  Under Title VII, an employer is under a duty to _____ _____ the religious observances, practices, or beliefs of its employees.

10. Disparate impact discrimination is often proven through _____ data about the employer's employment practices.

11. If a male applicant is not hired by an airline as a flight attendant because "women are more compassionate towards passengers," he is a victim of _____ _____.

12. Hanging a provocative male Chippendale's calendar in your office may be _____ _____.

13. Failing to accommodate an employee and forcing him or her to work on their Sabbath when it is not necessary is a form of _____ _____.

14. Seniority systems are lawful as long as they are not the result of _____ _____.

15. If two jobs are determined to be equal and _____, an employer cannot pay _____ wages to members of different sexes.

# Critical Thought Exercise

Carol Jones was employed with Richmond Components, Inc. (RCI), an electrical engineering and manufacturing company that supplied parts and guidance system development for the United States Air

Force. Jones was a public relations and communications manager for RCI at their facility located on Davis Air Force Base for over nine years. Of the 135 employees at the RCI facility at Davis AFB, only 9 women were in professional positions. Employees in the office where Jones worked used e-mail as the major form of communication between employees. Jones was sent sexually explicit material via e-mail, including pictures that had been downloaded from the Internet. Two male engineers in her work area used semi-nude swimsuit pictures as the screensaver on their computer. Pictures of nude women from magazines were cut out and put in her mailbox with notes, such as, "Will you pose like this for us?" When Jones requested that information for press releases be given to her by a stated deadline, she was told to, "Go have sex and chill out," along with other sexually demeaning comments about her anatomy. When Jones complained to the vice-president in charge of personnel, she was told that she worked in a high-stress 'boys' club" and she had better learn to accept the "give-and-take" environment at RCI. Jones quit her job and filed an action under Title VII. Will she prevail?

*Please compose your answer on a separate sheet of paper or on your computer.*

# Practice Quiz

## True/False

1. ___ The EEOC is not empowered to bring suit to enforce Title VII of the Civil Rights Act of 1964.

2. ___ Discrimination based on race, color, sex, national origin and religion are covered by Title VII.

3. ___ The requirements of Title VII also apply to state and local governments and their agencies.

4. ___ In an action for disparate treatment discrimination, the complainant need not prove that he or she applied for and was qualified for the employment position.

5. ___ When bringing an action under Title VII, it is not necessary for a private person to first file a complaint with the EEOC.

6. ___ Under title VII, race is not referred to in broad categories such as Black, Caucasian, Asian, and Native American.

7. ___ Conduct need not seriously affect the victim's psychological well-being to be actionable as abusive work environment harassment.

8. ___ When asserting an affirmative defense to sexual harassment, the employer need not prove that employees were informed of the employer's anti-harassment policy and the complaint procedure put in place by the employer.

9. ___ Many religious discrimination cases involve a conflict between an employer's work rule and an employee's religious beliefs.

10. ___ An employer has to accommodate an employee's request to have Saturday off from work for religious services even if the employer has no other employee that can work on that day.

11. ___ To be legal, a bona fide occupational requirement must be job related, and a business necessity.

12. ___ If an employer violated the Equal Pay Act, he must decrease the wages of the discriminated-against employee to eliminate the unlawful disparity of wages.

13. ___ Under the Equal Pay Act, an employer may not pay disparate wages to members of different sexes if the difference is based on a seniority system.

14. ___ Under the Equal Pay Act, an employer may not pay disparate wages to members of different sexes if one employee works the night shift for which higher wages are paid.

15. ___ Under the ADA, an employer may not inquire about the applicant's ability to perform job-related functions.

## Multiple Choice

16. The enforcement of federal antidiscrimination laws is the responsibility of the
    a. OWBPA.
    b. EEOC.
    c. ADEA.
    d. ADA.

17. The definition of what constitutes an "unlawful employment practice" was amended to Title VII by
    a. the Equal Employment Opportunities Act of 1972.
    b. a decision of the United States Supreme Court.
    c. the Americans with Disabilities Act.
    d. the Pregnancy Discrimination Act in 1978.

18. Title VII applies to employers with
    a. 8 or more employees.
    b. 12 or more employees.
    c. 15 or more employees.
    d. 33 or more employees.

19. Title VII prohibits discrimination in
    a. hiring.
    b. promotion or demotion.
    c. payment of compensation.
    d. all of the above.

20. To bring an action under Title VII, a private complainant must first file a complaint
    a. in federal district court.
    b. in the trial court in the state where they reside.
    c. with the EEOC.
    d. with the Commerce Department.

21. What do employers adopt to provide certain job preferences be given to minority racial and ethnic groups, females, and other protected-classes when an employer makes an employment decision?
    a. an international antidiscrimination law.
    b. employment quotas based on a specified number or percentage of minority applicants or employees
    c. affirmative action plans
    d. none of the above.

22. Which of the following are forbidden under Title I of the ADA?
    a. preemployment medical exams
    b. inquiring about the existence, nature and severity of a disability
    c. conditioning the job offer on passage of a medical exam only as to one entering employee
    d. all of the above

23. Which of the following is not a protected age category under the ADEA?
    a. persons under age 40
    b. persons over age 40
    c. persons over age 50
    d. persons over age 60

24. Which of the following remedies may a court award against an employer for violations of Title VII?
    a. punitive damages
    b. compensatory damages
    c. fictional seniority
    d. All of the above

25. Disparate-impact discrimination happens when
    a. an employer treats a specific individual less favorably than others based on that person's race, national origin, sex, religion or color.
    b. the EEOC issues a right to sue letter.
    c. an employer adopts a work rule that is neutral on its face but is shown to cause an adverse impact.
    d. when an employer adopts a work rule that is related to performance.

## Short Answer

26. List the five protected classes under Title VII.

    _____

27. Name three employment decisions that are subject to Title VII.

    _____

28. What is disparate-treatment discrimination?

    _____

29. What is disparate-impact discrimination?

    _____

30. What federal agency is responsible for enforcing most federal antidiscrimination laws?

    _____

31. What two things must happen before a claimant can sue their employer for a Title VII violation?

    _____

32. Which Act amended Title VII to forbid employment discrimination because of pregnancy, childbirth, or related medical conditions?

    _____

33. What duty does an employer have in regards to an employee's religious beliefs?

    _____

34. What are the three defenses that may be raised by an employer when faced with a Title VII suit?

    _____

35. What are the requirements for a BFOQ to be legal?

    _____

36. What does the Equal Pay Act prohibit?

    _____

37. What criteria justify a differential in wages?

    _____

38. Which Act amended the ADEA to prohibit age discrimination with regard to employee benefits?

    _____

39. On whom does the Americans with Disabilities Act impose obligations?

    _____

40. What is reverse discrimination?

    _____

## Answers To Refresh Your Memory

1. VII, Civil Rights Act [p 1011]
2. 15 [p 1012]
3. Disparate treatment [p 1012]
4. right to sue [p 1012]
5. National origin [p 1014]
6. childbirth, medical [p 1016]
7. sexual harassment [p 1017]
8. hostile work environment [p 1017]
9. reasonably accommodate [p 1021]
10. statistical [p 1012]
11. sex discrimination [p 1016]
12. sexual harassment [p 1017]
13. religious discrimination [p 1021]
14. intentional discrimination [p 1022]
15. similar, disparate [p 1024]

## Critical Thought Exercise Model Answer

Title VII applies to employers with 15 or more employees. With 135 employees at this facility, RCI will be covered by Title VII. Title VII prohibits harassment based on gender in the workplace. Sexual harassment may be based on lewd remarks, touching, intimidation, posting of sexually explicit pictures, and other unwanted verbal or physical conduct that is sexual in nature. Jones will argue that the activities of her co-workers have created a hostile work environment. To determine if the environment at RCI is hostile, a court will look at all the circumstances. These will include the frequency of the biased conduct;

its severity; whether it is physically threatening or humiliating, or a mere offensive utterance, and whether it unreasonably interferes with an employee's work performance.

The conduct of the male employees at RCI has created a hostile work environment. The acts are frequent and quite severe. Pictures are deliberately put in Jones' mailbox with notes that ask her to pose nude for fellow employees. Jones is berated verbally with sexual statements when she tries to do her job and get information for press releases. She is subjected to the sexually explicit pictures on computers on a daily basis because they have been installed as screensavers. Finally, there was no effort by RCI to stop or correct the harassment. Jones was told to accept it and no action was taken against the offending employees. Jones should prevail on a claim brought under Title VII for sexual harassment.

# Answers To Practice Quiz

## True/False

1.  False    The EEOC is empowered to conduct investigations, interpret statutes, encourage conciliation between employers and employees, and bring suit to enforce the law. [p 1012]
2.  True     Title VII prohibits discrimination on sex, national origin, race, color and religion. [p 1011]
3.  True     Title VII applies to state and local governments and their agencies and to most federal government employment. [p 1012]
4.  False    Applying for the job and being qualified is one of the four requirements to prove this type of discrimination. [p 1012]
5.  False    A private person must first file a complaint with the EEOC. If the EEOC decides to not sue on behalf of the claimant, the private person may then sue on their own. [p 1012]
6.  True     Race refers to broad categories like Black, Caucasian, Asian, and Native American. [p 1014]
7.  True     There is no requirement that the victim suffer any psychological injury to bring an action for abusive work environment harassment. [p 1018]
8.  False    In addition to this, the court will consider whether the employer had an anti-harassment policy and whether the employer had a complaint mechanism in place. [p 1020]
9.  True     Employer may require an employee work on their religious Sabbath, raising issue of whether or not the employer can offer reasonable accommodation of the employee's beliefs. [p 1021]
10. False    The courts must consider such factors as the size of the employer, the importance of the employee's position, and the availability of alternative workers. [p 1021]
11. True     A BFOQ must be both job related and a business necessity. [p 1022]
12. False    The employer may have to increase the wages of the discriminated against employee and pay back wages and liquidated damages. [p 1025]
13. False    It is lawful to pay disparate wages to long-term employees as an incentive for them to maintain employment with the employer. [p 1025]
14. False    An employer can pay disparate wages to members of different sexes if the disparity is based upon any factor other than sex, such as shift differentials. [p 1025]
15. False    The employer cannot ask an applicant about the existence, nature, and severity of a disability, but he can inquire as to the ability of the applicant to perform the job. [p 1028-1029]

## Multiple Choice

16. B    B is correct because the EEOC is the federal agency that is charged with enforcing federal anti-discrimination laws. Choices A, C, and D are all laws enforced by the EEOC. [p 1012]
17. A    A is the act passed by Congress that amended Title VII. B is incorrect because the definition of unlawful employment practice was added by legislation, not by case decision. Choices C and D are incorrect because they define discrimination as it pertains to disabilities and pregnancy, but were not the source of the broad language enacted under the EEPA. [p 1011]

18. C  Answer C is correct because it states the threshold number of employees needed to invoke the protection of Title VII. Choices A, B, and D all state incorrect numbers that cannot be located anywhere in Title VII. [p 1012]

19. D  Choice D is correct because choices A, B, and C correctly state areas of employment decisions where discrimination is prohibited by Title VII. [p 1012]

20. C  The claimant must file a complaint with the EEOC first. Only after getting a right to sue letter can the private claimant file suit in state or federal court. Choices A and B are incorrect because the complaint process with the EEOC is a prerequisite to an individual filing suit in a trial court. Choice D is incorrect because the EEOC is part of the Department of Labor. [p 1012]

21. C  Choice C is correct, employers adopt affirmative action plans, as these plans can be voluntarily adopted by employers, so as to settle a discrimination action, or ordered by the court. Answer A is incorrect, as employers do not adopt international antidiscrimination law in order to provide certain job preferences. Answer B is incorrect, as this is unlawful. Answer D is incorrect based on the reasoning given above. [p 1031]

22. D  D is correct, as A, B, and C are forbidden under Title I of the ADA. [p 1028-1029]

23. A  Choice A is correct, as persons under age 40 are not a protected age category under the ADEA. Answers B, C, and D are incorrect, as they are protected age categories under ADEA. [p 1025]

24. D  D is correct because the court may award any of the remedies given in answers A, B, and C against an employer based on violations of Title VII. [p 1013]

25. C  C is correct, as it properly describes the situation whereby disparate-impact discrimination results. Answer A is incorrect, as this is an example of disparate treatment. Answer B is incorrect, as it does not make any sense. Answer D is incorrect, as there does not appear to be any discrimination involved and presumably a rule that is related to performance may be a bona fide occupational job qualification. [p 1012]

## Short Answer

26.  Race, color, religion, sex, national origin. [p 1011]

27.  Name three of the following: hiring, promotion, demotion, payment of salaries, wages, fringe benefits, job training and apprenticeships, or work rules. [p 1012]

28.  It occurs when an employer treats a specific individual less favorably than others because of that person's race, color, national origin, sex, or religion. [p 1012]

29.  It occurs when an employer discriminates against an entire protected class. [p 1012]

30.  Equal Employment Opportunity Commission [p 1012]

31.  (1) the complainant must file a complaint with the EEOC and (2) the EEOC must refuse to bring suit and issue a *right to sue letter*. [p 1012]

32.  The Pregnancy Discrimination Act of 1978. [p 1016]

33.  A duty to reasonably accommodate an employee's religious beliefs if doing so does not cause an undue hardship on the employer. [p 1021]

34.  Merit, seniority, and bonafide occupational qualification. [p 1021-1022]

35.  It must be both job related and a business necessity. [p 1022]

36.  It prohibits pay discrimination for the same job based on the sex of the employee performing the job. [p 1024]

37.  Seniority, merit, quantity or qualify of work, any factor other than sex. [p 1025]

38.  The Older Workers Benefit Protection Act [p 1025]

39.  Employers and providers of public transportation, telecommunications, and public accommodations. [p 1028]

40.  It is discrimination against a person who is a member of a group that is usually thought of as a majority. [p 1032]

## Chapter 37

# PERSONAL PROPERTY, BAILMENT, AND INSURANCE

## Chapter Overview

Since private ownership of property is so important, a broad body of law has developed in the U.S. to protect property rights of owners to use, sell, dispose of, control, and prevent others from trespassing on their rights. Insurance is a means for individuals and businesses to protect themselves form the risk of loss. This chapter explores the kinds of personal property, methods of acquiring ownership, property rights in lost, mislaid, or abandoned property, and bailments. It also explores the formation of insurance contracts, types of insurance, and defenses to liability for insurance companies.

## Objectives

Upon completion of the exercises in this chapter, you should be able to:

1. Define personal property and discuss the methods for acquiring ownership in personal property.
2. Apply the rules relating to lost, mislaid, and abandoned property.
3. Discuss the elements of a bailment and the bailees liability for lost, damaged, or destroyed property.
4. Define an insurable interest and an insurance contract.
5. Identify the types of life, health, disability, and business insurance.

## Practical Application

Businesses are constantly transferring ownership of personal property or creating personal property for sale. Temporary use of property, whether by borrowing or renting, is a common commercial practice. Knowledge of the rights and duties relating to ownership and bailment of personal property helps anyone to make informed and reasoned choices when deciding how to deal with a personal property issue. The issue of insuring a property interest against loss is an important part of property ownership or possession, making an understanding of the rights and duties related to insurance very important.

## Helpful Hints

Once it is determined that something is personal property, it is wise to focus on the treatment of the property to determine who has rights in it and what duties may have arisen in regards to the property. The circumstances under which possession of property is accomplished from person to person or business to business will determine who may ultimately be responsible for damage to or loss of the property. The law differentiates the rights of people depending upon how they came into possession of the property and the circumstances surrounding the acquisition of possession. As you study this material, look at the status of the property as it changes possession. This will guide you in applying the correct law to solve a personal property issue and answer questions regarding insurable interests in property.

# Study Tips

## Personal Property

There are two kinds of property, real property and personal property. Real property is land and that which is permanently attached to the land. Personal property is everything that is not real property and can be acquired or transferred with little formality. Real property can become personal property if it is removed from the land.

- Personal property permanently attached to land or buildings is a fixture.
- Tangible property is property which is physically defined, like goods or animals.
- Intangible property represents rights that are not in physical form, like copyrights.

**Possession or Capture**. Unowned property can be acquired by taking possession or capturing it.

**Purchase**. The most common way to obtain property is to purchase it.

**Production**. Production is another common method for acquiring property.

- A manufacturer who turns raw materials into a product acquires ownership of the product.

**Gift.** A gift is a voluntary transfer of property without consideration. The person making the gift is the donor and the person receiving the gift is the donee. The three elements of a valid gift are:

- Donative intent. For a gift to be effective, the donor must have intended to make a gift.
- Delivery. Delivery must occur for there to be a valid gift. Delivery can either be physical or constructive (giving title documents to a car).
- Acceptance. This is usually not a problem unless the gift is refused.

*Gifts Inter Vivos and Gift Causa Mortis*. Gifts *inter vivos* are made during a person's lifetime, while a gift *causa mortis* is made in contemplation of death.

- Gifts causa mortis can be revoked up until the time of death and take precedence over a prior conflicting will.

*Uniform Gifts to Minor Act*. This act allow adults to make irrevocable gifts to minors.

- The custodian of the gift has broad discretionary powers to invest the money or securities for the benefit of the minor.

**Will or Inheritance**. If a person who dies has a valid will, the property is distributed to the beneficiaries, pursuant to the provisions of the will.

- If there is no will, the property passes to the heirs according to the relevant state statute.

**Accession**. Accession occurs when the value of personal property increases because it is added to or improved by natural or manufactured means.

- Wrongful improvement, the owner does not have to pay the improver.
- Mistaken improvement that can be removed, the improver must remove it and pay damages.
- Mistaken improvement that cannot be removed, the owner does not have to pay improver.

**Confusion**. Confusion occurs if two or more persons commingle fungible goods.

- The owners share ownership in the commingled goods to the amount of the goods contributed.
- Wrongful commingling, innocent party acquires title.

**Divorce.** Parties obtain property rights in the property of the marital estate.

# Mislaid, Lost, and Abandoned Property

People find property belonging to others and ownership rights to the property differ depending on whether the property was mislaid, lost, or abandoned.

**Mislaid Property.** Property is mislaid when the owner places it somewhere and forgets it. The owner will probably return when it is discovered that the property was mislaid.
- The owner of the property where it was found has the right to take possession.
- The owner of the premises becomes an involuntary bailee and must take reasonable care of the property until it is reclaimed.

**Lost Property.** Property is lost when the owner negligently, carelessly, or inadvertently leaves it somewhere.
- The finder of the property takes title against the world except the true owner.
- The finder must make efforts to return the property.

**Abandoned Property.** Property is classified as abandoned if the owner discards the property with the intent to relinquish his rights in it or he gives up all attempts to locate lost or misplaced property.
- The finder acquires title to the property, good against all, including the original owner.

**Estray Statute.** Most states have an estray statute, which dictates what the finder of lost or misplaced property must do to acquire title to the property.
- This usually includes turning the property over to the police, giving notice that the property was found, and waiting for a time period to pass.
- The finder can then claim ownership.

# Bailment

A bailment is a transaction where the owner transfers his or her personal property to another to be held, stored, delivered, or for some other purpose.
- Title to the property remains in the owner.
- The owner of the property is the bailor.
- The party who received the property is the bailee.

**Elements Necessary to Create a Bailment.** There are three essential elements to create a bailment:
- Personal Property. Only personal property can be bailed.
- Delivery of Possession.
  o The bailee has exclusive control over the personal property
  o The bailee must knowingly accept the personal property.
- Bailment Agreement. There must be a bailment agreement, either express or implied.

**Bailment for the Sole Benefit of the Bailor.** This is a gratuitous bailment that benefits only the bailor. The typical gratuitous bailment involves the bailee watching the bailor's property as a favor without compensation.
- The bailee only owes a duty of slight care.
- As long as the bailee is not grossly negligent, no liability will be incurred for loss or damage.

**Bailment for the Sole Benefit of the Bailee.** This is a gratuitous bailment for the sole benefit of the bailee. This is the typical "borrowing the lawnmower" situation.

- The bailee owes a duty of great care.
- The bailee is responsible for even the slightest negligence.

**Mutual Benefit Bailment.** This is made for the benefit of both the bailor and bailee.
- The bailee has a duty of reasonable care.
- The bailee is liable for any goods that are lost, damaged, or destroyed because of negligence.

**Duration and Termination of Bailments.** A bailment usually expires at a specific time or when a specific purpose is accomplished.
- A bailment for a fixed term terminates at the end of the term or by mutual consent of parties.
  - A party who wrongfully terminates the bailment is liable for damages.
- A bailment at will can be terminated at any time by either party.

**Warehouse Company.** These bailees contract for the storage of goods for compensation.
- They are held to a duty of reasonable case.
- They are not liable for the negligence of others that causes loss or damage.

*Warehouse Receipt.* This is a written document issued by a warehouseman, containing the terms of the bailment.
- The warehouse has a lien on the goods until all expenses incurred have been satisfied.

**Common Carrier.** These bailees offer transportation to the public. The delivery of goods to a common carrier creates a mutual benefit bailment.
- Common carriers are held to a duty of strict liability.
- If goods are lost, damaged, or stolen, the common carrier is liable even if it was not at fault.

*Bill of Lading.* This document of title is issued by a carrier when goods are received for shipment. Bills of lading are issued by common carriers, contract carriers and others engaged in the business of transporting goods.
- A carrier has a lien on the goods until all expenses incurred have been satisfied.

**Innkeeper.** An innkeeper owns a facility that provides lodging for compensation.
- Under common law, innkeepers are held to strict liability for the loss or damage to the property of guests.
- Most all states have innkeepers' statutes that limit the liability of innkeepers.
  - To limit their liability, the innkeeper must provide a safe and make guests aware of its availability for their use.

## Insurance

Insurance is a contract where one party undertakes to indemnify another against loss, damage, or liability arising from a contingent or unknown event. The risk of loss is pooled among all those insured.
- The insurance contract is a policy.
- The money paid to the insurance company is a premium, based on an estimate of those in the pool who will suffer losses.
- The insured pays a premium to the insurance company.
- The insurer, or underwriter, is obligated to pay insurance proceeds to those members of the pool who experience losses.

**Insurable Interest.** Any party who would suffer a monetary loss from the destruction of real or personal property has an insurable interest in that property.
- Ownership creates an interest.
- Life insurance requires a close family relationship or an economic benefit from the continued life of another.
- A person may insure his or her own life and name a beneficiary.

**Insurance Policy.** This insurance contract is governed by contract law. Some states mandate specific language and standardized forms.
- A modification is by endorsement or rider.

**Duties of Insured and Insurer.** The parties to the insurance contract are required to perform the duties imposed by the contract.
- The insured has the duty to pay the premiums, timely notify the insurer of an insured event, and cooperate in investigations.
- The insurer has the duty to defend against any suit involving a claim within the coverage of the policy, and to pay legitimate claims.

**Deductible Clause.** This clause provides that insurance proceeds are payable only after the insured has paid a certain amount of the damage or loss.

**Exclusions from Coverage.** Most policies include events that are excluded from coverage.

**Coinsurance Clause.** This clause requires the insured to pay a percentage of the cost of the insured loss.

**Misrepresentation and Concealment.** An insurer may avoid liability if its decision to insure was based on material misrepresentation of the applicant or if the applicant concealed material information.
- Incontestability clauses prevent insurers from contesting statement after a certain time.

**Life Insurance.** This "death insurance" obligates the insurer to pay on the death of the insured.
- The insurance company issues the policy.
- The owner contracts with the insurance company and pays the premiums.
- The insured is the person whose life is insured.
- The beneficiary is the person to receive the proceeds.

*Suicide Clause.* This clause states that if the insured commits suicide within a certain time after taking out the policy, the insurance company does not have to pay.

**Health Insurance.** This insurance helps cover the costs of medical treatment, surgery, or hospital care.

**Disability Insurance.** This insurance provides a monthly income to an insured who is disabled and cannot work.

**Fire and Homeowners' Insurance.** Two forms of insurance are generally available for residences: a standard fire insurance policy and a homeowners' policy.

*Standard Fire Insurance Policy.* This insurance protects real and personal property from loss from fire and some related perils.

*Homeowners' Policy.* This insurance is comprehensive coverage for the real and personal risks covered by a fire insurance policy and includes personal liability insurance, and coverage for theft.

*Personal Liability Coverage.* This insurance provides comprehensive personal liability insurance, which includes coverage for property damage, personal injuries, and medical expenses of those injured.

*Personal Articles Floater.* This is an addition to a homeowners' policy that provides coverage for specific valuable items and also provides the coverage while traveling.

*Renters' Insurance.* This insurance covers the possessions of a renter in the same way as a homeowners' policy and provides personal liability coverage.

**Title Insurance.** This insurance insures that the owners of real property have clear title to the property.
- It protects against defect in title and liens or encumbrances that are not disclosed on the policy.

**Automobile Insurance.** These insurance policies include property and liability insurance.

*Collision Insurance.* This insures the owner of an automobile against risk of loss or damage incurred if the car is involved in a collision.

*Comprehensive Insurance.* This insures the automobile from loss or damage due to causes other than collision.

*Liability Insurance.* This covers damage that the insured causes to third parties, both bodily injury and property damage.

*Medical Payment Coverage.* This covers medical expenses incurred by the owner, drivers, or passengers of the car who are injured in an automobile accident.

*Uninsured Motorist Coverage.* This provides coverage to the driver and passengers who are injured by an uninsured motorist or a hit-and-run driver.

*No-Fault Automobile Insurance.* Many states mandate that the driver's insurance company pay for any injuries or death suffered in an accident, no matter who caused the accident.

**Umbrella Insurance Policy.** This increases liability coverage beyond the original coverage of automobile and homeowners' insurance. It will pay when the basic policy limits have been exceeded.

**Business Insurance.** This insurance covers risks uniquely applicable to conducting business.

*Business Interruption Insurance.* This insurance covers lost revenue after the business property has been damaged or destroyed and time must be taken to repair or rebuild it.

*Workers' Compensation Insurance.* Many states require businesses to purchase this insurance to cover the risk of employees being injured while working and being compensated for those injuries.

*Key-Person Life Insurance.* This insurance compensates for the loss of owners or other important persons who work for the business.
- It can be used to fund buy-sell agreements among owners where the insurance proceeds are paid to the deceased's beneficiaries and the deceased's interest in the business reverts to the other owners or the business.

*Directors' and Officers' Liability Insurance.* This insurance protects directors and officers from liability for the actions they take on behalf of the corporation.

*Professional Malpractice Insurance.* This insurance protects against liability for injuries resulting from their negligence in practicing their profession.

*Product Liability Insurance.* This insurance protects against liability for injuries caused by defective products.

# Refresh Your Memory

The following exercises will help to test your memory regarding the principles given in this chapter. Read each question twice, then place your answer in the blank provided for each question. Review the chapter material for any questions you are unable to answer or remember.

1. A person can acquire ownership of a wild animal by _____ _____ of it or _____ it.

2. _____ property from its owner is the most common way of acquiring title to personal property.

3. A voluntary transfer of property without consideration is known as a(n) _____.

4. A gift made during a person's lifetime is a(n) _____ _____ gift that is a(n) _____ present transfer of ownership.

5. If a person dies with a valid will, the property is distributed to the _____. If there is not will, the property is distributed to the _____ as provided for in an inheritance statute.

6. When the value of personal property increases because it is added to or improved by natural or _____ means, this is known as _____.

7. When an owner voluntarily places his or her property somewhere and then inadvertently forgets it, the property is considered to be _____.

8. The finder of _____ property obtains title to the found property against everyone except the _____ owner.

9. The finder of lost or misplaced property can obtain title to the property if they follow the procedure set forth in _____ statutes.

10. If the owner discards the property with the intent to relinquish his or her rights in it, the property is considered to be _____.

11. A(n) _____ occurs when the owner of personal property delivers the property to another person to be held, stored, or delivered, or for some other purpose.

12. _____ is a contract where one party undertakes to _____ another against loss, damage, or liability arising from a contingent or unknown event.

13. A(n) _____ is an independent contractor and sells insurance for a number of companies.

14. The _____ is the person who purchases insurance to cover a risk.

15.   The _____ is obligated to pay insurance proceeds if an insured risk occurs.

# Critical Thought Exercise

Tom Cruel, chairman of the Central Republican Committee for Rashaw County, was transporting a valuable painting in his trunk to a friend's home where it was to be displayed during a fundraiser. Cruel stopped at the country club for lunch and left his Mercedes in the care of a parking attendant who worked for Jiffy Parking Service, Inc. The attendant left the key box unattended while taking a break. The car and its contents were stolen. The car was recovered by police using a global positioning system, but the trunk was empty upon its return. Cruel was missing the painting worth $30,000, a golf bag and clubs valued at $1,400, and a CD case containing 120 music compact discs worth an estimated $1,500. Cruel has filed suit against Jiffy for the value of all the items taken from the trunk, including the painting. Is Jiffy liable to Cruel? If so, for which stolen items must it pay damages to Cruel?

*Please compose your answer on a separate sheet of paper or on your computer.*

# Practice Quiz

## True/False

1.   ___   Intangible property includes stock certificates, bonds, and copyrights.

2.   ___   Taking possession or capturing property is not the most common method of acquiring property.

3.   ___   A constructive delivery will not be found for a gift despite such actions as giving the key to a safe-deposit box where the gift is located to the donee.

4.   ___   A gift *causa mortis* is made in contemplation of death.

5.   ___   The Uniform Gift To Minors Act is used by adults whenever they want to give a gift of money or securities to a minor.

6.   ___   If a person dies with a will, their property will be distributed to the beneficiaries.

7.   ___   A business owner who has an addition built on his building acquires ownership by accession.

8.   ___   If an improvement is made to the owner's property by mistake and the improvement cannot be removed, the owner obtains title to the improvement and does not have to pay for it.

9.   ___   Confusion does not occur if two or more persons commingle fungible goods.

10.   ___   The owner of premises where personal property is mislaid is not entitled to take possession of the property against all except the rightful owner.

11.   ___   The finder of lost property does not obtain title to such property against the whole world.

12.   ___   Most estray statutes require that the property be turned over to a government agency.

13. ___ If an owner of mislaid or lost property does not give up any further attempts to locate the property, the property is abandoned.

14. ___ In a bailment, the owner of the property is the bailor.

15. ___ A bailment is different than a sale or a gift as title to the goods does not transfer to the bailee.

## Multiple Choice

16. Animals and minerals are
    a. real property.
    b. a fixture.
    c. tangible property.
    d. intangible property.

17. Which of the following is method of acquiring ownership in personal property?
    a. By possession
    b. By purchase or production
    c. By gift
    d. All of the above

18. A gift made in contemplation of death is a gift
    a. inter vivos.
    b. causa mortis.
    c. by will or inheritance.
    d. by accession.

19. When a person cuts a car in half, adds a middle section, and creates a limousine, he has acquired ownership to the limousine by
    a. purchase or production.
    b. gift.
    c. confusion.
    d. accession.

20. If Janice hangs her jacket in a coatroom at a restaurant and forgets to take it home, her jacket will be considered
    a. mislaid property.
    b. lost property.
    c. abandoned property.
    d. intangible property.

21. If Sue put her purse on top of her car and it is blown off the roof as she drives to work, the purse is
    a. mislaid property.
    b. lost property.
    c. abandoned property.
    d. intangible property.

22. Which of the following can be bailed?
    a. promissory notes
    b. jewelry
    c. animals
    d. all of the above

23. Which of the following is true with respect to bailments?
    a.  The creation of a bailment requires certain formalities.
    b.  A bailment may not be implied.
    c.  A bailment must be in writing if it is for more than one year.
    d.  A bailment may not be expressed.

24. What type of care does a bailee owe when the bailment is for the sole benefit of the bailee?
    a.  slight care
    b.  utmost care
    c.  reasonable care
    d.  ordinary care

25. What type of care does the bailee owe in a mutual benefit bailment situation?
    a.  duty of reasonable or ordinary care
    b.  duty of utmost care
    c.  duty of slight care
    d.  none of the above.

## Short Answer

26.  What is tangible property?

27.  What are the seven ways to acquire personal property?

28.  What makes property "abandoned."

29.  What is a bailment?

30.  What must a bailee do at the termination of a bailment?

31.  Provide an example of a bailment for the sole benefit of the bailee.

32.  What sort of duty of care is owed by someone who borrows a power tool from a neighbor?

33.  What is a mutual benefit bailment?

34.  When are warehouses liable for loss or damage to the bailed property?

35.  What is an innkeeper?

_____

36.  What are the duties of the insured in an insurance contract?

_____

37.  What are the duties of the insurer in an insurance contract?

_____

38.  What is a "suicide clause" in a life insurance policy?

_____

39.  What are two types of insurance policies that cover damage or destruction to residences?

_____

40.  What are two types of insurance policies that cover damages related to automobiles?

_____

## Answers to Refresh Your Memory

1.   taking possession, capturing  [p 1042]
2.   purchasing  [p 1042]
3.   gift  [p 1042]
4.   inter vivos, irrevocable  [p 1043]
5.   beneficiaries, heirs  [p 1044]
6.   manufactured, accession  [p 1045]
7.   mislaid  [p 1045]
8.   lost, true  [p 1046]
9.   estray  [p 1046]
10.  abandoned  [p 1046]
11.  bailment  [p 1049]
12.  Insurance, indemnify  [p 1055]
13.  broker  [p 1055]
14.  Insured  [p 1055]
15.  Insurer  [p 1055]

## Critical Thought Exercise Model Answer

For liability to be created, a bailment must exist.  A bailment is created when personal property is delivered into the possession of a bailee by a bailor for a stated purpose for some period of time.  The bailee has the right of exclusive possession, but the bailor retains ownership of the bailed property.  Delivery may be accomplished by actual physical delivery of the property or constructive delivery of an item that gives control of the property, such as delivery of a car key to a parking lot attendant.  By delivering his car key to the employee of Jiffy Parking, Cruel created a bailment agreement.  Mutual benefit bailments are bailments that benefit both parties.  The bailee (Jiffy) owes a duty of reasonable care to protect the bailed goods.  The bailee is liable for any goods that are lost, stolen, damaged, or destroyed because of his or her negligence.  The law presumes that if bailed property is lost, damaged, destroyed, or stolen while in the possession of the bailee, it is because of lack of proper care by the bailee.  The typical commercial bailment where someone pays to have his property watched for a fee is this type of bailment.

A bailee accepts responsibility for unknown contents of a bailed automobile when the presence of those contents is reasonably foreseeable based on the factual circumstances surrounding the bailment of the automobile. It cannot be said that a country club parking attendant should reasonably foresee the presence of a valuable painting in a member's car trunk. Unless the bailee accepts possession of the property, either expressly or impliedly, there can be no bailment. Therefore, Jiffy Parking had no duty of care to protect the painting in the trunk. The other items lead to a different result. It is quite foreseeable that a club member would have golf clubs in his trunk. Car owners often have cases to carry an assortment of music for them to play in their car. Jiffy Parking will be liable to Cruel for $2,900, the cost of the golf clubs and compact discs.

# Answers to Practice Quiz

## True/False

1. True    Stocks, bonds, and copyrights are intangible property. [p 1042]
2. True    Taking possession or capturing property is not the most common method of acquiring property. Purchasing is the most common method of acquiring property. [p 1042]
3. False   Control has been given to the donee by delivering the key. [p 1043]
4. True    A gift *causa mortis* is a gift made in contemplation of death. [p 1043]
5. True    This statute applies only to gifts of money or stock. [p 1044]
6. True    If a person dies with a will, their property will be distributed to the beneficiaries. If a will does not exist, the property is distributed to the heirs by statute. [p 1044]
7. True    Accession occurs when the value of property increases because it is added to or improved by natural or manufactured means. [p 1045]
8. True    This is ownership by accession; the owner does not have to pay for the improvement.[p 1045]
9. False   Confusion occurs if two or more persons commingle fungible goods. [p 1045]
10. False  The owner of premises where personal property is mislaid is entitled to take possession of the property against all except the rightful owner and becomes an involuntary bailee. [p 1046]
11. True   The finder of lost property obtains title to the property against the whole world except the true owner. [p 1046]
12. True   Most statutes require that the property be turned over to a government agency. [p 1046]
13. False  An owner of mislaid or lost property must give up any further attempts to locate the property, for the property to be abandoned. [p 1046]
14. True   The owner is the bailor. [p 1049]
15. True   Instead, the bailee must follow the bailor's directions concerning the goods. [p 1049]

## Multiple Choice

16. C   Tangible property includes physically defined property. A is incorrect because real property is land. Choice B is incorrect because a fixture is personal property that has become real property by being permanently attached to land. Choice D is incorrect because intangible property represents rights that can't be reduced to a physical form, such as a copyright. [p 1042]
17. D   D is correct because all three choices are methods for acquiring personal property. [p 1042]
18. B   The gift may be revoked anytime before death. Choice A is incorrect because this is an irrevocable gift that does not contemplate death. Choice C and D are incorrect because they are not types of gifts. [p 1043]
19. D   When goods are improved by manufacture, this is accession. A is incorrect because production is from scratch, and the limousine was added to an already existing piece of property. Choice B is incorrect because there is no indication that the limousine was given to the new owner. Choice C is incorrect because this is not a fungible good that has been commingled. [p 1045]

20. A   Property that is voluntarily placed somewhere and then inadvertently forgotten is mislaid property. B is not correct because lost property is carelessly left somewhere, not intentionally placed somewhere. C is incorrect because Janice had no intent to relinquish her ownership rights. D is incorrect, as a coat is physical property, not representative of some other property. [p 1045]

21. B   Sue has negligently let the purse be blown off and it is now in an unknown location. A is incorrect because Sue did not intentionally place her purse in the road. C is incorrect because she did not intend to relinquish her ownership interest in the purse. D is not correct because the purse is tangible property. [p 1046]

22. D   Answer D is correct, as answers A, B, and C all may be bailed, since tangible and intangible personal property may be bailed. [p 1049]

23. C   Answer C is correct as it is the only true statement with respect to bailments. Answers A, B and D are all incorrect as they are false statements regarding bailments. [p 1050]

24. B   Answer B is correct, as the bailee owes a duty of utmost (or great care) when the bailment is for the sole benefit of the bailee. Answers A, C, and D are incorrect as they do not state the correct duty of care required of a bailee under these circumstances. [p 1052]

25. A   Answer A is correct, as the bailee owes a duty of reasonable or ordinary care when a mutual benefit bailment is involved. Answers B, C, and D are incorrect as they do not state the correct duty of care required when there is a mutual benefit bailment situation. [p 1052]

## Short Answer

26. It is all real property and physically defined personal property such as buildings, animals, minerals, automobiles, and equipment. [p 1042]

27. Capture or possession, purchase or production, gift, will or inheritance, accession, confusion, divorce. [p 1042-1045]

28. Property becomes abandoned if an owner discards the property with the intent to relinquish rights in it or an owner of mislaid or lost property gives up any further attempts to locate it. [p 1046]

29. A transaction where an owner transfers his or her personal property to another to be held, stored, or delivered. Title to the property does not transfer. [p 1049]

30. The bailee is obligated to do as the bailor directs with the property. Usually, the bailee is obligated to return the identical goods bailed. [p 1053]

31. A typical situation would be where the bailor is watching the property as a favor. [p 1052]

32. This is a bailment for the sole benefit of the bailee, which requires a duty of great care. [p 1052]

33. A bailment for the mutual benefit of the bailor and bailee. It is typified by the equipment rental agreement. The bailee owes a duty of ordinary care to protect the bailed property. [p 1052]

34. Warehousers are liable only for loss or damage to the bailed property caused by their own negligence. They owe a duty or reasonable care. [p 1053]

35. An innkeeper is owner of a facility that provides lodging to the public for compensation. [p 1054]

36. To pay premiums, to notify the insurer of the occurrence of an insured event, to cooperate in the investigation of claims. [p 1056]

37. To defend against suits brought against the insured that involve a claim within the coverage of the policy, and to pay legitimate claims up to the policy limit. [p 1056]

38. This clause states that if an insured commits suicide within a certain time after taking out the policy, the insurer does not have to pay the proceeds. [p 1058]

39. Name two: Standard fire insurance policy, homeowners' policy, personal liability coverage homeowners' policy, personal articles floater, and renter's insurance. [p 1060-1061]

40. Name two: Collision insurance, comprehensive insurance, liability insurance, medical payment coverage, uninsured motorist coverage, no-fault automobile coverage. [p 1062-1063]

# Chapter 38
# REAL PROPERTY AND LANDLORD-TENANT LAW

## Chapter Overview

Important facets of the U.S. culture and economy are ownership rights in real property, which concentrate on the rights to the property rather than the physical attributes of the land. Over half of the population, and many businesses, rent or lease real property through a landlord-tenant relationship, with rights and duties governed by real estate and contract law. Federal, state, and local governments have authority to regulate the ownership, possession, lease, and use of real property, and may also take private property for public use under eminent domain. The ownership and transfer of real property, landlord-tenant relationships, and government regulation of real estate are introduced in this chapter.

## Chapter Objectives

Upon completion of the following exercises you should be able to:

1.    Describe the different types of ownership interests in real property.
2.    Discuss how ownership interests in real property can be transferred.
3.    Describe the different types of tenancy.
4.    Understand landlord and tenant duties and their respective tort liability.
5.    Understand how zoning laws regulate the use of land.

## Practical Application

You should be able to recognize how a piece of real property is held by the owner and what effect that has upon its use, transfer, and value. You should be able to understand the duties and rights of landlords and tenants in the leasing of real property. Failure to meet the duties imposed at common law and by statute may cause a tenant to lose their tenancy or subject a landlord to damages and sanctions. A businessperson who is leasing a storefront or commercial building must understand the restrictions on the use of the building and what affirmative tasks must be undertaken to keep them out of breach of contract.

## Helpful Hints

The following questions about rights in real property can help assess factual and hypothetical cases:
- Is this real or personal property?
- In what form is the real property currently owned?
- Does anyone hold a future interest in this land?
- Is anyone a co-owner of this real property?
- Was there a legal transfer of an ownership interest?
- Was the transfer of the ownership interest properly recorded by deed?
- Does anyone own a nonpossessory interest in this real property?
- Is any legal action being taken against the real property?

# Study Tips

## Real Property

Real property is the land itself and any buildings, trees, soil, minerals, timber, plants and other things that are permanently affixed to the land.

**Land and Buildings.** The owner usually purchases surface rights to the land, or the right to use, enjoy, and develop the property as he or she sees fit.
- Any building or permanent structure that is built on the land becomes part of the real property.

**Subsurface Rights.** The owner of the property also owns the subsurface rights to any minerals, oil, gas, or other commodity that may be under the surface.
- These subsurface rights may be sold separate from the rest of the real property.

**Plant Life and Vegetation.** Both natural and cultivated plants are part of the real property.
- They become personal property if the owner severs them from the land.

**Fixtures.** These are items that are permanently affixed to the land or a building and become part of the real property if they cannot be removed without causing substantial damage to the realty.

**Air Rights.** An air space parcel is the air space above the surface of realty.
- This space may be sold or leased separate from the realty like a subsurface right.

## Estates in Land

The ownership rights one possesses in real property is called an estate in land.
- The bundle of legal rights that the owner has to possess, use, and enjoy the property.
- The type of estate an owner possesses is determined by the deed, will, lease or other document that created or transferred ownership rights.

**Freehold Estate.** An estate where the owner has a present possessory interest in the real property.

*A Fee Simple Absolute (Fee Simple).* This is a type of ownership of real property that grants the owner the fullest bundle of legal rights that a person can hold in real property.
- It is infinite in duration, has no limits on inheritability, does not end at occurrence of an event.

*Fee Simple Defeasible (Qualified Fee).* This estate grants the owner all the incidents of a fee simple absolute except that it may be taken away if a specified condition occurs or does not occur.

*Life Estate.* This is an interest in land for a person's lifetime.
- Upon that person's death, the interest will be transferred to another party.

## Concurrent Ownership

Concurrent ownership occurs when two or more persons own a piece of real property.

**Joint Tenancy.** Upon the death of one owner, the property passes to the other joint tenants automatically under the right of survivorship.

**Tenancy in Common**. The interest of a surviving tenant in common passes to the deceased tenant's estate and not to the co-tenants.

**Tenancy by the Entirety**. This form can only be used by married couples. This also has a right of survivorship, but unlike a joint tenancy, one tenant cannot sell their interest in the realty.

**Community Property**. Upon the death of one spouse, one-half of the community assets automatically pass to the surviving spouse, while the other half passes by will or by the state's intestate statute.
- Property acquired through gift or inheritance remains separate property.
- Neither spouse can sell, transfer, or gift community property without consent of other spouse.

**Condominium.** A form of ownership in a multiple-dwelling building where the purchaser has title to an individual unit and owns the common areas as a tenant in common.

**Cooperative.** A form of ownership of a multiple-dwelling building where a corporation owns the building and the residents own shares in the corporation.

## Future Interests

A person may be given the right to possess property in the future rather than in the present.

**Reversion**. A right of possession that returns to the grantor after the expiration of a limited or contingent estate.

**Remainder**. If the right of possession returns to a third party upon the expiration of a limited or contingent estate.

## Transfer of Ownership of Real Property

An owner may transfer their interest in realty by one of the following methods:

**Sale of Real Estate.** The passing of title from a seller to a buyer for a price, also called a conveyance.

*Deeds*. These are used to convey property by sale or gift.
- The seller or donor is called the grantor.
- The buyer or recipient is the grantee.
- A warranty deed has the greatest number of warranties or guarantees.
- The quitclaim deed provides no protection for the buyer, granting only the interest possessed.

*Recording Statute*. This statute provides that copies of the deed and other documents, such as mortgages and deeds of trust, may be filed with the county recorder's office to give constructive notice of ownership.
- Intended to prevent fraud and to establish certainty in the ownership and transfer of property.

*Quiet Title Action.* Lawsuit to have a court determine the extent of ownership rights in a parcel of realty.

*Marketable Title.* This means that the title is free from encumbrances, defects in title, or other defects that would affect the value of the property. A seller is obligated to transfer marketable title to the grantee.

- Attorney's opinion is where an attorney examines an abstract of title and renders an opinion on the status of the title.
- Torrens system is a judicial proceeding where everyone claiming an interest may appear and be heard. The court issues a certificate of title to the person determined to be the rightful owner.
- Title insurance requires the title insurer to reimburse the insured for any losses caused by undiscovered defects in the title.

**Tax Sale.** The government may obtain a tax lien against property for unpaid property taxes. If the lien remains unpaid, a tax sale is held to satisfy the lien.

**Gift, Will, or Inheritance**. These forms of transfer involve granting title to another without the payment of any consideration.

**Adverse Possession**. When a person openly possesses the property of another, they may acquire title if certain statutory requirements are met.

- The owner must have notice that his or her land is being wrongfully possessed and take no steps to eject the adverse possessor.

## Nonpossessory Interests

Nonpossessory interests exist when a person holds an interest in another person's property without actually owning any part of the property.

**Easement.** An easement is a given or required right to make limited use of someone else's land without owning or leasing it.

- Easements may be expressly created by
  - grant – where the owner gives another party an easement across his or her property
  - reservation – where an owner sells his or her land but keeps an easement on the land
- Easements may be implied by
  - implication – where an owner subdivides a piece of property with a well, path, road or other beneficial appurtenant that serves the entire parcel, or by
  - necessity – where a landlocked parcel must have egress and ingress

*Easements Appurtenant.* A situation created when the owner of a piece of land is given an easement over an adjacent piece of land.

- The land over which the easement is granted is the servient estate.
- The land that benefits from the easement is the dominant estate.

*Easements in Gross.* An easement that authorizes a person who does not own adjacent land the right to use another's land.

- The easement holder owes a duty to maintain and repair the easement.

**License.** A license grants a person the right to enter upon another's property for a specified and usually short period of time.

**Profit.** Profit a'pendre grants a person the right to remove something from another's real property.

## Landlord-Tenant Relationship

This relationship is created when the owner of a freehold estate transfers a right to exclusively and temporarily possess the owner's property. The tenant receives a nonfreehold estate.

- The tenant's interest in the property is the leasehold estate, or leasehold.
- The owner who transfers the leasehold estate is the landlord, or lessor.
- The party to whom the leasehold estate is transferred is the tenant, or lessee.

**Lease.** The rental agreement between the landlord and tenant, which must contain the essential terms of the agreement. Leases must meet the requirements of the Statute of Frauds.

*Tenancy for Years.* A tenancy created when the landlord and the tenant agree on a specific duration for the lease. Terminates automatically on expiration of the stated term.

*Periodic Tenancy.* A tenancy created when a lease specifies intervals at which payments are due but does not specify how long the lease is for. May be terminated at the end of any payment interval with notice.

*Tenancy at Will.* A lease that may be terminated at any time by either party.

*Tenancy at Sufferance.* A tenancy created when a tenant retains wrongful possession of property after the expiration of another tenancy or a life estate without the owner's consent.

**Landlord's Duty to Deliver Possession.** The landlord is obligated to deliver possession of the lased premises to the tenant on the date the lease term begins.

**Landlord's Duty Not to Interfere with the Tenant's Right to Quiet Enjoyment.** The law implies a covenant of quiet enjoyment in all leases. The landlord may not interfere with the tenant's quiet and peaceful possession, use, and enjoyment of the leased premises.

**Landlord's Duty to Maintain the Leased Premises.** The landlord must comply with the requirements imposed by building and housing codes.

**Tenant's Duty to Pay Rent.** A tenant owes a duty to pay the agreed-upon amount of rent for the leased premises to the landlord at the agreed-upon time and terms.
- Gross lease, the tenant pays a gross sum and the landlord pays taxes and assessments.
- Net lease, the tenant pays rent and taxes.
- Double net lease, the tenant pas rent, taxes, and utilities.
- Net, net, net lease (or triple net lease), the tenant pays rent, taxes, utilities, and insurance.

**Tenant's Duty Not to Use Leased Premises for Illegal or Nonstipulated Purposes.** A tenant may use the property for any lawful purposes permitted by the lease.

**Tenant's Duty Not to Commit Waste.** Waste occurs when a tenant causes substantial and permanent damages to leased premises that decrease value of the property and the landlord's reversionary interest.

**Tenant's Duty Not to Disturb Other Tenants.** A landlord may evict the tenant who interferes with the quiet enjoyment of other tenants.

**Implied Warranty of Habitability.** Under this warranty, the leased premises must be fit, safe, and suitable for ordinary residential use.

**Premises Liability.** A tenant owes a duty of reasonable care to persons who enter upon leased premises.
- Landlords owe a duty of reasonable care to tenants and third parties not to negligently cause them injury.

**Transfer of Rights to Leased Property.** Landlords may sell, gift, devise, or otherwise transfer their interests in leased property. The new landlord cannot alter the terms of an existing lease.

- The tenant's right to transfer possession of leased premises depends on the terms of the lease.

*Assignment of Lease.* The tenant may transfer all of his or her rights under a lease to another by way of an assignment.

- The new tenant is the assignee, obligated to perform the duties the assignor had under the lease.
- The assignor remains responsible for obligations under the lease unless released by landlord.

*Sublease.* If a tenant transfers only some of his or her rights under the lease, it is a sublease.

- The sublessor is still responsible under the lease.
- The sublessee does not obtain any rights under the original lease.

## Zoning

Zoning ordinances are local laws that are adopted by municipalities and local governments to regulate land use within their boundaries.

- Zoning ordinances are adopted and enforced to protect the health, safety, morals, and general welfare of the community.
- A landowner may obtain a variance that permits a type of building or use that would not otherwise be allowed by a zoning ordinance

## Civil Rights Acts and Real Estate

Federal and state laws guarantee civil rights in the purchase, sale, and leasing of real estate and in the use of public property.

**Civil Rights Act.** This Act prohibits racial discrimination in the transfer of real property, including housing, commercial, and industrial property.

**Fair Housing Act.** This Act makes it unlawful for a party to refuse to rent or sell a dwelling to any person because of race, color, national origin, sex, or religion.

- It prohibits discrimination by real estate brokers, mortgage lenders, and advertisers.

**Title III of the Americans with Disabilities Act.** This legislation prohibits discrimination on the basis of disability in places of public accommodation operated by private entities.

- It requires facilities to be designed, constructed, and altered in compliance with accessibility requirements.

## Eminent Domain and the "Taking" of Real Property

The government may use its power of eminent domain to obtain private property for public purposes.

- The Due Process Clause of the Fifth Amendment to the U.S. Constitution requires that the government only take property for "public use."
- The Just Compensation Clause of the Fifth Amendment requires that the government compensate the property owner when it exercises its right of eminent domain.

# Refresh Your Memory

The following exercises will help to test your memory regarding the principles given in this chapter. Read each question twice, then place your answer in the blank provided for each question. Review the chapter material for any questions you are unable to answer or remember.

1.    Houses, farms, and buildings are all forms of _____ property.

2.    Items of personal property that are affixed to real property are called _____.

3.    Rights to minerals and other things under the surface of land are called _____ rights.

4.    A person's ownership rights in real property are called a(n) _____ _____ _____.

5.    The highest form of ownership of real property is a(n) _____ _____ _____.

6.    An estate that may be taken away if a specified condition occurs or does not occur is a(n) _____ _____ _____.

7.    A landlord holds a(n) _____ estate that he or she can transfer to a tenant for their use.

8.    The tenant's interest in property is called a(n) _____ _____.

9.    The rental agreement between the landlord and tenant is called the _____.

10.    When the landlord and tenant agree on a specific duration for the lease, it is a(n) _____ _____ _____.

11.    The _____ _____ Act makes it unlawful for a party to refuse to rent or sell a dwelling to any person because of his or her race, color, national origin, sex, or religion.

12.    The government may use _____ _____ to acquire private property for public purposes.

13.    The _____ _____ Act prohibits racial discrimination in the transfer of real property.

14.    A(n) _____ _____ _____ authorizes a person who does not own adjacent land the right to use another's land.

15.    A(n) _____ _____ is created when the owner of one piece of land is given an easement over an adjacent piece of land.

# Critical Thought Exercise

Jim Lewis and Dale Tingle decided to form a partnership for the purpose of entering the restaurant business. Prior to forming the partnership, Lewis and Tingle purchased a large Victorian house in Sacramento with the idea that they would convert the first floor into a restaurant and the upper floors into office space. Lewis contributed $90,000 to the purchase and Tingle contributed $10,000. Lewis and Tingle took title as joint tenants with the right of survivorship. The partnership was formed five months later and the Sacramento property was converted into a restaurant and offices as planned. When Lewis and Tingle purchased another house in Davis, California, they took title as tenants in common. Tingle contributed $100,000 as the down payment for the Davis property. When the partnership was dissolved, the court ordered that both properties be sold. Lewis was given a reimbursement for the Sacramento property in the amount of $80,000. The Davis property was sold for $320,000 and the proceeds of the sale were divided equally between Lewis and Tingle. Did the court divide the proceeds from the sale of the two properties properly?

*Please compose your answer on a separate sheet of paper or on your computer.*

## Practice Quiz

### True/False

1. ___ Buildings constructed on land are not personal property.

2. ___ Subsurface rights may not be sold separately from surface rights.

3. ___ Natural plants such as trees are real property, as are cultivated plants such as a corn crop.

4. ___ Door knobs are not fixtures and are part of the realty.

5. ___ An easement is the bundle of legal rights the owner has to possess, use, and enjoy the property.

6. ___ A life estate is an interest in real property that lasts forever.

7. ___ When a life estate or contingent estate terminates, the right of possession does not revert to the grantor.

8. ___ A remainder is not a right of possession that returns to the grantor after the expiration of limited or contingent estate.

9. ___ If the right of possession returns to a third party upon the expiration of a limited or contingent estate, it is called a remainder.

10. ___ Tenancy in common is not a form of co-ownership that includes the right of survivorship.

11. ___ In a tenancy in common, the interests of a surviving tenant in common pass to the deceased tenant's estate.

12. ___ Tenancy by the entirety is a form of co-ownership of real property that can be used by anyone.

13. ___ A nonconforming use is a permission from a zoning board that permits an owner to make a nonzoned use of his or her property.

14. ___ The government is required to compensate the owner of property when it uses eminent domain.

15. ___ The Civil Rights Act prohibits discrimination on the basis of disability in places of public accommodation operated by private entities.

## Multiple Choice

16. Which of the following is real property?
    a. The tables and chairs in a restaurant
    b. A portable hot tub
    c. A camper in which a family is living
    d. An in-ground swimming pool

17. The rights to natural gas under Sue's home are her
    a. easement rights.
    b. profit.
    c. personal property.
    d. subsurface rights.

18. Larry conveys Blackacre to "Jim Smith and Greg Brown, as tenants in common." Jim Smith has a will that leaves his entire estate to Ned Green. If Smith dies, his interest in Blackacre will pass to
    a. Smith's heirs under the state's intestate statute.
    b. Green.
    c. Brown.
    d. none of the above.

19. The owner of a condominium
    a. has title to their individual unit.
    b. owns the common areas as tenants in common with the other owners.
    c. may sell or mortgage their unit without the permission of the other owners.
    d. all of the above.

20. Gus has a home on a 10-acre parcel that he subdivides into two 5-acre parcels. Gus builds a new house on the subdivided parcel. The only way for the new homeowner to get to the main road is to drive across Gus's parcel. The new homeowner has acquired an
    a. easement by express grant.
    b. easement by implication.
    c. license.
    d. profit a'pendre.

21. The government must compensate a property owner when the government takes his or her property by eminent domain under the mandate of the
    a. Just Compensation Clause.
    b. action to quiet title.
    c. Statute for the Regulation of Open Property.
    d. profit a'pendre.

22. Kyle, a landlord, has always rented his apartments to female schoolteachers. Kyle believes that schoolteachers, especially women, are neat and quiet and make the best tenants. Does Kyle have the right to discriminate against others in favor or female schoolteachers in this manner?
    a. Yes, because Kyle owns the premises and is free to contract with whomever he pleases.
    b. Yes, because Kyle is free to rent his freehold estate to anyone he desires.
    c. No, because there is no proof that schoolteachers are neat.
    d. No, because Kyle is prohibited by the Civil Rights Act from discriminating against tenants on the basis of their sex.

23. The Country Inn rents efficiency suites by the day, week, and month. The Inn has staircases and steps leading into all suites as part of its Victorian architecture. The Inn tells all disabled persons that it is unable to accommodate physical handicaps. The policy of the Country Inn
    a. is lawful because private businesses do not have to accommodate handicapped persons.
    b. is lawful because an owner may design their hotel to fit their own style and budget.
    c. is unlawful because the Americans with Disabilities Act prohibits discrimination on the basis of disability in places of public accommodation operated by private entities.
    d. is unlawful because it violates the Fair Housing Act.

24. The form of co-ownership that can be used only by a married couple, which has the right of survivorship for the surviving spouse, is
    a. joint tenancy.
    b. tenancy in common.
    c. tenancy by the entirety.
    d. community property.

25. Under adverse possession, a person who occupies another's property acquires title to the property if the occupation has been
    a. open, visible, and notorious.
    b. actual and exclusive.
    c. hostile and adverse.
    d. All of the above.

## Short Answer

26. What are three examples of buildings that would be considered to be real property?
    _____

27. Give four examples of things that may be removed from the earth or sold as part of an owner's subsurface rights.
    _____

28. Give four examples of things in a home that are fixtures and cannot be removed upon a sale of the real property.
    _____

29. What are the three types of freehold estates?
    _____

30. What is a life estate that is measured in the life of third party?
    _____

31. What is the interest that the grantor retains for him- or herself or a third party?
    _____

32. Name and define two future interests.
    _____
    _____

33. What is a joint tenancy and how should it be created in a deed?
    _____
    _____

34. What is a cooperative?

_____

35. What is adverse possession?

_____

36. What is a marketable title?

_____

37. How do zoning ordinances usually regulate land use?

_____

_____

38. What is the premises liability of a landlord and a tenant?

_____

_____

39. What does the Due process Clause of the Fifth Amendment provide for eminent domain?

_____

40. What does the Just Compensation Clause of the Fifth Amendment provide?

_____

## Answers to Refresh Your Memory

1.  real [p 1077]
2.  fixtures [p 1078]
3.  subsurface [p 1078]
4.  estate in land [p 1078]
5.  fee simple absolute [p 1078]
6.  fee simple defeasible [p 1079]
7.  freehold [p 1091]
8.  leasehold estate [p 1091]
9.  lease [p 1091]
10. tenancy for years [p 1091]
11. Fair Housing [p 1102]
12. eminent domain [p 1104]
13. Civil Rights [p 1102]
14. easement in gross [p 1089]
15. easement appurtenant [p 1089]

## Critical Thought Exercise Model Answer

The deed to the Sacramento property created a joint tenancy in the real estate. When a joint tenancy is created, each tenant acquires an equal right to share in the enjoyment of the land during his or her lives. A joint tenancy confers equivalent rights on the tenants that are fixed and vested at the time the tenancy is created. These do not change just because an additional agreement is executed to form a partnership. Once a joint tenancy is established between two people and a partition action is undertaken to divide the property, each person owns a one-half interest and they are entitled to one half of the total proceeds without reimbursement for an unequal down payment. When parties hold property as tenants in common, each tenants share is fully divisible and fully transferable to a purchaser or an heir upon death. The Davis property was subject to equitable adjustments for the large down payment made by Tingle. When the property is sold, the court must determine the percentage of equity that is attributable to the original down payment. Tingle will be entitled to a substantially greater share of the proceeds from the Davis property. However, the court may consider the Davis property as just one asset in the partnership. The adjustments to the division of the proceeds will consider the partnership contributions and assets as a whole.

# Answers to Practice Quiz

## True/False

1. True    Buildings are real property. [p 1077]
2. False    Owners may sell mineral rights, oil rights, etc., without selling their surface land. [p 1078]
3. True    All plant life and vegetation are considered real property. [p 1078]
4. False    They are fixtures as they cannot be removed without causing substantial damage. [p 1078]
5. False    This is the definition of an estate. [p 1089]
6. False    When the specified person dies, the property reverts to the grantor or the grantor's estate or other designated person. [p 1079]
7. False    This is called the right of reversion. The conveyance terminates and reverts to the grantor at the end of the individual's life estate. [p 1079]
8. True    This is a reversion, not a remainder. [p 1083]
9. True    The person who is entitled to the future interest is called a remainderman. [p 1083]
10. True    Joint tenancy includes the right of survivorship. [p 1080]
11. True    In a tenancy in common, the interest passes to the deceased tenant's estate. [p 1080]
12. False    It can only be used by spouses, as it has the right of survivorship for the spouse. [p 1080]
13. False    A variance is a permission from a zoning board that permits an owner to make a nonzoned use of his or her property. [p 1099-1100]
14. True    The government is required to compensate the owner of property when it uses eminent domain. [p 1104]
15. False    The Americans with Disabilities Act prohibits discrimination on the basis of disability in places of public accommodation operated by private entities. [p 1102]

## Multiple Choice

16. D    An in-ground pool cannot be removed without causing substantial damage to property. Choices A, B, and C are all portable and their movement or removal will not damage the land. [p 1077]
17. D    The owner or land owns the rights to whatever is under the surface of his or her land, including minerals, gas, and oil. A is incorrect because an easement is a right to use or cross another person's land. B is not correct because a profit is the right to remove something from another person's land. C is not correct because gas and minerals are a form of real property until they are removed from the land. [p 1078]
18. B    Green will receive the interest in Blackacre because Smith's interest may be passed through a will. A is incorrect because Smith has a will and did not die intestate. C is incorrect because a tenancy in common does not have a right of survivorship. D is incorrect because B is a correct answer. [p 1080]
19. D    D is correct because A, B, and C are all rights of a condominium owner. [p 1081]
20. B    It is implied by Gus's action that he would allow the new owner to have a driveway across his property. A is incorrect because Gus never expressly granted the right to cross his land to the new

owner. C is not correct because a license is usually for a short specified period of time. D is incorrect because nothing is being removed from Gus's land. [p 1089]

21. A  If the owner is not satisfied with the government's offer for compensation, the owner may bring an action to have a court determine the amount of compensation. B is not correct because it is an action to settle ownership of property, not the compensation to be paid by the government. C is not correct because it concerns ownership rights in Germany. D relates to compensation for taking something (timber) from the owners land. [p 1104]

22. D  The Fair Housing Act makes it unlawful for a party to refuse to rent or sell a dwelling to any person because of his or her race, color, national origin, sex, or religion. A, B and C are incorrect because the mandates of the Fair Housing Act control the renting of property. [p 1102]

23. C  ADA requires facilities to be designed, constructed, and altered in compliance with accessibility requirements. A is incorrect, as the ADA applies to private businesses. B is incorrect because the ADA has design and construction guidelines that must be followed. Choice D is incorrect because accommodations for disabilities are not covered by the Fair Housing Act. [p 1102-1103]

24. C  Answer C is correct, a tenancy by the entirety is a form of co-ownership that can be used only by a married couple, which has the right of survivorship for the surviving spouse. Answer A is incorrect, as a joint tenancy is a form of co-ownership where the interest of a deceased owner passes to the other co-owner. Answer B is incorrect, as a tenancy in common is a form of co-ownership where the interest of a deceased owner passes to his or her estate. Answer D is incorrect, as community property is a form of co-ownership where the surviving spouse receives one-half of the community property. [p 1080]

25. D  Answer D is correct, as answers A, B, and C are all vital for adverse possession. [p 1086-1087]

## Short Answer

26.  Answers will vary: Houses, apartment buildings, manufacturing plants, office buildings, radio towers, bridges, and grain silos. [p 1077]

27.  Answers will vary: Oil, gas, coal, gold. [p 1078]

28.  Answers will vary: Carpeting, doors, lights, sinks, cabinets. [p 1078]

29.  Fee simple absolute, fee simple defeasible, life estate. [p 1078]

30.  Estate pour autre vie. [p 1079]

31.  Future interest of either a reversion or a remainder. [p 1083]

32.  A reversion is a right of possession that returns to the grantor after the expiration of a limited or contingent estate. A remainder is when the right of possession returns to a third party upon the expiration of a limited or contingent estate. [p 1083]

33.  It is a form of co-ownership that includes the right of survivorship. It is created when the property is conveyed "to Mike and Sue as joint tenants, with the right of survivorship." [p 1080]

34.  A cooperative is a form of co-ownership of a multiple-dwelling building where a corporation owns the building and the residents own shares in the corporation. [p 1082]

35.  It is when a person who wrongfully possesses someone else's real property obtains title to that property if certain statutory requirements are met. [p 1086-1087]

36.  It is title that is free from any encumbrances or other defects that are not disclosed but would affect the value of the property. [p 1086]

37.  They establish use districts within the municipality, restrict the height, size, and location of buildings on a building site; and establish aesthetic requirements or limitations for the exterior of buildings. [p 1099]

38.  A landlord owes a duty of reasonable care to tenants and third parties not to negligently cause them injury. A tenant owes a duty of reasonable care to persons who enter on leased premises. [p 1096]

39.  It requires that the government only take private property for "public use". [p 1104]

40.  It requires the government to compensate the property owner when it exercises the power of eminent domain. [p 1104]

# FAMILY LAW, WILLS, AND TRUSTS

## Chapter Overview

Family law and domestic relations covers areas of marriage and its dissolution, spousal and child support, child custody, prenuptial agreements, and other related issues. Wills transfer property after a person dies, directing how property will be distributed. Trusts transfer property to be held and managed for the benefit of another person or persons. A living trust can be used for estate planning. This chapter explores family law and domestic relations, and the use of wills and trusts to transfer and protect property.

## Objectives

Upon completion of the exercises in this chapter, you should be able to:

1. Define marriage and discuss the legal requirements of marriage.
2. Define divorce and discuss how assets are distributed upon termination of marriage.
3. Describe the requirements for making a valid will.
4. Describe the application of an intestacy statute.
5. Define trust, living trust, living will, and health care directive and identify the parties to each.

## Practical Application

When a businessperson acquires assets, it is wise to know how marriage and the dissolution of marriage will affect those assets, and how the assets will be distributed upon their death. The fruits of years of hard work may be wasted if a person does not take adequate steps to protect and preserve their estate and ensure that the estate will be distributed as they wish. A business may have to be dissolved if the owners do not take estate planning into account.

## Helpful Hints

The main purpose of entering into business is to acquire wealth and provide the necessities of life for yourself, family, and others that depend upon you. Regardless of the amount of current assets held by a person, everyone should have an estate plan. It may be as simple as a will or may involve complex estate planning with the use of trusts, tax consultation, and use of joint tenancy. If an estate plan is in place, it will provide the distribution of assets as desired by the businessperson.

## Study Tips

### Premarriage Issues

Some issues may arise prior to marriage: promises to marry, engagement and prenuptial agreements.

**Promise to Marry.** In the 19th century, many courts recognized breach of a promise to marry as a breach-of-contract. Generally, is no longer recognized because of current social norms.

**Engagement.** A time leading up to marriage, generally beginning with a marriage proposal.
- Some states follow the fault rule if the engagement is broken off.
    - If the groom breaks the engagement, the bride keeps the engagement ring.
    - If the bride breaks the engagement, she must return the ring to the groom.
- The modern rule adopts an objective rule.
    - If the engagement is broken off, the bride must return the ring, regardless of fault.

**Prenuptial Agreement.** These are contracts entered into before the marriage that specify how property will be distributed upon termination of the marriage or death of a spouse.
- The Statute of Frauds requires these agreements to be in writing.
- Courts enforce these properly negotiated agreements, even if they provide unequal distribution of assets and eliminate financial support of a spouse on termination of the marriage.
- Courts will not enforce these agreements in some circumstances:
    - One party was not represented by an attorney.
    - One party failed to fully disclose all of his or her assets or liabilities.
    - The agreement was "last moment', immediately prior to marriage.
    - The terms are unfair or unconscionable.
    - The agreement violates public policy.
- An antenuptial agreement is a contract entered into during the marriage, setting forth the distribution of property on death or termination of the marriage.

# Marriage

Marriage grants certain legal rights and duties on the spouses, and on children born of the marriage.

**Marriage Requirements.** State law has certain conditions to be met before two people can be married.
- Most states require that the parties be a man and a woman, unmarried, and are of a certain age.
    - Younger persons may be married with parental consent.
    - Persons under a certain age may not be married.
    - Closely related persons cannot be married.

**Marriage License.** State law requires that parties obtain a marriage license, which may have certain conditions such as a blood test.
- Some states require that there must be a marriage ceremony.
- After the ceremony, the marriage license is recorded.

**Financial Support.** Most states require that a spouse financial support the other spouse and their children during their marriage, up to the level he or she is able to provide, even if they are living apart.

**Common Law Marriage.** This is a marriage where the parties have not obtained a valid marriage license and have not participated in a legal marriage ceremony.
- Recognition of this type of marriage requires
    - That the parties be eligible to marry.
    - That the parties voluntarily intend to be husband and wife.
    - That the parties must live together.
    - That the parties hold themselves out as husband and wife.
- Cohabitation alone is not sufficient to establish a common law marriage.
- The length of time the parties live together is not sufficient alone to establish this marriage.

- The couple must obtain a decree of divorce to end this marriage.

## Parents and Children

Couples who have children have certain legal rights and duties that stem from their parental status.

**Parents' Rights and Duties.** Parents must provide food, shelter, clothing, medical care, and other necessities until a child reaches the age of 18 or is emancipated.
- Parents must see that the child attends school, or is home-schooled, up to the state required age.
- Parents may be legally responsible beyond the child's age of majority if the child is disabled.
- Parents have the right to control the child's behavior.
  o Parents can select the school the child attends and the religion he or she will practice.
  o Parents can use corporal punishment, so long as it is not child abuse.
- Child neglect occurs when a parent fails to provide a child with the necessities of life or other basic needs.
  o Refusal to obtain medical care can be punished as a crime.

**Paternity Actions.** These are legal actions to determine the true identity of the father of a child.
- Brought by mothers to seek financial assistance from the father.
- Brought by the government when the mother is receiving government assistance, to recover payments from the father and establish future financial responsibility.
- Brought by the father to seek legal rights.

**Parent's Liability for a Child's Wrongful Act.** Generally, parents are not liable for their child's negligent acts, but are liable if their own negligence caused the child's act.
- About half the states have statutes that make parents liable for their child's intentional torts.

**Surrogacy.** A situation where a woman agrees to be artificially inseminated with the sperm of a male and to give the baby up to the sperm donor upon the birth of the child.

**Adoption.** This occurs when one becomes the legal parent of a child who is not one's biological child.
- The adoption process is complicated but generally requires that all state law procedures be met, the rights of the biological parents be legally terminated, and the court gives formal approval.

*Agency Adoption.* This occurs when a person adopts a child from a social service organization of a state.
- Many states now allow for disclosure of identities of biological parents in some circumstances.
- Open-adoption is used more often, where the biological and adoptive parents are introduced, the biological parents may screen prospective parents and may have visitation rights.

*Independent Adoption.* This occurs when there is a private arrangement between the biological and adoptive parents.
- A stepparent may formally adopt the child or children of a new spouse if the other biological parent relinquishes legal rights over the child.

*Court Approval of Adoption.* The court must approve the adoption, agency or independent, before it is legal, and bases its approval on the best interests of the child.
- There is a probation period following approval where the state investigates whether the adoptive parents are properly caring for the adopted child.

**Foster Care.** The primary means for caring for children under the state's jurisdiction is to place them in foster care, a temporary arrangement where the state pays foster families to care for foster children.

# Marriage Termination

Once a state has recognized the marital status of a couple, only the state can terminate this marital status. Until the marriage is terminated, the spouses have legal rights and duties to each other.

**Annulment.** An order of the court declaring that a marriage did not exist, based on grounds such as lack of capacity to consent or that there was duress or fraud.
- Children born of the marriage are considered legitimate.

**Divorce.** A legal proceeding where the court issues a decree that legally orders a marriage terminated.
- Traditionally, the person seeking a divorce had to prove the other person at fault, grounds for which were adultery, abuse, abandonment, substance or alcohol abuse, or insanity.
- No-fault divorce merely requires an assertion of irreconcilable differences, with no assignment of fault. Every state recognizes no-fault divorce, but fault may be a factor in dividing property.

*Divorce Proceedings.* These begin when a spouse files a petition for divorce with the proper state court.
- If the spouses do not settle issues such as property division, child custody, and spousal and child support, the case will go to trial.
- Many states require a waiting period between filing a petition and granting of the divorce.
- The court will enter a decree of divorce, a court order terminating the marriage.

*Pro se Divorce.* A "do-it-yourself" divorce; the parties represent themselves in the divorce proceeding.

*Settlement Agreement.* An agreement between the divorcing parties regarding the division of assets, child custody, spousal and child support, and other pertinent issues.
- Negotiations, with the assistance of attorneys, is a common manner of reaching agreement.
- Mediation can be used, and is sometimes court ordered, to reach an agreement.
- The agreement will be accepted by the court if it is fair and the rights of the parties and minor children are properly addressed.
- If an agreement is not reached, the case will go to trial.

# Division of Assets

Upon termination of a marriage, the parties must reach a settlement as to how these assets are to be divided. Without a settlement agreement, the court will order the division of assets.

**Separate Property.** This property includes property owned by a spouse prior to the marriage, and inheritances and gifts received during the marriage.
- Separate property is usually awarded to each spouse on termination of a marriage.
- If separate property is commingled with marital property, or if title has been changed to include the other spouse, the property is considered marital property.

**Marital Property.** This is property acquired during the course of the marriage using income earned by the spouses during the marriage, and separate property that has been converted to marital property.

*Equitable Distribution.* The court may order the fair distribution of property, which considers factors such as the length of the marriage, occupation of each spouse, standard of living, wealth and income-earning ability of each spouse, which party has custody of the children, and health of the parties.
- The house is usually awarded to the spouse granted custody of the children.

*Community Property.* All property acquired during the marriage is considered marital property and is divided equally between the spouses.

**Division of Debts.** In most states, each spouse is personally liable for his or her own premarital debts and the other spouse is not liable for these debts.
- Debts incurred during the marriage for necessities and other joint needs are the joint responsibility of each spouse.
- Spouses are jointly liable for taxes incurred during their marriage.
- If a debt is not paid by the spouse to whom the debt is distributed by the court, the third-party creditor may recover payment from the other spouse.

## Spousal Support, Child Support, and Child Custody

On the termination of a marriage, spousal support and child support may be awarded, and custody of children must be decided.

**Spousal Support.** Sometimes called alimony, this is court ordered support payable in monthly payments.
- The court decides, absent agreement, if payment of alimony is warranted and the amount.
- Temporary alimony, or rehabilitation alimony, is paid for a specific period of time and is designed to allow the recipient to gain the education or job skills to enter the job force.
- Lifetime, or permanent, alimony is usually awarded to one of an older age with few job skills.
- These payments usually end if the former spouse dies, remarries, or becomes self-sufficient.

**Child Support.** The obligation of a non-custodial parent to contribute to the expenses of his or her natural and adopted children, including food, shelter, clothing, medical expenses, and other necessities. The parents can agree to the amount, or the court can determine the payment.
- The court considers several factors, such as number of children and needs of the children, in determining child support.
- These payments continue until the child reaches the age of majority or graduates high school, or is emancipated.

*Family Support Act.* This Act provides that all original or modified child support orders require automatic wage withholding from a non-custodial parent's income.

**Child Custody.** On termination of a marriage, the issue of who is legally and physically responsible for raising the children must be decided, either by agreement or by the court.
- The courts consider several factors in determining what is in the best interests of the child.
  - o Ability to provide for the emotional needs, ordinary needs, and special needs of the child.
  - o Ability to provide a stable environment for the child.
  - o Desire to provide for the needs of the child.
  - o The wishes of the child.
  - o The religion of each parent.
- Custody is not permanent and may be changed as circumstances change.
- Custody can, if deemed appropriate, be awarded to persons other than the parents.

*Joint Custody.* Both parents are responsible for making major decisions concerning the child.
- Joint physical custody means that the child spends a certain portion of time being raised by each parent.

*Visitation Rights.* The non-custodial parent is usually awarded visitation rights, allowing the parent to visit the child for limited periods of time as determined by agreement or court order.

- If the safety of the child is an issue, the court may order supervised visitation.

# Wills

A will is a declaration of how a person wants his or her property distributed upon death.
- The person who makes this testamentary disposition of property is the testator or testatrix.
- The persons designated to receive the property are the beneficiaries.

**Requirements for Making a Will.** Every state has a Statute of Wills that sets forth the requirements for a valid will.
- Testamentary capacity. The testator must be of legal age and of sound mind.
- Writing. The will must be in writing, except for noncupative wills.
- Testator's signature. The will must be signed, usually at the end.

**Attestation by Witnesses.** Wills must be attested to by two or three objective and competent persons.
- The person need not live in the same state, but all the parties must be present when the will is attested to by all witnesses and signed by the testator.
- A formal will meets the requirements of the Statute of Wills.

**Codicil.** A separate document that changes an existing will, which must be executed with the same formalities as a will and incorporate by reference the will it is amending.
- The Will and Codicil are read as one instrument.

**Revoking a Will.** Any act that shows a desire to revoke a will shall be deemed a revocation.
- Making a new will, burning, tearing, or crossing out the pages are all forms of revocations.
- Wills may also be revoked by operation of law, such as when people get divorced or a spouse is convicted of the murder of the other spouse.

**Videotaped Wills.** Electronic wills and videotaped wills do not have any legal force by themselves. A written will is still required.
- The videotaped or electronically recorded will can be used to supplement the written will to show that the testator had testamentary capacity.

**Joint and Mutual Wills.** This occurs if two or more testators execute the same instrument as their will.
- Mutual, or reciprocal, will occur where two or more testators execute separate wills that make testamentary disposition of their property to each other on the condition that the survivor leaves the remaining property on his or her death as agreed by the testators.
  o Because of their contractual nature, these wills cannot be unilaterally revoked.

**Special Types of Wills.** The law recognizes several types of wills that do not meet the usual standards.
- Holographic wills are entirely handwritten by the testator, dated, and signed. They need not be witnessed.
- Noncupative wills are oral wills made before witnesses during a final illness. They are sometimes call deathbed wills.

**Simultaneous Deaths.** If it is impossible to determine which person died first when those persons would have inherited from each other, the questions becomes one of inheritance.
- The Uniform Simultaneous Death Act provides that each deceased person's property is distributed as though he or she survived.

**Undue Influence.** Undue influence occurs when one person takes advantage of another person's mental, emotional, or physical weakness and unduly persuades that person to make a will. The persuasion by the wrongdoer must overcome the free will of the testator.

- It can be inferred from the facts and circumstances surrounding the making of the will.
- A will may be invalidated if it was made as a result of undue influence upon the testator.

**Probate.** Probate is the process of a deceased's property being collected, debts and taxes being paid, and the remainder being distributed.

- A personal representative must be appointed to administer the estate.
    o If the person is named in a will, they are called an executor.
    o If the court appoints the representative, they are an administrator.
- A probate proceeding is administered and settled according to the state's probate code.
    o Almost half of the states have adopted most or all of the Uniform Probate Code.

**Testamentary Gifts.** A gift of real property is a devise; a gift of personal property is a bequest or legacy.

- Specific gifts are specifically named items of personal property, such as a ring.
- General gifts do not specify the source, such as a cash gift.
- Residuary gifts are established by a residuary clause that leaves the portion of the estate left over after all distributions and costs are satisfied.

**Lineal Descendents.** When the will leaves the estate to the testator's lineal descendants, it will be distributed either per stirpes or per capita.

*Per Stirpes Distribution.* The lineal descendants inherit by representation of their parents, in that they split what their deceased parent would have received.

*Per Capita Distribution.* The lineal descendants equally share the property of the estate without regard to the degree of relationship to the testator. Children share equally with grandchildren.

**Ademption and Abatement.** The Doctrine of Ademption states that the beneficiary receives nothing when the testator leaves a specific gift and that gift is not in the testator's estate when he or she dies.

- The Doctrine of Abatement applies if the testator's estate is not large enough to pay all of the devises and bequests.
    o If the will has general and residuary gifts, the residuary gift is abated first.
    o If the will only has general gifts, each gift is reduced proportionately.

## Intestate Succession

If a person dies without a will, or a will fails for some legal reason, the property is distributed to his or her relatives pursuant to the state's intestacy statute.

- Relatives who receive property under these statutes are called heirs.
- If there are no heirs, the property escheats (goes) to the state.

## Trusts

A trust is a legal arrangement established when one person, the settlor or trustor, transfers title to property to another person to be held and used for the benefit of a third person.

- The property held in trust is called the trust *corpus* or trust *res*.
- A trust can be created and become effective during a trustor's lifetime, or can be created to become effective upon the trustor's death.

**Beneficiaries.**  Trusts often give any trust income to an income beneficiary and the *corpus* is distributed to a remainderman upon termination of the trust.

**Express Trust.**  A trust created voluntarily by the settlor.
- An *inter vivos* trust is created while the settlor is alive.
- A testamentary trust is created by will.

**Constructive Trust.**  A trust that is implied by law to avoid fraud, unjust enrichment, and injustice.

**Resulting Trust.**  A trust created by the conduct of the parties.

**Special Types of Trusts.**  Trusts can be created for special purposes.
- A Charitable trust is created for the benefit of a segment of society or society in general.
- A Spendthrift trust is designed to prevent a beneficiary's personal creditors from reaching his or her trust interest.
- A Totten trust is created when a person deposits money in a bank in their own name and holds it as trustee for the benefit of another.

**Termination of a Trust**.  A trust is irrevocable, unless the settler reserves the right to revoke it.
- A trust contains a specific termination date or terminates on the happing of an event.
- On termination, the trust *corpus* is distributed as provided in the trust agreement.

## Living Trusts

A living trust, or grantor's trust or revocable trust, is a legal entity used for estate planning because one can hold property during one's lifetime and distribute the property upon death.

**Benefits of a Living Trust.**  The primary purpose of using a living trust is to avoid probate associated with using a will.
- When the grantor dies, property is owned by the living trust and is not subject to probate.
- If real property is owned in more than one state, then ancillary probate is avoided.
- The living trust does not reduce estate taxes or income taxes, or avoid creditors, or avoid being part of divorce settlement, or avoid controversies upon grantor's death.

**Funding and Operation of a Living Trust.**  The grantor transfers title to his or her property to the trust as the trust *corpus*.
- It is revocable during the live of the grantor.
- The trust names a trustee, usually the grantor, who is responsible for maintaining, investing, buying, or selling trust assets.

**Beneficiaries.**  A living trust names a beneficiary or beneficiaries entitled to receive income from the trust and to receive the *corpus* when the grantor dies.
- Grantor is usually income beneficiary.
- Assets are distributed to the remainder beneficiary or beneficiaries when the grantor dies.

**Pour-Over Will.**  This will is necessary to distribute any property acquired in the name of the grantor after the living trust is established or any property that was not transferred to the trust in the first place.
- This will transfers this property to the trust upon the grantor's death so that it can be distributed to the named beneficiaries of the trust.
- This will is subject to probate.

## Living Will and Health Care Directive

People who do not want their lives prolonged indefinitely by artificial means should sign a living will that stipulates their wishes before catastrophe strikes and they become unable to express it themselves.

- The living will should state which life-saving measures the signor does and does not want.
- The living will, or a separate document called a health care directive or health care proxy, the maker should name someone to be his or her health care agent to make all health care decisions in accordance with his or her wishes in the living will.

**The Right to Die.** The idea that an individual has the right to choose to die when he or she is terminally ill and has less than a certain time to live.

- The Oregon Death with Dignity Act, which exempts from civil or criminal liability physicians who administer or dispense or prescribe a lethal dose of drugs upon the request of a terminally ill patient, was upheld in *Gonzales v. Oregon*, 546 U.S. 243, 126 S.Ct. 904, 163 L.Ed.2d. 748, Web 2006 U.S. Lexis 767 (2006).

# Refresh Your Memory

The following exercises will help to test your memory regarding the principles given in this chapter. Read each question twice, then place your answer in the blank provided for each question. Review the chapter material for any questions you are unable to answer or remember.

1. A(n) _____ _____ is a contract entered into by prospective spouses prior to marriage, specifying how property will be distributed upon termination of the marriage or death of a spouse.

2. A(n) _____ _____ is a contract entered into by spouses during marriage, specifying how property will be distributed upon termination of the marriage or death of a spouse.

3. _____ is a legal union between a male and female that confers certain duties and rights upon the spouses.

4. _____ occurs if a child leaves the parents and voluntarily lives on his or her own.

5. A(n) _____ _____ is a legal proceeding in which a court identifies the father of a child.

6. _____ occurs when one becomes the legal parent of a child who is not one's biological child.

7. A(n) _____ is an order of the court declaring that a marriage did not exist.

8. A(n) _____ is an order of the court that terminates a marriage.

9. A(n) _____ _____ is the written document signed by the divorcing parties that shows their agreement to settle property rights and other issues of their divorce.

10. _____ _____ is the property owned by a spouse prior to marriage, as well as inheritances and gifts received by the spouse during the marriage.

11. _____ _____ is the property acquired during the course of marriage using income earned during the marriage, plus property that has been converted into this type of property.

12. A(n) _____ is a declaration of how a person wants his or her property to be distributed upon his or her death.

13. A will may be invalid if it was made under _____ _____, where one takes advantage of another's mental, emotional, or physical weakness and unduly persuades that person to make a will.

14. A(n) _____ is a legal arrangement where one delivers and transfers legal title to property to another to be held and used for the benefit of a third person.

15. A(n) _____ _____ is a document signed by a person that stipulates his or her wishes to not have his or her life prolonged by artificial means.

## Critical Thought Exercise

Jane Simpson and Steven Smythe were high-school sweethearts, attended the same university, and married shortly after graduating from university. They settled into great jobs in Great Falls and purchased a house in both their names with money given to them by Steven's parents. Over the next ten years, they had two children, traded up on their house three times, adopted a dog and a cat, bought and traded in several cars and minivans, struggled up their respective career ladders, and built up an average amount of debt. Eight years into the marriage, Steven's parents died, leaving him several million dollars in cash, investments, and property. Jane's parents died shortly thereafter, leaving her $220 in a savings account after the estate was settled. After ten years of marriage, Jane and Steven have agreed to divorce.

Their current major assets consist of the following: A house in both their names valued at $1,250,000; two cars and a minivan in both their names valued at $120,000; household goods valued at $500,000; two retirement accounts valued at approximately $1,200,000 each; a joint checking account of $10,000, including the $220 from Jane's parents; a joint savings account of $50,000; 2 joint CDs of $75,000 each, stocks, bonds, real estate, and other investments in Steven's name worth approximately $3,200,000 left him by his parents.

Which of these assets are separate property and which are marital property?

*Please compose your answer on a separate sheet of paper or on your computer.*

## Practice Quiz

### True/False

1. ____ Under the objective rule, if a prospective groom breaks off the engagement, the prospective bride may keep the ring.

2. ____ A prenuptial agreement is a contract entered into by prospective spouses prior to marriage, specifying how property will be distributed on termination of the marriage or death of a spouse.

3. ____ A divorce decree is a legal document issued by the state, certifying that two people are married.

4. ____ A surrogacy is a legal proceeding in which the court identifies the father of a child.

5. ____ A divorce is an order of the court declaring that a marriage did not exist.

6. ____ A marriage license is issued by the court to terminate the marriage.

7. ___ A *pro se* divorce is one in which the parties represent themselves in the divorce action.

8. ___ Equitable distribution is a method where the court orders an equal distribution of marital property to the divorcing spouses.

9. ___ The persons designated to receive the property under a will are the beneficiaries.

10. ___ A will must be signed by the testator or testatrix.

11. ___ Written documents are the only way to show a desire to revoke a will.

12. ___ A specific gift is an item of personal property, such as your great-grandmother's ring.

13. ___ Abatement is applied if the property the testator leaves is not sufficient to satisfy all the beneficiaries named in a will.

14. ___ When two people who would inherit property from each other die simultaneously, each deceased person's property is distributed as though he or she had not survived.

15. ___ A will may be found to be valid if it was made as a result of undue influence on the testator.

## Multiple Choice

16. Which of the following statements is accurate?
    a. A prenuptial agreement is executed by prospective spouses prior to marriage.
    b. An antenuptial agreement is executed by prospective spouses prior to marriage.
    c. A prenuptial agreement is executed by spouses during marriage.
    d. None of the above.

17. A legal document issued by the state, certifying that two people are married is
    a. A marriage.
    b. A marriage license.
    c. A marriage ceremony.
    d. A common-law marriage.

18. When a child leaves the parents and voluntarily lives on his or her own, it is called
    a. An annulment.
    b. A surrogacy.
    c. An emancipation.
    d. None of the above.

19. The written agreement signed by the divorcing parties that shows their agreement to settle property and other rights is
    a. The decree of divorce.
    b. The settlement agreement.
    c. A *pro se* divorce.
    d. Equitable distribution.

20. The property owned by a spouse prior to marriage, as well as inheritances and gifts received by the spouse during the marriage is
    a. Marital property.

    b.  Permanent alimony.
    c.  Spousal support.
    d.  Separate property.

21. The person who makes a will is the
    a.  testator.
    b.  executor.
    c.  beneficiary.
    d.  administrator.

22. When a testator leaves a specific devise of property to a beneficiary, but the property is no longer in the estate when the testator dies, the beneficiary receives nothing under the principle of
    a.  abatement.
    b.  ademption.
    c.  intestacy.
    d.  per capita distribution.

23. An oral will made by a dying person before witnesses is
    a.  a holographic will.
    b.  a joint will.
    c.  a nuncupative will.
    d.  a reciprocal will.

24. The person who is entitled to receive the trust *corpus* upon the termination of the trust is
    a.  the trustee.
    b.  the beneficiary.
    c.  the income beneficiary.
    d.  the remainder beneficiary.

25. The trust *res* is
    a.  The trust beneficiary.
    b.  The person who establishes a trust.
    c.  The party responsible for maintaining, investing, buying, or selling trust assets.
    d.  None of the above.

## Short Answer

26.    What is the difference between a prenuptial agreement and an antenuptial agreement?

_____

_____

27.    What is the difference between an annulment and a divorce?

_____

28.    How does separate property become marital property?

_____

29.    What is the difference between equitable distribution and equal distribution of assets in a divorce?

_____

_____

30. Mary and Marty were granted a decree of divorce after the court approved their agreed-upon property settlement and division of debts. As part of the settlement, Marty was given a debt for Stellar Loans. Marty loses his job and cannot pay the debt. Stellar demands payment from Mary. Can Stellar collect this debt from Mary?

     _____

     _____

31. What is the difference between joint custody and joint physical custody?

     _____

     _____

32. What are visitation rights?

     _____

33. What is child support?

     _____

34. What are the three main requirements of a valid will?

     _____

35. What is per stirpes distribution?

     _____

     _____

36. What happens to property when it escheats?

     _____

37. What is a remainder beneficiary?

     _____

38. What is a pour-over will?

     _____

39. What is a living will?

     _____

40. What is a health care agent?

     _____

# Answers to Refresh Your Memory

1.  prenuptial agreement  [p 1117]
2.  antenuptial agreement  [p 1117]
3.  Marriage  [p 1117]
4.  Emancipation  [p 1119]
5.  paternity action  [p 1119]
6.  Adoption  [p 1120]
7.  annulment  [p 1122]
8.  divorce  [p 1122]
9.  settlement agreement  [p 1123]

10. Separate property  [p 1124]
11. Marital property  [p 1124]
12. will  [p 1129]
13. undue influence  [p 1133]
14. trust  [p 1140]
15. living will  [p 1144]

# Critical Thought Exercise Model Answer

Separate property for Steven consists of the stocks, bonds, real estate, and other investments in his name from property left him by his parents valued at approximately $3,200,000.

Jane has no separate property. The $220 she received after the settlement of her parents' estate has been deposited into their joint checking account, therefore it has been commingled with marital property and has become marital property.

Marital property for the couple consists of the following: the house, despite their first house being purchased with money from Steven's parents, it is titled in both their names; the cars and minivan are titled in both of their names; the household goods were purchased as joint property with money earned during the marriage; the retirement accounts were begun and contributed to from money earned during the marriage; the checking and savings accounts are held jointly; the CDs are held jointly, despite their being purchased with money from Steven's parents' estate.

# Answers to Practice Quiz

## True/False

1. False  Under the fault rule, if a prospective groom breaks off the engagement, the prospective bride may keep the ring. [p 1117]
2. True  A prenuptial agreement is a contract entered into by prospective spouses prior to marriage, specifying how property will be distributed upon termination of the marriage or the death of a spouse. [p 1117]
3. False  A marriage license is a legal document issued by the state, certifying that two people are married. [p 1118]
4. False  A paternity action is a legal proceeding where the court identifies a child's father. [p 1119]
5. False  An annulment is an order of the court declaring that a marriage did not exist. [p 1122]
6. False  A decree of divorce is issued by the court to terminate the marriage. [p 1122]
7. True  A *pro se* divorce is where the parties represent themselves in the divorce action. [p 1123]
8. False  Equal distribution is a method where the court orders an equal distribution of marital property to the divorcing spouses. [p 1124]
9. True  The persons designated to receive the property under a will are the beneficiaries. [p 1129]
10. True  The will must be signed by the testator or testatrix; most states require the signature at the end to prevent fraud. [p 1130]
11. False  A will may be revoked by tearing, burning, or defacing the will. [p 1131]
12. True  A specific gift is an item of personal property, like your great-grandmother's ring. [p 1136]
13. True  Abatement is applied if the property the testator leaves is not sufficient to satisfy all the beneficiaries named in a will. [p 1138]
14. False  When two people who would inherit property from each other die simultaneously, each deceased person's property is distributed as though he or she had survived. It is a question of inheritance that is decided by the Uniform Simultaneous Death Act. [p 1132]
15. False  A will may be found to be invalid if made through undue influence on the testator. [p 1133]

## Multiple Choice

16. A  Answer A is correct, as it correctly states the fact that a prenuptial agreement is executed prior to marriage. Answer B is incorrect, as an antenuptial agreement is executed during marriage. Answer C is incorrect, as a prenuptial agreement is executed before marriage. Answer D is incorrect for the above reasons. [p 1117]

17. B  Answer B is correct, as a marriage license is a legal document issued by the state, certifying that two people are married. Answer A is incorrect, as a marriage is the legal union between a male and a female that confers certain duties and rights upon the spouses. Answer C is incorrect, as a marriage ceremony is where a couple exchanges marriage vows. Answer D is incorrect, as a common law marriage is a marriage recognized despite the fact that the parties did not meet the requirements of an official marriage. [p 1118]

18. C  Answer C is correct, as emancipation is when a child leaves the parents and voluntarily lives on his or her own. Answer A is incorrect, as an annulment is an order of the court declaring that a marriage did not exist. Answer B is incorrect, as a surrogacy is where a woman agrees to be artificially inseminated with the sperm of a male and to give up the baby to the sperm donor upon the birth of the child. Answer D is incorrect for the above reasons. [p 1118]

19. B  Answer B is correct, as a settlement agreement is the written agreement signed by the divorcing parties that shows their agreement to settle property and other rights. Answer A is incorrect, as the decree of divorce is a court order terminating the marriage. Answer C is incorrect, as a *pro se* divorce is one where the parties represent themselves in the divorce action. Answer D is incorrect, as equitable distribution is a method of dividing marital property in a divorce. [p 1123]

20. D  Answer D is correct, as separate property is the property owned by a spouse prior to marriage, as well as inheritances and gifts received by the spouse during the marriage. Answer A is incorrect, as marital property is the property acquired during the course of marriage using income earned during the marriage, plus property converted into this property. Answer B is incorrect, as permanent alimony is spousal support ordered by the court to be paid to one divorcing spouse to the other for life or until remarriage. Answer C is incorrect, as spousal support is money ordered by the court to be paid by one divorcing spouse to the other. [p 1124]

21. A  Answer A is correct, as the testator is the person who makes a will. A few states still maintain the additional designation of testatrix for a female testator. Answer B is incorrect, as the executor is the person named in the will to serve as personal representative for the administration of the will. Answer C is incorrect because the beneficiary receives the property upon disbursement. Answer D is incorrect because the administrator is the personal representative who is appointed when an executor is not named in the will. [p 1129]

22. B  Answer B is correct, as under ademption the gift lapses and is not granted from other estate assets. Answer A is incorrect because abatement is a method for dividing an estate that does not have enough assets to satisfy all the gifts and taxes. Answer C is incorrect because intestacy applies when there is no will. Answer D is incorrect because per capita distribution is a method for dividing the estate equally among all the living descendants. [p 1138]

23. C  Answer C is correct, as a nuncupative will is an oral will made by a dying person before witnesses. Answer A is incorrect, as a holographic will is entirely handwritten and signed by the testator. Answer B is incorrect, as a joint will is where two ore more testators execute the same instrument as their will. Answer D is incorrect, as a reciprocal will is where two or more testators execute separate will that leave property in favor of the other on condition that the survivor leave the remaining property on his or her death as agreed by the testators. [p 1132]

24. D  Answer D is correct, as a remainder beneficiary is the person who is entitled to receive the trust *corpus* upon the termination of the trust. Answer A is incorrect, as the trustee is one to whom legal title of the trust assets is transferred and who is responsible for the management of the trust. Answer B is incorrect, as the beneficiary is one for whose benefit a trust is created. Answer C is incorrect, as the income beneficiary is the person to whom trust income is to be paid. [p 1141]

25. D  Answer D is correct, as the trust *res* is the trust *corpus*, thus Answers A, B, and C are all incorrect. [p 1140]

## Short Answer

26. A prenuptial agreement is a contract entered into by prospective spouses prior to marriage, specifying how property will be distributed upon termination of the marriage or death of a spouse. An antenuptial agreement is essentially the same contract executed by the spouses during the marriage. [p 1117]
27. An annulment is an order of the court declaring that a marriage did not exist. A divorce is an order of the court that terminates a marriage. [p 1122]
28. If separate property is commingled with marital property or if the owner of the separate property changes title to the property by placing the other spouse's name on the title. [p 1124]
29. Equitable distribution is where the court orders fair distribution of assets, which does not mean equal distribution. Equal distribution of assets means that the assets are split equally. [p 1124]
30. Yes. Even though the couple agreed on the division of debt and the court approved, the third party creditor can seek payment from the other divorced spouse in the event that the spouse awarded the debt does not pay. [p 1125]
31. Joint custody means that both divorcing parents are responsible for making major decisions concerning the child. Joint physical custody means that the child of divorcing parents spends a certain amount of time being raised by each parent. [p 1129]
32. Rights for the non-custodial parent to visit his or her child for limited periods of time. [p 1129]
33. Payments made by the non-custodial parent to help pay for the financial support of his or her children. [p 1127]
34. Testamentary capacity, a written will, testator's signature. [p 1130]
35. In per stirpes, the lineal descendants (grandchildren and great-grandchildren of the deceased) inherit by representation of the parent. They split what their deceased parent would have received. If their parent is alive, they receive nothing. [p 1137]
36. Intestacy statutes provide that if there are no heirs, the deceased's property goes (escheats) to the state. [p 1140]
37. A person who is entitled to receive the trust corpus upon the termination of the trust. [p 1141]
38. A will that is necessary to distribute property of the grantor that is not in the living trust. [p 1143]
39. A document signed by a person that stipulates his or her wishes to not have his or her life prolonged by artificial means. [p 1144]
40. A person named in a living will or other document to make health care decisions for the maker of the living will or other document in accordance with the maker's wishes. [p 1144]

# Chapter 40

# ACCOUNTANT'S LIABILITY

## Chapter Overview

The major functions of accountants in business are to audit financial statements and to render opinions about those audits. Accountants will prepare financial statements, render tax advice, prepare tax forms, and provide consulting and other services. Accountants are usually sued for breach of contract, misrepresentation, and negligence or for statutory violations. They can be held liable to clients and to third parties. This chapter looks at the legal liability of accountants.

## Objectives

Upon completion of the exercises in this chapter, you should be able to:

1. Discuss an accountant's liability to his or her client for beach of contract and fraud.
2. Explain an accountant's liability to third parties under the *Ultramares* doctrine.
3. Discuss an accountant's liability to third parties under the *Restatement (Second) of Torts* and the foreseeability standard.
4. Explain an accountant's civil liability and criminal liability under federal securities laws.
5. Identify the duties of accountants under the Sarbanes-Oxley Act.

## Practical Application

You should be able to recognize whether an accountant is liable to his or her client for breach of contract or fraud. You should be able to discuss the liability of an accountant to third parties and the foreseeability standard. You should be able to understand the duties of an accountant under federal securities laws and the Sarbanes-Oxley Act.

## Helpful Hints

It may be helpful to organize the liability of accountants under the different categories, such as liability to clients and liability for violations of securities laws. Within these categories you can list the specific duties and how the accountant is held liable for violating those duties.

## Study Tips

### Public Accounting

A certified public accountant (CPA) is an accountant who has met certain educational requirements, passed the CPA examination, and has a certain number of years of audit experience. One who is not certified is referred to as a public accountant.

**Accounting Standards and Principles.** Certified public accountants must abide by two uniform standards of professional conduct.

- GAAPs. Generally Accepted Accounting Principles are standards for the preparation and presentation of financial statements.
- GAASs. Generally Accepted Auditing Standards specify the methods and procedures that must be used in conducting audits.

**Audits.** An audit is a verification of a company's books and records.
- An independent CPA must review the financial records, check for accuracy, and investigate the financial position of the company.
- Failure to follow GAASs is negligence.

**Auditor's Opinions.** A report about how fairly the financial statements of the client company represent the company's financial position, results of operations, and change in financial position.

*Unqualified Opinion.* This opinion states that the company's financial statements fairly represent the company's financial position, results of its operations, and changes in its financial position.
- The most favorable opinion an auditor can give.

*Qualified Opinion.* This opinion states that the financial statements are fairly represented except for a departure from GAAPs, a change in accounting principles, or a material uncertainty.

*Adverse Opinion.* This opinion determines that the financial statements do not fairly represent the company's financial position, results of operations, or changes in financial position.
- Usually there is a material misstatement of certain items on the financial statements.

*Disclaimer of Opinion.* This expresses the auditor's inability to draw a conclusion as to the accuracy of the company's financial records, usually because of insufficient information on hand.

**Limited Liability Partnership (LLP).** This is the business form chosen by most public accounting firms because of the limited liability of all partners.

## Liability of Accountants to Their Clients

Accountants are hired to perform certain accounting services for their clients and may be found liable to those clients for breach of contract, fraud, and negligence.

**Breach of Contract.** An accountant who fails to perform as specified in the terms of engagement may be sued for damages caused by the breach of contract.

**Fraud.** Actual fraud is an intentional misrepresentation or omission of a material fact that is relied on by the client and causes the client damage.
- Constructive fraud, or gross negligence, happens when the accountant acts with "reckless disregard" for the truth or the consequence of his or her actions.

**Negligence.** An accountant who fails to meet the standard of a reasonable accountant when providing services may be sued for negligence, or accountant malpractice.
- Violations of GAAPs or GAASs are *prima facie* evidence of negligence.

## Liability of Accountants to Third Parties

In lawsuits against accountants, the plaintiffs are third parties – such as shareholders and bondholders, trade creditors, or banks – who relied on information supplied by the auditor.

**The *Ultramares* Doctrine.** This doctrine states that an accountant cannot be held liable for negligence unless the plaintiff was either in privity of contract or a privity-like relationship with the accountant.
- A relationship would occur where a client employed an accountant to prepare financial statements to be used by a third party for a specific purpose.

**Section 552 of the Restatement (Second) of Torts.** This section provides that an accountant is liable for negligence to any member of a limited class of intended users for whose benefit the accountant has been employed to prepare the client's financial statements or to whom the accountant knows will be supplied copies of the financial statements.

**The Foreseeability Standard.** This standard holds an accountant liable to any foreseeable user of the client's financial statements.

**Fraud.** An injured third party who relies on the accountant's fraud may sue for damages.

**Breach of Contract.** Third parties generally cannot sue accountants for breach of contract because they are incidental beneficiaries and do not have privity of contract with the accountant.

**Accountant's Duty to Report Client's Illegal Activity.** Section 10A of the Securities Exchange Act imposes reporting duties on accountants regarding illegal acts of clients.
- The client's management and audit committee must be informed.
- If management fails to take timely and appropriate action, the board of directors must be informed if the act would materially affect the financial statements and the auditor expects to issue a nonstandard audit report or intends to resign.
- The board must report act to the SEC; if they fail to, the auditor must notify the SEC.

## Liability of Accountants for Violations of Securities Laws

Accountants can be held liable for violation of federal and state securities laws.

**Section 11(a).** Under this section of the Securities Act of 1933, accountants are considered to be experts and the financial statements they prepare to be included with the registration statement with the SEC are considered an expertised portion of the registration statement.
- Accountants have civil liability in fraud or negligence for making – or failing to find – misstatements or omissions of material facts in a registration statement.
- The due diligence defense states that the accountant can escape liability if he or she had reasonable grounds to believe and did believe that the statements made were true and there was no omission of a material fact that would make the statements misleading.

**Section 10(b) and Rule 10b-5.** Section 10(b) of the Securities Exchange Act of 1934 prohibit any manipulative or deceptive practice in connection with the purchase or self of any security. Rule 10b-5 makes it unlawful to defraud, make misstatements or omission of material fact, engage in fraud or deceit upon any person in connection with the purchase or sale of any security.

- Only intentional conduct and recklessness of accountants and others, but not ordinary negligence, violates these requirements.

**Section 18(a).** This section of the Securities Exchange Act imposes civil liability on anyone who makes false or misleading statements of material fact in any application, report, or document filed with the SEC.
- Requires a showing of fraud or reckless conduct; negligence is not actionable.
- Defendant can defeat liability by showing good faith actions or the plaintiff knew of the false or misleading statement when the securities were purchased or sold.

**Private Securities Litigation Reform Act of 1995.** This Act changed the liability of accountants and other securities professionals.
- Pleading and procedural requirements make it more difficult to bring class action securities lawsuits.
- The Act replaces joint and several liability of defendants with proportionate liability.
  - This limit is not available if the defendant acted knowingly.

## Criminal Liability of Accountants

Many statutes impose criminal penalties on accountants who violate their provisions.

**Section 24.** This section of the Securities Act makes it a criminal offense to willfully make any untrue statement of material fact or to omit any material fact that would cause one to be misled in a registration statement filed with the SEC.
- Penalties include fines, imprisonment, or both.

**Section 32(a).** This section of the Securities Exchange Act makes it a criminal offense to willfully and knowingly make or cause to be made any false or misleading statement in any application, report, or other document required to be filed with the SEC.
- Penalties include fines, imprisonment, or both.

**Criminal Liability Regarding Tax Preparation.** The Tax Reform Act of 1976 imposes criminal liability on accountants and other who prepare tax returns for negligent understatement of the tax liability, willful understatement of a client's tax liability, and aiding and assisting in the preparation of a false tax return. Penalties include fines, imprisonment, or both.
- Accountants can be enjoined from further federal income tax practice.

**Racketeer Influenced and Corrupt Organizations Act (RICO).** Securities fraud falls under this Act. If defendant is criminally convicted in connection with securities fraud, injured persons can bring a civil suit and collect treble damages.

**State Securities Laws.** Many states have enacted all or part of the Uniform Securities Act, which under section 101 makes it a criminal offense for accountants and others to willfully falsify financial statements and other reports.

## Sarbanes-Oxley Act

The Sarbanes-Oxley Act imposes new rules to improve financial reporting, eliminate conflicts of interest, and provide government oversight of accounting and audit services.

**Establishment of the Public Company Accounting Oversight Board.** This oversight board has authority to adopt rules concerning auditing, accounting quality control, independence, and ethics of public companies and public accountants.

**Public Accounting Firms Registering with the Board.** To audit a public company, a public accounting firm must register with the board and are subject to audit and discipline by the board.

**Separation of Audit and Nonaudit Services.** The Act makes it unlawful for a registered public accounting firm to concurrently provide audit and certain nonaudit services to a public company.

*Audit Report Sign-Offs.* Each audit is assigned an audit partner to supervise the audit and approve the audit report. The Act requires that a second partner must review and approve audit reports prepared by the firm.

*Prohibited Employment.* Any person employed by a public accounting firm that audits a client cannot be employed by that client as the CEO, CFO, controller, chief accounting officer, ore equivalent position for one year following the audit.

## Accountant's Privilege and Work Papers

In the course of their work, accountants obtain information about their clients and prepare work papers which, in the event of a lawsuit, may be sought by the court.

**Accountant-Client Privilege.** The U.S. Supreme Court has held that there is no accountant-client privilege under federal law. About 20 states have an accountant-client privilege.

**Accountants' Work Papers.** Some states provide work product immunity, which means an accountant's work papers cannot be discovered in a court case against the accountant's client.
  * Most states, and federal law, do not provide this protection.

## Refresh Your Memory

The following exercises will help to test your memory regarding the principles given in this chapter. Read each question twice, then place your answer in the blank provided for each question. Review the chapter material for any questions you are unable to answer or remember.

1. GAAPs are _____ for the preparation and presentation of financial statements.

2. GAASs specify method and procedures to be used to _____ _____.

3. A(n) _____ is a verification of a company's books and records.

4. A(n) _____ _____ states that the company's financial statements fairly represent the company's financial position.

5. A(n) _____ _____ states that the company's financial statements are fairly represented except for a departure from generally accepted accounting standards.

6. A(n) _____ _____ states that the company's financial statements do not fairly represent the company's financial position.

7. A(n) _____ _____ _____ expresses the auditor's inability to draw a conclusion as to the accuracy of the company's financial records.

8. The _____ _____ states that an accountant is not liable for negligence to a third party unless the third party was either in privity of contract or a privity-like relationship with the accountant.

9. The _____ _____ states that an accountant is liable to any foreseeable user of the client's financial statements.

10. The _____ _____ _____ _____ Act makes it more difficult for plaintiffs to bring class action securities lawsuits and imposes proportional liability for violations of securities laws.

11. The _____ _____ Act of 1976 imposes criminal liability on accountants for aiding or assisting in the preparation of a false tax return.

12. The _____ _____ Act establishes the Public Company Accounting Oversight Board (PCAOB).

13. It is unlawful for a registered public accounting firm to simultaneously provide _____ and certain _____ services to a public company.

14. The federal government does not recognize the _____ _____ _____ so that an accountant can be called as a witness against his client in a federal proceeding.

15. Some states provide _____ _____ _____, which means that an accountant's work papers cannot be discovered in a court case against the accountant's client.

## Critical Thought Exercise

Leo is a partner in a public accounting firm and the reviewing partner for the audit of a client. He has reviewed their financial statements and the audit report that was prepared by the audit supervisor. He has no reason not to sign off on the audit and audit report. However, at about the time he was ready to sign off on the report, one of the firm's newest interns asked to speak with him, bringing forth several concerns regarding the business practices of the client. She alleges that she overheard employees speaking about off-shore companies the client was using to obtain loans for the primary business, and that she came across a memo in a stack of paperwork that seemed to verify the existence of these companies and loans. But neither the companies nor the loans were reflected in the financial statements of the client, and she was not able to obtain a copy of the memo. The intern is worried that she is overstepping her authority by coming to a senior partner, but she really thought it was important and the audit supervisor never had to time listen to her concerns; he just told her to go make him some coffee and do her assigned tasks.

Under Section 10A of the Securities Exchange Act of 1934, is Leo obliged to make a report?

*Please compose your answer on a separate sheet of paper or on your computer.*

# Practice Quiz

## True/False

1. ___ GAAPs specify the method and procedures to be used to conduct audits.

2. ___ An unqualified opinion states that the company's financial statements fairly represent the company's financial position.

3. ___ A qualified opinion states that the company's financial statements do not fairly represent the company's financial position.

4. ___ An adverse opinion expresses the auditor's inability to draw a conclusion as to the accuracy of the company's financial records.

5. ___ A disclaimer of opinion states that the company's financial statements are fairly represented except for a departure from generally accepted accounting standards.

6. ___ A limited liability partnership provides partners with limited liability.

7. ___ Accountants cannot be held liable to their clients for breach of contract.

8. ___ Clients can hold accountants liable for fraud.

9. ___ Negligence of accountants is also called accountant malpractice.

10. ___ The Ultramares Doctrine states that an accountant is liable to any foreseeable user of the client's financial statements.

11. ___ A third party who relies on the accountant's fraud and is injured may not bring an action against the accountant to recover damages.

12. ___ RICO imposes civil treble damages against defendants previously criminally convicted of securities fraud.

13. ___ Accounting firms that audit public companies need not register with the PCAOB.

14. ___ The accountant-client privilege prevents the accountant from being called as a witness against his or her client.

15. ___ The federal government does not recognize the accountant-client privilege, but does recognize work paper immunity for accountants.

## Multiple Choice

16. Standards for the preparation and presentation of financial statements are the
    a. GAAPs
    b. GASPs

    c.  GAASs

    d.  GAPSs

17. The specifications for the method and procedures to be used to conduct audits are the
    a.  GAAPs
    b.  GASPs
    c.  GAASs
    d.  GAPSs

18. An auditor's opinion that states that the company's financial statements fairly represent the company's financial position is
    a.  An unqualified opinion.
    b.  A qualified opinion.
    c.  An adverse opinion.
    d.  A disclaimer of opinion.

19. Which of the following is true about the accountant-client privilege?
    a.  It protects the accountant from being called as a witness against a client.
    b.  The federal government does not recognize the privilege in federal proceedings.
    c.  About 20 states have enacted statutes that create this privilege.
    d.  All of the above.

20. An auditor's opinion that states that the company's financial statements are fairly represented except for a departure from generally accepted accounting standards is
    a.  An unqualified opinion.
    b.  A qualified opinion.
    c.  An adverse opinion.
    d.  A disclaimer of opinion.

21. Which of the following are true about the Sarbanes-Oxley Act?
    a.  It establishes the Public Accountant Responsibility Oversight Board (PAROB).
    b.  It exempts accounting firms that audit public companies from registering with the board.
    c.  It compels public accounting firms to concurrently provide audit and nonaudit services.
    d.  None of the above.

22. An auditor's opinion that states that the company's financial statements do not fairly represent the company's financial position is
    a.  An unqualified opinion.
    b.  A qualified opinion.
    c.  An adverse opinion.
    d.  A disclaimer of opinion.

23. Which of the following is false regarding the Securities Act of 1933?
    a.  It imposes civil liability on accountants for misstatements or omissions of material fact.
    b.  It imposes civil liability on accountants who employ manipulative or deceptive practices.
    c.  It makes it criminal for an accountant to willfully make untrue statements of material fact
    d.  None of the above.

24. An auditor's opinion that expresses the auditor's inability to draw a conclusion as to the accuracy of the company's financial records is
    a. An unqualified opinion.
    b. A qualified opinion.
    c. An adverse opinion.
    d. A disclaimer of opinion.

25. Which of the following is false regarding the Securities Exchange Act of 1934?
    a. It makes accountants liable who make false or misleading statements of material fact.
    b. It exempts auditors from reporting illegal acts committed by their clients.
    c. It makes it criminal for an accountant to willfully and knowingly make or cause to be made any false or misleading statements.
    d. None of the above.

## Short Answer

26. What does GAAPs signify?

_____

27. What does GAASs signify?

_____

28. What are the four types of auditor's reports that can be issued?

_____

29. What is the primary reason that accounting firms organize as a Limited Liability Partnership?

_____

30. What are the three primary grounds under which accountants can be liable to their clients?

_____

31. What are the three doctrines under which an accountant can be liable for negligence?

_____

32. Under which three federal securities laws can accountants be held liable?

_____

33. What are the two main provisions of the Private Securities Litigation Reform Act of 1995?

_____

34. What does Section 10A of the Securities Exchange Act of 1934 mandate?

_____

35. What are the five statutes that impose criminal liability on accountants?

_____

_____

36. What oversight board does the Sarbanes-Oxley Act establish?

_____

37. What simultaneous activity does the Sarbanes-Oxley Act make unlawful?

_____

38. What is the accountant-client privilege?

_____

39. What courts recognize the accountant-client privilege?

_____

40. What is work product immunity for accountants?

_____

# Answers to Refresh Your Memory

1.  standards  [p 1160]
2.  conduct audits  [p 1160]
3.  audit  [p 1160]
4.  unqualified opinion  [p 1160]
5.  qualified opinion  [p 1161]
6.  adverse opinion  [p 1161]
7.  disclaimer of opinion  [p 1161]
8.  Ultramares Doctrine  [p 1164]
9.  foreseeability standard  [p 1166]
10. Private Securities Litigation Reform  [p 1169]
11. Tax Reform  [p 1170]
12. Sarbanes-Oxley  [p 1172]
13. audit, nonaudit  [p 1172]
14. accountant-client privilege  [p 1173]
15. work paper immunity  [p 1173]

# Critical Thought Exercise Model Answer

Under Section 10A, Leo is required to report illegal acts committed by his client. Leo has financial reports and an audit report that appear to be legitimate and show no irregularities. He also has the report of hearsay evidence from a new intern that purports to show that there are irregularities in the client's business practices. However, the tangible evidence the intern claims to have seen was not copied to substantiate her allegations.

On their own, the intern's unsubstantiated allegations would not appear to be sufficient to trigger a SEC mandated report under Section 10A. He has no proof that there is any criminal activity on the part of his client. However, these allegations should be sufficient for Leo to hold off on signing off on the audit report for the client until more investigation can be made into the allegations made by the intern. If further investigation provides some substantiation for the allegations, then Leo will be required to make the SEC mandated report. If the investigations do not provide support to the allegations, then there has been a delay to the delivery of the audit report but no premature triggering of the reporting requirement.

# Answers to Practice Quiz

## True/False

1. False   GAASs specify the method and procedures to be used to conduct audits.  [p 1160]
2. True   An unqualified opinion states that the company's financial statements fairly represent the company's financial position.  [p 1160]
3. False   An adverse opinion states that the company's financial statements do not fairly represent the company's financial position.  [p 1161]
4. False   A disclaimer of opinion expresses the auditor's inability to draw a conclusion as to the accuracy of the company's financial records.  [p 1161]
5. False   A qualified opinion states that the company's financial statements are represented fairly except for a departure from generally accepted accounting standards.  [p 1161]
6. True   A limited liability partnership provides partners with limited liability.  [p 1161]
7. False   Accountants can be held liable to their clients for breach of contract.  [p 1162]
8. True   Clients can hold accountants liable for fraud.  [p 1162]
9. True   Negligence of accountants is also called accountant malpractice.  [p 1162]
10. False   The foreseeability standard states that an accountant is liable to any foreseeable user of the client's financial statements.  [p 1163-1166]
11. False   A third party who relies on the accountant's fraud and is injured may bring an action against the accountant to recover damages.  [p 1167]
12. True   RICO imposes civil treble damages against defendants previously criminally convicted of securities fraud.  [p 1170]
13. False   Accounting firms that audit public companies must register with the PCAOB.  [p 1172]
14. True   The accountant-client privilege prevents the accountant from being called as a witness against his or her client.  [p 1173]
15. False   The federal government does not recognize the accountant-client privilege, nor does it recognize work paper immunity for accountants.  [p 1173]

## Multiple Choice

16. A   Answer A is correct, as GAAPs refers to generally accepted accounting principals. Answer B is incorrect, as it is nonsense.  Answer C is incorrect, as GAASs refers to generally accepted auditing standards.  Answer D is incorrect, as it is nonsense.  [p 1160]
17. C   Answer C is correct, as GAASs refers to generally accepted auditing standards.  Answer A is incorrect, as GAAPs refers to generally accepted accounting principals.  Answers B and D are incorrect, as they are nonsense.  [p 1160]
18. A   Answer A is correct, as an unqualified opinion states that the company's financial statements fairly represent the company's financial position.  Answer B is incorrect, as a qualified opinion states that the company's financial statements are fairly represented except for a departure from generally accepted accounting standards.  Answer C is incorrect, as an adverse opinion states that the company's financial statements do not fairly represent the company's financial position.  Answer D is incorrect, as a disclaimer of opinion expresses the auditor's inability to draw a conclusion as to the accuracy of the company's financial records.  [p 1160]
19. D   Answer D is correct, as all of the answers A, B, and C are correct statements.  [p 1173]

20. B   Answer B is correct, as a qualified opinion states that the company's financial statements are fairly represented except for a departure from generally accepted accounting standards. Answer A is incorrect, as an unqualified opinion states that the company's financial statements fairly represent the company's financial position. Answer C is incorrect, as an adverse opinion states that the company's financial statements do not fairly represent the company's financial position. Answer D is incorrect, as a disclaimer of opinion expresses the auditor's inability to draw a conclusion as to the accuracy of the company's financial records. [p 1161]
21. D   Answer D is correct, as all answers A, B, and C are incorrect statements. [p 1172]
22. C   Answer C is correct, as an adverse opinion states that the company's financial statements do not fairly represent the company's financial position. Answer A is incorrect, as an unqualified opinion states that the company's financial statements fairly represent the company's financial position. Answer B is incorrect, as a qualified opinion states that the company's financial statements are fairly represented except for a departure from generally accepted accounting standards. Answer D is incorrect, as a disclaimer of opinion expresses the auditor's inability to draw a conclusion as to the accuracy of the company's financial records. [p 1161]
23. D   Answer D is correct, as all of the answers A, B, and C are true. [p 1168-1170]
24. D   Answer D is correct, as a disclaimer of opinion expresses the auditor's inability to draw a conclusion as to the accuracy of the company's financial records. Answer A is incorrect, as an unqualified opinion states that the company's financial statements fairly represent the company's financial position. Answer B is incorrect, as a qualified opinion states that the company's financial statements are fairly represented except for a departure from generally accepted accounting standards. Answer C is incorrect, as an adverse opinion states that the company's financial statements do not fairly represent the company's financial position. [p 1161]
25. B   Answer B is correct, as it imposes a duty on auditors to report illegal acts committed by their clients. Answers A and C are incorrect, as they are both true. Answer D is incorrect for the above reasons. [p 1168-1170]

## Short Answer

26. It stands for Generally Accepted Accounting Principals. [p 1160]
27. It stands for Generally Accepted Auditing Standards. [p 1160]
28. Unqualified opinion, qualified opinion, adverse opinion, and disclaimer of opinion. [p 1160-1161]
29. All of the partners have limited liability. [p 1161]
30. Breach of contract, fraud, and negligence or accountant malpractice. [p 1162]
31. Ultramares doctrine, Section 552 of the Restatement (Second) of torts, and the Foreseeability standard. [p 1163]
32. Section 11(a) of the Securities Act of 1933, Section 10(b) of the Securities Act of 1933, and Section 18(a) of the Securities Exchange Act of 1934. [p 1168]
33. It makes it more difficult for plaintiffs to bring class action securities lawsuits and it imposes proportional liability for violations of securities laws. [p 1169]
34. It imposes duties on auditors to detect and report illegal acts committed by their clients. [p 1167]
35. Section 24 of the securities Act of 1933, Section 32(a) of the Securities Exchange Act of 1934, Tax Reform Act of 1976, Racketeer Influenced and Corrupt Organizations Act, state securities laws. [p 1170-1171]
36. The Public Company Accounting Oversight Board (PCAOB). [p 1172]

37. For public accounting firms to simultaneously provide audit and certain nonaudit services to a public company.  [p 1172]
38. It protects the accountant from being called as a witness against his or her client.  [p 1173]
39. State courts in about 20 states recognize this privilege.  Federal courts do not recognize it.  [p 1173]
40. Work product immunity means that an accountant's work papers cannot be discovered in a court case against the accountant's client.  [p 1173]

# Chapter 41

# INTERNATIONAL AND WORLD TRADE LAW

## Chapter Overview

International law is unique in that it has no single legislative source to enact it, there is no single world court to interpret it, and there is no world executive branch to enforce it. Nations choose to obey international law enacted by other countries or international organizations. This chapter introduces broad concepts of international law, sources of international law, and administrative organizations.

## Objectives

Upon completion of the exercises that follow, you should be able to:

1. Recognize the function of the federal government's power under the Foreign Commerce and Treaty Clauses of the U.S. Constitution.
2. List and differentiate between the different sources of international law.
3. Understand the functions and importance of the United Nations.
4. Be familiar with the North American Free Trade Agreement and other regional economic organizations.
5. Discuss how the World Trade Organization's dispute resolution procedure works.

## Practical Application

You should be able to appreciate the importance of the Foreign Commerce and Treaty Clauses of the U.S. Constitution as well as the impact of sovereign immunity. You should be familiar with the names and functions of the various regional organizations. You should be able to state how international disputes are arbitrated and how the World Trade Organization's dispute resolution procedure works.

## Helpful Hints

You should focus on the fact that the chapter involves the international spectrum of business. The study tips below are organized first by sources of international law, then by regional organization, followed by procedure for resolving international disputes. It is very beneficial to understand the functions of the various organizations in order to better understand the cases discussed in the text.

## Study Tips

### The United States Foreign Affairs

The power to regulate the internal affairs of this country is divided between federal and state governments. The federal government is given most of the power in international affairs.

**Foreign Commerce Clause.** The Foreign Commerce Clause allows Congress to regulate commerce with foreign nations. States cannot unduly burden foreign commerce.

**Treaty Clause.** The Treaty Clause gives the president the power to make treaties as long as two-thirds of the senators present agree. State and local laws cannot conflict with treaties.

## Sources of International Law

Article 38(1) of the Statute of the International Court of Justice lists sources of international law that international tribunals use in deciding international disputes.

**Treaties and Conventions.** These are like legislations published by the United Nations and whose subject matter involves human rights, commerce, dispute settlements, foreign aid and navigation.
- A treaty is an agreement or contract between two or more nations, formally signed and ratified by the supreme power of each nation.
- Conventions are treaties sponsored by international organizations, signed by several signatories

**Custom.** A separate source of international law which defines a practice followed by two or more nations when interacting with one another.
- Requirements for a practice to become a custom include a repetitive action by two or more nations over a long period of time and acknowledgment that the custom is followed.
- Customs that have been followed for a considerable amount of time may become treaties.

**General Principles of Law.** Many countries depend on general principles of law that are used in civilized nations in order to resolve international disputes.
- These principles may be derived from statutes, common law, regulations or other sources.

**Judicial Decisions and Teachings.** This fourth source of law refers to the judicial teachings and decisions of scholars from the nations in dispute.
- There is no precedent for international courts, but courts can choose to refer to past decisions.

## United Nations

A very important international organization dedicated toward maintaining peace and security in the world, espousing economic and social cooperation and protecting human rights.

**General Assembly.** It is comprised of all member nations. The assembly adopts resolutions regarding human rights, trade, finance and economics.

**Security Council.** A council made up of fifteen member nations, of which five are permanent. The council's main duty is to maintain international peace and security and is allowed to use armed forces.

**Secretariat.** It administers the day-to-day operations of the UN. It is headed by the secretary-general and may use his office to help settle international disputes.

**UN Agencies.** The United Nations is made up of many agencies to handle a variety of economic and social agencies. UNESCO, UNICEF, IMF, IFAD, and the World Bank are among these agencies.

*The International Monetary Fund (IMF).* This agency was established to help promote the world economy, with its main focus on promoting sound monetary, fiscal and macroeconomic policies worldwide by giving aide to needy countries.

*The World Bank.* The World Bank is made up of over 180 nations, and financed by developed countries. It provides money to developing countries to fund humanitarian projects and to help relieve poverty.

*The International Court of Justice.* A court located in The Hague, the Netherlands which is also called the World Court. Only nations may have this court decide cases. A nation may however seek redress on behalf of a business or individual who has a claim against another country.

## Regional International Organizations

Several significant regional organizations have agreed to work together to promote peace and security as well as economic, social, and cultural development.

**The European Union (EU).** Formerly the European Community or Common Market, it represents more than 300 million people in several countries of Western Europe.
- Customs duties have been abolished among member nations and customs tariffs have been enacted for European Union trade with the rest of the world.
- A single monetary unit, the euro, and a common monetary policy have been introduced.

**The North American Free Trade Agreement (NAFTA).** An agreement signed by Mexico, Canada and the United States that created a free-trade zone stretching from the Yukon to the Yucatan.
- This agreement dispensed with or reduced most of the quotas, tariffs and duties as well as other barriers to trade among these three countries.
- Some economists feel that NAFTA is more of a managed trade agreement.

**Asian Economic Communities.** Several Asian countries have created the Association of South East Asian Nations (ASEAN). China and Japan are not members of this association. However, Japan has given financing for the countries that comprise this organization. China may one day become a member.

**Organization of Petroleum Exporting Countries (OPEC).** The Organization of Petroleum Exporting Countries is the best-known Middle Eastern economic organizations. OPEC sets quotas on the output of oil production by member nations.

**Other Regional Economic Organizations.** There are several Latin American and Caribbean countries that have founded many regional organizations to further economic development and cooperation.
- Mexico has entered into free trade agreements with all countries of Central America, Chile, Colombia, and Venezuela.
- Central and South America countries have formed regional economic organizations.
- Several regional economic communities have been formed in Africa.

**Central America Free Trade Agreement.** An agreement where the US and several Central American countries lowered tariffs and reduced trade restrictions, which is seen as a stepping stone to the Free Trade Area of the Americas (FTAA).

## World Trade Organization (WTO)

The WTO was created as part of the Uruguay Round of trade negotiations concerning the General Agreement on Tariffs and Trade. It is located in Switzerland.
- The WTO is also known as the "Supreme Court of Trade."
- Its jurisdiction is the enforcement of comprehensive and important world trade agreements.

**WTO Dispute Resolution.** The function of the WTO is to hear and decide trade disputes between nations that are members.
- A three-member panel hears the dispute, which then generates a report that is given to the dispute settlement body.
- There is an appellate body to appeal the dispute settlement body.
  - Only issues of law, not fact may be appealed.
- If a violation of a trade agreement is found, the offending nation may be ordered to stop participating in the violating practice, as well as to pay damages to the other party.
  - If the violating nation does not comply with the order, retaliatory trade sanctions by other nations may be assessed against the offending nation.

**Nationalization of Private Property.** This international law allows nations to nationalize private property owned by foreigners if it is for a public purpose.
- This can occur by expropriation whereby the owner is paid just compensation by the government that took the property or it can be accomplished by confiscation in which case the owner either receives an insufficient payment or no payment at all for the property seized.
- The Overseas Private Investment Corporation was created to help insure U.S. businesses and citizens against losses incurred from confiscation by foreign governments. The American businesses and citizens may purchase an insurance policy to protect their property.

## National Courts Decide International Disputes

National courts of individual nations hear the bulk of disputes involving international law.

**Judicial Procedure.** The main problems a party seeking judicial resolution of an international dispute faces are which court will hear the case and which law will be applied.
- Most cases are heard in the plaintiff's home country.
- Many international contracts provide for a forum-selection clause and/or choice of law clause.

**Act of State Doctrine.** This act proclaims that judges of one country cannot question the authority of an act committed by another country that occurs within that country's own borders.

**Doctrine of Sovereign Immunity.** This doctrine states that countries are granted immunity from suits in courts in other countries, which is absolute immunity. Most Western countries use restricted immunity.
- U.S. qualified, or restricted, immunity is codified in the Foreign Sovereign Immunities Act.

*Exceptions to the Sovereign Immunities Act.* The Foreign Sovereign Immunities Act provides a qualified or restricted immunity in two situations.
- The first instance in which a foreign country is not immune from lawsuits in the U.S. courts is if the foreign country has waived its immunity, either explicitly or by implication.
- The second instance is if the action is based upon a commercial activity carried on in the U.S. by the foreign country or carried on outside the U.S. but causing a direct effect in the U.S.

**International Arbitration.** International Arbitration is a nonjudicial method of resolving disputes whereby a neutral third party decides the case.
- An arbitration clause should specify the arbitrator ore the means of selection one.
- The arbitrator will issue an award, not a judgment.
- The award wining party may attach property of the losing party regardless of which country the property is located in.

- Over fifty countries are signatories to the United Nations Convention on the Recognition and Enforcement of Foreign Arbitral Awards.

**Jewish Law and the Torah.** In addition to abiding by the criminal and civil laws of their host countries, the Jews also obey the legal principles of the Torah.
- The Torah is an thorough set of religious and political rules formulated from Jewish principles.
- The base of the Torah is to determine the truth.

**Islamic Law and the Koran.** Saudi Arabia has Islamic law as its only law.
- It is mainly used in matters of divorce, marriage and inheritance with some criminal law.
- One main characteristic of Islamic law is it prohibits making unjustified or unearned profit.

**Hindu Law – *Dharmasastra*.** The Hindu law is religious based, using scholarly decisions that have been handed down from century to century.
- It embodies the doctrine of proper behavior.
- Outside of India, Anglo-Hindu law applies in many countries with Hindu populations.

# Refresh Your Memory

The following exercises will help to test your memory regarding the principles given in this chapter. Read each question twice, then place your answer in the blank provided for each question. Review the chapter material for any questions you are unable to answer or remember.

1. There is no individual source of _____ law.

2. The _____ _____ _____ of the United States Constitution gives Congress the power to regulate commerce with foreign nations.

3. The _____ _____ of the U.S. Constitution gives the president authority to enter into treaties with foreign nations, subject to a two-thirds vote of the Senate.

4. _____ and _____ are the equivalent of legislation at the international level.

5. A(n) _____ is a practice followed by two or more nations when dealing with each other.

6. Courts and tribunals that decide international disputes often rely upon _____ _____ _____ to make their decisions.

7. _____ _____ and _____ of the most qualified scholars of the nations that are involved in the dispute are known as the fourth source of international law.

8. The International Court of Justice also known as the _____ _____.

9. The purpose of the NAFTA was to create a(n) _____ _____ zone.

10. One of the main functions of the _____ _____ _____ is to hear and decide trade disputes between member nations.

11. The _____ _____ _____ _____ states that judges of one country cannot question the validity of an act committed by another country within that other country's borders.

12. The _____ _____ _____ _____ states that countries are granted immunity from suits in courts in other countries.

13. Some countries provide for _____ immunity, and other countries, like the U.S., provide _____ immunity.

14. A foreign country is not immune from lawsuits in U.S. court if it has _____ its immunity, or if it has engaged in _____ _____ in the U.S. or outside the U.S. that causes a direct effect in the U.S.

15. A(n) _____ _____ is included in many international contracts that require arbitration of disputes arising from the contract.

# Critical Thought Exercise

Scientists at Cornell University engaged in genetic engineering and created a pear called the New York Sweetie that is resistant to bruising, browning, and insect infestation. The Sweetie grows approximately 30% larger than known pears and has both a higher water and sugar content, making the Sweetie highly desired by consumers worldwide. The only pear that can compete with the quality of the Sweetie is the Favlaka Beauty, grown exclusively in Favlaka. Favlaka is a large European nation with a population of over 300 million people. The country of Favlaka is a member of the European Union and the World Trade Organization. The residents of Favlaka consume over $1.2 billion worth of pears each year. All pears that are eaten on Favlaka are grown in Favlaka or a neighboring EU country. Favlaka will not allow the importation of fruit that has undergone any genetic engineering. The Favlaka Pear Cartel argues that the introduction of genetically engineered pears into their markets jeopardizes the Favlakan pear industry and the health of all Favlakans. They fear that future crops will become susceptible to insect infestation and attacks by mold and fungus. The U.S. Pear Growers argue that there is no scientific evidence that the Sweetie will cause damage to any other variety of pear or humans when it is grown or consumed. They further argue that the actions of the Favlakan government in banning the Sweetie are unfair trade practices under WTO agreements. It is argued that the Favlakan government is only motivated by the goal of preventing international competition for the Favlakan Beauty.

In what forum should this dispute be resolved? What procedure should be used to resolve this international dispute? What law should control the issues in this case? How should the WTO rule?

*Please compose your answer on a separate sheet of paper or on your computer.*

# Practice Quiz

## True/False

1. ___ The Security Council for the United Nations is mainly responsible for maintaining national peace and security.

2. ___ The Educational, Scientific, and Cultural Organization, the United Nations International Children's Emergency Fund and the International Monetary Fund are among the agencies that are included from the United Nations due to the Economic and social problems involved with these agencies.

3. ___ Nations that have a claim against another country may have their cases decided by the International Court of Justice.

4. ___ The European Union treaty opened borders for trade by providing for the free flow of capital, labor, goods and services among member nations.

5. ___ In order to admit a new member to the European Union, there need not be a unanimous vote by existing European Union members.

6. ___ When a foreign government nationalizes property, there are many legal remedies available to the owners of the nationalized property.

7. ___ The U.S. Government and several private companies offer political risk insurance that covers loss from uncompensated nationalization of property.

8. ___ The North American Free Trade Agreement provides for the addition of duties, tariffs, quotas and other various trade barriers between Canada, the United States and Mexico.

9. ___ An important characteristic of the World Trade Organization is the elimination of the blocking power of member nations.

10 ___ The World Trade Organization has competed with the "Supreme Court of Trade."

11. ___ A general principle of international law is that a country has authority over what takes place within its own territory.

12. ___ Rabbi-judges sitting as Beis Din are more concerned with the truth than its adversarial process.

13. ___ Islamic law provides for the making of unearned or unjustified profit.

14. ___ An arbitrator issues a judgment, not an award.

15. ___ If there is no agreement providing where an international dispute will be brought, the case will not be brought at all.

## Multiple Choice

16. What types of matters are treaties and conventions concerned with?
    a. Statutes banning state governments from purchasing goods and services
    b. Human rights, foreign aid, navigation, commerce and dispute settlement
    c. Consistent and recurring action by two or more nations over a long period of time
    d. General principles of law that are recognized by civilized nations

17. Custom is often defined as
    a   an agreement between two nations.
    b. a principle of law that is common to the national law of the parties in dispute.
    c. a practice followed by two or more nations when dealing with each other.
    d. a goal to maintain peace and security in the world.

18. Which of the following is not a true statement?
    a. Nations must obey international law enacted by other countries or international organizations.
    b. There is no world executive branch to enforce international laws.
    c. There is no individual world court that must interpret international laws.
    d. There is no individual legislative source of international law.

19. A choice of forum clause in an international contract is a clause that
    a. states that commercial disputes between the United States and foreign governments or parties may be brought in federal district court.
    b. an agreement that designates which nation's laws will be applied in deciding the case.
    c. a trade pact giving nations much easier access to the United States' marketplace.
    d. designates which nation's court has jurisdiction to hear a case arising out of the contract.

20. The act of state doctrine states that
    a. the restraint on the judiciary is not justified under the doctrine of separation of powers.
    b. a country has no authority over what transpires within its own territory.
    c. judges of one country cannot question the validity of an act committed by another country within its own borders.
    d. the courts may sit in judgment upon the acts of the government of another, done within its own borders.

21. Which of the following is true with respect to the goals of the United Nations?
    a. One of its goals is to maintain peace and security in the world.
    b. It was created to promote economic and social cooperation.
    c. It functions to protect human rights.
    d. all of the above

22. Which of the following is not an agency associated with the United Nations?
    a. United Nations International Children's Emergency Fund
    b. the World Bank
    c. the International Monastery Fund
    d. the International Fund for Agricultural Development

23. Which of the following is the United Nations governed by?
    a. the General Assembly
    b. the Secretariat
    c. the Security Council
    d. all of the above

24. Which doctrine states that an act of a government in a foreign country is not subject to suit in the foreign country?
    a. the World Trade Organization Act
    b. the Sovereign Immunity Doctrine
    c. the Act of State Doctrine
    d. none of the above

25. Which of the following are agreements between nations that are formally ratified by the supreme power of each signatory nation?
    a. customs
    b. judicial decisions and teachings
    c. treaties and conventions
    d. general principles of law

## Short Answer

26. What are the two constitutional provisions that give power to the federal government to regulate international affairs?

27. What is the name of the international organization that was created by a multinational treaty to promote social and economic cooperation among nations and to protect human rights?

28. What is the most well known Middle Eastern economic organization?

29. Which organization has become the world's most important trade organization?

30. Which courts hear most of the international disputes?

31. What is the most litigated aspect of the Foreign Sovereign Immunities Act?

32. What are the benefits of an arbitrator deciding a dispute that arises between parties to a contract?

33. If Rachel had an international dispute that she needed to have resolved, which two sources of international law would she encourage the court to rely on when making its decision?

34. If Sue, an exporter from the U.S., has an excessive tariff placed on her goods when they enter one of the WTO's member countries, what multilateral treaty might she rely on to help limit the tariff?

35. If a violation of a trade agreement is found, what can the general report and appellate decision order the offending nation to do?

36. What are the four sources of international law in the Statute of the International Court of Justice?

37. Under what situations does the U.S. not allow a foreign country immunity from suit in the U.S.?

38. What three organs govern the United Nations?

39. What is the purpose of the International Monetary Fund (IMF)?

40.    What is the purpose of the World Bank?

_____

## Answers to Refresh Your Memory

1.    international  [p 1183]
2.    Foreign Commerce Clause  [p 1183]
3.    Treaties Clause  [p 1184]
4.    Treaties, conventions  [p 1185]
5.    custom  [p 1185]
6.    general principles of law  [p 1185]
7.    Judicial decisions, teachings  [p 1185]
8.    World Court  [p 1189]
9.    free-trade  [p 1192]
10.   World Trade Organization  [p 1195]
11.   Act of State Doctrine  [p 1198]
12.   Doctrine of Sovereign Immunity  [p 1201]
13.   absolute, qualified or restricted  [p 1201]
14.   waived, commercial activity  [p 1201]
15.   Arbitration clause  [p 1203]

## Critical Thought Exercise Model Answer

Both Favlaka and the U.S. are members of the United Nations (UN) and signatories to the General Agreement on Tariffs and Trade that created the World Trade Organization (WTO). One of the functions of the WTO is to hear and decide trade disputes between member nations. Any member nation that believes a trade agreement has been breached can initiate a proceeding that is first heard by a three-member panel of the WTO. The panel issues a report that is referred to a dispute settlement body of the WTO. A seven-member appellate body hears any appeal from the dispute settlement body. The dispute between Favlaka and the U.S. involves a trade barrier imposed by Favlaka. A nation may protect its food sources and livestock from foreign threats that are scientifically proven to exist, but cannot create a barrier that favors its domestic sources of goods over foreign sources for the sole purpose of economic advantage. Favlaka will have to show that the threat of crop destruction from the Sweetie is real. According to the facts, there is no scientific proof that the Sweetie poses any danger to the Favlaka Beauty. This issue has been decided before. Japan tried to prevent the importation of U.S. apples into Japan by creating apple-testing regulations that acted as a form of tariff or trade barrier. The WTO ruled that the lack of scientific evidence that the U.S. apples posed any threat to the Japanese crops meant that the apple-testing regulations were without merit and improperly impeded entry of foreign-grown apples. The situation with Favlaka is very similar. A judge would likely follow the same reasoning and order Favlaka to receive the Sweetie for sale in its country.

# Answers to Practice Quiz

## True/False

1.  False   The Security Council of the United Nations is made up of fifteen member nations whose main responsibility is to maintain international peace as well as security. The members may also use armed forces if necessary to accomplish this goal. [p 1187]

2.  True    UNESCO, UNICEF, IMF and the IFAD are agencies that not only are a part of the United Nations, but who deal with a variety of economic as well as social problems. [p 1187]

3.  True    Only nations can have cases decided by the International Court of Justice. However, a nation may bring a claim on behalf of an individual or business that wants to seek redress against another country. [p 1189]

4.  True    The European Union treaty opens borders for trade by providing for the free flow of capital, services, goods and labor among the member nations. [p 1191]

5.  False   Unanimity among European Union members is required to admit a new member. [p 1191]

6.  False   When a foreign government nationalizes property, there are few legal remedies available to the owners of the nationalized property. [p 1198]

7.  True    The U.S. Government and several private companies offer political risk insurance that covers loss from uncompensated nationalization of property. [p 1198]

8.  False   The North American Free Trade Agreement was created and signed by these three countries in order to create a free-trade zone between them. [p 1192]

9.  True    Prior to the World Trade Organization being created, the General Agreement on Tariffs and Trade ruled over trade disputes. If a party lost under a panel report, it would vote to block the implementation of a panel's findings against it. However, with the creation of the World Trade Organization, the blocking power of member nations has been eliminated. [p 1197]

10. False   Many call the World Trade Organization the "Supreme Court of Trade" because of the power given it to peaceably solve trade disputes among its more than 130 member nations. [p 1195]

11. True    A country has absolute authority over what occurs within its own territory. [p 1198]

12. True    Due to the active involvement of the rabbi-judges, the Beis Din is more concerned with the truth than the adversarial process. [p 1203]

13. False   Making a profit from providing services or the sale of goods is allowed. However, making an unearned or unjustified profit is not. [p 1204]

14. False   An arbitrator issues an award, not a judgment. [p 1203]

15. False   Though the decision of which nation's courts will hear a case involving an international dispute is often a problem, if there is no agreement providing otherwise, the case will usually be brought in the national court of the plaintiff's home country. [p 1198]

## Multiple Choice

16. B   Answer B is correct, as their provisions address such things as the settlement of disputes, human rights, foreign aid, navigation and commerce. Answer A is incorrect, as treaties and conventions both involve agreements often involving trade versus abolishing the purchase of goods and services. Further, treaties and conventions involve agreements between nations, not states. Answer C is incorrect, as this indicates one of the two elements necessary to show that a practice has become a custom. Answer D is incorrect, as this refers to what courts and tribunals depend on to resolve international disputes, not what treaties and conventions center around. [p 1185]

17. C  Answer C is correct, as consistent and recurring action by two or more nations over a significant period of time as well as recognition of the custom's binding affect is what is needed to show a custom exists between two or more nations. Answer A is incorrect, as this is the definition of a treaty. Answer B is incorrect, as a custom is not a principle of law, but rather a practice. Answer D is incorrect, as this states one of the goals of the United Nations. [p 1185]

18. A  Answer A is correct, as nations do not have to obey international law enacted by other countries or international organizations. Answers B, C, and D are all true statements and therefore they are not the correct answers. [p 1183]

19. D  Answer D is correct, as the forum-selection clause, also known as the choice of forum clause chooses which nation's court has jurisdiction to hear a case arising out of the contract. Answer A is incorrect because, even though this is a true fact, it had nothing to do with which court has jurisdiction to hear cases arising out of an international contract. Answer B is incorrect, as this is referring to the choice of law clause not the choice of forum clause. Answer C is incorrect, as a trade pact granting easier access to the U.S. has little or no bearing on the choice of forum to hear an international contract case. [p 1198]

20. C  Answer C is correct, based on the principle that a country has absolute authority over what transpires in its own country but, cannot question the validity of an act committed by another country within that other country's own borders. Answer A is incorrect, as it is not a true statement, since the restraint on the judiciary is justified under the doctrine of separation of powers. Answer B is incorrect, as a country has absolute authority over what transpires within its own territory. Answer D is incorrect, as the courts of one country will not sit in judgment upon the acts of the government of another, done within its own territory. [p 1198]

21. D  Answer D is correct as, answers A, B, and C are all true and all express goals of the United Nations. [p 1186]

22. C  Answer C is correct, as the International Monastery Fund is not an agency associated with the United Nations. Answers A, B and D are all incorrect as the answers expressed in these choices are all agencies associated with the United Nations. [p 1187]

23. D  Answer D is correct, as answers A, B, and C all govern the United Nations. [p 1186]

24. B  Answer B is correct, as the Sovereign Immunity Doctrine states that an act of a government in a foreign country is not subject to suit in the foreign country. Answer A is incorrect, as there is no such act as the World Trade Organization Act. Answer C is incorrect, as the Act of state doctrine states that an act of a government in its own country is not subject to suit in a foreign country's court. Answer D is incorrect for the reasons given above. [p 1201]

25. C  Answer C is correct, as treaties and conventions are agreements between nations that are formally ratified by the supreme power of each signatory nation. Answer A is incorrect, as a custom is a practice followed by two or more nations over a period of time when dealing with each other. Answer B is incorrect, as judicial decisions of national courts and teachings of the most qualified legal scholars of the nations of the parties involved in a dispute are sources of international law. Answer D is incorrect, as general principles of law that are principles that are common to the nations of the parties involved in the dispute. [p 1185]

## Short Answer

26.  The Foreign Commerce Clause and the Treaty Clause. [p 1183]
27.  The United Nations. [p 1186]
28.  The Organization of Petroleum Exporting Countries. [p 1194]
29.  The World Trade Organization. [p 1195]
30.  National courts of individual countries. [p 1198]
31.  Deciding what constitutes, "commercial activity" is the most litigated aspect of the FSIA. [p 1201]
32.  Arbitration is faster, less formal, less expensive and more private than litigation. [p 1203]
33.  Treaties and conventions. [p 1185]

34. She might rely on the General Agreement on Tariffs and Trade. [p 1194]
35. The general report and the appellate decision can order the offending nation to cease from engaging in the violating practice and to pay damages to the other party. [p 1197]
36. Treaties and conventions, custom, general principles of law, judicial decisions and teachings. [p 1185]
37. When it has waived its immunity, or when it has engaged in commercial activity in the U.S. or outside the U.S. that causes a direct effect in the U.S. [p 1201]
38. The General Assembly, the Secretariat, and the Security Council. [p 1186]
39. It helps promote the world economy, with its main focus on promoting sound monetary, fiscal and macroeconomic policies worldwide by giving aide to needy countries. [p 1188]
40. It provides money to developing countries to fund projects for humanitarian purposes and to help relieve poverty. [p 1188-1189]